Volume I

Wooden Planes in 19th Century America

Second Edition
[Second printing, December 1982]

by

Kenneth D. Roberts

FITZWILLIAM, NEW HAMPSHIRE - USA - 1982

Published by
Ken Roberts Publishing Co.
Fitzwilliam, NH 03447
Copyright © 1978 by Kenneth D. Roberts
Printed in the United States of America
First Published 1975
Second Edition 1978, Second Printing, Vol I, 1982
ISBN 0-913602-53-1

All Rights Reserved

No part of this publication may be reproduced
or transmitted in any form or by any means,
electronic or mechanical, including
photocopy, recording or any information storage
and retrieval system, without permission
in writing from the Publisher.

Dust jacket, title page and chapter headings
Designed and type-set by Jane W. Roberts
Old Time Printing, Fitzwilliam, NH

Printed by
Bond Press, Inc.
Hartford, Connecticut

Bound by
Riverside Book Bindery, Inc.
Rochester, New York

Cover Material *Skivertex-Wombati*
Furnished by Whitman Products, Ltd., Johnston, RI

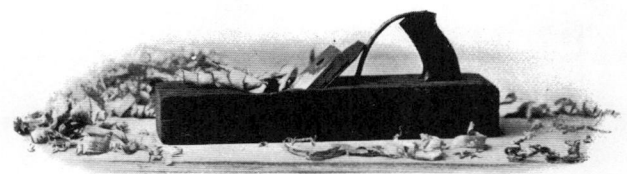

If you'd help make this world a desirable place,
And smooth its rough edges of care,
Keep planing away with a smile on your face,
And give of your savings with generous grace,
And take no more room than your share.

[Collection of Ruben Morrison]

Preface

An interest in antique furniture and house joinery led to my collecting wood working tools early in the 1950's. In 1965 my wife and I began a study of imprints on wooden planes. Antique shows and flea markets were excellent sources of information. At that time most dealers were amazed to learn that names were imprinted on such artifacts of the manufacturers. We were judged a little odd in approaching dealers: "May we look at the imprints on your planes?"; then proceeding to pick up the tools, rub the ends and record the data. To the casual observer this appeared very mysterious. Two things surely resulted from our studies. The prices began to soar and planes became more difficult to acquire. After our listing became substantial, we approached the Directors of the Early American Industries Society and offered to compile this data for publication in their *Chronicle*. Raymond Townsend, then Editor, was very enthusiastic about these studies, and presented our results in a four page *Supplement to the Chronicle*, Volume XIX, June 1966. My series of articles concerning identification and classification of planes and coopers' tools appeared in various issues of the *Chronicle*, Dec. 1966 through September 1969, which included four supplementary listings of imprints of planemakers.

This book is a revision of these previous writings with corrections and substantial additional material that has since come to my attention. This is intended to be a general purpose guide for collectors, museum personnel, historical societies and antiquarians. While I have a sincere interest in both historical technology and industrial research, I do not consider myself a craftsman having any expertise using his tools. Fortunately I have many friends competent in these crafts who have been of invaluable assistance to my learning process and writings. These studies have taught me that for the most part answers to the riddles of "who, when, where, why and how" are found from examination and discussion with others concerning tools with persistent research of primary material rather than from secondary historical writing.

This book is not as detailed in historical research as our previous work: *Planemakers and Edge Tool Enterprises in New York State in the Nineteenth Century*. It is more of a compilation of material and sources, noted in the Introduction. Hopefully this will be helpful for others to undertake additional research and produce writings in further depth.

The chapter concerning 18th Century New England planemaking was written by Anne and Donald Wing from their research, studies of both their own collection and others, correspondence and travels in England. Their contribution to this text is gratefully acknowledged. Elliot M. Sayward and William Streeter allowed me to study their manuscript: "Planemaking in the Valley of the Connecticut River and Hills of Western Massachusetts," previous to its publication in the *Chronicle*, for which I am very much appreciative. William Hilton has also shared material concerning Boston Planemakers.

The staffs of many libraries and historical societies have been helpful in my requests for information. The following are noted: American Antiquarian Society, Worcester, Mass.; Connecticut Historical Society and Connecticut State Library, Hartford, Conn.; New York State Historical Association, Cooperstown, N.Y.; New York Historical Society, New York, N.Y.; New York State Library, Albany, N.Y. and Ohio State Historical Society, Columbus, Ohio.

Reproduction of the 1858 *Arrowmammett Works Trade Catalogue* was through loan from the Connecticut Historical Society. Study of this important catalogue has been the principal basis for revision of my former classification of wooden planes published in the *Chronicle*.

R. A. Salaman of Harpenden, England kindly sent me an advance copy of his monumental and important recently published work, *Dictionary of Tools*, which has been very helpful in writing the commentaries concerning various types of planes and differences between English and American practices. I also wish to acknowledge helpful correspondence with both William Goodman and Philip Walker.

In writing the section concerning the Stanley Rule and Level Co.'s products, I principally used my own collection of Catalogues, many of which I have republished. Additionally I wish to acknowledge material and correspondence during the last ten years with the Product Engineering Department of this firm. Regretfully the recent book by Alvin Sellens, *The Stanley Plane (A history and descriptive inventory)* was not yet available when I wrote this section.

Acknowledgement is made to the Directors and Members of Early American Industries Association for their co-operation, assistance and interests in sending data concerning the listing of planemakers and arranging for its original publication. Contributing Members were mentioned in the *Supplement to the Chronicle*, Volume XX, June 1967. A listing of these persons, with others who have since contributed, appears at the end of the revised Check List in the Appendix.

Collections of planes from several museums and historical societies have been examined. These are noted in the section concerning where planes may be seen, listed in the Appendix.

Unless otherwise noted the planes photographed are from my own collection. In these instances professional photography was done either by Edward H. Goodrich of Bristol, Conn. or John Abbott of Keene, N.H.

Acknowledgement is made to my wife Jane W. Roberts for assistance making three different contributions to this book. 1. Design and type setting the chapter headings, title page and dust jacket. 2. Recording the names and research data of the plane makers on file cards. 3. Constructive and helpful suggestions concerning the manuscript. I sincerely appreciate her willingness to help and understand without complaint the frustrations experienced by the author during the last year while writing and publishing this book.

Finally, I would like to dedicate this book to my late uncle, Donald Adair Roberts, of Cheyenne, Wyoming, who was not the slightest interested in planes, but without whose financial assistance this work could not have been undertaken.

Kenneth D. Roberts, September 30, 1975

Preface to Volume I, the second printing of the Second Edition

The preface to the first printing of the second edition appears on page 188. This unorthodox arrangement was the most economical presentation of 88 pages of new material and 31 pages of a revised check list in the form of a *SUPPLEMENT* to the 1975 first edition, which was also combined with that work. Approximately 400 *SUPPLEMENTS* and 1,230 copies of this second edition were published in 1978. These were out of print by December 1981. Numerous requests have accumulated for another printing.

Since publishing this second edition, I have additionally published and marketed 27 reprint trade tool catalogues with documentaries, a major text [*SOME 19th CENTURY ENGLISH WOOD WORKING TOOLS*], and a monograph concerning rules. During this period research by others has resulted in considerable new information concerning wooden and transitional planes. Much of this has been published, either privately or in existent journals of tool societies. In operating my one-person publishing company, I regret it has not been possible for me to continue to research and compile newly reported imprints of possible planemakers. Fortunately, a great deal of useful data has been reported in *PLANE TALK*, the Bulletin of the British-American Rhykenological Society [BAR-S] and Roger Smith's comprehensive study, *PATENTED TRANSITIONAL & METALLIC PLANES IN AMERICA, 1827-1927*. The forthcoming work by Emil and Marty Pollak will consist of imprints, brief biographies and dates of many planemakers, as well as an up-dated check list in book form. This will be a welcome publication.

My own continued research on planes has been principally concerned with Hermon Chapin at his Union Factory at Pine Meadow, Connecticut. This operation was carried on by three generations of Chapins, 1826-1929 at New Hartford, the longest tenure of any American planemaking firm. Machinery for mass-producing planes, superseding hand methods, was first developed there in 1826. It is my intent to publish this study as Volume II, *WOODEN PLANES IN 19th CENTURY AMERICA*. Among the subjects considered will be: apprentice agreements and training; production methods; excerpts from trade catalogues, 1839-1920; broadside advertisements; competitive firms; costs and pricing methods; agreements among competitors to fix prices and production quotas, 1869-1890; rule making, and other products. Technical difficulties in reproduction of significant original data from account journals have delayed publication, but hopefully this will be completed during 1983.

Kenneth D. Roberts, December 1982

Table of Contents

First Edition

Preface		iii
	List of Illustrations	vi
	List of Plates	viii
	List of Tables	viii
Chapter I	Introduction	1
Chapter II	New England Planes of the 18th Century	7
Chapter III	Historical Survey of 19th Century Planemaking	16
Chapter IV	The Demise of the Wooden Plane	47
Chapter V	Classification and Identification of Wooden Planes	62

Appendicies

I	Arrowmammett Tool Co. 1858 Trade Catalogue of Bench Planes, etc.	141
II	Section from Nicholoson's *MECHANIC'S COMPANION*, 1849	154
III	Section from Holtzapffel's *MECHANICAL MANIPULATION & TURNING*, 1856	168
IV	Some Museums where Planes may be Seen	182

Second Edition

Preface		188
	List of Illustrations	309
	List of Plates	310
	List of Tables	310
Chapter VI	New Insights into 18th Century Planemaking	189
Chapter VII	More about 19th Century Planemaking	201
Chapter VIII	Ohio Planemaking and Sandusky Tool Co.	223
Chapter IX	Window Sash Planes	247
Chapter X	Moulding and Miscellaneous Wooden Planes	259
Appendix V	Check List of 19th Century American and Canadian Makers and/or Firms [also Great Britain makers of Planes imported or brought to the United States and Canada during the 19th Century.]	279
Index		311

LIST OF ILLUSTRATIONS

Figure Number	Title	Page
1	18th Century Moulding Planes	9
2	18th Century Bench Plane	11
3	18th Century Plow Plane	11
4	Imprints of 18th Century Moulding Planes	13
5	Planemakers' Floats	30
6	Jack Planes and Irons	50
7	T. D. Worrall Patent Planes	53
8	"Bailey's Patent" Wood Planes	58
9	Stanley Adjustable "Liberty Bell" Wood & Rabbet Planes	58
10	Stanley-Bailey Transitional Wood Soled Adjustable Planes	60
11	Jenny Handle Smooth No. 37 Bailey Patent SR&L Co. Plane	61
12	Wood and Transitional Block and Mitre Planes	61
13	Gage's Self-Setting Planes	63
14	'Double Razee' Long Jointer Plane	67
15	Transitional Type Wooden Sole Bench Planes	69
16	T. D. Worrall Patent No.18,312, September 29,1857 Plane	70
17	"Phillips' Plough Plane"	70
18	Miller's Patent Metallic Plow	71
19	SR&L Co. "45" Traut's Patent Adjustable Combination Plane	73
20	SR&L Co. "55" Universal Plane	75
21	E. T. Burrowes' Screen Grooving Plane	76
22	Bench Plane	81
23	Jointer Planes	81
24	Single and Double Plane Irons	83
25	Mitre Plane	85
26	Bull Horn Smoothing Planes	85
27	Smoothing Plane with Handle	86
28	Toothing Plane	86
29	Toy Plane	87
30	Instrument Maker's Smoothing Planes	87
31	English Music Maker's Planes	88
32	English Instrument Maker's Planes	88
33	Razee Jack Plane [17"]	89
34	Group of Recess Handle Planes	89
35	Set of Plow Irons	91
36	Beech Plow with Slide Arms	92
37	Beech Screw Arm Plows	92
38	Empire Rosewood Screw Plow	93
39	All Boxwood, Ivory Tipped Screw Plow	93
40	Board Match Planes	94
41	Closed Handle Board Match Planes	95
42	Plank Match Planes	96
43	Set Of Moving Match Planes	96
44	Moving Filletster	97
45	Moving Filletster with Screw Arms	98
46	Common Rabbet Planes	99
47	Rabbet Plane with Integral Fence	99
48	Rabbet Planes with Closed Handles	100
49	"Jack" Rabbits	100
50	Panel Plane [14"]	101
51	Adjustable Width Raising Jack Plane	102
52	Raising Plane with Screw Arm Fence	103
53	Panel Jack Plane	103

54	Side Rabbet Planes	104
55	Dado Planes	105
56	Bead Plane [1"]	108
57	Section, Cutting Iron and Cove or Scotia Moulding Plane	108
58	Various Methods of Boxing Bead and Snipe Bill Planes	109
59	Oblique Boxed Bead Planes	110
60	Simple Moulding Planes	111
61	Double Iron Moulding Planes	111
62	Pair of Hollow and Round Planes [1"]	112
63	Set of Nine Round Irons	113
64	Sets of Hollows and Rounds [1-1/2"]	113
65	Group of Complex Moulding Planes [1/2" - 1" widths]	114
66	Plain and Reverse Ogee Moulding Planes	115
67	Grecian Ogee Moulding Planes	116
68	Grecian Ovolo Planes	116
69	Various Complex Moulding Planes [1" - 2" widths]	117
70	Complex Moulding Plane with Iron Removed	117
71	Complex Moulding Planes [2" - 3"] Widths	118
72	Moulding Planes with Closed Handles	118
73	Full Boxed Snipe Bill	119
74	Pair of Single Boxed Snipe Bill Planes	119
75	Sash Planes	120
76	Double Iron Sash Plane with Handle and Boxed Splines	120
77	Adjustable Double Iron Sash Planes	121
78	Adjustable Screw Arm Sash Plane	121
79	Single Ogee Coping Plane	122
80	Double Coping Plane [Ovalo Section]	123
81	Various Double Coping Planes	124
82	Saddle-type Sash Templates	124
83	Cornice Plane [5-3/4" wide]	125
84	Crown Moulding Plane by E.W.Carpenter [6-1/2"] Wide	126
85	Cornice Plane by C.Fuller, Boston, Mass. [3" width]	126
86	Crown Moulding Plane with Adjustable Fence	127
87	Gothic Bevel Cornice Plane [4" width]	128
88	Pump and Gutter Planes	129
89	Spar, Mast or Rounding Planes	130
90	Compass Planes	131
91	Patented Chamfer Plane	131
92	Core Plane [Pattern Maker's]	132
93	Slitting Plane	133
94	English Router Planes	133
95	Two Wooden and a Cast Iron Router Planes	134
96	Coopers' Jointer Planes	136
97	Coopers' Levelers	136
98	Chamfer Plane and Chamfer Iron	137
99	Coopers' Howel Planes	137
100	Coopers' Crozes	138
101	Various Forms of Croze Irons for Coopers' Planes	138
102	Carriage Makers' Plane	139
103	Carriage Makers' Compass and "T" Rabbet Planes	140
104	Exhibit at Delaware State Museum	183
105	Cabinet Maker's Shop at Farmers Museum NYSHA	183
106	Cabinet Maker's Shop at Pennsylvania Landis Valley Museum	184
107	Cabinet Maker's Shop at Old Sturbridge Village	184
108	Carriagemaker's Planes at Heritage Plantation	185
109	Shipmaker's Planes at Mystic Seaport	185
110	Exhibit at Sloane-Stanley Museum	186
111	Exhibit at Shelburne Museum	186

LIST OF PLATES

Figure Number	Title	Page
I	James H. Wells' Joiner's Tools	17
II	Broadside - John Denison's Joiners' Planes	21
III	Advertisements in *1850 Connecticut Business Directory*	22
IV	Title and Front Page from 1869 Greenfield Tool Co. Catalogue	29
V	Broadside - Philip Chapin's Catalogue & Prices of Planes	30-31
VI	Broadside - Isreal White's Patent Plow	33
VII	Utica Directory Advertisement of 1828 by L. Kennedy & Co.	35
VIIIa-d	Pages from *1885 Sandusky Tool Co. Catalogue*	38-41
IX	The Story of the Plane, SR&L Co. Chart No. 131	54-55
X	Transcription of Hazard Knowles 1827 Cast Iron Plane Patent	51
XI	Page 39 from *1870 SR & L Co. Catalogue of Tools*	56
XII	Page 40 from *1879 SR & L Co. Price List of Tools*	57
XIII	Summaries of Gage Plane Patents	62
XIV	Gage's Self-Setting Planes from *1896 H., S. & Co. Catalogue*	64
XV	Page 9 from *1911 Sargent & Co. Catalogue*	65
XVI	"Double Razee Planes" - Advertised in *Ohio Tool Co. Catalog*	67
XVII	Longitudinal Half-Section of a Jack Plane	82
XVIIIa	Types of Rectilinear Grooves Made by Planes	90
XVIIIb	Types of Board Joints	95
XIX	Types of Cabinet Joints	97
XX	Section of Moving Filletster	98
XXI	Simple Square Framed Panel Construction	101
XXII	Halving Plane	104
XXIII	Sketches of Simple Mouldings	107
XXIV	Methods of Boxing Moulding Planes	109
XXV	Sketch of Hollow & Round Planes	112
XXVI	Construction of OGee & Moulding Plane	114
XXVII	Variations of Ogee and Grecian Mouldings	115
XXVIII	Sections of Coping Planes	122
XXIX	Cross-sections of Cornice Planes	129
XXX	SR & L Co. Advertisement of Router Plane, 1884	134
XXXI	Coopers' Jointers listed in *1909 L & IJ White Catalogue*	135

LIST OF TABLES

I	New England Eighteenth Century Plane Makers	14
II	Early 19th Century United States Plane Makers	16
III	1850 Connecticut Planemakers Reported in 1850 & 1860 Census	23
IV	Data from 1855 Massachusetts Compendium of Census	27
V	Trade Marks of Greenfield Tool Co.	27
VI	Movement of Planemaking through New York State	34
VII	Principal Wooden Plane Firms in United States after 1870	42
VIII	Plane Iron Manufacturers During 19th Century	44
IX	Sequence Significant Iron Bench Plane Patents in U.S.	50
X	Patent Improvements in Securing & Adjusting Plane Bits	53
XI	Total Sales of "Bailey" Planes, 1870 - 1898 by SR & L Co.	76
XII	Classification of 19th Century American Wooden Planes	80
XIII	Shapes of Moulding Planes listed in *Arrowmammett Catalogue*	106
XIV	Sizes of Simple Moulding Planes	110

FRONTISPIECE

From Back Cover of *1857 Illustrated Supplement to the Catalogue and Invoice Price List of BENCH PLANES, Moulding Tools, &c..Manufactured at the ARROWMAMMETT WORKS, Middletown, Conn.*

[Courtesy of the Connecticut Historical Society, Hartford, Connecticut]

x

| Copeland & Co. Warranted | J. Killam | J. Denison | M. Copeland Hartford |

| ARROWMAMMETT WORKS Middletown | A. & E. Baldwin/New York [over stamped] Arrowmammett Works/Middletown,Ct. | C.W.Holden NORWICH | M.COPELAND & CO. Warranted |

IMPRINTS from 19th CENTURY PLANES made in UNITED STATES
[actual size, (see page 188)]

Chapter I

Introduction

The wooden plane during the nineteenth century was an important tool in the trades of: carpentry, joinery, cabinetmaking, coopering and coachmaking. The distinction between carpentry and joinery is explained in Nicholson, (see Appendix: N87) Cabinetmaking was considered a subdivision of joinery. Tomlinson has briefly described these trades as practiced in England in 1860.[1] Kilby has written an excellent text concerning cooperage.[2]

Those readers not presently familiar with planes are referred to the chapter concerning this subject in *The History of Woodworking Tools* by W.L. Goodman.[3] The same author has written a more detailed study: *British Plane Makers from 1700*.[4] Mercer's *Ancient Carpenter's Tools*, while offering some interesting photographs, unfortunately has some inaccuracies naming planes and relied on English terminology, both of which may confuse the reader.[5] R.A. Salaman's recently published *Dictionary of Tools: used in woodworking and allied trades c.1700-1970*, is most highly recommended for those desiring additional technical details.[6]

Prior to the nineteenth century the majority of joiners' and carpenters' tools were imported from England. Since the colonies were essentially English, the terminology, with some exception, continued to follow that used in the Mother country. Joseph Moxon's *Mechanick Exercises* became the eighteenth century doctrine. The first part of this appeared as early as 1678.[7] The so-called third edition published in 1703, became the definitive work of such crafts as: "Smithing, Joinery, Carpentry, Turning and Bricklaying".[8] The section concerning "The Art of Joinery" described *'Bench Plains'* "of several sorts, as: Fore Plain, the Joynter and the Smoothing Plane. Also descriptions were presented for the Rabbet-Plane, the Plow and Moulding-Planes: as the Round, the Hollow, the Ogee, the Snipes-bill, the Grooving-plane, &c."

Concerning the Fore Plane Moxon stated: -

> "It is called the *Fore Plane* because it is used before you come to work either with the *Smooth Plane*, or with the *Joynter*. The edge of its Iron is not ground upon the straight, as the *Smooth Plane*, and the *Joynter* are, but rises with a Convex-Arch in the middle of it; for its Office being to prepare the Stuff for either the *Smoothing Plane* or the *Joynter*, Workmen set the edge of it Ranker. ."[9]

However in his section of House-Carpentry Moxon stated: -

> "*Jack-Plane*, called so by Carpenters, but is indeed the same that Joyners call the *Fore-Plane*.[10]

The derivation of the term "jack" in reference to this plane is believed to have conveyed the meaning "short" as in "jack-rafter". Hummel has commented on the confusion regarding the terms jack and fore planes, indicating the probability that the former became preferable near the end of the eighteenth or beginning of the nineteenth century.[11] However these controversial terms continued in England late into the nineteenth century. The index and glossary of *The Carpenter and Joiner's Assistant*,[12] c.1880, defined: -

> "Jack-Plane: One of the bench-planes. It is about eighteen inches long, and is used in reducing inequalitites in the timber preparatory to use of the trying plane."

> "Fore-Plane: The first plane used after the saw or axe."

Goodman has listed in tabular form the names of the common bench planes by various authorities 1673/1958 and commented on such differences.[13]

The 1736 *The City and Country Purchaser's and Builder's Dictionary*[14] [London], did not mention the Jack-Plane, but offered the following: -

> "PLANE, is also a well-known Instrument used by Carpenters and Joiners to shave or smooth Boards, &c. There are several sorts according to the Uses to which they are put; as first: -
> The Fore-Plane, which is about 18 inches long, and set rank, and the iron ground with kind of Convexity, to take off the rough Surface of the Board, to prepare it for The Long Plane, about two Foot in Length, which smooths the Work after the rough Stuff is taken off by the Fore-Plane, and prepares the Way for the Smoothing Plane; or, if for the Edge of a Board, the Jointer, which is about 6 inches larger than the Long-Plane, as is so called, being set very fine, from its being used to make the Joints of two Boards, even and smooth, and fit for being glew'd together. The Strike-Block is a sort of a Plane used to join Mouldings and short Work; and may be reckon'd a short Jointer, being about 14 inches long. The Smoothing Plane, so called from its Use, to smooth or finish the Planing-Work, the Iron of which is set fine for that Purpose; is about 6 or 7 inches in length. The Rabbet-Plane, is used to make a kind of Gutter or Rabbet, as it is called by Workmen, on the Edge of a Board, in order for a Door or Window to shut close into, as also for Fillets in Mouldings, &c. This Plane is about 10 or 11 inches long, about 4 inches deep, and about an inch wide in the Face, and the Iron as broad as the Stock, that the Rabbet may be cut strait and regular. The Plow, so called from its Shape, and from its plowing a Gutter or Groove in the Edge of a Batten of whole Deal, to admit a Pannel of slit Deal into it. Round and Hollow Planes; curious Artists have 16 Sorts of these Planes, of different Sizes, from half a quarter of an inch to more than two inches, wherewith, by the Assistance of Snipes-Bill, and Rabbet-Plane above mentioned, they make the various sorts of Mouldings. Snipes-Bill, a plane used in striking Mouldings. Lastly there are Moulding Planes, of different Breadths, some 4 or 5 inches, which require two Mem, one to shove it forward, and the other, by means of a round Piece of Wood thro' the Head of the Plane, to pull it to him, to strike a Moulding, and the Iron is consequently indented with Rounds and Hollows, and shap'd for that Purpose."

Peter Nicholson, an architect, was the author of *The Carpenters' Guide: Joiners' Assistant, &c.*, [London, 1793]. He was also the author of *Mechanical Exercises*, first published in London in 1812. Subsequently this work was re-published in America, first in 1832 as *The Mechanic's Companion, etc.*, but identical in content to the 1812 English title.[15] A second American edition appeared in 1849 [16] and a third in 1856.[17] The title page and the section concerning planes from the 1849 work is reproduced in the Appendix. This text was based in part on Moxon and late eighteenth century practice. It became the definitive work for the crafts mentioned on the title page: Carpentry, Joinery, Bricklaying, Masonry, Slating, Plastering, Painting, Smithing and Turning. It was widely used both in England and America through the first sixty years of the nineteenth century. There were no revisions of the materials presented on the crafts in any of the editions that followed the original of 1812. Therefore, it is not surprising that this text strongly influenced the terminology of crafts for the first half of the nineteenth century.

While Nicholson grouped Bench Planes according to their order of usage: jack, fore, trying, long, jointer and smoothing, he did not define the fore-plane He stated "trying-up" or reducing the ridges following the jack-plane was accomplished using the Trying Plane. If further trying-up "very straight" was required, this was accomplished by the Long Plane. This terminology was seldom used in America.[18] Here, the 22 inches long plane employed after the jack was usually called either the fore or the short jointer. While the trying plane was not included in Moxon, he did note: "The Joynter is also used to try tables".[19] (i.e., to make straight the entire length)

Abraham Rees' monumental work: *The Cyclopedia or Universal Dictionary of Arts, Science and Literature,* [thirty-nine volumes of text and four of illustrations],[20] was re-published in 1822 at Philadelphia. Rees defined bench planes according to Nicholson as: "Jack, trying long, jointer (or shooting) and smoothing". In lengths these respectively were: 17, 22, 26, 30, and 7½ inches.

Volume II of *Turning and Mechanical Manipulation. . . on the Lathe, etc.* by Charles Holtzapffel was published in 1856.[London][21] Chapter XXIII. concerning planes is reproduced in the Appendix. This important study not only defined and described planes, but additionally explained how these tools were used and gave procedures for sharpening their irons. Holtzapffel divided planes into three groupos: Bench for smoothing and leveling (jack, trying, long, jointer and smoothing); Grooving for rectilinear channels (plough, rebate and fillister);and Moulding for curved surfaces.

While 'plough' and 'rebate' were apparently preferred spellings used in England during the nineteenth century,(also used by Nicholson) in America 'plow' and 'rabbet' were more comonly employed. Actually these American spelling were eighteenth century English as they were used by Moxon. In America 'filletster' (or sometimes: filetster or fillitster) was followed rather than the English 'fillister'.

In a true sense Moulding Planes should be called 'moulding tools' as they form curved surfaces, not the flat or rectilinear surface formed by a true plane. It was their similarity of operation by which these tools became known as 'moulding'planes.

Broadsides advertising types and sizes of various planes and moulding tools and listing their prices were issued in America in increasing quantitites after 1825. These were outgrowths of earlier English practice of issuing 'pattern' books, such as Joseph Smith's 1816, Key to the Manufactories of Sheffield. Trade catalogues illustrating, describing and pricing such American tools commenced being published in America soon after 1850. To a certain degree these earlier broadsides and catalogues were influenced by English terminology. However, soon after 1850, the terminology for tools in America definitely became independent of England. Within the next twenty-five years United States assumed world leadership in such tool manufacturing. This accomplishment was a fortuitous combination of technological advances, enterprise and free competion.

In America by 1850 Bench planes were defined in progressively longer lengths as: smooth, 8"; jack, 17"; fore or short jointer, 22"; and long jointers of sizes between 24"- 30". Grooving planes became: plow, rabbet (sometime rabbit), dado, filletster, and match sets. (a match set being a tongue and groove combination for same size of board) Moulding tools were named according to their shaping form.

When Knight's *American Mechanical Dictionary* was published in 1882, the section describing planes unfortunately was taken directly from Holtzapffel's 1856 work.[22] Not only were these English terms, but by this date this data was mostly obsolete in America. The all metal plane and the wood sole with cast iron fixtures('transitional') bench planes then being produced in quantity by the Stanley Rule & Level Co. under the L.Bailey patents were rapidly replacing the former styles and sizes of wooden bench planes.[23] All metal combination planes for grooving and moulding operations were soon to follow.[24] Knight did illustrate and describe a 'transitional' bench type plane of Smith & Carpenter patent and an iron plane with flexible sole patented by Evans. (circular plane)[25] However, these varieties[26] were not as important as those then being made by Stanley R&L Co. under the L.Bailey patents.[27]

Types of Planes
Listed in Knight's
American Mechanical Dictionary
[see note 22]

	Length in Inches.	Width in Inches.	Width of Irons.
Modeling-plane	1 - 5	¼ - 2	3/16 - 1½
Smoothing-plane	6½ - 8	2⅜ - 3⅛	1¾ - 2⅓
Rabbet-plane	9½	⅜ - 2	⅜ - 2
Jack-plane	12 - 17	2½ - 3	2 - 2¼
Panel-plane	14½	3½	2½
Trying-plane	20 - 22	3¼ - 3⅜	2⅜ - 2½
Long-plane	24 - 26	3⅝	2⅝
Jointer-plane	28 - 30	3¾	2¾
Cooper's jointer-plane	60 - 72	5 - 5¼	3½ - 3¾

Angle-plane.
Astragal-plane.
Badger-plane.
Banding-plane.
Bead-plane.
Bench-plane.
Border-plane.
Break-iron.
Capping-plane.
Carpenter's plane.
Compass-plane.
Concave-plane.
Cooper's plane.
Core-box plane.
Cornice-plane.
Counter-check.
Covetta.
Cutting-plane.
Cutting-thrust.
Dovetail.
Dovetail box-plane.
Edge-plane.
Fillet-plane.
Fillister.
Fluting-plane.
Fore-plane.
Forkstaff-plane.
Grooving-plane.
Hand-rail plane.
Hollows and rounds.
Hollow-sash plane.
Howel.
Ice-plane.
In-shave.
Jack-plane.
Joiner's plane.
Jointer.
Jointing-plane.
Lamb's-tongue.
Long-plane.
Matching-plane.
Metal-plane.
Miter-plane.
Modeling-plane.
Molding-plane.
Ogee-plane.
Overshave.
Ovolo-plane.
Panel-plane.
Panel-plow.
Pistol-router.
Plane-guide.
Plane-iron.
Plane-table.
Plow.
Quarter-round.
Quirking-plane.
Rabbet-plane.
Reed-plane.
Reglet.
Rounding-plane.
Round-nose plane.
Router.
Sash-fillister.
Sash-plane.
Scaleboard-plane.
Scraping-plane.
Shooting-plane.
Side-fillister.
Side-plane.
Side-rabbet plane.
Side-round plane.
Side-snipe.
Single and three reed planes.
Skew-plane.
Skew-rabbet plane.
Slat-plane.
Slitting-plane.
Smoothing-plane.
Snipe-bill plane.
Splint-plane.
Spokeshave.
Spout-plane.
Square-rabbet plane.
Stock-shave.
Sun-plane.
Table-plane.
Tonguing-plane.
Toothing-plane.
Try-plane.
Whisk.
Witchet.

In this present study the following broadsides and trade catalogues have been consulted:-

BROADSIDES

1. Joiners' Tools, Manufactured by D. & M. Copeland, Hartford, Conn., c.1825
2. List of Joiners' Tools, Manufactured and Sold Wholesale & Retail by F.K. Collins at Ravenna, Portage County, Ohio, July 5, 1838
3. Joiners' Tools, Manufactured by John J. Bowles, Hartford, Conn., c.1840
4. Manufacturer of Joiners' Planes, John Denison, Winthrop, Conn., c.1845/55
5. Plane Manufacturer, Samuel H. Bibighaus, Successor to John Bell No.311 Willow Street, near Forth, Philadelphia,, c.1852

TRADE CATALOGUES

1. Catalogue and Invoice Prices of Rules, Planes, Gauges, &c., 1853
   Hermon Chapin, Union Factory, Pine Meadow (New Hartford), Conn.
2. Invoice Price List of Carpenters' and Joiners' Bench Planes & Moulding Tools. Manufactured and Sold at Arrowmammett Works, Middletown, Conn. 1858, (Reproduced in Appendix)
3. Illustrated Catalogue and Price List... Mechanic's Hardware, 1861
   Pratt & Co., Buffalo, New York
4. Illustrated Catalogue of American Hardware, 1865,
   Russell Erwin and Manufacturing Co., New Britain, Conn.
5. Invoice Price List and Illustrated Catalogue, 1862; also 1872
   Greenfield Tool Co., Greenfield, Mass.
6. Price List and Illustrated Catalogue of Rules, Planes, Gauges, &c., 1874
   H. Chapin's Son, (E.M. Chapin), Pine Meadow (New Hartford), Conn.
7. Price List of Planes, Edge Tools, 1875
   D.R. Barton Tool Co., Rochester, N.Y.
8. Price List and Illustrated Catalogue of Hardware, 1871
   Sargent & Co., New Haven, Conn.
9. Illustrated Price List and Catalogue of Hardware, 1873
   J.B. Shannon, Philadelphia, Pa.
10. Planes, Plane Irons, etc., 1885
    Sandusky Tool Co., Sandusky, Ohio
11. Price Lists and Tool Catalogues: 1870, 1874, 1877, 1879, 1884, 1888, 1892, & 1898. Stanley Rule & Level Co., New Britain, Conn.

CATALOGUE & BROADSIDE

1. Catalogue & Prices of Planes, c.1850
   P. Chapin, 44 Light Street, Baltimore, Md.

ENGLISH 'PATTERN' BOOK

1. Explanation or KEY to the Various Manufacturies of Sheffield, Sheffield, 1816. Published by Joseph Smith. [28]

Acknowledgement is also made to Maynard Mitchell, Director Leeds City Museums for consultation and use of *John Willey, Saw Maker & Joiners' & Cabinet Makers' Tool Warehouse*, Broadside Price List, c.1864/1881, Leeds, England. Displayed at Abbey House Museum, Leeds

Note: Throughout this book the English spelling *moulding* is used, which was the spelling most comonly used in United States during the 19th century.

Notes - Introduction

1. Charles Tomlinson, *Illustrations of Trades*, [London,1860], Reprinted EAIA,1972
2. Kenneth Kilby, *The Cooper and His Trade*, [London,England, 1971]
3. W.L. Goodman, *The History of Woodworking Tools*,[London,1964], pp.39-109
4. W.L. Goodman, *British Planemakers from 1700*, [London, 1968]
5. H.C. Mercer, *Ancient Carpenters' Tools*, [Doylestown,Pa., 1951], pp.98-133
6. R.A. Salaman, *Dictionary of Tools*, [London, 1975]
7. Joseph Moxon, *Mechanick Exercises*, [Praeger Publisher's Reprint of 1703 Edition, New York, 1970], Introduction, ix
8. *Ibid*, Introduction xxv
9. *Ibid*, p.65
10. *Ibid*, p.161
11. C.F. Hummel, *With Hammer in Hand*, [Winterthur, Del.,1968], p.106
12. James Newland, *The Carpenter and Joiner's Assistant,* [London, c.1880] This is not to be confused with similar titles by Peter Nicholson [London,1793] and revised by his son Michael A. Nicholoson [London, 1826, revised 1835]
13. W.L. Goodman, *HWT*, op. cit.,Table IV, p.102, commentary, p.103
14. Richard Neve, *The City and Country Purchaser's and Builder's Dictionary or The Complete Builder's Guide,* [London, 1736], 3rd. Ed.
15. Peter Nicholson, *Mechanic's Companion,* [Philadelphia,Pa., 1832]
16. *Ibid*, [Philadelphia, 1849]
17. *Ibid*, [Philadelphia, 1856], Addition:"An Essay on the Steam Engine"
18. A Broadside-Catalogue by P.Chapin,Baltimore,Md.,c.1850, notes a trying plane.
19. Joseph Moxon, *op. cit.,*[Praeger Reprint], p.69
20. Rees' original *Cyclopedia* was published over the period 1802-1819 in London. The section concerning planes ,Vol27,Section II, is believed to have been published March 1814.See: Attempt to Ascertan Actual Dates of Publication of Rees' Cyclopedia, B.A.Jackson, [London, 1895]
21. Charles Holtzapffel had planned on publishing this work in six volumes, which began in 1843. He died in 1847, age 41. He had completed the manuscripts for Volumes II & III, which were respectively published in 1856 & 1864.[London, by Holtzapffel & Co.] Vols. IV and V were completed by his son,John J.Holtzapffel and published respectively in 1879 and 1884. See: Introduction by Robert Austin, *The Principles & Practice of Ornamental or Complex Turning,*by J.J.Holtzapffel, Volume V, [Dover Publication Reprint, New Nork,N.Y.,1973]
22. Edward H. Knight, *American Mechanical Dictionary,*[Boston,1882],Vol.II,p.1724. Ninety-two varieties of plane are listed on page 1725. E.S.Ferguson reported a New York,N.Y. Edition of this work [3 volumes, 1874-1876],*Bibliography of the History of Technology,* [Cambridge,Mass, 1968],p.65. This earlier work of Knight was not consulted in this study.
23. These were first advertised in *Stanley Rule & Level Co.'s Catalogue of Tools and Hardware* , [New Britain,Ct.,1870], pp.38-40.(See 1973 Reprint,K.R.Pub.Co.)
24. Miller's"Patent Adjustable Metallic Plow,Filletster,Rabbet, and Matching Plane" manufactured by SR&L Co. was first advertised in 1871 Supplement to above noted 1870 SR&L Co.'s *Catalogue*. Also see: *SR&L Co.'s Combination Planes* [Fitzwilliam,N.H.,1975], pp.7-11.
25. E.H.Knight, *op. cit.,* p.1724
26. U.S.Pat.#81,425; F.Smith & I.Carpenter, Aug.25,1868,Lancaster,Pa. - "stock stiffened by an upper metallic frame"['transitional' type]& G.F. Evans U.S.Pat.#41,993, Mar.22,1864, Norway, Maine, "metallic plane with flexible sole".
27. Leonard Bailey's Patents were: U.S.Pat.#67,398,Aug.6,1867 [reissue June 22,1875] for Bench Plane ['transitional'type] & U.S.Pat.#113,003,Mar.28,1871 for iron plane with flexible sole.
28. The title page and various plates concerning plane irons have been reproduced in: KD. & J.W. Roberts, *Planemakers and Other Edge Tool Enterprises in New York State in the Nineteenth Century,* [Cooperstown,N.Y.],Plates 9-11,pp.8&9.

Chapter II

New England Planes of the Eighteenth Century

[by Donald B. and Anne C. Wing]

Plane making in 19th-century America was well-established, with large factories employing many men. The industry, however, had its origins in the small, individual shops of makers of the 18th-century. While the large later factories tended to be concentrated in western Massachusetts, Connecticut, New York State, and Ohio (with exceptions, of course), the known 18th-century makers seem to have originated mainly in the southeastern New England area. This section is intended to show the state of current research on these early New England makers, and to point out the common characteristics of 18th-century American planes which distinguish them from their later counterparts.

If one looks at a row of wooden planes, those made in the 18th-century stand out from the rest like the proverbial sore thumb. Perhaps the most telling characteristic of 18th-century planes is the shape of the body. The early moulding planes were non-standard in length, almost always longer than the later-standard 241 mm. (9½"), anywhere up to 268 mm. (10½"). The bodies are often quite shallow or quite high in proportion to the length, tending to look short and squatty or tall and thin.

A sharp, wide chamfer is common in many planes of this period. While most 19th-century planes have a more rounded and/or more narrow slope between their tops and sides, those of the 18th-century usually had a well-defined chamfer. On the bottom half of the fore end and heel of the 18th-century planes are often found decorative indentations, or fluting. This is particularly true of moulding planes. (See Figs 1 through 4.)

Wedges of these planes are often noticeably odd-shaped and proportioned, and with rounded tops. Some of the makers (Joseph Fuller of Providence, R.I., and Aaron Smith of Rehoboth, Mass., for example) relieved, or notched, the top back of the wedge, presumably so that the blade could be tapped easily without mashing the wedge in the process. (See Fig. 1, center row left.) The Sandusky Tool Company of Ohio used the same style a century later.

Handles on large bench planes and crown mouldings were often offset in the early planes. They had flatter sides and were shorter, thicker, and not as rounded as the later models. (See Fig. 2.)

Blades, (commonly referred to as 'irons') of course, were often hand-forged in the 18th-century. This is another clue to the age of a plane. The hand-forged blades were seldom signed, although planes of the late 18th-century sometimes had British blades signed by James Cam (1787 - 1833) or Newbould (1787 -1881). [1]

Blades on the bench planes were usually single (i.e., without the cap iron).

The makers' name stamps on these planes are quite different from later ones. Letters are often both upper and lower case and in some instances appear to have been stamped individually, as they can be rather uneven. The letters tend to be fairly large. "I" was often used where today we would expect a "J," as in "Ion Ballou, Providence." (See Fig. 4.) The signatures on the fore end of early planes have intrigued many people, and some facts are now beginning to come to light regarding the makers of these first American planes.

Also characteristic of the name stamps on early New England planes is the presence of the words "living in" or "in" before the name of the maker's town. Cesar Chelor used the same "living in" and "Wrentham" stamps as had his master, Francis Nicholson.[2] Planes by Joseph Fuller have been found marked "Jo. Fuller, living in, Providence," "Jo. Fuller, in, Providence," and "Jo. Fuller, Providence." He also used a very distinctive anchor in his stamp. This usage of "living in" seems to occur primarily in the area of southeastern Massachusetts and northeastern Rhode Island, and it may possibly indicate some sort of connection among those who used it. An exception to this is "Briggs, in Keen," (New Hampshire); perhaps he moved northward after learning the trade in southern New England.

Although this section is concerned primarily with American 18th-century planes, it is interesting to compare them with early British planes, which were, after all, their direct ancestors and cousins. The British planes had many of the same features as the American ones; yet there are some strong differences. The vast majority of British planes were of beech, while yellow birch was most common in early American planes, with beech and mahogany used occasionally. The British chamfers were less pronounced, and the wedges tended to be less extreme. The British planes generally looked more refined and uniform, as might be expected of a then more technically advanced country.

A Britisher, Christopher Gabriel, and his contemporaries, working about 1770, began the manufacture of planes at the now-standard length of 241 mm. (9½").[3] After this date, almost all British planes were made to conform with that length, and American makers followed suit. In fact, many 18th-century planes found today show evidence of having been sawn off to a 241 mm. length, to fit standing on end in a tool chest with other planes - a most frustrating fact when it was the signed fore end that was cut off.

While much research remains to be done on early makers, we know from the excellent history of British plane makers by W. L. Goodman[4] that plane-making in Britain was not a casual trade; the maker learned his craft usually as an apprentice and set up his own shop only after years of studying under the eye of his master. That this same type of system was developed in the colonies is substantiated by the 1789 charter of the Providence (R.I.) Association of Mechanics and Manufacturers, which included plane makers. New members of this organization had to be approved by the Select Committee of the group or be certified as a member in good standing from another association, and to pay a fee, be at least 21 years

Fig. 1. 18th Century Moulding Planes. Varied length, wedged shapes, heavy chamfers, and fluting are characteristic of these American planes. Left to right, top row: C.E. Chelor[Wrentham,Mass]; Ion Ballou [Providence,R.I.]; F.Nicholson [Wrentham,Mass.]. Second Row: A.Smith[Rehoboth,Mass.]; I.Walton[Reading,Mass.]; E.Clark [Middleboro,Mass.]. Bottom Row: Phillipson [British]; C.Brett [s.e. Mass.]; Tho. Grant [New York - plane possibly a British import].

old, and "No person who is a journeyman, shall be admitted unless he has served a regular apprenticeship of seven years to a mechanic or manufacturing business, and can be well-recommended."[5] Planes made by two or three different makers that have strikingly similar wedges, handles, or shapes indicate that several master-apprentice relationships are awaiting our discovery.

With the similarities between British and American planes, and the obvious fact that most of the settlers of New England were British, some plane makers must have come to the New World from England. Only one maker has been established as a link between the two continents; Thomas Napier was listed in an Edinburgh directory as a tool maker in 1774-5 and in a 1786 Philadelphia newspaper was advertising as a plane maker.[6] Certainly there were others.

Plane-making in the New World did not spring up overnight, obviously. Evidence has been found that at least two men were importers of British planes. Planes have been found bearing the name "Tho. Grant, N. York," and some without the city name. Thomas Grant was on the New York poll lists in 1761 and 1768, but not in 1769 or later.[7] Grant's planes have a somewhat British appearance to them, the refined look, and beech wood. A plane has come to light[8] bearing both the stamps "Tho. Grant, New York," and "I. Cogdell." John Cogdell was a maker in London from 1750 to 1770.[9] Thus, we may assume that Grant was importing planes made by Cogdell and possibly others, and stamping his own name on them. Whether he actually made planes himself is unclear. Henry Wetherell was another apparent importer. The Norton, Mass., Vital Records show his marriage in 1760. He next appears in the 1790 Census as a resident of Chatham, Connecticut. His death date is uncertain.[10] Planes are known stamped "H. Wetherell, in Norton," "H. Wetherell, Chatham," and "H. Wetherell, Middletown" (Conn.).

Those planes marked Norton are very much in the American style, and in fact are quite similar to those of "E. Clark, Middleboro" (Mass.), who is, to date, a question mark but who also may have moved to Connecticut. However, Wetherell's Chatham planes appear much more refined and bear strongly British characteristics. Some of his later planes also bear the stamp of a crown nearly identical to a crown found on some of Grant's planes. Might this be a symbol for exports? Did Wetherell begin to import British planes when he moved to Connecticut?

A report in 1790-91 of the Providence, R.I., products of industry states that the total value of "Joiners' bench and moulding tools" annually was $1000.00. It goes on to state that "The particular prices, by reason of the great variety, cannot be ascertained, but are at present sold at something higher than those imported; the workmen not having full employ. But as the materials are so easily obtained. the prices might be reduced upon par with imported tools, if there was vent for large quantities."[11] This report was done in connection with the Providence Association of Mechanics and Manufacturers, an organization chartered in March, 1789, to promote domestic industry, spread technical knowledge, regulate quality, give aid to members, and the like.[12] Men in all phases of manufacturing became members, and among them were at least two plane makers. Perhaps because imported planes were cheaper in Providence, and probably elsewhere as well, men like Grant and Wetherell turned from manufacture to import.

Joseph Fuller was listed as a charter member in 1789, but his name then disappears and does not occur on the list of 1798. Whether he had a falling out with the group or just what happened is not certain. A Joseph Fuller was listed as a blockmaker in Providence directories up to 1832 and without an occupation to 1843.[13]

John Lindenberger (some planes are known marked simply "I. Lindenberger," and some "I. Lindenberger, Providence") was voted a member of the Association in April, 1789, and so he was an early, though not a charter, member. His name is also on the membership list of 1798. He died in 1817 at the age of 64.[14] His origins are uncertain, as he does not appear in the Providence birth or marriage records.

The inventory of Lindenberger's estate, done for the Probate Court, is a researcher's dream come true: three pages, listing the tools in his shop. Among those listed are; "3 Groving Ploughs," "962 Moulding Plane Irons," "14 float files," and "1500 feet Beach [sic] and Birch Stuff," to "1 Mahogany Secretary," "2 pr. Pantaloons," and "1 Cow."[15] Interestingly, there is no mention made of any so-called "mother planes," concerning which there is now a controversy. (A 'mother' plane is defined as a master plane used for mass production of a specified shape of moulding plane. It is in

Fig. 2. 18th Century Bench Planes

Offset and distinctively-shaped handles typical of 18th-c. bench planes. Note also heavy chamfers, fluting, and wedge design. Top to bottom: unsigned birch jointer; another unsigned birch jointer; crown moulding plane by E. Clark [Middleboro,Mass.]; panel plow by H.Wetherell.[Norton,Mass.]

Unsigned. Has typical 18th-c. characteristics: wood thumb-screws locking fence arms; wood depth stop; arms riveted to fence and the steel plate riveted to the body; heavy chamfer; fluting; and relieved wedge.

Fig. 3. 18th Century Plow Plane

fact opposite in contour to the desired finished shape). Neither is there a mother plane mentioned in the equally complete inventory of Aaron Smith of Rehoboth, Mass., who died in 1822.[16] Presumably then, mother planes came into use later in the 19th-century makers simply did not use them. The discovery of more such inventories of early plane makers should shed a great deal of light on the subject of the actual processes used in the manufacture of wooden planes.

A summary of other documented information to date concerning the various 18th-century plane makers follows. It is curious to note the large number of New England makers who worked in the southeastern Massachusetts-northeastern Rhode Island area. Infact, this area was evidently a center of early plane-making, with the craft spreading from there. 18th-century style planes have been found bearing the following Massachusetts town names: Dedham, Medway, Mendon, Middleboro, Norton, Reading, Rehoboth, and Wrentham; and in Rhode Island, Cumberland and Providence - all within about a 25-mile radius, with the exception of Reading.

The earliest documented American plane maker to date is Francis Nicholson of Wrentham, Mass. ("F. Nicholson, living in, Wrentham"). In his will, filed in December of 1753, Deacon Francis Nicholson set free his "Negro-man Caesar Chelo" and bequeathed to him "his Bedstead, Bed & Bedding, his Chest and Cloathing, his Bench & common bench-tools, a Sett of Chizells, one Gouge, one Vise, one Scythe & tackling, & ten Acres of land . . . & one third part of my timber."[18] To his only son John, Francis Nicholson left "all my Tools & timber, except what is being excepted," land, and other items.[19] In the inventory of his estate, the tools were lumped together at a value of £ 32.00.[20]

Francis Nicholson was in his 70th year when he died in 1753 and so was born about 1683. His birth is not to be found in the Wrentham Vital Records, and just where he came from is not yet known. Nicholson is reported to have approval in the church records of Rehoboth, Mass., in 1713.[21]

John Nicholson, the son of Francis, is more elusive. Planes are known stamped simply "I. Nicholson," "I. Nicholson, Wrentham," "I. Nicholson, living in, Wrentham," and "I. Nicholson, in, Cumberland." The "living in, Wrentham" stamps are the same as those used by both Francis Nicholson and Cesar Chelor.[22] John Nicholson is not in the 1790 Census in either Wrentham or Cumberland, and his final resting place is not known.[23]

Cesar Chelor, the freed slave of Francis Nicholson, made planes on his own bearing the marks "CE Chelor, living in, Wrenthem," "Cesar Chelor, living in, Wrentham," and "CE Chelor, Wrentham." Chelor married in 1758 and had 9 children, all born in Wrentham.[24] He died intestate in 1784, and in the inventory of his estate is referred to as "Tool-maker," with the lump value of his tools at 424 shillings, 4 pence.[25]

Next chronologically comes Jonathan Ballou of Providence, R.I. "(Ion Ballou, Providence"). He died on October 2, 1770, and the inventory of his estate[26] is much less complete than those of Lindenberger and Smith and simply lists "a large Number of Tooles of all

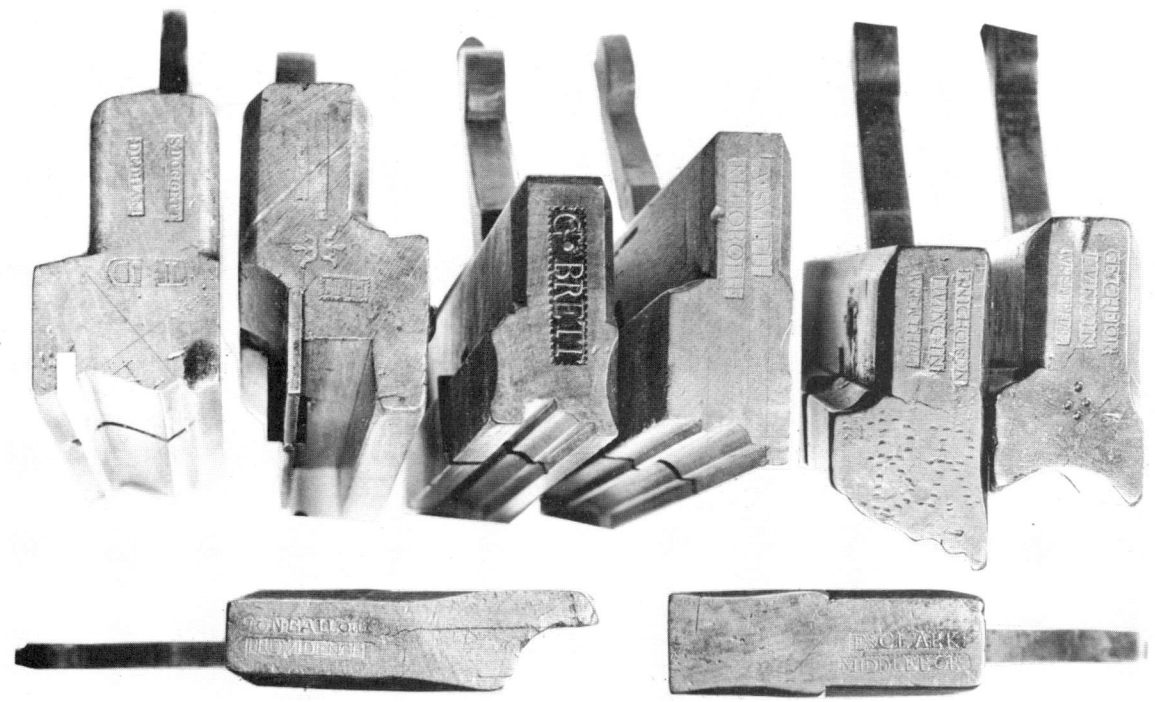

Fig. 4. Imprints on 18th Century Moulding Planes. Varied styles of fluting & chamfers, along with stamps of some 18th-c. American makers. Left to right, top row: S. Doggett, Dedham[Mass.](note whale-bone insert spline on sole); H. Wetherell, Chatham[Conn.](note crown stamp discussed in text); C. Brett (s.e. Mass. style); A. Smith, Rehoboth[Mass.]; F. Nicholson living in Wrentham[Mass.]; C.E. Chelor living in Wrentham[Mass.]. Bottom row: Ion Ballou, Providence[R.I.]; E. Clark, Middleboro[Mass.].

Kinds new and old with some Stock," valued at £19/4. This statement, however, shows that this is the man who made the planes. He was born in 1723 in the part of Providence that is now Lincoln, R.I.[27] In his will, dated August, 1770, he refers to himself as a "Shop Joiner" and leaves everything, unspecified, to his wife. They had no children.[28] With the proximity of Lincoln to Wrentham and Cumberland, one wonders whether there may have been a connection between Ballou and the Nicholsons.

Aaron Smith of Rehoboth is important for two reasons. The before mentioned inventory of his estate is a valuable reference, and he is a transition man, between the 18th and 19th-centuries. One can see a change in his planes from birch to beech and from the wide chamfer and fluting to a more simple 19th-century style. Smith's birth does not appear in the Rehoboth Vital Records, but his marriage in 1792 (and again in 1811) does. Perhaps he moved to Rehoboth upon his marriage, as he is not listed there in the 1790 Census. Of course, at age 21 in 1790 (he died at age 53 in 1822, thus having been born in 1769), he may not yet have been the head of a household and so not counted even though he could have been in Rehoboth at the time of the Census. He was counted in the Census of 1800.[29]

Smith's son, Aaron Mason Smith, died only twelve years after the father, in 1834. He had moved to New Bedford, Mass., and the inventory of his estate shows that he also made planes.[30] Thus, he is probably the maker of those planes stamped "A.M. Smith, Warranted." Aaron Smith also had a son named Ezekiel, who inherited his workshops.[31] A few planes are known stamped "E. Smith, Rehoboth," the town stamp being identical to the one used by Aaron. Thus we can be sure that Aaron's son Ezekiel did indeed make planes on his own, showing a vertical, father-to-son relationship between plane makers. Further, an Ezekiel Smith taught the trade of tool-making about 1845 in Blackstone, Mass., which is in the same area.[32] Much later an Ezekiel Smith appears in Worcester, Mass., making planes in the 1860's and '70's; planes marked "E. Smith, Warranted" are quite common. With further research, these two E. Smiths may be found to be the same man, or perhaps father and son.

Another transition man, and one who also left his business to his sons, is Nicholas Taber of New Bedford, Mass. ("N. Taber"). According to the Taber genealogy[33] he was born in 1761 and died in 1839 and had a son named John Marshall Taber. However, in the Bristol County Probate records, N. Taber's will was dated 1844 and proved in 1855. In his will, he left his shop to his son, John Marshall Taber, who became a prolific mid-19th-century maker.

A summary list of known 18th-century New England plane makers, with documented information to date, is presented in Table I.

TABLE I - NEW ENGLAND EIGHTEENTH-CENTURY PLANE MAKERS

Maker	Location Worked	Documented Dates
Jonathan Ballou	Providence, RI	b.1723, d.1770
C. Brett		
Briggs	Keene, NH	
Cesar Chelor	Wrentham, MA	freed 1753, d.1784
David Clark	Cumberland, RI	
E. Clark	Middleboro, MA	
B. Dean		
S. Doggett	Dedham, MA	
Benjamin Alford Edwards	Northampton, MA	b.1757, d.1822
Joseph Fuller	Providence, RI	b.1746, d.1822, Member PAMM 1789
J. Holmes		
I.[J.?] Jones	Medway, MA	
John Lindenberger	Providence, RI	-1789-, d.1817, joined PAMM 1790
L. Little,	Boston, MA	
Francis Nicholson	Wrentham, MA	b.1683, d.1753
John Nicholson	Wrentham, MA & Cumberland, RI	[son of Francis]
I. Pike	Dedham, MA	
I. Sleeper		
Aaron Smith	Rehoboth, MA	b.1769, d.1822
Nicholas Taber	New Bedford, MA	d.1761[?], d.1855
E. Taft	Mendon, MA	
I. Walton	Reading, MA	
H. Wetherel	Norton, MA	m.1760
	Chatham, Ct.	1790 Census, d.1797
H. Wetherell	Chatham & Middletown, CT	[son of above]

NOTES - CHAPTER II

1. W.L. Goodman, *BPM, op. cit*, pp. 118-119
2. John S. Kebabian, "More Eighteenth Century American Planemakers", *Chronicle of EAIA,* Vol. xxiv, No.2, p.25   (June 1971)
3. W.L. Goodman, *BPM, op. cit.*, p.33.
4. *Ibid,* pp. 28-36.
5. Charter of the Providence Association of Mechanics and Manufacturers, March 1789, printed by Bennett Wheeler, 1789.
6. W.L. Goodman, *BPM, op. cit.*, pp. 24-25.
7. Kenneth D. & Jane W. Roberts, *Planemakers and Other Edge Tool Enterprises in New York State*, [hereafter referred to as *Planemakers*], [Cooperstown,N.Y.,1971] (New York State Historiacal Association & EAIA), p.166
8. Elliot M. Sayward, "A Letter on Other Matters", *Chronicle of EAIA,* Vol. XXVII, No.4, December 1974, p.74.
9. W.L. Goodman, *op. cit, BPM,* p.65
10. J.S. Kebabian, *Chronicle of EAIA,* Vol. XXIV, No.2, June 1971, pp.25-26,*op.cit.*
11. Report on the Products of Industry in Providence, Jan. 1,1790 - Oct.10,1791,p.98
12. Charter of Providence Association . . *op. cit.* (Note No.5, above)
13. *Providence Directory,* Brown & Danforth. 1824, 1826, 1828, 1830, 1832, 1836-37, 1838-39, 1841-42, 1844, 1847-48, 1950, 1852-53.
14. Providence Vital Records.
15. Probate Records, Providence, R.I. Vol. 12, p.367-69.
16. Bristol County Probate Records, Vol. 60, p. 168.
17. J.S. Kebabian,"More on the 18th Century Planemakers of Wrentham, Mass.", *Chronicle of EAIA,* Vol. XXV, No.1, March 1972, pp. 15-16.
18. *Ibid*, p. 15.
19. *Ibid*, p. 16.
20. *Ibid*, p. 15
21. J.S. Kebabian, Unpublished research.
22. J.S. Kebabian, *op. cit.,Chronicle of EAIA, Vol.XXIV, No.2,*June 1971, p. 25.
23. J.S. Kebabian, Unpublished Research
24. Vital Records, Wrentham, Mass.Vol.I,p.42-43; Vol.2,p.266
25. J.S. Kebabian, *op. cit.,Chronicle of EAIA, Vol.XXV, No.1, March 1972, p.16.*
26. Probate Records, Providence, R.I. Vol. 5, pp. 537-39.
27. Adin Ballou, *An Elaborate History & Genealogy of the Ballous in America,* [Providence, R.I., 1888], p. 98.
28. *Ibid.*
29. R.L. Bowen, *Early Rehoboth,* [Rehoboth, Mass., 1950], p. 138.
30. Bristol County Probate Records, Vol.74,p.55
31. *Ibid,* Vol. 61, p. 373-79.
32. *Representative Men and Old Familiies of Rhode Island,* [Chicago,Ill.,1908],p.2304.
33. G.L. Randall, *Taber Genealogy, Descendants of Thomas, Son of Philip Taber,* [New Bedford, Mass., 1924], p.30.

The authors acknowledge the research and writings of John S. Kebabian published in the *Chrongile of EAIA,* referred to in the above Notes. His discovery of Francis Nichloson's will and subsequent research concerning both Francis and John Nicholson and Cesar Chelor has been a significant contributuion to the study of 18th century American planemakers.

Chapter III

Historical Survey of 19th Century Plane Making

Until at least 1820 the majority of joiners' tools were imported from England. At the beginning of the nineteenth century there were several planemakers working at Philadelphia.[1] While their individual production must have been relatively small, they were probably able to supply a substantial amount of tool requirements for local cabinetmakers and carpenters operating within twenty miles of the city. Documented planemakers listed in the available city directories are cited in Table II. Undoubtedly there were several others. Only a few of the larger cities published such directories before 1825. Except in these more populated cities annual publication was not generally common until after 1840.[2]

TABLE II

Listing of Planemakers working in United States during early part of 19th Century Documented from Directories

Name	Place of Work	Working Dates
Consider Alford	New York City	1812 - 1817
Enos Baldwin	Albany	1807 - 1817
	New York City	1817 - 1829
William Brooks	Philadelphia	1791 - 1807
George Butler	Philadelphia	1819 - 1835
John Butler	Philadelphia	1795 - 1830
Jo. Fuller	Providence	18thC.-1824
George Goldsmith	Philadelphia	1809 - 1853
Thomas Goldsmith	Philadelphia	1801 - 1837
Samuel Kennedy	New York City	1817 - 1822
Leonard Kenney	Albany	1818 - 1819
James W. Massey	Philadelphia	1808 - 1830
Samuel Massey	Philadelphia	1818
Thomas Napier	Philadelphia	1785 - 1810
R. A. Parrish	Philadelphia	1807 - 1845
Simeon Rowell	Albany & Troy	1820 - 1832
Elias Safford	Albany	1813 - 1821
William Vance	Baltimore	1804 - 1833
George White	Philadelphia	1818 - 1833

The first city directory published at Hartford, Connecticut was in 1825.[3] After 1838 directories were published there annually. Planemaking had become a significant trade at Hartford by 1820. At that date it is believed that at least two firms: Leonard Kennedy and D. & M. Copeland were in operation. Both firms are listed in the 1825 *Business Directory of the City of Hartford*. The brothers, Daniel and Melvin Copeland, born in Sturbridge, Mass. late in the 18th century, came to Hartford and probably learned planemaking there from Leonard Kennedy, Sr.[4] The latter may have made planes at Hartford late in the 18th century. The types of planes made by Kennedy at Hartford in 1810 are noted in an advertisement that appeared in the *Connecticut Mirror*. (See: Plate I) The Copelands remained in Hartford associated in various tool making firms until removing to central Massachusetts in 1842. At the latter location, Huntington, they continued engaged in planemaking, but on a much smaller scale. While planemaking at Hartford did not materialize into a large center, the trade was continued there by at least one firm until 1848. A very significant development did however result from the Copeland enterprise. This was the formation of H. Chapin's UNION FACTORY, established in 1826 at Pine Meadow.

Plate I

Newspaper Advertisement from:
Connecticut Mirror November 26, 1810
[page 3, column 5]
Connecticut State Library, Hartford, Conn.

[Announcement of sale of Leonard Kennedy's Sr. Shop with Stock of Tools.

JOINERS' TOOLS.
JAMES H. WELLS
HAS purchased the whole of Mr. Kennedy's stock of JOINERS' TOOLS forming a large assortment of:
Long and short Joiners, Jack and smoothing Planes, hollows and rounds, cavettos, O.G. Beads, moving Philisters, reeding, sash Philisters, Dados, Rabbit Planes, nosing, ogees, ovalos, quarter rounds, quirk ogees, astragals, cavetto and beads, quirk ogee beads, spring planes, band moulding tools, quirk ovaolos, cock beads, quirk ovalo beads, match planes, braces, gauges, and a great variety of other Tools, which will be sold at the old prices, and the assortment kept as complete as possible by frequent supplies from the manufacturers.
ALSO JUST RECEIVED
An addition to his assortment of imported Goods — best Braces with bright & black Bits, Plane Irons, Chisels, Squares, Saws, Files, Knives and Forks, Barlow Penknives, Razors, Scissors, &c.
Hartford, Nov. 26.

Hermon Chapin (1799-1866) began his apprenticeship at plane making in 1822 with D. &. M. Copeland in Hartford. Apparently he developed into an exceptionally good craftsman. It is believed that the Copeland brothers dissolved their partnership in 1825. Daniel then went into partnership with H. Chapin under the firm name of Copeland & Chapin. They leased a mill with water power on the Farmington River at New Hartford. This was located in Litchfield County, Connecticut, at a district known as Pine Meadow, about twenty miles northwest of Hartford. Daniel Copeland remained in Hartford where he operated a tool store selling both his own products and planes produced by Chapin. In 1828 this partnership was dissolved. Chapin maintained a business relationship with the new Hartford firm of M. & A. Copeland with whom he continued to supply planes.[5] The UNION FACTORY under the capable management of three generations of Chapins became one of the largest, most important, and certainly the longest continuously operating wooden plane manufacturing firm in the United States, 1826-1929.

Early in the nineteenth century Connecticut had achieved national leadership in industry and manufacturing.[6] This reputation for industrial supremacy was held by Connecticut manufacturers, at least until the close of the War Between the States in 1865. The mass production system of interchangeable parts using "jigs and fixtures" was developed here at Plymouth by Eli Terry in producing four thousand wooden tall clock movements on a contract dated 1807.[7] Until recently, unfortunately, Eli Whitney has been given total credit for initiating this system of manufacturing.[8] Other important Connecticut manufacturing during the 19th-century in addition to guns and clocks included pewter, buttons, tinware and brass products. Wrought brass was first produced in United States at Waterbury in 1802.[9]

It will not be surprising that documentation will emerge to the effect that planemaking in England was performed employing mass production techniques sometime late in the eighteenth century. The earliest documented mass produced wooden article was a system designed for making pulley blocks for ships. A block mill was perfected at Portsmouth, England in 1803.[10] Marc Brunel, a naturalized American and former Chief Engineer of New York City, held an English patent concerning the design of this machinery. It was Sir Samuel Bentham, originator of the circular wood cutting saw, who recommended Brunel's proposed system for block machinery to the English Admiralty in 1802.

Quite co-incidentally, the same year that H. Chapin commenced at his Union Factory in 1826, approximately six miles down the Farmington River at another grist mill site at the adjacent town of Canton, Samuel Collins began making axes with the establishment of the Collins Co.[11] Sales of the products were then also carried out at Hartford offices. Manufacturing was accomplished at Canton for the following one-hundred and forty years. This part of the village became known as Collinsville, where the firm achieved recognition as among the leading quality producers of axes, machetes and other edge tools.

The training of apprentices at the UNION FACTORY was perhaps as important as the manufactured tool products. This led to new establishments of joiner' tool firms, as well as supplying trained talents to other industries. L. C. Stephens learned rulemaking under Chapin and formed his own firm in 1854. William Winship, later a partner in the Springfield, Mass. planemaking firm of Hills & Winship, served his apprenticeship under Chapin. William Warner, later a partner in the Phoenix Factory, under the firm name of Warner & Driggs, planemakers at New Hartford, also learned the trade under Chapin. Nathaniel Chapin, an older brother by seven years, served as foreman at the UNION FACTORY in 1837. Later he established the Eagle Factory at New Hartford. Subsequently he removed to Westfield, Mass. making planes there under this firm name. Another brother, Philip Chapin, six years younger than Hermon, established a planemaking firm at Baltimore about 1833. He remained there until the Civil War at which time he returned to work at the Union Factory for a short period. It would appear likely that Philip probably received his training at the Union Factory.

The next largest plane manufactory in Connecticut was the Baldwin Tool Co. at Middletown, 1841-1857. This firm was established by Austin Baldwin who had formerly been in the plane business with his half-brother, Elbridge G. Baldwin, at New York City, 1830-1841.[12] Published information concerning Baldwin's plane business at Middletown has been extremely limited. The following brief account is transcribed from a history of Middlesex County, which concerned the industries at Middletown: - [13]

". . . Once more taking our note book, we will extend observations along the Arrowmammett River[14] which rises at Durham, flows through Middletown and empties into the Connecticut, affording many excellent water privileges yet unoccupied, besides those already in use. . . . And at last, though by no means least, the plane factory of Austin Baldwin. Mr Baldwin has long been extensively known as a maker of joiners' planes and none better than those who have had occasion to to experience the advantages of a good plane over a poor one. Planes of all patterns are here made to the amount of $25,000 a year, by twenty-eight workmen. . . " [Products of Industry in the 1850 U.S. Census recorded this value for their manufacture of 40,000 planes.]

Austin Baldwin became prominent in Connecticut politics.[15] After selling his interests in the Baldwin Tool Co. in 1857, he returned to New York, where he died in 1886.[16] The Baldwin Tool Co. is believed to have been taken over by the Globe Manufacturing Co. This firm was organized in 1849 locating on the West River in Middletown. "The goods manufactured at this establishment include builder's hardware and an extra fine quality of edge tools, said to be equal in temper and finish to any imported on the market."[17] Imprints on plane irons used by H. Chapin's UNION FACTORY and others have been observed: "GLOBE M'F'G Co./BALDWIN/Warranted/Middletown, Ct., U.S.A." Testimonials regarding the quality of these irons by such plane manufactures as: Robert Harron of New York; A.B.Seidenstricker of Baltimore; W.H.Pond of New Haven; Arnold & Crouch of Northampton; G.Roseboom of Cincinnati; E.W.Carpenter of Lancaster, Pa.; Obed Andrus, South Glastenbury, Conn.;

and B.Sheneman & Bros. of Philadelphia, Pa. are noted in the 1858 *Arrowmammett Works Trade Catalogue*. (See: Appendix) This advertisement acknowledges that "the Plane Irons were manufactured from W.S.Butchers, Superior Cast Steel" a product of Great Britain. While the Globe Manufacturing Co. continued to use the firm name of Baldwin Tool Co. at least through 1860,[18] soon after this became the Middletown Tool Co. At that time it is believed that wooden planes were discontinued in favor of making only plane irons.

Further down the Connecticut River at Saybrook on Long Island Sound planemaking was carried on from 1845 - 1884 by a succession of Denison firms: John Denison, L.Denison, J. & L.Denison (possibly not in that order) and finally G.W.Denison & Co.[19] A broadside, c.1845/1855, notes the variety and prices of "joiner planes" produced by John Denison. (See: Plate II) While these Denison firms were all relatively small operations, surviving planes, particularly attractive rosewood plows and sash filletsters, prove that a high quality product was manufactured by these concerns. The operations of the final firm, G.W.Denison & Co., 1868-1890 has been described from surviving records by Carlson.[20] This partnership consisted of Gilbert Wright Denison (assumed last name), Gideon K. Hull and Jedediah Harris who operated in the Winthrop section of Deep River (formerly Saybrook). A bill head printed during the 1870's noted: "G.W.Denison & Co., Manufacturers of Joiner's Plows and Moulding Planes, of SUPERIOR Quality".

Among many interesting imprints observed on Connecticut planes is: *"PHOENIX COMPANY/ Warranted/ Warner & Driggs"*. This firm is noted among planemakers in the 1849 *NEW ENGLAND MERCANTILE DIRECTORY*. located at New Hartford. Soon thereafter in 1853 they moved to the adjacent district of Barkhamstead, known as "Hitchcockville".[21] They occupied the former factory building used by Lambert Hitchcock, maker of famed stencilled chairs. Hitchcock had recently undergone bankrupcy. Their imprint was then changed to: *PHOENIX FACTORY/ Hitchcockville/ Warranted"*. Also then sharing the factory at the same date and manufacturing planes were the brothers, Arba and Alfred Alford, operating as the Alford Plane Co. They were brothers-in-law to Lambert Hitchcock and had formerly worked with him at the Hitchcock Chair Co.[22] On October 23, 1861 Alfred Alford bought out the Phoenix Company and continued the business alone until 1864, when he sold out the entire establishment to Stephens & Co.[23] They manufactured rules there until combining with Chapin interests in New Hartford in 1901 as Chapin-Stephens Co.[24] Another planemaking firm of relatively short duration and operating near New Hartford was the Winsted Plane Co., established in 1851, but becoming insolvent in 1856.[25]

Data from the 1850 and 1860 Products of Industry Sections of the U.S. Censuses, listed in Table III, provides an indication of the sizes of some of these Connecticut planemaking firms. During this ten year period H.Chapin slightly decreased the number of his employees by about 10%, but the production increased by about 10%. In 1850 a steam engine had been obtained rated at 10HP to run their machinery. James Killam at Glastenbury with only two employees was the smallest firm. The record for William H. Pond for 1850, who was established by 1847 at New Haven, could not be located. He became a relatively larger producer of planes. Advertisements for Sawheag Works in Wallingford and Wm. Warner in New Hartford, which

Plate II

JOHN DENISON,
MANUFACTURER OF
JOINERS' PLANES,
WINTHROP, CONN.

	Price.
Smooth Planes, Cast Steel Irons,	$0.55
Jack " " "	65
Fore " " "	90
Jointer " " "	1.05
Smooth " Double, "	80
Jack " " "	90
Fore " " "	1.35
Jointer " " "	1.60
Astrigals, 3/8 to 3/4 inch,	42
" 7/8 to 1 inch,	50
Beads, 1/8 to 3/8 inch,	45
" 1/2 to 3/4 inch,	55
" 7/8 to 1 inch,	65
" 1 1/8 to 1 1/4 inch,	75
" Double Box, to 3/8 inch,	55
" " " 1/2 to 3/4 inch,	62
" " " 7/8 to 1 inch,	75
" " " 1 1/8 to 1 1/4 inch,	85
" Full Box, 1/8 to 1/4 inch,	60
" " " 5 1-6 to 3/8 inch,	66
" " " 1/2 to 3/4 inch,	75
" " " 7/8 to 1 inch,	95
Coves, 3/8 to 5/8 inch,	42
" 3/4 to ? inch,	50
Center Beads, 1/8 to 1/2 inch,	62
Dado Wood Stops, 1/4 to 1 inch,	90
" Screw Stops, 1/4 to 1 inch,	1.34
Fillisters, with Cut and Boxed,	1.25
" drop stop, Cut and boxed,	1.88
" screw stop, Cut and boxed,	2.25
" screw, all Boxwood,	2.62
Ogees, 3/8 to 1/2 inch,	66
" 5/8 to 3/4 inch,	75
" 7/8 to 1 inch,	90
Reversed O. G., 3/8 to 1/2 inch,	66
" O. G., 5/8 to 3/4 inch,	75
" O. G., 7/8 to 1 inch,	90
Grecian Ovolos, 3/8 to 1/2 inch,	66
" " 5/8 to 3/4 inch,	75
" " 7/8 to 1 inch,	90
Hollows and Rounds, (setts, 9 pair,)	6.75
" " " pair, 1/4 to 1/2 inch,	65
" " " pair, 5/8 to 7/8 inch,	75
" " " pair, 1 to 1 1/2 inch,	85

	Price.
Match Planes, pair, 3/8 to 5/8 inch,	1.06
" " " 3/4 to 1 inch,	1.10
" " plated, 3/8 to 5/8 inch,	1.30
" " plated, 3/4 to 1 inch,	1.35
" " handles plated, 3/4 to 1 inch,	2.10
" " handles plank,	1.87
" " handles plank, plated,	2.12
" " handles plank, moving,	2.37
Plows, wedge arms, (no bitts,)	3.00
No. 2, " " "	2.62
Plows, screw arms, all box, (no bitts,)	4.50
" No. 2, fence and arms box, do.	4.12
" 3, arms box, do.	3.75
" 4, Dogwood arms, do.	3.37
" 1, Rosewood, do.	4.50
" 1, all box handle, do.	6.00
" 2, fence and arms box, do.	4.87
" 3, arms box, do.	4.50
" 4, Dogwood arms, do.	4.12
" 1, Rosewood, do.	6.00
Sash Planes, one iron,	60
" " two irons,	85
" " to move, two irons,	1.32
" " half box,	1.42
" " full box,	1.70
" " all boxwood,	2.25
Side Rabbets, per pair,	80
Square Rabbets, to 1 inch,	50
" " 1 1/4 to 1 1/2 inch,	65
" " 1 3/4 to 2 inches,	75
Skew " 1/2 to 1 inch,	50
" " 1 1/4 to 1 1/2 inch,	65
" " 1 3/4 to 2 inches,	75
" " Extra, for boxing,	25
" " " for Cut,	25
Torus Beads, to 3/4 inch,	60
" " 7/8 to 1 inch,	70
Table Planes, per pair,	85
Cutting Guage,	37
" " with handle,	75
" Common Marking Guage,	12
" " " all box,	18
" " " pannel,	25

BENHAM, STEAM PRINTER, 55 ORANGE STREET, NEW HAVEN, CONN.

Reproduced from an original broadside courtesy of John S. Kebabian.
[95% of original size, i.e. 5% size reduction]

Plate III. Advertisements from the *1850 Connecticut Business Directory*
[top, page 240; bottom, page 241]

Courtesy of Connecticut State Library, Hartford, Connecticut

appeared in the 1850 CONNECTICUT BUSINESS DIRECTORY [26] are illustrated in (Plate III).

TABLE III - PRODUCTS OF INDUSTRY DATA REGARDING
CONNECTICUT PLANEMAKING FIRMS FROM 1850 and 1860 U.S. CENSUS

1850

FIRM	Amount Capitalized	Number of Employees	Monthly Payroll	Annual Production Number of Planes	Annual Production Value of Products
A. Baldwin, Middletown	$15,000	30	$600	40,000	$25,000
H. Chapin, New Hartford	28,500	40	1000	-	30,000
J. Denison, Saybrook	2,500	5	150	1,750	3,300
J. Killam, Glastenbury	300	2	50	-	1,200
Sawheag, Wallingford	10,000	10	400	-	15,000
Wm. Warner, New Hartford	3,000	5	-	-	2,500

1860

Baldwin Tool, Middletown	60,000	75	1750	60,000*	36,000*
H. Chapin, New Hartford	46,000	36	1080	-	33,000
J. Denison, Saybrook	5,000	8	370	12,000	6.000
W. H. Pond, New Haven	4,000	6	240	18,780	15,000

* Also produced 2000 irons valued at $7,000

During the period of 1840 through 1860 there was considerable activity in planemaking at various towns in central Massachusetts in the Connecticut River valley. An account of this subject has been recently prepared by Sayward and Streeter.[27] It was at Amherst where several firms became prominent. The earliest of these is reported to be Hills, Wolcott & Co. They were succeeded by Samuel and Harvey Hills, operating as S. & H. Hills on March 16, 1829. Later these partners removed to Springfield. There subsequently the planemaking firm of Hills & Winship was formed, which were awarded a prize for tool products at the Boston Mechanic Exhibition in 1837.

The names of Luther Fox, George Burnham, Jr. and James Kellogg became prominent in planemaking at Amherst. Also Truman Nutting had established a plane factory in Amherst in 1831, operating there until 1852. His account books for this period survive.[28] About the time that Nutting started at this business, Luther Fox is believed to have soon followed. On June 29, 1831 he purchased "a water shop and land flowed by a pond and also the privileges that belong"[29] Subsequently, according to a town history report,[30] Luther Fox engaged George Burnham, Jr., an apprentice planemaker from East Hartford, Conn. to work at his shop as a journeyman. However soon after in 1843 he sold out to Burnham and others and left for Baltimore around 1847.

On April 13, 1841 Burnham formed a partnership with Aaron Ferry, Benoni Thayer and Hiram Fox, each owning a common quarter interest in Hiram Fox's shop and water privilege at East Amherst: "beginning at the Bridge on the road leading from Amherst to Pelham, running northwardly on the River. ."[31] Subsequently, as mentioned previously, the business of Luther Fox was added.[32] Soon after

Burnham bought out his partners and managed the business under his own name until selling out his shop and equipment on February 15, 1853. Details of this sale are recorded in a land deed,[33] partially transcribed: -

> ". . . land bounded by a butternut tree at the North bank of the River containing 11 acres with all the buildings thereon, including the mill, known as the PLANE SHOP, with all the machinery and fixtures therein and also the new SHOP or upper privilege, so called, with all the machinery and fixtures now in the same. . together with canals & dams connected. . . "

James Burnham, thought to have been a brother of George, subsequently sold the machinery, which was removed to Middletown, Conn.,[34] presumably the Baldwin Tool Co.

Examination of planes made by George Burnham during his tenure, 1844-1853, making these products at East Amherst positively reveal high quality workmakship, certainly the equal of any competitor manufactured at that time. A detail, recorded in Hampshire County Deed,[35] dated July 27, 1848, of peripheral interest noted: -

> ". . . I, Luther Fox of Baltimore in the State of Maryland in consideration of fifty dollars paid to me by George Burnham of Amherst. . .PLANEMAKER . . . receipt which I do hereby acknowledge do hereby give, grant, bargain, sell and convey unto the said Burnham, his heirs and assigns, PEW No. 36 on the lower floor of the East Meeting House in said Amherst. . "

After selling his planemaking machinery to James Burnham, George remained in Amherst and later formed a partnership with Stephen W. Gilbert making axe-handles. However, before this enterprise he equipped the former plane shop with presses and manufactured straw hats. James Burnham of Middletown, Conn., where presumably he had gone to work in the plane factory there, sold back the property of the former East Amherst plane shop to George Burnham on August 3, 1858.[36]

Details concerning James Kellogg's connections with the plane business remain as obscure as those for Burnham and Fox. The following account regarding Kellogg is transcribed from a history of Amherst published in 1896:[37] -

". . . . Perhaps the most important, certainly the most sucessful in its day, was the manufacture of planes at East Amherst. About 1835, James Kellogg bought from Eli Dickinson a shop at South Amherst . . . there he engaged in the making of bench planes and molders' planes. The business prospered, and a partnership was formed under the name of *Kellogg, Washburne & Fox* for its devolpment. This firm was dissolved in April, 1839, and immediately thereafter James Kellog and Hiram Fox formed a partnership "for the merchandising and manufacturing of joiners' tools in Amherst." [*Kellogg & Fox*] The firm was dissolved in 1840, Mr. Kellog continuing the business. [*J.Kellogg*] In 1839 the business was removed to that part of Amherst, which subsequently acquired the name of "*Kelloggville*". Here two factories were erected, one of brick and one of wood, which were stocked with machinery of the latest pattern. Success attended the new venture, the business increasing so rapidly that the factories were frequently unable to fill the orders which came from all parts of the country and even from abroad. Experts declare that better planes were never made than those sent out from Kellogg's factory [sic: undocumented statement probably influenced by local pride of authors] in Amherst, and that many years after the business was suspended orders for the goods continued to come in. When the works were in full operation some twenty men were employed and planes of all kinds were manufactured. The operatives were well paid and residing near the factories they formed a flourishing little community, which, as stated above, was christened "*Kelloggville*". . . A sketch of the business written in 1869, states that the woodwork of the planes was made from beech, box and rosewood, and that the irons were brought from New Haven and fitted at the factory. The average daily output from the factory was 150 to 200 planes. In 1886 the dam of the pond that furnished power for the factories was carried away and for several years the works remained idle. . . . "

It is suggested that Kellogg only had financial interests in the plane business, not being personally engaged in the actual manufacturing, other than being a manager. Previous to 1830 James Kellogg is listed in various Hampshire County Deeds as being a "trader" or "merchant". A deed dated March 17, 1831 noted Samuel Hills, "gentleman", selling property in Amherst to James Kellogg, "trader"[38] This may have been the date that Kellogg acquired Hills' plane business. In any event throughout his career with planemaking he also operated a mercantile store in Amherst. While local history reported that it was in 1835 that he entered the planemaking business in a partnership with Fox and Washburn at South Amherst, after 1840 from land deeds he apparently operated as sole proprietor at East Amherst, near the site of Burnham's factory. The earliest documented date as a planemaker is his listing at Amherst in the 1849 *New England Mercantile Union Business Directory*.[39] This same source incidentally listed George Burnham at East Amherst and Truman Nutting at South Amherst as planemakers. A similar directory for 1865 listed the firm James Kellogg and Son, planemakers at Amherst. On February 8, 1867 James Kellogg retired from business selling both his Amherst store[40] and his plane factory[41] to his Son, William. The latter deed noted: -

> ". . . on the Highway leading to Belchertown from East Amherst all buildings on the premises & water power, including the right of use of canal. . the shops and all the stock therein. . . "

William Kellogg continued the business at least until 1875.[42] No imprints on wooden planes for this firm or the previous, James Kellogg & Son, have yet been reported. The peak of Amherst planemaking was apparently between 1845-1853. After that it declined rapidly, as noted in the following report.[43]

> ". . . The following statistics show the rise and decline of this industry: In 1837, the value of planes manufactured was $8000, the number of employes 10, the amount of capital invested $3000. In 1845 the value of tools manufactured was $14,975, the numbers of employes 22. In 1855, the value of tools manufactured was $18,000, the number of employes 20. In 1865, the value of the product had declined to $3,000 and the number of employes to 3. . . "

Melvin Copeland, as previously noted, left Hartford, Connecticut in 1842 and settled in Norwich, Mass. This became the town of Huntington in 1855.[44] He was joined there by his brothers, Daniel, who died there in 1852 and Alfred, who died there in 1858. The firm of Copeland & Co., producing planes, is believed to have been in operation there until about 1856. Charles R. Copeland, a half-brother who was listed in 1839 and 1840 Hartford directories as a planemaker, was granted a mortgage from Alfred and Melvin on property in Amherst October 20, 1848.[45] Apparently Charles was working then as a planemaker at Amherst, possibly with George Burnham, Jr. Three years later when Charles pleaded to be an "Insolvent Debtor", Burnham was appointed "Assignee".[46] Subsequently, April 1, 1852, Burnham received a release from Alfred and Melvin Copeland on the mortgage they held on Charles' tenement and property in Amherst.[47]

Another Connecticut planemaker, who continued in this business at Westfield, Massachusetts sometime after 1837, was Nathaniel Chapin. He operated under the firm name of EAGLE FACTORY. Other than a listing in the 1849 previously mentioned *New England Business Directory*, the dates of his operation at Westfield are not known. He died at Westfield in 1876.

During the 1850's there were several planemaking concerns located in western Massachusetts that must have given considerable competition to the business of Amherst. Among these were: Arnold & Crouch at Northhampton; A. Kelley at Ashfield; Conway Tool Co. at Conway; H. Barrus at Goshen; H. Browning at Rowe; E. & T. Ring at Worthington and Greenfield Tool Co. at Greenfield. An indication of the extent of this business in 1855 at some of these towns is reported in Table IV. After 1855, except for the Greenfield Tool Co., planemaking in western Massachusetts declined in comparison to the expansion of this industry in New York and Ohio. In the 1875 Compendium of the Massachusetts Census reports for Franklin and Hampshire Counties, only three plane manufactures were listed at three towns. The values of these manufactured goods were reported: $1,000 at Amherst; $1,500 at Cummington; $25,000 at Greenfield. The decline from the data of Table IV is substantial.

TABLE IV
PLANEMAKING DATA FROM 1855 COMPENDIUM OF MASSACHUSETTS CENSUS

TOWN REPORTING	Number of Employees	Value of Product	Probable Firm Reporting (Author's suggestion)
Amherst	22	$18,000	2 - J.Kellogg & G.Burham
Ashfield	8	4,000	1 - A. Kelley
Goshen	14	9,500	1 - H. Barrus
Greenfield	80*	120.000*	Greenfield Tool Co.
Huntington	15	12,000	1 - Copeland & Co.
Williamsburg	43	25,000	1 - H.C. James
Worthington	8	4,000	1 - E. & T.Ring

* Estimated that 1/2 this figure applies to Planemaking as other toolmaking firms contributed to this amount.

Alonzo Parker is reported to have begun the manufacturing of joiner and carpenter tools at Conway in 1842.[48] This business apparently expanded rapidly. Parker soon affiliated with Horace Hubbard and others continuing the business as Parker, Hubbard & Co. In 1850 this was reorganized as the Conway Tool Co. The former owners were paid $18,000 for the property, building and one steam engine.[49] Eighty men were reported to have been employed at the factory.[50] A fire destroyed the factory in 1851.[51] The Directors with some residents of the neighboring village of Greenfield immediately reorganized as a joint stock corporation as the Greenfield Tool Co.[52] A factory was constructed at Greenfield[53] and tool manufacturing was started in 1852. The firm experienced financial difficulties throughout its tenure. The Greenfield Savings Bank assumed ownership of the plant by a mortgage deed granted June 29, 1876.[54] In 1880 the stockholders authorized a $60,000 Bond issue in an attempt to liquidate the indebtness.[55] The property, bounded by Arch Street and the Connecticut River Railroad, the machinery and the trade marks are described in detail within this Deed to the Trustee. From this information it is apparent that at this date the concern was also engaged in manufacturing cutlery in addition to joiner tools. Descriptions of the firm's trade marks are listed in Table V.

TABLE V
TRADE MARKS OF GREENFIELD TOOL CO. NOTED IN 1880 BOND DEED

Trade Mark	Remarks quoted from Bond Deed
Greenfield Tool Co. ⟨+⟩ Warranted Cast Steel	This mark is used on all our Diamond Stamp of Plane Irons and Extra Cast Steel Adzes & Hammers.
"Mason Bros" Cast Steel	Used on Plane Irons with Iron Caps
"Greenfield Tool Co." Greenfield, Mass.	Used on all First Grade Beech Planes
"New York"	Used on Second Grade Beech Planes

While the Bond Deed was recalled and cancelled Nov. 30, 1881, the liabilities of the company had not been discharged. An advertisement from the 1881 *Greenfield Directory* described the diversity of products being made at that date. Foreclosure of the mortgage by the Greenfield Savings Bank resulted in an auction of the property and factory. Henry Watson by virtue of a high bid of Twenty-thousand dollars acquired title to the Greenfield Tool Co. April 16, 1886. The demise of the firm occurred by fire: - [56]

> "Fire in Greenfield. . March 24,1887. . The old Tool Factory two hundred feet by twenty-five feet was totally destroyed by fire. It was owned by H.D.Watson Publishing Co. and occupied by Gorham D. Williams, a cutlery and plane factory. Mr Watson estimated losses on the building at $13,000 with $7000 insurance on the shop and $1050 on the machinery. . ."

During thirty odd years of planemaking by the firm it became the largest factory manufacturing this product in Massachusetts. At least three trade catalogues were published: 1861, 1869 and 1872. The title page and forward to the 1869 Catalogue are reproduced herewith. (Plate IV) This noted a total of 744 models and sizes of wooden planes. Other tool products included: rules, bevels, try squares, gauges and handles. After 1870 this operation was not profitable. Insufficient foresight to introduce new products to compete with the iron plane was likely a factor that contributed to financial failure in spite of apparent high quality manufacturing performed by this concern.

There were numerous other significant, but smaller plane firms in Massachusetts both in rural villages and cities throughout this state. Two examples of the former, operating after 1865 for about ten years, were H.L.Narramore at Goshen and J.F. & G.M. Lindsey at Huntington. Firms located at Boston, Lowell, Worcester, New Bedford, Springfield, New Bedford and Pittsfield, as well as many smaller towns, are noted in the Check List.

Documentation for operating dates of firms located in Boston has been accomplished by consulting directories. An excellent study of these concerns has been published, written by William Hilton.[57] Most of these firms were small operations and of short duration. Exceptions were: Thomas L. Appleton, 1878-1892; Porter A. Gladwin, 1865-1882; Charles Fuller, 1852-1887; James Stevens, 1836-1860; and Timothy Tileston 1820-1866. The successes of many of these Boston firms may be attributed to sales made in local hardware stores. Merchants as well as individuals from surrounding locations within a radius of fifty miles frequently visited Boston as a shopping center. Many hardware firms purchased planes from local makers and then applied their own imprints to these tools.

Numerous smaller and less important planemaking concerns were scattered throughout New England in New Hampshire, Maine, Vermont and Rhode Island. Addison Heald working at Milford, N.H., 1868-1895, was probably the most prolific manufacturer.[58] Wooden planemaking remained a significant industry in New England at least until 1870. While production was sufficient to take care of requirements from the residents of the states within this area, a general decline after 1855 resulted from competitive growth elsewhere. This began in New York state during the 1820's and shifted to Ohio early in the 1830's.

Illustrated Catalogue

AND

Invoice Price List

OF

Joiners' Bench Planes,

MOULDING TOOLS, HANDLES, &c.,

MANUFACTURED BY THE

Greenfield Tool Company,

GREENFIELD, MASS.

Greenfield:
FRANKLIN BOOK AND JOB PRINTING OFFICE.
1869.

WE take pleasure in presenting to our Customers, and the Trade generally, our NEW ILLUSTRATED CATALOGUE and INVOICE PRICE LIST of Mechanics' Tools. It has been revised and diligently compared with the other Lists now in use, and we believe it is as nearly perfect as any can be made. The Invoice numbers have *not* been altered from our List of 1861, and the prices are those adopted by *all* the leading manufacturers two years since.

We give special attention to the selection and packing of goods designed for shipment. Our long experience in supplying the California, South American and Australian trade with the kind of Tools manufactured by us, enables us to guarantee satisfaction in every particular. Our Moulding Planes are all made of first quality second growth split timber, thoroughly seasoned. Our premium Bench Planes are also made of split timber and straight grained, well seasoned and dry before being made up. All our work is done by good mechanics; we employ no convict labor, consequently are not obliged to receive work that is in the least defective in workmanship. We warrant all American Irons we use, except in common Bench Planes. If any Tools are wanted that are not mentioned in this list, we will make them from samples or drawings, on short notice. We are content to let our tools recommend themselves; the use of them will test their quality, and we are confident will give satisfaction. The Planes are all put up in good strong manilla paper and labeled.

Goods will be delivered at the Railroad Depot free of charge for package or cartage, and Insurance effected on the same, if desired. Boxes at cost.

All orders will receive prompt attention, and should be addressed to the

GREENFIELD TOOL COMPANY,
Greenfield, Mass.

Plate IV. Title and Front Page from Greenfield Tool Company's 1869 Invoice Price List and Catalogue.

Fig. 5. Planemakers' Floats

CATALOGUE
AND
PRICES OF PLANES,
MANUFACTURED BY
PHILIP CHAPIN,
Plane Manufactory 44 Light Street,
BETWEEN PRATT AND LOMBARD,
BALTIMORE.

BENCH PLANES.

Dbl Smooth,	To 2¼ Bit,	$1 12	Dbl Long,	To 2¾ Bit,	$2 75	Single Jack,	$0 87
Dbl Circular,	" " "	1 25	Dbl Coopers' Jointer,	To 3½ Bit,	4 00	Do. Fore,	1 38
Dbl Jack,	" " "	1 38	All Dbl Planes extra width per ¼ inch		12	Do. Long,	2 00
Dbl Fore,	" 2¼ " "	2 00	Single Smooth,		75	Do. Coopers' Jointer,	3 00
Dbl Trying,	" 2¾ " To 26 inch	2 50	Do. Circular,		88	Coopers' Crows,	75

Coopers' Hawksbill Crows,	$1 50
Do. Block Plane,	1 25
Tooth Plane,	1 00
Mitre do.	88

Plate V. Top Portion of Philip Chapin's Broadside [See following page.]

MOULDINGS.

Astragal. To ¾ inch,	$0 62
Do. Over "	75
Back Ogee, To ¾ inch,	62
Do. Over "	75
Back Ogee and Bead, To 1 inch,	1 12
Do. do. Over "	1 25
Back Ogee and Fillet, To ¾ inch,	87
Do. do. Over "	1 00
Do. and Dbl. Fillet,	1 00
Badger, per inch,	80
Band, Base or Bed Mould, per inch,	75
Extra for Handles in Moulding Planes,	50
Beads, To ½ inch,	62
Do. Over " per ¼ inch,	13
Do. Slip, To ¾ inch,	87
Do. Full or Key Box, Extra,	25
Do. 2 Tip do.	12
Belections, To 1 inch,	88
Do. Over "	1 00
Belections, Qk. To 1 inch,	1 12
Do. do. Over "	1 25
Book Case Plane,	1 25
Do. do. Box'd,	1 50
Centre Beads or Single Reeds,	87
Do. and Follower,	1 13
Chair, Front Plane,	87
Do. Scroll do. Mould,	75
Do. do. do. Bench,	1 00
Do. Tenanting,	1 50
Do. do. Box'd,	2 00
Coach Routers, Single,	1 25
Do. do. Dbl.	3 50
Do. Beading Hubs,	75
Do. do. do. Dbl. Iron Face,	1 50
Do. T Plane,	1 00
Cock Bead,	63
Coping Planes, Ovalo,	75
Do. do. Gothic,	87
Cornice and Cabinet Ogees, per inch,	80
Cove, or Scotia,	63

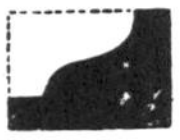

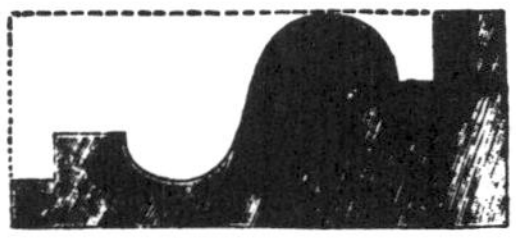

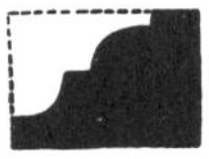

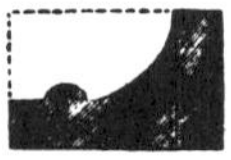

Cove and Beads, To 1 inch,	$0 87
Do. do. Over "	1 00
Cut Thrust,	1 25
Do. Brass Stop,	1 37
Do. Screw do.	1 75
Draw Plane,	75
Filletsters,	1 75
Do. Box and Cutter,	2 75
Do. do. Screw Stop,	3 75
Extra for Screw Arms, Apple,	75
Do. do. Box,	1 00
Gothic Bead,	1 00
Do. 2 Irons,	1 38
Gothic Reed,	1 12½
Do. 2 Irons,	1 50
Grecian Ogee, To 1 inch,	88
Do. do. Over to 1½,	1 00
Do. do. " per inch,	75
Grecian Ogee and Splay, To 1 inch,	1 25
Do. do. do. Over to 1½,	1 38
Do. do. do. " per inch,	87
Grecian Ogee and Square, To 1 inch,	1 25
Do. do. do. Over to 1½,	1 38
Do. do. do. " per inch,	87
Grecian Ogee and Square, To 1 inch,	1 25
Do. do. " Over to 1½,	1 38
Do. do. " " per inch,	87
Grecian Ovalo, To 1 inch,	87
Do. do. Over to 1½,	1 00
Do. do. " per inch,	75
Grecian Ovalo and Fillet, To 1 inch,	87
Do. do. do. Over to 1½,	1 00
Do. do. do. " per inch,	75
Grecian Ovalo and Bead or Square, To 1 in.	1 12
Do. do. do. Over to 1¼,	1 25
Do. do. do. " to 1½,	1 38
Do. do. do. " 1½ pr in.	87
Hand Rail Plane,	1 00

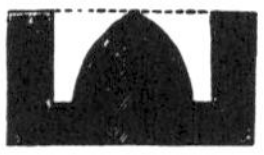

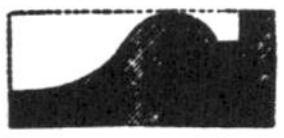

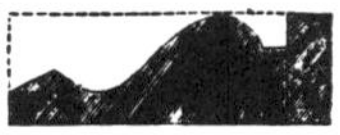

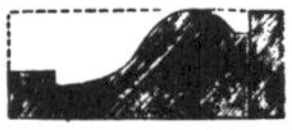

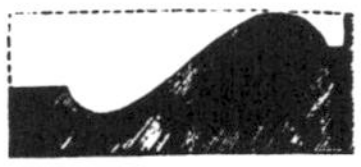

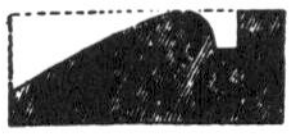

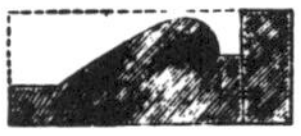

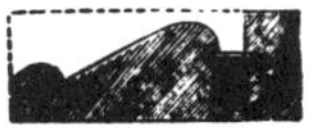

Hollows and Rounds, per pair to No. 10,	$1 13
Do. do. " Over to 18,	1 25
Do. do. " " 24,	1 50
Do. do. Circular,	1 50
Match Planes, To ½ inch,	1 37
Do. do. " ¾ "	1 50
Do. do. " ⅞ "	1 62
Do. do. " 1 "	1 75
Do. do. Extra for Plating,	37
Do. do. Over 1 inch, Standing,	2 50
Do. do. " 1 " Plated,	3 00
Do. do. " 1 " Slide Arms,	3 50
Do. do. " 1 " Screw do.	4 00
Do. do. Extra Boxing Groove,	50
Do. do. do. 2 set bits,	50
Meeting Rail Plane,	75
Moulding, To Drawing, per inch,	1 00
Nosing Planes,	75
Do. do. 2 Irons,	1 25
Do. do. Handle,	1 25
Do. do. do. 2 Irons,	1 50
Ogee, To 1 inch,	63
Do. Over to 1½,	75
Ogee, Feather Edge,	87
Ogee and Fillet,	88
Ogee Qk, To ¾ inch,	75
Do. Over to 1 inch,	87
Do. " to 1¼ "	1 25
Ogee Qk and Bead, To ¾ inch,	1 00
Do. do. Over to 1 inch,	1 12
Do. do. " 1¼ "	1 25
Ovalos, To 1 inch,	75
Do. Over to 1½ inch,	87
Do. " 1½ per inch,	75
Ovalos Qk, To ¾ inch,	87
Do. Over to 1 inch,	1 00
Do. " 1¼ "	1 25
Ovalos Qk and Bead, To ¾ inch,	1 12
Do. do. Over to 1 "	1 25
Do. do. " 1¼ "	1 50
Pilaster, No. 1,	1 75

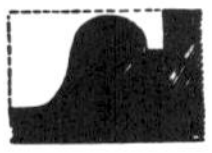

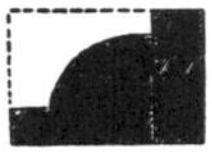

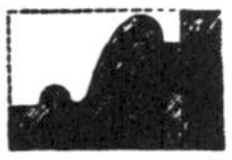

Pilaster, No. 2,	$1 88
Do. " 2, 2 Bits,	2 25
Plows, Wood Stop, Slide Arm,	3 50
Do. Screw Stop,	4 25
Do. do. Brass Cap,	5 00
Do. do. do. Tip'd,	5 50
Do. do. do. Riveted, do.	6 50
Do. Apple, Screw Arms, as above.	
Do. Box, do. Extra,	50
Do. do. Fence, "	75
Do. all Box, "	1 50
Do. half set Bits, less,	50
Rabbets, Skew, To 1 inch,	75
Do. do. " 1¼ "	87
Do. do. " 1½ "	1 00
Do. do. " 1¾ "	1 13
Do. do. " 2 "	1 25
Do. do. " 2¼ "	1 50
Do. Extra ea. Cutter and Handle,	25
Do. Square, To 1 inch,	87
Do. do. Over 1 "	1 00
Raising Plane, per inch,	1 00
Sash Planes, Belection, Slide Arm,	2 75
Do. do. Screw,	3 00
Do. Bevel, Slide,	2 50
Do. do. Screw,	2 75
Sash, Gothic, Slide,	2 75
Do. do. Screw,	3 00
Sash, Lambs Tongue, Slide,	2 75
Do. do. Screw,	3 00
Sash, Ogee, Slide,	2 75
Do. do. Screw do.	3 00
Sash, Ovalo, Slide Arms,	2 50
Do. do. Screw do.	2 75
Do. do. Extra for Full or Key Box,	50
Do. do. Self Regulating,	50
Do. do. do. Brass Arms,	75
Sash, Filletsters, Slide Arms,	2 50
Do. do. Screw do.	3 00
Side Rabbets, per pair,	1 50
Side Rounds, do.	1 50
Slat Planes,	62
Do. Box'd,	75
Do. for Blinds,	2 00
Snipe Bills, per pair,	1 50
Do. Shoulder Box,	2 00
Spar Plane,	1 12
Table Plane, per pair and Gage,	1 50
Traversing Planes,	2 00
Weather Board Plane,	62
Do. do. Handle,	1 00
Do. do. Moving Fence,	2 00
Spoke Jarvie,	1 50
Whip Makers Plane,	1 12

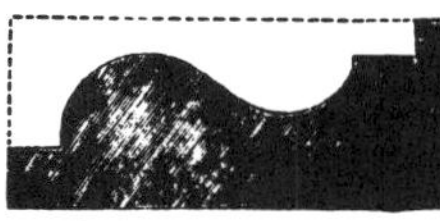

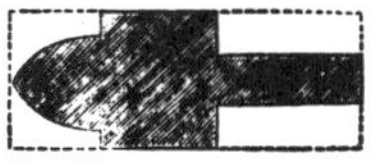

The Subscriber Manufactures and has for sale Tools of all kinds used by wood workmen, naming in part, Marking, Cutting, Mortice and Pannel Gauges; Wood Turning, and Wood Screws, all sizes, viz: Gage, Hand, Foot, Tail, Head and Clamp Screws; Sash Clamps, Mallets, Chissel and Auger Handles, Bevels, Squares. Rules, Saws, Hatchets; Braces and Bits, in sets and separate; Spirit Levels, Chissels, Augers, Gimblets, Oil-stone, Scrapers, Saw-sets, Screw Drivers, Hammers, Wrenches, Compasses, Files, Drawing Knives, Spoke Shaves, Mitre Squares, Venitian Blind Chissels, &c. in all their varieties.

PRINTED BY JOHN D. TOY, CORNER OF MARKET AND ST. PAUL STREETS, BALTIMORE.

Plate V. Philip Chapin's Broadside [continued from preceding page

At Newark, New Jersey two planemakers operated for several years: George W. Andrus, 1836-1861; Abraham Mockridge, 1836-1872. The latter was also connected with the firm Mockridge & Francis, 1835-1870 and also Mockridge & Son, 1870-1898. Both concerns also operated as tool and hardware stores.

Among several documented planemakers working at Baltimore, Maryland, R.W. Maccubbin operated the longest time, 1847-1871. A bead plane of "boxed and slipped" construction with his imprint has been observed. This is rare for American practice, and may indicate English training, for which technique is not uncommon. Philip Chapin, brother of Hermon Chapin of the UNION FACTORY at New Hartford, Conn., operated at 44 Light Street, Baltimore until about 1861, after which he returned to Connecticut. It is not certain as to his starting date at Baltimore, but he is listed there in an 1842 directory. A broadside, which P. Chapin called *"CATALOGUE and PRICE LIST of PLANES"* is illustrated, showing identifications of many mouldings. (See: Plate V) This is the only known reference in any American trade advertisement as to *"TRYING PLANE"* as a type of Bench Plane.

Planemaking in Pennsylvania did not become a major trade during the nineteenth century. At Philadelphia this was a significant business during the late eighteenth century. A sufficient number of planemakers worked there through 1850 to take care of local requirements, but after 1860 this trade rapidly diminished. Samuel H. Bibighaus, planemaker at Philadelphia, 1840-1867, noted on a price list, that he was: *"SUCCESSOR to JOHN BELL"*. This was published as a broadside and is dated c.1852, as the working dates for John Bell from Philadelphia Directories were 1829-1851. Israel White, working there 1831-1839, was granted a Letters Patent for a 'Pannel' Plow,[59] noted on the illustrated broadside. (Plate VI) Other than at Philadelphia the only location in Pennsylvania where planemaking achieved prominence was at Lancaster. Emanuel W. Carpenter, a planemaker working there, was granted three patents. These were: *Improvement in Tounge & Groove Planes, Jan.30,1830; #594, Plow Plane, February 6, 1838; and #6225, Adjusting the position of Plane Irons and Regulating the Throats of Planes, March 27, 1849.*[60]

The major growth of wooden planemaking in the 19th-century America after 1830 was not in New England, but occurred first in New York State and later in Ohio. This is not surprising in view of the completion of the Erie Canal, the migration westward and the resulting building requirements as settlements were established and expanded. Details of these developments regarding New York planemaking and edge tool manufacture have been previously published.[61] The Check List (See Appendix) notes some 214 firms in operation in New York State during the 19th-century that either made or sold wooden planes. The important centers and dates that this trade became a significant trade are noted in Table VI. While numerous New York firms contributed to planemaking, three enterprises are noted of major importance: D.R.Barton at Rochester, 1832-1875 (succeeded by Mack & Co, in business until 1924); L. & I.J.White, Buffalo, 1840-1940; and Auburn Tool Co., 1864-1893. (succeeded by Ohio Tool Co.)

ISRAEL WHITE,
PLANE MANUFACTURER,
CORNER OF
Callowhill & Fourth Sts.
PHILADELPHIA.

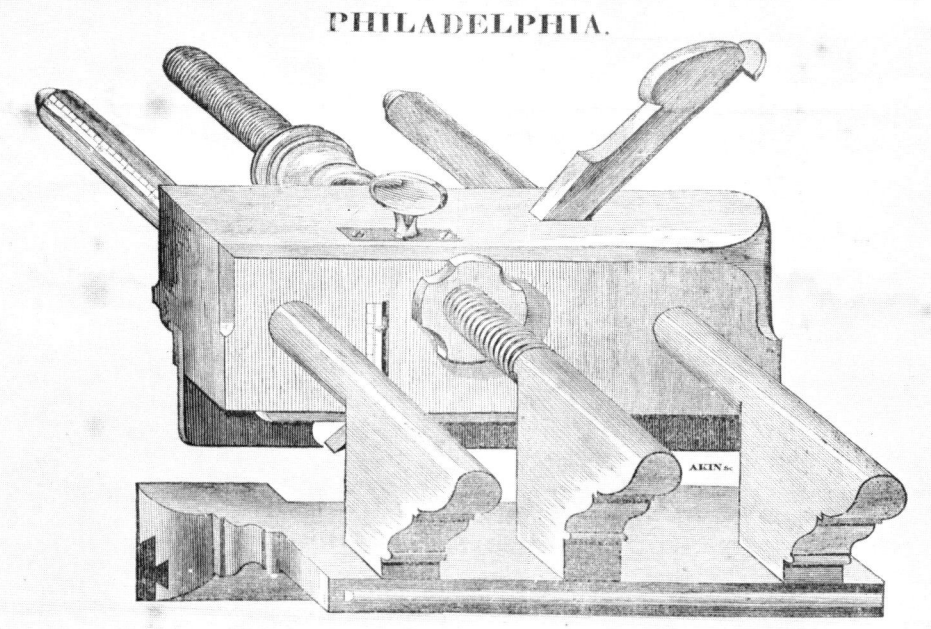

ISRAEL WHITE'S PATENT PLOW.

The following recommendations of the **PANNEL PLOW**, by Architects, House Carpenters, Cabinet Makers, and Mechanics, is a sufficient testimony of its utility; the price of which is nearly as low as Plows made on the old principle.

Grooving Planes, Sash Planes, and Fillisters, are also made on the above Patent, improved principle. A large assortment of all kinds of Planes are constantly on hand. A liberal discount made to Merchants and others.

All orders punctually and promptly executed.

PHILADELPHIA, November 12th, 1833.

WE, the undersigned, have examined a Plow, invented and made by Israel White, Plane Maker of this city. It possesses the following advantages over Plows on the old principle.

1st. It has three arms, the middle one being a screw arm, which acts as a self-regulator to the whole, and it can be fixed in half the time other Plows can.

2nd. The liability of either fence or arms to break is completely obviated.

3rd. The Plow can be fixed at any distance required, the fence being always parallel to the plate, lengthways.

4th. A rule is inserted on the first arm, and also one in the side of the Plow, which gives the distance of the fence from the plate, and the depth of the groove required. The trouble of measuring is saved by this method.

The Plow is of the usual size, and we cheerfully recommend it as a useful, as well as an ingenious invention; it is superior to any Plow we have ever seen. Great praise is due for the manner in which the article is executed.

ARCHITECTS.
John Haviland,
William Strickland,
Jesse Ford.
HOUSE CARPENTERS.
Daniel Smith,
Jonathan Johnson,
Philip Justus,
Preston C. Firth,
L. Coursaily,
Jesse Johnson,
Samuel Bowers,
Reuben Haines,
Joshua H. Coulter,
George Loudenslager,
Frederick F. Johnson,
George E. Lippincott,
G. F. Schell,
C. H. Winters,
W. H. Ellis,
William Thane,
Samuel Copeland,
David E. Hance,
John O'Neill,
George W. Wharton,
John M. Ogden,
Wm. H. Fulton,
Job Gibbs, Jun.

William Moulton,
George C. Roach,
Seth Hicks,
Benjamin Swager,
Francis Clinton,
David R. Hewes,
John A. Miskey,
William Thackary,
John Elwell,
P. Senneff,
Daniel Maule,
Joseph Smith,
Thomas Davis,
Moses Lancaster,
Lewis Bitteng,
John Longstreth,
Nicholas Mecker,
Job Gibbs, Sen.
Jesse Williamson,
Michael Baker,
John B. Cole,
Wm. Wagner,
James Weir,
George Link,
Jacob Beck,
D. Henry Flickeir,
Joseph Strahan,
Daniel Knight,

James Mitchell,
Egbert Sowerudeke,
John Kellock,
William A. Burns,
John W. McMahon.
Samuel B. Rudolph,
William Brown,
Henry Leides,
Hugh Donaldson,
David P. Lewis.
George F. Jackson,
Samuel Burr,
John Williams,
Gustavus S. Ford,
J. Hopper,
Edward Hatch,
Foster M. Savidge,
John Snyder,
David Ball,
Samuel D. Paynter,
William F. Reed,
Matthias Carr,
John Allen,
George Perry,
Joseph Wise,
John A. Miller,
N. Walton,
Pheneas H. Binch,

Jonathan Rubicam,
Edward Turner,
William Kyfor,
Charles Snyder,
B. Wily,
Thomas Sutton,
M. Garnett and Son,
E. Green,
Abraham Strickley.
CABINET MAKERS.
Cook & Parkins,
Chas. H. & John F. White,
Barry & Brickbaum,
James R. Ramsey,
C. L. Rowand,
Urban Lynch,
John Yard,
M. Bouveir,
S. Bouveir
PIANO FORTE MAKERS.
E. N. Scheer,
C. Roos,
George Pitsch,
Syle Seusevan,
O. Shaw,
E. Blakeman, Sash Maker,
Henry Keller, Coach Maker
John Underwood, Picture Frame Maker.

J. S. PAUL, Printer, 119, North Fourth Street,

Plate VI. Broadside of Israel White [from collection of Oliver W. Deming].
[approximately 40% reduction in size from original]

TABLE VI

Movement of Planemaking through New York State

City	Date First Established	Date Achieved Substantial Production
Albany	1807	1828
Utica	1820	1830
Auburn	1821	1834
Rochester	1827	1840
Buffalo	1828	1844
Troy	1828	1844

Both the Barton and White firms, respectively located at Rochester and Buffalo, established reputations as being among the leading manufacturers in the nation for cooper and other edge tools. Planes were probably an important, but not major, part of their productions. Both firms published extensive trade catalogues of their tools. The Auburn Tool Co. was established from a succession of firms, commencing with Dunham & McMaster, 1821, who employed contract labor at the New York State Prison located at this village. In 1893 the Directors of this concern purchased the Ohio Tool Co. at Columbus, Ohio and also continued in the plane business at Auburn until about 1914, but under the name of the Ohio Tool Co. Mention is made of Bensen & Crannell, at Albany, 1844-1862 and various firms at Troy of English-born Robert Carter, which he managed 1831-1861 as being smaller plane firms, but making high quality products. Leonard Kennedy, Jr. was among the numerous Connecticut planemakers that migrated to New York State. In 1825 he located in Utica. His advertisement appearing in the 1828 *Utica Directory* is illustrated. (Plate VII) This is the earliest directory advertising exclusively for the product of planes. In New York City during the nineteenth century there were at least 86 firms merchandising planes. The majority were wholesale operations and did not manufacture planes. Sales by these hardware dealers, many of whom stamped their own firm imprint name on these planes, were important contributions to the growth of this industry.

Early in the 1830's planemaking at Ohio became a well established business at Cincinnati. This city, located on the navigable Ohio River, had become both a prominent manufacturing center and an important distribution point for the growing west. Not only was the population composed of a large number of residents formerly from the east, but also had a substantial number of foreign born. Planemaking was no exception. John Creagh was a native of England; Thomas Fugate from Maryland; Joseph Lyon from Massachusetts.

CARPENTERS' & JOINERS'
Tool Manufactory

LEONARD KENNEDY & CO.

Having recently erected a large work-shop at the head of Broadway, they hope to have it in their power to supply all demands in "their line of business."— They manufacture all kinds of

MOULDING TOOLS,
AND
BENCH PLANES.

Their Tools are made from the best *second growth white beech,* and are warranted to work well. We are disposed to think that we can supply merchants with Tools as *good* and as *cheap* as they can be obtained at any other establishment. We pledge ourselves not to be undersold by any manufactory in the U. States, not excepting the one at Auburn.

All Tools manufactured by L. Kennedy & Co. Hartford, Conn. Kennedy & White, New-York, or L. Kennedy & Co. Utica, not proving good, will be repaired gratis.

The subscribers intend keeping on hand a few first rate

SAWS, BRACES & BITTS,
SQUARES, &C.

for retail customers.

L. KENNEDY & Co.

Utica, July, 1828.

Plate VII. Advertsiement of Leonard Kennedy & Co. from *1828 Utica Directory*

Two advertisements in the 1829 Cincinnati Directory noted:

PLANE and BRUSH MANUFACTORY
No. 231, Main Street, Cincinnati
CREAGH & RICKARD
Keep constantly on hand, *(of their own manufacture)*
a large and general assortment of
PLANES AND BRUSHES
warranted of the best materials and workmanship,
which they offer *wholesale* and *retail* on the most accomodating terms.
Together with a select assortment of *EDGE TOOLS, &c., &c.*
*N.B. Orders from any part of the Western County punctually
attended to and neatly packed, if addressed as above.*

PLANE MANUFACTORY

Thomas Fugate informs the *CITIZENS* of Cincinnati and Vicinity that he has established himself in the above business on Main Street, between Sixth and Seventh, where he keeps on hand PLANES and JOINER'S TOOLS of every Description and is prepared to fill orders on shortest notice.

(Advertisements from *The Cincinnati Directory for 1829*, Robinson & Fairbank)

An advertisement in the 1842 *Cincinnati Directory* noted "LYON, McKINNEL & CO., PLANE MANUFACTURERS & EDGE TOOLS, *successor to John Creagh*, Main Street between 5th & 6th." By 1841 there were reported to be four plane factories employing 34 hands and producing goods valued to the amount of $95,000.[62] *Sketches and Statistics of Cincinnati* reported that by 1851 this had increased to seven establishments employing 96 hands and producing goods valued at $167,000.[63] Accounts from this source stated:

> "E.F.Seybold, 207 Main St. (establashed 1836) is one of the oldest manufacturers in this line. His products are planes, squares, gauges and saws, to the annual value of $50,000. His sales rooms are depots also of truss hoops, Coopers' & Carpenters' edge tools are also made here or in the immediate vicinity of which are sold to the value of $60,000, fifty hands, raw materials 40%. Sells also extensively, mechanics tools of all descriptions."
>
> C.B. Shaefer & Co., salesrooms, 224 Main St., Factory on Miami Canal, manufactures planes, squares, gauges, bevels, etc. of all descriptions; value of planes, etc. $50,000, also edge tools, such as coopers' carpenters & edge tools. One factory. 25 hands employed, raw material 35%."

While Cincinnati continued to serve as an important hardware and tool distribution center, the manufacture of planes and other edge tools there declined after 1850. Competition from less costly goods at Columbus was likely a factor.

Previous to 1850 planemaking was performed by several other firms at various locations in Ohio. A broadside noted: *"List of JOINER'S TOOLS, Manufactured and Sold Wholesale and Retail by F.K.Collins at Ravenna, Portage County, Ohio"*[64] This is dated July 5, 1838 indicating an early business at this northeastern town. An imprint "WHITE & SPEAR" Warren, O. and is dated before 1852.[65] Warren is not very far from Ravenna.

Imprints from the firm "DENNING & CAMPBELL, Chillicothe,O." have been recorded. From advertisement published in the *Scioto Gazette,* printed at Chillicothe, this firm has been dated 1843-1856.[66] An advertisement from this source, dated September 29, 1847, noted the following:

> HARDWARE. DENNING & CAMPBELL. *Sign of the MILLSAW, PLANE and PADDOCK*, east side of Paint Street, Chillicothe, WHOLESALE and RETAIL DEALERS in American and English HARDWARE and Saddlery Goods, and although they do not boast of importations direct from Birmingham or Sheffield, England, (as do their neighbors) or offer to sell lower than can be bought in Eastern cities, they do assure their liberal patrons and generous public that they will sell the same style and quality goods in their line as low (if not a little lower) as they can be bought in this market. . . " [67]

The earliest record located of tool making at Columbus appeared in a *Report of the Directors and Warden of the Ohio State Penitentiary,* dated December 1841: - [68]

> ". . . There are in the employ of Messrs. Hall and Jenkins some thirty or forty convicts at tool making and cabinet work. Tools such as manufcatured by them are not made in this State, so far as we are advised, but have principally supplied from the Auburn Prison in the State of New York. . . "

From previous Ohio Penitentiary Reports it is learned that Peter Hayden had similar contracts for the manufacture of saddlery hardware. He had earlier such contracts at Auburn, N.Y., where the practice of using convict labor making planes had started about 1821. Use of prison labor by contract of highest bid dated as early as 1817 at Columbus.[69] It is possible that Peter Hayden was responsible for the initial tool contract at Columbus, The Ohio Tool Co. was incorporated in 1851, capitalized at $190,000.[70] George Gere, a retail and wholesale hardware dealer was elected president and Peter Hayden was among the seven Directors. Locally this firm was called the PLANE FACTORY, as the principal product was carpenters planes.[71] By 1865 this concern had become among the largest and most important plane manufacturers in the United States.[72] However competition from the Sandusky Tool Co. and the marketing of the iron Bailey plane by Stanley Rule & Level Co. after 1870 undoubtedly halted further growth. The use of prison labor is believed to have continued until Nov. 14, 1893 when the firm was purchased by the Auburn Tool Co. Operations were combined and incorporated under the name of the Ohio Tool Co. at Auburn, N.Y. Planes were manufactured at Columbus until 1914 when the operations were removed to South Charleston, West Virginia. In trade catalogues published by the Ohio Tool Co., after the merger with Auburn Tool Co., the founding date is noted as 1823. This is believed to refer to the Auburn Tool Co.'s predecessors, rather than operations at Columbus.

The Sandusky Tool Co., located about 100 miles due north of Columbus on Lake Erie, was organized in 1869. Within a short period this firm was among the five leading wooden plane manufacturers in the United States. In 1885 this concern published a 77-page *Illustrated Catalogue and Price List of Tools*. Four pages from this (Plate VIII) are reproduced which include a comparative listing of wooden planes made by the other then four leading manufacturers: Auburn Tool Co., H.Chapin's Co., Greenfield Tool Co. and the Ohio Tool Co. Planes were manufactured by this firm into the twentieth century, but the product was changed to forks and hoes, until the business was discontinued about 1926.

The principal wooden plane firms operating in the United States after 1865 are noted in Table VII. Advancing technology with the perfection of the iron plane, various combination metal planes and automated wood-forming machinery were the principal factors that brought the end and outmoded the wooden plane.

J. E. MARSHALL,	MOZART GALLUP,	C. B. LOCKWOOD,
President.	Treas. & Gen. Manager.	Secretary.

THE SANDUSKY TOOL COMPAMY.

SANDUSKY, OHIO, Jan. 1st, 1885.

GENTLEMEN:

We have the pleasure of presenting the Trade a new and enlarged edition of our Illustrated and Descriptive Catalogue.

This issue will be found more complete in every particular than any heretofore published.

Among other improvements in this edition, we take pleasure in calling the attention of the Trade to OUR NEW AND ORIGINAL COMPARATIVE LIST OF PLANES, showing at a glance the Number used by each of the manufacturing companies to designate the same Plane.

We desire to impress particularly upon the minds of all purchasers that every article sold by us IS FULLY WARRANTED.

In consequence of numerous changes having been made in list prices on some goods, we request that all former Lists be destroyed AND ORDERS MADE FROM THIS ONLY.

Soliciting your valued commands, we are,

Very Truly,

THE SANDUSKY TOOL COMPANY.

Plate VIII a. - Foreword from 1885 Sandusky Tool Co. Trade Catalogue
[courtesy of Library - The Ohio Historical Society]

SANDUSKY TOOL COMPANY.

Catalogue of 1885.

COMPARATIVE LIST OF NUMBERS OF THE DIFFERENT MANUFACTURERS OF PLANES.

S.T.Co. Cat. 1885.	Sandusky Tool Co.	Ohio Tool Company.	Auburn Tool Company.	Chapin Tool Company.	Greenfield Tool Co.	DESCRIPTION	
PAGE.	NO.	NO.	NO.	NO.	NO.		
7	1	1	1	104	5	Smooth Plane, Single Iron	$ .60
"	3	3	3	112	23	" " Double Iron	.90
"	4			1		Carriage Smooth Plane, Double Iron	.90
"	5	5	7	112½	98	Smooth Plane, Double Iron, Solid Handle	1.75
"	5½	5½	7½			Jack Handled, Smooth Plane	1.50
"	6	6				Slip Mouth " " Double Iron,	1.65
"	7	8	8	415	90	Boxwood " " " "	2.50
"	8	9	58	417	92	Rosewood " " " "	2.25
8	10	12	9	105	6	Jack Plane, Single Iron	.75
"	11	13	10			Jack Plane, Single Iron, with Bolted Handle	1.00
"	12	14	11	105½		Razee Jack Plane, Single Iron, with Start	1.00
"	13	15	12	113	24	Jack Plane, Double Iron,	1.00
"	14	16	14			Jack Plane, Double Iron, with Bolted Handle, extra timber	1.25
"	15	17	16	113½	24½	Razee Jack Plane, Double Iron, with Start	1.20
"	16	18	17	106	7	Fore Plane, Single Iron, with Start	1.00
"	17	19				" " " " Bolted Handle	1.30
"	18	20	19	106½		Razee Fore Plane, Single Iron, with Start	1.30
"	19	21	20	114	25	Fore Plane, Double Iron,	1.40
"	20	22	22			Fore Plane, Double Iron, Bolted Handle, extra timber	2.00
"	21	23	24	114½	26½	Razee Fore Plane, Double Iron, with Start	1.60
9	22	24	26	107	9	Jointer Plane, Single Iron, with Start	1.10 to 1.30
"	23	25				" " " " Bolted Handle	1.55 to 1.75
"	24	26	29	107½		Razee Jointer, " " " Start	1.40 to 1.60
"	25	27	30	115	28	Jointer Plane, Double Iron, 26 to 30 inch	1.50 to 1.75
"	26	28	35			Jointer Plane, Double Iron, Bolted Handle	2.30 to 2.55
"	27	29	37	115½	28½	Razee Jointer, " " with Start	1.75 to 2.00
"	28		55	411		Applewood Smooth Plane, Double Iron, 2 to 2¼ inch	1.50
"	29		194	411½	97½	" Smooth Plane, Solid Handle, Double Iron, 2 to 2¼ inch	2.25
"	30		56	412		" Jack Plane, Double Iron, 2 to 2¼ inch	1.75
"	31		57	413		" Fore " " " 2⅜ to 2⅝ inch	2.40
"	32		57½	414		" Jointer " " " 2½ to 2¾ inch	3.25
"	33					" Smooth " Single " " 2 to 2¼ inch	1.20
"	34					" Jack " " " 2 to 2¼ inch	1.40
"	35					" Fore " " " 2⅜ to 2⅝ inch	2.00
"	35½					" Jointer " " " 2½ to 2¾ inch	2.50
14	36	30	190	430	109	Tooth Plane, Single Iron	1.00
"	37					Applewood Tooth Plane	1.40
"	38	31 A	46	431	110	Mitre Plane, Square, Single Iron	.75
"	38½	31	47	432	110	" " Smooth Shape, Single Iron	.75
"	39	31¼	49	434	111	" " " " Double Iron	1.00
"	40				117½	Schuting Plane, for Picture Frames, with Box	14.00
"	41	32	196	442	118	Gutter Plane	1.25
"	42	32½	198	443	119	Pump Plane, for Chain Pumps	1.15
"	43	33				" " with Handle	1.65
"	44	34	192	436		Circular or Heel Plane, Single Iron,	1.00
"	45	35	193	437		" " " Double "	1.25
"	45½		200	446	120½	Box Makers' Plane, Jack Shape, Razee, Double Iron,	1.60
"	045½	29 D	199	446	119½	" " " " " Single "	1.10
"	045¾	29 C				" " " " Smooth Shape, " "	1.00
"	045 A			5		Carriage Makers' T Rabbet Plane	2.00

Plate VIII b. Comparative List of Numbers of the Different Manufacturers of Planes. [courtesy of Library – The Ohio Historical Society]

4 SANDUSKY TOOL COMPANY.

COMPARATIVE LIST—CONTINUED.

S.T.Co. Cat. 1885.	Sandusky Tool Co.	Ohio Tool Company.	Auburn Tool Company.	Chapin Tool Company.	Greenfield Tool Co.	DESCRIPTION.	
PAGE.	NO.	NO.	NO.	NO.	NO.		
15	46	36	102	122	139	Astragals	$ .75 to 1.00
"	47	37	105	123	147	Side Bead Planes, Single Boxed	.50 to .90
"	48	38	106	124	162	Side Bead Planes, Double Boxed	.60 to 1.10
16	49	39	107	125	177	" " " Boxed, Dovetailed	.70 to 1.00
"	50	40	159	222	136	Base Planes, with Handle	2.50 to 3.00
"	51	41	108	126	230	Center Bead Planes, Double Boxed	.60 to .65
17	52	42	108	127	181	Center Beads, Solid Boxed, Dovetailed	.75 to .90
"	52½		113	130		Torus Bead, to 1 inch	.75
"	53	43	156	219	210	Cove Planes	.50 to .65
18	54	43½	155	219	555½	Scotia, or Quarter Round	.50 to .65
19	54¾	43⅛	155½	217¾		Casing Moulding Plane, with Fence, to work on edge	.80 to 1.00
"	55	44	157	220	218	Cove and Bead	.65 to .80
20	56	45	174	202	208	Coping Plane, Double, for Sash Plane.	.75
"	57	45½		201		" " " Boxed for Sash Plane	.90
"	58	45¾				" " " for Doors	.90
"	60	47	176	138	252	Dado, Brass Side Stop	1.10
"	61	47½		139		" Screw Stop, Solid Handle	2.50
"	62	48	177	139	259	" " "	1.50
21	65	51	117	146	272	Fillister, without Cutter	1.10
"	66	52	118	147	273	" with Cutter	1.25
"	67	53	119	148	277	" " " and Brass Side Stop	1.40
"	68	54	120	149	278	" " " " " " " Boxed	1.85
"	69	55	121	150	280	" " " " " Screw " "	2.50
"	70	56	121½	150½		" " " B. S. Stop Boxed, and Boxwood Fence	3.00
"	71	57	123	154		" " " B. W. S. Arms, B. Screw Stop, Boxed	4.00
"	72	58	124	154½	292	" " " B. W. S. Arms, B. S. S. Boxed and Handle	4.75
"	73	58½		154¾		Back Fillister	3.50
"	74	59	128	204	444	Ogee	.65 to 1.00
22	75					Grecian Ogee, Quirk and Bead	1.25 to 2.00
"	76	59½		206½		Roman Ogee	.75 to .90
23	77	60	140	208	449	Grecian Ogee	.75 to 1.10
"	78		142	209	467	" " and Bead	.90 to 1.05
24	79	61	144	209	455	" " with Bevel and Fillet	.90 to 1.25
"	80	49	109	225	201	Cabinet Makers' Ogee, 2 to 4 inch,	per inch 1.00
"	80½	50		224		Cornice Ogee, 2 to 4 inch,	per inch 1.00
25	81	62	127	206	682	Reverse Ogees	.75 to 1.15
"	82	62½	126	206	682	Roman Reverse Ogees	.75 to 1.15
26	82½	62¼		207½		" " " with Fence, to work on edge	.80 to 1.20
"	83	63	145	212	320	Grecian Ovolo	.75 to 1.50
27	84	64	150	214	327	" " with Bevel or Fillet	1.00 to 1.25
28	85	65	147	214	343	" " and Bead	1.00 to 1.25
"	86	66				Gothic Bead, with one iron	1.00
"	87					" " " two Irons, Boxed	1.25
"	88	68		226	351	Halving Plane	.75
"	89	69		227	352	" " Plated	1.00
"	90	70		227	353	" " with Solid Handle	1.25
"	91	71			354	" " " " " Plated	1.40
29	92	72	180	163	379	Hollows and Rounds, ¼ to 2 inch	per pair, .75 to 1.50
33	94	73	180	167	373	" " " Nos. 10, 11 and 12, per set $3.30,	per pair 1.10
35	95	72½				Skewed Hollows and Rounds	per pair, 1.00 to 2.00
36	96	140	125	207		Reverse Ogee and Square	.75 to 1.00
"	97	141	114			Door Moulding Plane, Boxed	.90 to 1.05
"	98	151				Pilaster Moulding	3.50 to 4.00
37	98½					Board Match Planes, Twin or Separate, ¼ inch	net 3.00
"	99	75	69	171	382	" " " " " ⅜ to ⅞ inch	1.25
"	99½			173		" " " Separate, 1¼ and 1½ inch	1.75
"	99¾					" " " Twin or Separate, Plated, ¼ inch,	net 4.00
"	100	76	70	172	383	" " " Plated, ⅜ to ⅞ inch	1.50
"	100½			172		" " " Separate, Plated, 1¼ and 1½ inch	2.00
"	101	77	73	175	396	" " " Solid Handle, ⅜ to ⅞ inch	2.00
"	101½			175		" " " " " 1¼ and 1½ inch	2.50
"	102	78	74	176	397	" " " " " Plated, ⅜ to ⅞ inch	2.25
"	102½			176		" " " " " " 1¼ and 1½	2.75
"	103	79	75	177	406	Plank Match Planes	2.00
"	104	80	76	178	407	" " " Plated	2.25
"	105	81				" " " Boxed	2.25
38	106	82	80	181	414	" " " Screw Arms	3.50
"	106½	84	81	182		" " " " " Plated	3.75
"	107	83				" " " " " Boxed	4.00
"	108			183		" " " " " Plated and Boxed	4.25
"	109	85		184	415	" " " " " Full Plated	4.50
38	110	89	158		434	Nosing Mouldings	$ .80 to 1.00
"	111	90	189	132	435½	" One Iron	.80 to 1.25
"	112	90½	189	134	437	" " " with Handle	1.10 to 1.50

Plate VIII c. Comparative List of Numbers of the Different Manufacturers of Planes. [continued from Plate VIII b. Page 4 *1885 Sandusky Tool Co. Trade Catalogue*. Courtesy Library - The Ohio Historical Society.]

SANDUSKY TOOL COMPANY.

COMPARATIVE LIST—Continued.

S.T.Co. Cat. 1885.	Sandusky Tool Co.	Ohio Tool Company.	Auburn Tool Company.	Chapin Tool Company	Greenfield Tool Co.	DESCRIPTION.	
PAGE.	NO.	NO.	NO.	NO.	NO.		
38	113	91	189	133	438½	Nosing, Two Irons..	1.10 to 1.50
"	114	92	189	133½	440	" " " with Handle..	1.50 to 2.00
39	116	94	87	230	516½	Panel Plow, Beech, four Irons, Wood Stop..........................	3.00
"	117	95	89	232	509	" " " Screw Stop, Eight Irons............................	4.50
"	118	96	89½	233	510	" " " " " Boxed Fence............................	4.85
"	119	96½	90	234	526	" " " " " with Handle.............................	5.50
"	120	97	90½	235	527	" " " " " " Boxed Fence.........................	5.85
"	121	98	91	243		" " " " " :" Boxwood Arms..........................	5.25
"	122	99	93	244		" " " " " " Boxed Fence..........................	5.60
"	123	100	92	236		" " " " " Boxwood Arms, with Handle,..............	6.75
"	124	101	94	238		" " " " " " " Boxed Fence............	7.00
"	125	107 A				Applewood Panel Plow, Screw Stop, " " "................	6.75
"	126	106		244½		" " " " Boxwood Arms,.....................	6.50
"	127	107				" " " " " Boxed Fence..................	7.00
"	128	107 B		239½		" " " " " " with Handle..............	8.00
"	129	107 C				" " " " " " B. F. & Handle...........	8.25
"	130	102	95	245	518	Panel Plow, Box or Rosewood..	7.00
"	131	103	97			" " " " Ivory Tipped.....................................	8.00
"	132	104	96	240½	532	" " " " Screw Stop, with Handle.........................	9.00
"	133	105	98			" " " " Screw Stop, Handle, Ivory Tipped.........	10.00
"	134		99			" " " Ebony...	9.00
"	135					" " " " Ivory Tipped.....................................	10.00
"	136	108				" " " " with Handle.......................................	11.00
"	137	109	100			" " " " " " Ivory Tipped...........................	12.00
"	138					" " " Box or Rosewood, Self-Regulating................	10.00
"	139					" " " " " " " Ivory Tipped.........	11.50
"	140					" " " " " " " with Handle...........	11.50
"	141					" " " " " " " Handle, Ivory Tipped 13.00	
"	142					" " " Ebony, Self-Regulating, with Handle.............	17.50
"	143		101			" " " " " " " Ivory Tipped.........	20.00
40	144	114	60	162	663	Raising Planes, 2½ to 4 inches..	2.50 to 4.00
"	145	115	63			" " with Screw Arms, 2½ to 4 inches..................	2.80 to 4.50
"	146	116	181	157	597	Rabbet Planes, Skewed,..	.60 to .90
41	147	117	181	158	627	Rabbet Plane, Skew, with Cutter and Boxed...........................	1.05 to 1.35
"	149	119	51	160	651	Jack Rabbet, with Handle and Two Cutters............................	1.70 to 2.00
"	149	119	53	159		Jack Rabbet, with Handle on Side...	1.85
"	150	120	181	155	561	Rabbet Planes, Square,...	Same price as Skewed.
"	151	121		156		Rabbet Plane, Square, Boxed Face..	1.05 to 1.15
"	151½	123	183	161	730	Side Rabbets, Right and Left,.. per pair	1.25
"	152	122	182	131	675	Reeding Planes,... each, 1.00 to	2.60
42	153	124	184		728	Snipe Bills, Single,... per pair	1.25
"	154				729	Snipe Bills, Double,.. per pair	1.75
44	155	125	165	185	689	Sash Plane, One Iron, Bevel or Ovolo.....................................	.60
"	156	126	165	187	692	" " Two " " " ".................................	1.00
"	157	127	165	191	693	" " " " Boxed, Bevel or Ovolo................	1.25
"	164	131	165	193	704	" " Screw Arms, Self-Regulating, Bevel or Ovolo.....	1.75
"	165	131½	168	193	704	" " " " " " Gothic or Ogee........	1.75
"	166	132	166	195	705	" " " " " " Boxed, Bevel or Ovolo..	2.00
"	167	132½	169	195	703	" " Boxed, Gothic or Ogee, Screw Arms, Self-Regulating	2.00
"	168	133	167	192	706	" " Dovetailed Boxed, Bevel or Ovolo, " ".....	2.25
"	169	133½	168	192	706	" " " " Gothic or Ogee. " ".......	2.25
"	170	134				" " Brass Screws, Self-Regulating, Boxed, Bevel or Ovolo..	2.75
"	171	134½				" " " " " " Dovetailed Boxed, G. or O.	2.75
"	172	135		198		" " " " " " " " B. or O.	2.00
"	173	135¼				" " " " " " " " G. or O.	3.00
"	174	135½		198		" " Tuscan, in Two Parts..	1.50
"	174½	135¾				Meeting Rail Plane, for Sash...	2.00
45	175	136	185	168	733	Table Planes, with Gauge, ½ to ¾ inch....................................	1.10 to 1.25
"	176	137	186	169	738	" " " " Dovetailed Boxed............per pair 1.50 to	1.65
"	177	138	187	170	734	" " " Fence..	1.40 to 1.60
"	179	139¼	115	145	270	Door Plane, with Screw Arms and Fence..................................	1.75
"	180	139½	116	145	271	" " " Screw Arms and Bevel..............................	1.50
"	181	139¾	115	145	271	" " " " " " Ogee...............................	1.60

Plate VIII d. Comparative List of Numbers of the Different Manufacturers of Planes. [continued from Plate VIII c., Page 5 *1885 Sandusky Tool Co. Trade Catalogue*. Courtesy Library - The Ohio Historical Society.]

TABLE VII

PRINCIPAL WOODEN PLANE FIRMS IN UNITED STATES, after 1870

Firm Name	Date Organized	Date Dissolved	Location
Auburn Tool Co.	1864	1893*	Auburn, NY
H. Chapin's Son	1866	1901**	New Hartford, CT
Greenfield Tool Co.	1851	1887	Greenfield, MA
Ohio Tool Co.	1851	1913	Columbus, OH
Sargent & Co.***	1864	-	New Haven, CT
Sandusky Tool Co.****	1869	1931	Sandusky, OH

* After that date became part of Ohio Tool Co.
** After that date was part of Chapin-Stevens Co., until 1929
*** Purchased wooden planes from H. Chapin until 1890, then Sandusky Tool Co.
**** Became part of American Fork & Hoe Co. in 1929, dissolved in 1931.

In concluding this brief historical sketch of the industry, mention is made of four women plane makers noted in 19th-century directories who continued businesses established by their deceased husbands. These were: -

  Widow of William Brooks, Philadelphia, 25 King's Alley, 1808
  Charlotte White, (late Israel), Philadelphia,
        139 Callowhil, 1840
  Catherine Seybolt (Late, E.F.Seybolt), 207 Main St.
        Cincinnati, 1853-1855
  Sarah S. Carpenter, (widow of E.W.Carpenter), 73 S.Queen St.
        Lancaster, Pa. 1860

Details concerning the manufacturing process for making wooden planes are not reported in this study. Reference is made to excellent articles by the late Frank H. Wildung, (author of *Woodworking Tools at Shelburne Museum),* published several years ago in the *Chronicle of EAIA*.[73] Essentially this involved: 1. gang-sawing blanks from selected well-seasoned stock, usually beech wood; 2. routing the "gab" (opening in the body for the plane iron and mouth) employing bedding and cheeking chisels; 3. additional stock removal using specially shaped floats; and 4. finishing by sawing and sanding operations. A float is a form of a rasp having a series of sharp parallel cutting edges. (See: fig. 5) By 1865 automated machinery had replaced many of the former hand operations followed in planemaking.[74]

Throughout the nineteenth century plane irons, made from high carbon steel, were imported from England, principally from Sheffield. Invariably these were stamped "cast steel" with the imprint of the particular manufacturer. Among these Sheffield firms were: Wm. Ash, Wm. & Saml. Butcher, James Cam, Issac Greaves, Richard

Groves, Thos. Ibbottson, Philip Law, Moulson Brothers, Saml. Newbould and John Sorby.[75] The process of making such high carbon steel involved direct crucible melting of raw materials, casting the melt into a bar or ingot, mechanical working by hot forging on a trip-hammer and rolling into strip stock. The discovery of this process in 1740 is credited to Benjamin Huntsman, working at Sheffield in his effort to produce an improved product for watch and clock springs.[76] This process became known as "cast steel" and by 1750 was in general use at Sheffield. Steel produced by this method was of superior quality for cutlery applications compared to such formerly made from "blister" steel (i.e., 'shear', Newcastle or German steel).[77]

Advertisements appearing in early nineteenth century newspapers indicate that a large number of finished plane irons for bench planes, as well as soft blanks for moulding planes, were imported at the large seaport cities and then distributed to hardware merchants. Importers could make selections from English "pattern books", such as Joseph Smith's 1816 *Key to the Sheffield Manufacturies*. James Wells, a hardware merchant, advertised in 1806 at Hartford: " imports: 50 doz. cast steel and common plane irons; 80 doz. soft moulding irons".[78] With the establishment of plane manufacturing businesses and other competing edge tool enterprises in the mid-1820's, raw material of such cast steel in the form of bar stock was imported for processing into plane irons and other edge tools.

A plane iron, axe, draw knife or other large edge cutting surface was made then as a composite of inexpensive low carbon steel (sometimes employing wrought iron) as an extension handle for supporting the more costly "cast steel" cutting edge. The two materials were welded together by a blacksmith and then shaped or sheared into size. The cutting edge was then rough ground to almost final size, hardened, tempered and finished ground. Examination of such a plane iron readily reveals a line of demarcation where these two materials have been "scarf" welded together.

The trade of planemaking in United States was originally established by joiners who made the wooden parts of their own tools and purchased imported cutting irons. As business increased a market soon developed for such cutting irons and soon edge tool manufacturing enterprised followed to supply such demands. In New York State the important firms of D.R. Barton at Rochester and L. & I.J. White at Buffalo were originally established as suppliers and manufacturers of a general line of edge tools as 'smithing' concerns. Planemaking was subsequently added to their lines by hiring joiners to make the wooden bodies, thus supplemented their edge tool products. Perhaps larger markets for these firms were supplying plane irons to other concerns making only planes. In New England Providence Tool Co., Middletown Tool Co. and various New Haven 'smithing' firms supplied such irons to the trade. A partial listing of such American firms observed from imprints appearing on the plane irons is presented in Table VIII.

TABLE VIII

Plane Iron Manufacturers in United States during the 19th Century
[partial listing from imprints of firm name stamps]

FIRM NAME [imprint]	Location	Manufacturing Dates for Plane Irons
Auburn Tool Co.	Auburn, N.Y.	1864 - 1893
Baldwin Tool Co.	Middletown, N.Y.	-1850 - 1860
D.R. Barton	Rochester, N.Y.	-1835 - 1875
Barton Tool Co.	Rochester, N.Y.	1875
Boston Multiform Tool Co.	Boston, Mass.	-1857-
Charles Buck	Millbury, Mass.	1873 - 1900-
Buck Brothers	Millbury, Mass.	1853 - 1900-
Casey, Kitchell & Co.	Auburn, N.Y.	1847 - 1858
Dwight & Foster		
Excelsior Works	Auburn, N.Y.	
Bird French	Salisbury, Conn.	-1849-
Dwight French Co.	New Haven, Conn.	-1850-
Globe Manufacturing Co.	Middletown, Conn.	1881 -
Greenfield Tool Co.	Greenfield, Mass.	1852 - 1883
A. Howland	Auburn, N.Y.	1869 - 1874
Humphreysville Manufact. Co.	Seymour, Conn.	-1871 - 1873-
Lynch, Murray & Co.		
Mack & Co.	Rochester, N.Y.	1875 - 1900-
Middletown Tool Co.	Middletown, Conn.	1854 - 1876
New Haven Tool Co.	New Haven, Conn.	1850 - 1870-
New York Tool Co.	Greenfield, Mass.	-1880-
Ohio Tool Co.	Columbus, Ohio	1851 - 1900-
Providence Tool Co.	Providence, R.I.	1850 - 1870
Reynolds, Baker & Co.	Auburn, N.Y.	
Sandusky Tool Co.	Sandusky, Ohio	1869 - 1900-
Sargent & Co.	New Haven, Conn.	-1890 - 1900-
Snell Manufacturing Co.	Fiskdale, Mass.	-1890-
Stanley Rule & Level Co.	New Britain, Conn.	1869 - 1900-
James Swan	Seymour, Conn.	-1880 - 1900-
Underhill Edge Tool Co.	Derry, N.H.	-1877 - 1900-
Union Manufacturing Co.	New Haven, Conn.	
L. & I.J. White	Buffalo, N.Y.	1873 - 1900-

Undoubtedly there were many other smaller firms and in a few instances such irons were made from domestically produced high carbon steel Sheffield steel, whether in the form of finished irons or raw material, continued to dominate the market. Unquestionably some of the firms noted on this listing did not actually make their own cutting irons, but had these produced on contract and imprinted with their own firm name for sales promotion of their products.

After the Bailey plane was introduced with the thinner cutting iron (c.1870), the entire blade was made from a single piece of high carbon "cast steel". Stanley Rule & Level Co. manufactured and sold such irons with their line of planes. As late as the 1892 S.R. & L. Co.'s Price List noted: "The cutters are made of the best English Cast Steel, tempered and ground by an improved method." (Bailey's Iron Spoke Shaves, p.54)

Notes Chapter III

1. C.F.Hummel, *Winterthur Portfolio II,* (Winterthur,Del., 1965), "English Tools in America: The Evidence of the Dominys", p.29
2. D.N.Spear, *Bibliography of American Directories Through 1860,* (Worcester,Mass., 1961), This checklist notes American directories published through the year 1860.
3. *The Pocket Register for the City of Hartford,* (Hartford, 1825), 67pp.
4. Kennedy is noted as a "joiner" in [1799] *Business Men of the City of Hartford in the Year 1799.* An advertisement in *Hartford Courant,* Jan. 11,1809,p.3, col.5, noted: - "James H. Wells,hardware wholesale & retail carries an assortment of Kennedy's moulding tools and planes. . "
5. An early plow plane has been observed with imprint "H.Chapin/Union Factory" over which has been stamped the firm imprint: "M & A. Copeland/Warranted".
6. E.S.Grant, *Yankee Dreamers and Doers,* (Chester,Conn., 1975), 269 pp. Many interesting, but undocumented accounts of early Connecticut industries.
7. K.D.Roberts, *Eli Terry and The Connecticut Shelf Clock,* (Hartford,Conn.,1973), p27-28.
8. R.S.Woodbury, *Technology & Culture,*Dec. 1959, "The Legend of Eli Whitney and Interchangeable Parts".
9. W.G.Lathrop, *The Brass Industry in United States,* (Mt.Carmel,Ct,1926),p.40
10. K.R.Gilbert, *The Portsmouth Blockmaking Machinery* (London,1965), p.5
11. *Brief Account of the Development of the Collins Co.* (Collinsville,Ct.,1935),p.7
10. K.D. & J.W. Roberts,*Planemakers, etc.,* p.148
13. *History of Middlesex County,* (Middletown,Ct.,1884), p.92
14. *Beer's Atlas of Connecticut,* Middlesex County Map, 1874
15. C.C.Baldwin, *The Baldwin Genealogy from 1500 - 1881,* (Cleveland,O.,1881),p.724
16. C.C.Baldwin, *Supplement to the Baldwin Genealogy,* (Cleveland,O., 1889),p.1254
17. *History of Middlesex County,* (Middletown,Conn.,1884), p.104
18. U.S.Census 1860, Products of Industry Middlesex County
19. J.S.Kebabian, *(Chronicle of EAIA),*"Imprints of Various Denison Firms", Vol.27,No.1, April 1974, p.15
20. R.Carlson, *(Chronicle of EAIA),* "A Wooden Plane Maker of the 1870's - G.W.Denison & Co.", Vol. 26,No.4, Dec. 1973, pp. 58-60.
21. E.L.Smiley, *A Short History of Riverton,Connecticut,* (Riverton,Conn.,1934),p.8. "Hictchcockville"district of Barkhamstead, was renamed Riverton about 1865.
22. C.Tahk, *Chronicle of EAIA,*"The Phoenix Co.",Vol.27,No.2,June 1974, p.34
23. *History of Litchfield County,* (Philadelphia, 1881), p.241
24. *Chapin-Stephens Co. Catalogue No.114,* p2."Since our consolidation in 1901"
25. John Boyd, *Annals and Family Records of Winchester,Conn.,*(Hartford,1873),p.522
26. *The Connecticut Business Directory for 1851,* Published by J.H.Benham,New Haven
27. E.M.Sayward and W.W.Streeter,"Planemaking in the Valley of the Connecticut River and Hills of Western Massachusetts", Manuscript. Acknowledgement is made to these authors for sharing their information before publications. While this report includes details of planemaking in these areas, many of the conclusions are speculative and await doucumentation.
28. Amherst Historical Society, Amherst, Mass. Noted in unpublished manuscript by R.F.Grosse, Nov. 20, 1974
29. Hampshire County Deeds (hereafter referred to as HCD), Book 68. p.296
30. Carpenter & Morehouse, *History of the Town of Amherst,Massachusetts,* (Amherst, 1896), p.301
31. HCD, B.85, p.200
32. HCD, B.90, p.493
33. HCD, B.148, p.73
34. Carpenter & Morehouse, *op. cit.,* p.301
35. HCD, B.138, p.307

Notes Chapter III [continued]

36. HCD, B.180, p.162
37. Carpenter & Morehouse, *op. cit.*, p.294
38. HCD, B.66, p.512
39. Published by Pratt & Co., New York,N.Y.,1849
40. HCD, B.240, p.359
41. HCD, B.240, p.357
42. Listed as Planemaker,*New England Business Directory of 1875,* published by Sampson,Davenport & Co., (Boston, 1875)
43. Carpenter & Morehouse,*op. cit.*, p.295
44. *History of Connecticut Valley in Massachusetts,*(Philadelphia, 1879),V.I,p.518
45. HCD, B.125, p.398
46. HCD, B.138, p.25
47. HCD, B.143, p.130
48. *History of Connecticut Valley in Massachusetts,op.cit,*V.II, p.678
49. Franklin County Deeds,[Herefater FCD], B.160, pp. 255-256
50. *Conway 1767 - 1967,* (Conway,Mass., 1967), p.71
51. Thompson, *History of Greenfield,*(Greenfield,Mass.,1904), V.I,p643
52. FCD, B.170, p.306, March 3, 1852
53. FCD, B.170, p.142
54. FCD, B.323, p.77
55. FCD, B.348, p.33
56. F.M.Thompson,*History of Greenfield, op. cit.*, p.628
57. W.Hilton, *Chronicle of EAIA,* V.27,No.2,June 1974, pp.23-27
58. W.Hilton, *Chronicle of EAIA,* V.28,No.1.March 1975, p.14
59. Acknowledgement is made to Oliver Deming for use of this document.
60. The first two of these patents are illustrated by P.C.Welch, *Contributions from the Museum of History of Technology,* (Smithsonian Institution, Washington, D.C.) Paper No. 48, "New Uses for Old Tools", pp.128-129
61. K.D. & J.W. Roberts, *Planemakers, etc.,op. cit.*
62. C.Cist, *Sketches and Statistics of Cincinnati,* (Cincinnati, 1841),p.54
63. C.Cist, *Sketches and Statistics of Cincinnati,* (Cincinnati,1851),p.226-27
64. Ohio Historical Society Library, Columbus,Ohio
65. A.S.Kellog,*Memorial of Elder John White[Hartford,1860],* p.141
66. Correspondence with John Grabb, Chillicothe,O. from his studies at Chillicothe Historical Society.
67. The"neighbor" firm referred to in this advertisement has been identified as Gardner & Schutte by John Grabb. Upon the death of Gardner the firm then became   D.A.Schutte for whom plane imprints at Chillicothe have been reported. Studies indicate that Schutte made several trips to England to purchase hardware and advertises" "Importer of English, French, German and Belgium Hardware and Cutlery" . . "for sale at the Sign of the Paddock. . "
68. *Report of the Directors and Warden of the Ohio State Penitentiary,* (Columbus,Ohio, Dec. 28, 1841). The Directors were advised in error as planes were being made at that date at Cincinnati and elsewhere in Ohio.
69. H.L.Hunkey, *Industrial Evolution of Columbus,* (Columbus, 1958), p.3o
70. A.E.Lee, *History of the City of Columbus,*(Columbus,1892), p.327
71. W.T.Martin,*History of Franklin County,*(Columbus,1858), p.432
72. M. & G. Tuttle, *Ohio Tool Collectors Bulletin,* (Springfield,O.,1974), V.I,No.2, Notes regarding Ohio Tool Co.
73. F.H.Wildung,"Making Wooden Planes in America", *Chronicle of EAIA,* Vol.III,No.2,April 1955,pp.19-21; also Vol.III,No.3,July 1955, pp.28-30.
74. K.D. & J.W. Roberts,*Planemakers, etc.,op.cit.,*p.100; note #83,p.103; also see: F.H.Colvin,"Workmen's Skill vs Modern Machinery,*American Machinist,*Jan.30,1913
75. W.L. Goodman, *op.cit.,BPM,* Appendix I, p.118.
76. R.A. Mott,"The Sheffield Crucible Steel Industry and it Founder,Benjamin Huntsman",*Journ. of Iron & Steel Institute,* March 1955, p.227-237.
77. G.I.H. Lloyd, *The Cutlery Trade,*[London, 1913], p.74.
    J.R.Grabb,"Shear Steel,etc.",*Chronicle of EAIA,*Vol.28,No.1,March 1975,pp.8-11.
78. *Connecticut Courant,* Vol. XLII,No.2149,[Hartford,Conn.]Jan.22,1806,p.4.

Chapter IV

Demise of the Wooden Plane

Both the subjects of processing wood by machinery and introduction of the cast iron plane were reviewed in our previous work: Chapter IX, "Advancing Technology and the Decline of the Wooden Plane", *PLANEMAKERS, etc.*[1] However these details concerned developments and contributions principally occurred in New York State.

The Greek Revival period in America had become popular by 1825. Accompanying changes both in architecture and furniture styles affected practices in joinery and carpentry. The balloon system employing smaller vertical studs rather than the former heavier mortise and tenon framing simplified house construction. The thickness of planking for siding was reduced. New materials and techniques changed interior finishing. Wainscotting in the form of wooden panels was replaced by lath and plaster. Door and window construction followed simpler rectilinear moulding rather than the former fancier shaped moulded and beveled raised panels.[2] Many houses and buildings formerly constructed according to Colonial and Federal designs were altered to conform to the new "Greek" styles. This is particularly noticeable observing many conversions of doorways and window frames in older New England houses. The expanding population and migration westward brought increased demands for processed lumber. It was the areas of the Western Reserve in Ohio, southern Michigan and elsewhere in rural mid-western towns where house construction along the new Greek Revival fourished.

American Empire furniture may be dated 1805-1840.[3] Looking-glass frames using half-round columns, frequently gilded or decorated with stencilled patterns had come into popularity by 1825. Chairs of "country Windsor" designs with similar stencilled patterns, later known as "Hitchcock's", were in vogue 1826-1843.[4] Clock cases having stencilled half-round columns and top splates, comparable to the then popular looking-glasses, introduced in 1828, had by 1830 virtually replaced the Terry type "pillar and scroll" pediment design.[5] Bevel mouldings employed in furniture had become popular in American Empire styling early in the 1830's. This was first evidenced in looking-glass frames and soon after in clock cases. The "O.G." (Ogee - cyma recta) was soon to follow. The Victorian period, commencing in 1837, brought even fancier mouldings; Grecian O.G. with bevel, Grecian Ovolo with bead, and numerous other combinations that were to remain prominent through the end of the Civil War.

These cultural changes, associated with increased demands for wood as a structural material, quite naturally brought about improvements in both processing techniques and designs of tools. In 1843 the Commissioner of Patents, reviewing the important developments during that year concerning lumber processing ("including machines for sawing, planing, mortising, &c.") noted:[6] -

> "The inexhaustible supply of timber within the limits of the United States, in view of its scarcity in the territory of some of the most populous nations of Europe, soon rendered lumber an article of extensive consumption at home, and important as an article of export: and hence we find that the people of the United States have done more to improve machinery and tools employed in manufacturing and working lumber, than any other people in the world; and, from the magnitude of interests involved, every labor saving machine in this branch of industry become important to every section of the country."

His Report continued citing machinery for: saw-mills, cutting veneers, making staves for barrels, coach-making and forming irregular shapes. A similar report noted improvements in 1845 making shingles and clapboards by action of a circular saw; also modifications of Blanchard's lathe for turning such irregular forms as oars and scythes.[7] By this date much of the work formerly accomplished by hand planing was now being done by machinery.

William Woodworth of Poughkeepsie, N.Y. was granted a patent December 27, 1828 for a surfacing machine for planing boards following their being sawed from logs. Subsequently in 1829 an agreement was made to incorporate provisions of another planing machine patent into the Woodworth design.[8] While other planing machines were developed, with the exception that patented by Daniels, the Woodworth machinery virtually monopolized the field until 1856. T.E. Daniels of Worcester, Mass. was granted a patent December 25, 1834 for his planing machine. The stock was mounted on a long movable bed, which operated through rack and pinion gearing, and moved under fixed cutters. The Woodworth machine had cutters mounted on a circular drum and was more rapid in removing stock. However the Daniels machine did have an advantage in surfacing thicker stock, was excellent for straightening planks and was used in many pattern shops.[9] An advertisement in the 1845 *Worcester Directory* noted:[10]-

> T H O M A S E. D A N I E L S,
> Court Mill, Worcester, Mass.
> Builds to order, if not on hand, his
> Improved Patent PLANING Machine
>
> Which is very useful for Squaring out stuffs for Machinery, so that no Jointer is used about it; all kinds of mill work; floor and other kinds of boards; bedstead, table, bureau, door and spoke stuff; hollowing out drum laggs, water-wheel lining, &c, &c. He has patterns to plane all widths, from 8 to 24 inches, and from 4 to 22 feet long. The small MACHINE may be used to good advanyage by hand power.
>
> Also, MACHINES FOR MATCHING BOARDS, and GROOVED PLANK for flooms and factory floors, so as to receive Mortar between the floors to prevent fire.
>
> This Machine is too well known to need recommendation. Suffice it to say, that Eighteen are in use in Worcester. Eight in different Shops belonging to the United States Government, and many others in all parts of the country, from Maine to Louisiana; and they are used for planing all kinds of work, from the United States Ship timbers, to a Connecticut wooden clock; -
> and in all cases they give entire satisfaction.

In addition to planing the Woodworth patent covered simultaneous tongue and grooving, as well as forming sash and moulding stock. In the original design only one surface was planed in a pass through the machine. In preparing sawed lumber for flooring only one surface was planed. As considerable variation in thickness existed from the boards as sawn, even after planing and cutting a tongue or groove, to make a level floor, it was frequently necessary to adjust the surface of the joists with an adze.[11]

Boards cut from logs on a vertically driven "up and down" saw mill were left with a series of rough kerf marks, corresponding to the individual strokes of the saw across the width. The primary function of the "jack" plane was to remove such kerf bands, thus roughing out the sawn surface. The jack plane was recommended to be ground with considerable concavity. (Note: Nicholson, p.92N). The resulting planed surface, while rid of the saw kerf marks, had series of waves. This condition is frequently present on drawer bottoms or boards where such a rough planed surface was not objectionable. With the development of the planing mill, the degree of convexity across the jack plane iron was not required. Consequently American jack planes were soon offered with almost flat surfaces. Fig. 6 illustrates an eighteenth century jack plane with its iron at the right and a mid-nineteenth century jack plane on the left. The difference in convexity is self-evident. While machine planed boards were left with a series of ridges from chatter of the knives, the smount of work required to smooth such surfaces was greatly reduced.

During the tenure of the Woodworth patent, several other types of wood processing machines were developed. Among these were: C.B.Rogers, Norwich, Conn., sash and door moulding, 1840; George Page, Keene, N.H., mortising, 1830; Baxter Whitney, Winchendon, Mass., planing & moulding, 1846; and J.A.Fay of Keene, N.H., moulding, 1848.[12] In 1848 an association operated under the firm names of C.B.Rogers & Co. at Norwich, Conn. and J.A.Fay & Co. at Keene, N.H. for manufacturing door and sash machinery. In 1852 Fay, conducting business under his own name, built a factory in Cincinnati, which reportedly became the largest manufacture of wood working machinery in the world.[13]

Planing mills, usually driven by either water or steam power, literally sprung up all over the country at centers where the population was sufficient for the demands. At Hartford, Conn. such a mill driven by steam power was noted in an 1842 Directory. The Lawrence Wood Moulding Mill, patented in 1848, operating in New York City noted: "a large stock of Mouldings & any of required pattern. worked to order".[14] The *Boston Almanac* for 1853 listed three firms supplying machined mouldings.[15] The Boston Planing and Moulding Mill, established in 1854, published a 59 page catalogue in 1860 illustrating and pricing 579 varieties of machine made wood mouldings. The foreword to this stated that kept on hand were: "a good quantity of Pilasters, Cornices, Beads, Hand Rails. Pew Caps, Stair Posts, Balusters of all sizes; also Gutters for Wooden Buildings. Mouldings for Picture and Looking-Glass Frames. . ." In cities where such planing and moulding mills were in operation the demands for moulding planes must have been substantially reduced from previous times.

Fig. 6. 16" Jack Planes and Irons. 18th c. right; 19th c. left [See text]

Contrary to popular belief it was not Leonard Bailey who invented the iron sole plane. Goodman describes and illustrates such planes surviving from the late Roman Empire period found both in continental Europe and England.[16] A summary of the development of the iron plane, published by the Stanley Rule & Level Co. as advertising material:[17] "THE STORY OF THE PLANE", is reproduced as Plate IX. Unquestionably it was the successful marketing and sales, combined by competent manufacturing at Stanley Rule & Level Co., under the Bailey Patents licensed in 1869, that promoted the iron plane into prominence by 1890. A sequence of significant U.S. Patents for Iron Bench Planes that predated this development is listed in Table IX.

Table IX - Sequence of Significant U.S. Patents for Iron Bench Planes

Patentee	Number	Residence	Date of Pentent	Title
Hazard Knowles	-	Colcester, Conn.	Aug. 24, 1827	Cast Iron Plane Stock
W. Foster	3355	Washington, D.C.	Nov. 4, 1843	Bench Plane (iron stock)
C.S. Beardsley & S. Wood	6459	Auburn, N.Y.	May 22, 1849	Bench Plane (iron stock)
B. Holly	9094	Senaca Falls, N.Y.	June 6, 1852	Bench Plane (metal stock)
G.E. Davis	12787	Lowell, Mass.	May 1, 1855	Bench Plane (metal stock)
W.S. Loughborough	23928	Rochester, N.Y.	May 10, 1859	Bench Plane (iron stock)
N. Palmer	64790	Auburn, N.Y.	May 14, 1867	Bench Plane (iron stock)
E.G. Storke	96052	Auburn, N.Y.	Oct. 19, 1869	Bench Plane (iron stock)

Data from *Index of Patents from United States Patent Office from 1790 to 1873*, [Washington, D.C., 1873], pp. 1055-1056.

Since the 1827 Patent by Hazard Knowles is the earliest for which an extant record exists,[18] the specifications are presented in Plate X. A restored drawing of this plane has been illustrated by Welch.[19] Three advantages are cited for such a metal plane: durability and wear resistance of the iron sole, uniformity of opening, and "cheaper" to manufacture.

Plate X

LETTERS PATENT Granted to Hazard Knowles of Colchester, Connecticut [August 24,1827]

The Schedule referred to in these Letters Patent and in making part of the same containing a description in the words of the said Hazard Knowles himself of his improvement in Plane Stocks of Cast Iron.

The Stock is to be made of cast iron with the face and sides about one fourth of an inch in thickness, or the thickness of them may be so varied as to adopt it to any degree of heaviness or lightness that may be wished. The height of the sides where the Plane iron and wedge enters to be about the same as that in the common stock of wood and the sides from the place where the wedge and iron enters terminating at each end in a point. The Plane iron to be supported by projections from the two sides inclining towards the front end in an angle of about 45 degrees, which projections are cast at the same time with the sides and part of the same. A round socket to be placed in the front end in which a handle is to be inserted which may be shoved by the left hand and a long socket in the other end and for the insertion of a handle in the common form for jack Planes & Jointers and for the smooth Plane a round socket at each end. The peculiar excellency of this kind of stock consists in this, that it is more durable than the common stock of Wood, that the face of it unlike that of the wooden will always keep in the same condition and not be like that contantly subject to wear & hollowness in the centre and that the opening thro which the shaving passes will always retain the same width and that in can be afforded at a much cheaper price. Dated at Colchester, July 10th 1827. - Witnesses
    Newhall Tainter   *Hazard Knowles*
    E.W. Worthington

    The perfection of the metal plane awaited improvements in holding and adjustment device of the cutting iron. Strange as it may seem these improvements were first developed in connection with wood bench planes. This led to the "transitional design" with cast iron fixtures mounted on a wooden sole. These efforts were cumulative accomplishments of numerous inventors, occurring during the period 1856-1867. The most important of these patents are listed in Table X.

    The earliest of the so-called, "transitional", cast iron superstructure types, was a plane manufactured by the Lowell Plane & Tool Co. under the Patent of T.D. Worrall (No.14,979, dated May 27,1856), shown in Fig. 7. In the same illustration a wooden block plane is shown with this same firm imprint and method of holding the iron with a screw clamp, tightened from the back end. Later Worrall obtained a patent which provided for tightening the iron by driving together two oppositely inclined wedges (June 30, 1857; No.17,657), rather than by screw adjustment.[20]

It was the combining features from three different patents of Leonard Bailey (Nos. 21,311, 67,398 & 72,443) that led to the first practical and marketable iron plane. Sketches from these pertinent patents appear in Plate IX, *The Story of the Plane*. As pointed out by Goodman, the lever cap, providing for rapid release and securing the cutting iron, was illustrated in Bailey's earlier June 22, 1858 Patent, but not claimed.[21] The screw adjustment for depth control of the cutting iron, Patent #67,398, was first fixed on a vertical axis, which was later changed to a horizontal position. It was the construction of the cap iron with a bend, which when clamped together by tightening a screw and thus exerted sufficient pressure on the plane iron and prevented chattering, which enabled the latter to be made from thin hardened stock. This indeed was an important factor in the successes of the Bailey Patent Planes.[22]

Bailey had worked in Winchester, Mass. from 1861 - 1864.[23] In 1864 he removed to Boston, continuing to operate a tool store at 73 Haverill Street through 1868 as L.Bailey & Co., manufacturer of iron planes.[24] In 1868 at the same address he was in partnership with Jacob Chany as Bailey,Chany & Co., manufacturer of wood and iron planes. On May 19, 1869 the Stanley Rule & Level Co. signed an agreement with Leonard Bailey to license his patents, purchased the machinery and stock of the Bailey,Chany & Co., and brought Leonard Bailey to New Britain, Conn., as manufacturing superintendent in their newly organized plane department. The initial line of Bailey's Patent Planes produced by SR&L Co. consisted of eleven iron and seventeen wood ("transitional") models. These were first advertised in SR&L Co.'s *1870 Catalogue of Tools and Hardware*.[25] (See Plate XI). Testimonials appearing in this publication reported the superiority of these "Bailey Patent Planes".[26] The earliest of these was dated Aug. 16,1869, which indicated that the SR&L Co. certainly expedited manufacturing of this line of products, as this date was only three months after the agreement with Bailey.

George Warren of Bridgewater, Mass. was granted U.S. Patent #111,890, dated Feb.14,1871 for an improvement, illustrated as applied to a "Bailey Plane". This consisted of an eccentric plate which provided for lateral adjustment of the cutting iron through a circular screw mechanism. This patent was almost immediately acquired by SR&L Co. and incorporated into its designs. A later improvement for lateral adjustment was made by a SR&L Co. contract worker, Justus A. Traut.[27] This patent #386,509, dated July 24, 1876, assigned to SR&L Co., concerned a lever mechanism in back of the cutting iron mounted at the top section of the frog.

A less expensive line of iron and wood planes was introduced by SR&L Co. in 1876 and exhibited at the Centennial at Philadelphia.[28] The regulation for depth of the cutting iron was accomplished by action of a thumb lever.[29] This device was patented by J.A.Traut and Henry Richards, Dec. 27,1875, U.S.Pat. #176,152. A distinctive feature was the "Liberty Bell" cast on the lever cap. These were referred to as "The Stanley Adustable Planes" and were first illustrated in the 1877 SR&L Co. Catalogue. (See Plate XII).

Table X

Patents for Improvements is Securing & Adjusting Plane Bits

Patentee & Residence	Patent Number & Date	Title
T.D.Worrall	14,979 May 27,1856	Method of Securing Plane Bits
Lowell, Mass.	16,309 Dec.23,1856	Method of Adjusting Plane Bits
	17,657 Jun.23,1857	Improved Bench Plane
	17,951 Aug. 4,1857	Bench Plane
M.B.Tidey	16,889 Mar.24,1857	Improved Carpenter's Plane
Ithaca,N.Y.		
Leonard Bailey	20,615 Jun.22,1858	Adjustmanet Device for Plane Iron
Winchester,Mass.	21,311 Aug.31,1858	Securing Plane Iron to Stock
Boston,Mass.	67,398 Aug. 6,1867	Improvement in Bench Planes
	72,443 Dec.24,1867	Improvement in Carpenter's Plane
Seth Howes	37,694 Feb.17,1863	Bench Planes
South Chatham,Mass.	40,483 Nov. 3,1863	Bench Planes

Fig. 7. T.D. Worrall Patent Planes. Left: Early transitional wood sole plane with cast iron super-structure[8-1/2" x 2-5/8", 2" iron]; Right: Block plane [7-1/2" x 1-7/8", 1-1/2" iron]. İmprint on fore end of planes: *Lowell Plane & Tool Co./Worrall Patent/May 27,1856 [U.S.Pat. #14.979]*; Imprint on Plane Iron: *Multiform Moulding Plane Co./ Boston*.

Plate IX

THE STORY OF THE PLANE

The modern Plane is the product of Evolution. In this short story you can follow the stages of improvement and realize what man has accomplished through the centuries.

We must go to the very beginning of civilization, as our present day Plane has evolved from the Chisel. The Chisel in its earliest form was nothing more than a stone sharpened at one end. Tools of this kind have been discovered in use as far back as 4000 B.C.

It is probable that the Hebrews developed the first Plane as they have been credited with the placing of a sharp stone through a block of wood made smooth on the bottom. The stone was held by a wedge. Fig. 1.

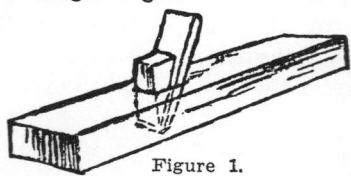

Figure 1.

Later metal became known to the Hebrews which they substituted for the sharp stone.

The Romans used a Plane about 50 A.D., which had an open mouth to allow shavings to come out. This was the first Plane to have this feature.

In the ruins of Pompeii (about 79 A.D.) a Plane of this type was discovered.

Very little improvement was made in the Plane until the early part of 1700, when an iron was placed in front of the cutter which served to break the chips or curl the shavings. This without question was an important advancement. A little later a convenient handle was added. Fig. 2.

Figure 2.

This type of Plane was used for many years and we know of the manufacture of such a Plane in the United States in 1828.

The first invention of importance occurred in 1827 and was made by H. Knowles. His patent was a Plane of cast iron. This Plane had the advantage of lightness, no warping, a true working surface and less wear on the sole. It also used the old method of fastening the cutter by the wooden wedge. Fig. 3.

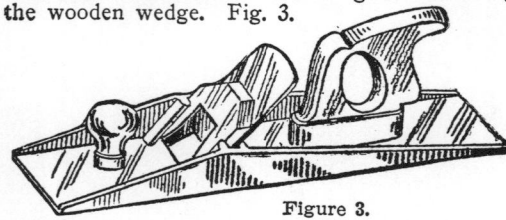

Figure 3.

In 1843 a patent was issued to W. Foster for an improvement on the Knowles cast iron Plane. This was an attempt to provide an adjustment to vary the thickness of the shaving. A block connected to a threaded screw held in a square pocket was intended to regulate the shaving.

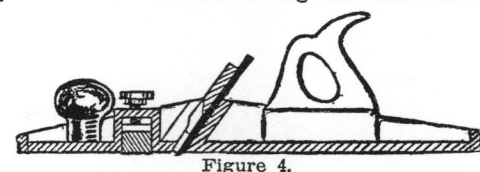

Figure 4.

A patent was awarded to L. Sanford in 1844 for a longitudinal adjustment of the Plane. Fig. 5.

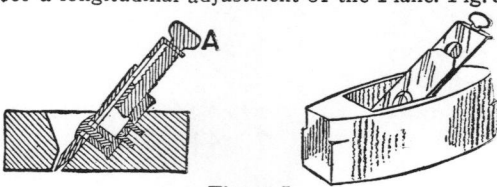

Figure 5.

In 1854 a patent was issued to W. S. Loughborough for an improved method of fastening the cutter. The first important departure from the age old method of fastening the cutter by wedge. Fig. 6.

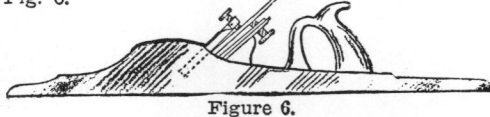

Figure 6.

To Leonard Bailey is due more credit than to any other person for improving the Plane to its present day usefulness.

The first patent was awarded to him in 1858. This invention was on a wooden bottom Plane having a cammed lever for fastening the cutter. Fig. 7.

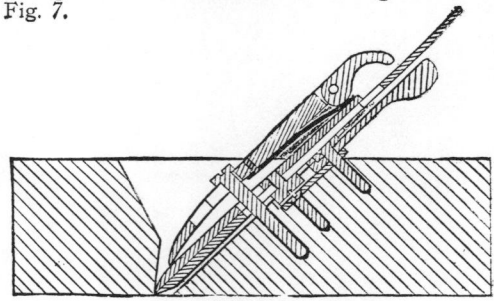

Figure 7.

In 1867 an important improvement was made by Leonard Bailey in his invention of the longitudinal adjustment. Fig. 8.

Figure 8.

Plate IX [continued]

The adjusting nut was in the vertical position but was soon changed to the horizontal position.

Soon after he invented a Plane with an iron body and an iron adjustable cutter seat or frog which supported the thin steel cutter.

At this time he was engaged in the manufacture of Planes on a small scale in Boston, Massachusetts, but in 1869 sold out his business and practically all his inventions to the Stanley Rule & Level Company of New Britain, Connecticut. He was thereafter employed by them as the head of their Plane Department.

A great number of inventions for new devices on Planes appeared the latter part of 1800 but although they are more or less important in showing the development of the Plane none were of a permanent nature.

Bailey's claim to distinction was that he saw clearly the desirability of a thin steel cutter of uniform thickness, which could be kept in condition by honing only and whose original bevel could therefore be more easily maintained. He was the first man to invent a Plane in which such a cutter could be used to advantage. His inventions while few in number were of practical value and are still to be found in the Plane that bears his name.

In 1871 a patent was issued to G. A. Warren for improvements of the Plane. The particular feature as stated in his patent was a lateral adjustment of the cutter by means of a circular knurled thumb nut and eccentric plate. His patent was later acquired by the Stanley Rule & Level Company. Fig. 9.

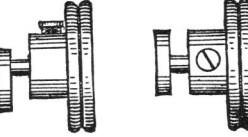

Figure 9.

The most important features of Mr. Warren's Plane were not even mentioned in the specifications of his patent. This was the first Plane to have correct balance, due to the proper placing of the cutter, and the knob, and the proper shaping of the handle. How accurately he satisfied the requirements of beauty and design and ease in handling is shown by the fact that the general design is followed today in the Stanley Bailey Plane.

Another feature of Mr. Warren's Plane was the use of a separable frog. Fig. 10.

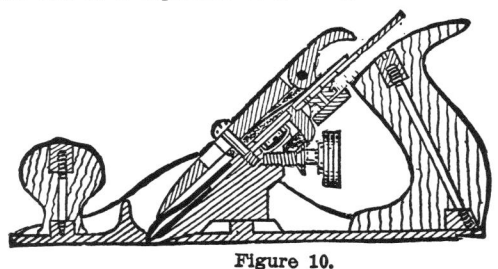

Figure 10.

A further improvement was made by J. A. Traut who was associated with the Stanley Rule & Level Company. In 1888 he was awarded a patent for the lateral adjustment of the Plane cutter. Fig. 11.

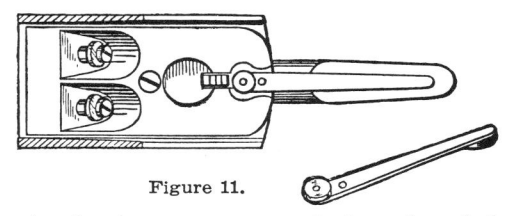

Figure 11.

Another improvement was the invention of the two step paralleled seating of the frog in 1902, by H. Richards, also associated with the Stanley Rule & Level Company. Fig. 12.

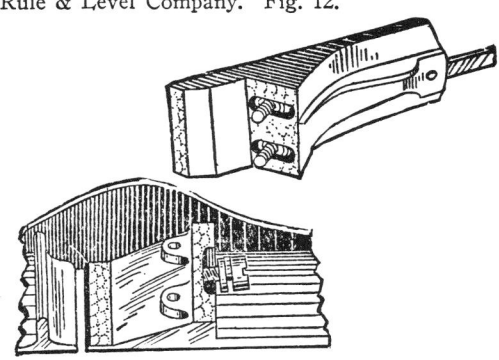

Figure 12.

The last major progress in the construction of the Stanley Bailey Plane was made by an employee of the same company, E. A. Schade, in 1910. His patent was an improved bearing on the bottom end of the frog which gave added strength to the frog base and prevented the slightest movement.

The most recent improvement in the Plane was the enlarging of the adjusting nut facilitating the adjustment of the cutter.

Another valuable addition is in having the knob fitted into an embossed ring in the casting which acts as a ferrule on the base of the Plane knob.

This is the story of the evolution of one of the most important tools for woodworking of our present day, the Stanley Bailey Plane.

It is not the invention of any one man but is a combination of the best features of many inventions of many men. It is a good example of that great Universal Law that applies to the mechanical as well as the natural world and decrees that only what is best and fittest shall survive.

STANLEY TOOLS
DIVISION OF THE STANLEY WORKS
NEW BRITAIN, CONN., U. S. A.

CHART No. 131

PRINTED IN U.S.A

Courtesy of STANLEY TOOLS, Division of The Stanley Works, New Britain, Conn.

Plate XI. Page 39 from *1870 Stanley Rule & Level Co.'s Catalogue of Tools,* etc.

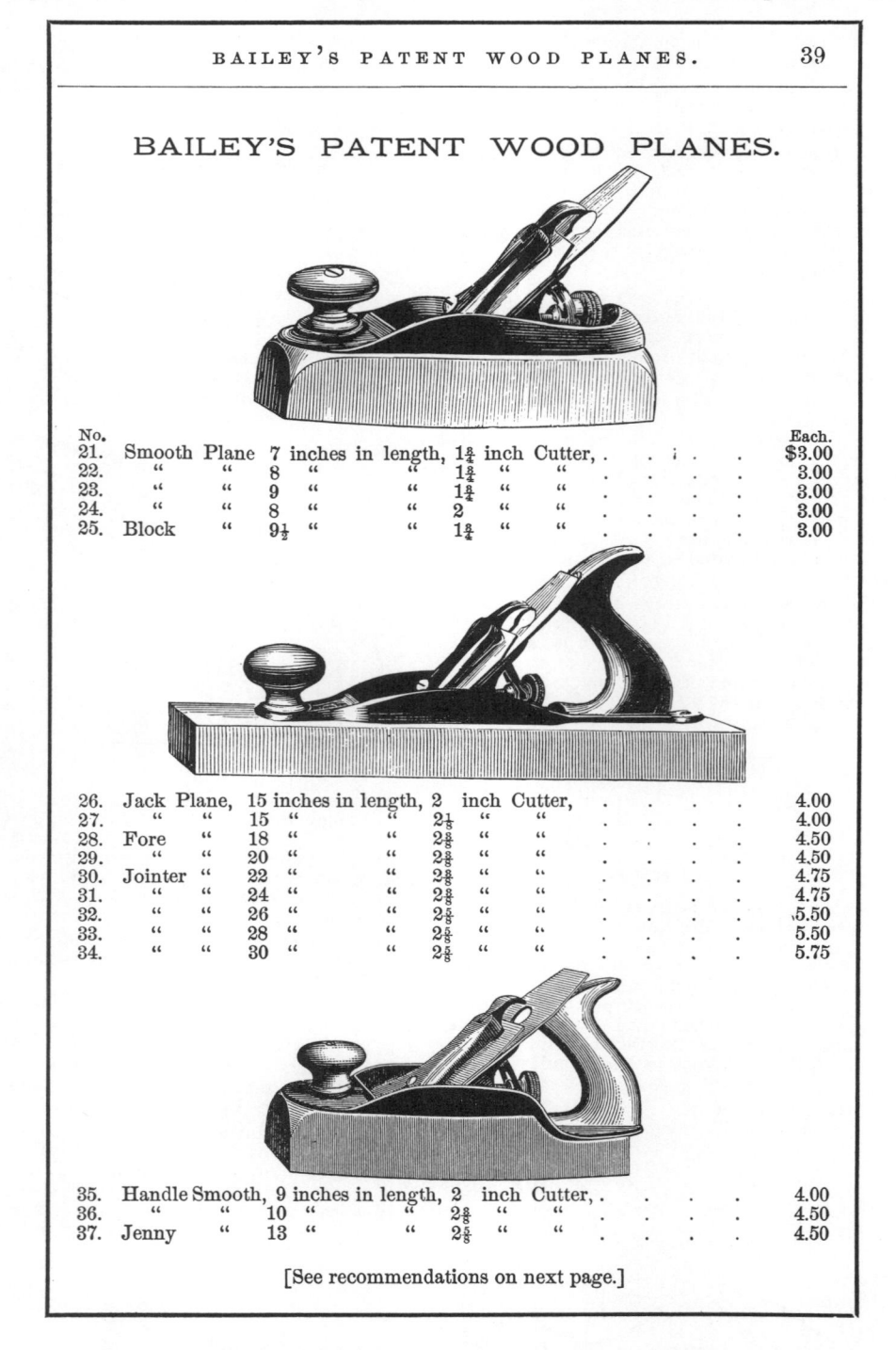

BAILEY'S PATENT WOOD PLANES. 39

BAILEY'S PATENT WOOD PLANES.

No.							Each.
21.	Smooth Plane	7 inches in length,	1¾ inch Cutter,				$3.00
22.	" "	8 "	1¾ " "				3.00
23.	" "	9 "	1¾ " "				3.00
24.	" "	8 "	2 " "				3.00
25.	Block "	9½ "	1¾ " "				3.00

26.	Jack Plane,	15 inches in length,	2 inch Cutter,				4.00
27.	" "	15 "	2¼ " "				4.00
28.	Fore "	18 "	2⅜ " "				4.50
29.	" "	20 "	2⅜ " "				4.50
30.	Jointer "	22 "	2⅜ " "				4.75
31.	" "	24 "	2⅜ " "				4.75
32.	" "	26 "	2⅝ " "				5.50
33.	" "	28 "	2⅝ " "				5.50
34.	" "	30 "	2⅝ " "				5.75

35.	Handle Smooth,	9 inches in length,	2 inch Cutter,				4.00
36.	" "	10 "	2⅜ " "				4.50
37.	Jenny "	13 "	2⅜ " "				4.50

[See recommendations on next page.]

These tools meet with universal approbation from the best mechanics. For beauty of style and finish they are unequaled, and the great convenience in operating renders them the cheapest Planes in use; they are *self-adjusting* in every respect, and each part, being made *interchangeable*, can be replaced at a trifling expense. Both the Iron and Wood Planes are entirely independent in themselves, requiring neither hammer, screw driver, or wrench, to remove, replace, or adjust the Cutter, which is secured firmly in its place, or may be instantly released therefrom, by use of the cam with a Thumb-piece at upper end of the Cap over the same. Without removing the Plane from the work, or either hand from the Plane, by simply turning a Thumb-screw, located under the bed-piece on which the Plane-Iron rests, the Cutter may be accurately adjusted to any thickness of shaving desired.

☞ Each Plane is fitted in working order, and cannot fail to give entire satisfaction.

Plate XII - Page 40 from *1879 SR&L Co. Price List of Tools and Hardware*

40   THE STANLEY ADJUSTABLE PLANES.

Wood Planes.

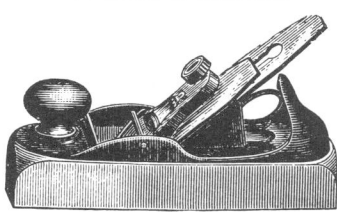

No.		Each.
122.	Smooth Plane, 8 inches in Length, $1\frac{3}{4}$ in. Cutter......	$1 50
135.	Handle Smooth, 10 inches in Length, $2\frac{1}{8}$ in. Cutter...	2 00
127.	Jack Plane, 15 inches in Length, $2\frac{1}{8}$ in. Cutter.....	2 00
129.	Fore Plane, 20 inches in Length, $2\frac{3}{8}$ in. Cutter.....	2 25
132.	Jointer Plane, 26 inches in Length, $2\frac{5}{8}$ in. Cutter.....	2 50

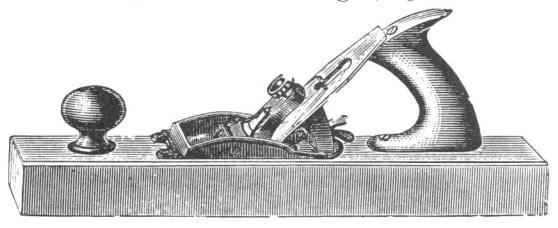

☞ The STANLEY PLANE IRONS are the same prices, for corresponding widths, as per list of Bailey's Plane Irons—See page 37.

PATENT IMPROVED RABBET PLANES.

WITH STEEL CASE.

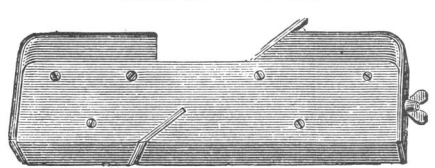

No.		Each.
80.	Rabbet Plane, Skew, 9 inches in Length, $1\frac{1}{2}$ in. Cutter.	$1 10
90.	Rabbet Plane, Skew, 9 inches in Length, with Spur, $1\frac{1}{2}$ in. Cutter...	1 25

TESTIMONIALS.

"The best Plane now in use."—CHICKERING & SONS, Piano Forte Manufacturers, Boston, Mass.

"I have used a set of Bailey's Planes about six months, and would not use any other now."—EDWARD CARVILLE, Sacramento, Cal.

"The best plane ever introduced in carriage-making."—JAS. L. MORGAN, at J. B. Brewster & Co.'s Carriage Manufactory, New York.

"From the satisfaction they give would like to introduce them here."—J. ALEXANDER, at Bell's Melodeon Factory, Guelph, Canada.

"Bailey's planes are used in our factory. We can get only one verdict, and that is, the men would not be without them."—STEINWAY & SONS, Piano Forte Manufacturers, New York.

"I have owned a set of Bailey's Planes for six months, and can cheerfully say that I would not use any others, for I believe they are the best in use."—C. C. HARRIS, Stair Builder, St. Louis, Mo.

"A Boston Mechanic says: "I always tell my shopmates, when they wish to use my Plane, not to borrow a Bailey Plane unless they intend to buy one, as they will never be satisfied with any other Plane after using this."

Fig. 8. SR&L Co.'s "Bailey's Patent Wood Planes. Top to Bottom: No.30 Jointer,22"; No.27 Jack,15"; No. 35 Handle Smooth, 9"; No.22 Smooth,8".

Fig. 9. Stanley Adjustable "Liberty Bell" Wood Planes & Patent Rabbet. Top to Bottom: No.127 Jack,15"; No.135 Handle Smooth,10"; No.122 Smooth, 8"; No. 90 Skew Rabbet Plane, 9" length, 1-1/2" Cutter with Spur.

Also illustrated for the first time was the No. 80 Patent Improved Rabbet Plane, shown below the "Liberty Bell" wood planes. This patent also by Traut and Richards (U.S.Pat.#168,431), dated Oct. 5, 1875, claimed the feature of fabricating a steel case for such a wood plane.

Illustrations of various Bailey and Stanley Adjustable Planes appear in Fig. 8 & 9. The entire Bailey line is shown in Fig. 10. This includes the No.27½,15" Jack, which was the only addition made to the group, other than the "Liberty Bell" series, and this was not made until early in the twentieth century. The #35 - 9" Smooth Plane shown in Fig. 9 has the Traut lateral adjustment feature, added after 1876; the other three planes appearing in this photograph predate this.

Perhaps the most unusual of the original seventeen Bailey "transitional" planes is the No. 37 "Jenny" Smooth, illustrated in Fig. 11. It has the rectangular shape of the larger fore and jointer, but a "Razee" effect in the frame casting. The cutter is 2-5/8" wide; the equal to the largest jointers. Floyd J. Locher has suggested the derivation of this name: -

> "The term 'JENNY' is the feminine of 'JACK' as applied most commonly to the jackass. Leonard Bailey may have had a good streak of humor in using this term to describe a plane that was shorter and broader in the beam than the Jack plane. . . . The plane was probably used for fast finishing of soft wood. . . "

Another unique item in this series was the #25 - 9½" Block Plane. This was originally offered with a single 1-3/4" width iron set at an angle of thirty seven degrees, lower than the forty-two degree angle of the other planes. Soon after this appeared with the double iron and with the Traut lever lateral adjustment. This plane is illustrated at the lower right in Fig. 12. Directly in back of this is shown a conventional 9-1/2" wood block mitre. At the left front in this same photograph is seen the #122 - 8" Smooth Plane with an ordinary wood smooth plane to the rear. At the center is seen an 8" smoothing plane with imprint "C.Fuller/Boston". Instead of the conventional wooden wedge, this has the L.Bailey spring-actuated cap iron, imprinted with his name and patent date, Aug. 31,1858.

The first of several competitive 'transitional' planes were developed and manufactured by the Gage Tool Co. of Vineland, N.J. What became known as "Gage's Self-setting Plane" developed from three patents noted in Plate XIII. The earliest under patent dated April 17,1882, by David A. Bridges was assigned in three-quarters part to John Gage. Subsequently John Porcius Gage was granted patents for improvements in 1885 and 1886. Five of these planes are illustrated in Fig. 13. Nine sizes are noted in the 1896 *Hammacher, Schlemmer & Co. Catalogue*, Plate XIV. Other models appear in other trade catalogues.[31] While these planes were generally supplied with beechwood soles, they are also known to have been furnished in both rosewood and applewood. Numerous advertisements of these Gage Planes in trade catalogues indicate that considerable competition must have resulted. Experienced craftsmen however report it debatable as to whether these products were superior to the Stanley-Bailey line. In any event SR&L Co. purchased the business of Gage Tool Co. in 1920.[32]

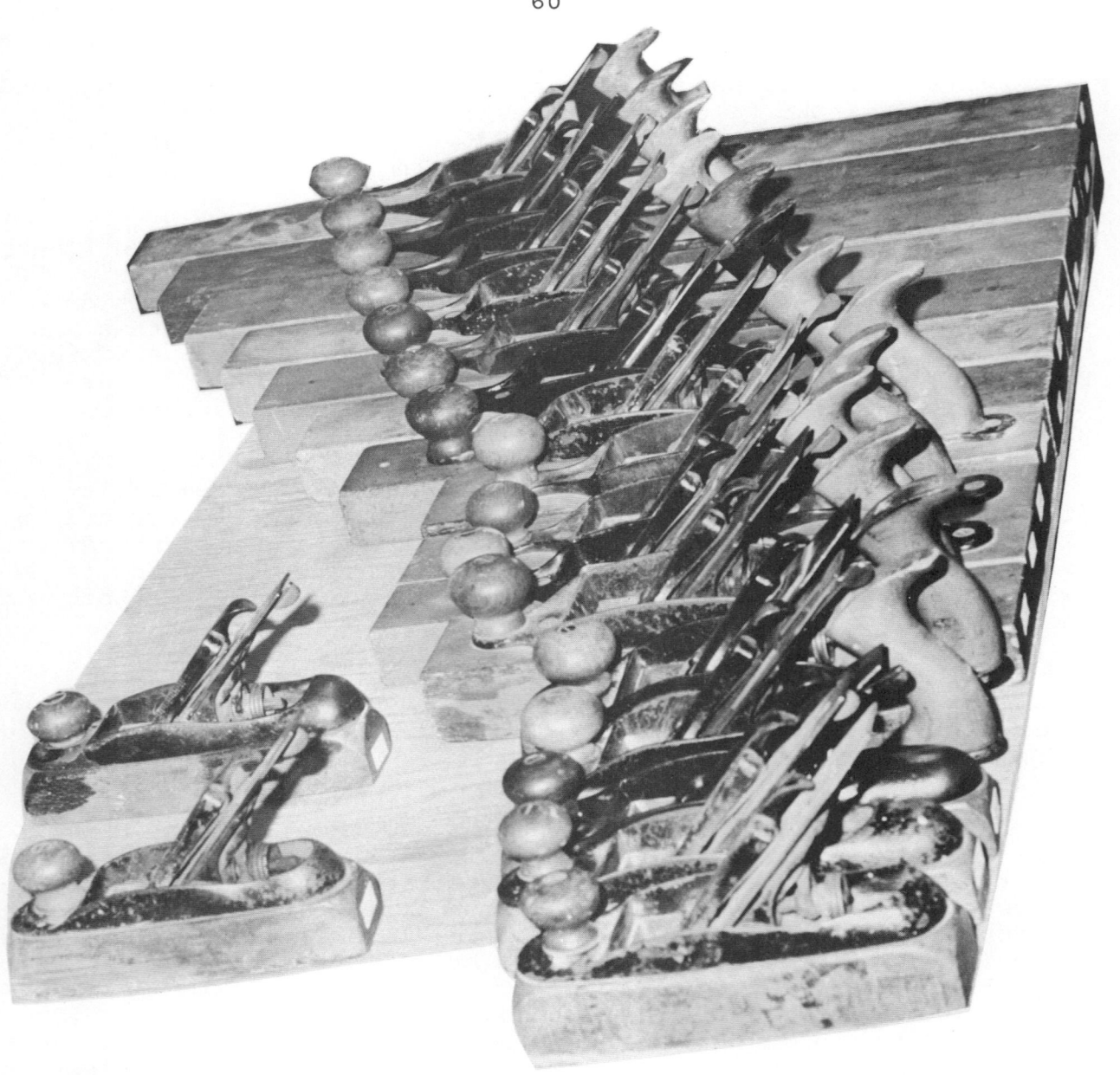

Fig. 10. The Stanley-Bailey Transitional Wood Soled Adjustable Bench Planes: Top to Bottom. Left Row: No.22, 8" long, 1-3/4" iron; No.21, 7" long, 1-3/4" iron. Right row. No. 34 Jointer 30" long, 2-5/8" iron; No.33 Jointer, 28" long, 2-5/8" iron; No.32 Jointer; 26" long, 2-5/8" iron; No. 31 Jointer, 24" long, 2-3/8" iron; No. 30 Jointer, 22" long, 2-3/8" iron; No. 29, Fore Plane, 20" long, 2-3/8" iron; No. 28 Fore Plane, 18" long, 2-3/8" iron; No. 27-1/2 Jack Plane, 15" long, 2-1/4" iron; No. 27 Jack Plane, 15" long, 2-1/8" iron; No. 26 Jack Plane, 15" long, 2" iron; No. 37 Jenny Smooth Plane, 13" long, 2-5/8" iron; No. 36 Handled Smooth Plane, 13" long, 2-3/8" iron; No. 35 Handled Smooth Plane, 9" long, 2" iron; No. 25 Block Plane, 9-1/2" long, 1-3/4" iron; No. 24 Smooth Plane, 8" long, 2" iron; No. 23 Smooth Plane, 9" long, 1-3/4" iron,

From the Collection of Floyd J. and Phyllis C. Locher. [Photo courtesy of Floyd J. Locher]

Fig. 11. Jenny Handle Smooth No. 37 Bailey Patent SR&L Co. Wood Plane. 13" long, 2" iron. [Photo Courtesy of Floyd J. Locher from his Plane Collection.]

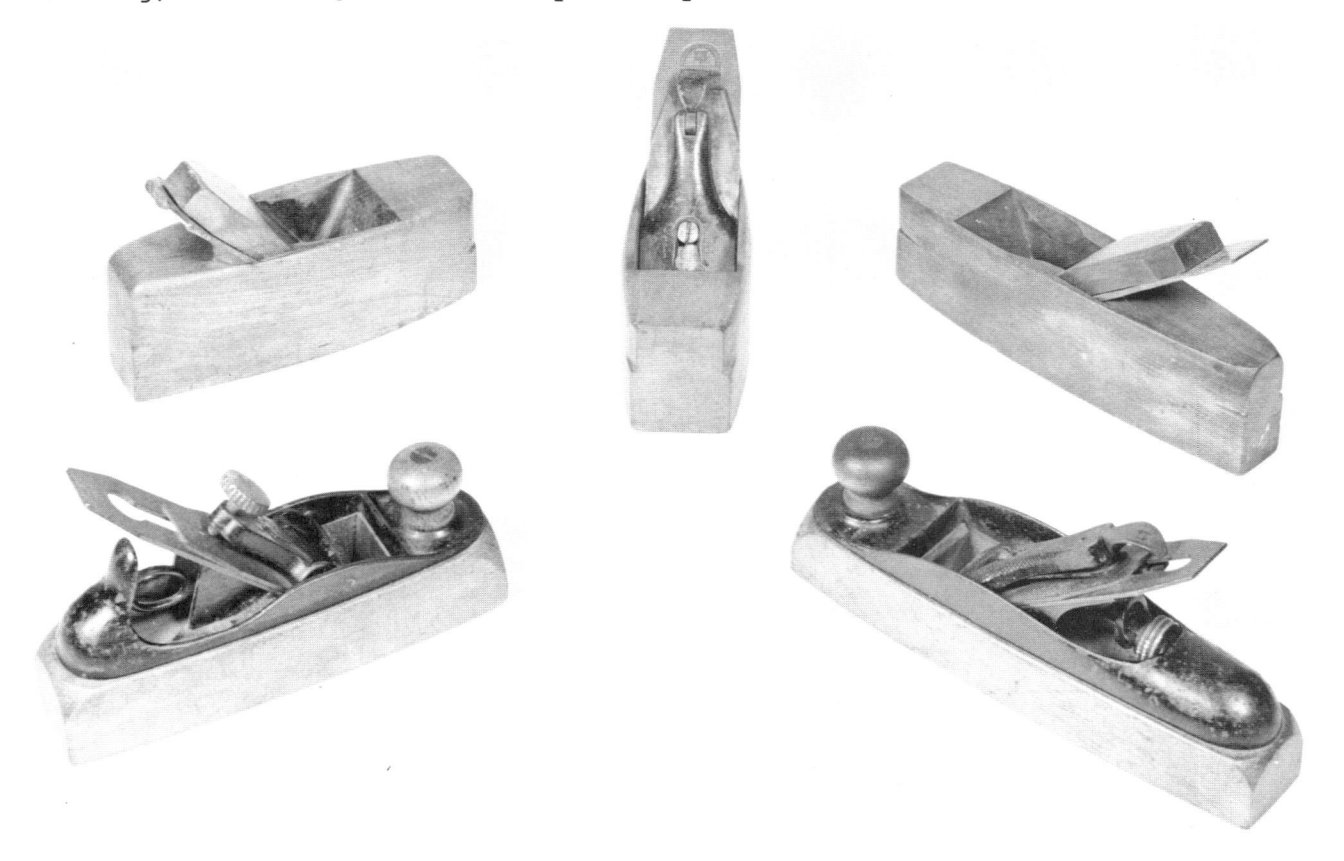

Fig. 12. Wood and Transitional Block and Mitre Planes. From left to right: Rear row: 8" wooden smoothing plane; C.Fuller imprint on 8" wood smooth plane with L.Bailey cast iron patented wedge; 9-1/2" wooden mitre plane.
Front Row: No.122 SR&L Co. 8" smooth plane; No. 25 SR&L Co. 9-1/2" Block Plane.

271,569. BENCH-PLANE. DAVID A. BRIDGES, Vineland, N. J., assignor of three-fourths to John Gage, same place. Filed Apr. 17, 1882. (No model.)

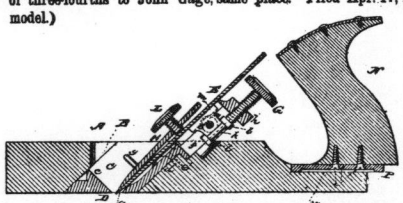

Claim.—1. In a bench-plane having fixed bearings in its throat for the cap-iron, the combination, with a cap-iron having lateral notches to engage said fixed bearings, of the independently-adjustable bit-plate E, adapted to be moved in the direction of its length without moving the cap-iron, substantially as specified.

2. The combination, with the oblique throat-iron and its adjusting-screw G, of the bit-plate E, its clamp-sections having lugs n, and the transverse connecting-screw, substantially as shown and described.

3. The combination with the oblique throat-iron and adjusting-screw G, seated therein, of the bit-plate E, having lugs n, engaging the said adjusting-screw, and the stationary cap-iron and its adjusting-screw, substantially as and for the purposes specified.

Volume 23, 1883, p.430

Plate XIII

Summaries of Gage Plane Patents

Copied from U.S. Patent Office
OFFICIAL GAZETTE

323,804. BENCH-PLANE. JOHN P. GAGE, Vineland, N. J. Filed Apr. 23, 1885. (Model.)

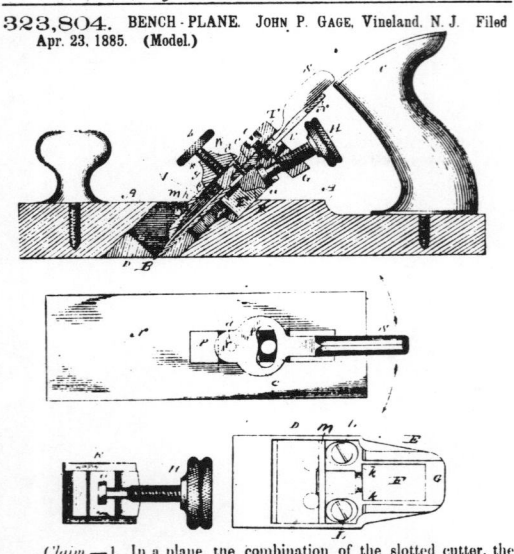

Claim.—1. In a plane, the combination of the slotted cutter, the under bearing, R, having a stud, d, and operated by means of the adjusting-screw, the fellow plate, screw connecting the fellow plate and bearing R, lever S, and its fulcrum-bearing c, arranged in the slot of the cutter, substantially as specified.

2. The combination of the slotted cutter, a bearing arranged beneath the same, with a stud passing through the slot of the said cutter a fellow plate connected with the said under bearing, the finger-lever and its fulcrum-bearing, as c, arranged in the slot, whereby lateral deviations of the cutting-edge may be corrected, substantially as specified.

3. A plane having a lever adapted to correct deviations in the edge of the cutter, which lever has its lower end pivoted in a longitudinal slot of the cutter, and provided with a stud to engage and move laterally a fulcrum-bearing in the said slot, substantially as specified.

Volume 32, 1885, p.625

339,872. BENCH-PLANE. JOHN P. GAGE, Vineland, N. J. Filed Jan. 16, 1886. (No model.)

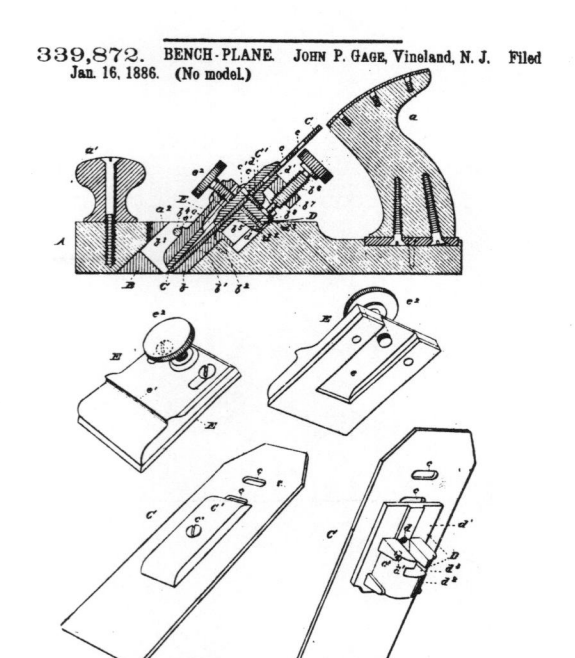

Claim.—1. In a bench-plane, the combination, with the plane-stock, the tool-holder, slotted as described, and the adjusting-screw b, moving in a threaded opening in said tool-holder, of the tool C, the clamping-plate C' on the outer side of the tool, and the clamp D on the under side thereof, the said clamp being provided with the block d^2, passing through the slot b^5 of the tool-holder and having the recess d^3, which engages the disk b^3 of the screw b, and the screw holding the clamp to the tool, substantially as specified.

2. In a bench-plane, the combination, with the plane-stock and tool-holder, constructed as described, of the clamps C' and D, the tool C, arranged between the said clamps and having the transverse slots c, and the screw c', for securing the clamps to the tool, substantially as specified.

Volume 35, 1886, p.205

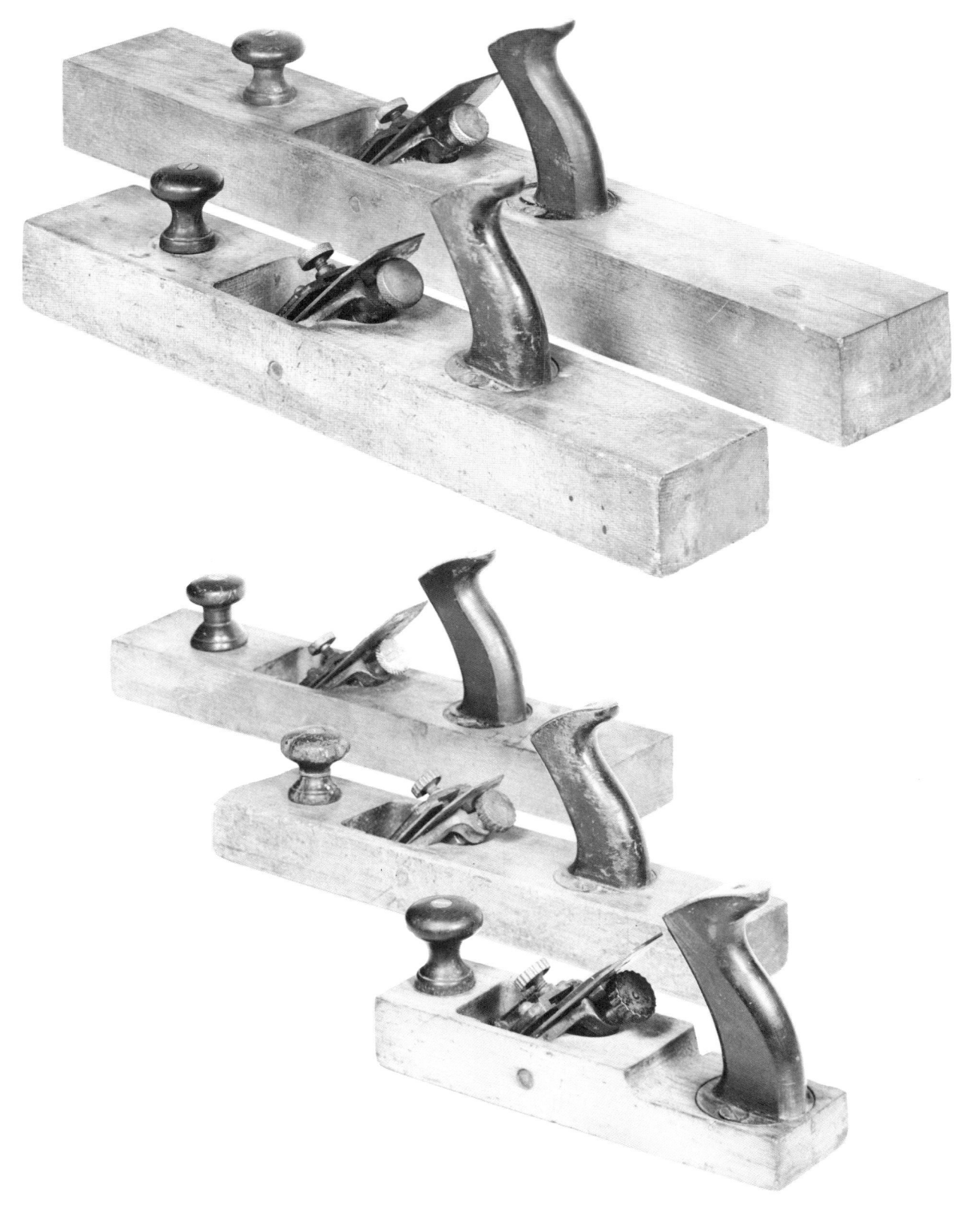

Fig. 13. Gage's Self-Setting Planes. From top to bottom; No. 21 Jointer, 24" long, 2-1/2" cutter; No. 12 Fore, 18" long, 2" cutter; No. 11 Jack, 16" long, 2" cutter; No. 7 Jack, 14" long, 1-3/4" cutter; No. 2 Smooth, 9" long, 1-3/4" cutter.

GAGE'S SELF-SETTING PLANES.

HAMMACHER, SCHLEMMER & CO.

Are self-setting in every respect, and can be perfectly set for the finest work with the eyes closed; the bit simply dropped into position, sets the plane with the most minute accuracy.

When properly adjusted, they cannot be set wrong. The cap and cutter may be removed, replaced and accurately set in five seconds, by actual trial; this alone would save many days in the course of a year usually spent in setting the cutter.

The adjustment is such that the cutting-iron may be set square with the face of the plane, even if the cutter is not ground square with itself.

The throat is prevented from wear by being within the adjustable iron bit-holder which extends through the plane.

The cap is not attached to the cutter, but remains stationary while the cutter is moved up or down by a thumb-screw; thus, even while at work the thickness of a shaving can be changed by a simple movement of the thumb and finger.

This tool can be changed from a double to a single iron, or from a single to a double iron plane in two seconds.

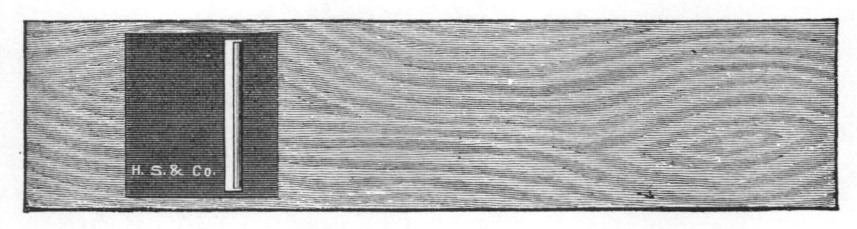

43

Bottom View. (Showing Adjustable Iron Throat.)

No.								Each,
No. 2.	Smooth Plane,	9 inches long	1¾ inch Cutter	....	Each,	$2.28
No. 4.	"	" 9 "	2 "	....	"	2.47
No. 4½.	"	" 10 "	2¼ "	....	"	2.67
No. 7.	Jack	" 14 "	1¾ "	....	"	2.47
No. 11.	"	" 16 "	2 "	....	"	2.66
No. 12.	Fore	" 18 "	2 "	....	"	2.85
No. 16.	"	" 20 "	2¼ "	....	"	3.04
No. 17.	Jointer	" 22 "	2¼ "	....	"	3.23
No. 21.	"	" 24 "	2½ "	....	"	3.42

Plate XIV. Gage's Self-Setting Planes. [*Hammacher, Schlemmer & Co. 1896 Catalogue, TOOLS for All Trades*, 209 Bowery, New York, N.Y., page 43].

Sargent V·B·M Adjustable Wood-Bottom Planes.

Patented February 3, 1891.

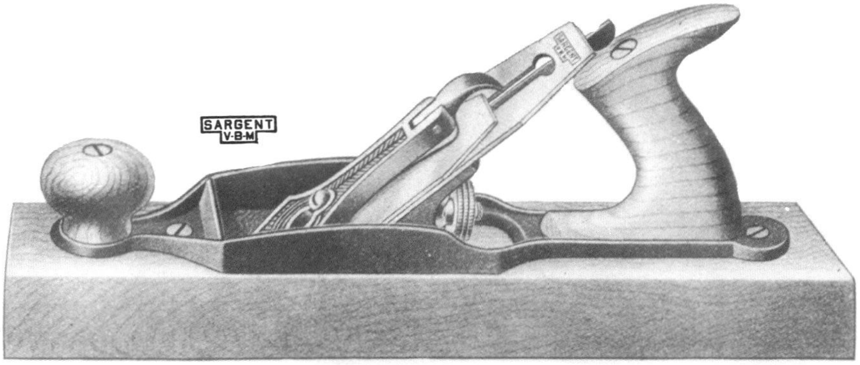

With Screw Adjustment.

With Patent Side Adjustment for exact adjusting of the Cutter with the face of the Plane.

Jack and Fore.

No. **3415**,	Jack Plane,	15 Inches,	2 Inch Cutter .	each, net	$1 60
No. **3416**,	" "	15 "	2⅛ " " .	" "	1 80
No. **3417**,	" "	15 "	2¼ " " .	" "	1 85
No. **3418**,	Fore "	18 "	2⅜ " " .	" "	2 00
No. **3420**,	" "	20 "	2⅜ " " .	" "	2 05

Jointer.

No. **3422**,	Jointer Plane,	22 Inches,	2⅜ Inch Cutter	each, net	$2 15
No. **3424**,	" "	24 "	2⅜ " "	" "	2 20
No. **3426**,	" "	26 "	2⅝ " "	" "	2 35
No. **3428**,	" "	28 "	2⅝ " "	" "	2 4(
No. **3430**,	" "	30 "	2⅝ " "	" "	2 5(

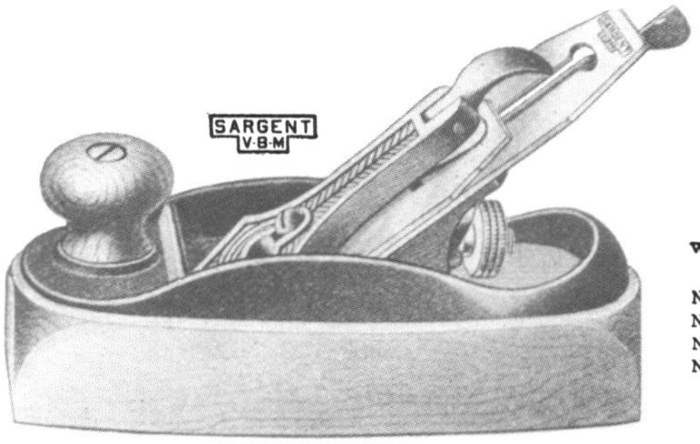

Smooth.

With Screw Adjustment.

With Patent Side Adjustment for exact adjusting of the Cutter with the face of the Plane.

No. **3407**,	7 Inches,	1¾ Inch Cutter . . .	each, net	$1 45
No. **3408**,	8 "	1¾ " " . . .	" "	1 50
No. **3409**,	9 "	1¾ " " . . .	" "	1 55
No. **3410**,	8 "	2 " " . . .	" "	1 60

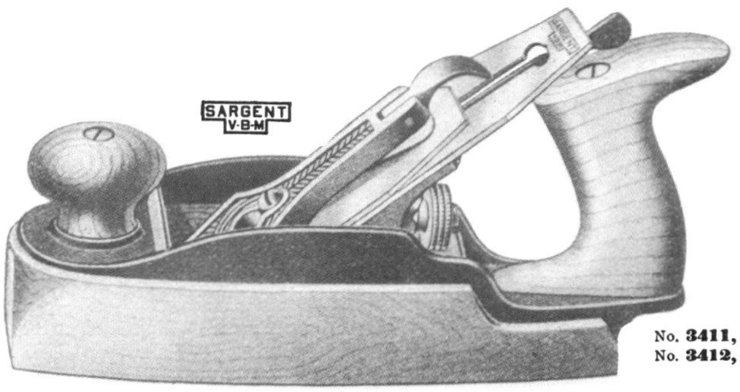

Handled Smooth.

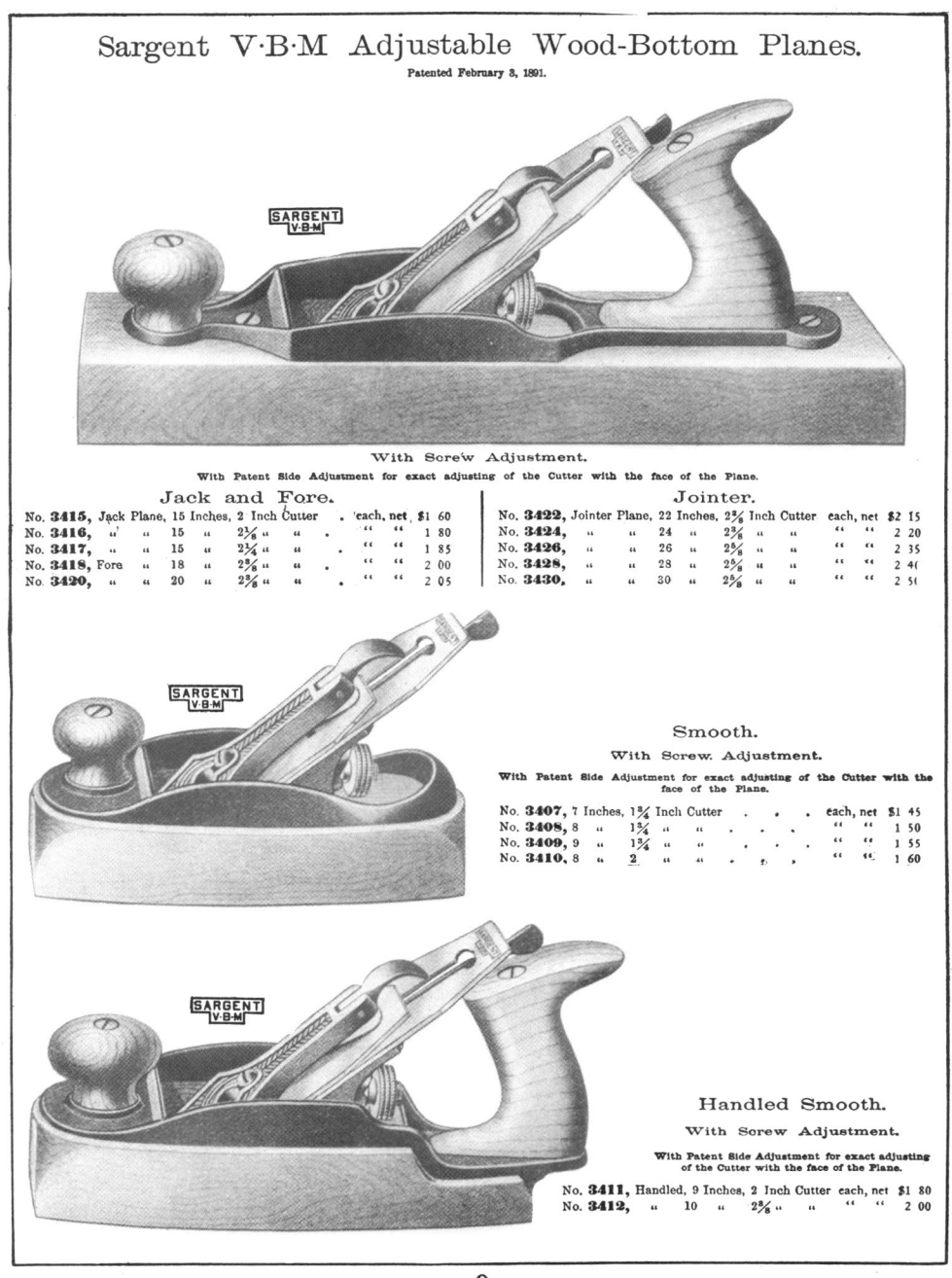

With Screw Adjustment.

With Patent Side Adjustment for exact adjusting of the Cutter with the face of the Plane.

No. **3411**,	Handled,	9 Inches,	2 Inch Cutter	each, net	$1 80
No. **3412**,	"	10 "	2⅜ " "	" "	2 00

9

Plate XV. Page 9 from *1911 SARGENT & Co. Book of Mechanic's Tools*. New Haven,Ct.

Noted in the above book: - *"All Tools bearing the* V-B-M *stamp are the Very Best Made and can be depended on as being made from the Very Best Tool Steel. They have just obtained an enviable reputation for excellence of material, temper and workmanship. They are fully guaranteed, and all dealer are authorized to take back or exchange if found defective in any particular"*

"The Cutter is made from the very best double refined ENGLISH cast steel and is tempered by the very best improved process, then highly polished and sharpened ready for use and is WARRANTED. To avoid the possibility of quivering in hard wood the cutter is now made from heavier steel than formerly." . . ."On the SARGENT wood bottom planes observe that: 1. The bottom is highly finished. 2. The wood is quarter sawed. 3. The frog is set into the iron framework with machine screws. These will not work loose. On other makes wood screws hold the frog to the wood bottom".

Upson Nut Co. located in Unionville district of Farmington, Conn., adjacent to New Britain, produced a 'transitional' line of planes made under the patent of G.Karrmann, #41,710, dated Sept. 10, 1889. This was a small operation and no match for the giant Stanley organization. About the turn of the century, after experiencing financial difficulties, this concern was bought out by SR&L Co. which eliminated this competition.

Sargent & Co. was established in New Haven, Conn. in 1864.[33] While they manufactured a line of hardware, initially they retailed tool products from other concerns. Planes and rules were obtained from the Chapin's Union Factory at New Hartford.[34] After Bailey's patents for the spring lever cap had expired, the Sargent firm acquired a patent dated February 3, 1891 for a lateral adjustment, competitive with the Stanley-Bailey line and commenced manufacturing planes of both iron and combination wood body with cast iron frames. The latter type is shown in Plate XV. Their trade mark "V-B-M" signified VERY BEST MADE. This line became the principal competition to Stanley and was continued until the beginning of World War II.

Union Manufacturing Co. was established in New Britain in 1866. Initially the stockholders were local manufacturers, including many of the officers of the SR&L Co.[35] The purpose was to provide a cast iron foundry for accomplishing work required by many New Britain firms. Among the numerous products were the cast iron plane beds and other parts for SR&L Co. In 1900 this firm acquired the Derby Plane Co. A line of both metal and 'transitional' planes was begun at New Britain.[36] The imprint UNION MANUFACTURING CO. on these planes includes "Pat. Oct. 28, 1889". This was a patent acquired from the Derby Plane Co.[37] This line was discontinued in 1920 when the Union Manufacturing Co. was acquired by the SR&L Co.

The Ohio Tool Co. brought out a line of 'transitional" planes of identical sizes as the SR&L Co.'s line. In fact the same numbering sequence was used as in the SR&L Co.'s catalogues, except that an "0" was placed before each number.[38] These appeared about the turn of the century. However the irons employed by the Ohio firm were the old type of heavy tapered construction. Apparently SR&L Co. did not mind its designs being copied, as long as they controlled the patent for the thin hardened steel irons.

A distinctive type of "double razee" wooden bench plane was manufactured by the Ohio Tool Co. either late in the nineteenth or early in the twentieth century. This was made in jack, fore and jointer sizes as noted on page 30 of their *Catalogue No. 25, "Ohio" Guaranteed Tools,* 1914. (See: Plate XVI) The firm was then located at Charleston, W. Virginia. These planes were also advertised in their *Catalogue No. 23,* c.1910, but it is not known whether these were made before 1900. The 30-1/2" jointer shown in Fig. 14, does not have an imprint, but the 2-1/4" cutter is stamped "Auburn Tool Co., Auburn, N.Y." Apparently this line of planes was exported to England as they appeared in a Melhuish (London, 1912) listing. (D-304)

WOOD BENCH PLANES--Continued.
IMPROVED WOOD PLANES.

Carefully made, faced, finely varnished with pure shellac varnish, and put in perfect working order before leaving the factory. The Wooden Wedge, nicely fitted, which many mechanics prefer to the Iron Holder, is used. They occupy a position in price between the iron and cheap wood Planes, and are in many respects very desirable. *The Bits are fully warranted, nicely blued at the upper end, whetted and tested.* Packed one each in a paper box.

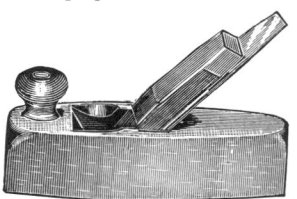

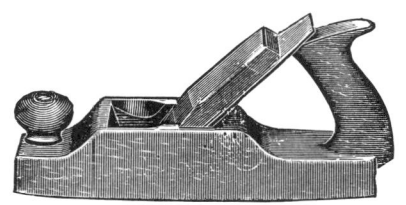

No. 280.   No. 282.

Invoice Nos.		Price Each
280	Smooth Plane, without Handle, 8 inches in length, 2 inch cutter	$1.50
281	Smooth Plane, without Handle, 8 inches in length, $2\frac{1}{8}$ inch cutter	1.60
282	Smooth Plane, with Handle, $10\frac{1}{4}$ inches in length, 2 inch cutter	1.90
283	Smooth Plane, with Handle, $10\frac{1}{4}$ inches in length, $2\frac{1}{8}$ inch cutter	2.00

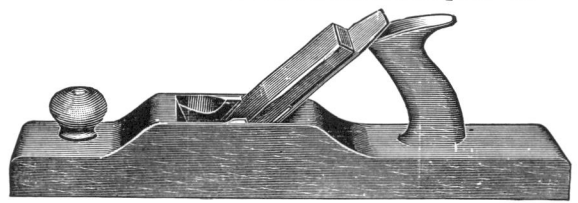

No. 284.

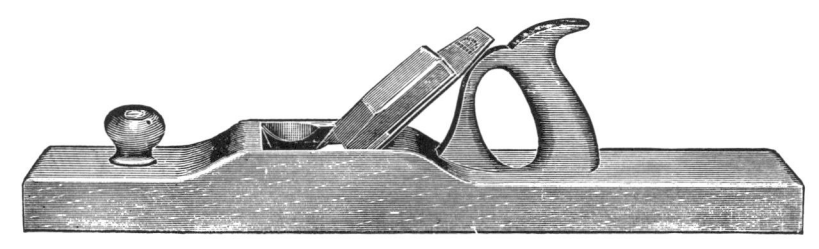

No. 286.

Invoice Nos.		Price Each
284	Jack Plane, 16 inches in length, $2\frac{1}{8}$ inch cutter	$1.80
286	Fore Plane, 22 inches in length, $2\frac{3}{8}$ inch cutter	2.65
288	Jointer Plane, 26 inches in length, $2\frac{1}{2}$ inch cutter	3.00
290	Jointer Plane, 28 inches in length, $2\frac{1}{2}$ inch cutter	3.15

Plate XVI. 'Double Razee Planes' Advertised in Ohio Tool Co. Catalogue No.25

Fig. 14. Double Razee Long Jointer Plane. ($30\frac{1}{2}$" x 3"). [see text]

Both SR&L Co. and Sargent wholesaled their planes to mail order houses and hardware retail sales companies. Hammacher, Schlemmer & Co. published a tool catalogue in 1896 listing 'transitional' "Stanley Patent Planes" with imprint "H.S.& Co." : -[39]

"Nos. 21 - 24 Smooth; Nos. 35 & 36 Handled Smooth;
Nos. 26 & 27 Jack; Nos. 28 - 29 Fore; Nos. 30 -34 Jointer"

These were the same numbers listed in the SR&L Co.'s Catalogue and at about 60% less than in the latter's 1897 price list. Montgomery Ward & Co. offered SR&L Co.'s products, while Sears Roebuck & Co. offered Sargent planes with irons supplied by Fulton Hardware Co. of New York City. Transitional bench planes made by SR&L Co., Sargent, Union Manufacturing Co., Upson Nut Co., Ohio Tool and probably a Sargent with Fulton iron for Sears, Roebuck & Co. are illustrated in Fig. 15.

The development of the metal combination plane parallels the time period of the transitional and cast iron bench plane. A combination plane is capable of interchanging cutting irons so that multiple operations may be performed using the same stock.[40]

Thomas Worrall, while residing at Mount Holly, N.J. was granted U.S. Patent #11,635, dated Aug. 29, 1954, for a "Multiform Molding Plane". His claim was for a "plane capable of working all kinds of grooves, fillets and mouldings". On Dec. 23,1856 he was granted reissue No. 418 for this patent, announcing that he was then residing at Lowell, Massachusetts. The particular patent concerned separate dovetailed slides fitted and held in a common stock. Each slide performed a different function for such separate operations as sash fillister, plow, rabbet or various mouldings. Hilton has described and presented a sketch of such a plane from the patent drawing.[41] As previously mentioned in connection with the development of the 'transitional' bench planes, Worrall may have had some connection with both the Lowell Tool and Plane Co. and the Multiform Plane Co. of Boston. On September 29, 1857 Worrall was granted another patent, #18,312, for a method of attaching an adjustable handle on planes. The idea was to interchange the same handle for separate stocks, thus reducing the space required in the tool chest for carrying planes. Such a plane is illustrated in Fig. 16 showing the brass wing nut with washer in the T-slot for attaching the handle. The sketch from the *Patent Journal* illustrating this feature is also included.[42] Peculiarly planes of this construction bear the imprint: "MULTIFORM/MOULDING CO./Patented/ Aug.29,1854". The date of the patent referred to the interchangeable bottom inserts of three years previous and not to the feature of the handle. Further confusion results from a plane of this construction, bearing the patent date of Aug. 29,1854, but with imprint of OHIO TOOL CO.[43] It would appear that either Worrall or Multiform Tool Co. offered such planes to the Ohio firm for their retail sales.

William S. Loughborough of Rochester, N.Y. was granted patent #23,928, dated May 3,1859. He stated: "...I have invented a new and useful IRON Fillister Plane, the principles of which are applicable, with slight modifications, to panel-plows, match-planes, dados, rabbets and to bench planes."[44] This was manufactured by a relatively small firm in Rochester. Due to limited marketing and promotional advertising, this plane did not become widely known.

Fig. 15. Transitional Type Wooden Sole Bench Planes. Left to right. - SR&L Co. "Bailey" No. 27, 15" long, 2-1/8" cutter; Ohio Tool Co. (Auburn,N.Y.imprint on both plane and iron); 15" long, 2-1/8" cutter; Union Manufacturing Co.. No. 27, Pat. Oct. 22, 1889, 15" long, 2-1/8" cutter; Upson Nut Co. (Unionville,Conn.) No.27, 15" long, 2" cutter; Probably Sears, Roebuck & Co. (iron stamped Fulton Co.,New York,N.Y.), 20" long, 2-1/4" cutter; Sargent V-B-M, No. 3418, 18" long, 2-1/4" cutter.

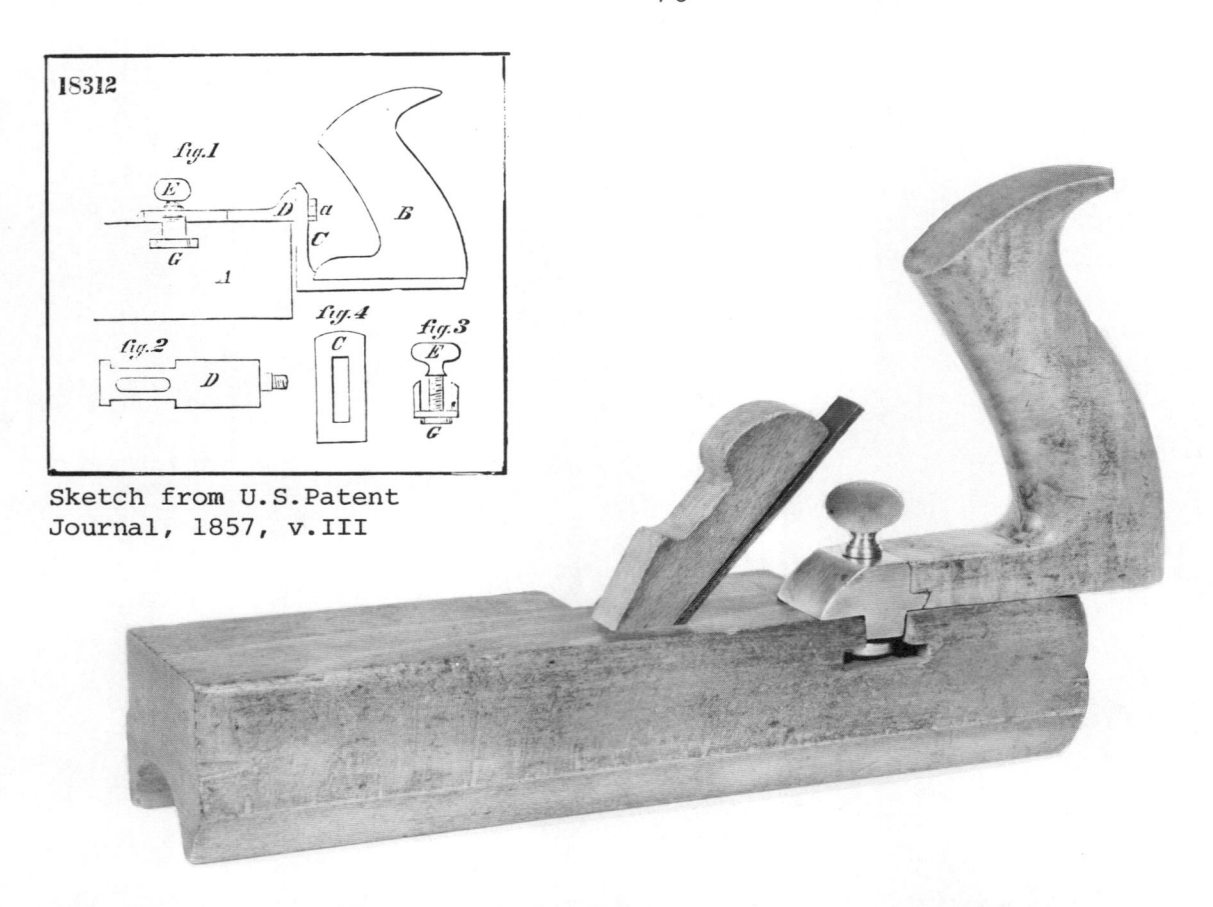

Fig. 16. T.D. Worrall Patent No.18,312, Sept. 29,1857 Plane. Imprint: *Multiform Moulding Plane Co.* 9-1/2" long. Collection of James C. Tillinghast.

Fig. 17. "Phillips' Plough Plane" Pat'd. Aug.31,1867: also imprint of Babson & Repplier, 7 Doane St.,Boston. C.C.Harlow/Maker/Bridgewater/Mass. 9-1/2" long.

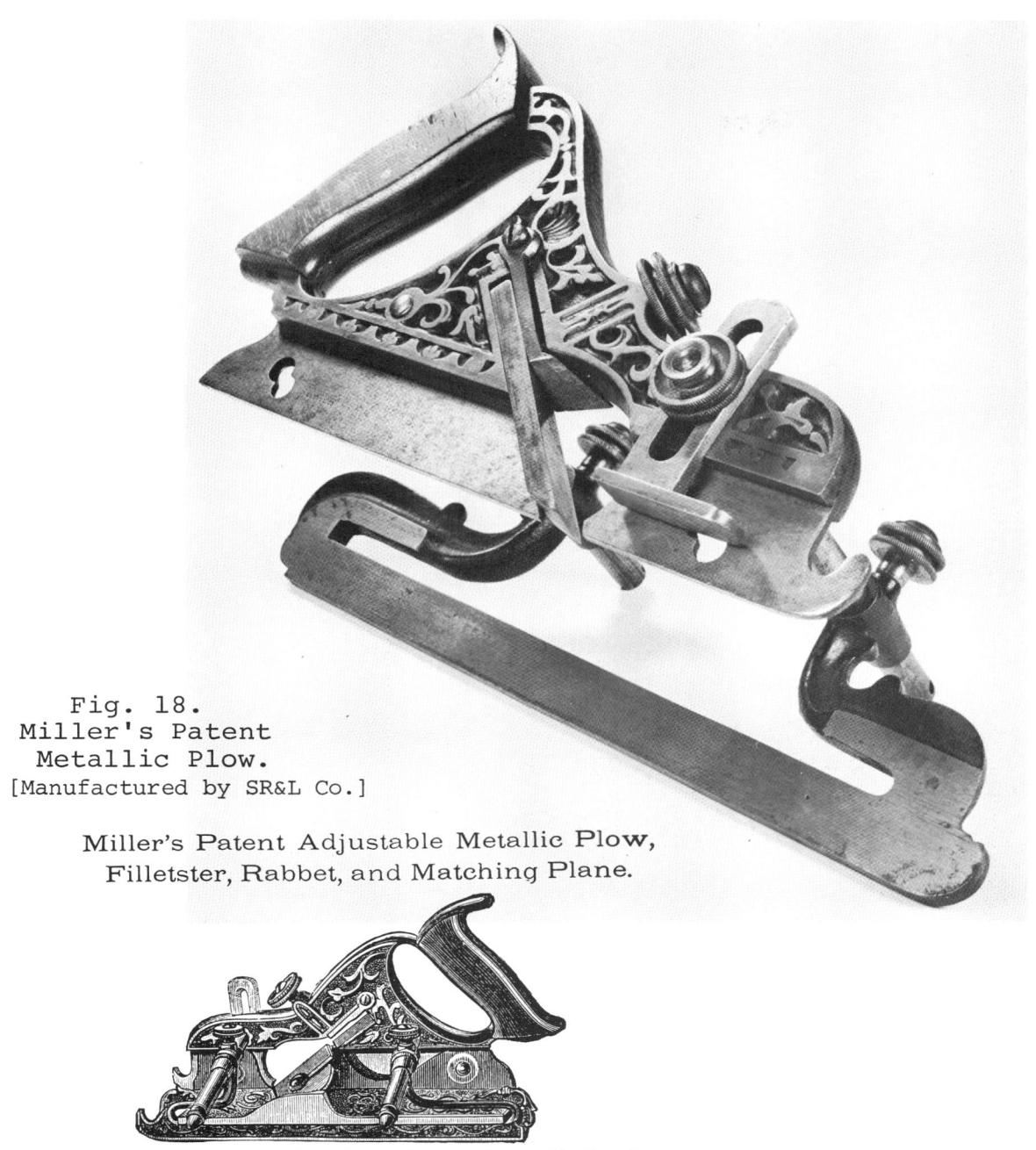

Fig. 18.
Miller's Patent
Metallic Plow.
[Manufactured by SR&L Co.]

Miller's Patent Adjustable Metallic Plow,
Filletster, Rabbet, and Matching Plane.

This tool embraces, in a most ingenious and successful combination, the common Carpenters' Plow, an adjustable Filletster, and a perfect Matching Plane. The entire assortment can be kept in smaller space, or made more portable, than an ordinary Carpenters' Plow.

Each Tool in this combination is complete in itself, and is capable of more perfect adjustment, for its specific uses, than the most improved form of the same Tool as manufactured separately by any other party.

Announcements in 1871 Supplement
to 1870 SR&L Co. 1870 *Catalogue
of Tools and Hardware,*

The above drawing represents the FILLETSTER, which may be readily adjusted to cut any required width, by regulating the horizontal Guage which slides upon the two bars on the front side of the Stock. The depth to be cut can be adjusted by use of the upright Guage, with a Thumb-screw, on the back side of the Stock.

Russell Phillips of Boston invented a combination plow and filletster plane for which he was granted patent #67,671, August 6, 1867. Subsequently Philips was granted Letters Patent #106,868, dated August 30, 1870: "Improvement in Carpenter's Planes", stating:

> "This invention combines in one implement elementary features found in several independent tools, the result being a great saving in space in transportation, as well as in stores and carpenters' shops and enabling a mechanic to obtain, at small comparative cost and in a compact and efficient form, the substitutes for several classes of planes. . . . While this invention consists primarily of the combination of a rabbeting-plane and an expansible matching plane, the latter, in turn will be found to consist of several members, so organized as to enable one to produce a "tongued grooved-connection", called "matching stuff", a "cross-channel", or a "plowed groove of any desired dimensions."

This latter plane was very elaborate in design and more costly to produce than the Miller combination plane manufactured then or shortly thereafter by SR&L Co. An illustration of the earlier Philips' patented plane is shown in Fig. 17.

Charles Miller of Brattleboro, Vermont invented a combination plane specified in his U.S.Patent #104,753, dated June 28, 1870.[45] At that date SR&L Co. was manufacturing the line of Bailey patent iron and wood bench planes. Charles Mead, formerly manager of the Stearns Rules at Brattleboro, had come to New Britain with SR&L Co. as a production manager. It was likely Mead who persuaded Miller to license his plane patent to SR&L Co. and also to join the firm at New Britain. While the title of the Miller patent was "Improvement in Carpenter's Planes", the specification stated:

> "My invention relates to a carpenter's plane, and consists in certain improvements for making it convertible into a *grooving, rabbeting, or smoothing plane*, as hereinafter described."

This was the first advertised in the 1871 Supplement to the 1870 *SR&L CO. Catalogue* in which this was referred to as: "Miller's Patent Adjustable Metallic Plow, Filletster, Rabbet, and Matching Plane". An illustration of this plane as first made by SR&L Co. and the "cut" appearing in the 1871 Supplement Catalog are shown in Fig. 18. Later Miller collaborated with Leonard Bailey, obtaining joint dado plane patent, as well as his own tonguing & grooving plane patent which were both assigned to SR&L Co.[46]

Further improvements in such combination planes were soon achieved by Justus A. Traut, a contractor at SR&L Co.[47] His patent #136,469, dated March 4, 1873, "Improvement in Carpenters' Planes" first approved in *SR&L Co.'s 1874 Catalogue*.[48] This became models Nos. 46 & 47, called "Traut's Patent Adjustable, DADO, FILLETSTER, PLOW ETC." [48] Traut continued to offer new ideas and designs with the famed SR&L Co.'s *"FORTY-FIVE"* appearing in 1884.[49] The advertisement with cut appearing in this SR&L Co. Catalogue as well as an illustration of this plane are shown in Fig. 19. Six different operations: beading; rabbeting; dado; plow; matching and slitting are noted. Soon after an attachment was offered for this plane for hollow and round operations. The most sophisticated of all combination planes was developed at SR&L Co. by J.A.Traut & E.A.Schade, Letters Patent #582,892, dated Jan.22,1895.[50] This became "STANLEY'S PATENT UNIVERSAL PLANE, No. 55". The cut illustrating

Fig. 19. SR&L Co. "45" - Traut's Patent Adjustable Combination Plane.

TRAUT'S PATENT ADJUSTABLE
BEADING, RABBET AND SLITTING PLANE.

This Plane embraces in a compact and practical form (1) Beading and Center Beading Plane ; (2) Rabbet and Filletster ; (3) Dado ; (4) Plow ; (5) Matching Plane ; and (6) a superior Slitting Plane.

In each of its several forms this Plane will do perfect work, even in the hands of an ordinary mechanic—its simplicity of construction and adaptation of parts (as described in the Directions which accompany each Tool) being easily understood.

☞ Each Plane is accompanied by seven Beading Tools (1-8, 3-16, 1-4, 5-16, 3-8, 7-16 and 1-2 inch), nine Plow and Dado Bits (1-8, 3-16, 1-4, 5-16, 3-8, 7-16, 1-2, 5-8 and 7-8 inch), a Slitting Tool and a Tonguing Tool.

Price, including Beading Tools, Bits, Slitting Tool, etc.,
No. 45. Iron Stock and Fence.. $8 00

Advertisement Announced in *1884 Stanley Rule & Level Co. Tool Catalogue.*

this as a moulding plane, which first appeared as an insert in 1897 to the 1892 Catalogue,[51] is shown in Fig. 20. This plane was furnished with fifty-two standard cutters. Special cutters were made to order. Blanks were available from which a workman could file any required form of moulding. While numerous combination planes were patented and manufactured by other firms after 1880 through the turn of the century, it was those made by SR&L Co. that were most effective in the demise of the wooden plane.[52]

Perusal of the 1895 *Montgomery Ward & Co. Catalogue No. 57* shows the decline of both wood bench and moulding planes.[53] A set of four wooden bench planes (smooth, jack, fore and jointer) made by the Ohio Tool Co. was offered for $1.80; a higher quality set from Barton Tool Co. of Rochester, N.Y. at $3.00. A set of these four planes of the Stanley "Liberty-bell" series at $3.25. This incidentally was less than 40% of the price listed in SR&L Co.'s 1897 catalogue. Seven types of wooden shaping and moulding planes were listed: hollow & rounds; rabbet; nosing; beading; moulding; dado and match were offered, totaling about seventy-five different sizes and items. Far more space was devoted to advertising bench and combination planes made of iron. The wooden plane industry was indeed sick and near its death bed.

The last known special wood-forming plane appeared about the end of the nineteenth century. This was offered by E.T. Burrowes of Portland, Maine for use in his patented sliding wooden window screen.[54] This is illustrated in Fig. 21. Instructions were printed on the side of this plane: "Use this tool for fitting Burrowes' Patent Sliding Screens. If screens do not run easily, groove out the shallow groove a little with this plane."

Wooden planes were still made by a few of the larger firms during the early years of the twentieth century. Among these were Ohio Tool Co., Sandusky Tool Co., and Chapin-Stephens. Honeyman Hardware Company of Portland, Oregon noted wood bench planes in their 1910 catalogue: -

> "There is still a demand for the old fashioned wood plane. We therefore stock the various styles and sizes commonly used. We do not show a cut of the Razee Jack plane, but we do carry it in stock. It is built on a similar line to the Ship Jack Plane."

Specific reasons for superiority of the "Bailey" wood plane over the "old fashion wood plane" are clearly stated in this same "Book of Tools" of Honeyman Hardware Co.: -

> "Every carpenter needs two or more wood planes in his kit for rough outside work. "Bailey" wood planes supply the demand for a wood plane of superior quality. The bottom, handle and knob are made from selected and well seasoned beech. The cutters are the regular "Bailey" type and are adjustable both endwise and sidewise. The frog is held in place by two machine screws which pass through the top iron and screw into the brass lugs. These lugs are screwed and securely pinned into the wood bottom. This is far superior to other methods of fastening, and it holds together firmly the wood bottom, the top iron which strengthens the wood bottom and frog."

75

Stanley Patent Universal "55" Plane

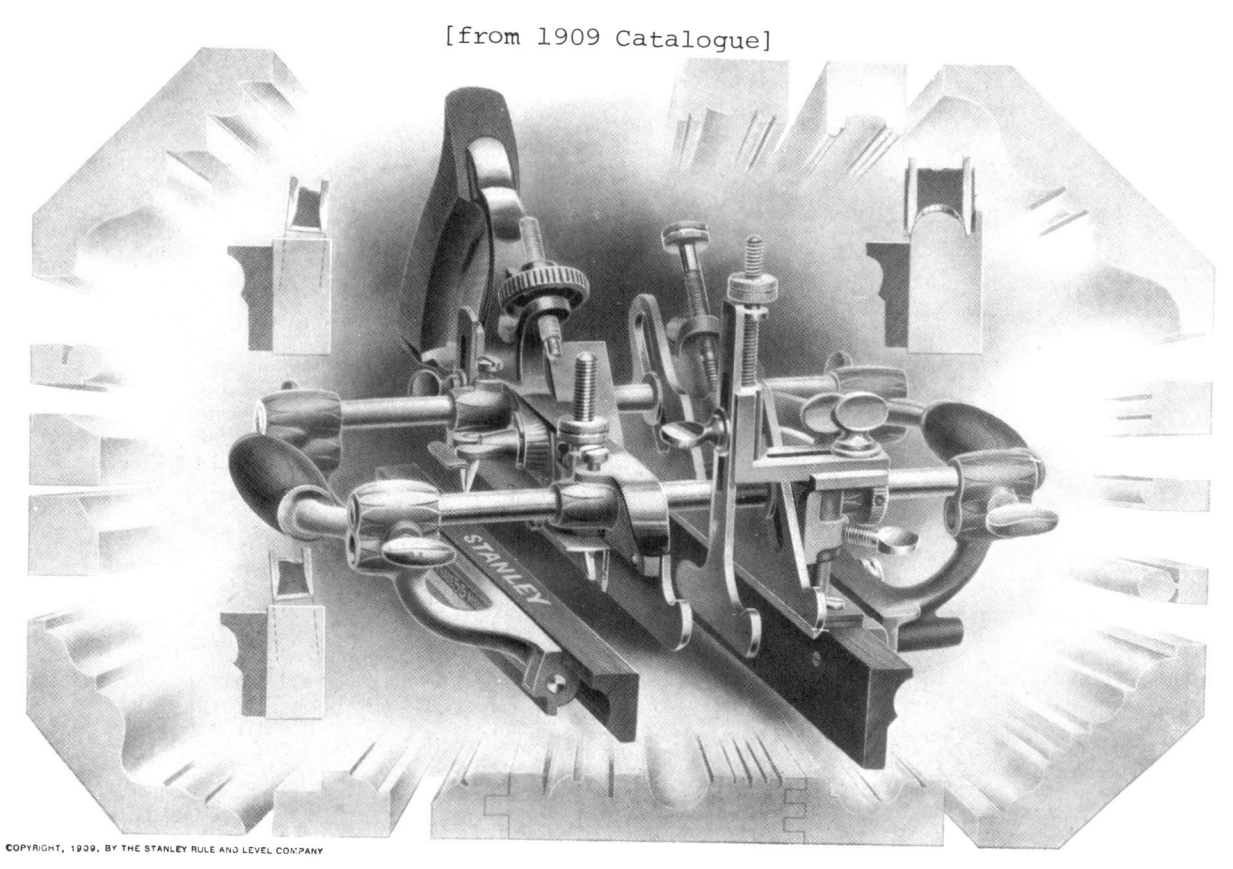

[from 1909 Catalogue]

ILLUSTRATION OF NO. 55 WITH SPECIMENS OF WORK DONE BY PLANE

Fig. 20. SR&L Co.'s "No. 55" [Advertisement from *Stanley Rule & Level Co. Catalogue No. 102 [1909]*, page 66.

STANLEY'S PATENT UNIVERSAL PLANE.

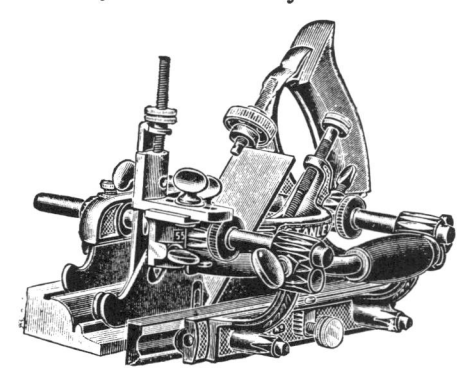

DIRECTIONS.

MOULDING PLANE.—Insert a Cutter, and adjust bottom of Sliding Section (B) to conform to the shape of the Cutter; then, by means of the two Check-nuts on the transverse arms, fasten this section firmly—*before tightening* the Thumb-screws which secure the sliding section to the arms.

When needed, adjust Auxiliary Center Bottom (C) for an additional support in front of the Cutter. By tilting the rosewood guides on Fences D and E, mouldings of various angles may be formed.

Advertisement of "55" Plane as a MOULDING PLANE. *1897 Supplement to SR&L 1892 Cat.*

The old style wooden bench and moulding planes were the dying victims of advancing technology.

Sales of "Bailey" planes reported by Stanley Rule & Level Co. in their various trade catalogues are noted in Table XI.[55]

Table XI

Total Sales of "Bailey" Planes, 1870 - 1898
noted in *STANLEY RULE & LEVEL CO.'S Trade Catalogues*

Year Reported	Cumulative Total Sales
1871	6,500
1874	80,000
1877	100,000
1879	175,000
1884	450,000
1888	900,000
1892	1,500,000
1898	3,000,000

This spectacular growth in sales of iron planes and successes at SR&L Co. was the combination of several factors: excellent management, sensitive to importances of new designs and products; high quality manufacturing with control of materials; effective sales organization with retail stores in principal cities throughout the country; promotional advertising and marketing of products with frequent publishing of trade catalogues.

The funeral services of the wooden plane industry were held at New Hartford in 1929 on which date the SR&L Co. purchased the Chapin-Stephens Co. This concluded 103 years of management by three generations at this site.[56]

Fig. 21. E.T. Burrowes' Screen Grooving Plane.

Notes Chapter IV

1. K.D. & J.W. Roberts, *PLANEMAKERS, etc.*, op. cit., pp. 124-139
2. *The Rules of Work of the Carpenters' Company. . .Philadelphia,1786*, Sketches:IX[Door Frames];X[Window Frames];XVI[Paneled Door Details], Reprint by Pyne Press,Princeton,N.J., 1971
3. E.G.Miller, Jr., *American Antique Furniture*, (New York,1937),V.II,p.60
4. *Ibid*, p.226
5. K.D.Roberts, *Eli Terry & Connecticut Shelf Clock*, (Bristol,Ct.,1973),p.137
6. *United States Patent Reports*,(Washington,D.C.,1843),Document #177, p.299
7. *U.S. Patent Reports for 1845*, (Washington,D.C.,1845), Document #75,pp.504-505
8. The historical development of the Woodworth Planing Machine is discussed in *Planemakers [op.cit]*, pp.126-129,(For details see Notes 8 & 10,p.139)
9. "Early Progress Made in the Manufacture of Woodworking Machinery",*WOOD CRAFT*, (Cleveland,O., Jan.1911), Vol. XIV, p.114
10. *The Worcester Almanac,Directory and Business Advertiser for 1845*, (Worcester,Ma., 1845), p.116
11. *op. cit.[Reference Note #9 above]*, p.112
12. H.Hjorth, *Machine Woodworking*, (Milwaukee,Wi.,1937), pp.11-14
13. *Ibid*, p.13. [Chapter I of this text,pp.1-23 Development of Machinery] Excellent!
14. *New York State Business Directory for 1859*, (New York,N.Y.,1859), p.105
    Also see: *Planemakers, op. cit.*, Plate 111, p.130
15. *Boston Almanac for 1853*, (Damrell and Moore & Coolidge)(Boston,Ma.1853),p.104
16. W.L.Goodman, *The History of Woodworking Tools*, (London,England,1964),pp.43-56
17. Originally this is believed to have been published sometime 1930/1935 as Chart. No. 131 by The Stanley Works,New Britain,Conn. as advertising material. The material was condensed from an article published in *Hardware Magazine*, (New York,N.Y., June 1913). This information was also published by the Stanley Works Ltd.,Sheffield,England, in a bulletin: *Brief History of the Plane*.
18. A photostat of this restored Patent by Knowles was sent to me by P.Welch when he was curator of the Growth of the United States in the Smithsonian Institution's Museum of History and Technology,Washington,D.C. Acknowledgement is made of use.
19. P.C.Welch, "United States Patents 1790 to 1870; New Uses for Old Ideas", *Contributions from the Museum of History and Technology [U.S.National Museum Bulletin]*, [Washington,D.C.,1965], Paper 48, p. 122, Fig. 12
20. Specifications of Patent #17,657,*Patent Office Report for 1857*,(Washington,D.C., 1857), V.II, p.270. Illustration, V.III, p.601. Some illustrations and descriptive material regarding these Worrall Patents are reported by W.B.Hilton, "The Boston Multiform Moulding Plane Co.", *CHRONICLE of EAIA*,V.28,No.2,pp.19-20.
21. W.L.Goodman, *HWT, [op.cit.]*, p.97
22. Details regarding "Bailey's Patent Plane Irons" with an illustration appear on page 41 of SR&L Co. *Catalogue of Tools & Hardware*. [See: 1973 Reprint] of *1870*.
23. W.B.Hilton, "A Checklist of Boston Plane Makers", *CHRONICLE of EAIA*,V.27,No.2, July 1974, p.24. This article additional has an excellent brief review of Bailey's tool patents 1855/1867 presented with very fine sketches.
24. *Boston Business Directories; 1864/1867;* also *Boston Almanacs*
25. Documentary and references published in *SR&L Co. 1870 Catalogue* [1973 Reprint]
26. *Ibid, 1973 Reprint SR&L Co. Catalogue & Price List of Tools & Hardware for 1870*, [Ken Roberts Publishing Co.], p.40.
27. A contract worker was not actually an employee, but agreed with the management to produce a given number of finished articles on a contracted price. The contractor was provided materials, equipment, power and a place in the factory to work, but he hired his own work force. A deduction from payments to the contractor was made for spoilage of material and unsatisfactory products. This system of manufacturing was common in the 19th century.

Notes Chapter IV [continued]

28. This line consisted of two iron plane(#104-9" smooth & No.105-14" jack) and the five varieties noted in the 1877 *SR&L Co. Catalogue*.[wooden planes]
29. This Thumb lever device was indeed less expensive, but the regulation was not as accurately controlled as the screw device used on the "Bailey" line. This line was discontinued at SR&L Co. during the 1932 depression.
30. Correspondence from F.J.Locher, April 18, 1975
31. No.1-8" smooth with overhanging handle; No.6-12" jack; (both with 1-3/4" cutters); No.8-12" jack; No.13-20" fore (both with 2" cutters);No.18-24" joiner with 2-1/4" cutter; and No.19-2-1/2" cutter are illustrated in *Montgomery & Co.* (105 Fulton Street, New York,N.Y.,1897)Catalogue p.446 Presumably there was at one time a full line of from Nos.1-21.
32. SR&L Co. also manufactured after that date the Gage design for at least five different iron planes. SR&L Co. discontinued the Gage line about 1935, but continued to advertise these for a few years after to use up stock. See note No.4 in Documentary for my Reprint *SR&L Co. Catalogue No.102, 1909*.
33. "History of the Sargent & Co.", *Connecticut Circle*, (Hartford,Ct.), Jan.1954, V.17, p.31
34. *Sargent & Co. Catalogue of Hardware & Tools,*(New Haven,Ct., 1871)
35. "History of Union Manufacturing Co.", *Hardware*, (New Britain,Ct.) June 1926, Vol. VI, No.9, p.8-9, 23.
36. A line of eight"Union Adjustable Iron Planes.Bailey Pattern" and sixteen "Union Adjustable Wood Smooth and Bench Planes. Bailey Pattern." was advertised in the *Albany Hardware & Iron Co. Catalogue,*(Albany,N.Y., c.1901, p.194
37. Other patents acquired were by Charles F. Young; Bench Plane #455,957 and Plane Bit Fastening #456,104, both dated July 14,1891 and assigned to Union.
38. *Ohio Tool Co. Catalogue & Price List, No.23,* (Columbus,O.,c.1910)
39. *Tools for All Trades,* Hammacher, Schlemmer & Co.,(New York,N.Y.,1896),p.45
40. *SR&L Co.'s COMBINATION PLANES,* (hereafter,SCP) (Fitzwilliam,N.H.,1975),p.2
41. W.B.Hilton, *op.cit., Chronicle of EAIA,* V.28,No.2,July 1975, p.19,Fig.4.
42. *Patent Reports,* (Washington,D.C.,1857) Vol.III,#18312; Specifications,V.II,p.273
43. "Moulding Plane from the Collection of George Tuttle", *Chronicle of EAIA,* V.26,No.2,June 1973, p.32
44. *Planemakers, op. cit.,* Patent and commentary, pp.133-134
45. This patent with drawings is reproduced. See: *SCP, op. cit.,* p.10-11.
46. *Ibid,* pp. 5, 16-17.
47. J.A.Traut became one of the most prolific inventors in 19th century America. He was granted 128 patents in his own name and 21 joint with others. Note reference #11, *SCP, op. cit.,* p.11
48. *SCP, op. cit.,* pp. 12-15
49. *Ibid,* pp. 19-25
50. *Ibid,* pp. 48-59
51. *Ibid,* pp. 40-43
52. *Ibid,* See listing of patents. Inside of back cover.
53. Republished by Dover Publications,Inc., New York,N.Y., 1969
54. W.B.Hilton,"E.T. Burrowes", *Chronicle of EAIA,* V.26,No.4,Dec.1973,p.57
55. Shown graphically. Next to last page. *1888 SR&L Co.'s Price List,*[1975 Reprint]
56. It is doubtful whether planes were being produced by Chapin-Stephens Co. at that date. Their last known published Catalogue, dated Jan.1,1922 listed planes. SR&L Co. is believed to have purchased the Chapin-Stephens Co. to eliminate the competition of low priced rules manufactured at the latter firm. At that time F.M.Chapin and H.M.Chapin grandsons of the founder Hermon Chapin, were respectively President and Vice-president of Chapin-Stephens Co.

Chapter V

Classification and Identification of Wooden Planes

The "Wooden Plane Classification", published in the *Supplement* to the *Chronicle of EAIA*, (Vol. XIX, June 1966, p.1) was based on my earlier studies and research. Admittedly I was then unaware that considerable differences in spelling and terminology existed between Great Britain and United States. That classification was strongly influenced by Nicholson's, *Mechanic's Companion*. After considerable studies since 1966 of American trade catalogues and discussions with fellow collectors, a revised Classification of 19th Century Wooden Planes is suggested and presented in Table XII. These tools are divided into four basic groups: -

- A. Leveling or Smoothing
- B. Grooving
- C. Moulding
- D. Special Shaping

Groups A. & B., listed in the left column have flat cutting irons and are indeed true planes. Most of the tools listed in the right column, Groups C. & D., have shaped irons and therefore produce contours. In reality these are moulding tools rather than true planes, but have been called the latter name as they operate similarly. While this Classification is incomplete, as there exist several special tools regarded as planes, Table XII is believed to include the majority of types of planes used by the trades of carpentry, joiner, cabinetmaking, coopering and coach making.

The photographs that follow will correspond to this Table. The descriptions will be a revision of those previously published in my articles in the *Chronicle of EAIA*, referring to this material as: C. (Volume, Number and Page). References to the material appearing in the Appendix respectivly from: *Arrowmammett Tool Catalogue*, (A-page); Nicholoson's *Mechanic's Companion*, (N-page); Holtzapffel's *Mechanical Manipulation, etc.*, (H-page) and R.A. Salaman's recently published *Dictionary of Tools*, (D-page) will be with these initials and to the original page number in each text.

I. <u>Common Bench Planes</u>. As the name implies these are the common varities of leveling and smoothing planes used by craftsmen on the work bench for preparing "stuff" from board lumber for either further "shooting moulding" or finishing or jointing. Definitions and terminology of such planes were given in Chapter I. With exception of the short smoothing plane which was generally used on short pieces of work, this series of planes was employed in order of succession of increasing lengths to render the work more straight, level or smooth. The jack plane (14" - 18") used first to rough-out the saw kerf surface on the lumber resulting from the saw-mill.

CLASSIFICATION of 19th CENTURY AMERICAN WOODEN PLANES – Table XII

A. **Leveling or Smoothing**

I. Common Bench (length in inches)
  1. smooth (8")
  2. jack (16")
  3. fore [short jointer] (22")
  4. jointer (26"; 28"; 30")

II. Special Bench Planes
  1. mitre [smooth shaped or straight block]
  2. Bull horn smooth [German]
  3. Smooth with handle
  4. Toothing [veneer]
  5. Toy [boy] (smooth & jack)
  6. Instrument maker's [musical & technical]

III. Ship Planes [Razee]
  1. jack (16")
  2. fore (22")
  3. jointer (26"; 28'; 30")

B. **Grooving**

IV. Plow
  1. wedge arm
  2. screw arm
  3. premium types

V. Match (tongue & grooving)
  1. board [without/with handle]
  2. plank [usually "   "]
  3. moving [wedge/screw arms]

VI. Rabbet
  1. filletster
  2. common [square & skew iron]
  3. fixed fence
  4. handle ["Jack" Rabbet]
  5. Raising or Panel
  6. halving
  7. side

VII. Dado [skew iron]
  1. wood stop
  2. brass stop
  3. screw stop

C. **Moulding or Shaping**

VIII. Simple moulding
  1. hollows & rounds
  2. astragals
  3. beads, torus, quarter round
  4. reeds
  5. scotia, covetta, & ovalo, &c.

IX. Complex Moulding
  1. simple Ogee
  2. Grecian Ogee
  3. Grecian Ovalo
  4. Combination [numerous styles]
     example: Grecian OG & Bevel (complex & simple)
  5. Snipe's Bills

X. Sash [combination rabbet & moulding]
  1. single iron
  2. double iron [plain, box screw regulating & brass pad types]
  3. coping [single & double]

XI. Cornice [single & double iron]

D. **Special Shaping Planes**

XII. Carpenter, Joiner & Cabinetmaker
  1. Gutter or Pump
  2. Spar or Mast
  3. Stair [nosing]
  4. Compass
  5. Chamfer
  6. Corebox [pattern maker's]
  7. Slitting
  8. Routing

XIII. Coopers'
  1. jointer [single & double irons]
  2. leveling [sun]
  3. howell
  4. croze

XIV. Carriage Maker's
  1. smooth [flat & circular]
  2. plain rabbet [flat & curved]
  3. T-Rabbet [flat & curved]

Next the 22" fore plane removed the wavy surface left from the jack or produced a straighter edge. This was followed by selecting a jointer plane (24' - 30"), the length being chosen according to the degree of straightness or levelness required for the finished work. Illustrations of bench planes are shown in Figs. 22 and 23.

Fig. 22 - BENCH PLANES   [front to rear: 8" smooth,16" jack,22" fore and 26" jointer]

Fig. 23 - JOINTER PLANES   [front to rear: 26", 28" and 30"]

A sectional drawing of a jack plane with names of the principal parts is shown in Plate XVII. (Also see: H-477) Most jack planes have a single handle (tote), while the longer fore and jointer types have double handles for improved support in guiding these planes. The bodies (stocks) of planes were generally made from seasoned white beech, but occasionally applewood, rosewood or some other hard fancier woods were employed. The 'knock-out pin', called the "start", was tapped with a mallet to loosen the wedge for removal, adjustment cleaning or sharpening the cutting iron. This was an optional feature furnished with the better grade planes and was either a pin made from boxwood or iron. (See: A-4) The most frequent pitch of the iron was at 45 degrees angle with the sole, used for soft woods and called "Common Pitch". For harder woods the pitch was slightly steeper (See: H-482) The bodies of the bench planes were usually rectangularly shaped, with exception of the smoothing plane, and increased slightly in breadth and height in proportion to increasing lengths. Smoothing planes were usually 'coffin' shaped being widest at the mouth (2-1/2") and tapered toward each end. (2" wide)

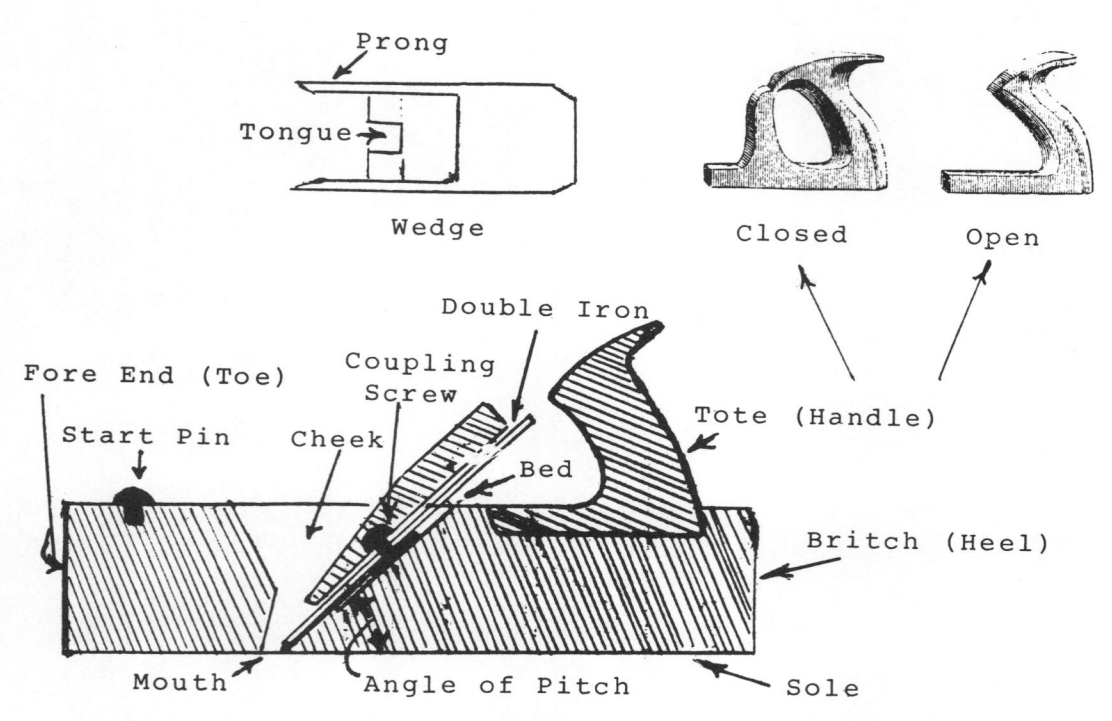

Plate XVII - LONGITUDINAL HALF-SECTION of a JACK PLANE

The best bench planes were furnished with double irons, a practice which became increasingly common after 1800. A single iron and various views of a double iron are illustrated in Fig. 24. Such irons, as previously mentioned for economy, were generally composed of a high-carbon steel cutting edge scarf welded to a low carbon extension. The two parts forming a double iron are respectively called the 'cutting' and the 'break' irons, and are joined together by a coupling screw. (See: H-480'81) The break iron formed a steep slope for the rising shaving and also stiffened the cutting iron. Accordingly both tearing and chatering were minimized in comparison to a single iton, thus accomplishing a smoother surface. The cutting iron was made with a longitudinal slot which allowed the coupling screw to pass through and attach the former to the break iron and provided for easy adjustment and removal.

| Single Iron | Break-iron on on top of Cutting-Iron | Break-iron (left) Cutting-iron (right) | Cutting-iron on top of Break iron |

Fig. 24 Single and Double Plane Irons

    The angle, or taper (called 'basil') to which the cutting edge was ground depended on the nature of the material being planed. In the jack, sometimes in the fore, plane iron were ground with a degree of convexity across the width. (See: Fig.6) This prevented tearing or gouging the surface at the edges of the iron on the planed surface during heavy cuts and rapid stock removal. This subject is discussed in detail in both Nicholson and Holtzapffel. (see: N-92-93 & H-479-481). The degree of convexity was less in a fore plane than the jack. Jointer and smoothing planes were usually ground straight across the entire width. Additional references to Bench Planes and their irons may be found in: C-V.XIX,No.4,Dec.1966,pp.49-51; also: D-305, 329, 332, 333, 368-69.

II. <u>Special</u> <u>Bench</u> <u>Planes</u>. (C., V.XX,No.1,March 1967,pp.4-5)

1. *MITRE* (Fig. 25; N-97). A mitre [British spelling, preferred American, *miter*] joint consists of two pieces cut at 45 degrees and fitted together to form a right angled joint. This was commonly used in making looking glasses [mirrors], picture frames, clock cases and cabinet doors. Since the cut was invariably across the grain the mitre plane, used for trimming and fitting the adjacent edges of the joint, had the iron set at a lower angle. (usually about 40 degrees) Such mitre planes were made in two basic shapes. (See: A-5) The *Smooth Shape*, shown in between the other two in Fig. 25, is similar to a 'coffin' type smooth plane, but slightly narrower. The illustrated plane, 9" long, tapers from a width of 1-1/4" at each end to a maximum width of 2-1/8" at the mouth. The other two planes illustrated in Fig. 25 (right and left) are called *Square Mitre* or *Straight block Mitre*. Most mitre planes were furnished with a single iron. Note the plane shown on the right has a "start" (knock-out pin)

2. *Bull Horn Smoothing Plane* (Fig. 26; H-478) was a type predominantly used in continental Europe, frequently referred to as a *German Plane*. The horn functioned as a front handle and was dovetailed into the stock. Such planes are not believed to have been commercially made by American plane manufacturers until the mid-1870's; then probably to satisfy sufficient demands of immigrant European craftsmen. Three bull horn planes are illustrated in Fig. 26: (8½" x 2-5/8" x 2-3/4"); at the front are two views of a plane bearing the label "Josiah King, New York,N.Y.", which was made in the United States, possibly by H.Chapin's Son, c.1874. The two shown in the rear are imported planes, probably made in Germany. Distinct differences in construction are noted in the wedges, mouths and shape of horns. This type of plane is still being manufactured at this date in European countries and imported into the United States.

3. *Smoothing Plane with Handle*. (Fig. 27; A-4, item-41) Some workers apparently preferred smoothing planes with handles. The illustrated plane, made from beech wood (10½" x 2½" x 2½") is compared to a conventional shaped boxwood smoothing plane shown in front in Fig.27.

4. *Toothing Plane*. (Fig. 28; A-5,item 88; D-368) The function of this plane was to rough a smooth surface preparatory for applying glue for veneer work. The plane is named after its serrated cutting iron which is pitched at an angle of 85 degrees in this example. Such a tool was also called a *Veneering Plane*.

5. *Toy Planes*. (Fig. 29; A-4, items,55-56) These were used by boys, probably principally by sons of carpenters and joiners and were smaller types of smoothing, jack and fore planes. The jacks shown in Fig. 29 are 12"x 2" x 1½", while the smoothing planes are 6" x 2" x 2". In as much as the toy smoothing plane was made sometimes of boxwood, and furnished with a double iron, it is difficult to distinguish from an intrument maker's plane.

6. *Instrument Maker's Planes*. These were miniature planes of many types, usually made by the individual craftsman for his particular work in cleaning and smoothing small items. A group of smoothing planes are illustrated in Fig. 30, the smallest at the extreme left (1" x 2¼") and the largest at the extreme right (6½" x 2-3/4"). For comparative purposes a conventional size smoothing plane is shown in the center. English types [called 'thumb' planes] are shown in Figs.31 & 32.

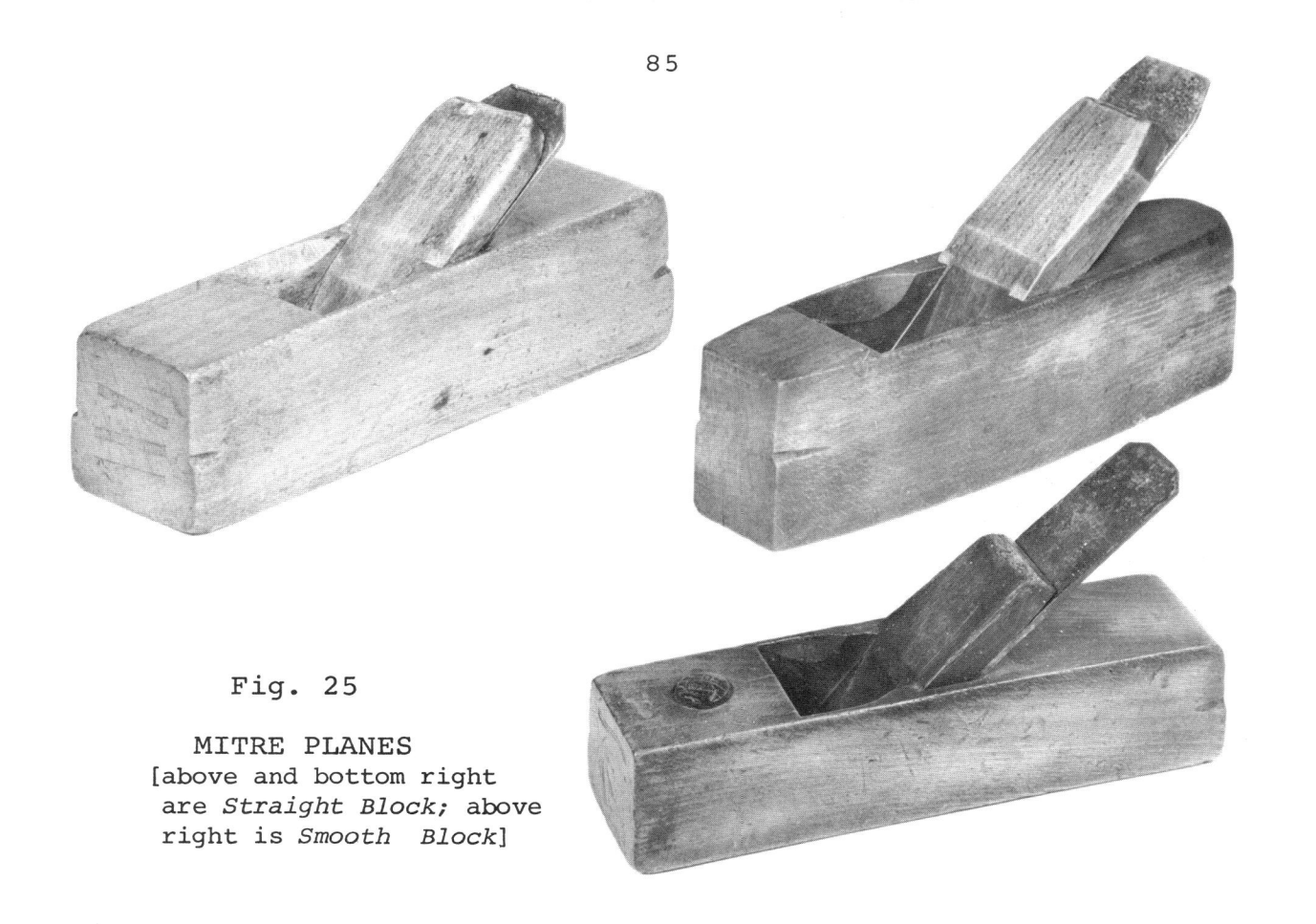

Fig. 25

MITRE PLANES
[above and bottom right are *Straight Block*; above right is *Smooth Block*]

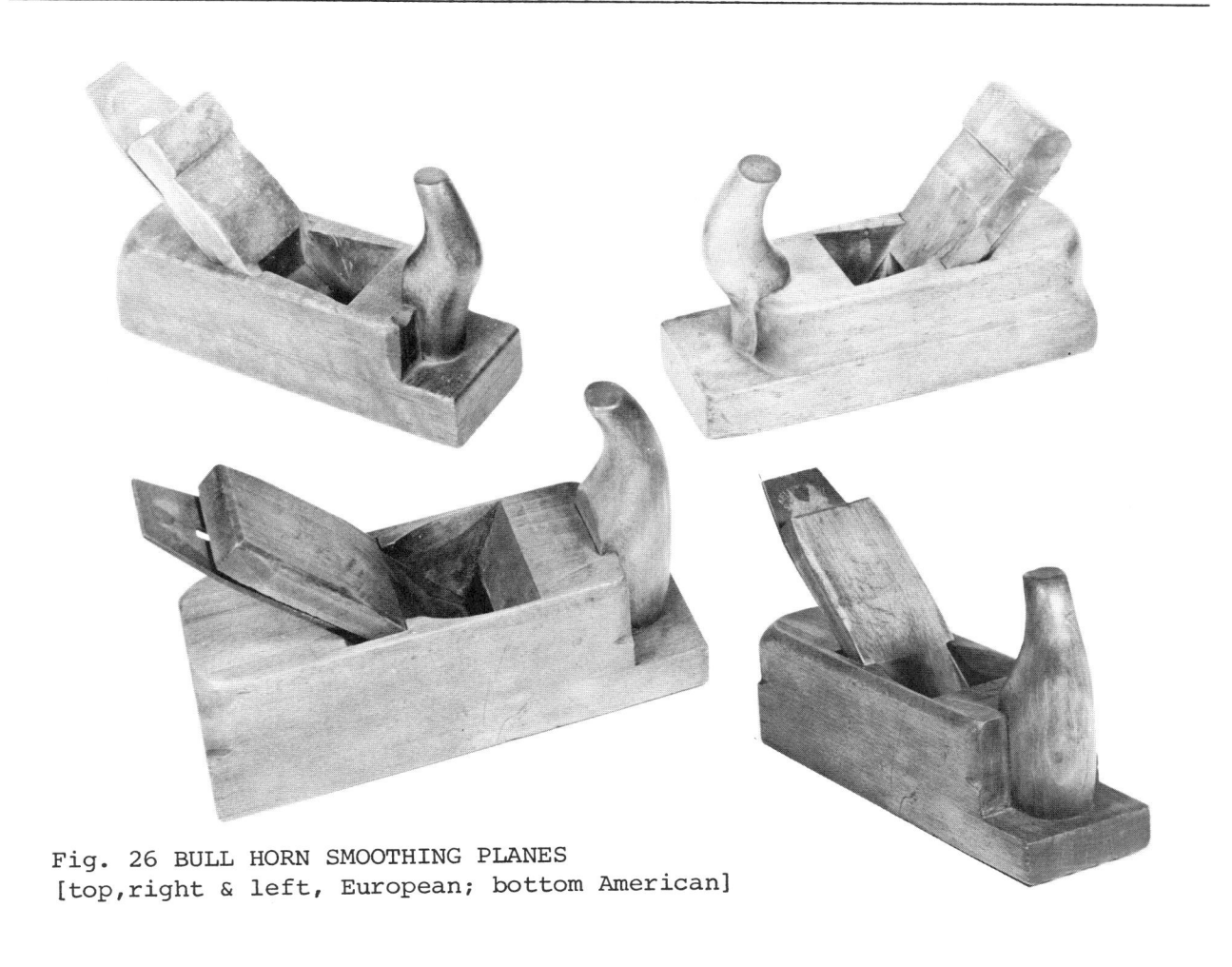

Fig. 26 BULL HORN SMOOTHING PLANES
[top, right & left, European; bottom American]

Fig. 27

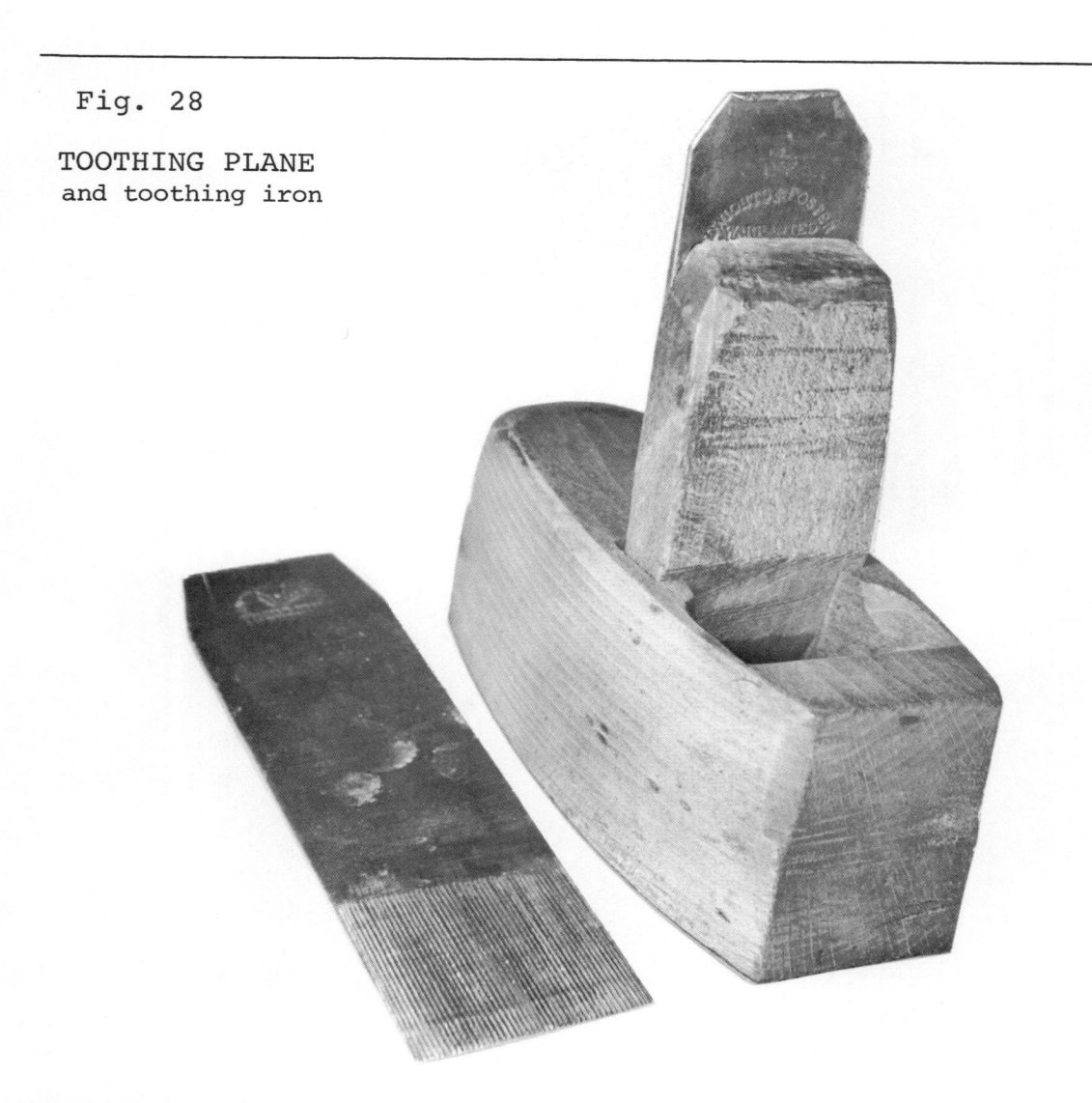

SMOOTHING PLANE WITH HANDLE
[Sandusky Tool Co.]

Compared with
Conventional Boxwood
Smoothing Plane

Fig. 28

TOOTHING PLANE
and toothing iron

Fig. 29

TOY PLANES [6" Smooth & 12" Jack]

Fig. 30 INSTRUMENT MAKER'S SMOOTHING PLANES [2" to 6-1/2" lengths from left to right compared with 8" conventional size in center]

Fig. 31 ENGLISH MUSIC MAKER'S PLANES [Photograph Courtesy of the Science Museum, London. Planes lent to Science Museum, London by Mrs. A. T. Scott, Harrow" Note: Scale in front at bottom is in centimeters. (2.54 cms = 1 inch)]

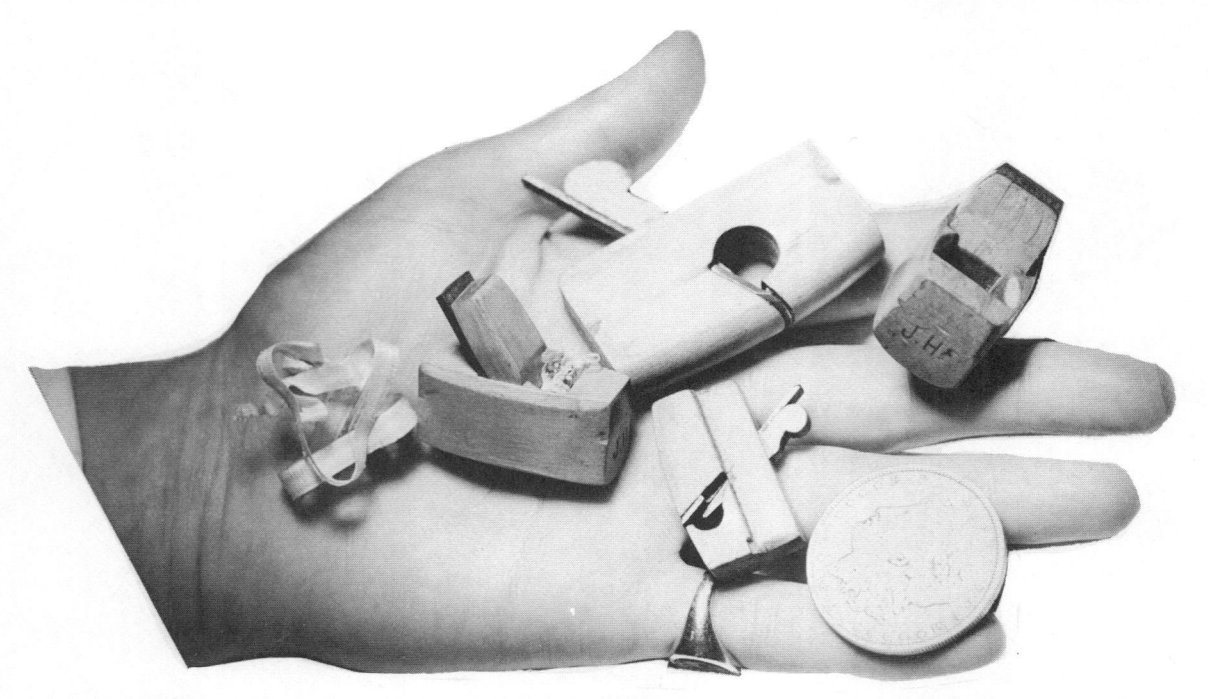

Fig. 32. ENGLISH INSTRUMENT MAKER's PLANES. [Planes and Photograph from the collection of James E. Ayres, Bath, ENGLAND.]

III. Ship Planes (Razee). (C.,V.XX,No.1,March 1967,p.4)(Figs.33-34)

[below, open handle]

Fig. 33
17" RAZEE JACK PLANES
 [above, closed handle]

Ship Planes were available in jack, fore and jointer sizes [see; A-4. items 49-51]. These were also known as *Razee* or *Recess*. The cut-away section permits support of the britch from the operator's wrist. This is advantageous for a shipbuilder worked above the curved surface of the side of a boat and planing in a downward direction. Additionally it reduces the weight of the plane. The jack plane shown above with a closed handle is unsual for a jack, but much easier for a ship builder to hold while working from above than the open handle plane. While ship planes were apparently not used in England, a similar type called a "technical jack" was used at schools for beginners.(D-333)

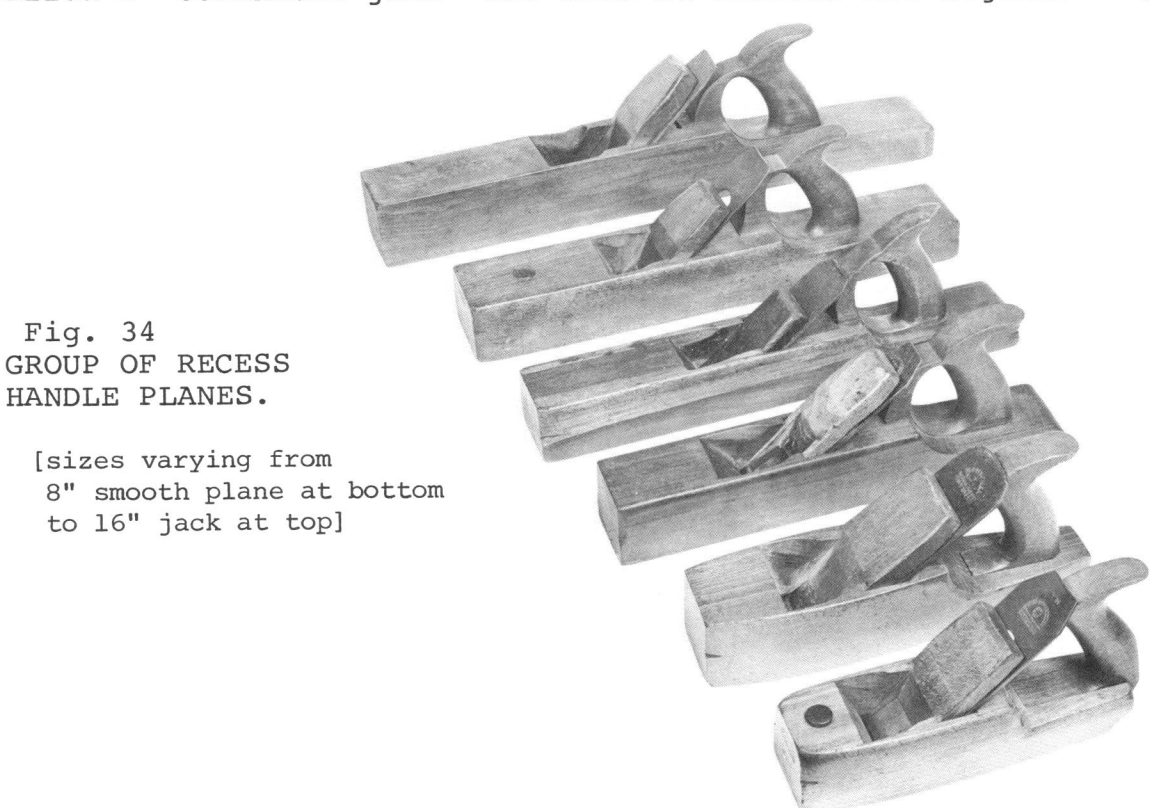

Fig. 34
GROUP OF RECESS
HANDLE PLANES.

 [sizes varying from
  8" smooth plane at bottom
  to 16" jack at top]

B. <u>Grooving Planes</u>. IV <u>Plow</u>

A rectangular groove formed in a piece of wood had many purposes in joinery, carpentry and cabinet work. When such a channel was formed longitudinally (along or with the grain) and usually within 6" from the edge, along a piece of "stuff", the plane used was known as a *plow* [in England called a *plough*]. This designation was probably derived from the resulting furrow conforming to the rectilinear shape of the groove formed by the plane iron. Among applications for grooving were: preparing edges of boards for joints and panels, slots for shelves of cabinets or drawer bottoms, etc. Types of grooves are indicated in Plate XVIIIa.

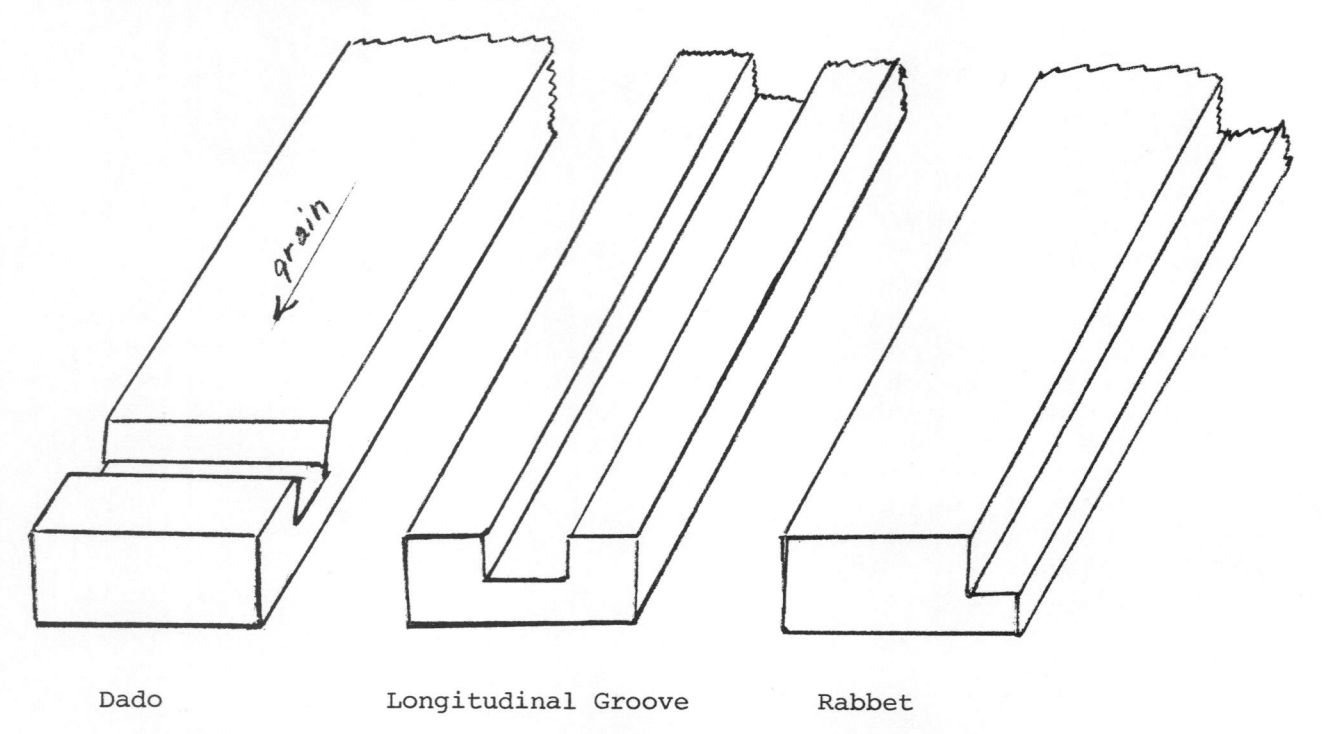

Dado   Longitudinal Groove   Rabbet

Plate XVIIIa - Types of Rectilinear Grooves made by Planes

A *Plow Plane* is composed of two parts: the stock (body) and a movable fence. (See: N-107; H-486; D-346; C-V.XX,No.3,Sept.1967,pp.36-37) These were made in several varieties and arrangements of fence construction, stop or depth regulation and with or without handles. The price varied accordingly depending on the sophistication of arrangement and finish. (See: A-6, items 108-131) An iron keel, inserted longitudinally and screwed into the right side, extended about 1" below the sole and guided the cutting iron. A cutting iron selected according to the desired width of the groove was inserted through a slot into the body and held firmly against the iron keel by a wooden wedge. Cutters were furnished in a set of eight in increments of 1/16" between 1/8" to 9/16" (Fig. 35).

The overall length of these irons is about 8", but only the bottom cutting end (about 3") was made from tool steel. The remaining upper end (5") formed a shank and was made from low carbon or wrought iron and scarf welded to the cutting portion. The latter was then forged to proper shape, ground, hardened and tempered. The shank remained soft and was formed with a quarter round tip for tapping with a mallet to adjust to proper depth and to provide and edge for striking upwardly to loosen the wedge during removal. Two additional irons are illustrated at the bottom of Fig. 35. The upper of these, lying on its top surface, has a longitudinal slot about 2½" long cut into the back of the tip. The purpose of this slot was to center the cutting iron on the keel before being secured by the wedge. The iron below shows the side profile to which these irons were forged and ground. The leather case is a reproduction, made by J. W. Roberts.

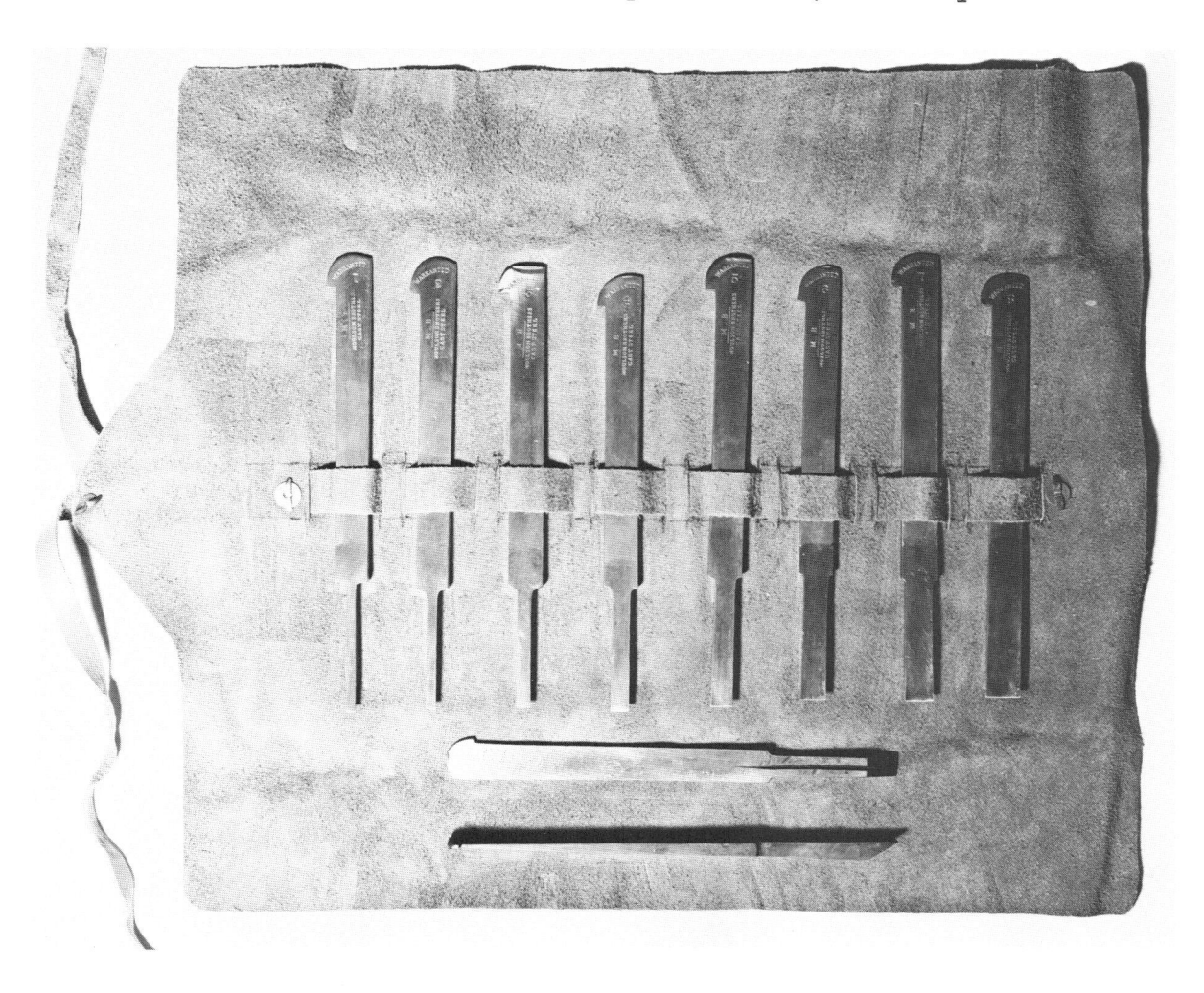

Fig. 35. Set of Plow Irons, Nos. 1 - 8.(1/8" - 9/16") Made by Moulson Brothers, Sheffield, England. Similar sets were made in United States.

Control of the grooving depth was accomplished by a 'stop' morticed through the body of the stock. The simplest form and least expensive was a rectangular shaped piece of hard wood, tapped to proper depth and held firmly by a wooden screw through the side. (See: Figs. 3 & 36) An improved adjustable stop consisted of an iron plate, morticed into the sole, actuated by a screw mechanism from a brass wing nut, held in an escutcheon screwed into the top. (Figs. 37-39) The fence which controlled the position of the groove from the edge of the board was attached to the stock through two arms which passed through the sides at right angles. There were two types of arms: sliding and screw regulated. Sliding arms were both earlier and less expensive and were locked into place by wedges morticed into the sides (Fig. 36) or by wooden screws from the top. (Fig. 3) The latter arangement was sometime furnished with ferruled arms to prevent the locking screws from indenting into the top surface of the arms. The screw arm type, referred to as the "German Plow' by Holtzapffel (H-486), became the preferred plow used in the United States by 1850. The helical screw arms were made from box imported from Turkey, as were the circular lock nuts. There were at least four basic grades of such screw arm plows available from the Arrowmammett Toool Co. in 1858: 1. common beechwood, no handle (A-6, #121,top Fig.37); 2. common beechwood with handle (A-6,#125,bottom Fig. 37); 3. Empire Plow (A-6,#128, Fig.38; 4. Premium Plow, (A-6,#124, all boxwood and ivory tipped (Fig. 39).

Fig. 36

Beech Plow with Slide Arms, wedge locks and wood stop.

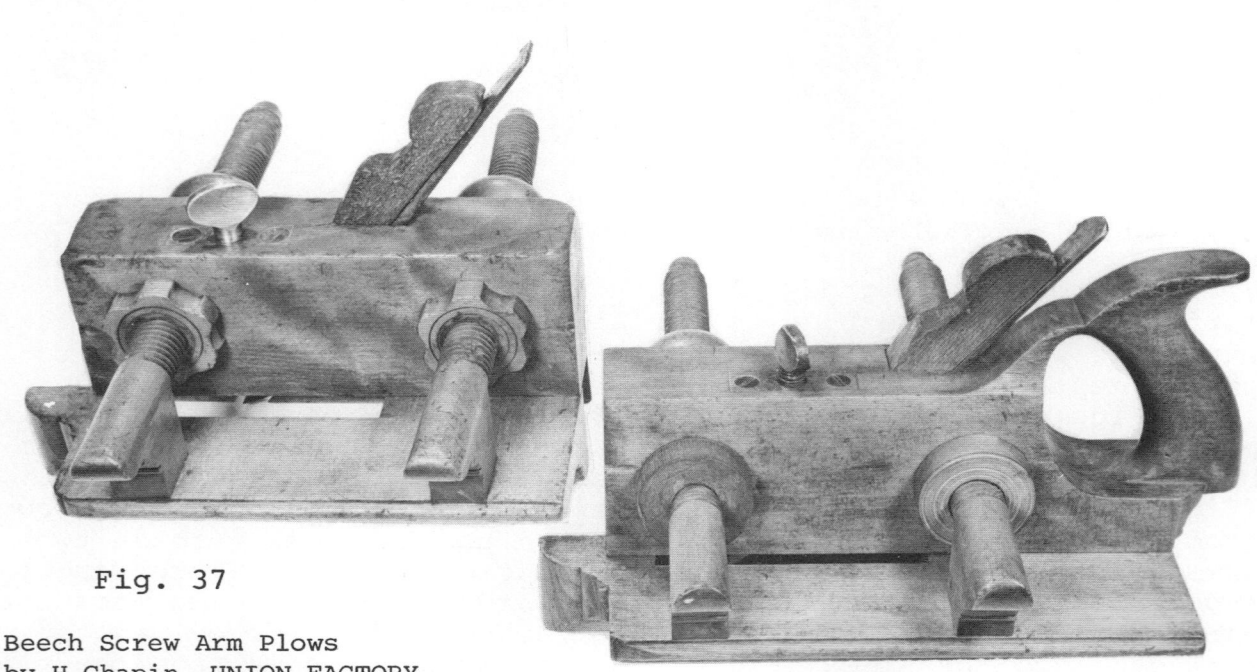

Fig. 37

Beech Screw Arm Plows
by H.Chapin, UNION FACTORY
Top: no handle; Bottom: Handle

Fig. 38

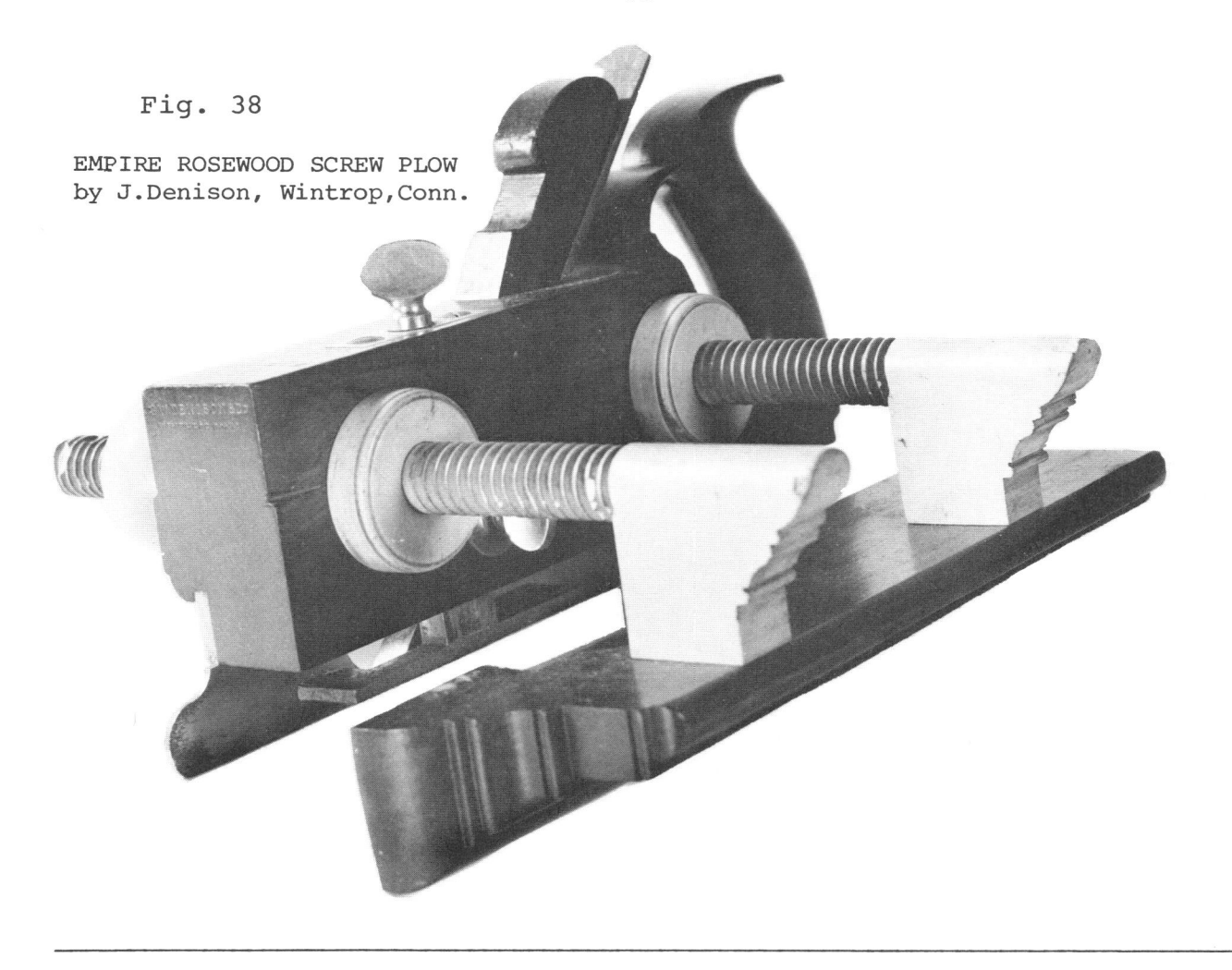

EMPIRE ROSEWOOD SCREW PLOW
by J.Denison, Wintrop,Conn.

Fig. 39

ALL BOXWOOD, IVORY TIPPED SCREW PLOW by Hall,Case & Co.,Columbus,Ohio,c.1850

V. Match Planes (Tongue & Groove) C. v.XX,No.3,April 1967,pp37-38.

A set of two planes respectively for forming the tongue and groove on the edges of two boards of the same thickness were known as a *"Match Planes"*. (D-334-35)(See Plate XVIIIb) The 'grooving' plane may be regarded as a plow with a fixed fence. Matched sets were available for boards of sizes 3/8" to 1" thickness in increments of 1/8" [*Board Match*: See - A-7; items 132-137] and for planks of thickness 1¼" & 1½". [*Plank Match* : A-7,items 138-39] Board match planes without handles were made the same size as conventional moulding planes; i.e., 9-3/8" long x 3½" high) The better grades were reinforced with a thin strip of iron on the sole to prevent wear. A single plane furnished with oppositely set cutters each respectively forming the tongue and groove on the same thickness board is called *Combination Match Plane*. Board "match planes" were also available with closed handles. While these latter planes were usually 11½" long x 3½" high, (Fig. 40) these were also made in 10½" and 9½" lenths. (Fig.41)

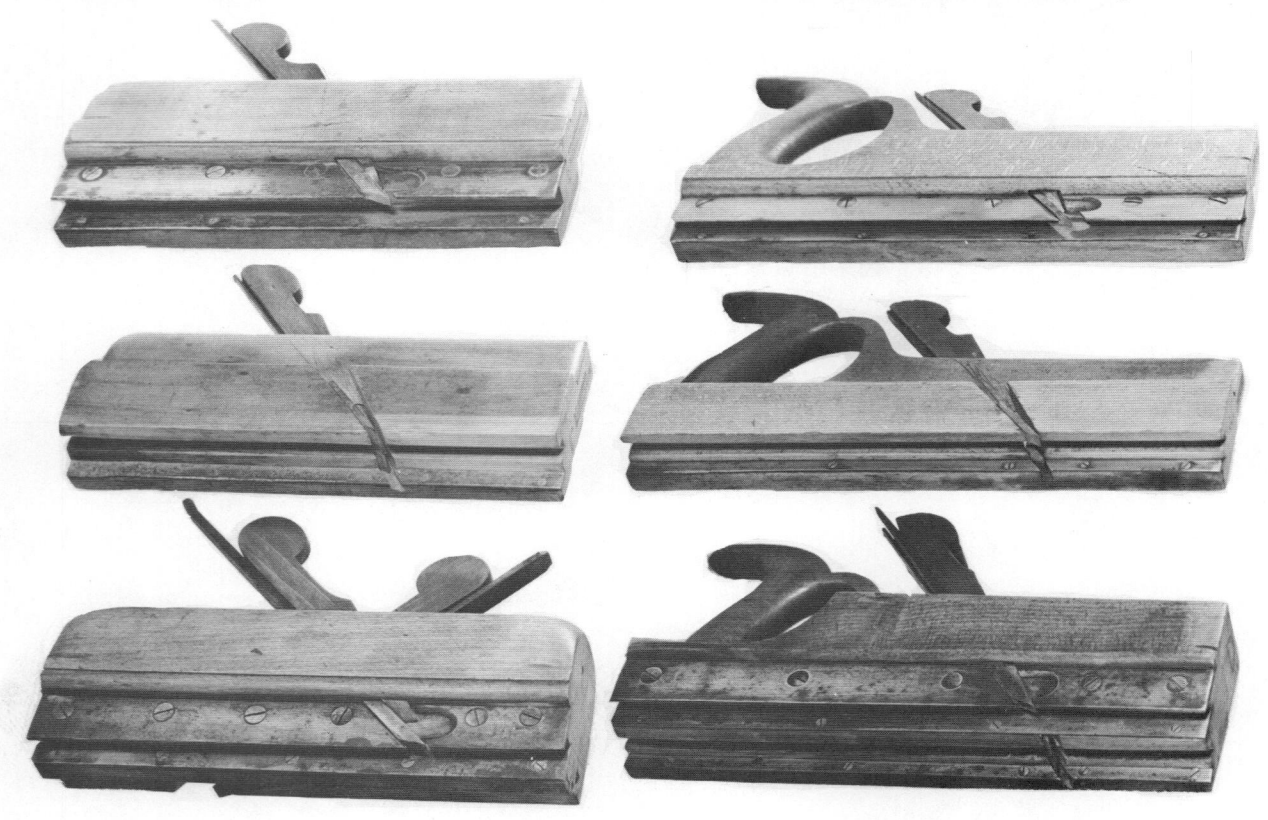

Fig. 40. BOARD MATCH PLANES: 3/4" size. Left, no handle; Right, closed handles. Top, grooving;middle, tongue; botton,combination.

The combination match plane with handle (bottom right, Fig. 40) cut a tongue on the inner surface and a groove on the outer. P.A.Gladwin of Boston, Mass. received a U.S. Patent #17,541, dated June 9,1857, for this arrangement.

A set of *Plank Match* planes for 1½" planks are illustrated in Fig. 42. (14" long x 4" high). Sets of plank match were also made with adjustable fences, *Moving Match,* in wedge or screw arm (Fig. 43) arrangements. (A-7; items 140-141).

Plate VIIIb - Type of Board Joints

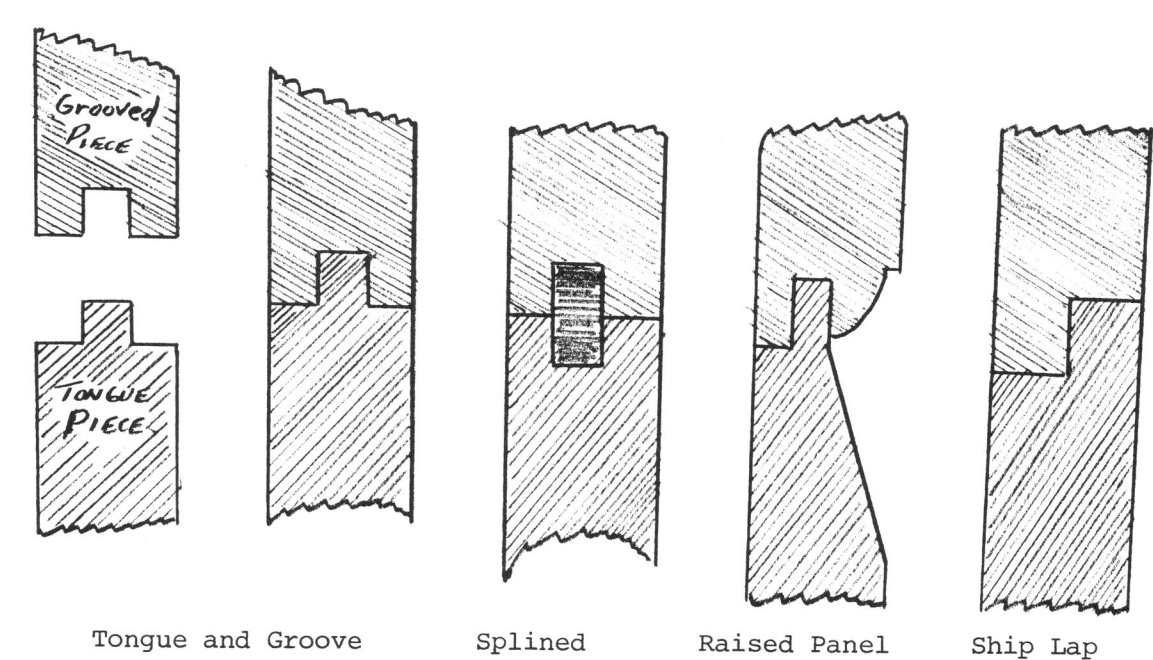

Tongue and Groove   Splined   Raised Panel   Ship Lap

Fig. 41

CLOSED HANDLE
Board Match Planes
3/4" Board Thickness
Top   Tounging
Bottom: Grooving

Lengths:

Top: 11-1/2"
Middle: 10-1/2"
Bottom: 9-1/2"

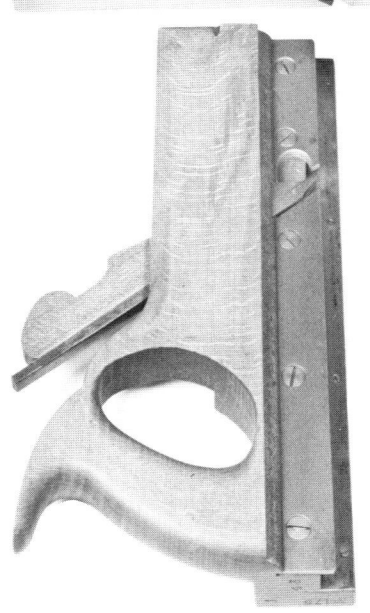

Fig. 42. Plank Match Planes for 1½" thicknes boards (14" long)

Fig. 43. Set of Moving Match Planes (Screw Arm Type) (14" long)

VI. Rabbet Planes

The process of removing a rectilinear section along the edge of a board is known as "rabbeting". The function of a rabbet is either decorative or as part of a joint. Types of rabbet joints are shown in Plate XIX. Note the increased support and rigidity as compared to a lap joint.

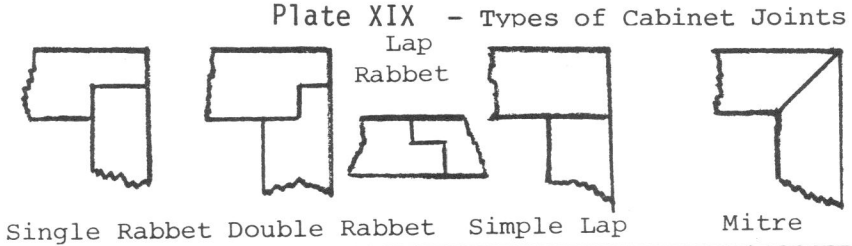

Plate XIX - Types of Cabinet Joints

Single Rabbet   Double Rabbet   Simple Lap   Mitre

Fig. 44
Moving Filletster
Top: View from Side

Bottom: View of Bottom and Adjustable Fence

VI - 1. Moving Filletster [C.,v.XX,No.2,June 1967,pp.22-23; N-104; H-485; D-327-28; A-7; items 145-162]

The *Moving Filletster*, is an adjustable rabbet plane, illustrated in Fig. 44. (9-3/8" x 2¼" x 3½") The width of the rabbet cut may be regulated up to 1½" by positioning the fence mounted on the bottom of the sole. Set screws in two slotted brass castings, inserted at right angles to the length of the fence, provide for this adjustment. The brass casting fixture, positioned on the cutting side of this plane, functioned as a stop for regulating the depth of cut up to a maximum of 7/16". Adjustment of this stop was through screw control from a wing-nut at the top. The operations of these mechanisms will be apparent from examination of the sketch in Plate XX and viewing Fig. 44. The plane iron was set "skew", i.e. at an oblique angle, across the sole. In this manner rabbets could be conveniently cut both with and across the grain. The wedge shaped knife-cutter, called a 'spur' or 'scoring tooth', mounted on the side and directly in front of the plane cutting iron, marked the edge as the plane was advanced. This was particularly helpful in preventing tearing during cross-grain rabbeting. The depth of the scoring could be regulated by tapping the top of this knife with a mallet. In order to provide for wear resistance along the working edge a boxwood insert was splined 3/8" along the corner of the side and sole. The type of box noted in Fig. 44 is 'shoulder box'; a less expensive form was 'single box'. The most expensive type of *Moving Filletster* was furnished with screw arms for fence adjustment. (Fig. 45)

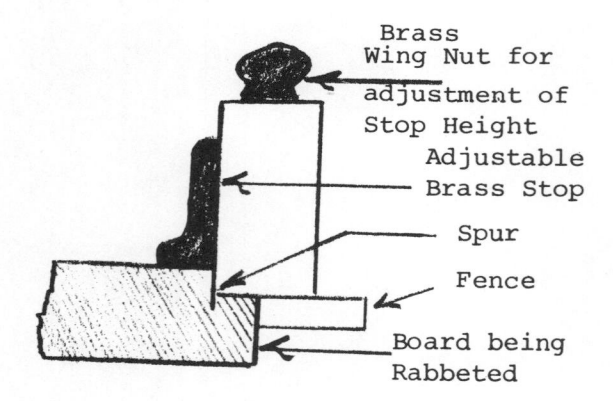

Plate XX
Section of a Moving Filletster
Plane Cutting a Rabbet

Fig. 45

Moving Filletster with Screw Arms

Common Rabbet Planes (VI-2) were available in both square and skew irons without fences in sizes from 1/2" to 1" widths in increments of 1/8" (see: A-9) and in sizes from 1" to 2" in increments of ¼". In Fig. 46 the top plane has a square iron (for longitudinal with grain work) and the bottom plane has a skew iron (for cross grain work) with a spur-cutter and a boxed edge. The middle plane shows a temporary fence nailed to the sole for regulation of width of the particular rabbet cut. For special work in larger quantities a few sizes of rabbet planes were available with integral fences rabbeted into the sole. (Fig. 47.)

Fig. 46 Common Rabbet Planes. Top: Square Iron; Bottom Skew Iron.

Fig. 47. Rabbet Plane with Integral Fence.

100

Left:
3/4" Rabbet Plane with
Handle and Integral Fence
[12" x 1"]

Above:
Skew Rabbet [12" X 2"]

Right: Moving Filletster
[10" x 2-1/4"]

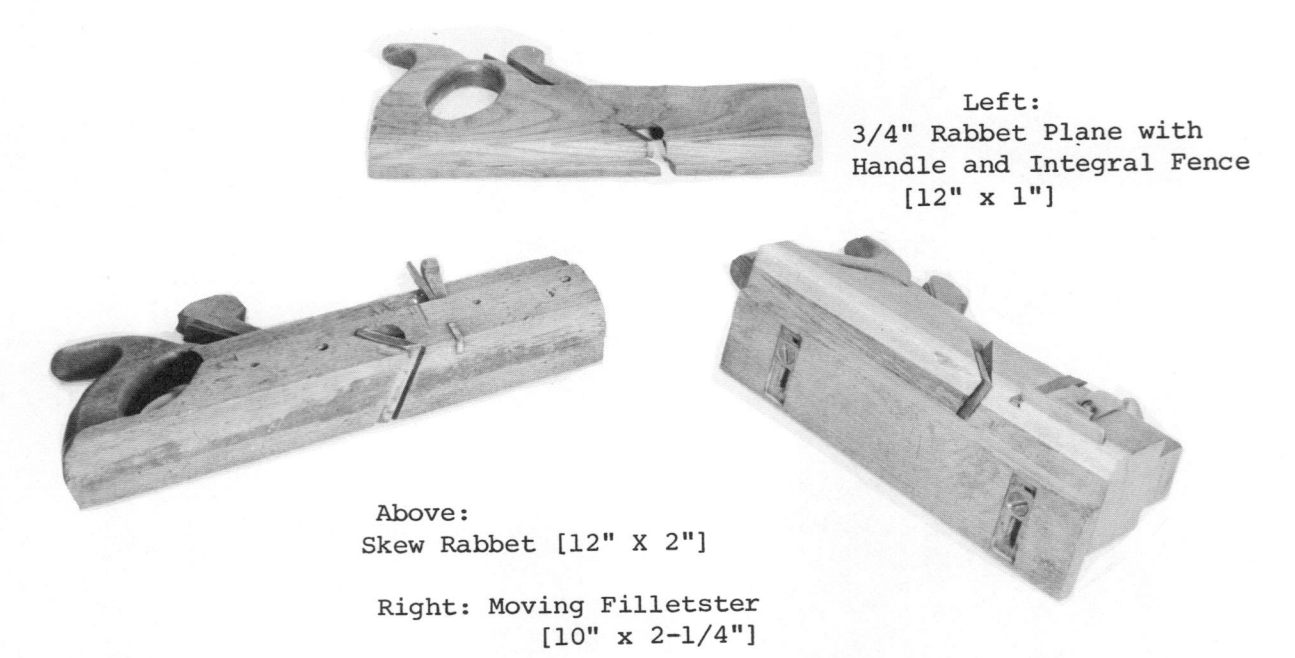

Fig. 48 Rabbet Planes with Closed Handles

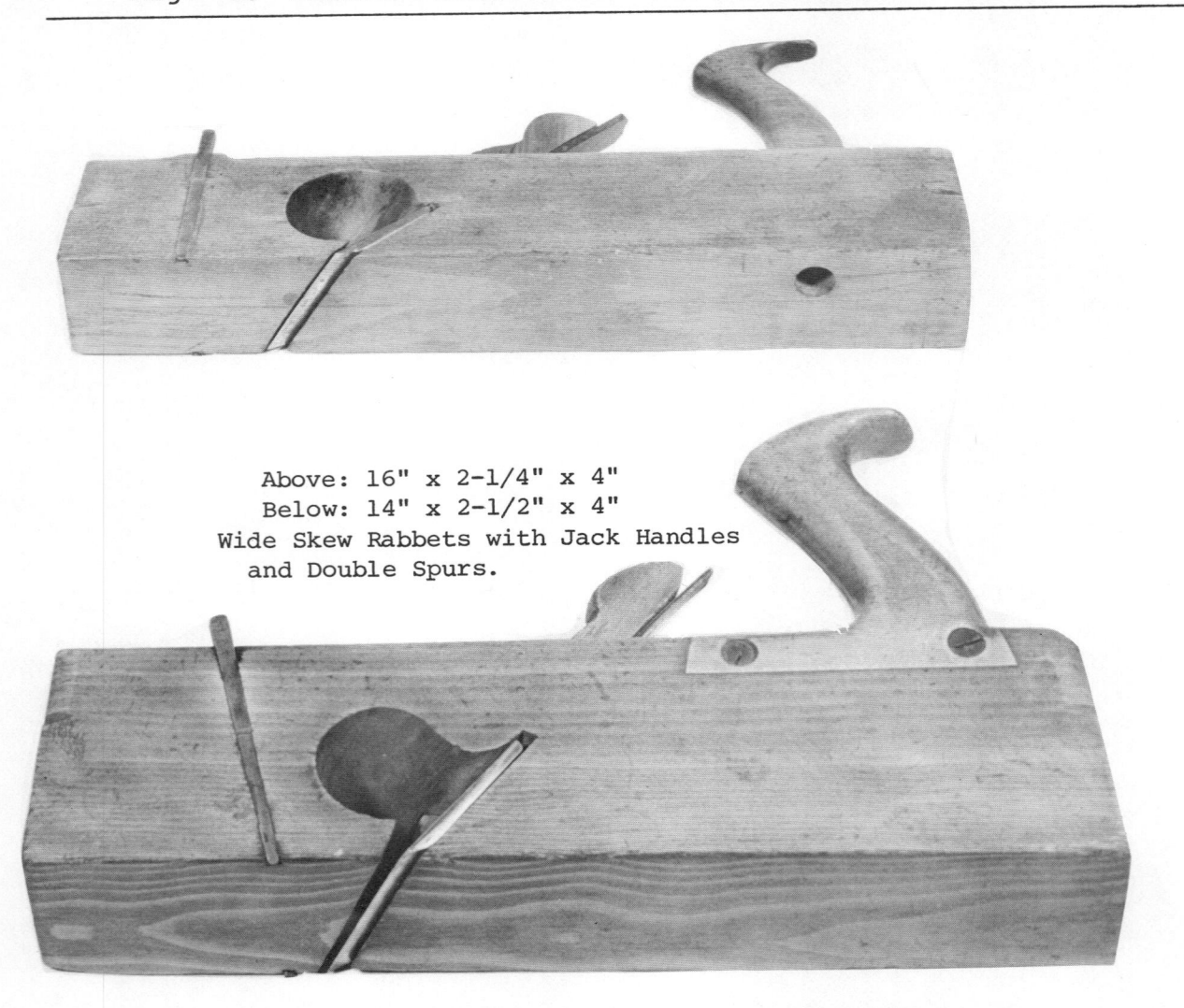

Above: 16" x 2-1/4" x 4"
Below: 14" x 2-1/2" x 4"
Wide Skew Rabbets with Jack Handles
and Double Spurs.

Fig. 49 "Jack" Rabbits [so called, *1875 D.R.Barton Tool Catalogue*]

VI - 5. Raising or Panel Planes. (A-5, items 92-97; D-344)

The shaping of a raised (fielded) panel by a *Panel Plane* may be regarded as forming a wide rabbet. The construction of a simple square framed panel is shown in Plate XXI. The beveled surface, called the cant, was formed during the eighteenth and early nineteenth centuries with a special bench plane having a skewed cutting iron, a fixed integral fence and a rabbeted surface on the inside opposite edge which acted as a depth stop. Such planes usually had open (jack) handles and were 14" in length. (See: Fig.50) By the middle of the nineteenth century these *Panel Planes* were mass produced and became known as *Raising Jacks* and were often made with adjustable fences, stops and spur cutters. (Figs. 51 & 52).

Plate XXI

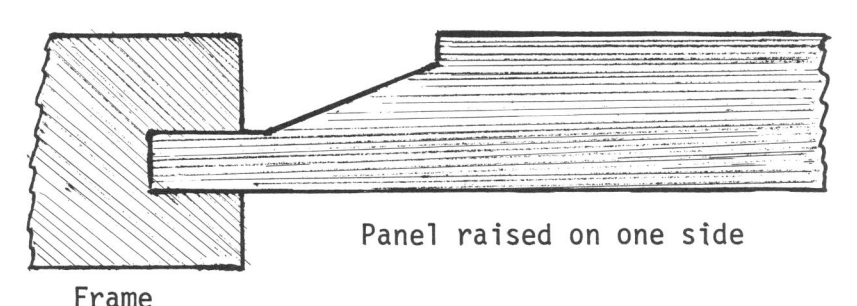

Frame — Panel raised on one side

SIMPLE SQUARE FRAMED PANEL CONSTRUCTION

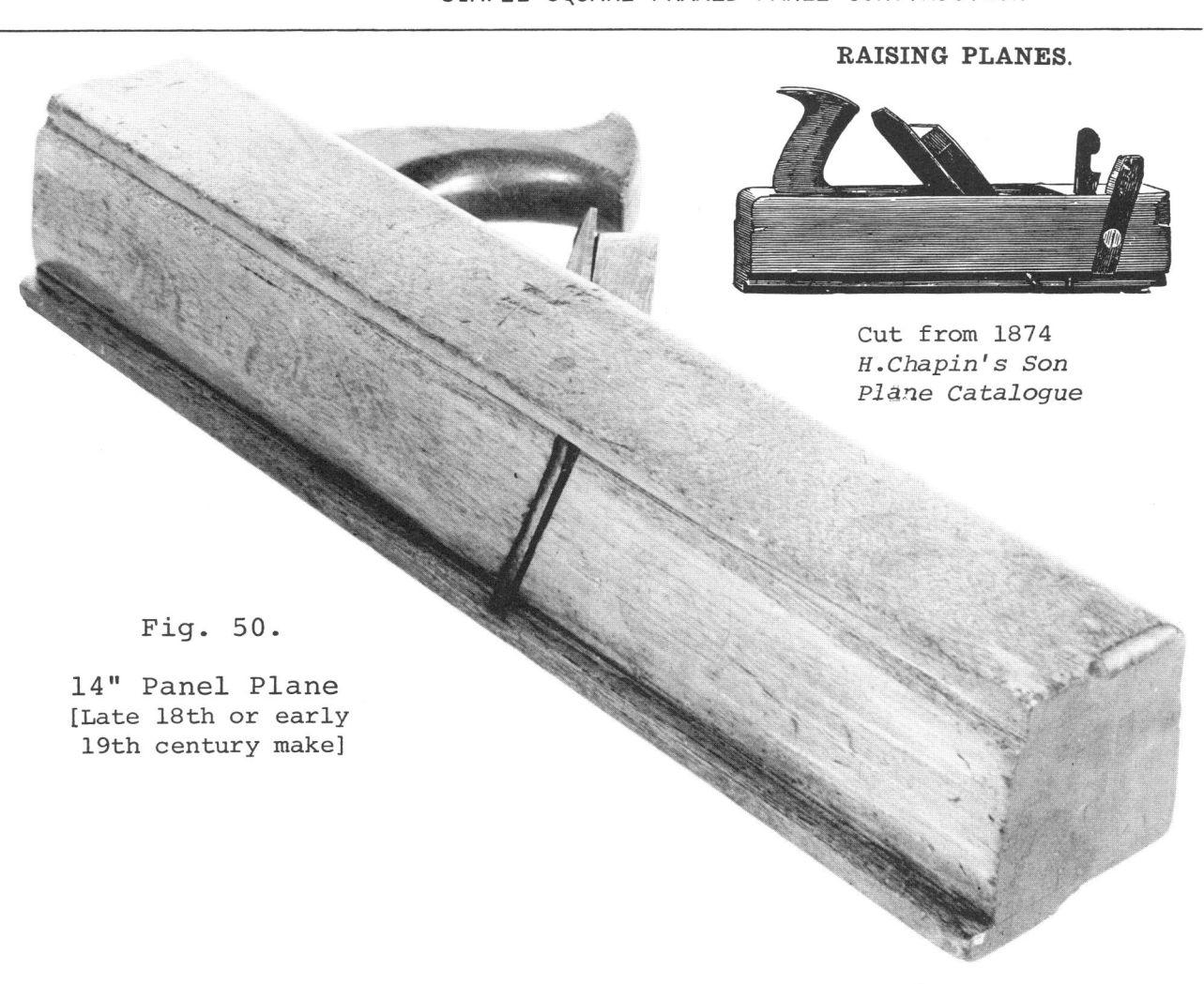

RAISING PLANES.

Cut from 1874
*H.Chapin's Son
Plane Catalogue*

Fig. 50.

14" Panel Plane
[Late 18th or early
 19th century make]

Fig. 51.

Adjustable Width
Raising Jack Plane, c.1850

Imprint: *H.Chapin/UNION FACTORY*
16" x 4" x 3"; 3" width iron
Adjustable Fence on Sole and Side
   similar to Moving Filletster

Used for Large Door Panels

Fig. 52.

Raising Plane with
Screw Arm Fence: [16" x 4' x 3"]

For cleaning up wide rabbet cuts a jack plane with skew iron and generally having a boxed edge was used to complete wide panels. In Great Britain such a plane was frequently called a *Badger Plane*. (D-304) Side and bottom views of such a plane are shown below in Fig. 53.

Fig. 53

Panel Jack Plane
 [14" x 3" x 3"]
 Side and Bottom Views
Note: Skew Iron and
 Boxed Edge.

Plate XXII

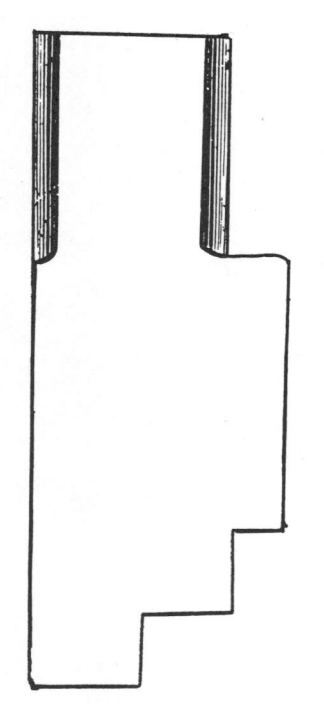

VI - 6. Halving Plane.

This was a special rabbet plane for 1" thick boards for cutting a rabbet half the thickness; hence the term *Halving Plane*. (See: Plate XXII) The right edge serves as a fence and the rabbet cut into the left edge serves as a stop equal to the width of the middle step. This is believed to be the only size made. Probably the principal use of such a plane was for making ship lap rabbet cuts on 1" boards for flooring. The cut shown in Plate XXII appeared in *H.Chapin - Union Factory Tool Catalogue 1853*. This is a cross-sectional view from the back end of the plane.

Halving Plane Section

VI - 7. Side Rabbeting Planes [A-10, item 249; N-106; D-358]

Side Rabbet Planes (Fig. 54) were furnished in pairs (right & left) and used for trimming and smoothing the side surface of rabbet cuts. The cutting edge is on one side only and extends about 1¼" above the sole at a fixed angle of between 75 and 90 degrees. Three different angles of the cutting iron are noted in Fig. 54. The plane shown in the middle left (side opposite cutting edge) and the bottom plane (cutting side) are respectively a *right* and *left pair of side rabbet planes*.

Fig. 54 Side Rabbet Planes. [note: three different cutting angles]

VII. Dado Planes [C.,v.XX,No.3,Sept.1967,p38; A-10; N-108; D-324-325]

A dado is defined as a rectilinear channel cut across the grain for such applications as supports for cabinet shelves or drawer supports. *Dado Planes* were furnished with skew irons in sizes from ¼" to 1¼" in increments of 1/8" and also the special size of 5/16". Since these were essentially for cross-grain work, a double spur marking the edges of the cut was placed in front of the cutter in order to prevent tearing during planing. Three varieties of stops were furnished: *1. boxwood* (least expensive) *2. slotted brass* (manual adjustment with side screw); *3. brass wing-nut screw adjustment* (most expensive). A temporary fence was attached across the work and the plane first pulled backwardly against the fence to scribe the extremities of dado width. The plane was then advanced forward against the fence a number of passes until sunk to the depth regulated by the stop.

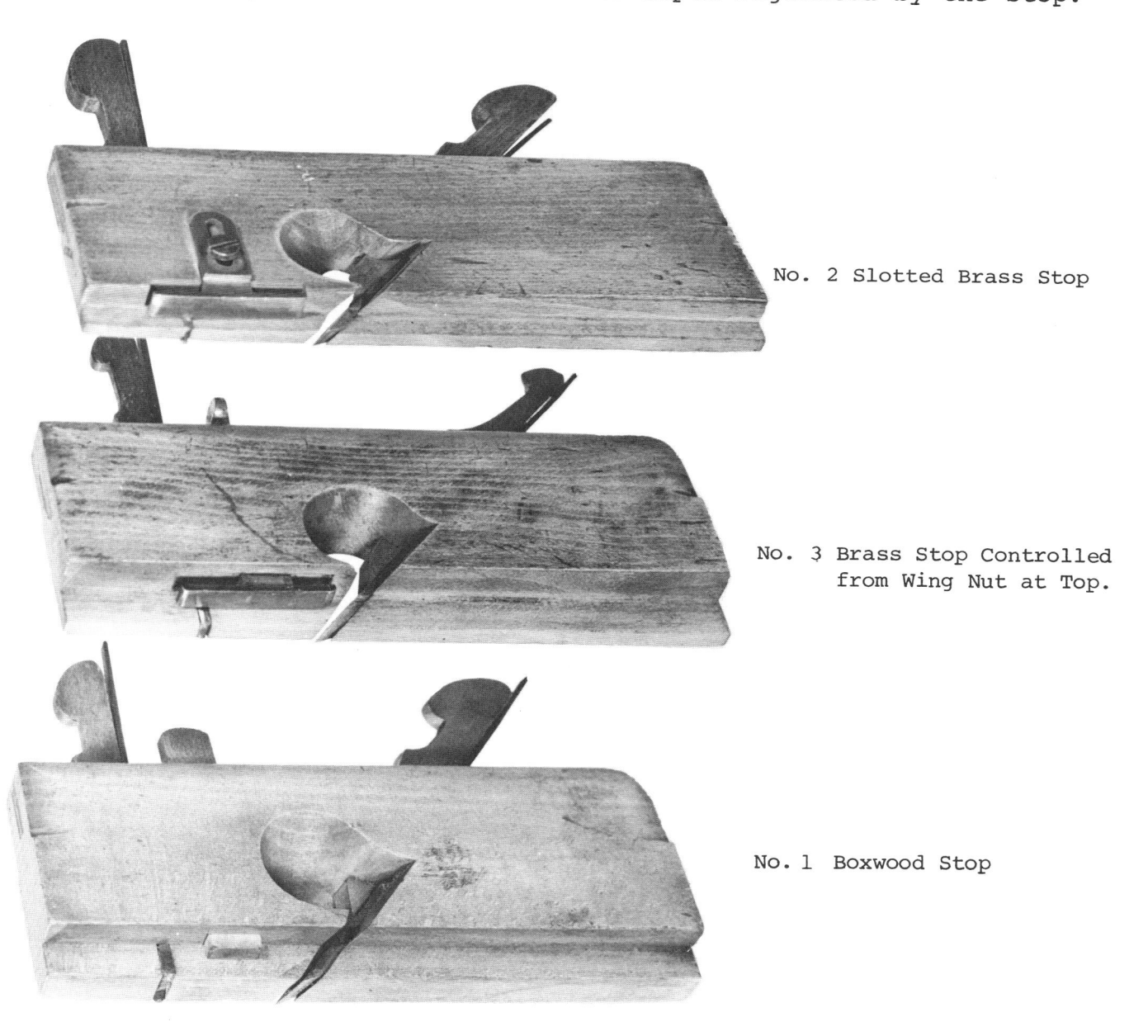

No. 2 Slotted Brass Stop

No. 3 Brass Stop Controlled from Wing Nut at Top.

No. 1 Boxwood Stop

Fig. 55. Dado Planes [conventional sizes of moulding planes]

C. Moulding or Shaping Planes

The function of a moulding is essentially decorative. While the present preferred spelling in the United States is *molding*, as stated previously in this study, *moulding* is used throughout this work in conformity to that followed during most of the nineteenth century, and still used in England. Applications for such mouldings are: the cornice strip below a ceiling along the top of a wall; above a floor base board; adjacent to a window casement; borders for panels in doors, cabinets, frames, etc.

Shaping mouldings by wooden planes was common joinery practice in England during the seventeeth and eighteenth centuries. About 1770 this form of plane, without a handle, became standardized in size: 9½" long by 3½" high with width varying according to the particular moulding between ¼" to 2". (D-338) As planemaking became an established trade in United States about 1800, it was only natural that sizes and shapes followed previous practice in the Mother country. Late in the eighteenth century there was a change in architectural designs from classical Roman to Grecian. Mouldings of the former designs were based on segments of a circle or continuous curvatures frequently in combination with rectilinear fillets. The latter had more abrupt profiles with marked turning points and employed quirks and bevels. A 'quirk' is a narrow groove, usually in the form of a rectilinear channel adjacent to and terminating a curved moulding. About 1820 in United States a style of architecture developed, known as "American Empire' that was bolder and departed to a marked degree from classical forms followed in Europe.

The shapes and forms of mouldings are indeed almost infinite. A recently reprinted section of Alex. Mathieson & Son, Ltd. *1899 8th Edition, Catlogue of Woodworking Tools* illustrates 526 shapes and sizes of mouldings. Many of these were used and identified by the same name in the United States throughout the nineteenth century. The 1858 *Arrowmammett Works Catalogue* (Appendix) notes 298 items of moulding planes Thirty-two shapes of moulding planes noted are listed in Table XIII. Another source of identification of plane moulings is *Tools of the Woodworker* [J.I.Rempel, Technical Leaflet No.25, American Association of State & Local History, *History News*, v.19,No.12,October 1964, Nashville, Tenn.]

Table XIII

Shapes of Moulding Planes List in 1858 Arrowmammett Works Catalogue (See: Appendix)

Simple Shapes	Complex Shapes				
Astragal	Grecian OGee			Gothic Bead	
Center Bead	"	"	& Astragal	Plain OGee	
Cock Bead	"	"	& Bead	Quirk OGee	
Edge Bead	"	"	& Bevel	Quirk Oges	& Bead
Cove	"	Ovalo		Reverse OGee	
Cove & Bead	"	"	& Astragal	Reverse Ogee	& Astragal
Hollow & Round	"	"	& Bead	" "	& Bead
Quirk Ovalo	"	"	& Fillet	" "	& Flat
Reed	"	"	& Square	" "	& Square
Scotia				" "	& 2 Squares
Torus Bead				Snipe Bill	
				Torus Cove & Bead	

In Appleton's *Cyclopaedia of Drawing* [1869, edited by W.E.Worthington] it is stated that in as much as mouldings are essential parts of an edifice, they should be classed as necessary, rather than ornamental members: "The regular mouldings are eight in number: Fillet or Band, Torus, Astragal or Bead, Ovalo, Cavetto, Cyma Recta or Ogee, Cyma Reversa or Talon and Scotia"

In this study a simple moulding is defined as being formed from a continuous curve, such as an arc of a cirle, and may include a rectilinear quirk. A complex moulding consists of an irregular curvature, usually having a definite turning point and may be combined with simple mouldings and quirks. Shapes of simple mouldings are shown in Plate XXIII. A *fillet* is a simple rectilinear strip, comparable to that portion removed by a rabbet. A *bead* is usually composed of one-half a circle (180 degree of arc), but may be as much as three-quarters of a circle (270 degrees arc). An *astragal* (A) is a semi-circlular bead flanked on each side by a fillet. When the bead projects beyond the surface it is said to be *cocked* (B). Perhaps the most common bead is one with a *quirk* (C). Less frequent is a bead with a *bevel* (D). A *return bead* is composed of three-quarters of a circle on the edge with a fillet or quirk on each side. (E). A *torus bead* has an outside fillet, an arc of 215 degrees (5/8 of circle circumference) and an inside quirk of depth about one-half the fillet width. (F) A *center bead*, also known as a *read*, or a *sunk bead*, is formed on the inside surface away from the edge. (G) A *double read* is formed by sinking parallel beads. (H) *Fluted reads* are formed by sinking portions of a series of inverted beads. (I & J) The sizes of beads and reads are expressed in the diameter of the circle forming their composition. A quarter circle on the outside edge forms an *ovalo*. (K) The reverse of an ovalo is *cavetto* (also called *cove* or *scotia*). (L) Both of the latter forms are frequently accompanied by fillets.

Plate XXIII - Sketches of Simple Mouldings

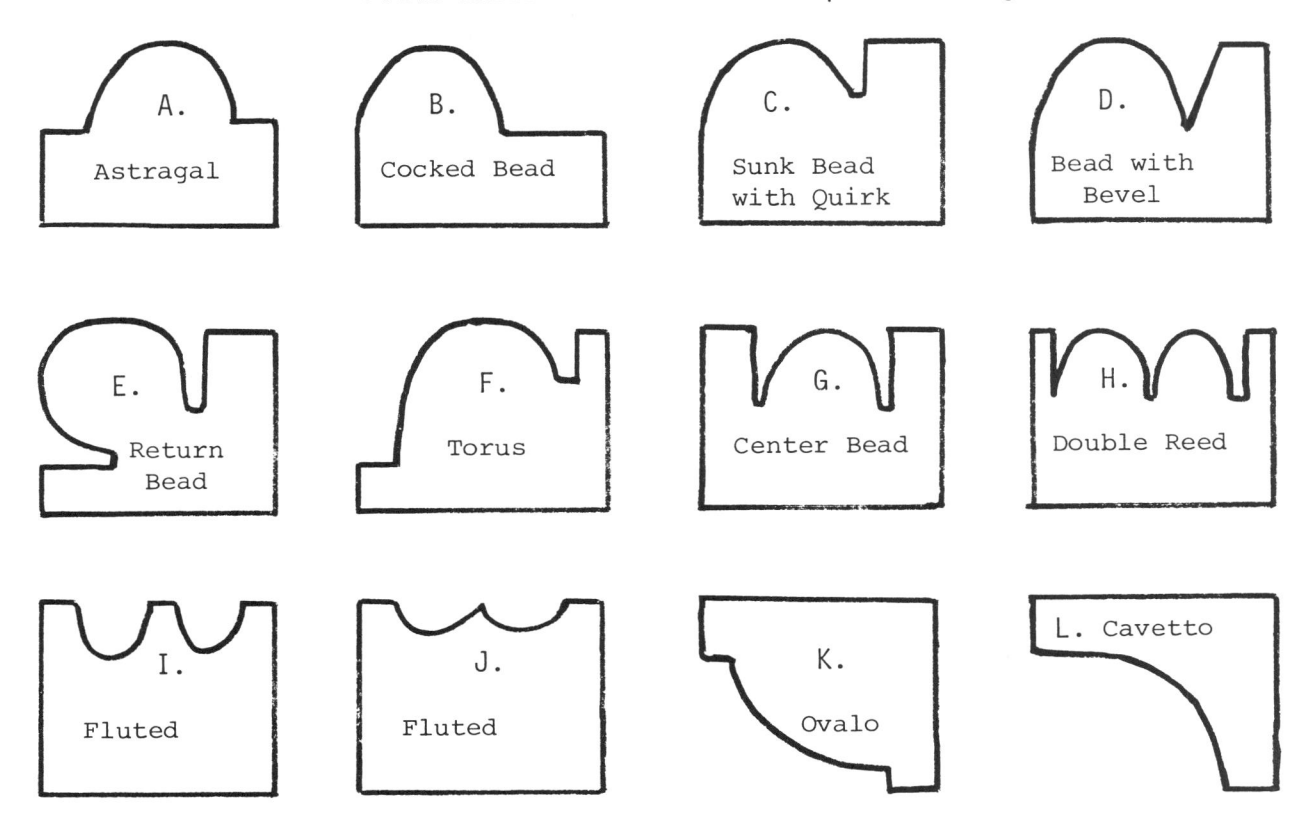

A. Astragal
B. Cocked Bead
C. Sunk Bead with Quirk
D. Bead with Bevel
E. Return Bead
F. Torus
G. Center Bead
H. Double Reed
I. Fluted
J. Fluted
K. Ovalo
L. Cavetto

The fore end of a 1" *bead* plane with imprint of Randall & Cook, Albany, N.Y., c.1837, is illustrated in Fig. 56. The rabbet section defined to the left of the boxwood spline and the sole served as a stop during planing. Note that a line drawn *parallel* to the base of the sole to the left of the insert is tangent with the top of the bead circle. The function of the boxed spline was to provide for increased wear resistance at the point of forming the quirk.

A *scotia* or *cove* plane is illustrated in Fig. 57. The cutting iron has been removed and placed along side of this plane to the left.

Fig. 56. 1" Bead Plane
Plane and photograph from the Collection of John R. Grabb.

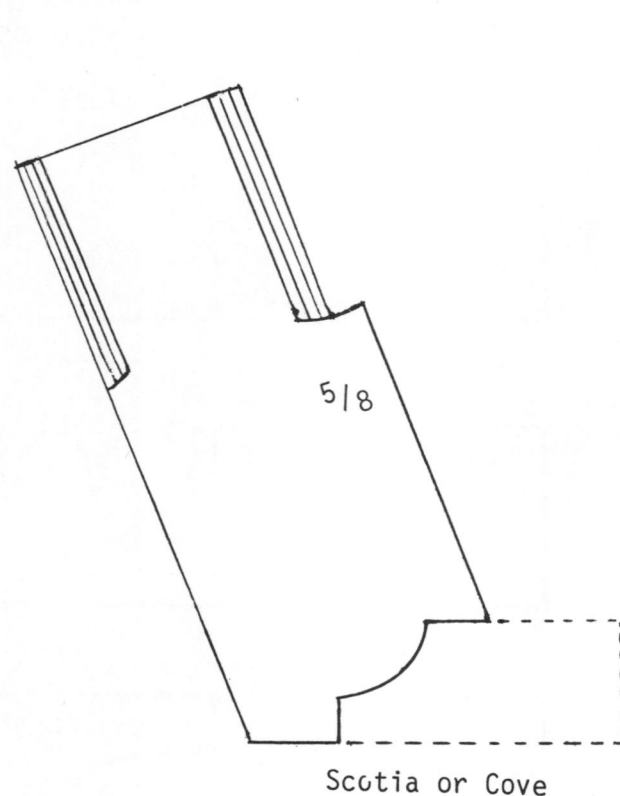

Scotia or Cove

Fig. 57 Section, Cutting Iron and Cove or Scotia Moulding Plane

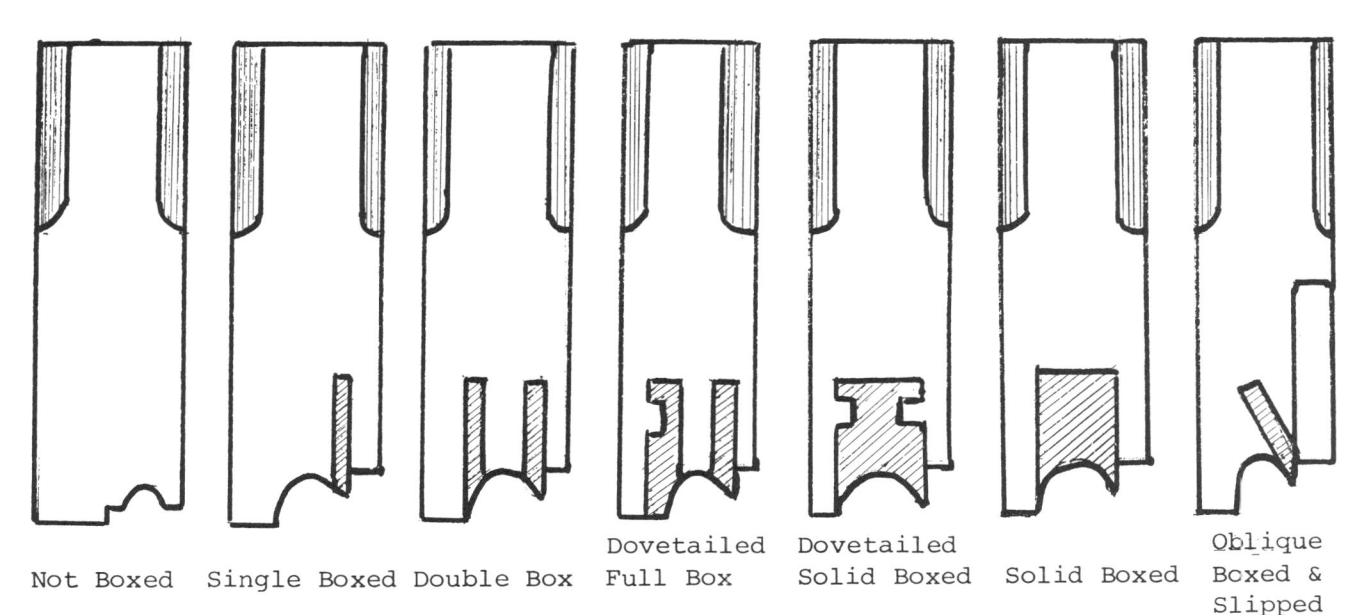

Plate XXIV - Methods of Boxing Moulding Planes

(left to right: Not Boxed; Single Boxed; Double Box; Dovetailed Full Box; Dovetailed Solid Boxed; Solid Boxed; Oblique Boxed & Slipped)

Various methods of boxing bead planes are illustrated in Plate XXIV. At slightly increased costs double box, full box or solid dovetailed box grades were available in most sizes of bead planes. A series of bead planes showing different box constructions appear in Fig. 58. Two different methods of boxing snipe bill planes are also illustrated. Common sizes of simple moulding planes available during the middle of the nineteenth century are listed in Table XIX.

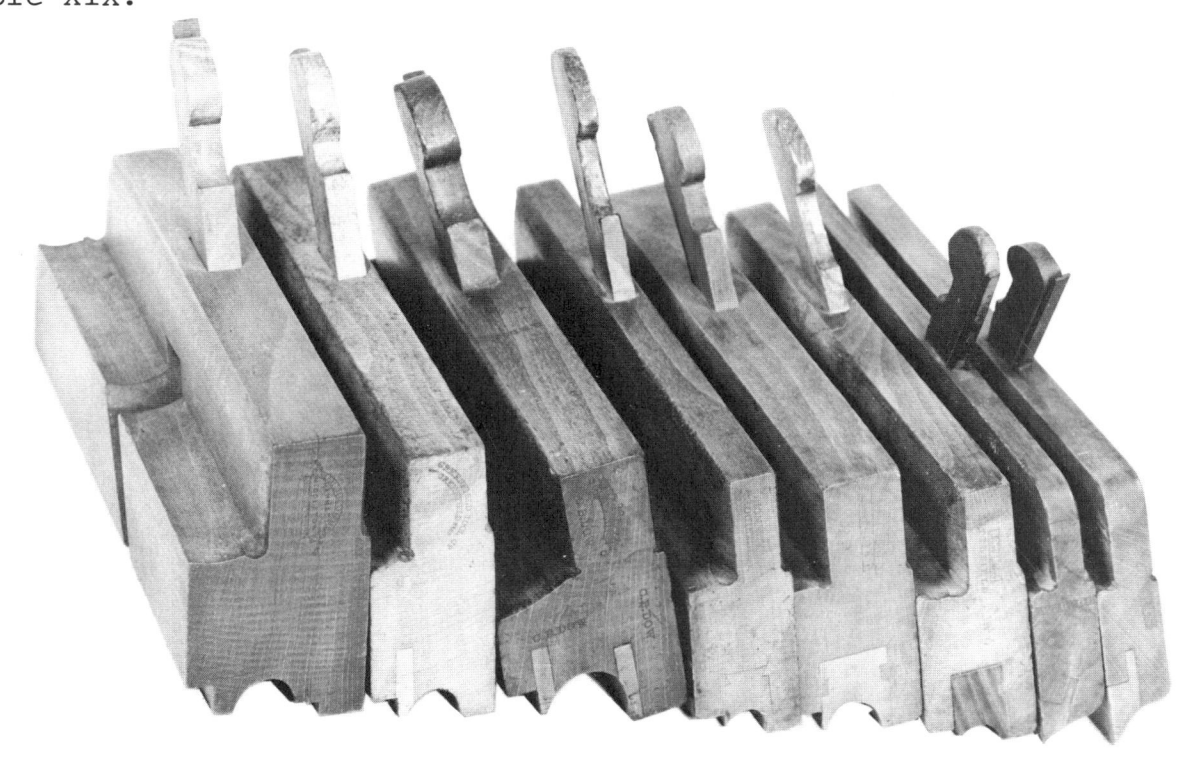

Fig. 58. Various methods of boxing bead and snipe bill planes. [from left to right: 3/4" astragal, plain with no boxing; 3/4" single boxed bead; 1" double-boxed bead; 1/2" dovetailed solid box bead; 1/2" dovetailed solid box bead; 3/8" solid boxed bead; snipe bill, full boxed; snipe bill full boxed (another method) (snipe bill planes were also single boxed)]

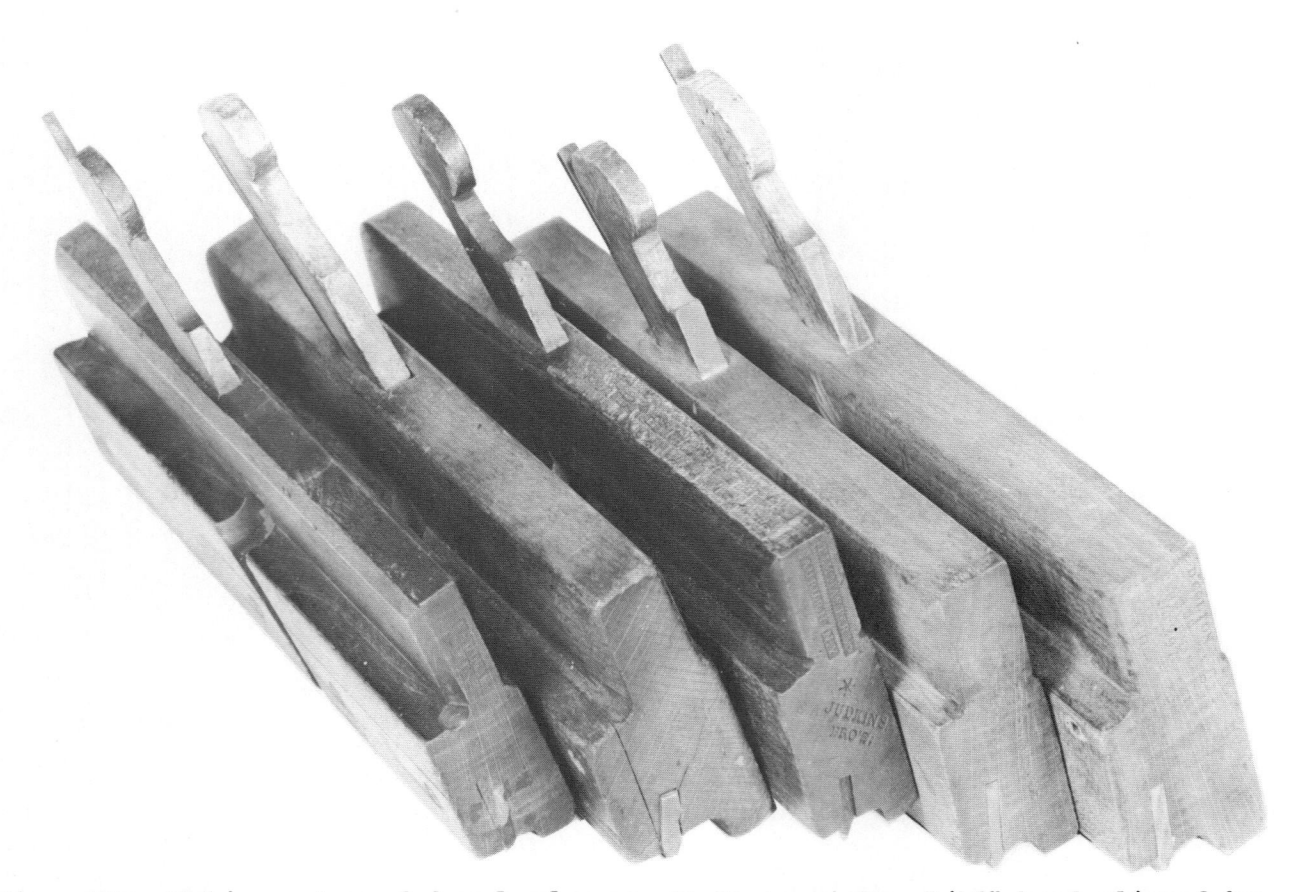

Fig. 59. Oblique boxed bead planes. [left to right: 5/16" bead, slipped by Robert Bewley, Leeds, England (1798-1845); 5/8" bead, slipped by R.W. Maccubbin, Baltimore, Md (-1847-71-); 5/8" bead, T.J. McMaster, Auburn, N.Y.: 7/16" bead, H. Chapin, Pine Mead, Ct.; D.R. Colton, Philadelphia, Pa.; 5/8" bead]

In England some bead and other moulding planes were fitted with a replaceable strip along the cutting side attached with screws. In this manner the strip could be replaced when worn to the point that the plane would normally be no longer serviceable. In making such 'slipped' planes the single boxed spline was inserted obliquely to the sole in order not to fall out in replacing the side strip. While the majority of single boxed planes made in United States were splined at right angles to the sole, in some instances these were set oblique. (Fig. 59.) Consequently it is erroneous to assume that all planes boxed obliquely were made in England. A 'slipped' bead plane made by R.W. Maccubbin of Baltimore, a practice rare in America, is shown in Fig. 59.

Table XIV
Sizes of simple moulding planes

Type of plane	1/8	5/32	3/16	1/4	5/16	3/8	7/16	1/2	5/8	3/4	7/8	1	1-1/8	1-1/4	1-3/8	1-1/2
Astragal	x	-	-	x	-	x	-	x	x	x	x	x	x	x	x	x
Bead, Single Box	x	x	x	x	x	x	x	x	x	x	x	x	x	x	x	x
Bead, Double Box	x	x	x	x	x	x	x	x	x	x	x	x	x	x	x	x
Bead, Solid Box	x	-	x	x	x	x	x	x	x	x	x	x	x	-	-
Center Bead	x	-	x	x	x	x	x	x	x	x	x	-	-	-	-
Reed	-	-	x	x	x	x	-	x	x	x	x	x	-	-	-	-
Nosing	-	-	-	-	-	-	-	-	x	x	x	x	x	x	x	x
Torus	x	-	x	x	x	x	x	x	x	x	x	x	-	-	-	-
Ovalo	-	-	-	-	-	x	-	x	x	x	x	x	-	x	-	x
Cavetto	-	-	-	-	-	x	-	x	x	x	x	x	-	x	-	x

Diameter in inches of cut bead

- denotes not manufactured   x denotes manufactured

Fig. 60. Simple Moulding Planes [left to right: 3/4" center bead; 5/8" reeding plane; 1-1/8" nosing plane; double iron 1" bead plane]

The *nosing* (alternatively known as *step* or *stair plane*) shown with the other simple moulding planes of group VIII is classified as Group XII-3 (special carpenter plane). However since its shape is a semi-circle, it is described with the group of simple moulding shapes. The use of this plane was for preparing the front surface of a stair step. In the larger sizes of above 1" both nosing and edge bead planes were supplied with double irons. (Fig.61) The probable advantage of this construction was ease of sharpening a shorter arc. The double iron *ovalo plane* (7/8" right and left) shown in Fig. 61) was a convenience to have both contours contained in a single plane.

Fig. 61. Double Iron Moulding Planes [left to right: torus, ovalo & nosing]

Hollows & Rounds. VIII-6. [C.v.XX, No.4, Dec.1967, p61; N-111; H-492; A-17-18; D-331]

HOLLOWS AND ROUNDS.

Fig. 62. Pair of One Inch Hollow and Round Planes. [worked 2" dia. circle]

    A *hollow plane* has a hollow or concave surface and forms a round or convex surface; while a *round plane* forms a hollow or concave surface. In other words these planes produce surfaces opposite their names. These planes were sold in pairs, a hollow and round, of each size for working circular surface from 1/8" to 3-1/2" diameters. The contour of arc of each plane is one-sixth of a circle, the chord of which denotes the radius of the circle worked. Note sketch in Plate XXV. In Great Britain these were sometimes called *casement planes*. A problem resulted in United States with different manufactures assigning a different system of numbers to the various sizes. [See: Alvin Sellens, "Hollows and Rounds", *Chronicle of EAIA*, v.XXV, No.1, Mar.1972, pp12-13] A carpenter's ordinary requirements might be satisfied with nine pairs in 1/4" increments for working circles 1/4" to 2-1/4" diameter. An experienced joiner on the other hand might require the entire set of twenty-four pairs (see: A-18-19, item 567).

Plate XXV.
(right)
Sketch of Hollow & Round
Pair of Planes for
Working 2" dia. circle

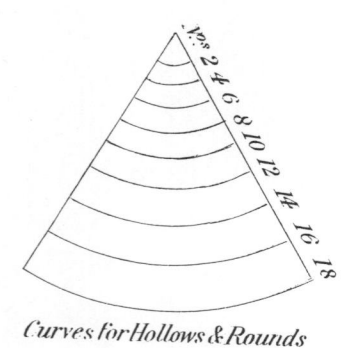

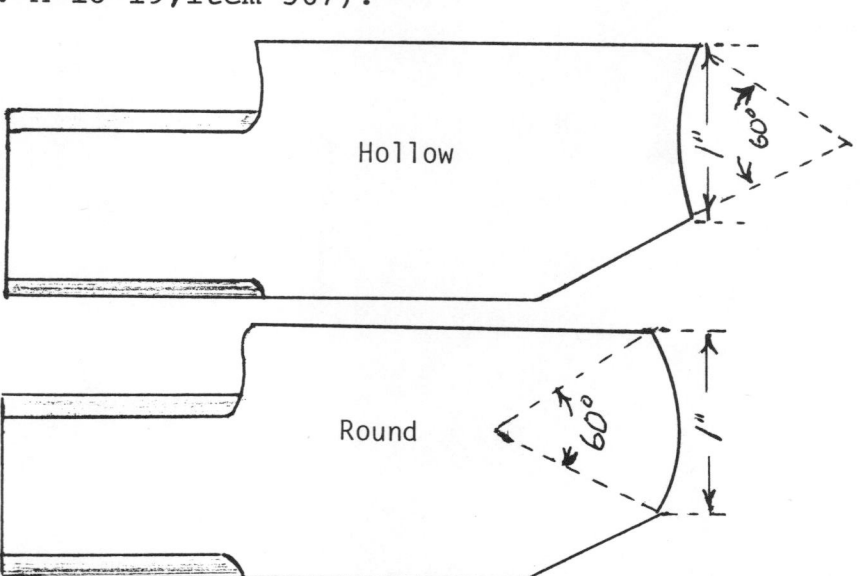

Curves for Hollows & Rounds

Fig. 63. Set of Nine Round Irons [1/8" - 1-1/2" widths] & Triangular Box

In order to protect the cutting irons from rusting, these were sometimes stored in a box. Such a set of nine irons and a triangular shaped storing box are illustrate in Fig. 63. These were usually set 60 degrees pitch and square across the sole. On special order sets of skew planes were available for cross-grain work. An experienced joiner with a full set of hollows and rounds, supplemented by a pair of snipe bill planes, could work or reproduce almost any shape of moulding by shaping small increments and accordingly changing slope of curvature by selecting different sizes to match a given curve. The majority of hollows and rounds were furnished without handles. A rather uncommon matching set of 1-1/2" size with handles is shown in Fig. 64, together with a set of the same size without handles and irons removed.

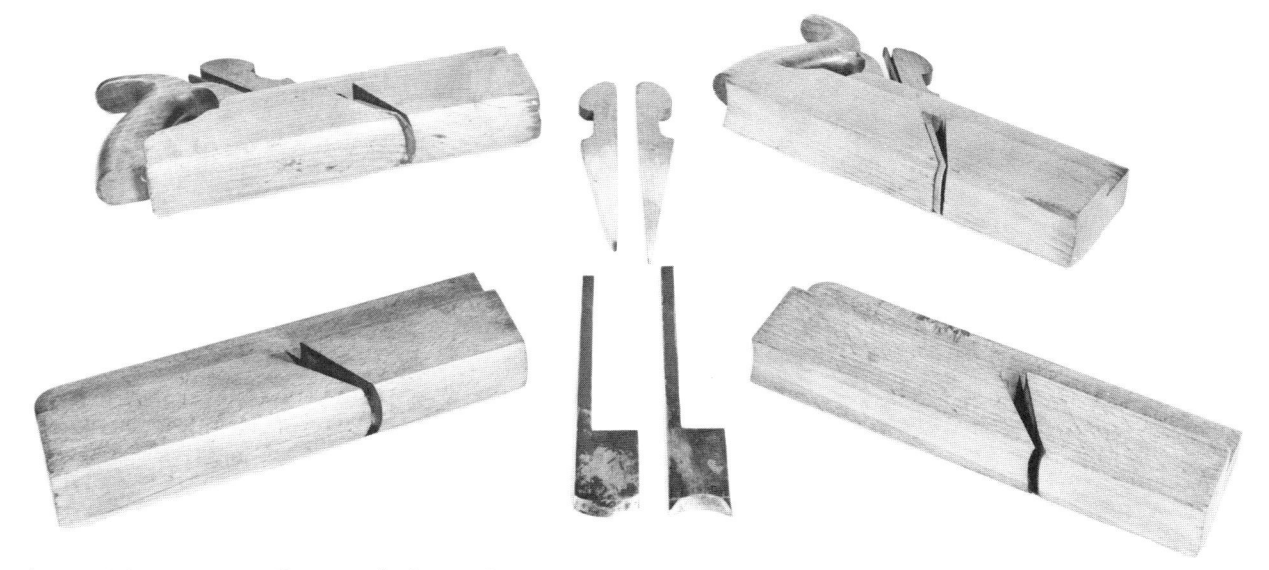

Fig. 64 Sets of 1-1/2" Hollows and Rounds. [Bottom set: no handles with irons and wedges removed and shown at center: top with handles]

IX. Complex Mouldings. C.,v.XXI,No.1,Mar.1968,pp.4-6; N-108; H-492-93.

Group of Complex Moulding Planes (½" - 1" widths) Fig. 65.

Complex mouldings have been defined as contours with irregular curvature having definite turning point, which may be combined with simple mouldings. Several designs were based on variations of the 'Ogee'(O.G.), formally known as *Cyma Recta*. This classical architectural form is composed of joining members of a concave (upper surface) and a convex curve (lower surface). The geometrical construction of a plain Ogee is shown in Plate XXVI. When these surfaces have the uppermost convex and the lower concave a *Cyma Recta* or *Talon* is formed, which is called 'reverse Ogee'.

Plate XXVI Construction of Cyma Recta (Ogee) & Moulding Plane

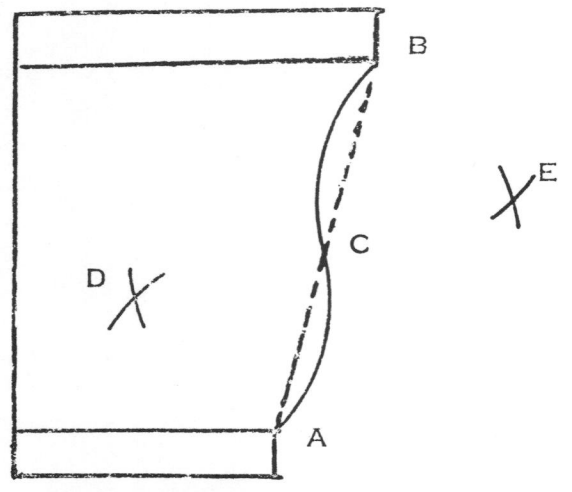

Construction: Join A and B, the extremities of the curve, and bisect AB at C. On A & C as centers with radius AC, described arcs, meeting at E. On D & E as centers decribe the arcs AC & CB composing the Moulding.

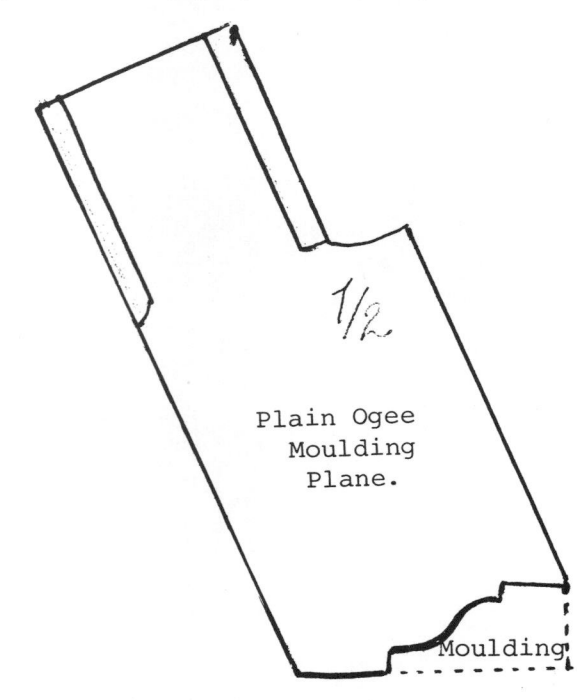

Plain Ogee Moulding Plane.

Reverse Ogee — Grecian Ogee — Grecian Ovalo

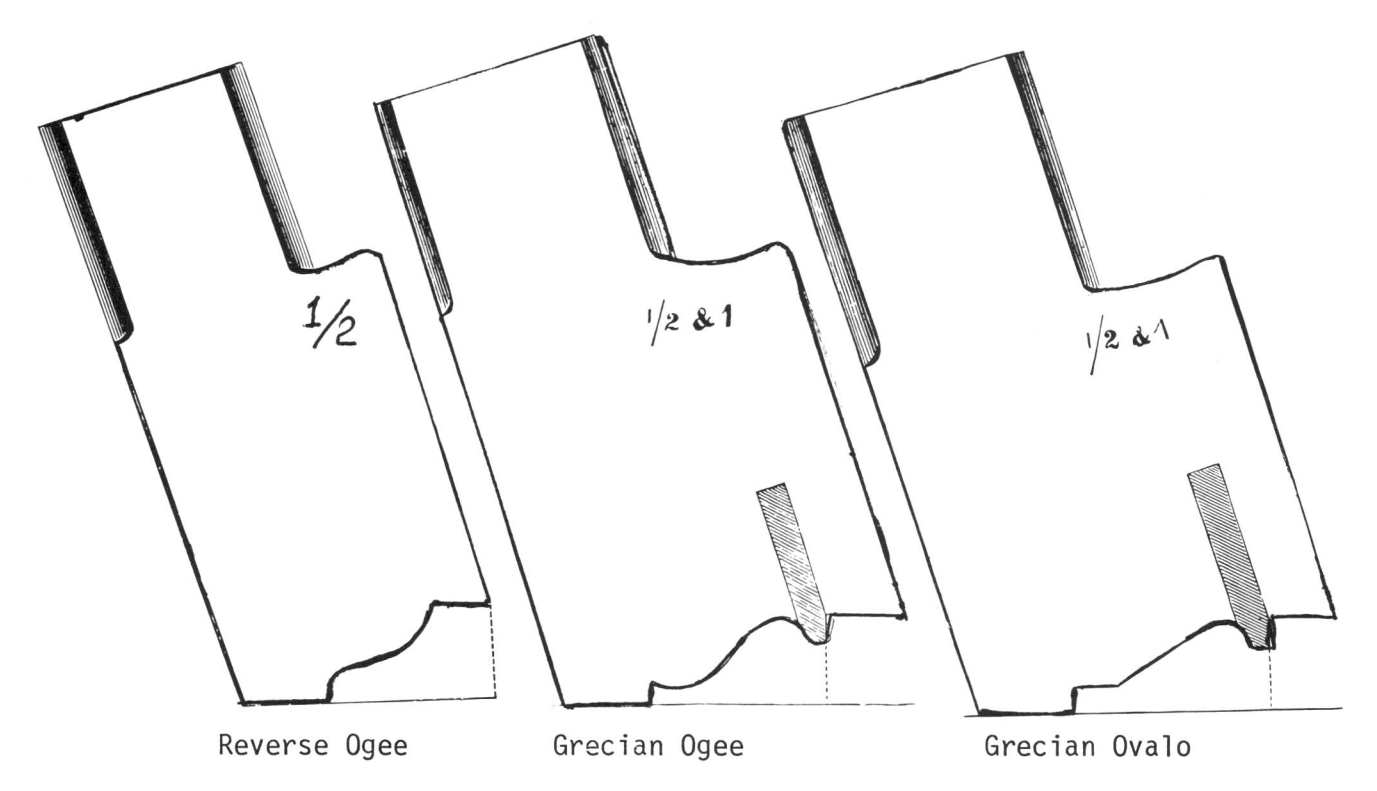

Plate XXVII - Variation of Ogee and Grecian Mouldings

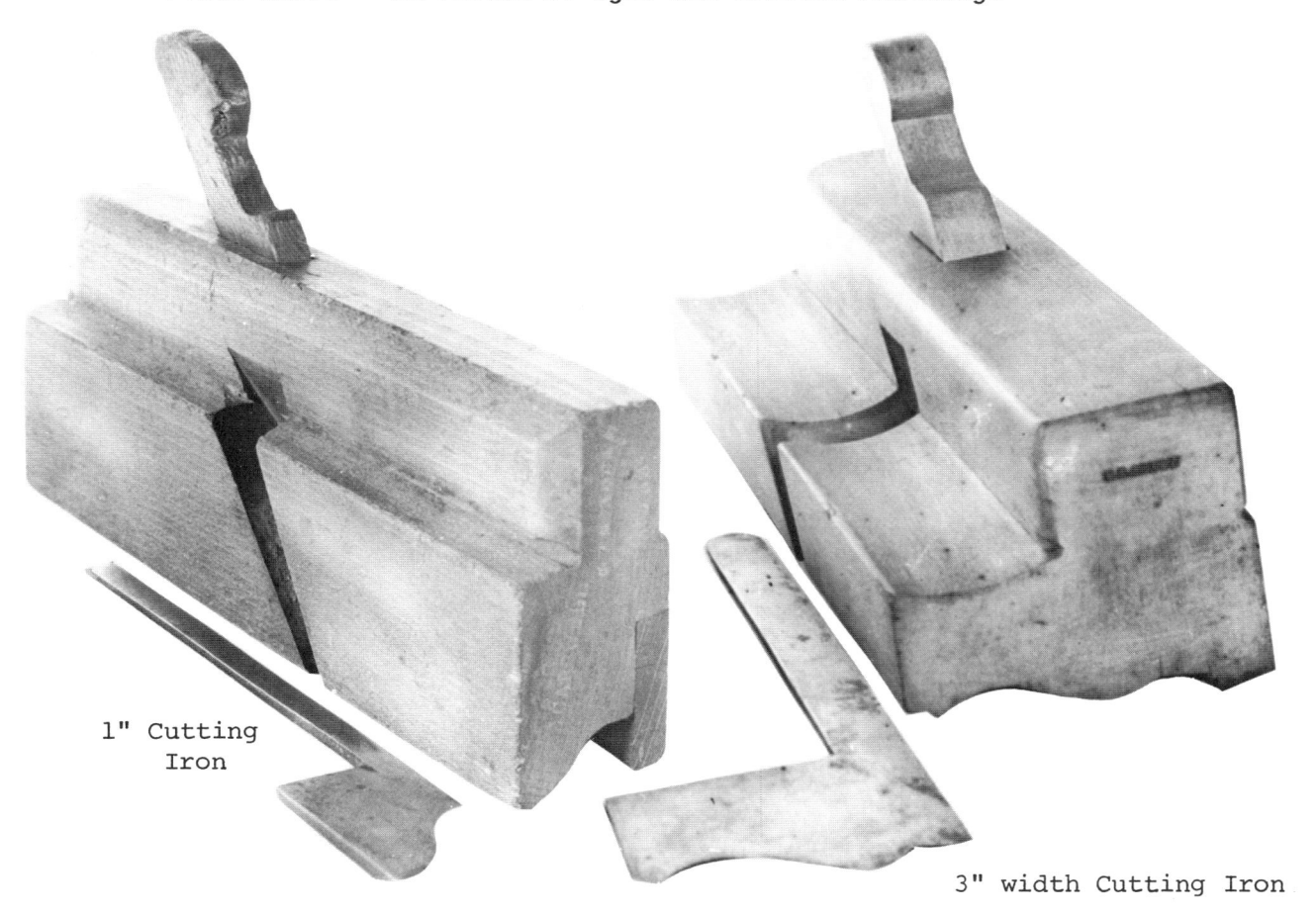

1" Cutting Iron

3" width Cutting Iron

Fig. 66. Plain (left) and Reverse (right) Ogee Moulding Planes.

Fig. 67. Grecian Ogee Moulding Planes

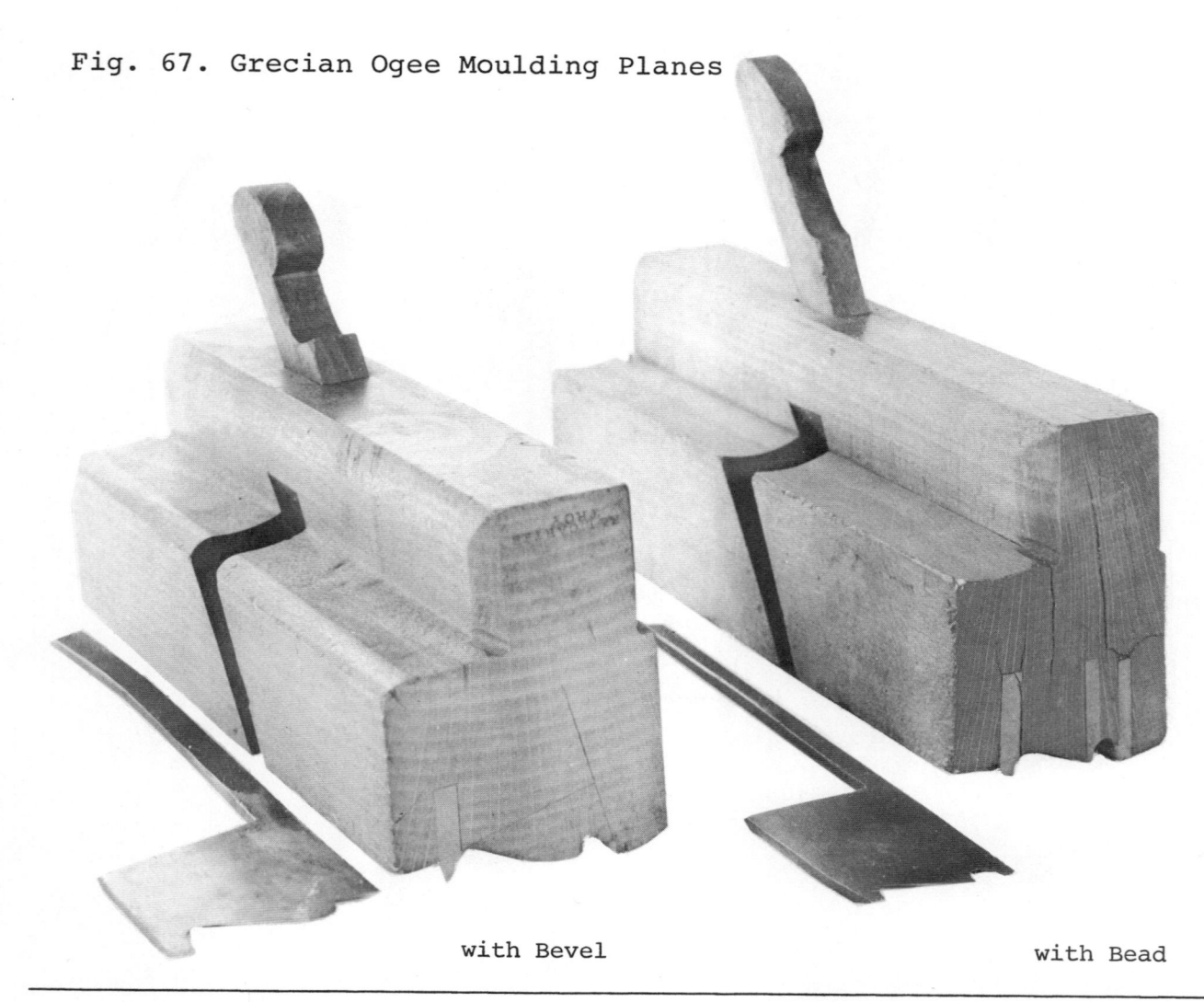

with Bevel   with Bead

with Square   with Bevel

Fig. 68. Grecian Ovolo Planes

Fig. 69. Various Complex Moulding Planes. [1" - 2" widths]

A *Grecian Ogee* moulding has a 'quirk' on the inside surface and generally a fillet, square, bevel or a bead accompannying on the outside edge. (See:Plate XXVII & Fig. 67) A *Grecian Ovolo* consists of an eliptical curve rather than a circular arc and also has an inside 'quirk' and is combined with outside edge mouldings. (See: Plate XXVII & Fig. 68) Numbers stamped on the back end of such moulding planes indicated the size that a given tool worked and the depth (height of the moulding. As noted from the numbers on the planes in Plate XXVII the depth was generally half the width. A single number denoted the width that the tool worked.

Many complex moulding planes were furnished with boxwood splines similar to bead planes to reduce wear at the points of change of slope to prolong the life of the plane. Frequently on the front end of complex moulding planes two lines have been scribed at right angles to each other by an owner. These served as guide lines to indicate the vertical and horizontal holding positions during planing. (Se: Fig. 70)

Fig. 70 (right)

Complex Moulding Plane with iron removed to show operating position.

Note scribed guide lines marked on front end.

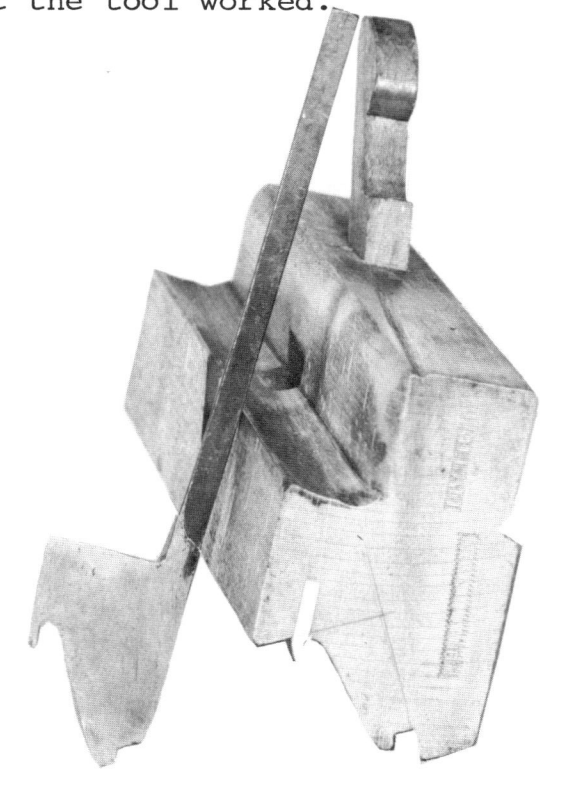

Fig. 71. Complex Moulding Planes[2" - 3" widths]

Various shapes of complex moulding planes are listed in Table XIII which appear in the *Arrowmammett Works Catalogue*.(Appendix, pp. 12-17). A number of these are labeled on the P. Chapin Broadside. (See:Plate V) Such moulding planes were normally supplied without handles, but these were available on special order. (Fig. 72.)

The operation of preparing a moulding from a strip of planed wood, usually from 8 to 10 feet long, was referred to as "Striking a moulding", also some times called "sticking". (See: H-352). It required a series of cuts for the surface of the moulding plane to be fully developed. The piece of prepared wood which was worked into the moulding was referred to as a"piece of stuff". One end was held rigid at the far left end of the bench. The worker would start at the far right end and walk along the bench toward the left in a continuous stroke shaving the entire length. Generally the plane was held at an angle, rather than perpendicularly; hence the scribed reference mark noted in Fig. 70. In making wide or complicated items often the surface would first be planed to a bevel using a jack or jointer plane. The number of passes required depended on the complexity of the design, the nature of the wood and the condition of the cutting edge.

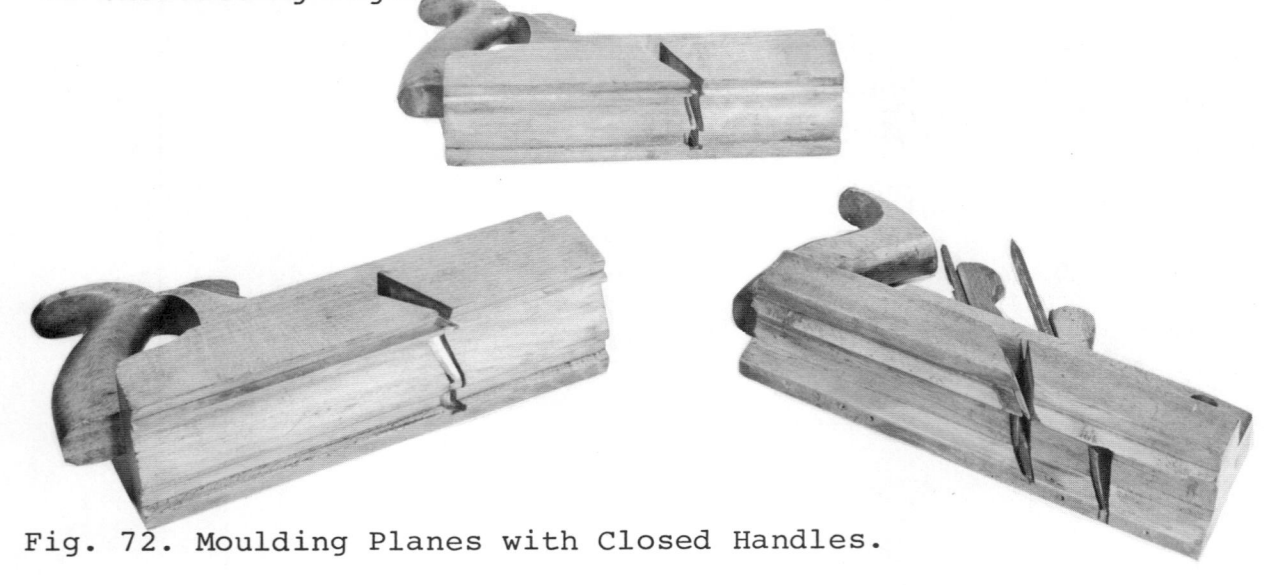

Fig. 72. Moulding Planes with Closed Handles.

Snipe Bill Planes. IX - 5.
[C.,v.XX,No.4,Dec.1967,p.60; N-111; D-359-360]

Single Boxed

Full Boxed

Fig. 73 Full Boxed Snipe Bill

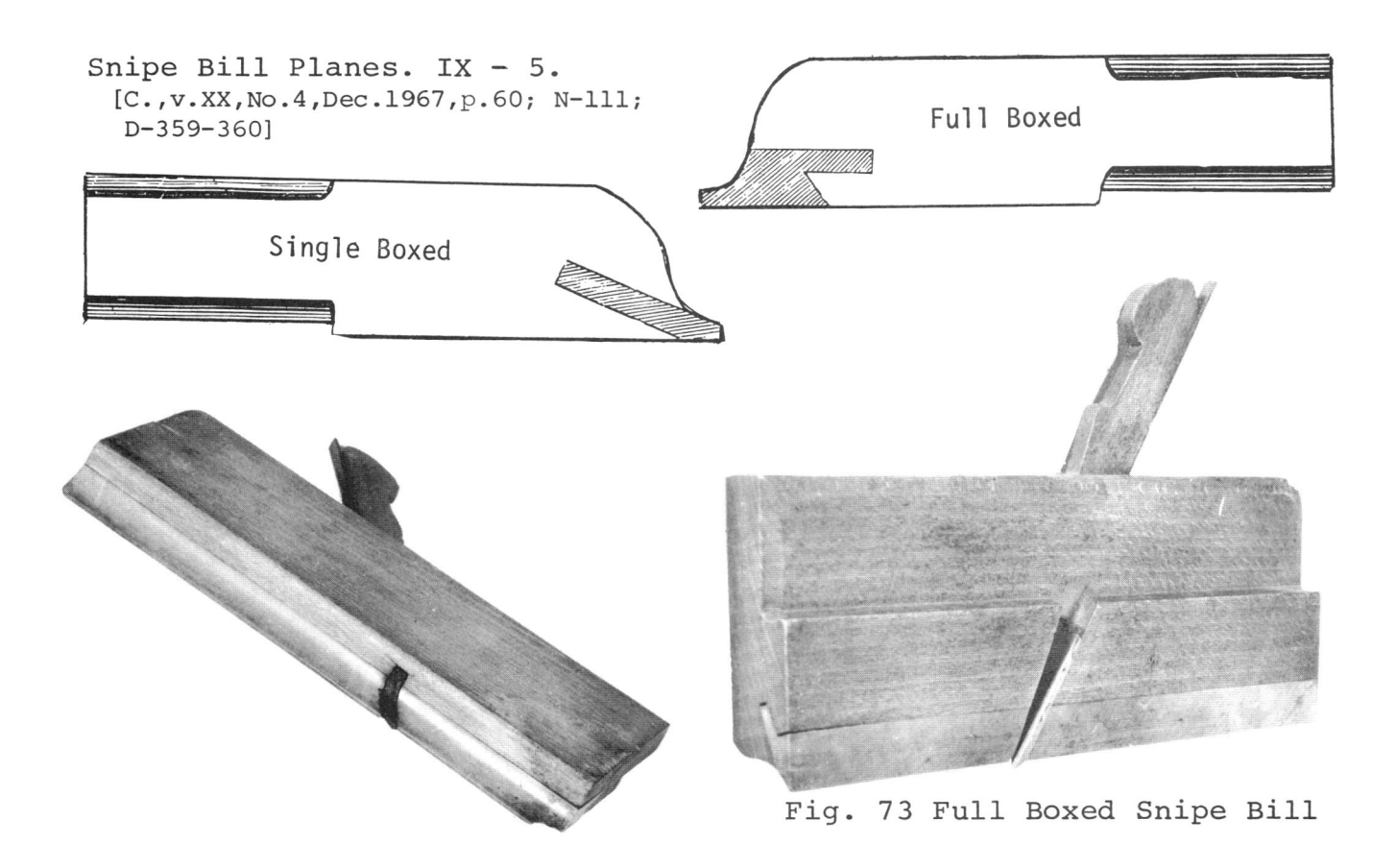

Snipe Bill Planes were furnished in pairs (right & left). These were so named because of the similarity of the Ogee shaped cutting iron and sole to the bill of a snipe. Actually these are associated with hollow & round planes, but because their shapes are complex in design and these were also used to clean out quirks and corners of cut mouldings, their description is included with the group of complex moulding planes.

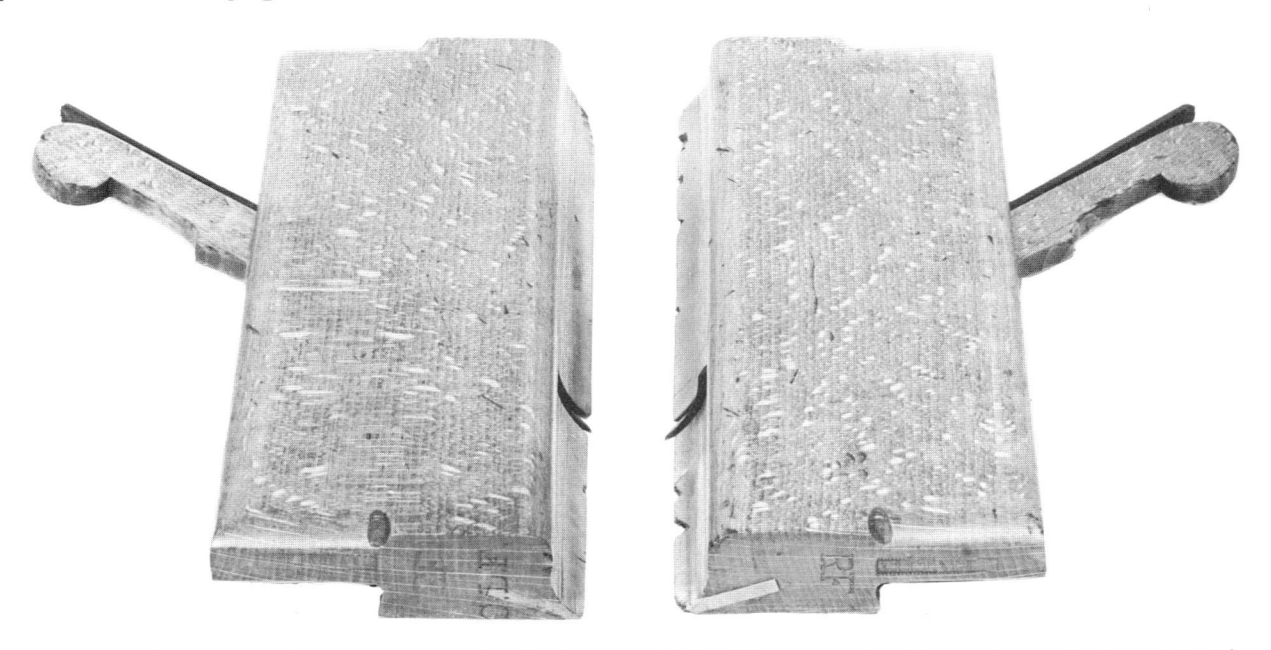

Fig. 74. Pair of Single Boxed Snipe Bill Planes [collection of Donald Wing]

Sash Planes - X. [C.,v.XX,No.2,June1967,p.24; N-102-4; D-354-55; A-7-8]

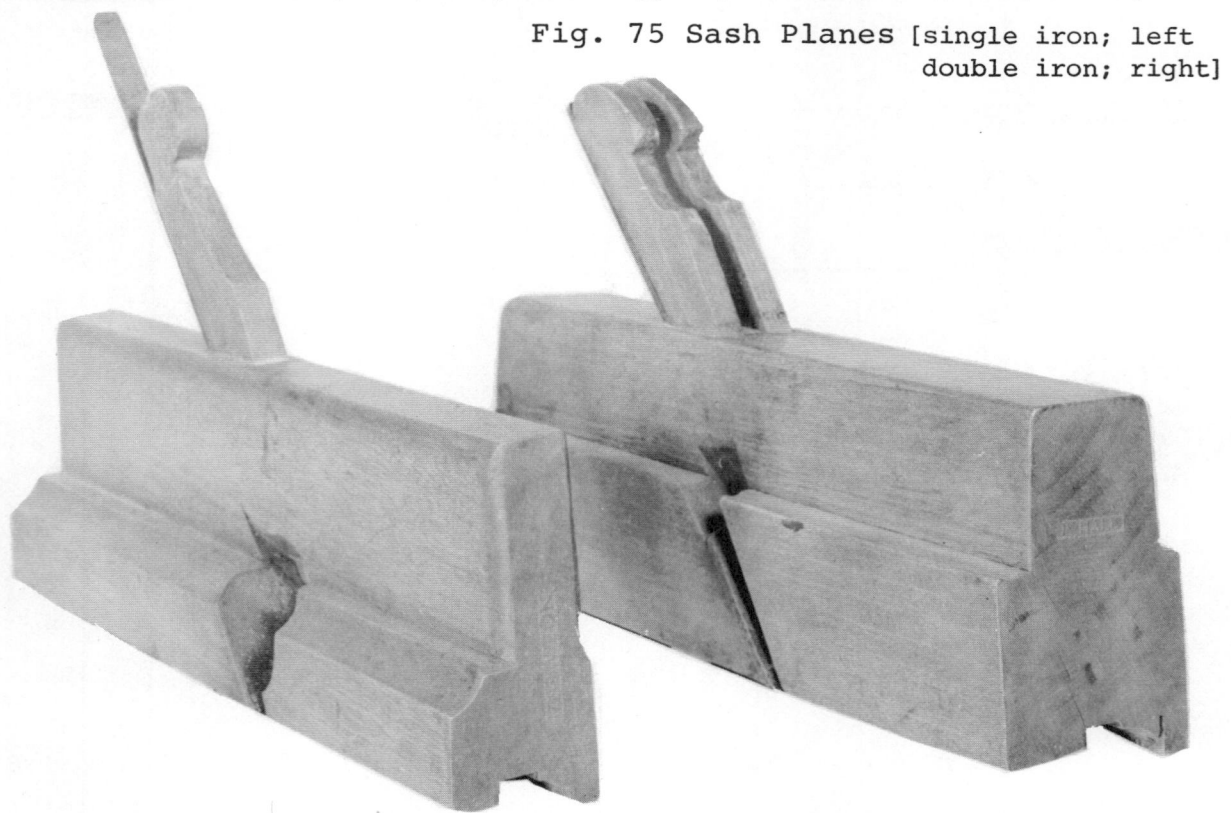

Fig. 75 Sash Planes [single iron; left double iron; right]

Sash Planes, used in window frame making, may be regarded as combination planes. A rabbet was cut on one side of the section for holding a pane of glass, while the other side was decoratively cut with a moulding section; such as an ovolo, Gothic, Ogee,etc. The least expensive plane, used only for a single size, had a single iron. (Fig. 75, left). At slightly higher cost a double iron plane was sold. (Fig. 75, right) One iron was for the rabbet cut and the other for the moulding, thus permitting easier sharpening.

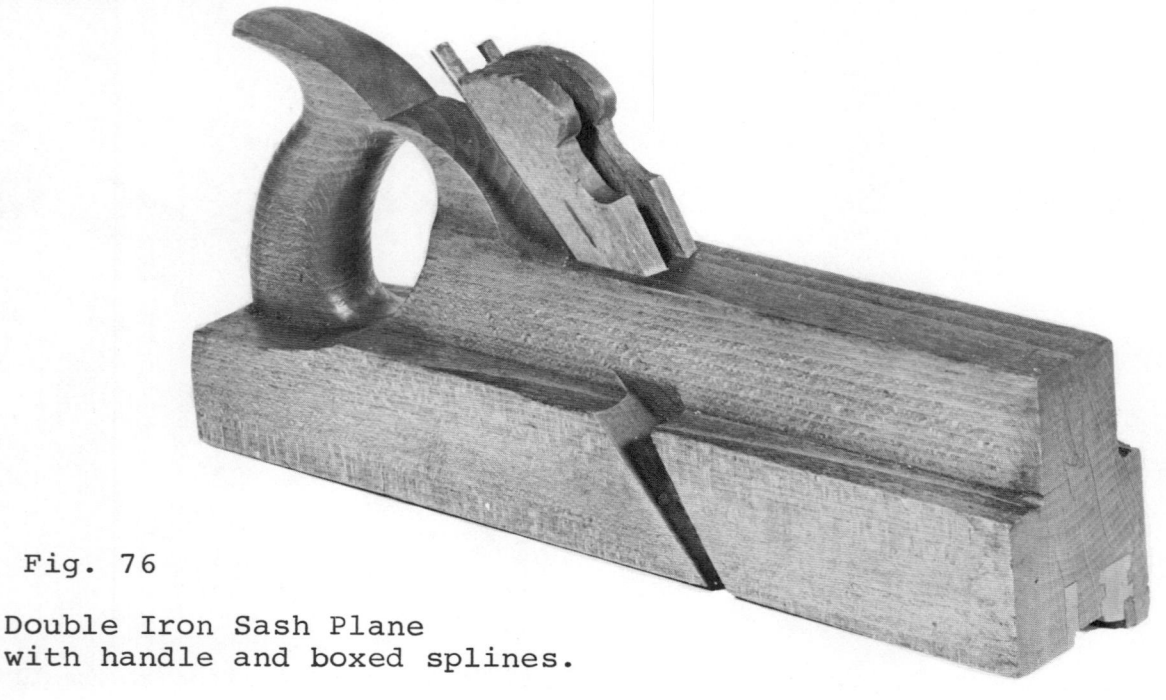

Fig. 76

Double Iron Sash Plane with handle and boxed splines.

Fig. 77. Adjustable Double Iron Sash Planes.[Diamond Pad;top left, Brass Pad; top right]

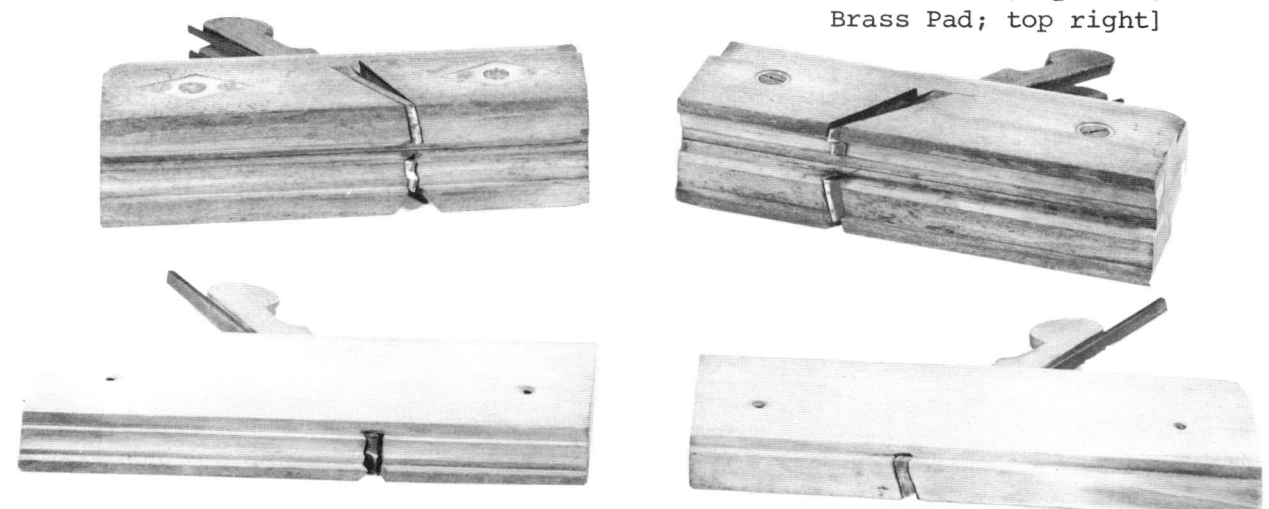

A double iron,boxed and with handle sash plane could be purchased at a higher price. (A-189, Fig. 76). The best grades of sash planes were made up with the two individual rabbet and moulding components assembled together with a screw adjustment which provided for variable spacing between the two planes. The two different types of iron-screw self-regulating double iron sash planes are illustrated in Fig. 77. The more expensive,*diamond pad*, is shown at the top left, while the *brass-pad* arrangement is shown at the top right. At the bottom the component planes from a screw-type arrangement are shown separated; at the left an ovolo moulding plane and at the right the rabbet plane. The most expensive and best type of adjustable sash plane was made with box screw arms, called an *adjustable screw arm sash plane*. Fig. 78.

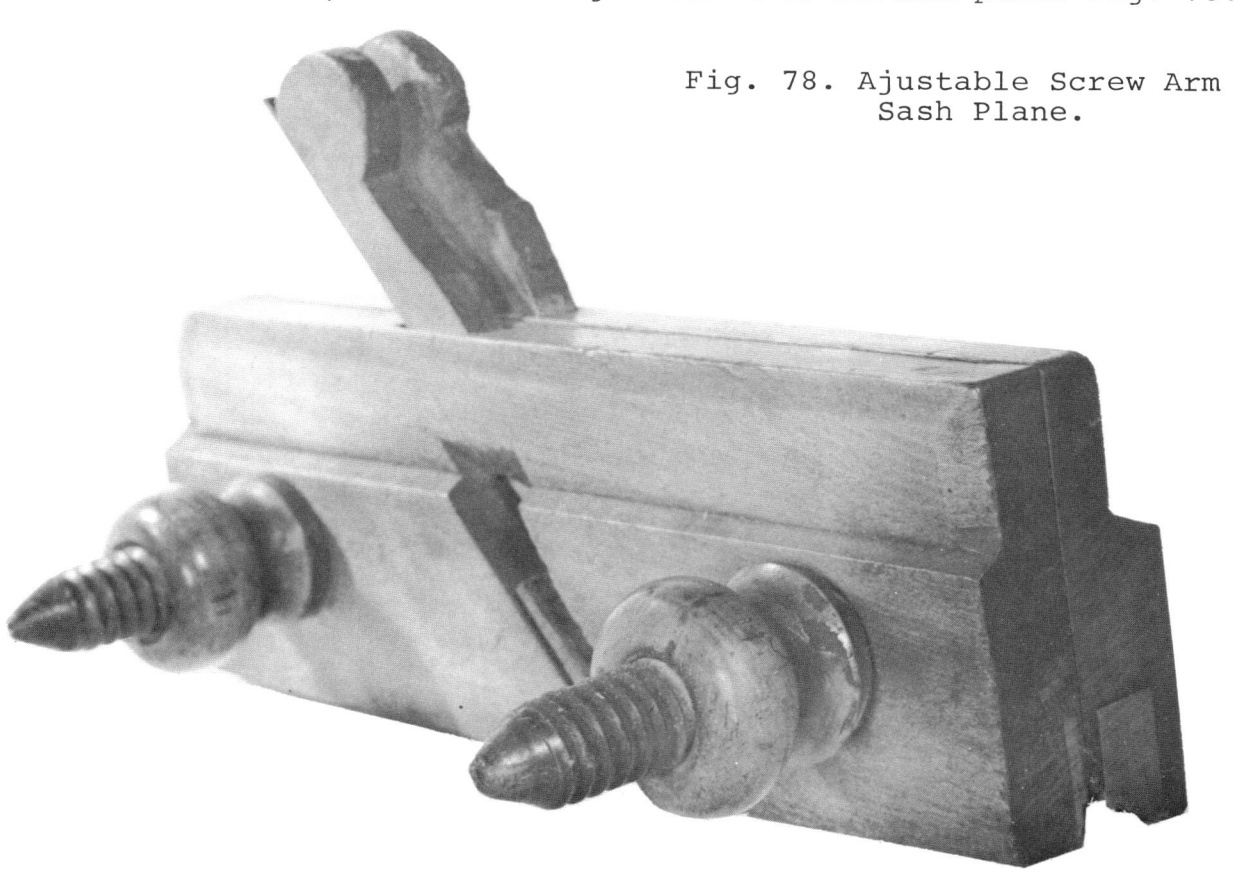

Fig. 78. Ajustable Screw Arm Sash Plane.

Sash Coping Planes. X - 3.

Fig. 79

Single OGee Coping Plane

Associated with sash planes were various *coping planes* for forming the section adjacent to window frames. These were commonly offered in four moulding sections: ovolo, gothic, bevel and ogee. (Plate XXVII.) Such planes were sold as single (Fig. 79) [A-197] or double. (Figs. 80 & 81)

Plate XXVIII - Sections of Coping Planes

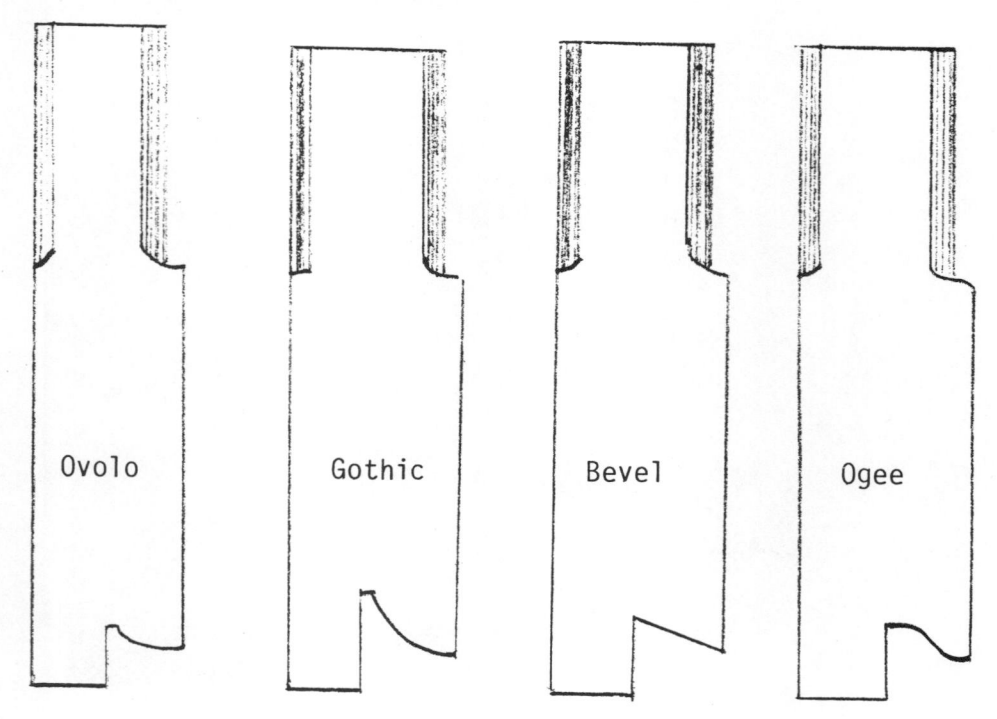

Ovolo   Gothic   Bevel   Ogee

Fig. 80.

Double Coping Plane
Ovolo Section By M. Copeland
   [top view; imprint on plane
      shown below]

The right angle fence screwed into the sole of the double coping plane functioned both as a stop and a guide for assuring a straight cut on such a narrow moulding.

Fig. 81. Various Double Coping Planes

Various saddle-type templates or gauges for duplicating and checking the contour of sash mouldings are illustrated in Fig. 82.

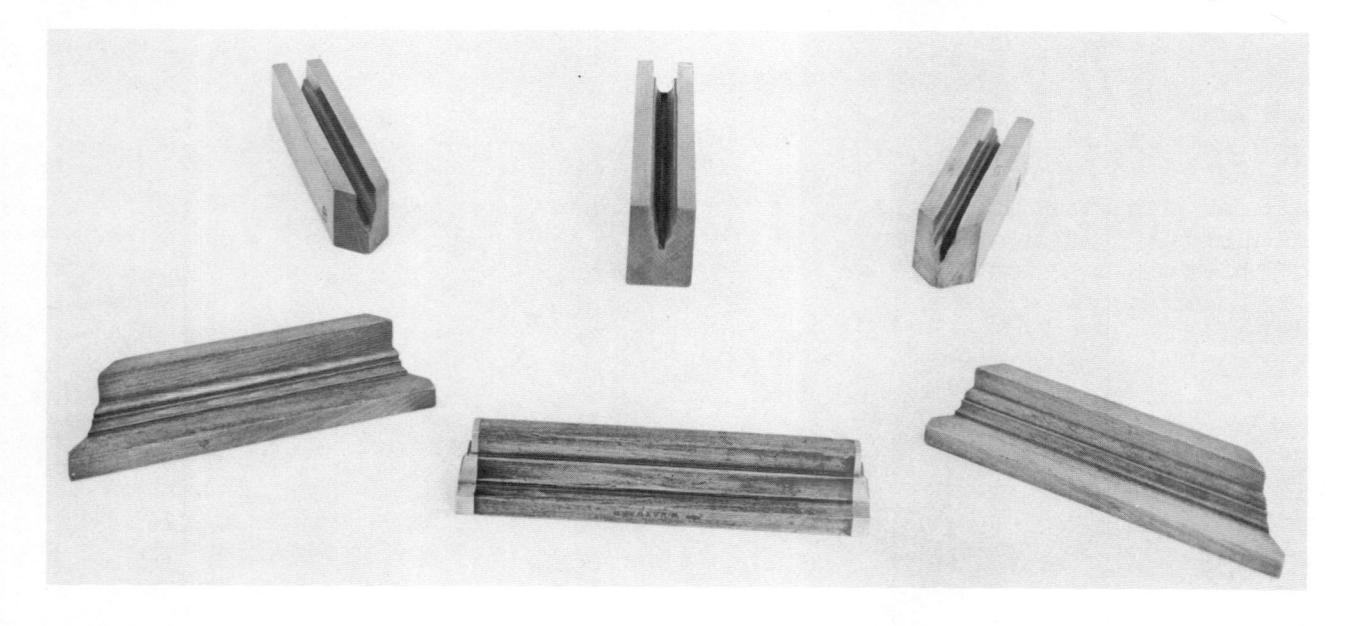

Fig. 82. Saddle-type Sash Templates.

XI - Cornice Planes. [C..v.XXI,No.2,June 1968,pp.22-25; D-323; A-5,items 97-100]

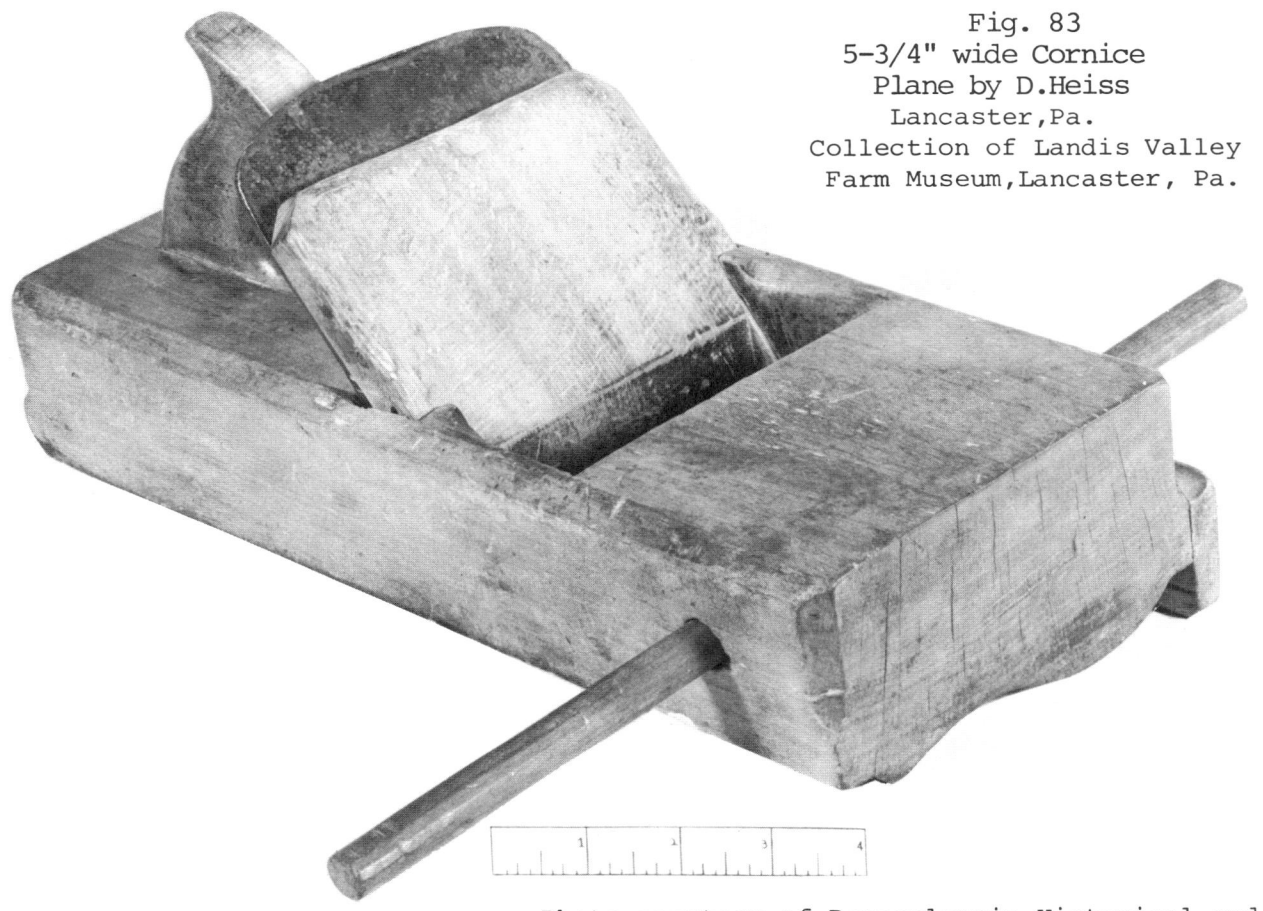

Fig. 83
5-3/4" wide Cornice
Plane by D.Heiss
Lancaster,Pa.
Collection of Landis Valley
Farm Museum,Lancaster, Pa.

Photo courtesy of Pennsylvania Historical and
Museum Commission, Harrisburg, Pa.

A *cornice* is defined architecturally as a decorative aggregate of mouldings which crown or finish a composition (entablature) internally or externally. Such a combination usually consists of either a bed moulding, composed usually of a bead, and ovolo and fillet, or a plain member sometimes cut into dentils with a bead, cyma recta (Ogee) or ovolo and fillet. In house construction the cornice is applied externally below the roof eave and horizontally across the front plate, called the facia. During both Colonial and Federal Periods extensive use of inside raised panels on walls, frequently extending from the floor to the ceiling, was common practice. The juncture of such paneling with the ceiling was dressed with a broad hand planed cornice moulding, referred to as the *crown moulding*. Such mouldings of widths from 4" to 6" were shaped with a single plane. Occasionally this operation required the efforts of two men simultaneously working the plane. One man pushed and guided the plane, while the other pulled a rope attached to the front end. (H-493) Such a *crown moulding plane* having a single iron 5-3/4" in width is illustrated in Fig. 83. The pull bar to which the rope was attached at the front end of this plane is evident in this illustration. A fence was attached to the left side for guiding the cut.

A later variety *crown moulding plane* with double irons is shown in Fig. 84. The width of the entire contour is 6½". The wider iron on the right [stamped W.Butcher (English manufacture] is 4" in width; while the left iron [stamped Providence Tool Co.] is 2½".

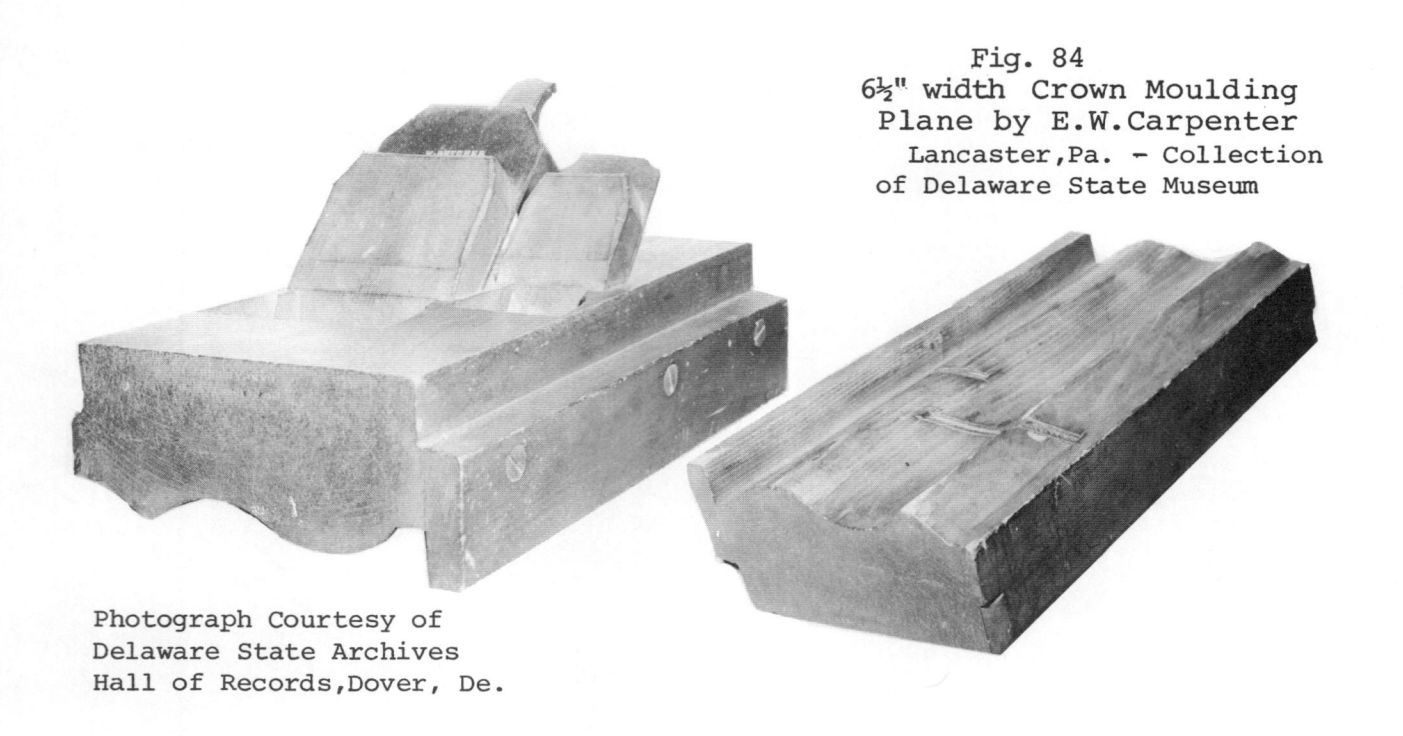

Fig. 84
6½" width Crown Moulding
Plane by E.W.Carpenter
Lancaster,Pa. - Collection
of Delaware State Museum

Photograph Courtesy of
Delaware State Archives
Hall of Records,Dover, De.

Fig. 85
3" width Cornice Plane
by C.Fuller,Boston,Mass.

The probable purpose of double irons was for ease in sharpening. It is essential in using such a plane to have both irons cutting simultaneously to allow the entire contour to develop across the entire width. This plane has the imprint of E.W. Carpenter of Lancaster, Pa., who was known to have been working there in 1859 which is compatible with the date of Providence Tool Co. The fence was screwed to the left side and could be readily removed.

A shorter, 10" long, crown moulding plane is shown in Fig. 85, also illustrating the iron removed from the plane and the sole. The width of the iron is 3", and the imprint is C.Fuller/Causeway/Boston, Mass., who was at that address 1852-1856. The iron was made by Humphreyville Manufacturing Co. at Seymour, Conn. The weld of the steel cutting section to the iron extension is clearly noticed at the middle. The hole in one side is believed to have been for hanging or supporting the plane in a rack after use. Since this does not extend through both sides, it obviously was not for a peg for attachment of a pull rope.

An unusual 14" length crown moulding plane with an adjustable fence is illustrated in Fig. 86. The 3" width cutting iron is shown at the left and a view of the sole appears below the plane. No imprints appear on either the plane or iron.

Fig. 86
Crown Moulding Plane with
 Adjustable Fence.
   [3" width x 14" length]

A double iron Gothic bevel cornice plane (15½" long x 4" wide) with front pull pin is illustrated in Fig. 87. While there is no imprint on the plane to indicate the maker, the irons are stamped: SWINSCOW & MANUAL/ S & M/Cast Steel/Warranted. The plane is believed to be an American make, c.1840. The wedge is a single piece.

Fig. 87
4" width Gothic
Bevel Cornice Plane

A later development in the manufacture of wide cornice planes was producing these in matched pairs of single iron with a fence, each plane to form approximately one half the width of the contour. This obviously reduced the effort required in planing the section. Such pairs for "Ogee cornices", 4" to 5½" widths, are noted in the *Arrowmammett Works Catalogue*, (Appendix A-5, items 97-100). A sketch from 1874 *H.Chapin's Son Price List* for a pair of cornice planes for forming a 5½" section is shown in Plate XXIX. The plane forming the left section is shown with solid lines. The dotted outline in the middle indicates the right edge of the plane forming the right section of this moulding. The price quoted for such planes was $1.00 per inch of moulding, which in this instance of the plane in the sketch would amount to a cost of $5.50. The section of base and band moulding, also appeared in the 1874 Chapin Catalogue, shows such a moulding with a 3" width and a 7/8" rise. The price of these planes were $0.70 per inch of width, including handle.

Plate XXIX

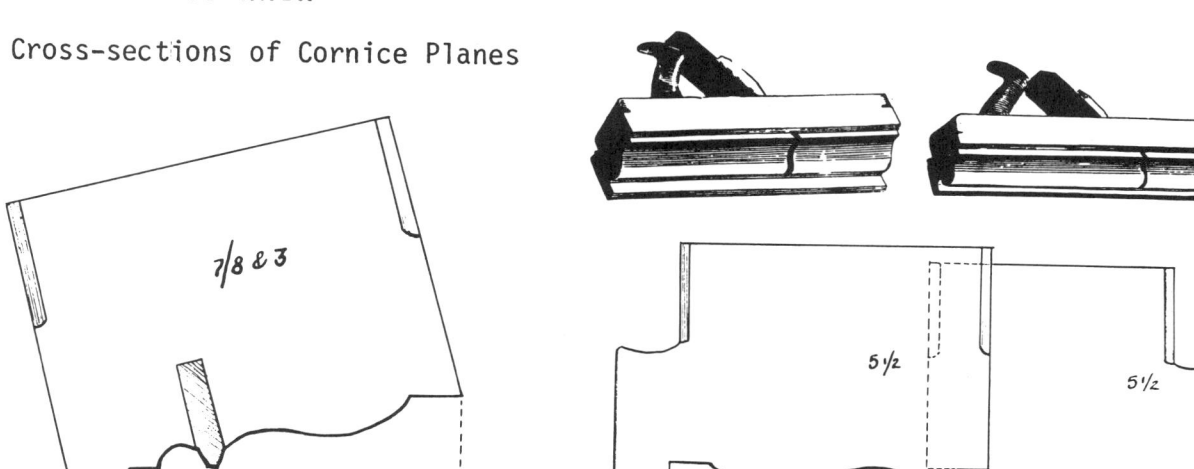

Cross-sections of Cornice Planes

Base and Band Moulding Plane

Pair of Cornice Planes

D. Special Shaping Planes. - XII. 1. Gutter or Pump Planes

Fig. 88. Pump (left) and Gutter (right) Planes.

Planes for hollowing out troughs or a similar semi-cirular section for making a water pump were respectively known as *gutter* and *pump planes*. (Fig. 88) The sizes of both are similar to common jack planes and usually had similar open handles. In fact many such planes were probably converted into these special uses from ordinary jack planes. The gutter plane had a semi-circularly shaped sole without a fence. (Item No.77; A-5) Pump planes had soles shaped similar to astragal mouldings (i.e., a fillet either side of a central semi-circle of either 1½" or 1½" diameter[items Nos. 86&87,A-5]). Two matching sections of 2" x 4" stock worked with a pump plane and attached together formed a hollow pipe for a chain pump.

The final rounding of square stuff first shaped with a draw knife was accomplished with a plane having a concave sole in the shape of a circular arc. In England these were sometimes referred to as *forkstaff planes*. (N-97; D-329) In America these were usually defined according to intended use; i.e. mast, spar or rounding planes. Frequently such planes were convered from common jack or smoothing planes. (Fig. 89)

Fig. 89. Spar, Mast or Rounding Planes.

Fig. 90. Compass Planes.

    A *compass plane* has a convex longitudinally shaped sole in the form of a circular arc. The purpose of this tool is to shape a longitudinally rounded section. (N-96; D-315). While such planes were available from manufacturers [items 75&76, A-5], many were converted from 8½" smoothing planes A compass plane with a sole to which an iron plate has been attached to minimize the wearing surface is among the three illustrated in Fig. 90.

Fig. 91. Patented Chamfer Plane. [imprint of Mander & Dillon: 7" long x 3"]

A chamfer is defined as a bevel, usually 45 degrees, cut along an edge. An adjustable depth chamfer plane, 7" long x 3" wide, is illustrated in Fig. 91. This particular plane bears the imprint of Mander & Dillon/ Philadelphia, Pa. U.S. Patent #314,338 was granted to James Mander and Maurice R. Dillon on March 24, 1885 for the feature of the adjustable block, sliding within the "V" shaped sole to regulate the depth of the chamfer during planing along the top and one edge surfaces. (See: D-309-310)

An unusual wooden plane, 14½" long with a "v" shaped sole, 3" wide, is illustrated in Fig. 92. This plane was used by a pattern maker for making a mould for a core, and therefore called a *core plane*. [See: W.B.Hilton,*Chronicle of EAIA*,v.XXVI,No.2,June1973,p.26; also D-345] There is no imprint for identification of the maker of this plane.

Fig. 92. Core (Pattern Maker's) Plane. 14½" long x 3" width sides.

[22" long x 3" wide]

Fig. 93. Slitting Plane (Gauge).

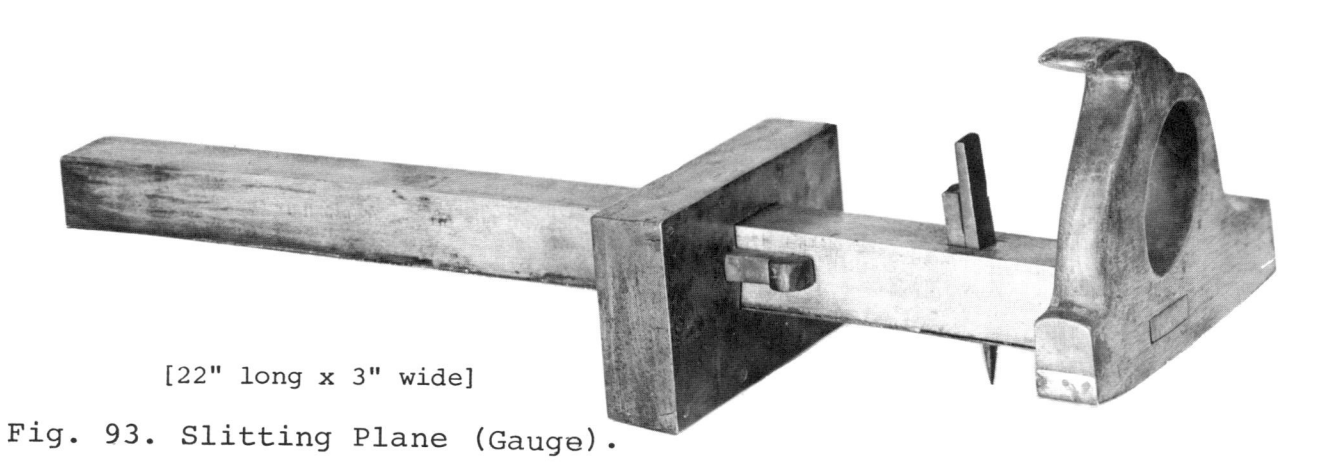

A *slitting plane* for cutting thin boards to appropriate widths up to 20" is illustrated in Fig. 93. This particular plane has a sliding gauge 6" x 3½" with a wedge lock. The sole is brass bound for minimizing wear. [item No. 67, A-19)

Wooden router planes do not appear to been commercially made for resale in United States. Since these were relatively simply tools to make, it is possible that they were made individually by cabinet makers or perhaps imported from England, where they were called *old woman's tooth* (H-487) or *granny's tooth* (D-353). Three English *router planes* are illustrated in Fig. 94. The iron may have been from a plow (lower right), or a forge "L" shaped cutter. (lower left). The iron projected below the surface, adjusted and locked by a wedge, and the plane was held with both hands and pulled forward to remove stock from a channel. Two *wooden router planes* illustrated at the front of Fig. 95 may have been made in United States. A cast iron"*Woodworker's Handy Router Plane*", made by Stanley Rule & Level Co., who were assigned a patent dated March 4,1884 for this tool, is shown in the center of Fig. 95. The advertisement for this plane first appeared as a supplement page [40-1/2]to the 1884 *SR&L Co. Catalogue*. (See Plate XXX)

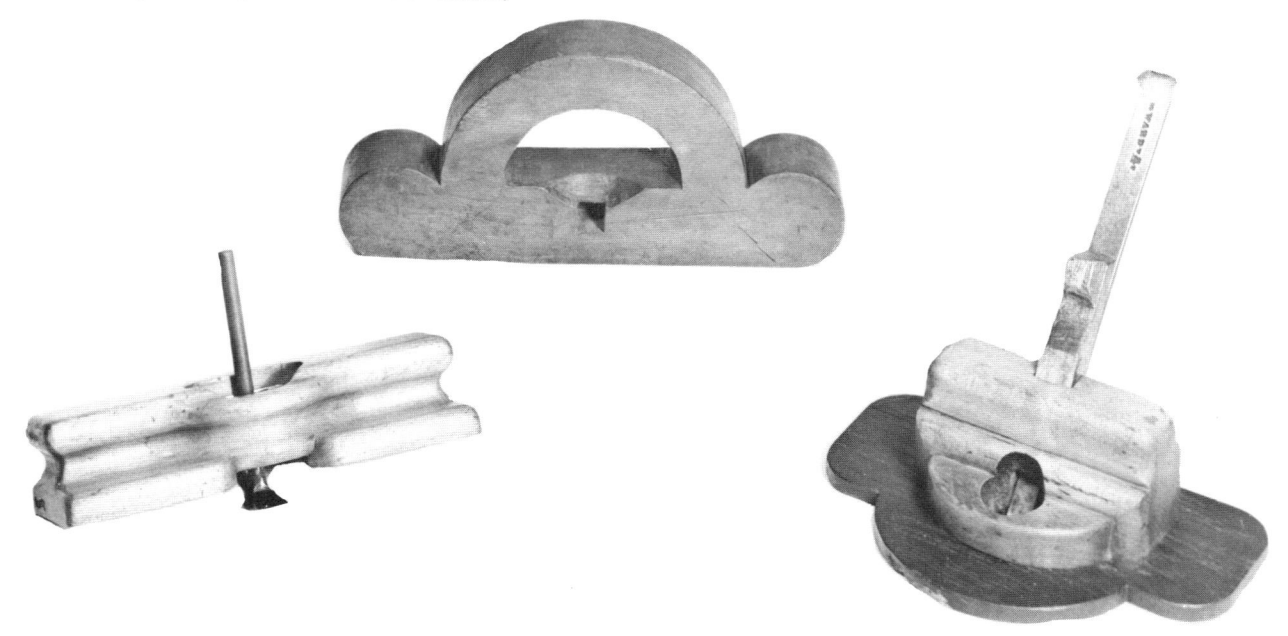

Fig. 94. English Router Planes. (Old Woman's Tooth")

Plate XXX - Advertisement from 1884 SR&L Co. Catalogue, page 40-1/2

WOODWORKER'S HANDY ROUTER PLANE.

This tool should be added to the kit of **every skilled** Carpenter, Cabinet Maker, Stair Builder, Pattern Maker or Wheelwright.
When in the form shown in the illustration it is perfectly adapted to smooth the bottom of grooves, panels, or all depressions below the general surface of any woodwork.
The Bits can also be clamped to the backside of the upright post, and outside of the stock. In this position they will plane into corners, or will smooth surfaces not easily reached with any other tool, as the form of the shank enables the Bit to work either parallel with the stock lengthwise, or at a right-angle with it.

PRICE.

No. 71. Iron Stock, with Steel Bits (¼ and ½ inch) $1.50

Fig. 95. Two Wooden (front) and a Cast Iron (center) Router Planes.

Cooper's Planes. XIII.

It is assumed that persons interested in this section have a general familiarity with the process of making barrels and kegs. This subject was reviewed in a three part article published in the *Chronicle of EAIA,* [K.D.Roberts, "Some Cooper's Tools", Part I, v.XXI, No.4, Dec.1968; Part II, v.XXII, No.1, Mar.1969; Part III, v.XXII, No.3, Sept.1969]. The following texts are recommended: J.Geraint Jenkins, *Traditional Country Crafsmen* [London,1965]; Kenneth Kilby, *The Cooper and His Trade,* [London, 1971]; R.A.Salaman, *Dictionary of Tools,* [London,1975] The latter source has excellent sketches of these tools. There were two major differing trades of coopering: wet (liquid containers) and dry (grain or solids). The tools differed slightly.

Cooper's Jointers were made in two basic sizes: *short* for head staves, 3 to 4½ feet in length; *long* for barrel staves: 4½ to 6 feet in length. The cross-section of planes containing only one iron was generally 4" square, but those containing parallel double slots for two irons were larger, 4" x 6". Fig. 96 illustrates two stave jointers of different arrangement against a saw horse and a double iron head jointer in the foreground. Cooper's jointers were made of beech, maple and applewood. Sizes and prices of such jointers are listed in Plate XXXI. While this data is actually 20th Century, there was not a great deal of differences in the prices noted in the *Arrowmammett Works Catalogue* of 1858. (Appendix: A-5; items 69 - 74.

Plate XXXI - Coopers' Jointers listed in 1909 L & I J White Trade Catalogue.

No. 133

Coopers' Jointers

Single Irons

3 to 3½ feet long, maple, 2½ inch iron, Per doz.,	$19.20
4 to 4½ feet long, maple, 2⅝ inch iron, Per doz.,	24.00
5 to 5½ feet long, maple, 2¾ inch iron, Per doz.,	33.00
6 feet long, maple, 2¾ inch iron, Per doz.,	37.20

Double Irons

3 to 3½ feet long, maple, 2½ inch iron, Per doz.,	$24.00
4 to 4½ feet long, maple, 2⅝ inch iron, Per doz.,	30.00
5 to 5½ feet long, maple, 2¾ inch iron, Per doz.,	37.80
6 feet long, maple, 2¾ inch iron, Per doz.,	52.80

Single Irons

3 to 3½ feet long, applewood, 2½ inch iron, Per doz.,	$33.00
4 to 4½ feet long, applewood, 2⅝ inch iron, Per doz.,	38.40

Double Irons

3 to 3½ feet long, applewood, 2½ inch iron, Per doz.,	$37.80
4 to 4½ feet long, applewood, 2⅝ inch iron, Per doz.,	42.00

A pair of Coopers' Jointers consist of one single iron heading and one double iron stave jointer. When ordering, state what kinds are wanted, single iron heading, double iron heading, or double iron stave, and maple or applewood.

Photograph Courtesy of Farmer,s Museum
New York State Historical Association
Cooperstown, New York

Fig. 96. Coopers' Jointer Planes.

Fig. 97. Coopers' Levelers. Top: Combination Sun & Howel Plane. Bottom: Sun.

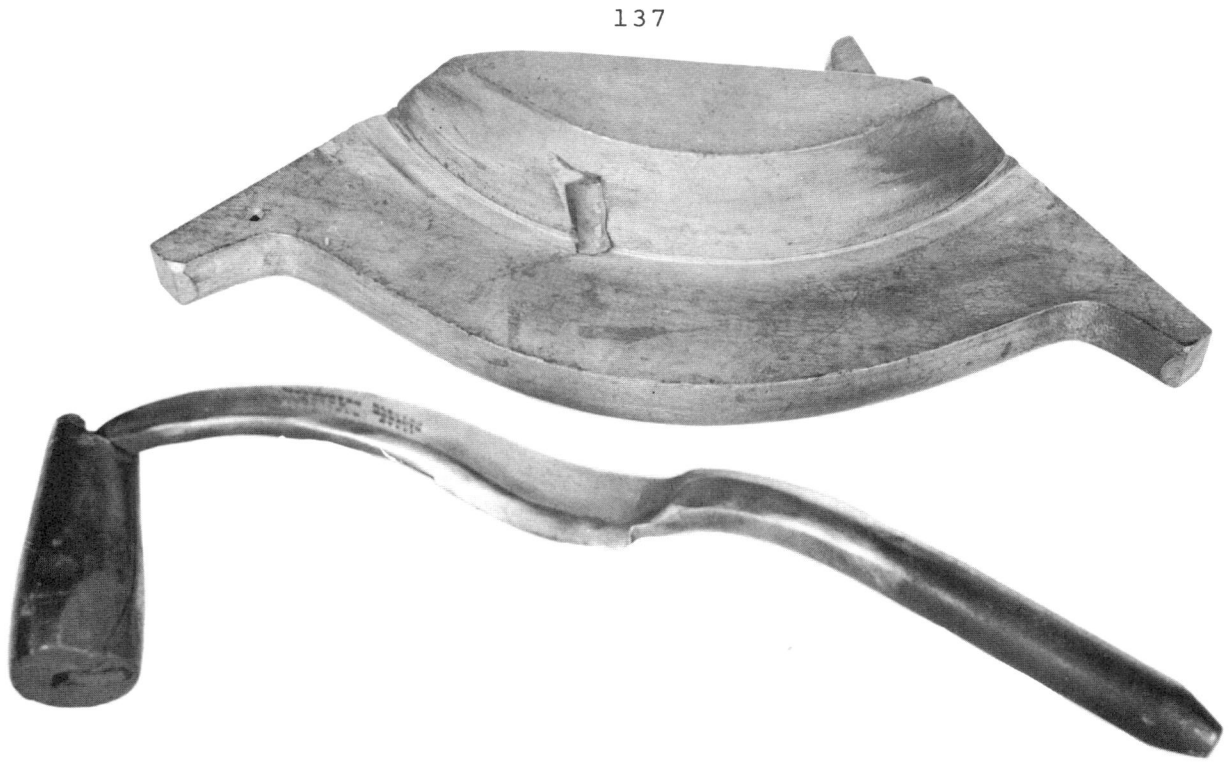

Plane from the Collection of James Cooley
Fig. 98. Chamfer Plane (top) and Chamfer Iron (bottom)

Fig. 99. Coopers' Howel Planes.

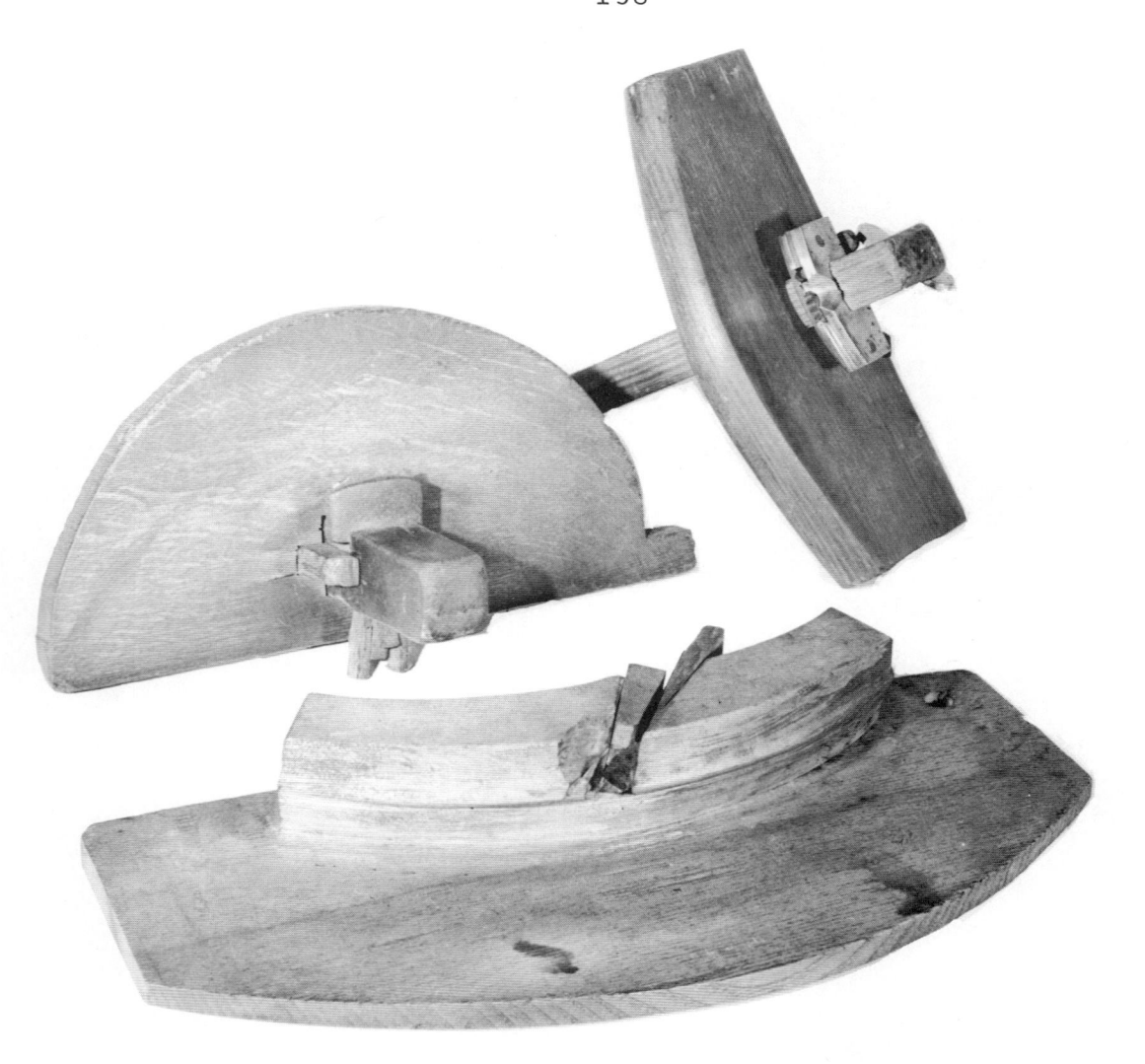

Fig. 100. Coopers' Crozes

Fig. 101. Various Forms of Croze Irons for Coopers' Planes.

After the staves had been assembled into a barrel, the top was trimmed with a cooper's adze and final leveling accomplished with a *sun plane*, also called *leveler*, and in England known as a *Topping plane*. Such planes were usually 12" to 14" in length. A sun plane is illustrated in Fig. 97 which also shows a rare combination *sun-howel plane*.

After leveling the top, a bevel, called the chime, was cut around the inside circumference of the barrel. This was accomplished by: cutting with a cooper's adze, a chamfer knife (Fig. 98), or a *chamfer* plane, in England called a *chime plane*. (Fig. 98).

Below the chime around the inside of the barrel an arc shaped cut about 2" wide was cut with a *howel plane*, (Fig. 99), in England called a *chiv*. The purpose of shaping the howel was to obtain a uniform surface for the groove for holding the cover or barrel head. This recess was cut with a *croze plane*, Fig. 100. Variations in croze cutters were used for different types of barrels: i.e. dry or wet cooperage. (Fig. 101).

XIV. Carriage Makers' Planes.

Fig. 102

Carriage Makers' Planes

Fig. 103 Carriage Makers' Compass (bottom left) and "T-Rabbet" Planes.

Carriage makers' tools included a large variety of special routers and draw knives. The planes employed in this trade were generally smaller varieties of those used by cabinetmakers. (See: R.A.Salaman, *Dictionary of Tools,* [London, 1975], Coachbuilder's Planes, pp. 312-314] Smoothing and rabbet planes were usually less than 7" in length. (Fig. 102) In some instances these planes were probably cut down from ordinary joiners' planes. Frequently the sole was lined with a brass plate to reduce wear.

A special form of rabbet plane was made for this trade, known as "*T-Rabbet*" due to the shape of the sole being about 1-3/4" wide and the body only 1", thus forming a T-shape. The function of this was to permit grasping with one hand and working down into deep recesses. These were made in both curved and straight shapes. (Fig. 103). A small brass-lined sole compass plane, 5" x 2", used in this trade is also illustrated in Fig. 103.

A group of carriage planes is illustrated from the exhibit at Heritage Plantation of Sandwich in the section concerning Museums.

Appendices

I - Arrowmammett Tool Co.
Trade Catalogue of Bench Planes and Moulding Tools

CATALOGUE AND INVOICE PRICE LIST

OF

BENCH PLANES

AND

MOULDING TOOLS,

ALSO, A LIST OF

BOY'S AND GENTLEMEN'S TOOL CHESTS,

MANUFACTURED AND FOR SALE AT THE

ARROWMAMETT WORKS,

MIDDLETOWN, CONN.

MIDDLETOWN:
CHARLES H. PELTON, PRINTER.
1858.

INVOICE PRICE LIST

OF

CARPENTERS' AND JOINERS'

BENCH PLANES AND MOULDING TOOLS,

MANUFACTURED AND SOLD AT THE

Arrowmamett Works,

Middletown, Conn.

BENCH PLANES.

1	SMOOTH, Cast Steel, single Iron, Common	$ 45
2	JACK, " " " "	55
3	FORE, 22 inch " " "	85
4	JOINTER, 26 in. do " "	95
5	do 28 do " "	1 05
6	do 30 do " "	1 20
7	SMOOTH, Cast Steel, Double Iron, Common	70
8	JACK, " " "	80
9	FORE, 22 inch " "	1 15
10	JOINTER, 26 in. " "	1 30
11	do 28 " "	1 40
12	do 30 " "	1 55
13	SMOOTH, Best Cast Steel, Single Iron	55
14	JACK, " " "	65
15	FORE, 22 inch " "	95
16	JOINTER, 26 in " "	1 05
17	do 28 " "	1 15
18	do 30 " "	1 30
19	SMOOTH, Best Cast Steel, Double Iron	80
20	JACK, " " "	85
21	FORE, 22 in " "	1 25
22	JOINTER, 26 in. " "	1 40
23	do 28 " "	1 50
24	do 30 " "	1 60

No.	Description	Price
25	SMOOTH, Best C S, Double Iron, & Boxwood Start,	$ 90
26	Jack, " " " -	1 00
27	Fore, " " " -	1 35
28	Jointer, 26 in. " " " -	1 45
29	do 28 " " " " -	1 55
30	do 30 " " " " -	1 70
31	Smooth, Best C S Double Iron, with Iron Start -	95
32	Jack, " " " -	1 05
33	Fore, " " " -	1 40
34	Jointer, 26 in. " " "	1 50
35	do 28 " " " " -	1 60
36	do 30 " " " " -	1 75
37	Smooth, 9 inch Best C S Double Iron, 2¼ inch Iron	1 25
38	Jack, 18 " " " 2½ "	1 25
39	Fore, 20 " " " 2½ "	1 30
40	Jointer, 24 " " " 2⅝ "	1 40
41	do 32 " " " 2¾ "	2 00
42	SMOOTH, Best C S double Iron, all Boxwood,	1 75
43	Jack, " " Bolt with Handle & Start	1 50
44	Fore, " " " "	1 50
45	Jointer, 26 in. " " " "	1 60
46	do 28 " " " " "	1 70
47	do 30 " " " " "	1 85
48	Smooth, Solid Handle, Best Cast Steel Double Iron,	1 75
49	Jack, Recess, " " "	1 20
50	Fore, " " " "	1 50
51	Jointer, 26 inch, " " "	1 60
52	Smooth, Single Iron for Boys - - -	50
53	Jack, " " - - - - -	60
54	Fore, " " - - -	75
55	Smooth, Best Cast Steel, Double Iron for Boys -	70
56	Jack, " " " -	80
57	Fore, " " " -	1 20
58	Smooth, all Boxwood C S Single Iron for Boys, -	1 25
59	do " " Double " -	1 50
60	Smooth, Best db'l C S Iron for Ship carpenters, 9 in.	1 00
61	Jack, " recess, for " 16 "	1 20
62	Fore, " " " 22 "	1 50
63	Jointer, " " " 24 "	1 60

No.	Description	Price
64	Smooth, upright Iron, double C. S. for Cabinet Makers	$1 00
65	Jack, " " "	1 10
66	Fore, 20 in. " " "	1 40
67	Jointer, 24 in " " "	1 60
68	do 26 " " " "	1 75
69	Coopers' Jointer, 5 feet long, Single Iron, -	2 10
70	do 5½ " " - -	2 35
71	do 6 " " - -	2 60
72	do 5 " Double Iron -	2 75
73	do 5½ " " - -	3 00
74	do 6 " " - -	3 25

MISCELLANEOUS PLANES.

No.	Description	Price
75	Compass Plane, Best C. S. Single Iron - -	65
76	do " Double " - -	1 05
77	GUTTER PLANE - - - -	1 00
78	Hand Rail Plane, Single Iron - - -	1 05
79	do do Double " - - -	2 00
80	do do right and left, per pair, short, -	4 00
81	do do do do handled -	4 50
82	Miter Planes, Single - - - -	60
83	do do Smooth Shape - - -	65
84	Block Miter Planes, 2½ inch Iron - -	1 00
85	Step Planes with Handle, Single Iron - -	1 50
86	Pump Planes, 1¼ inch - - - -	1 50
87	do 1½ " - - - - -	1 75
88	Tooth Planes - - - - -	95
89	Levelling Planes - - - - -	1 75
90	Crows Stocks - - - - -	1 75
91	Howell Plane and Stock - - - -	3 75
92	Raising Jack Plane or Pannel Plane, stop & cut, 2¼ in.	2 25
93	do do do 2½ "	2 50
94	do do do 3 "	3 00
95	do do do 3½ "	3 50
96	do do do 4 "	4 00
97	Cornice Planes, per pair, O. Gee, 4 inches - -	2 75
98	do do do 4½ " - -	3 25
99	do do do 5 " - -	3 75
100	do do do 5½ " - -	4 50

INVOICE LIST.

101	Cabinet O. Gee Planes, 2½ inches	$2 10
102	do 2¾ "	2 60
103	do 3 "	2 85
104	do 3½ "	3 25
105	do 4 "	3 75
106	do 4½ "	4 50
107	do 5 "	5 00

GROOVING PLOWS.

108	PLOWS, wedge arm, Box stop, side screw, 8 irons,	2 90
109	do do Brass stop, 8 "	3 90
110	do do Best plate, 8 "	4 25
111	do Ferruled arms do do 8 "	5 00
112	do do do side screw do	5 25
113	do do do boxed fence	5 50
114	do do do side screw, all boxwood	7 50
115	do do do solid handle	10 00
116	Plows, screw arm, Box stop, side screw, 8 Irons	3 00
117	do do Brass stop, do	4 00
118	do do do best plate do	4 25
119	Plow, Box Screw Arm, do do	4 90
120	do do do with side screw	5 25
121	Plow, Box screw arm, boxed fence, best plate, brass stop, and side screw, 8 irons	5 50
122	Plow, screw arm, all boxwood, brass stop, best plate, side screw, 8 irons	6 75
123	Plow, screw arm, all boxwood, best plate, brass stop, side screw, ivory tips upon arms, 8 irons	8 00
124	Premium Plow, screw arm, all boxwood, best plate, brass stop, side screw, arms ivory tipped plated fence, screws in brass escutcheons, 8 irons	12 00
125	Plow, screw arms, solid handle, brass stop, 8 irons	5 50
126	Plow, box screw arms, " best plate	6 00
127	Plow, box screw arms, solid handle: brass stop, best plate boxed fence	6 25
128	EMPIRE PLOW, box screw arms, solid handle brass stop, best plate, plated fence, side screw, 8 irons	7 50
129	Empire Plow, all boxwood	9 50
130	do do with ivory tipped arms	10 00
131	Plow, solid handle, all boxwood, plated fence, ivory tips, with best plate and brass side screw, screws in escutcheons, best stop, premium pattern	15 00

INVOICE LIST.

MATCH PLANES.

132	BOARD MATCH, per pair, ⅜, ½, ⅝, ¾, ⅞, 1 inch,	$1 05
133	do " faced,	1 30
134	do solid handles "	1 80
135	do " " faced,	2 10
136	do double, "	1 05
137	do " "	1 30
138	PLANK MATCH, per pair, from 1¼ to 1½ inch	1 85
139	do " faced,	2 10
140	MOVING MATCH, per pair	2 90
141	do do wedge arm	3 50
142	do do do ferruled	6 00
143	do do screw arm	3 50
144	do do box screw arm	4 50

FILLETTSTERS.

145	Fillettsters, brass side stop and moving fence,	1 25
146	do do do and cutter	1 35
147	do do do single box	1 55
148	do do do shoulder box	1 85
149	Fillettsters, screw stop, shoulder box and cutter	2 50
150	do all boxwood do	5 00
151	do with screw arms side stop and cut	2 40
152	do do do single boxed	2 50
153	do do do shoulder boxed.	3 00
154	do do do screw stop	3 75
155	do do do wedge arms, side stop and cut	2 50
156	do do do ferruled do screw stop and cut	4 50
157	Sash Fillettster or Back Fillettster, wd'g arms, wood stop	2 10
158	do ferruled arms, brass stop	4 00
159	do screw arms, wood stop	2 10
160	do box do brass stop	4 25
161	do do do box corner	4 50
162	do do do box faced	4 75

SASH PLANES.

163	SASH PLANES, 1 iron, Ovalo pattern,	60
164	do do Bevel do	60
165	do do Gothic do	60
166	do do 2 irons, Ovalo do	1 00

INVOICE LIST.

167	Sash Planes, 2 irons, Bevel pattern,	-	$1 00
168	do do Gothic do	-	1 00
169	do do Ogee do	-	1 25
170	do do Nosing do show case		1 25
171	do do Ovalo do iron fence		1 50
172	do double, box screw arms, Ovalo pattern		1 45
173	do do do Gothic do	-	1 45
174	do do do Bevel do	-	1 45
175	do do do Ogee do	-	1 60
176	do do do Ovalo, self-regulating		2 60
177	do do do Bevel do		2 60
178	do do do Gothic do		2 65
179	do do do Ogee do		2 75
180	do round, brass pad, iron screw, Ovalo		1 45
181	do do do do Bevel		1 45
182	do do do do Gothic		1 45
183	do do do do Ogee		1 60
184	do do diamond pad, iron screw, self-regulating, Ovalo		1 75
185	do do do diamond pad, iron screw, self-regulating, Bevel		1 75
186	do do do diamond pad, iron screw, self-regulating, Gothic		1 75
187	do do do diamond pad, iron screw, self-regulating, Ogee		2 00
	Extra for Double Box in Sash	-	20
	do for Full do do	-	30
188	Sash Plane, solid handle, single iron	-	1 30
189	do double, solid handle, 2 irons		1 60
190	do do do double screw arm		2 75
191	do do do self-regulating		4 00
192	do do do diamond pad		3 75
193	do do do full Box		2 60
194	do do do screw arm, full box		3 00
195	do do do self-regul'g full box		4 25
196	do do do diamond pad do		4 00
197	Sash Coping Planes, single to suit planes		40
198	do do double to do	-	75
199	Bevel Door Planes, single	-	1 00
200	do do double, with screw arms		1 50

INVOICE LIST.

RABBETT PLANES, (or REBATE.)

201	RABBETT PLANES, square iron, ½ inch	$ 45
202	do do ⅝ "	45
203	do do ¾ "	45
204	do do ⅞ "	50
205	do do 1 "	50
206	do do 1¼ "	55
207	do do 1½ "	65
208	do do 1¾ "	75
209	do do 2 "	85
210	do skew iron ½ "	50
211	do do ⅝ "	50
212	do do ¾ "	50
213	do do ⅞ "	50
214	do do 1 "	50
215	do do 1¼ "	55
216	do do 1½ "	60
217	do do 1¾ "	70
218	do do 2 "	80
219	do do 2¼ "	90
220	do do 2½ "	1 00
221	Rabbett Planes, box corners, 1 inch skew iron,	70
222	do do 1¼ "	75
223	do do 1½ "	80
224	do do 1¾ "	90
225	do do 2 "	1 00
226	do do 2¼ "	1 10
227	do do 2½ "	1 20
228	do box faced, ½ "	80
229	do do ⅝ "	80
230	do do ¾ "	80
231	do do ⅞ "	80
232	do do 1 "	80
233	do do 1¼ "	90
234	do do 1½ "	1 00
235	do do 1¾ "	1 10
236	do do 2 "	1 20
237	Rabbet Planes, skew iron, with handles, 2 inch	1 35
238	do do do 2¼ "	1 45
239	do do do 2½ "	1 55
240	do do box corner, 2 "	1 60

INVOICE LIST.

241	Rabbett Planes, skew iron, box corner 2¼ inch,	$1 70
242	do do do 2½ "	1 80
243	do do with screw arms, 2 "	2 00
244	do do do 2¼ "	2 25
245	do do do 2½ "	2 50
246	do do do and handles, 2¼ in.	3 00
247	do do do do 2½ "	3 50
248	Extra for Cutters, each	15
	Ship Carpenter's Rabbett Planes, 22 inches long, 2 in.	1 50
249	Side Rabbett Planes, per pair	90

DADO PLANES, or (Cut & Thrusts.)

251	DADO PLANES, box wood stop, side screw, ¼ inch	90
252	do do do 5-16 "	90
253	do do do ⅜ "	90
254	do do do ½ "	90
255	do do do ⅝ "	90
256	do do do ¾ "	90
257	do do do ⅞ "	90
258	do do do 1 "	90
259	do do do 1⅛ "	1 00
260	do do do 1¼ "	1 10
261	Dado Planes, brass side stop, ¼ inch	95
262	do do do 5-16 "	95
263	do do do ⅜ "	95
264	do do do ½ "	95
265	do do do ⅝ "	95
266	do do do ¾ "	95
267	do do do ⅞ "	95
268	do do do 1 "	1 05
269	do do do 1⅛ "	1 15
270	do do do 1¼ "	1 40
271	Dado Planes, brass screw stop, ¼ inch,	1 40
272	do do do 5-16 "	1 40
273	do do do ⅜ "	1 40
274	do do do ½ "	1 40
275	do do do ⅝ "	1 40
276	do do do ¾ "	1 40
277	do do do ⅞ "	1 40
278	do do do 1 "	1 40
279	do do do 1⅛ "	1 50
280	do do do 1¼ "	1 60

INVOICE LIST.

Moulding Planes.

281	ASTRAGALS, ⅜ inch wide,	$ 40
282	do ½ do	40
283	do ⅝ do	45
284	do ¾ do	45
285	do ⅞ do	50
286	do 1 do	50
287	do 1¼ do	55
288	do 1½ do	60

BEADS.

289	BEADS, single box, ⅛ inch,	45
290	do do 3-16 "	45
291	do do ¼ "	45
292	do do 5-16 "	45
293	do do ⅜ "	50
294	do do ½ "	50
295	do do ⅝ "	55
296	do do ¾ "	55
297	do do ⅞ "	60
298	do do 1 "	65
299	do do 1¼ "	75
300	do do 1½ "	85
301	Beads, double box, ¼ inch,	55
302	do do 5-16 "	55
303	do do ⅜ "	55
304	do do ½ "	55
305	do do ⅝ "	60
306	do do ¾ "	60
307	do do ⅞ "	70
308	do do 1 "	70
309	do do 1¼ "	85
310	Beads, full box, ⅛ inch,	60
311	do do 3-16 "	60
312	do do ¼ "	60
313	do do 5-16 "	60
314	do do dove tailed, ⅜ inch,	75
315	do do ½ "	75
316	do do ⅝ "	80
317	do do ¾ "	85

318	Beads, full box, dovetailed 7/8 inch	$	90
319	do do do 1 "		95
320	do do do 1 1/4 "	1	10
321	Center Beads, 1/8 inch,		60
322	do 3-16 "		60
323	do 1/4 "		60
324	do 5-16 "		60
325	do 3/8 "		60
326	do 1/2 "		60
327	do 5/8 "		65
328	do 3/4 "		65
329	Cock Bead, 1/8 "		50
330	do boxed, 1/8 "		60
331	Reeding Planes, 1/8 "		80
332	do 3-16 "		80
333	do 1/4 "		80
334	do 3/8 "		85
335	do 1/2 "		90
336	do 5/8 "	1	00
337	Torus Beads, 1/2 "		60
338	do 5/8 "		55
339	do 3/4 "		70
340	do 7/8 "		75
341	do 1 "		80

GRECIAN MOULDING PLANES.

342	GRECIAN OVALO, to work, 3/8 inch × 3/4 inch		60
343	do do 1/2 " × 1 "		5
344	do do 5/8 " × 1 1/4 "		70
345	do do 3/4 " × 1 1/2 "		75
346	do do 7/8 " × 1 3/4 "		80
347	do do 1 " × 2 "		90
348	Grecian Ovalo, with handle, 7/8 inch × 2 inch	1	50
349	do do 7/8 " × 2 1/4 "	1	55
350	do do 1 " × 2 1/2 "	1	75
351	do do 1 " × 2 3/4 "	2	00
352	do do 1 1/4 " × 3 "	2	15
353	Grecian Ovalo & Square, 3/8 inch × 3/4 inch		60
354	do do 1/2 " × 1 "		65
355	do do 5/8 " × 1 1/4 "		70

356	Grecian Ovalo & Square, 3/4 " × 1 1/2 "	$	75
357	do do 7/8 " + 1 3/4 "		80
358	do do 1 " × 2 "		90
359	Grecian Ovalo & Square, with handle, 7/8 in. × 2 in.	1	50
360	do do do 7/8 " × 2 1/4 "	1	55
361	do do do 1 " × 2 1/2 "	1	75
362	do do do 1 " × 2 3/4 "	2	00
363	do do do 1 1/4 " × 3 "	2	15
364	Grecian Ovalo & Fillet, 3/8 inch × 3/4 inch		70
365	do do 1/2 " × 1 "		75
366	do do 5/8 " × 1 1/4 "		80
367	do do 3/4 " + 1 1/2 "		85
368	do do 7/8 " × 1 3/4 "		90
369	do do 1 " × 2 "	1	05
370	Grecian Ovalo & Fillet, with handle, 7/8 inch × 2 inch	1	50
371	do do do 7/8 " × 2 1/4 "	1	60
372	do do do 1 " × 2 1/2 "	1	80
373	do do do 1 " × 2 3/4 "	2	00
374	do do do 1 1/4 " × 3 "	2	35
375	Grecian Ovalo & Bead, 3/8 inch × 3/4 inch		75
376	do do 1/2 " × 1 "		80
377	do do 5/8 " × 1 1/4 "		85
378	do do 3/4 " × 1 1/2 "		90
379	do do 7/8 " × 1 3/4 "	1	00
380	do do 1 " × 2 "	1	15
381	Grecian Ovalo & Bead, with handle, 7/8 inch × 2 inch	1	60
382	do do do 7/8 " × 2 1/4 "	1	75
383	do do do 1 " × 2 1/4 "	2	00
384	do do do 1 " × 2 3/4 "	2	25
385	do do do 1 1/4 " × 3 "	2	50
386	Grecian Ovalo & Astragal. 3/8 inch × 3/4 inch		75
387	do do 1/2 " × 1 "		80
388	do do 5/8 " × 1 1/4 "		85
389	do do 3/4 " × 1 1/2 "		90
390	do do 7/8 " × 1 3/4 "	1	00
391	do do 1 " × 2 "	1	15
392	GRECIAN OGEE, to work, 3/8 inch × 3/4 inch		70
393	do do 1/2 " × 1 "		75
394	do do 5/8 " × 1 1/4 "		80
395	do do 3/4 " × 1 1/2 "		85

2

396	Grecian Ogee, to work,	⅞ inch × 1¾ inch	-	$	90
397	do do	1 " × 2 "	-	1	05
398	Grecian Ogee, with handle,	⅞ inch × 2 inch	-	1	50
399	do do	⅞ " × 2¼ "	-	1	55
400	do do	1 " × 2½ "	-	1	80
401	do do	1 " × 2¾ "	-	2	00
402	do do	1¼ " × 3 "	-	2	15
403	Grecian Ogee & Bevel,	⅜ inch × ¾ inch	-		75
404	do do	½ " × 1 "	-		80
405	do do	⅝ " × 1¼ "	-		85
406	do do	¾ " × 1½ "	-		90
407	do do	⅞ " × 1¾ "	-	1	00
408	do do	1 " × 2 "	-	1	15
409	Grecian Ogee & Bevel, with handle,	⅞ inch × 2 inch		1	60
410	do do do	⅞ " × 2¼ "		1	75
411	do do do	1 " × 2½ "		2	00
412	do do do	1 " × 2¾ "		2	25
413	do do do	1¼ " × 3 "		2	50
414	Grecian Ogee & Bead,	⅜ inch × ¾ inch	-		75
415	do do	½ " × 1 "	-		80
416	do do	⅝ " × 1¼ "	-		85
417	do do	¾ " × 1½ "	-		90
418	do do	⅞ " × 1¾ "	-	1	00
419	do do	1 " × 2 "	-	1	15
420	Grecian Ogee & Bead, with handle,	⅞ inch × 2 inch		1	60
421	do do do	⅞ " × 2¼ "		1	75
422	do do do	1 " × 2½ "		2	00
423	do do do	1 " × 2¾ "		2	25
424	do do do	1¼ " × 3 "		2	50
425	Grecian Ogee & Astragal,	⅜ inch × ¾ inch	-		75
426	do do	½ " × 1 "	-		80
427	do do	⅝ " × 1¼ "	-		85
428	do do	¾ " × 1½ "	-		90
429	do do	⅞ " × 1¾ "	-	1	00
430	do do	1 " × 2 "	-	1	15
431	Torus Cove & Bead,	⅜ inch × ¼ inch	-		75
432	do do	½ " × 1 "	-		80
433	do do	⅝ " × 1¼ "	-		85
434	do do	¾ " × 1½ "	-		90
435	do do	⅞ " × 1¾ "	-	1	00
436	do do	1 " × 2 "	-	1	15

437	Nosing, Bilection, (Torus Bead & Cove,)	½ inch × 1 in.	$		75
438	do do do	⅝ " × 1⅛ "			80
439	do do do	¾ " × 1¼ "			85
440	do do do	⅞ " × 1½ "			90
441	do do do	1 " × 1¾ "		1	05
442	do do do	1¼ " × 2 "		1	15
443	Quirk Ovals, to work	⅜ inch deep,	-		55
444	do	½ do	-		60
445	do	⅝ do	-		65
446	do	¾ do	-		70
447	do	⅞ do	-		75
448	do	1 do	-		80
449	Quirk O G's, to work	⅜ inch thick,	-		55
450	do do	½ do	-		60
451	do do	⅝ do	-		65
452	do do	¾ do	-		70
453	do do	⅞ do	-		75
454	do do	1 do	-		80
455	Quirk Ogee & Beads,	⅜ inch thick,	-		70
456	do do	½ do	-		75
457	do do	⅝ do	-		80
458	do do	¾ do	-		85
459	do do	⅞ do	-		90
460	do do	1 do	-	1	05
461	Reverse Ogee & Bead,	⅜ inch × ¾ inch	-		75
462	do do	½ " × 1 "	-		80
463	do do	⅝ " × 1¼ "	-		85
464	do do	¾ " × 1½ "	-		90
465	do do	⅞ " × 1¾ "	-	1	05
466	do do	1 " × 2 "	-	1	15
467	Reverse Ogee & Astragal,	⅜ inch × ¾ inch,	-		75
468	do do	½ " × 1 "	-		80
469	do do	⅝ " × 1¼ "	-		85
470	do do	¾ " × 1½ "	-		90
471	do do	⅞ " × 1¾ "	-	1	05
472	do do	1 " × 2 "	-	1	15
473	Reverse Ogees,	⅜ × ⅜ inch,	-		50
474	do	½ × ½ "	-		50
475	do	⅝ × ⅝ "	-		55
476	do	¾ × ¾ "	-		55
477	do	⅞ + ⅞ "	-		60

478	Reverse O G's, 1 × 1 inch,	$ 65
479	do 1¼ × 1¼ "	75
480	Reverse Ogee, flat, ⅝ × 1 inch,	65
481	do do ½ × 1¼ "	70
482	do do ⅝ × 1¾ "	75
483	do do ¾ × 2 "	80
484	do do ⅞ × 2⅜ " handled,	2 00
485	do do 1 × 3 " do	2 10
486	Reverse O'G & square, flat, ⅜ × 1 inch,	80
487	do do do ½ + 1¼ "	85
488	do do do ⅝ × 1¾ "	90
489	do do do ¾ + 2 "	95
490	do do do ⅞ × 2½ " handled,	2 00
491	do do do 1 + 3 " do	2 15
492	Reverse Ogee & 2 squares, ⅜ inch,	70
493	do do ½ "	70
494	do do ⅝ "	70
495	do do ¾ "	70
496	do do ⅞ "	80
497	do do 1 "	80
498	Plain Ogees, ⅜ inch,	45
499	do ½ "	45
500	do ⅝ "	50
501	do ¾ "	50
502	do ⅞ "	55
503	do 1 "	60
504	do 1¼ "	65
505	Coves, ⅜ inch,	40
506	do ½ "	40
507	do ⅝ "	45
508	do ¾ "	45
509	do ⅞ "	50
510	do 1 "	55
511	do 1¼ "	60
512	Cove & Beads, ⅜ inch,	65
513	do do ½ "	65
514	do do ⅝ "	70
515	do do ¾ "	75
516	do do ⅞ "	75
517	do do 1 "	80

518	Coves & Beads, 1¼ inch,	$ 90
519	Scotias do ⅜ "	60
520	do do ½ "	60
521	do do ⅝ "	65
522	do do ¾ "	65
523	do do ⅞ "	70
524	do do 1 "	75
525	do do 1¼ "	80
526	Gothic Bead with 2 irons, ⅜ inch × ½ inch,	1 00
527	do do ½ " + ⅝ "	1 10
528	do do ⅝ " × ¾ "	1 25
529	Step Nosings, double iron, 1¼ inch,	1 10
530	do do 1½ "	1 20
531	Halving Plane,	40
532	do with moving fences & stop,	1 25
533	Spar Planes, single iron,	1 00
534	do double iron,	2 00
535	TABLE PLANES, per pair,	95
536	do do with fence,	1 15
537	do do box faced,	1 50
	Guage extra,	15

HOLLOWS AND ROUNDS.

538	HOLLOWS & ROUNDS, 1 pr. No. 2, works ¼ in. circle,	70
539	do do do " 4, ½ do	70
540	do do do " 6, ¾ do	70
541	do do do " 8, 1 do	70
542	do do do " 10, 1¼ do	70
543	do do do " 12, 1½ do	75
544	do do do " 14, 1¾ do	80
545	do do do " 16, 2 do	85
546	do do do " 18, 2¼ do	90
547	do do do " 20, 2½ do	95
548	do do do " 22, 3 do	1 00
549	do do do " 24, 3½ do	1 10
550	Hollows & Rounds, even nos. per sett, 9 pr., No. 2*a*18	6 80
551	do do 10 do 2*a*20	7 75
552	do do 12 do 2*a*24	9 85
553	Hollows & Rounds, 1 pr. No. 1, to work ⅛ in. circle,	70
554	do do 3, do ⅜ do	70
555	do do 5, do ⅝ do	70

556	Hollows & Rounds, 1 pr. No. 7, to work $\frac{7}{8}$ in. circle,	$ 70
557	do do 9, do $1\frac{1}{8}$ do	70
558	do do 11, do $1\frac{3}{8}$ do	75
559	do do 13, do $1\frac{5}{8}$ do	80
560	do do 15, do $1\frac{7}{8}$ do	85
561	do do 17, do $2\frac{1}{8}$ do	90
562	do do 19, do $2\frac{3}{8}$ do	95
563	do do 21, do $2\frac{3}{4}$ do	1 00
564	do do 23, do $3\frac{1}{4}$ do	1 10
565	Hollows & Rounds, per sett, 18 pr. from 1 to 18, cmp'l	13 60
566	do do 20 do 1 to 20 do	15 50
567	do do 24 do 1 to 24 do	19 70
568	BEADS, left hand, $\frac{1}{4}$ inch, - - - - -	50
569	do do $\frac{3}{8}$ " - - - - -	50
570	do do $\frac{1}{2}$ " - - - - -	50
571	do do $\frac{5}{8}$ " - - - - -	60
572	do do $\frac{3}{4}$ " - - - - -	60
573	Beads, double right & left, $\frac{1}{4}$ inch, - -	1 00
574	do do $\frac{3}{8}$ " - - -	1 00
575	do do $\frac{1}{2}$ " - - -	1 00
576	do do $\frac{5}{8}$ " - - -	1 10
577	do do $\frac{3}{4}$ " - - -	1 10
578	SNIPE BILLS, Single box, per pair - -	1 25
579	do shoulder box, do - -	1 75

MISCELLANEOUS.

650	PLANE HANDLES Jack, per dozen, - -	90
651	do Fore, do - -	1 50
652	Saw do do - -	4 00
653	Chisel Handles, per dozen, - - -	50
654	do ferruled, per dozen, - -	75
655	do box wood, ferruled, - -	1 75
656	Brad Awl Handles, - - - -	40
657	do do box wood, ferruled, - -	1 00
658	Scribe Awl Handles, do do - -	1 00
659	Chalk Spools, common, per dozen, - -	60
660	do box wood, do - - -	1 80
661	Malletts, Beech, round, per dozen, - -	3 00
662	do do small size, - - - -	2 00
663	do do do box, - - -	3 00

664	Mallets, Carpenters, round, all box, - -	$ 4 50
665	Bung Starts, per dozen, - - - - -	2 50

GUAGES.

666	MARKING GUAGES, with box screws, per dozen,	1 50
667	do do plated, do do	2 50
668	do do all box wood do	3 00
669	do do do with inches, do	3 50
670	Cutting Guages, with box screws, per dozen, -	2 25
671	do plated, with box screws, per dozen,	3 00
672	do box wood screws, per dozen, -	3 75
673	Pannel Guages, per dozen, - - -	4 50
674	Slitting do do - - - -	7 50
675	do do with Roller Handle, - -	10 50

TURNING WEBB SAWS.

676	Turning Webb Saws, frames complete, per doz., 12 in.	10 00
677	do do do do 14 "	11 00
678	do do do do 16 "	12 00
679	do do do do 18 "	13 50
680	do do do do 20 "	15 00

BENCH SCREWS.

681	Walnut Bench Screws, per doz 2 inch, - -	5 00
682	do do do $2\frac{1}{2}$ " - -	9 50

HAND SCREWS.

683	Hand Screws, $\frac{3}{4}$ inch, - - - - -	2 25
684	do 1 " - - - - -	3 00
685	do $1\frac{1}{4}$ " - - - - -	4 50

BOY'S TOOL CHESTS.

598 BOY'S TOOL CHESTS, 16 inch, with: — Net.
1 Jack Plane, 1 Guage,
1 Mallet, 1 Rule,
6 Handles for Chisels, &c - - - 2 50

599 BOY'S TOOL CHESTS, 18 inch, with:
1 Jack Plane, 1 Mallet,
1 Smooth Plane, 1 Rule,
1 Guage, 8 Handles for Chisels, &c. 3 50

INVOICE LIST.

600 BOY'S TOOL CHESTS, 19 inches, with:
1 Single Jack, 1 Mallet,
1 Double Smooth, 1 Rule,
1 Guage, 1 Chalk Spool,
12 Handles for Chisels, &c. - - $4 00

611 GENT'S TOOL CHESTS, 21 inch. of black walnut, with:
1 Single Jack plane, 1 Rule,
1 do Smooth do 1 Mallet,
1 Guage, 1 Chalk Spool,
15 Handles for Chisels, &c. - - 5 50

602 GENT'S TOOL CHESTS, of black walnut, with drawer, 22 inch., containing:
1 Single Jack plane, 1 Guage,
1 Single Smooth plane, 1 Mallet,
1 Double Smooth plane, 1 Rule,
1 Rabbett plane, 18 Chisel & file Handles,
1 pr. Hollow & Rounds, 1 Chalk Spool, &c. - 7 00

603 GENT'S TOOL CHESTS of black walnut with drawer, and raised feet, 24 inch. with:
1 Single Jack plane, 1 Single Smooth plane,
1 Double do 1 Double do
1 Double Fore, 1 Rule,
1 Rabbett plane, 24 Handles for Chisels,
1 pair Hollows & Rounds, Brad Awls, &c.
1 Guage, 1 Chalk Spool,
1 Mallet, 1 Oil Stone, boxed, - 10 00

604 BOY'S TOOL CHESTS, 16 inch, fitted up complete, containing:
1 Jack plane, 1 pr. Pincers,
1 Mallet, 1 Chisel,
1 Try Square, 2 Brad Awls,
1 Small Saw, 1 Hammer,
1 pr. Compasses, 1 Screw Driver,
2 Gimlets, 1 Guage,
Tacks, Nails, Screws, &c. - - 4 50

INVOICE LIST. 21

605 BOY'S TOOL CHEST, 18 in. fitted up complete, containing:
1 Jack plane, 1 pr. Compasses,
1 Smooth plane, 1 pr. Pincers,
1 Mallet, 1 Knife,
1 Guage, 2 Chisels,
1 File, 1 Screw Driver,
1 Saw, 2 Brad Awls,
1 Guage, 1 Rule,
1 Try Square, Nails, Brads. Tacks, &c. $5 75

606 BOY'S TOOL CHESTS, 19 in. fitted up complete, containing:
1 Jack plane, 1 pr. Pincers,
1 Double Smooth plane, 1 Try Square,
1 Hammer, 2 Chisels,
1 Mallet, 1 Gouge,
1 Tack Hammer, 1 Screw Driver,
1 Guage, 2 Brad Awls,
2 Files, 1 Oil Stone,
1 pr. Compasses, 1 Rule,
2 Gimlets, Nails, Screws, Brads, &c. - 6 50

607 GENT'S TOOL CHESTS, 21 inch, fitted up complete, containing:
1 Single Jack plane, 1 Mallet,
1 Double Smooth plane, 1 Saw,
1 pr Compasses, 2 Chisels,
2 Gimlets, 1 Gouge,
1 Knife, 1 Screw driver,
1 pr Pincers, 2 Brad Awls,
1 Nail Hammer, 1 Saw file,
1 Tack Hammer, 1 Half round file,
1 Guage, 1 Oil Stone,
1 Rule, Nails, Screws, Tacks,
Brads, &c. - 9 00

608 GENT'S TOOL CHESTS, 22 inch, with drawer, fitted up complete, containing:
1 Jack Plane, single iron, 1 pr. Compasses,
1 Smooth Plane, do 1 pr. Pincers,
do double iron, 1 pr. Plyers,
1 Rabbett Plane, 1 Screw Driver,
1 Round file, 3 Chisels,
1 Half round file, 2 Gouges,

INVOICE LIST.

1 Saw file,
1 Back Saw,
1 Hand Saw,
1 Mallet,
1 Square,
1 Rule,
3 Brad Awls,
3 Gimlets,
1 Hammer,
1 Tack Hammer,
1 Chalk Spool,
1 Oil Stone,
Tacks, Screws, Brads, Brass nails, &c. - 13 50

609 GENT'S TOOL CHESTS, 24 inch, with drawer, double till fitted up complete, containing:

1 Jack plane, single iron,
1 Fore plane, double do
1 Smooth plane, do
1 Hand Saw,
1 Back Saw,
1 Compass Saw,
1 Hatchet,
1 Mallet,
1 Hammer,
1 Half Round file,
1 Half Round Rasp,
1 Round File,
1 Saw File,
3 Gimlets,
2 Augur Gimlets,
1 Small Brace,
1 Smooth plane, single iron,
1 Rabbett plane,
1 pr. Hollows & Rounds,
6 Bitts for Brace,
1 Hand Vice,
1 pr. Pincers,
1 pr. Plyers,
1 Try Square,
3 Brad Awls,
1 Oil Stone,
1 Screw Driver,
1 do Small,
1 Guage,
4 Chisels,
3 Gouges,
Nails, Screws, Brads, Brass Nails,
Glue, Sandpaper, &c. 20 00

610 GENT'S TOOL CHESTS, 26 inch, Extra of black walnut, double till, fitted up complete, containing:

1 Single Smooth Plane,
1 Single Jack Plane,
1 Double Smooth Plane,
1 Double Jack Plane,
1 Double Fore Plane,
1 Double Jointer,
1 Rabbett Plane,
1 pr Hollows & Rounds,
1 pr Match Planes,
1 Hand Saw,
1 Back Saw,
1 Compass Saw,
1 Hammer,
1 Small Hammer,
1 Draw Knife,
1 Set Brace and Bitts,
1 Flat File,
1 Round File,
1 Saw File,
1 Hand Vice,
1 pr. Nippers,
1 pr. Plyers,
1 Try Square,
1 Guage,
1 Oil Stone,
4 Brad Awls,
2 Screw Drivers,
5 Chisels,
3 Gouges,
1 Augur Gimlet,
4 Gimlets,
1 Hatchet,
1 Rule,
1 Knife,
1 Half Round File,
Nails, Screws, Sandpaper,
Tacks, Brads, &c. - 30 00

CERTIFICATES.

LANCASTER, JULY 1st, 1856.

Baldwin Tool, Co.
Middletown, Conn.

GENTLEMEN:—

I should have written sooner in reference to your PLANE IRONS, but wishing to give them a thorough trial, I have deferred writing until I find it necessary for me to order a further supply.

Thus far I have found them to be full as good as the best English Irons: they all cut beautifully, and some of them I tried over knots and they stood it well. My hands, as well as myself, are working upon hard wood with your Irons, and they do so well that we could not wish for any thing better.

I have formerly tried Irons of American Manufacture, and they have so far failed in the temper, that I was obliged to abandon the use of them altogether, and I acknowledge that it was with much reluctance that I was induced to try yours; but I have now sent Planes with your Irons to some of my most particular customers. I have ground up and tried all of them, without finding any deficiency, and have written that I was sure they were good and would warrant every one of them.

I am very happy to find as good a Plane Iron may be made in this country as in England, and as long as your Irons maintain their present standard, I shall not desire to use any other.

Yours, truly,

E. W. CARPENTER, Plane Manufacturer.

SOUTH GLASTENBURY, CONN.
FEBRUARY, 2d, 1858.

The Baldwin Tool Co.
MIDDLETOWN, CONN.

Your favor with enquiries respecting my opinion of your PLANE IRONS, was duly received. In reply, I would say, that I have been making Planes for the last fifteen years, for Carpenters themselves, and the retail trade. I have used both English and American Irons, with different degrees of success, often a complete failure, until eighteen months since, you induced me to try some of yours. I consider them in point of finish and temper, fully equal to any English Irons I have ever used, and they are ground with more precision than the generality of English Irons. I now use none but your Irons, which give entire satisfaction to my customers.

Yours, respectfully,

OBED ANDRUS, Plane Maker.

CERTIFICATES.

28

NORTHAMPTON, MASS. SEPT. 28, 1856

This is to certify, that we have used the Irons manufactured by the BALDWIN TOOL Co., for the past two years, and our experience fully warrants us in saying, that we consider the quality of those Irons superior to any other of American Manufacture, and fully equal to those of the most approved English stamps, and we can confidently recommend them as for their cutting quality and superiority of finish as equal to the best Plane Irons in market.

ARNOLD & CROUCH, Plane Manufacturers.

CINCINNATI, OHIO, JAN. 25th, 1858.

This is to certify, that I have used the BALDWIN TOOL. Co's Plane Irons in my factory for some length of time, and take pleasure in recommending them. I believe them to be the best Irons in market.

G. ROSEBOOM, Plane Manufacturer.

PHILADELPHIA, JANUARY 28th, 1858.

Baldwin Tool Co.
Middletown, Conn.

GENTLEMEN:—

I have been using your Plane Irons for the past two years, and as my business is exclusively a retail one, I have peculiar opportunities for testing them. I have no hesitation in recommending them as fully equal to any English Irons I have ever used.

PHILADELPHIA, JAN. 28, 1858.

This is to certify, that I have used, during the past two years, the Plane Irons manufactured by the "BALDWIN TOOL Co.," of Middletown, Conn., and consider them fully equally to any imported Irons, and superior to any of American Manufacture, with which I am acquainted.

B. SHENEMAN & BRO., Plane Makers.

CERTIFICATES.

24

This is to certify, that I have been for the past six months, using the Plane Irons of the BALDWIN TOOL Co., and have found them in all respects, equal in quality to the best imported Irons, having had ample opportunity of seeing them thoroughly tested by use.

ROBERT HARRON, Plane Manufacturer. New-York City.

New-York, June 21, 1856.

MIDDLETOWN. AUGUST 16, 1856.

We, the undersigned, Master Builders in the City of Middletown, hereby certify, that we have used during the past year, the PLANE IRONS manufactured by the BALDWIN TOOL Co., and have found them in every respect fully equal to the best English Irons we have heretofore used.

N SMITH & SON,
I. W. BALDWIN.

Baldwin Tool Co.
Middletown, Conn.

GENTLEMEN—

We had abandoned the use of American Plane Irons altogether, and with much hesitation consented to try those of your manufacture. We find them, after repeated trials, to be far superior to any other Plane Irons made in this country, and confidently recommend them to our customers, as being equal to the best English Irons.

Very respectfully, yours,
A. B. SEIDENSTRICKER & CO. Plane Manufacturers.

BALTIMORE, MD. February, 5th, 1858.

DEAR SIRS—

I have used your PLANE IRONS for the past two years, and it affords me pleasure to say, that I consider them, in every respect, fully equal to any imported Irons. My business is strictly retail, and as I get an extra price, I aim to furnish Planes that will give entire satisfaction. Your Irons are ground with great precision, are uniform in temper, and neatly finished.

Yours, respectfully,
W. H. POND, Plane Manufacturer.

NEW HAVEN, CONN. FEB. 2d, 1858.

INVOICE LIST OF PLANE IRONS,

MANUFACTURED FROM

W. & S. BUTCHERS, Superior Refined Cast-Steel,

BY THE

BALDWIN TOOL Co.

MIDDLETOWN, CONN.

SINGLE CAST STEEL PLANE IRONS, OR CUT IRONS, PER Doz

1½	1⅝	1¾	1⅞	2	2⅛	2¼	2⅜	2½	2⅝	2¾	3 In.
$ 1.75,	1.75,	1.75,	1.87½,	2.00,	2.12½,	2.37½,	2.62½,	2.87½	3.12½,	3.50,	4.50,

DOUBLE CAST STEEL PLANE IRONS, PER Doz

1½	1⅝	1¾	1⅞	2	2⅛	2¼	2⅜	2½	2⅝	2¾	3	3¼	3½	3¾	4 In.
$ 3.75,	3.75,	4.00,	4.00,	4.12½,	4.25,	4.50,	4.75,	5.25,	5.50,	6.50,	7.50,	9.00,	10,50,	12.00	15.00.

SINGLE CAST STEEL PLANE IRONS, assorted from 2 to 2½, PER Doz. $2.37½.
DOUBLE do do do do do 4.50.

CAST STEEL RAISING PLANE IRONS, PER Doz.

2	2¼	2½	2¾	3	3¼	3½	3¾	4 In.
$ 2.25,	2.75,	3.25,	3.75,	4.50,	5.00,	5.50,	6.00.	6 50.

CAST STEEL SOFT IRONS, PER Doz.

2	2⅛	2¼	2⅜	2½	2⅝	2¾	3	3¼	3½	3¾	4 In.
$ 2.00,	2.12½,	2.37½,	2.62½	2.87½,	3.12½,	3.50,	4.50,	4,75,	5.50,	6.00,	6 50.

CAST STEEL SINGLE COOPER'S JOINTER IRONS, 11 In. long, PER Doz.

2¾	3	3¼	3½	3¾	4	4¼	4½ In.
$ 6.00,	6.25,	6.75,	7.25,	8.00,	8.75,	9.50,	10-50.

CAST STEEL HOWELLING IRONS, PER Doz.

1¾	2	2⅛	2¼	2½ In.
$ 3.00,	3.25,	3.75,	4.00	4.50.

CAST STEEL TOOTH PLANE IRONS, PER Doz.

2	2⅛ In.
$ 2.75,	3.00,

CAST STEEL SOFT MOULDING IRONS, PER Doz.

¼	⅜	½	⅝	¾	⅞	1	1⅛	1¼	1⅜	1½	1⅝	1¾	1⅞	2	2⅛	2¼	2⅜	2½ In.
$ 0.69,	0.69,	0.69,	0.71,	0.71,	0.75,	0.81,	0.88,	0.96,	1 00,	1.06.	1.13,	1.25,	1.38,	1.50,	1.63,	1.75,	1.88,	2.06.

CAST STEEL RABBETT IRONS, SKEW OR SQUARE, PER Doz.

½	⅝	¾	⅞	1	1⅛	1¼	1⅜	1½	1⅝	1¾	1⅞	2	2⅛	2¼	2⅜	2½	2⅝ In.
$ 0.94,	1.00,	1.04,	1.10,	1 21,	1.25,	1.33,	1.38,	1.44,	1.50,	1.63,	1.69,	1.81,	1.94,	2.06,	2 19,	2.38,	2,75.

CAST STEEL GROOVING IRONS, FOR BOARD MATCH, PER Doz.

⅜	½	⅝	¾	⅞	1 In. Board Match.
$ 1.04,	1.10,	1.21,	1.25,	1.33,	1 .38.

CAST STEEL GROOVING IRONS, FOR PLANK MATCH, PER Doz.

1¾	1⅞	2 In.
$ 1 75,	1.87½	2.00.

CAST STEEL GROOVING PLOW BITTS, PER SETT, $ 1.00.

CAST STEEL MATCH PLOW BITTS, ⅛ 3/16 ¼ 5/16 ⅜ In. per Doz. $ 1.00.

CAST STEEL FILLETTSTER IRONS, 1½ In. per Doz. $ 1.50.

CAST STEEL DADO IRONS

3-16	¼	5-16	⅜	½	⅝	¾	⅞	1 In.
$ 1.00,	1,00,	1.00,	1.00,	1.00,	1.05,	1,10,	1.15,	1.25,

CAST STEEL DADO CUTTERS, per Doz.

3-16	¼	5-16	⅜	½	⅝	¾	⅞	1 In
$ 1.25,	1.25,	1.25,	1.25,	1.25,	1.30,	1.35,	1.40,	1.50.

FILLETTSTERS CUTTERS, per Doz $ 1.00.

RABBETT PLANE CUTTERS, per Doz. $ 0.60.

II - Section from Nicholson's Mechanic's Companion, 1858

THE

MECHANIC'S COMPANION,

OR, THE

ELEMENTS AND PRACTICE

OF

CARPENTRY, JOINERY, BRICKLAYING, MASONRY, SLATING, PLASTERING, PAINTING, SMITHING, AND TURNING,

COMPREHENDING THE LATEST IMPROVEMENTS

AND CONTAINING A FULL DESCRIPTION OF

THE TOOLS

BELONGING TO EACH BRANCH OF BUSINESS;

WITH COPIOUS DIRECTIONS FOR THEIR USE.

AND AN EXPLANATION OF THE

TERMS USED IN EACH ART;

ALSO AN

Introduction to Practical Geometry.

BY PETER NICHOLSON.

Illustrated with forty Copperplate Engravings.

PHILADELPHIA:

PUBLISHED BY JOHN LOCKEN,

NO. 311 MARKET STREET.

......

1849.

JOINERY.

§ 1. JOINERY is a branch of Civil Architecture, and consists of the art of framing or joining together wood for internal and external finishings of houses; as the coverings and linings of rough walls, or the coverings of rough timbers, and of the construction of doors, windows, and stairs.

Hence joinery requires much more accurate and nice workmanship than carpentry, which consists only of rough timbers, used in supporting the various parts of an edifice. Joinery is used by way of decoration only, and being always near to the eye, requires that the surfaces should be smooth, and the several junctions of the wood be fitted together with the greatest exactness.

Smoothing of the wood is called planing, and the tools used for the purpose, planes.

The wood used is called stuff, and is previously formed into rectangular prisms by the saw; these prisms are denominated battens, boards, or planks, according to their dimensions in breadth or in thickness. For the convenience of planing, and other operations, a rectangular platform is raised upon four legs, called a bench.

§ 2. *The Bench.* PL. 12. FIG. 12.

Consists of a platform A B C D called the top, supported upon four legs, E, F, G, H. Near to the further or fore end A B is an upright rectangular prismatic pin a, made to slide stiffly in a mor-

JOINERY. 125

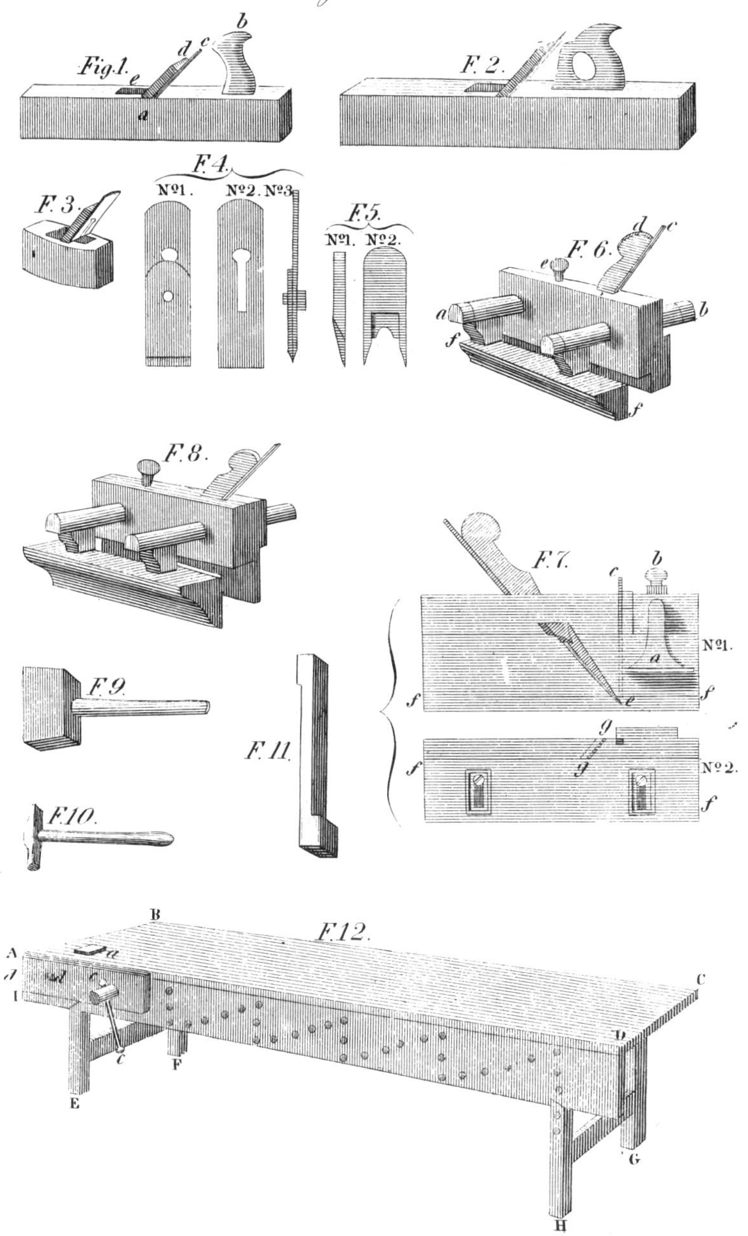

§ 67. EXPLANATION OF THE PLATES IN JOINERY.

PLATE XII.

TOOLS.

Fig. 1 the jack plane, *a* the stock, *b* the tote or handle, being a single tote, *c* the iron, *d* the wedge for tightening the iron, *e* the orifice or place of discharge for the shavings.

Fig. 2 the trying plane, the parts are the same as the jack plane, except that the hollow of the tote is surrounded with wood, and is therefore called a double tote.

Fig. 3 is the smoothing plane without a tote, the hand-hold being at the hind end of the plane.

Fig. 4 the iron, No. 1. the cover for breaking the shaving, screwed upon the top of the iron, in order to prevent the tearing of the wood, in a front view: No. 2. front of the iron without the cover, showing the slit or the screw which fastens the cover to the iron: No. 3. profile of iron and cover screwed together.

Fig. 5 the wedge for tightening the iron: No. 1. longitudinal section of the wedge: No. 2. front, showing the hollow below for the head of the screw.

Fig. 6 sash fillister, for throwing on the bench, *a* head of one stem, *b* tail of the other, *c* iron, *d* wedge, *e* thumb screw for moving the stop up and down, *ff* fence for regulating the distance of the rebate from the arris.

Fig. 7 the moving fillister for throwing the shaving on the bench: No. 1. right hand side of the plane, *a* brass stop, *b* thumb screw of do. *c d e* tooth, the upper part *c d* on the outside of the neck, and the part *d e* passing through the solid of the body with a small part open above, *e*, for the tang of the iron tooth, *ff* the guide of the fence: No. 2. bottom of the plane turned up, *a* the guide of the stop, *ff* the fence, showing the screws for regulating the guide, *g g* the mouth and cutting edge of the iron.

Fig. 8 the plow, the same with regard to the stem fence and stop, and also in other respects as the sash fillister, except the sole, which is a narrow iron.

tise through the top. This pin is called the bench hook, which ought to be so tight as to be moved up or down only by a blow of a hammer or mallet. The use of the bench hook is to keep the stuff steady, while the joiner, in the act of planing, presses it forward against the bench hook. D I a vertical board fixed to the legs, on the side of the bench next to the workman, and made flush with the legs: this is called the side board. At the farther end of the side board, and opposite to it, and to the bench hook, is a rectangular prismatic piece of wood $b\,b$, of which its two broad surfaces are parallel to the vertical face of the side board: this is made moveable in a horizontal straight surface, by a screw passing through an interior screw fixed to the inside of the side board, and is called the screw check. The screw and screw check are together called the bench screw; and for the sake of perspicuity, we shall denominate the two adjacent vertical surfaces of the screw check, and of the side board, the checks of the bench screw. The use of the bench screw is to fasten boards between the checks, in order to plane their edges; but as it only holds up one end of a board, the leg H of the bench and the side board are pierced with holes, so as to admit of a pin for holding up the other end, at various heights, as occasion may require. The screw check has also a horizontal piece mortised and fixed fast to it, and made to slide through the side board, for preventing it turning round, and is therefore called the guide.

Benches are of various heights, to accommodate the height of the workman, but the medium is about two feet eight inches. They are ten or twelve feet in length, and about two feet six inches in width. Sometimes the top boards upon the farther side are made only about ten feet long, and that next the workman twelve feet, projecting two feet at the hinder part. In order to keep the bench and work from tottering, the legs, not less than three inches and a half square, should be well braced, particularly the two legs on the working side. The top board next to the workman may be from one and a half to two inches thick: the thicker, the better for the work; the boards to the farther side

may be about an inch, or an inch and a quarter thick. If the workman stands on the working side of the bench, and looks across the bench, then the end on his right hand is called the hind end, and that on his left hand the fore end. The bench hook is sometimes covered with an iron plate, the front edge of which is formed into sharp teeth for sticking fast into the end of the wood to be planed, in order to prevent it from slipping; or, instead of a plate, nails are driven obliquely through the edge, and filed into wedge-formed points. Each pair of end legs are generally coupled together by two rails dovetailed into the legs. Between each pair of coupled legs, the length of the bench is generally divided into three or four equal parts, and transverse bearers fixed at the divisions to the side boards, the upper sides being flush with those of the side boards, for the purpose of supporting the top firmly, and keeping it from bending. The screw is placed behind the two fore legs, the bench hook immediately before the bearers of the fore legs, and the guide at some distance before the bench hook. For the convenience of putting things out of the way, the rails at the ends are covered with boards; and for farther accommodation, there is in some benches a cavity, formed by boarding the under edges of the side boards before the hind legs, and closing the ends vertically, so that this cavity is contained between the top and the boarding under the side boards; the way to it is by an aperture made by sliding a part of the top board towards the hind end: this deposit is called a locker.

§ 3. *Joiners' Tools.*

The bench planes are, the jack plane, the fore plane, the trying plane, the long plane, the jointer, and the smoothing plane; the straight cylindric plane, the compass and forkstaff planes; the straight block, for straightening short edges. Rebating planes are the moving fillister, the sash fillister, the common rebating plane, the side rebating plane. Grooving planes are the plough and dado grooving planes. Moulding planes are sinking snipebills, side snipebills, beads, hollows and rounds, ovolos and ogees. Boring tools are, gimlets, brad-awls, stock, and bits. Instruments for dividing the wood, are principally the ripping saw, the half ripper, the hand saw, the panel saw, the tenon saw, the carcase saw, the sash saw, the compass saw, the keyhole saw, and turning saw. Tools used for forming the angles of two adjoining surfaces, are squares and bevels. Tools used for drawing parallel lines are guages. Edge tools, are the firmer chisel, the mortise chisel, the socket chisel, the gouge, the hatchet, the adze, the drawing knife. Tools for knocking upon wood and iron are, the mallet and hammer. Implements for sharpening tools are the grinding stone, the rub stone, and the oil or whet stone.

§ 4. *Definitions.*

If a plane be set with the under surface upon the wood it is intended to operate upon, and placed before the workman, and if four surfaces are perpendicular to the under surface, each of these surfaces is said to be vertical; the one next the workman is called the hind end, and the opposite one, the fore end, and the two in the direction which the plane works, the sides: the under surface is called the sole, the side of the plane next to the workman is called the right hand side, and the opposite side to that, the left hand side of the plane.

The depth of a plane is the vertical dimension from the top to the under surface; the length of a plane is the horizontal dimension in the direction in which the plane is wrought; the breadth or thickness of a plane is the horizontal dimension at right angles, to the length and depth.

In order to make a distinction between the tool, the under surface is called the sole of the plane.

The reason for being so particular in defining these common place terms which might be supposed to be known to every one, is from a desire of the author to prevent ambiguity; as in the term depth, which implies a distance from you in whatever direction it runs, as the depth of a well is the vertical or plumb distance; but the depth of a house is the distance from the front to the rear wall, and consequently is a horizontal distance

§ 5. *The Jack Plane,* Pl. 12. Fig. 1.

Is used in taking off the rough and prominent parts from the surface of the wood, and reducing it nearly to the intended form, in coarse slices, called shavings; this plane consists of a block of wood called the stock, of about seventeen inches in length, three inches high, and three inches and a half broad. All the sides of the stock are straight surfaces at right angles to each other. Through the solid of the stock, and through two of its opposite surfaces is cut an aperture, in which is inserted a thin metal plate called the iron, one side of the plate consisting of iron, and the other of steel. The side of the opening which joins the iron part, is called the bed, which is a plane surface, making an angle of forty-five degrees with the hind part of the underside of the plane.

The end of the iron next to the bottom is ground to an acute angle off the iron side, so as to bring the steel side to a sharp edge, having a small convexity. The sloping part thus formed, is called the basil of the iron. The iron is fixed by means of a wedge, which is let into two grooves of the same form, on the sides of the opening; two sides of the wedge are parallel to each other, and to the vertical side of the plane, and consequently to two of the sides of the groove; the two sides of the grooves, parallel to the vertical sides of the plane are called cheeks, and the two other sides inclined to the bed of the iron are called the abutments or abutment sides: the wedge and the iron being fixed, the opening must be uninterrupted from the sole to the top, and must be no more on the sole side of the plane, than what is sufficient for the thickest shaving to pass with ease; and as the shaving is dis charged at the upper side of the plane, the opening through must expand or increase from the sole to the top, so as to prevent the shavings from sticking. In conformity to analogy, the part of the opening at the sole, which first receives the shaving, is called the mouth. In order for the shaving to pass with still greater ease, the wedge (Pl. 12. Fig. 5.) is forked to cut away in the middle, leaving the prongs to fill the lower parts of the aforesaid grooves. On the upper part of the plane, behind the iron, rises a protuberance, called the tote, so formed to the shape of the hand, and direction of the motion, as to produce the most power in pushing the plane forward.

The bringing of the iron to a sharp cutting edge is called sharpening. The cutting edge of the iron must be formed with a convexity, and regulated by the stuff to be wrought, whether it is hard or soft, cross grained or curling, so that a man may be able to perform the most work, or to reduce the substance most, in a given time. To prevent the iron from tearing the wood to cross grained stuff, a cover is used with a reversed basil, (Pl. 12. Fig. 4.) and fastened by means of a screw, the thin part of which slides in a longitudinal slit in the iron, and the head is taken out by a large hole near the upper end of it. The lower edge of the cover is so formed, as to be concentric or parallel to the cutting edge of the iron, and fixed at a small distance above it, and to coincide entirely with the steel face. The basil of the cover must be rounded, and not flat, as that of the iron is. The distance between the cutting edge of the iron, and the edge of the cover, depends altogether on the nature of the stuff. If the stuff is free, the edge of the cover may be set at a considerable distance, because the difficulty of pushing the plane forward becomes greater, as the edge of the cover is nearer the edge of the iron, and the contrary when more remote.

The convexity of the edge of the iron depends on the texture of the stuff, whether it is free, cross grained, hard or knotty. If the stuff is free, it is evident that a considerable projection may be allowed, as a thicker shaving may be taken: the extreme edges of the iron must never enter the wood, as this not only retards the progress of working, but chokes and prevents the regular discharge of the shavings at the orifice of the plane.

§ 6. *To Grind and Sharpen the Iron.*

When you grind the iron, place your two thumbs under it, and the fingers of both hands above, laying the basil to the stone, and holding it to the angle you intend it shall make with the steel side of it, keeping it steady while the stone is turning, and pressing the iron to the stone with your fingers; and in order to prevent the stone from wearing the edge of the iron into irregularities, move it alternately from edge to edge of the stone with so much pressure on the different parts, as will reduce it to the required convexity; then lift the iron to see that it is ground to your mind: if it is not, the operation must be repeated, and the steel or basil side placed in its former position on the stone, otherwise the basil will be doubled; but if in the proper direction it will be hollow, which will be more as the diameter of the stone is less. The basil being brought to a proper angle, and the edge to a regular curvature, the roughness occasioned by the gritty particles of the grindstone may be taken away, by rubbing on a smooth flat wet stone or Turkey stone, sprinkling sweet oil on the surface; as the basil is generally ground something longer that what the iron would stand, for the quicker despatch of wetting it, you may incline the face of the iron nearer to the perpendicular, rubbing to and fro with the same inclination throughout: having done it to your mind, it may be fixed. When there is occasion to sharpen it again, it is commonly done upon a flat rub stone keeping the proper angle of position as before, then the edge may be finished on the Turkey stone as before: and at every time the iron gets dull or blunt, the sharpening is produced by the rub stone and Turkey stone, but in repeating this often the edge gets so thick that it requires so much time to bring it up, that recourse must be had again to the grindstone.

§ 7. *To Fix and Unfix the Iron.*

In fixing the iron in the plane, the projection of the cutting edge must be just so much beyond the sole of the plane, as the workman may be able to work it freely in the act of planing. This projection is called iron, and the plane is said to have more or less iron as the projection varies: when there is too much iron, knock with the hammer on the fore end of the stock; and the blows will loosen the wedge, and raise the iron in a certain degree, and the head of the wedge must be knocked down to make all tight again: if the iron is not sufficiently raised, proceed again in the same manner, but if too much, the iron must be knocked down gently by hitting the head with a hammer: and thus, by trials, you will give the plane the degree of iron required. When you have occasion to take out the iron to sharpen it, strike the fore end smartly, which will loosen the wedge, and consequently the iron.

§ 8. *To Use the Jack Plane.*

In using the jack plane, lay the stuff before you parallel to the sides of the bench, the farther end against the bench hook: then proceed to take off the rough parts throughout the whole breadth, by laying the forepart of beginning at the hind end of the stuff, by laying the forepart of the plane upon it, lay hold of the tote with the right hand, and pressing with the left upon the fore end, thrust the plane forward in the direction of the fibres of the wood and length of the plane, until you have extended the stroke the whole stretch of your arms; the shaving will be discharged at the orifice: draw back the plane, and repeat the operation in the next adjacent rough part: proceed in this manner until you have taken off the rough parts throughout the whole breadth, then step forward so much as you have planed, and plane off the rough of another length in the same manner: proceed in this way by steps, until the whole length is gone over and rough planed; you may then return and take all the protuberant parts or sudden risings, by similar operations

§ 9. *The Trying Plane*, Pl. 12. Fig. 2.

Is constructed similar to the jack plane, except the tote of the jack plane is single, and that of the trying plane double, to give greater strength; the length of this plane is about twenty-two inches, the breadth three and a quarter, and the height three and an eighth. Its use is to reduce the ridges made by the jack plane, and to straighten the stuff: for this purpose it is both longer and broader, the edge of the iron is less convex, and set with less projection: but as it takes a broader though finer shaving, it still requires as much force to push it forward.

§ 10. *The Use of the Trying Plane.*

The sharpening of the iron, and the operation of planing is much the same as that of the jack plane; when the side of a piece of stuff has been planed first by the jack plane, and afterwards by the trying plane, that side of the stuff is said to be tried up, and the operation is called trying.

When the stuff is required to be very straight, particularly if the broad and narrow side of another piece is to join it, instead of stopping the plane at every arm's length, as with the jack plane, the shaving is taken the whole length, by stepping forwards, then returning, and repeating the operation throughout the breadth, as often as may be found necessary.

§ 11. *The Long Plane*

Is used when a piece of stuff is required to be tried up very straight; for this purpose it is both longer and broader than the trying plane, and set with still less iron; the manner of using it is the same. Its length is twenty six inches, its breadth three inches and five eighths, and depth three inches and one eighth.

§ 12. *The Jointer*

Is still longer than the long plane, and is used principally for planing straight edges, and the edges of boards, so as to make them join together; this operation is called shooting, and the edge itself is said to be shot. The length of this plane is about two feet six inches, the depth three inches and a half, and the breadth three inches and three fourths. The shaving is taken the whole length in finishing the joint, or narrow surface.

§ 13. *The Smoothing Plane*, Pl. 12. Fig. 3.

Is the last plane used in giving the utmost degree of smoothness to the surface of the wood: it is chiefly used in cleaning off finished work. The construction of this plane is the same with regard to the iron wedge and opening for discharging the shaving, but is much smaller in size, being in length seven inches and a half, in breadth three, and in depth two and three quarters, and differs in form, on account of its having convex sides, and no tote.

There is also this difference in giving the iron a finer set, that you may strike the hind end instead of the fore part.

§ 14. *Bench Planes.*

The jack plane, the trying plane, the long plane, the jointer and the smoothing plane, are denominated bench planes.

§ 15. *The Compass Plane*

is similar to the smoothing plane in size and shape, but the sole is convex, and the convexity is in the direction of the length of the plane. The use of the compass plane is to form a concave cylindrical surface, when the wood to be wrought upon is bent with the fibres in the direction of the curve, which is in a plane surface perpendicular to the axis of the cylinder. Consequently compass planes must be of various sizes, in order to accommodate different diameters.

§ 16. *The Forkstaff Plane*

Is similar to the smoothing plane in every respect of size and shape, except that the sole is part of a concave cylindric surface, having the axis parallel to the length of the plane. The use of the forkstaff plane is to form cylindric surfaces, by planing parallel to the axis of the cylinder. Planes of this description must likewise be of various sizes, to form the surface to various radii: these two last planes are more used by coach-makers than by joiners.

§ 17. *The Straight Block*

Is used for shooting short joints and mitres, instead of the jointer, which in such cases would be rather unhandy; this plane is also made without the tote, and as it is frequently used in straightening the ends of pieces of wood perpendicularly to the direction of the fibres, the iron is inclined more to the sole of the plane, that is, it forms a more acute angle with it: in order that it may cut clean, the inclination of the basil, and the face of the iron, is therefore less on this account: the length of the straight block is twelve inches, its breadth three and one eighth, and depth two and three quarters.

REBATE PLANES IN GENERAL.

§ 18. *The Rebate Plane*

Is used after a piece of stuff has been previously tried on one Nos. 7 & 8.

JOINERY.

side and shot on the other, or tried on both sides, in taking away a part next to one of the arises of a rectangular or oblong section, the whole part therefore taken away is a square prism, and the superfices formed after taken away the prism is two straight surfaces, forming an internal right angle with each other; so that the stuff will now have one internal angle and two external angles. The operation of this reducing the stuff is called rebating. Rebating is either used by way of ornament, as in the sinking of cornices, the sunk facias of architraves, or in forming a recess for the reception of another board, so that the edge of this board may coincide with that side of the rebate, next to the edge of the rebated piece. The length of rebating planes is about nine inches and a half, the vertical dimension or depth is about three and a half, they are of various thickness, from one and three quarters to half an inch. Rebate planes are of several kinds, some have the cutting edge of the iron upon the bottom, and some upon the side of the plane. Of these which have the cutting edge on the bottom, some are used for sinking, and some for smoothing or cleaning the bottom of the rebate; and these which have the cutting edge upon one side are called side rebating planes, and are used after the former in cleaning the vertical side of the rebate. Rebate planes differ from the bench planes, before mentioned, in their having no tote; the cavity is not open to the top, but the wedge is made to fit completely, and the shaving is discharged on one side or other, according to the use of the plane.

§ 19. *Sinking Rebating Planes*

Are of two denominations, the moving fillister and sash fillister: the moving fillister is for sinking the edge of the stuff next to you, and the sash fillister the farther edge; consequently these planes have their cutting edges on the under side.

JOINERY.

§ 20. *Of the moving Fillister*, Pl. 13. Fig.

Upon the bottom of the moving fillister is a slip of wood, so regulated by two screws as one of the vertical sides of the slip may be fixed parallel to the edge of the sole; then the breadth between this side of the slip and the edge of the sole of the plane is equal to the breadth of the rebate. This slip is called a fence, and the vertical side of it next to the stock, the guide; as the rebate is made upon the right edge of the stuff, the fence is always upon the left side of the sole. The iron between the guide and the right hand edge of the sole of the plane must project the whole breadth of the uncovered part of the sole, otherwise the plane will not sink, so long as it is kept in one position; the right hand point of the cutting edge of the iron must stand a small degree without the vertical right hand side of the plane; for if this point of the iron stood within, the situation of the point would also prevent the sinking of the rebate; it is also necessary that the cutting edge of the iron should stand equally prominent in all parts out of the sole, otherwise the plane cannot make shavings of an equal thickness, and consequently instead of keeping the vertical position, will turn round and incline to the side on which the shavings are thickest, and thus the part cut away will not have a rectangular section, for the bottom of the rebate will not then be parallel to the upper face of the stuff; and the side which ought to have been vertical, will be a kind of ragged curved surface, formed by as many gradations or steps as the depth consists of the number of shavings. Observe, that whatever regulates any plane which takes away a portion of the stuff next to the edge, to cause the part taken away on the upper face of the stuff from the edge to be of one breadth, is called a fence: in like manner, whatever prevents a plane working downwards beyond a certain distance, is called a stop. Therefore the fence regulates the horizontal breadth of what is taken away, and the stop the vertical dimension or depth, and this is to be understood, not only of rebate planes, but of moulding planes, where the moulding is regulated in its horizontal

100   JOINERY.

dimension, in the breadth or thickness of the stuff, and the vertical on the adjacent vertical side.

Returning to the moving fillister, the guide is the bottom surface of a piece of metal which is regulated by a screw, so as to move it to the required distance from the sole. Though the bottom of this piece of metal is properly the stop, yet it is altogether called a stop by plane makers and carpenters; but to avoid a confusion of words, we shall call the bottom of the stop the vertical guide. The stop moves in a vertical groove in the side of the fillister, and has a projection with a vertical perforation, which goes farther into the groove, or into the solid of the stock. The stop is placed on the right hand side of the fillister, between the iron and the fore end of the plane, and is moved up and down by a screw, which is inserted in a vertical perforation from the top of the plane to the groove, and passes through the perforation in the projecting part of the stop, which has a female, or concave screw adapted to that cut on the convex screw. The convex screw is always kept stationary by a plate of metal, let in flush with the upper side of the plane; below this plate, and on the same solid with the screw, is a collar, and above, another which projects still farther upwards by way of a lever, for the ease of turning the screw. This part which turns round, is called the thumb screw. It is evident, as the axis of the thumb screw can neither move up or down as it turns round its axis, the inclination of the threads will rise or fall according to the direction of the thumb screw, and cause the stop to move up and down in the groove on the side of the plane, and thus the stop may be fixed at pleasure. In this plane, the opening for discharging the shaving is upon the right side of the fillister, and in this case the shaving is said by workmen to be thrown on the bench, that is, upon the right side of the plane; but when the orifice of discharge is upon the left, and consequently the shaving thrown upon the left, the plane is said to throw the shaving off the bench; and these expressions are applied to all planes which throw the shavings to one side.

In the moving fillister, as well as in several other planes, the

JOINERY.   101

upper part on the sides of the stock is thinner than the lower part; this part is called the hand-hold, and the thick part the body. In the moving fillister, the reduction made for the hand-hold is equally upon both sides of the plane, that is, the rebates are of equal depth. The edges of these rebates, which is the upper surface of the body, are called shoulders; this plane is therefore double shouldered. The same appellation is given to the iron, when a part is taken from one or both sides, so as to make the upper part equally broad, but the sides parallel to the sides of the bottom part. The part of the iron so diminished, is called the tang of the iron, and the broad part at the bottom, which has the cutting edge, is called the web, and the upper narrow surfaces of the web are called the shoulders of the iron, in analogy to those of the plane. The iron of the moving fillister is only single shouldered. Besides the above-mentioned parts, the moving fillister has another, which is a small one-shouldered iron, inserted in a vertical mortise, through the body, between the fore end of the stock and the iron. The web of this little iron is ground with a round basil, from the left side, so as to bring the bottom of the narrow side of the iron to a very convex edge. This little iron is fastened by a wedge, upon the right side of the hand-hold, passing down the mortise in the body. The use of this little iron is principally for cutting the wood transversely when wrought across the fibres, and by this means it not only cuts the vertical side of the rebate quite smooth, but prevents the iron from ragging or tearing the stuff. The whole of this little iron is called a tooth, and the bottom part may be distinguished by the name of the cutter. The cutter must, therefore, stand out a little farther on the right hand side of the plane than the iron, but must never be placed nearer to the fence than the narrow right hand side of the iron. In this plane, the steel side of the iron, and consequently the bedding side of it, is not perpendicular to the vertical sides of the plane, but makes oblique angles therewith, the right hand point of the cutting edge of the iron being nearer to the fore end of the plane than the left hand point of the cutting edge. By this obliquity, the bottom of the rebate is cut smoother, particularly in a transverse direction to the fibres, or where the stuff is cross grained, than could otherwise be done when the steel face of the iron is perpendicular to the vertical sides of the plane. The principal use is, however, to contribute, with the form of the cavity, to throw the shaving into a cylindrical form, and thereby making it issue from one side of the plane.

§ 21. *Of the Sash Fillister in general.* Pl. 12. Fig. 6.

The sash fillister is a rebating plane for reducing the right hand side of the stuff to a rebate, and is mostly used in rebating the bars of sashes for the glass, and is therefore called a sash fillister. The construction of this plane differs in several particulars from the moving fillister. The breadth of iron is something more than the whole breadth of the sole, so that the extremities of the cutting edge are, in a small degree, without the vertical sides of the stock. In the moving fillister, the fence is upon the bottom of the plane, and always between the two vertical sides of the stock; but in this it may be moved to a considerable distance, the limit of which will be afterwards mentioned. The fence is not moved, as in the moving fillister, by screws fixed in the bottom, but by two bars, which pass through the two vertical sides of the stock at right angles to their sides, fitting the two holes exactly through which they pass in the stock. Each of the bars which thus passes through the stock, is called a stem, and is rounded on the upper side, for the convenience of handling. That part of each stem, projecting from the left hand side of the plane, has a projection downwards, of the same thickness as the parts which pass through the stock; the bottom sides of these projections are flat surfaces, parallel to the sole of the plane; the other two sides of the said projections are also straight surfaces, parallel to the vertical sides of the plane, and are called the shoulders, so that each stem has three vertical straight surfaces. The left end of each stem, viz. the end on the left side of the stock, opposite to the shoulder, may be of any fanciful form. The end of each stem which contains the projection, is called the head of the stem. To each of the heads of the stem, and under each of the lower flat surfaces of the projecting parts, is fixed a piece of wood by iron pins, passing vertically through each head, and through this piece; one of the sides of this piece, next to the stock of the plane, is vertical, and goes about half an inch lower than the sole. The small part of each stem, from the head to the other extremity on the right hand of the stock, is called the tail. The prismatic part is by workmen called the fence. The surface of the fence next to the stock of the vertical plane, and parallel to the vertical faces, is called the guide of the fence. The pins which connect the stem and fence, have their heads on the under side of the fence; the heads are of a conical form; the upper ends of the pins are rivetted upon a brass plate on the round surface of the stem. These pins fix the two stems and the fence stiffly together, but not so much as to prevent either stem from turning round upon the fence, or to make oblique angles with the guide. The upper surface of each stem is rounded, and the two ends ferruled, to prevent splitting when the ends are hit or struck with a mallet, in order to move the guide of the fence either nearer or more remote from the stock, as may be wanted. On the most remote opposite, or vertical sides of the stem, and close to these sides, are cut two small wedge-formed mortises, in which are inserted two small tapering pieces of wood called keys; so that when driven in, or towards the mortise, they will stick fast, and press against the stem, and keep it fast at all points of the tail, and thereby regulate the distance of the fence from the left vertical side of the stock. In order to prevent the keys from being drawn out, or loosing, each has a small elliptic nob at the narrow end, which is also of greater breadth than the mortise upon the left vertical side of the stock. There are two kinds of sash fillisters, one for throwing the shaving on the bench, and the other for throwing it off: their construction is the same so far as has been described.

JOINERY.

§ 22. *The Fillister which throws the Shavings on the Bench,* Pl. 12. Fig. 6.

Has its discharging orifice in course upon the right hand vertical side of the stock, and the left extremity of the cutting edge of the iron is nearer to the fore end of the plane, than the right hand extremity of the said edge. On the left side of the stock, and from the sole, is a rebate, the depth of which is equal to the depth of the rebate made on the stuff. The upper side of the fence ranges exactly with the side of the rebate which is parallel to the sole of the plane; and by this means, the guide of the fence may be brought quite close to the vertical side of the rebate, or as far upon the side of the rebate, parallel to the sole of the plane, as may be found necessary. The depth of the rebate to be made in the stuff, is regulated by a stop, which coincides vertically with the vertical side of the rebate; the guide of the stop is parallel to the sole of the plane, and the stop is moved up and down by a thumb screw, in the same manner as that of the moving fillister, but not in a groove on the side of the plane, but in a mortise: the side of the rebate parallel to the sole of the plane, is mortised upwards, that the guide may be screwed up so as to be flush with that side of the rebate. The iron of this plane is single shouldered, and the projection of the web at the bottom, beyond the tang, is on the right hand side of the plane, and consequently the narrow side of the tang and web parts of the iron are in the same straight line.

§ 23. *Of the Sash Fillister for throwing the Shavings off the Bench.*

The sash fillister which throws the shavings off the bench, differs only from the last, in having no rebate on the left hand side of the plane; the stop slides in a vertical groove on the left hand verticle side of the stock, in the same manner as the stop of the moving fillister, and not in a vertical mortise cut in the vertical

JOINERY.

side of the body of the plane: it has also a cutter on the left side, in order to cut the vertical side of the rebate clean. One extremity of the cutting edge of the iron, on the right hand side of the plane, is nearer to the fore end than the other; consequently the steel face of the iron makes angles with the vertical sides of the plane the contrary way to the sash fillister, which throws the shavings on the bench.

§ 24. *Rebating Planes without a Fence.*

Rebating planes which have no fence, are of two kinds; in both, the cutting edge of the iron extends the whole breadth of the sole; and the upper part of the stock is solid on the two vertical sides, but the lower part is open on both sides; the opening increases from the sole regularly upwards, until it comes to a large cavity, which opens abruptly into a curved form on the side next to the fore end of the plane. The web of the iron is equally shouldered on both sides of the tang.

§ 25. *Skew-mouthed Rebating Plane.*

The thickest stocks, or broadest sole planes, of this description, are made with the face of the iron standing at oblique angles with the vertical sides. The right hand extremity of the cutting edge of the iron, stands nearer to the fore end of the plane than the left hand extremity of the said cutting edge, and the large cavity is greater upon the left side of the plane than upon the right. The shaving is therefore thrown off the bench. The use of this plane is not for sinking the rebate, but rather for smoothing the bottom, after the moving fillister, or after the sash fillister, next to the vertical edge of the rebate. In this manner it is used in cleaning the bottom **entirely** of rebates which do not exceed the breadth of its sole: but **where** the rebate exceeds this breadth, it is only used next to the vertical side of the rebate as before, and the

N

remaining part of the bottom of the rebate is cleaned off with the trying and smoothing planes. When the iron is set at oblique angles to the vertical sides of the plane, the cutting edge of the sole is said to stand askew, that is, at oblique angles with the sides of the plane. This is therefore called a skew rebating plane. The thickness of this rebating plane is about one inch and five eighths.

§ 26. Square-mouthed Rebating Planes.

The common rebating planes have the steel side of the iron, or the bed, perpendicular to the vertical sides of the stock, and throw the shaving off the bench; the cavity for the discharge of the shaving is much the same as the skew rebating plane; and since the shaving is thrown off the bench, the widest side of the cavity is on the left hand side of the stock, to clean the internal angles of fillets, and the bottoms of grooves, &c.

§ 27. Side Rebating Planes

Are those which have their cutting edge on one side of the plane, and discharge the shaving at the other; the lower part of the stock is therefore open upon both sides. The use of this plane is to clean or plane the vertical sides of rebates, grooves, &c.: for this purpose, they are made both right and left: a right hand side rebating plane has its cutting edge on the right hand side of the plane, and consequently throws the shaving off the bench, and the contrary of the left hand rebating plane. The side of the plane containing the mouth, is altogether vertical; but the opposite side is only in part so, from the top downwards to something more than half the height, then recessed and beveled with a taper to the sole; the orifice of discharge for the shaving is beveled. The iron stands askew, or at oblique angles with the mouth side, but perpendicular with regard to the sole or top of the plane; the cut-

ting edge stands nearer to the fore end than the opposite edge. The mortise for the wedge of the iron is without a cavity, as in the other rebating planes, and the iron shouldered upon one side. The web is cut sloping to answer the beveling of the stock.

§ 28. The Plough, Pl. 12. Fig. 8.

Is used in taking away a solid in the form of a rectangular prism, by sinking any where in the upper surface, but not close to the edge, and thereby leaving an excavation or hollow, consisting of three straight surfaces, forming two internal right angles with each other, and the two vertical sides, two external right angles with the upper surface of the stuff. The channel cut is called a groove, but the operation is called grooving or plowing. The plow consists of a stock, a fence, and a stop. There are two kinds of plows, one where the fence and stop is immoveable, and the other which is universal, of which, both fence and stop are moveable, and will admit of eight or ten irons of various breadths, from one eighth of an inch to three fourths. This is what I shall chiefly describe. The fence has two stems with keys and a stop, moved by a thumb screw, as in the moving fillister for throwing the shaving on the bench. The sole of this plane is the bottom narrow side of two vertical iron plates, which are something thinner than the narrowest iron. The wedge and iron are inserted in the same manner as in the rebating planes, the fore end of the hind plate forms the lower part of the bed of the iron, and has a projecting angle in the middle, and the bed side of each angle has an external angle adapted to the same. This prevents the iron from being removed by the resistance of knots or such sudden obstacles: the fore iron plate is cut with a cavity similar to the common rebate planes. The stop is placed between seven inches and three eighths, and this plane is in length about seven inches and three eighths, and in depth three inches and five eighths, and the length of each stem eight inches and a half.

§ 29. *Dado Grooving Plane,*

Is a channel plane, generally about three eighths of an inch broad on the sole, with a double cutter and stop, both placed before the edge of the iron which stands askew; it throws the shaving off the bench. The best kind of dado grooving planes have screw stops of brass and iron; the common sort are made of wood, to slide stiffly in a vertical mortise, and are moved by the blow of a hammer or mallet, by striking the head, when the groove is required to be shallow: but when required to be deep, and consequently the stop to be driven back, a wooden punch must be placed upon the bottom of the stop, and the head of the punch struck with the hammer or mallet, until the guide of the stop arrives at the distance from the sole of the plane that the groove is to be in depth: the use of this plane is for tongueing dado at internal angles, for keying circular dado, grooving for library shelves, or working a broad rebate across the fibres.

§ 30. *Moulding Planes*

Are used in forming curved surfaces of many various fanciful prismatic sections, by way of ornament; these surfaces have therefore this property, that all parallel sections are similar figures. Single mouldings or different mouldings in assemblage have various names, according to their figure, combination, or situation; mouldings are formed either by a plane reversed to the intended section, by a fence and stop on the plane, which causes them to have the same transverse section throughout, or otherwise, by several planes adapted as nearly as possible to the different degrees of curvature; this is called working mouldings by hand. All new or fanciful forms are generally wrought by hand, and particularly in an assemblage of mouldings, where it would be too expensive to make planes adapted to the whole section, or to any particular member or members of that section. The length of moulding planes is nine inches and three eighths, and the depth about three inches and three eighths. Mouldings are said to be stuck when formed by planes, and the operation is called sticking. In mouldings, all internal sinkings which have one flat side, and one convex turned side, are called quirks.

§ 31. *Bead Plane*

Is a moulding plane of a semi-cylindric contour, and is generally used in sticking a moulding of the same name on the edge, or on the side close to the arrise: when the bead is stuck upon the edge of a piece of stuff, so as to form a semi-cylindric surface to the whole thickness, the edge is said to be beaded or rounded. When a bead is stuck on, and from one edge on the upper surface of a piece of stuff, so that the diameter may be contained in the breadth of that surface, but not to occupy the whole breadth: then the member so formed has a channel or sinking on the farther side, called a quirk, and is therefore called bead and quirk. When the edge of a piece of stuff has been stuck with bead and quirk; then the vertical side turned upwards and stuck from the same edge in the same manner, another quirk will be formed upon this side provided the breadth of this side be equal to that of the bead; then the curved surface will be three fourths of a cylinder, this is called bead and double quirk or return bead. The fence is of a solid piece with the plane. The guide of the fence is parallel to the sides of the plane, and tangential to the concave cylindric surface, and its lower edge comes about one fourth or three eighths of an inch below the cylindrical part, the other edge of the cylindrical part forms one side of the quirk, and is on a level with the top of the guide of the fence. The other side of the quirk is a vertical straight surface, and reaches as high as the most prominent part of the cylindric surface of the bend. From the upper edge of this flat side of the quirk, and at right angles to the vertical sides of the plane, proceeds the guide of the stop, which prevents the bead from sinking deeper than the semi-diameter of the cylinder, and the guide of the fence prevents the plane from taking more of the breadth than the diameter. When one, two, or more, contiguous semi-cylinders are sunk within the surface of a piece of wood, with the prominent parts of the curved surface of each, in the same surface as that from which they were sunk, this operation is called reeding, being done in imitation of one or a bundle of a reeds, and each little cylinder is called a reed. In this case, the axis of the reed is in the same straight surface: but this is not always the case, they are sometimes disposed round a staff or rod. Bead planes are sometimes so constructed, as to have the fence taken off or on at pleasure, by screws, for the purpose of striking any series of reeds. When the fence is taken off, the two sides form quirks, and are exactly similar and equal to each other.

The least sized bead is about one eighth of an inch, the next $\frac{5}{32}$, the regular progression stands thus: $\frac{1}{8}$, $\frac{5}{32}$, $\frac{3}{16}$, $\frac{1}{4}$, $\frac{5}{16}$, $\frac{3}{8}$, $\frac{1}{2}$, $\frac{5}{8}$, $\frac{3}{4}$, $\frac{7}{8}$, the first two only differ $\frac{1}{32}$, the next three $\frac{1}{16}$, and from $\frac{3}{8}$ to $\frac{7}{8}$ of an inch, they differ by $\frac{1}{8}$ of an inch each, the $\frac{3}{4}$ and $\frac{7}{8}$ inch beads are torus planes as well as bead planes. The torus only differs from the bead in having a fillet upon the outer edge of the stuff: consequently the torus consists of a fillet and semi-cylinder. It may be observed, that whether there be one or two semi-cylinders stuck on the edge of a piece of stuff, that without there is a fillet upon the edge they only take the name of beads. The torus is in general much larger than the bead: but when there are two semi-cylinders with a fillet upon the outer edge, the combination is called a double torus, and if there is no fillet, it is called a double bead, even though the one should be much larger than the other.

§ 32. *A Snipesbill*

Is a moulding plane for forming a quirk: snipesbills are of two kinds, one for sinking the quirk, called a sinking snipesbill, and the other for cleaning the vertical flat side of the quirk, called a side snipesbill. Each of these two kinds are right and left.

In the sinking snipesbill the cutting edge is on the sole, and the extremity of the iron comes close to the side of the plane, which forms the vertical side of the quirk; the sole consists of two parts of a cylindric surface of contrary curvature: one next to the edge which forms the quirk, is concave, and the part more remote, is convex.

The side snipesbill has its iron placed very nearly perpendicular, with regard to the sole of the plane, the top of the iron leaning about five degrees forward: this plane has its cutting edge upon one side or the other, according to the side or to the hand it is made for. The iron stands askew to the vertical sides of the plane.

§ 33. *Hollows and Rounds*

Are mouldings for striking convex and concave cylindrical surfaces, or any segment or parts of these surfaces; they have therefore their soles exactly the reverse of what is intended. Hollows and rounds are not confined to cylindric surfaces, but will also stick those of cylindrical forms, or those which have elliptic sections, perpendicular to the direction of the motion by which they are wrought. Mouldings depressed within the surface of a piece of wood, or those which form quirks, must first be sunk by the snipesbill, and formed into the intended shape by hollows and rounds. The hollow is only used in finishing a convex moulding; the rough is generally taken off with the jack plane, when there is room to apply it, if not, with the firmer chisel. In making a hollow, a rough excavation is first made with a gouge, and then finished with the round, and sometimes with two rounds, of which the sole of the one that comes first is a little quicker, and the iron set more rank.

III - Section from Holtzapffel's Mechanical Manipulation and Turning, Volume II, 1856

CHAPTER XXIII.

CHISELS AND PLANES.

SECT. I.—INTRODUCTION; BENCH PLANES.

If we drive an axe, or a thin wedge, into the center of a block of wood, as at *a*, fig. 318, it will split the same into two parts through the natural line of the fibres, leaving rough uneven surfaces, and the rigidity of the mass will cause the rent to precede the edge of the tool. The same effect will partially occur, when we attempt to remove a stout chip from off the side of a block of wood with the hatchet, adze, paring or drawing knife, the paring chisel, or any similar tool. So long as the chip is too rigid to bend to the edge of the tool, the rent will precede the edge; and with a naked tool, the splitting will only finally cease when the instrument is so thin and sharp, and it is applied to so small a quantity of the material, that the shaving can bend or ply to the tool, and then only will the work be *cut* or will exhibit a true copy of the smooth edge of the instrument, in opposition to its being *split* or *rent*, and consequently showing the natural disruption or tearing asunder of the fibres.

In fig. 318 are drawn to one scale several very different paring-tools, which agree however in similitude with the type, *b*, fig. 316, page 460, and also corroborate the remark on page 462, that "in the paring-tools, the one face of the wedge or tool is applied nearly parallel with the face of the work." In tools ground with only one chamfer, this position not only assists in giving direction to the tool, but it also places the strongest line of the tool exactly in the line of resistance, or of the work to be done.

For example, the axe or hatchet with two bevils, *a*, fig. 318, which is intended for hewing and splitting, when applied to *paring* the surface of a block, must be directed at the angle *a* which would be a much less convenient and less strong position than *b*, that of the *side hatchet* with only one chamfer; but for paring either a very large or a nearly horizontal surface, the side

hatchet in its turn is greatly inferior to the adze *c*, in which the handle is elevated like a ladder, at some 60 or 70 degrees from the ground, the preference being given to the horizontal position for the surface to be wrought.

The instrument is held in both hands, whilst the operator stands upon his work in a stooping position, the handle being from twenty-four to thirty inches long, and the weight of the blade from two to four pounds.

The adze is swung in a circular path almost of the same curvature as the blade, the shoulder-joint being the center of motion, and the entire arm and tool forming as it were one inflexible radius; the tool therefore makes a succession of small arcs, and in each blow the arm of the workman is brought in contact with the thigh, which thus serves as a stop to prevent accident. In coarse preparatory works, the workman directs the adze through the space between his two feet, he thus surprises us by the quantity of wood removed; in fine works, he frequently places his toes over the spot to be wrought, and the adze penetrates two or three inches beneath the sole of the shoe, and he thus surprises us by the apparent danger yet perfect working of the instrument, which in the hands of the shipwright in particular, almost rivals the joiner's plane; it is with him the nearly universal paring instrument, and is used upon works in all positions.

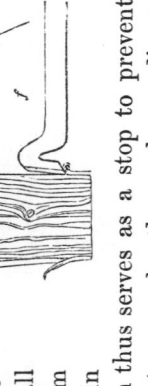

The small Indian adze or Bassōōlāh *d*, fig. 318, in place of being circular like the European adze, is formed at a direct angle of about 45 or 50 degrees; its handle is very short, and it is used with great precision by the nearly exclusive motion of the elbow joint.*

---

* "This very useful instrument (says Sir John Robison), varies a little in different districts, in weight and in the angle which the cutting face forms with the line of the handle, but the form shown is the most general, and the weight averages about

474   MODIFICATIONS OF THE CHISEL.

chisels, it is necessary to remove the handle, which is easily accomplished as the eye of the tool is larger externally as in the common pickaxe, so that the tool cannot fly off when in use, but a blow on the end of the handle easily removes it.

The chisel *e*, admits of being very carefully placed, as to position, and when the tool is strong, very flat, and not tilted up, it produces very true surfaces as seen in the mouths of planes. The chisel when applied with *percussion*, is struck with a wooden mallet, but in many cases it is merely *thrust* forward by its handle. It will shortly be shown that various other forms of the handle or stock of the chisel, enable it to receive a far more defined and effective thrust, which give it a different and most important character. The *paring-knife*, fig. 8, p. 26, Vol. I, exhibits also a peculiar but most valuable arrangement of the chisel, in which the thrust obtains a great increase of power and control; and in the *drawing-knife*, the narrow transverse blade and its two handles form three sides of a rectangle, so that it is actuated by *traction*, instead of by violent percussion or steady thrust.

The most efficient and common paring-tool for metal, namely *f*, has been added to fig. 318 for comparison with the paring-tools for wood; its relations to the surface to be wrought are exactly the same as the rest of the group, notwithstanding that the angle of its edge is doubled on account of the hardness of the material, and that its shaft is mostly at right angles, to meet the construction of the slide rest of the lathe or planing machine.

The chisel, when inserted in one of the several forms of stocks or guides, becomes the plane, the general objects being, to limit the extent to which the blade can penetrate the wood, to provide a definitive guide to its path or direction, and to restrain the splitting in favour of the cutting action.

In general, the sole or stock of the plane is in all respects an

---

GENERAL FORMS OF PLANES.   475

accurate counterpart of the form it is intended to produce, and it therefore combines in itself the longitudinal and the transverse sections, or the two guides referred to in the theoretical diagram, page 464, and the annexed figure 319, the parts of which are all drawn to one scale, may be considered a parallel diagram to 317, page 464, so far as regards planes.

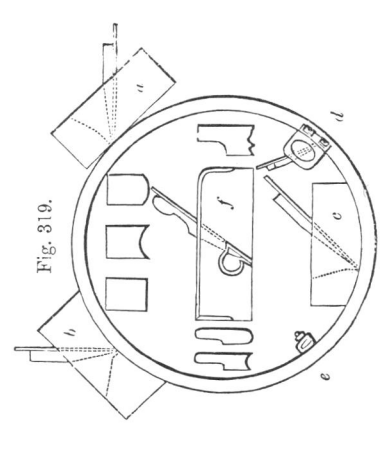

Fig. 319.

Thus, although convex surfaces, such as the outside of a hoop, may be wrought by any of the straight planes, applied in the direction of a tangent as at *a*, it is obvious the concave plane, *b*, would be more convenient. For the inside of the hoop, the radius of curvature of the plane must not exceed the radius of the work: thus *c*, the *compass plane*, would exactly suit the curve, and it might be used for larger diameters, although in a less perfect manner. For the convenience of applying planes to very small circles, some are made very narrow or short, and with transverse handles such as *d*, the plane for the hand-rails of staircases, the radius of its curvature being three inches; it resembles the spokeshave *e*, as respects the transverse handles, although the hand-rail plane has an iron, wedge, and stop, much like those of other planes.

The sections of planes, are also either straight, concave, convex, or mixed lines, and suited to all kinds of specific mouldings, but we have principally to consider their more common features, namely, the circumstances of their edges and guides; first, of those used for flat surfaces, called by the joiners, *bench planes*; secondly, the *grooving* planes; and thirdly, the *moulding* planes.

---

1 lb. 12 oz. The length of handle is about twelve or thirteen inches, and in use it is grasped so near the head, that the forefinger rests on the metal, the thumb nearly on the back of the handle, the other fingers grasp the front of it, the nails approaching the ball of the thumb. The wrist is held firmly, the stroke being made principally from the elbow, the inclination of the cutting face being nearly a tangent to the circle described by the instrument round the elbow joint as a center, the exact adjustment being made by the grasp and the inclination of the wrist, which is soon acquired by a little practice. In this way very hard woods may be dressed for the lathe with a degree of ease and accuracy not attainable with the small axe used in this country."

476 SURFACING, OR BENCH PLANES.

The various surfacing planes are nearly alike, as regards the arrangement of the iron, the principal differences being in their magnitudes. Thus the maximum width is determined by the average strength of the individual, and the difficulty of maintaining with accuracy the rectilinear edge. In the ordinary bench planes the width of the iron ranges from about 2 to 2½ inches.*

The lengths of planes are principally determined by the degree of straightness that is required in the work, and which may be thus explained. The joiner's plane is always either balanced upon *one* point beneath its sole, or it rests upon *two* points at the same time, and acts by cropping off these two points, without descending to the hollow intermediate between them. It is therefore clear, that by supposing the work to be full of small undulations, the spokeshave, which is essentially *a very short plane*, would descend into all the hollows whose lengths were greater than that of the plane, and the instrument is therefore commonly used for curved lines. But the greater the length of the plane, the more nearly would its position assimilate to the general line of the work, and it would successively obliterate the minor errors or undulations; and provided the instrument were itself *rectilinear*, it would soon impart that character to the edge or superficies submitted to its action. The following table may be considered to contain the ordinary measures of surfacing planes.

Names of Planes.	Lengths, in inches.	Widths, in inches.	Widths of Irons.
Modelling Planes, like Smoothing Planes	1 to 5	¼ to 2	⅜ to 1½
Ordinary Smoothing Planes	6¼ to 8	2⅜ to 3⅜	1¼ to 2⅜
Rebate Planes	— 9½	⅜ to 2	⅜ to 2
Jack Planes	12 to 17	2½ to 3	2 to 2¼
Panel Planes	14½	3½	2½
Trying Planes	20 to 22	3¼ to 3⅜	2⅜ to 2½
Long Planes	24 to 26	3⅜	2½
Jointer Planes	28 to 30	3¾	2¾
Cooper's Jointer Planes	60 to 72	5 to 5¼	3½ to 3¾

The succession in which they are generally used, is the jack plane for the coarser work, the trying plane for finer work and trying its accuracy, and the smoothing plane for finishing.

* The "iron," is scarcely a proper name for the *plane-iron*, which is a *cutter* or *blade*, composed partly of iron and steel; but no confusion can arise from the indiscriminate use of any of these terms.

GENERAL STRUCTURE OF PLANES. 477

The diagram, fig. 320, is one quarter the full size, and may be considered to represent the ordinary surfacing planes, the mouths of which are alike, generally about one-third from the front of the plane, and thus constituted. The line a, b, is called the *sole*; c, d, upon which the blade is supported, is the *bed*, and this, in planes of common pitch, is usually at an angle of 45° with the perpendicular.

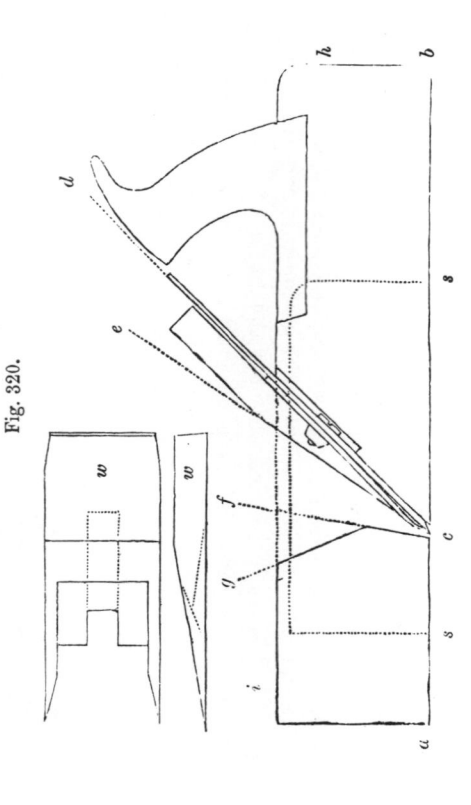

Fig. 320.

The *mouth* of the plane is the narrow aperture between the face of the iron, and the line c, f, which latter is called the *wear*: the angle between these should be as small as possible, in order that the wearing away of the sole, or its occasional correction, may cause but little enlargement of the mouth of the plane; at the same time the angle must be sufficient to allow free egress for the shavings, otherwise the plane is said to *choke*. The line g, is called the *front*, its angle is unimportant, and in practice it is usually set out one quarter of an inch wider on the upper surface than the width of the iron.

The *wedge* of the plane which fixes the iron is commonly at an angle of 10°, and it is slightly driven between the face of the iron and the shoulder or *abutment*, c, e. It is shown by the two detached views, that the wedge w, is cut away at the central part, both to clear the screw which connects the double iron, and to allow room for the escape of the shavings. The wedge is loosened by a moderate blow, either on the end of the plane at h, on the

478   GENERAL STRUCTURE OF PLANES.

top at i, or by tapping the side of the wedge, which may be then pulled out with the fingers; a blow on the front of the plane at j, sets the iron forward or deeper, but it is not resorted to.

In all the bench planes, the iron is somewhat narrower than the stock, and the mouth is a wedge-formed cavity; in some of the narrow planes the cutting edge of the iron extends the full width of the sole, as in the rebate plane f, fig. 319, page 475; in these and others, the narrow shaft of the iron and the thin wedge alone proceed through the stock, and there is a curvilinear mouth extending through the plane; the mouth is taper, to turn the shavings out on the more convenient side. When the planes only cut on the one part of the sole, as in fig. 332, page 485, the angular mouth extends only part way through the plane, and the curvilinear perforation is uncalled for.

In the diagram, fig. 320, when the stock terminates at the dotted line, s, s, it represents the smoothing plane; when it is of the full length, and furnished with the handle or *toat*, it is the jack plane or panel plane; the still longer planes have the toat further removed from the iron, and it is then of the form shown in fig. 330, page 483.

Fig. 321 represents, one-eighth the full size, a very effective plane, which is commonly used on the continent for roughing out, or as our jack plane, the *horn h*, being intended for the left hand, whilst the right is placed on the back of the stock. The Indians and Chinese bore a hole through the front of the plane for a transverse stick, by which a boy assists in pulling the plane across the work. When the plane is very large, it is by the Chinese, and others, placed at the end of the bench at an angle, and allowed to rest on the ground, whilst the work is slid down its face; and a similar position is employed by the coopers in our own country, for planing the staves of casks, the plane being in such cases, five or six feet long and very unwieldy, the upper part is supported on a prop, and the lower rests on a transverse piece of wood or sleeper.

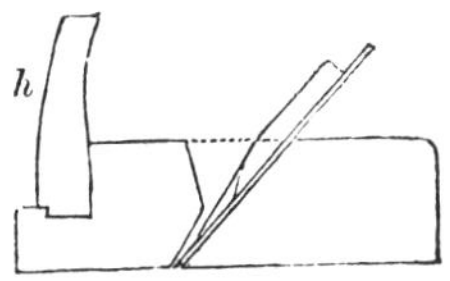

The amount of force required to work each plane is dependent on the angle and relation of the edge, on the hardness of the material, and on the magnitude of the shaving; but the required

ACTION OF THE PLANE-IRON.   479

force is in addition greatly influenced by the degree in which the shaving is *bent* for its removal in the most perfect manner.

The diagrams 322 to 326 represent, of their full size, parts of the irons and mouths of various planes, each in the act of removing a shaving. The sole or surface of the plane rests upon the face of the work, and the cutter stands as much in advance of the sole of the plane, as the thickness of the shaving, which is in each case so bent as to enable it to creep up the face of the inclined iron, through the narrow slit of the plane, called its mouth, the width of which determines the extent to which the fibre of the wood can tear up or split with the grain.

The spokeshave, fig. 322, cuts perhaps the most easily of all the planes, and it closely assimilates to the penknife; the angle of the blade is about 25 degrees, one of its planes lies almost in contact with the work, the inclination of the shaving is slight, and the mouth is very contracted. The spokeshave works very easily in the direction of the grain, but it is only applicable to small and rounded surfaces and cannot be extended to suit large flat superficies, as the sole of the plane cannot be cut away for such an iron, and the perfection of the mouth is comparatively soon lost in grinding the blade.

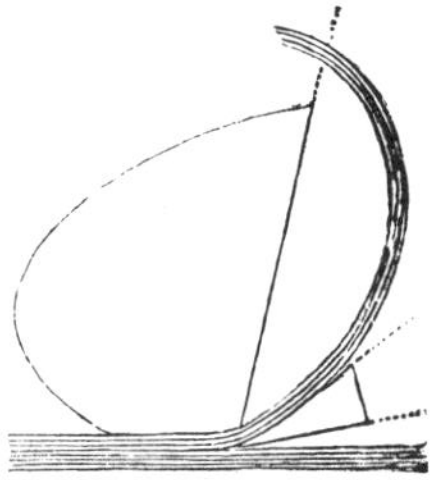

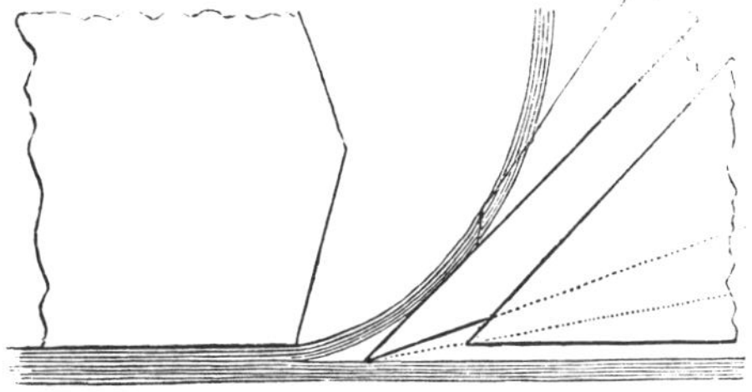

The diagrams, figs. 323, 4, and 5, suppose the plane irons to be ground at the angle of 25°, and to be sharpened on the more refined oilstone at 35°, so as to make a second bevil or slight facet, as shown by the dotted lines a, in each of the figures; the irons so ground are placed at the angle of 45°, or that of *common pitch*; it therefore follows, that the ultimate bevil which should be very narrow, lies at an elevation of 10° from the surface to be planed.

Fig. 323 represents the mouth of an old jack plane, from the sole of which about half an inch of wood has been lost by wear

480   ACTION OF THE PLANE-IRON.

and correction, which is no uncommon case. The wide mouth allows a partial splitting of the fibres before they creep up the face of the single iron; this plane works easily, and does not greatly alter the shavings, which come off in spiral curls, but the work is left rough and torn.

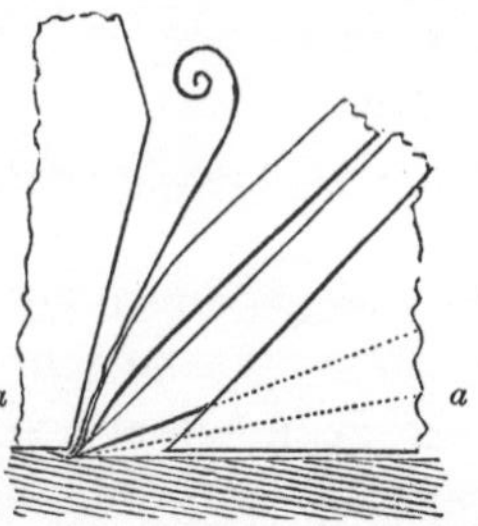

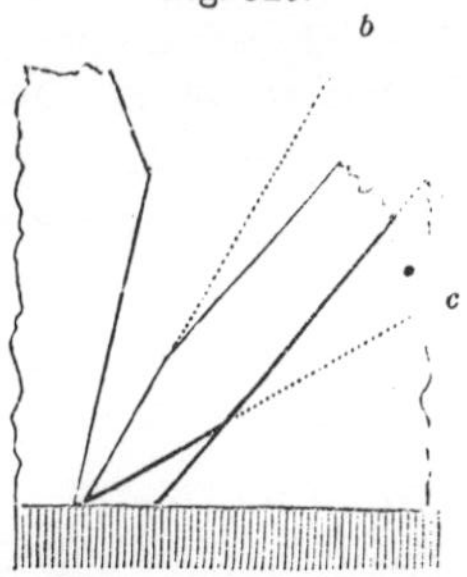

Fig. 324, a similar but less worn plane with a closer mouth, allows less of the splitting to occur, as the shaving is more suddenly bent in passing its narrower mouth, so that the *cutting* now begins to exceed the splitting, as the wood is held down by the closer mouth: the shaving is more broken and polygonal, but the work is left smoother.

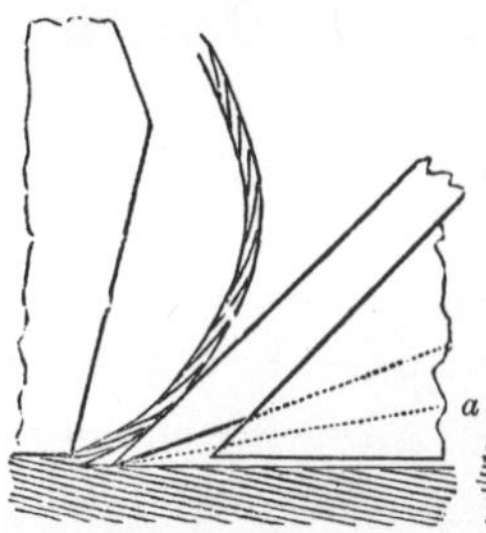

The same effects are obtained in a much superior manner in the planes with double irons, such as in fig. 325, the top iron is not intended to cut, but to present a more nearly perpendicular wall for the ascent of the shavings, the top iron more effectually *breaks* the shavings, and is thence sometimes called the *break iron*.

Now therefore, the shaving being very thin, and constrained between two approximate edges, it is as it were bent out of the way to make room for the cutting edge, so that the shaving is removed by absolute *cutting*, and without being in any degree split or rent off.

The compound or double iron is represented detached, and of half size in fig. 327: in this figure the lower piece c, is the one

Fig. 324.   Fig. 325.   Fig. 326.

Fig. 327.

ACTION OF THE PLANE-IRON.   481

edge, which is also moderately sharp, the top iron is placed from one-sixteenth to one-fiftieth of an inch from the edge of the cutter, the two are held together so closely by the screw which passes through a long mortise in c, and fits in a tapped hole in t, that no shaving can get between them.

The constant employment of the top iron in all available cases, shows the value of the improvement; and the circumstances of the plane working the smoother, but harder, when it is added, and the more so the closer it is down, demonstrate that its action is to *break* or *bend* the fibres. This is particularly observable in the coarse thick shavings of a double-iron jack plane, compared with those of the same thickness from a single-iron plane; the latter are simply spiral and in easy curves, whereas those from the double-iron are broken across at short intervals, making their character more nearly polygonal; and the same difference is equally seen in thinner shavings, although of course less in degree.

Fig. 326 represents the iron of a plane intended " for the use of cabinet-makers and others, who require to cut either hard or coarse-grained wood," the upper bevil given to the iron, being considered to dispense with the necessity for the top-iron; but it is obviously much more difficult to produce a true rightlined edge, by the meeting of two planes, each subject to error in sharpening, than when one exists permanently flat as in the broad surface e of the blade.*

The same edge may be obtained by a blade with a single chamfer, the flat side of which is placed in either of the dotted positions of fig. 326. The first, or b, is that previously in common use in the ordinary moulding planes for mahogany, and c is almost the position of the bed for the iron of the mitre-plane, also previously common: in all three planes, the ultimate angle of the face of the cutter is just 60 degrees from the horizontal.

Fig. 328 represents the mouth of the mitre plane full size, and fig. 329 the entire instrument one-eighth size. The stock is much less in height than in ordinary planes, and the iron lies at an angle of about 25°, and is sharpened at about the ordinary angle of 35°, making a total elevation of 60°, which, together with the delicate metallic mouth, render the absence of the top

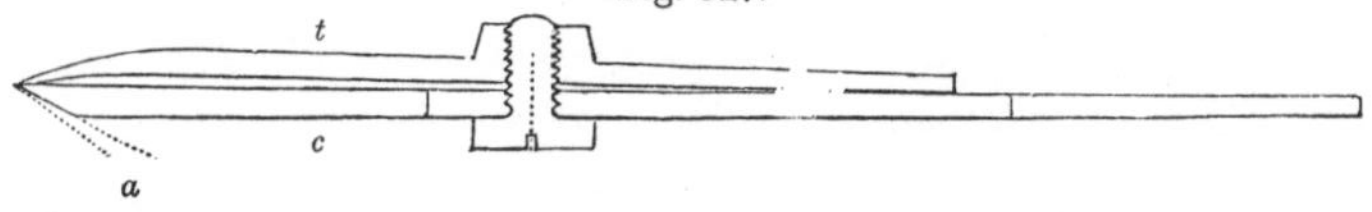

used for cutting, the upper piece t or the top iron, has a true

---

* See Transactions of the Society of Arts, 1825, vol. xliii. p. 85.

482   MITRE PLANE. ANGLES OF PITCH.

iron unimportant, even when the plane is used lengthways of the fibres, although its ostensible purpose is to plane obliquely across their ends, as in the formation of mitre joints.

Fig. 328.

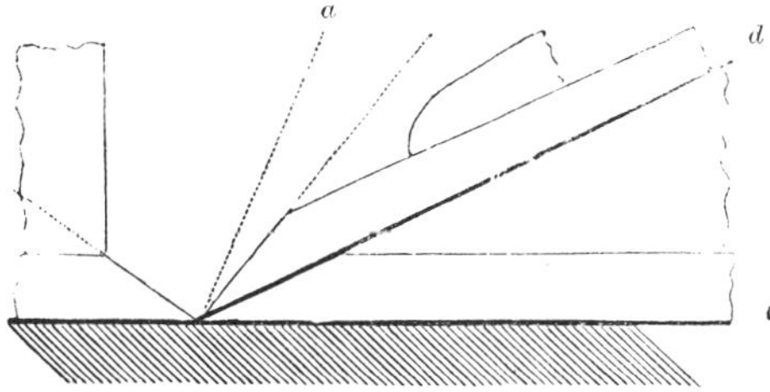

Fig. 329.

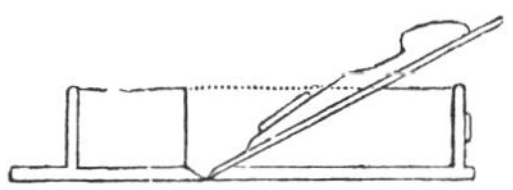

In all ordinary planes the mouth gets wider as the iron is ground away, because of the unequal thickness or taper form of the blade as seen at *c*, fig. 327. In the mitre plane this is avoided by placing the chamfer upwards, now therefore the position of the blade is determined by its broad flat face which rests on the bed of the instrument *d*, and maintains one constant position as regards the mouth, uninfluenced by the gradual loss of thickness in the iron.

The smoothing and trying planes are also made with metal soles, and with single irons of ordinary angles, as one great purpose of the top iron is to compensate for the enlargement of the mouth of the plane by wear, this defect is almost expunged from those with iron soles, and which are gradually becoming common, both with single and with double irons. See Appendix, Note A.H., page 978.

Some variation is made in the angles at which plane irons are inserted in their stocks. The spokeshave is the lowest of the series, and commences with the small inclination of 25 to 30 degrees; and the general angles, and purposes of ordinary planes, are nearly as follows. *Common pitch*, or 45 degrees from the horizontal line is used for all the bench planes for deal, and similar soft woods. *York pitch*, or 50 degrees from the horizontal, for the bench planes for mahogany, wainscot, and hard or stringy woods. *Middle pitch*, or 55 degrees, for moulding planes for deal, and smoothing planes for mahogany, and similar woods. *Half pitch*, or 60 degrees, for moulding planes for mahogany, and woods difficult to work, of which bird's-eye maple is considered one of the worst.

PLANES OF UPRIGHT PITCH.   483

Boxwood, and other close hard woods, may be smoothly *scraped*, if not cut, in any direction of the grain, when the angle constituting the pitch entirely disappears; or with a common smoothing-plane, in which the cutter is perpendicular, or even leans slightly forward; this tool is called a *scraping plane*, and is used for scraping the ivory keys of piano-fortes, and works inlaid with ivory, brass, and hardwoods; this is quite analogous to the process of turning the hardwoods.

The cabinet-maker also employs a scraping-plane, with a perpendicular iron, which is grooved on the face, to present a series of fine teeth instead of a continuous edge; this, which is called a *toothing plane*, is employed for roughing and *scratching* veneers, and the surfaces to which they are to be attached, *to make a tooth* for the better hold of the glue.

The smith's-plane for brass, iron, and steel, fig. 330, has likewise a perpendicular cutter, ground to 70 or 80 degrees; it is adjusted by a vertical screw, and the wedge is replaced by an end screw and block, as shown in the figure, which is one-eighth size. In the planes with vertical irons, the necessity for the narrow mouth ceases; and in the smith's plane some of the narrow irons, or more properly cutters, are also grooved on the faces, by which their edges are virtually divided into several narrow pieces; this enables the instrument to be more easily employed in roughing-out works, by abstracting so much of the width of the iron, and by giving it a greater degree of penetration, but the finishing is done with smooth-edged cutters, and those not exceeding from five-eighths of an inch to one inch wide.

Fig. 330.

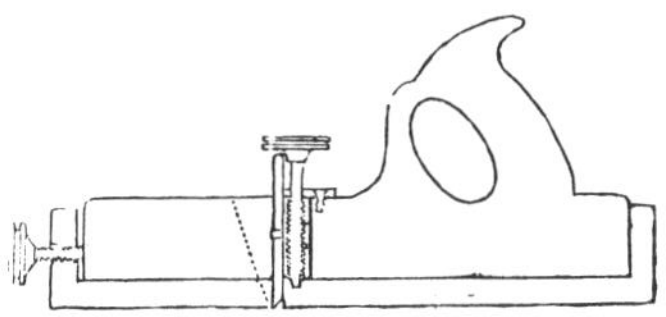

It is well known that most pieces of wood will plane better from the one end than from the other, and that when such pieces are turned over, they must be changed end for end likewise; the necessity for this will immediately appear, if we consider the shade-lines under the plane-irons *a*, *b*, fig. 331, to represent the natural fibres of the wood, which are rarely parallel with the face of the work. The plane *a*, working *with the grain*, would cut smoothly, as it would rather press down the fibres than otherwise; whereas *b* would work *against the grain*, or would meet the fibres cropping out, and be liable to tear them up.

It was explained in Chap. IV, Vol. I, that the handsome characters of showy woods, greatly depend on all kinds of irregularities in the fibres: so that the conditions *a* and *b*, fig. 331, continually occur in the same piece of wood, and in which we can therefore scarcely produce one straight and smooth cut in any direction. Even the most experienced workman will apply the smoothing-plane at various angles across the different parts of such wood according to his judgment; in extreme cases, where the wood is very curly, knotty, and cross-grained, the plane can scarcely be used at all, and such pieces are finished with the steel scraper.

This simple tool was originally a piece of broken window-glass, and such it still remains in the hands of some of the gun-stock makers; but as the cabinet-maker requires the rectilinear edge, he employs a thin piece of saw-plate, which is represented black and highly magnified at *s*, fig. 331. The edge is first sharpened at right angles upon the oilstone, and it is then mostly burnished, either square or at a small angle, so as to throw up a trifling burr, or wire-edge. The scraper is held on the wood at about 60°, and as the minute edge takes a much slighter hold, it may be used where planes cannot be well applied. The scraper does not work so smoothly as a plane in perfect order upon ordinary wood, and as its edge is rougher and less keen, it drags up some of the fibres, and leaves a minute roughness, interspersed with a few longer fibres.

SECT. II.—GROOVING PLANES.

We may plane *across the grain* of hard mahogany and boxwood with comparative facility, as the fibres are packed so closely, like the loose leaves of a book when squeezed in a press, that they may be cut in all directions of the grain with nearly equal facility, both with the flat and moulding planes. But the weaker and more open fibres of deal and other soft woods, cannot withstand a cutting edge applied to them *parallel with themselves*, or laterally, as they are torn up, and leave a rough unfinished surface. The joiner uses therefore, *for deal and soft woods*, a very keen plane of low pitch, and slides it across obliquely, so as to attack the fibre from the one end, and virtually to remove it in the direction of its length; so that the force is divided and applied to each part of the fibre in succession.

The moulding planes cannot be thus used, and all mouldings made in deal, and woods of similar open soft grain, are consequently always planed lengthways of the grain, and added as separate pieces. As however many cases occur in carpentry, in which rebates and grooves are required directly across the grain of deal, the obliquity is then given to the *iron*, which is inserted at an angle, as in the skew-rebate and fillister, and the stock of the plane, is used in various ways to guide its transit.

Many of these planes present much ingenuity and adaptation to their particular cases: for example fig. 332 is the side view, and fig. 333 the back of the *side-fillister*, which is intended to plane both with and across the grain, as in planing a rebate around the margin of a panel. The loose slip, or the fence *f*, is adjusted to expose so much of the oblique iron as the width of the rebate; the screw-stop *s*, at the side, is raised as much above the sole of the plane as the depth of the rebate, and the little tooth *t*, or scoring point (shown detached, in two views *a*, *b*), precedes the bevelled iron, so as to shear or divide the fibres as with the point of a penknife, to make the perpendicular edge keen and square. This plane is therefore a four-fold combination of two measures and two cutters. The oblique iron, and the tooth or cutter, are pretty constantly met with in the planes used across the grain.

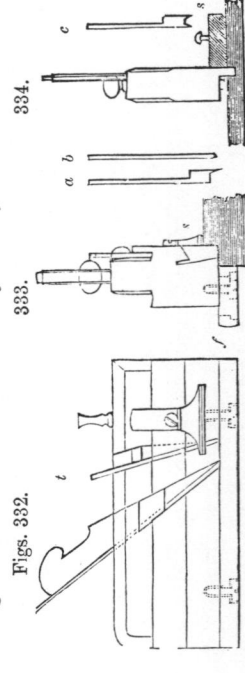

Others of these planes have less power of adjustment; for

486 GROOVING PLANES; PLOUGH, ETC.

instance the grooving-plane fig. 334, for planing across the grain, has two separate teeth, or else a single tooth with two points c, in addition to the cutting-iron which is commonly placed square across the face of the plane; the groove is only used for the reception of a shelf, its sides are therefore the more important parts, and the obliquity of the iron may be safely omitted. The fence can no longer be a part of the instrument, as it is often used in the middle of a long piece, a wooden straight-edge s, is therefore temporarily nailed down to guide the plane; and the stop is sometimes a piece of boxwood fitted stiffly in a mortise through the stock, at other times it is adjusted by a thumb-screw, as in the figure 334.

The *plough*, fig. 335, is a grooving-plane, to work *with the grain*; it has similar powers to the fillister, but with a greater horizontal range. The width of the groove is determined by that of the blade, of which each plough has several; they are retained in the perpendicular position by a thin iron plate, which enters a central angular groove in the back of the blade. The teeth or scoring points are now uncalled for, as the iron works perfectly well the lengthway of the fibre. The screw-stop is the same as before; but the *fence f*, is built upon two transverse *stems s s*, instead of the stems $s s$, and there are two wooden nuts to each screw, one on each side of the stock of the plough.

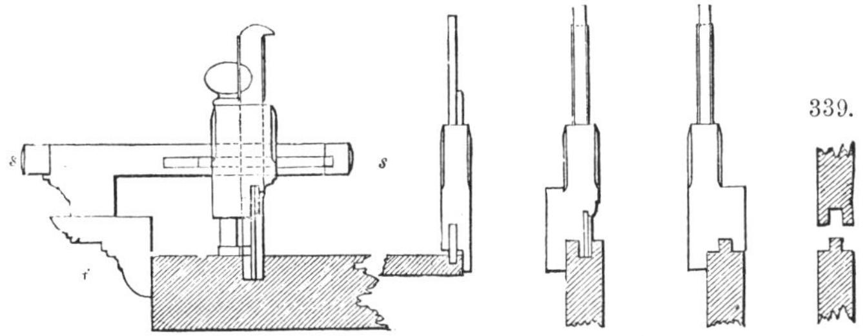

Other grooving-planes for working with the grain are also made without teeth, examples of which may be seen in the drawer-bottom plane 336, and the slit deal planes, of which 337 makes the groove, and 338 the tongue, used for connecting

Figs. 335. 336. 337. 338.

339.

REGLET PLANE, ROUTER, CARPENTERS' GAGES. 487

boards for partitions and other purposes, with the groove and tongue-joint 339. The planes of this class being generally used for one specific purpose and measure, are unprovided with loose parts, as they are worked until the sole of the plane, or some of its edges come in contact with the wood, and stop the further progress of the cutter.

Fig. 340, the reglet plane, is of this kind, it derives its name from being employed in making the parallel slips of wood, or *reglet*, used by the printer for the wide separation of the lines of metal type; the adjustable fences are screwed fast, as much in advance of the sole of the plane as the required thickness of the reglets or rules, which are then planed away until, from the slips resting on the bench, the tool will cut no longer.

Figs. 340.

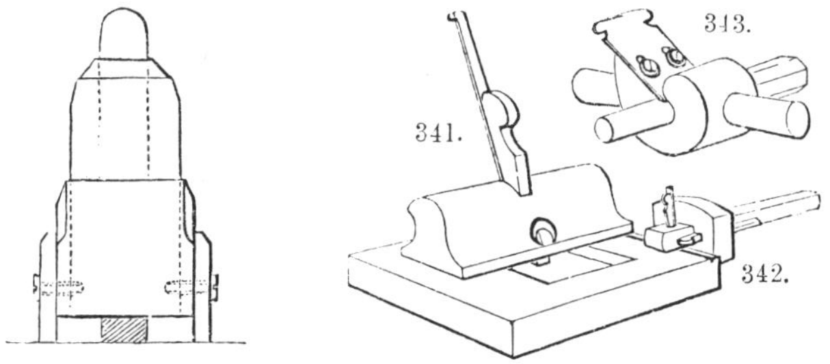

Fig. 341 is a router plane; it has a broad surface carrying in its centre one of the cutters belonging to the plough, it is used for levelling the bottoms of cavities, the stock must be more than twice the width of the recess, and the projection of the iron determines the depth, the sides of the cavities are prepared before-hand with the chisel and mallet. The ordinary name for this plane is not remarkable for its propriety or elegance, it is generally called the "*old woman's tooth.*" See Appendix, Note A.I, page 979.

The carpenters' gages, for setting out lines and grooves parallel with the margin of the work, are closely associated with the system of fences or rails. The *stem* of the gage, fig. 342, is retained in the *head*, or stock, by means of a small wedge, and the cutter is fixed in a hole at right angles to the face of the stem, by another wedge. The *marking-gage*, for setting out lines, has a simple conical point; the *cutting-gage*, for cutting veneers and thin wood, has a lancet-shaped knife, and is a

488   GAGES, BANDING PLANE, AND ROUNDER.

very effective tool; the *router-gage*, for inlaying small lines of wood and brass, has a tooth like a narrow chisel.

There are other forms of gages, some of these have screw adjustments; in the most simple, the stem is a wooden screw, flattened on one side, and the head of the gage consists of two wooden nuts, which become fixed when screwed fast against each other. The *mortise-gage*, which is much used, has two points that may be adjusted to scribe the widths of mortises and tenons. In the *bisecting gage* there are two sliding pieces or heads, which are made to embrace the object to be bisected, and the scribing point is in the center of two equal arms jointed respectively to the two sliding heads.*

The *cooper's croze* is used for making the grooves for the heading of casks, after the ends of the staves have been levelled by a tool called a *sun plane*, like a jack-plane, but of a *circular* plan. The croze is similar to the gages, except that it is very much larger; the head is now nearly semicircular, and terminates in two handles; the stem, which is proportionally large, is also secured by a wedge, but the cutter is composed of three or four saw-teeth, closely followed by a hooked router, which sweeps out the bottom of the groove.

The *banding-plane*† is allied to the gages, and is intended for cutting out grooves, and inlaying strings and bands in straight and circular works, as in the rounded corners of piano-fortes and similar objects. It bears a general resemblance to the double plough, fig. 335, but it is furnished in addition with the double tooth *c*, of the grooving plane, fig. 334. In the banding plane, the central plate of the plough is retained as a guide for the central positions of the router and cutter, which are inserted, so as to meet in an angle of about 80 degrees, between two short projections of the central plate; the whole of the parts entering the groove are compressed within the length of one inch, to pass through curvatures of small radius; there are various cutters and fences, both straight and circular, according to the nature of the work. See Appendix, Note A.J., page 979.

Fig. 343 is a plane which is the link betwixt carpentry and

---

* See H. R. Palmer's gage for marking center lines.—Trans. Soc. of Arts, 1813, vol. xxxi. p. 248.
† Mr. R. Onwin's banding plane.—Trans. Soc. of Arts, 1817, vol. xxxv. p. 122.

MOULDING PLANES, AND THEIR IMPERFECTIONS.   489

turning; the conical hole in the plane is furnished with a cutter placed as a tangent to the circle, so that the wood enters in the rough octagonal form, and leaves it rounded, fit for a broom, an umbrella handle, or an office ruler; sometimes either the work or plane is driven by machinery, with the addition of one or two preparatory gouges, for removing the rougher parts.

SECT. III.—MOULDING PLANES.

All the planes hitherto considered, whether used parallel with the surfaces, as in straight works, or as tangents to the curves, as in curved works, are applied under precisely the same circumstances, as regards the angular relation of the mouth, because the edge of the blade is a right line parallel with the sole of the plane; but when the outline of the blade is curved, some new conditions arise which interfere with the perfect action of the instrument. It is now proposed to examine these conditions in respect to the semicircle, from which the generality of mouldings may be considered to be derived.

In the astragal, a, b, c, d, e, fig. 344, a small central portion at c, may be considered to be a horizontal line; two other small portions at b, and d, may be considered as parts of the vertical dotted lines, b, f, and d, g; and the intermediate parts of the semicircle are seen to merge from the horizontal to the vertical line.

The reason why one moulding plane figured to the astragal cannot, under the usual construction, be made to work the vertical parts of the moulding with the same perfection as the horizontal, consists in the fact, that whereas the ordinary plane iron presents an angle of some 45 to 60 degrees to the *sole* of the plane, which part is meant to cut, it presents a right angle to the *side* of the plane, which part is not meant to cut. Thus if the parts of the iron of the square rebate plane, which protrude through the sides of the stock, were sharpened ever so keenly, they would only *scrape* and not *cut*, just the same as the scraping plane with a perpendicular iron.

When, however, the rebate plane is meant to *cut at the side*, it is called the *side-rebate plane*, and its construction is then just reversed, as shown in the three views, fig. 346; that is, the iron is inserted perpendicularly to the sole of the plane, but at a horizontal angle $x\ x$, or *obliquely to the side of the plane*, so either numerous positions of the plane, or an iron of such a kind as to combine these several positions.

Theoretically speaking therefore, the face of the cutter suitable to working the entire semicircle or bead, would become a cone, or like a tube of steel bored with a hole of the same diameter as the bead, turned at one end externally like a cone, and split in two parts. Fig. 347 would represent such a cutter, and which just resembles a half round gouge applied horizontally and sharpened externally. But this theoretical cutter would present all the difficulties of the spokeshave iron; as to the trouble of fixing it, its interference with the sole of the plane, and the difficulty of maintaining the form of the mouth of the instrument, if made as a spokeshave, owing to the reduction of the cutter in sharpening.*

But as the iron 3, and also the side-rebate, fig. 346, work perfectly well in their respective positions, or when the cutters are inclined *horizontally*, whilst the central iron 2, only requires to be inclined *vertically*, it occurred to me that by employing a cutter *in all respects as usual*, except that its face should be *curved as in the arc connecting the three irons* in fig. 345, the one tool would cut equally well at every point of the curve; and experience proved the truth of the supposition. The precise form of the iron will be readily arrived at, by cutting out in card the diagram, fig. 348, and bending it to a circular sweep, until the parts exterior to the dotted lines $bf,—dg$, just meet the spring of the bead, at about the angle of half or middle pitch, or 30 or 35 degrees from the right angle, and it will be then found necessary to cut away the corners to the lines $bs,—ds$, or so much of them as dip below the straight surface of the fillet, as seen in fig. 349.

The author had a plane constructed exactly in agreement with the above particulars, that is, with an iron curved to about the third of a circle, the mouth of the plane was curved to correspond, and in every other respect the instrument was as usual; it was found entirely successful.

The inclination of the tool to each part of the work is very

* The cutter 347, is used for making the cylindrical rollers upon which ribbons are wound; the cutter is fixed at the end of a slide, and is worked by a lever, the cylinders are made at two cuts in lengths of 8 or 10 inches, and afterwards divided.

that the cut is now only on the one side zz, of the plane, and which side virtually becomes the sole. A second plane sloped the opposite way, is required for the opposite side, or the planes are made in pairs, and are used for the sides of grooves, and places inaccessible to the ordinary rebate plane.

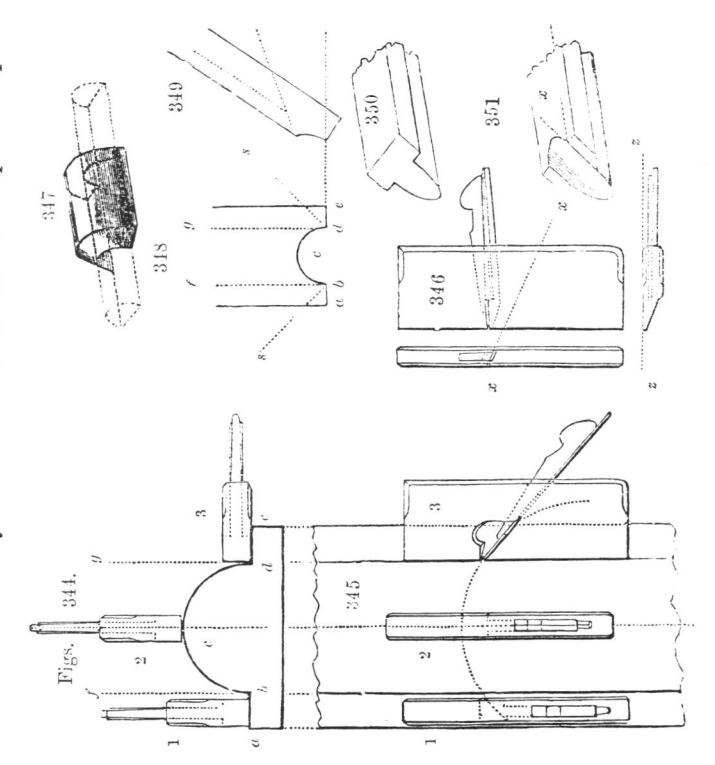

In the figures 344 and 345, the square rebate planes 1 and 2, will cut the horizontal surfaces a, b, and c, perfectly, because the irons present the proper slopes to these surfaces; but in attempting to plane the vertical line bf, with the side of 1, we should fail, because the cutter is at right angles to that superficies, and it would only scrape, or be said to *drag*. The plane 3, when laid on its side, would act perfectly on the vertical face, but now it would be ineffective as regards the horizontal. The square rebate plane, if applied all around the semicircle, would be everywhere effective so long as its shaft stood as a radius to the curve, in fact as at 2, and 3, as then the angle of the iron would be in the right direction in each of its temporary situations. But in this mode a plane to be effective throughout, demands

492 IMPERFECTIONS OF

nearly alike, and it assimilates at different parts to each of the ordinary rebate planes, all of which work well. Namely, at the crown of the moulding c, to the square rebate plane; at the spring b and d, to the side rebate planes; and at the fillets $a\,b$, $d\,e$, to the skew rebate. And notwithstanding the fluted form of the iron, no greater difficulty is experienced in sharpening the iron in the new form like a gouge, than in the old like a chisel, the figure of the end being nearly alike in each case.*

As all the imperfections in the actions of moulding-planes occur at the vertical parts, there is a general attempt to avoid these difficulties by keeping the mouldings flat or nearly without vertical lines. For example, concave and convex planes, called *hollows and rounds*, include generally the fifth or sixth, sometimes about the third of the circle; and it is principally in the part between the third and the semicircle that the dragging is found to exist; and therefore, when a large part of the circle is wanted, the plane is applied at two or more positions in succession.

In a similar manner large complex mouldings often require to be worked from two or more positions with different planes, even when none of their parts are undercut, but in which latter case this is of course indispensable. And in nearly all mouldings the plane is not placed perpendicularly to the moulding, but at an angle so as to remove all the nearly vertical parts, as far towards the horizontal position as circumstances will admit.

---

* The above forms of cutters suggested for mouldings, are each applicable to most mouldings, but from their nature they are too troublesome for ordinary use. For instance, we may employ a cutter such as 347, the lower surface of which, as in 350, is the astragal or any other moulding, the general slope or chamfer, will cause the tool to cut at the fillets and at c, which parts are horizontal; but nearly the sections of the mouldings, and to be sharpened always in front, in the spokeshave form of iron; but partly in front and partly behind in the sloping irons; but these conditions are far too complex except in some favourable cases. The cutters are always made flat on the face, and to lessen the difficulty, the mouldings are drawn shallow, with but few or no vertical parts, or else they are wrought by two or more different planes.

MOULDING PLANES. 493

Thus the plane for the moulding, fig. 352, would have its stock perpendicular to the dotted line $a\,b$, connecting the extreme parts of the moulding, the angular deviation being generally called the *spring*. The spring is also partly determined by the position which is most favourable to the maintenance of the form of the cutter in sharpening it; as the obliquity of the sole of the plane causes the cutter, when advanced through it, also to shift sideways, and cause a disagreement between their figures.

Fig. 352.

In the act of working, or as it is called in *sticking* the moulding, the wood is always first accurately squared to its dimensions to serve as a guide, and it is then sometimes roughly bevelled nearly to the line $a\,b$; the plane is applied in the dotted position, the blank edge o, of the plane, rests against the edge of the prepared wood, and determines what is called the "*on*" of the moulding, that is, how far the plane can proceed upon the wood; and the planing is continued vertically until the blank edge d stops the further action, or determines the "*down*," by resting upon the solid wood beneath it. In some cases where the planes are unprovided with fences or blank edges, or that they are applied in places where fences in the ordinary form are inapplicable, a slip of wood is nailed down for their guidance, as in fig. 334, page 485.

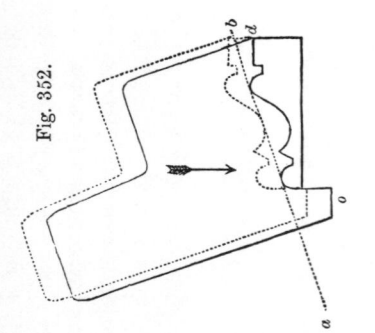

Wide moulding planes have been occasionally worked by two individuals, one to guide and thrust as usual, the other to pull with a rope. The top iron is however absent from the whole of the group, if we except the *capping plane* used for the upper surfaces of staircase rails, which are faintly rounded. The absence of the top iron is partly compensated for, by the pitch of moulding planes being as stated on page 482, about 10 degrees more upright than in bench planes for the same materials. The angles and edges of many of the small planes are *box slipped*, that is, slips of boxwood are inlaid in the beech-wood, in order that the projecting edges or the *quirks* may possess greater durability.

CABINET-MAKER'S BENCH.

SECT. IV.—REMARKS ON THE BENCH, AND USE OF THE PLANE.

It is not the present intention to resume the consideration of the joiner's planes in this work, it therefore appears desirable before quitting the subject to add a few instructions respecting the modes of keeping them in order, and of using them, in which some kind of bench or support for the work is always required.

The benches are made in various ways, from a few rough boards nailed together, to the structure shown in fig. 353, which represents one of the most complete kind of cabinet-makers' benches, carefully connected by screw-bolts and nuts: its surface is a thick plank planed very flat and true, with a trough to receive small tools, without interfering with the surface of the bench.

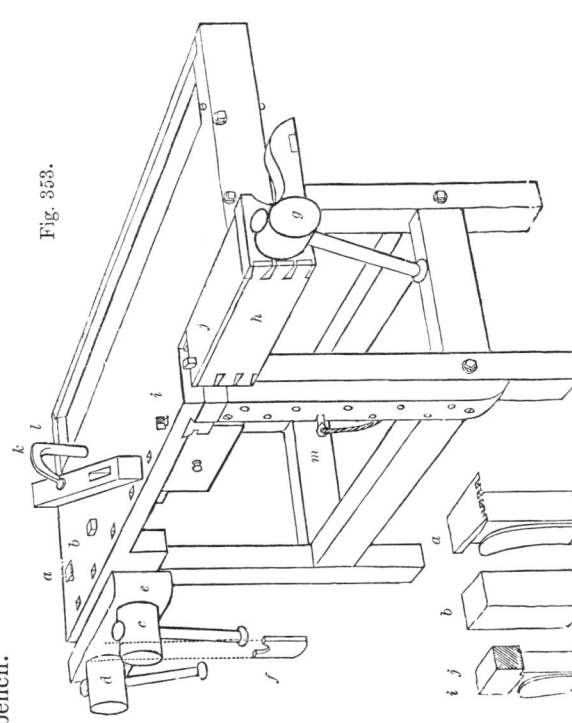

Fig. 353.

The wood to be planed is laid on the bench, and is stayed by an iron bench-hook a, which is fitted in a mortise, so that it may be placed at any required elevation, or flush with the surface of the bench. The bench-hook has teeth projecting from its face, intended to stick into the wood, and retain it from moving sideways; but to avoid the injury which would be inflicted by the teeth on nearly finished works, there is also a square wooden stop b, fitted tight into a square mortise. These are shown

removed, and on a much larger scale, at the foot of the engraving, the same letters of reference being repeated.

The two side screws c, d, constitute with the chop e, a kind of vice; the screw c, simply compresses, the screw d, has a piece f, called a *garter* (shown detached), which enters a groove in the cylindrical neck of the screw d, so that when the screws are both opened, d serves to bring the chop e outwards. The chops are greatly used for fixing work by the sides or edges, and as they open many inches, small boxes, drawers, and other works, may be pinched between them.

There are other constructions of benches which it is unnecessary to describe; some have only one of the screws c, d, the other being replaced by a square bar fixed in e, and many are not furnished with the end screw g, which draws out the sliding piece h, that is very carefully fitted. The end screw serves also as a vice for thin works which are more conveniently held at right angles to the position of the side screws; but its more valuable purpose is for holding work by the two ends, which mode is exceedingly convenient, especially in making grooves, rebates, and mouldings, as the work is in no danger of slipping away from the tools. There are several square holes along the front of the bench, for an iron stop i, which has a perpendicular and slightly roughened face, and a similar stop j, is also placed in h, and as the latter slides a quantity not less than the interval between the holes, pieces of any length below the longest may be securely held.

For holding squared pieces of wood upon the bench, as in making mortises or dovetails, the holdfast k, is used in the manner shown, it is an **L** formed iron, the straight arm of which fits loosely in a hole in the bench; the work is fixed by driving on the top at k, and it is released by a blow on the back at l. Sometimes also the holdfast is made in two parts jointed together like the letter **T**, with a screw at the one end of the transverse piece, by which the work can be fixed without the hammer, but the former mode is far more common and is sufficiently manageable. And m is a pin which is placed in any of the holes in the leg of the bench, to support the end of long boards, which are fixed at their other extremity by the screws, c, d. We will now proceed to the management of the planes. See Appendix, notes A K, A L, and A M, pp. 978 and 980.

496 SHARPENING AND ADJUSTING.

Of the bench planes enumerated in the list on page 476, the following are most generally used, namely, the jack plane for the coarser work, the trying plane for giving the work a better figure or trying its straightness and accuracy, and the smoothing plane for finishing the surface, without detracting from the truth obtained by the trying plane. Sometimes when the wood is very rough and dirty, two jack planes are used still more to divide the work, and these instruments are managed in the following manner.

The remarks on pages 477-8 explain that, for long planes, the iron is released by a blow of the hammer on the top of the plane at the front; the smoothing, and all short planes, are struck at the back of the plane, and never on the top, or the wedge may be tapped sideways, and pulled out with the fingers.

The top iron is then removed, by loosening the screw, and sliding it up the mortise, until its head can pass through the circular hole in the cutting iron.

The plane iron having been ground to an angle of some 25 degrees, with the stone running towards the edge, it is next sharpened at an angle of about 35 degrees on the oilstone. The iron is first grasped in the right hand, with the fore finger only above and near the side of the iron, and with the thumb below; the left hand is then applied with the left thumb lapping over the right, and the whole of the fingers of that hand on the surface of the iron; the edge should be kept nearly square across the oilstone, as when one corner precedes the other the foremost angle is the more worn.

When the iron is required to be very flat, as for the finishing planes, the surface of the oilstone should be kept quite level, and the blade must be held at one constant angle; but when it is required to be round on the edge, a slight roll of the blade is required edgeways; lastly, the flat face of the iron is laid *quite flat* on the oilstone, to remove the wire edge, and if required, the edge is drawn through a piece of wood to tear off this film, after which the iron is again touched on the oilstone, both on the chamfer and flat surface, as the edge when finished should be perfectly keen and acute.

The iron is frequently held too high to expedite the sharpening; it is clear, that should it be elevated above 45°, or the pitch of the plane, the bevil would be in effect reversed, and it could only

THE PLANE IRONS. 497

act as a burnisher; exactly at 45° the keen edge would be soon worn away, and the condition of the burnisher would remain; and, within certain limits, the lower or thinner the edge is sharpened the better. Perhaps the angle of 35° which is assumed, is as favourable as any, as if the edge be too acute the durability greatly decreases, and therefore some regard is also shown to the degree of wear and fatigue the iron is called upon to endure.*

The edge of the iron is likewise ground to different *forms* according to the work; thus, the jack plane is found to work more easily when the iron is rounded as an arc, so that whether it project in the center more or less than one-sixteenth of an inch, the common measure, the angles of the iron should sink down to the sole of the plane at the corners of the mouth.

The ease thus afforded appears more or less due to three causes. The rounded iron makes its first penetration more easily, as it commences as it were with a point, or very narrow edge: the iron has to penetrate the wood as a wedge, first to *cut* and then to *bend* the shaving; and it is likely that the reduction of labour in the *cutting*, by the narrow portion of the edge being employed, is greater than the increase, in *bending* a thicker but narrower shaving; and lastly, the curved iron distantly approaches the condition of the skew-iron, and in all inclined blades there is a partial sliding or saw-like motion, which is highly favourable to cutting. The irons for the finishing planes, although sharpened as flat as possible at other parts, are faintly rounded at the corners to prevent their leaving marks upon the wood.

The cutting iron having been sharpened, the top-iron is screwed fast at the required distance from the edge, say for coarse works one-sixteenth, and for fine work, one fortieth or fiftieth of an inch. The compound iron is placed in the mouth of the plane, and the eye is directed from the front along the sole, to see that it projects uniformly and the required quantity; the wedge is then put in with the right hand, and slightly tapped with the hammer. If this should by chance carry forward the iron also, a blow on the back of the plane at *h*, fig. 320, p. 477,

---

* When the minute chamfer of the plane-iron is almost parallel with the sole of the plane, it will for a short time be entirely effective. Thus, as an experiment, drive the iron a very small quantity through the sole, and sharpen it by allowing the oilstone to rub both on the edge and on the wood behind; this will produce a very accurate edge, and the iron when set back, will cut beautifully.

K K

or on the upper surface of the long planes at i, partially withdraws the iron, and in this manner, by a few slight blows on the end or either edge of the iron, and on the end of the wedge, the adjustment is readily effected. Violence should be avoided, as the wedge if overdriven might split the plane, and long before that it would distort the sole and *drive the back wood up*, which means, that the wood behind the iron would be driven so as to stand slightly in advance of that before the iron, the two parts of the sole becoming slightly discontinuous or out of line. The iron should be always so slenderly held, that one or two moderate blows would release the iron and wedge.

There is a very ingenious modification of the double iron plane,* in which the cutter is a thin unperforated blade of steel placed between a brass bed and an iron top-piece; the cutter, instead of being fixed and adjusted in the ordinary manner by taps of the hammer, is managed by the quiet action of various screws.

In a plane patented in America, in 1832, the bottom or cutting iron is made as usual, but without any mortise; the top iron has a thumb-screw at its upper end, and moves on two lateral pins or fulcrums $\frac{3}{4}$-inch from its lower edge; the pins fit into two grooved pieces of metal let into the sides of the plane, the lengths of the grooves exactly determine the situation of the top iron. When therefore the cutter is placed in its required position, the thumbscrew is turned, it bears on the upper part of the cutter, and tilts the top iron, until its lower edge also bears hard against the usual part of the cutter, and thereby fixes it without a wedge.

The main hindrances to the general employment of these constructions appear to be their increased cost, and the great dexterity with which the required adjustments are accomplished by the accustomed hand with the apparently rude, yet sufficient, means of the hammer.†

---

rounding," these partial prominences are first removed with the jack plane; but in general the shavings should be of the full length of the work, or at any rate a yard long.

The toat of the plane is held in the right hand, the front being grasped with the left hand, the thumb towards the workman; the planes require to be pressed down on the work during the cut, this is done less by an exertion of the muscles, than by slightly inclining the body, to cause its weight to rest partly upon the plane. During the return stroke, the pressure should be discontinued to avoid friction on the edge, which would be thereby rounded, and there is just an approximation to lifting the heel of the plane off the work; or in short pieces it is entirely lifted. The general attempt should be to plane the work somewhat hollow, an effect which cannot however really occur, when the plane is proportionally long and quite straight.

The sole of a long plane is in a great measure the test of the straightness of the work; thus when the rough outside has been removed with the jack-plane, the trying-plane is employed, which is set with a much finer cut, and the workman will in a great measure tell the condition of the surface by the continuity and equality of the shavings. It is however also needful to examine its accuracy with a straight-edge; the edge of the plane applied obliquely across the board is in general the primary test, but as the work approaches to perfection, the straight-edge is laid parallel with the sides of the work, and also diagonally across it; and towards the last, the work if small is raised to the level of the eye, or in large pieces, the workman stoops to attain the same relative position.

The planes being respectively in good working condition, the board to be planed is laid on the bench, and if it should be obviously higher, either at the opposite corners from being "*in winding*," or in the middle, or at the edges from being "*cast and*

---

* Invented by Mr. H. Bellingham. See Trans. Soc. of Arts, 1836, vol. li.
† The same remark applies to Mr. F. E. Franklin's Screw Bench Hook, (idem, vol. liii,) intended to supersede a or j, fig. 353, page 494.

IV - Some Museums where Planes may be seen.

Many museums are seasonal and frequently closed one day during each week. If the visiting schedule is not known, it is best to either telephone or write in advance of a trip. Any written inquiry should include a self-addressed return envelope with a postage stamp for the reply. In the advent that special information is desired regarding items in storage or records concerning the collection, it is essential to arrange an appointment with the Curator or Director since their schedules involve both daily commitments and travel.

Eighteenth Century planes may be seen in use at both the Cabinetmaker's and Cooper's Shops at Colonial Williamsburg*, Williamsburg, Va.,23185. The Dominy Shop (1760-1840) at Henry Francis du Pont Winterthur Museum,* Wintherthur,De. 19735, exhibits tools used by three generations during this period. The collection is superbly described with documentation in Charles Hummel's book: *With Hammer in Hand* [1968, available at Winterthur Museum Book Store].

Both cabinetmakers' and coopers' tools are on exhibition at Farmers' Museum*, New York State Historical Association, Cooperstown, N.Y., 13326; Old Sturbridge Village*, Sturbridge, Mass., 01566; and Mystic Seaport, Inc.*, Mystic, Ct.,06355. The latter additionally displays ship-building tools. Other museums including ship-building tools are: Bath Museum, Bath,Me., 04530 and Strawbery Banke,Inc., Portsmouth, N.H., 03841.

Exhibits of significant collections of planes may also be seen at the following museums: Pennsylvania Farm Museum of Landis Valley*, Lancaster, Pa.,17601; Bucks County Historical Society Museum*, Doylestown, Pa.,18901; Center of Science and Industry,*[Edward Durell Collection] Columbus, Oh.,43211; Colonial Valley*, Menges Mills, Pa.,17346; Delaware State Museum,*Dover, De.,19901; Hadley Farm Museum,*Hadley, Ma.,01035; Heritage Plantation of Sandwich, Sandwich,Ma.,02563; New Canaan Historical Society, New Canaan, Ct.,06840; Old Water Mill Museum, Water Mill,L.I., N.Y.,11976; Ohio Historical Society*, Columbus, Oh.,43211; San Joaquin County Historical Society,[Floyd Locher Collection] Lodi. Ca.,95240; Shelburne Museum,*Shelburne, Vt.,05482; Shaker Museum,*Old Chatham, N.Y.,12136; Sloane-Stanley Museum,*Kent, Ct.,06757; Smith's Clove,*Monroe, N.Y., 10950; Vermont Guild of Old Time Crafts and Industry, Weston,Vt.,05161.

Excellent collections of planes and other tools may be seen in Canada at Upper Canada Village, Morrisburg, Ontario and Black Creek Village, Toronto, Ontario.

There are certainly more planes in private collections than in museums. Most collectors are very willing to show their collections to interested strangers upon appointment. There are several plane collectors who are members of Early American Industries Association. Applications for Membership in this Society may be obtained from the Membership Chairman: Earl Soles, Blaikley Durfee House, Williamsburg, Va., 23185.

Photographs of some of the most outstanding exhibits of planes from collections in Museums open to the Public are shown in Figs. 104 - 111. Grateful acknowledgement is made to these Museums for supplying these photographs. Museums noted above with an * indicates their collection of planes was studied by the author.

Fig. 104. Exhibit at Delaware State Museum, Dover, De. [Photo courtesy Division of Historical and Cultural Affarirs, Hall of Records, Dover, Delaware]

Fig. 105. Cabinetmaker's Shop at Farmers Museum. New York State Historical Association. [Photo Reproduced through Courtesy NYSHA]

Fig. 106. Cabinetmaker's Shop at Pennsylvania Farm Museum of Landis Valley, Lancaster, Pa. [Photo courtesy of Penn. Historical and Museum Commission]

Fig. 107. Cabinetmaker's Shop at Old Sturbridge Village, Sturbridge, Mass. [Old Sturbridge Village Photo by Donald F. Eaton, photographer.]

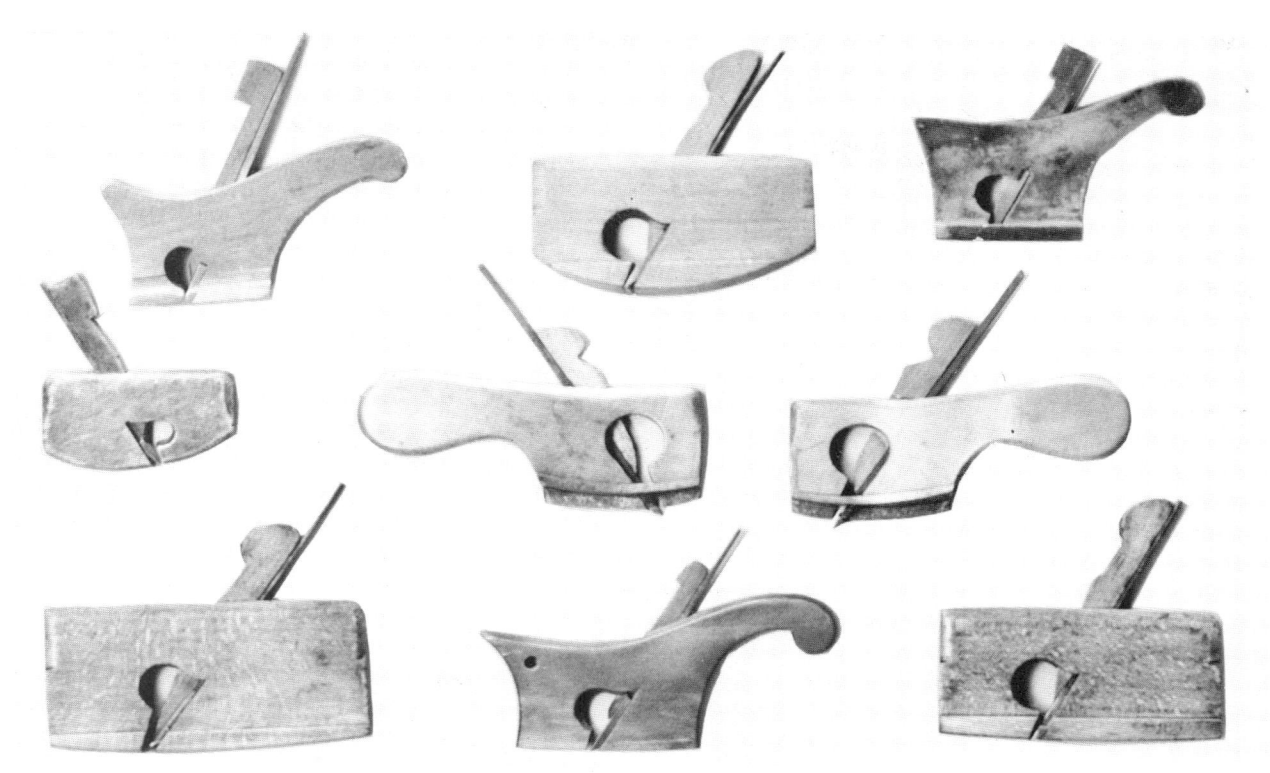

Fig. 108. Carriagemaker's Planes at Heritage Plantation of Sandwich, Sandwich, Mass. [Photo Courtesy of Heritage Plantation of Sandwich]

Fig. 109. Shipmaker's Plane Exhibit at Mystic Seaport Inc. Mystic, Conn. [Photo courtesy of William Downes]

Fig. 110. Exhibit at Sloane-Stanley Museum, Kent, Conn. [Photo courtesy of Sloane-Stanley Museum and Connecticut Historical Commision, Hartford, Conn.]

Fig. 111. Exhibit at Shelburne Museum, Shelburne, Vt. [Photo courtesy of Shelburne Museum] This is an outstanding collection of tools excellently displayed.

Fig. 112. Plane Exhibit. Peter Lowd House. Photo Courtesy Strawbery Banke, Inc.

The recently restored Peter Lowd House at Strawbery Banke historic preservation, Portsmouth, New Hampshire is exclusively devoted to exhibiting 18th and 19th century tools. These are principally related to woodworking trades; carpenter and joiner; cooper, shipwright and boat builder and cabinetmaker. These were all important trades at Portmouth. A nostalgic atmosphere exists at Peter Lowd, living there in 1833, was a cooper.

There are over 200 tools with identifying labels, grouped according to uses, shown in 15 cases with attractive varieties of colored backgrounds. The high legible lettering of the labels provides clarity and real meaning for the average visitor. The collection is supplemented by attractively produced silk screened illustrations from advertisements and directories.

The majority of tools are from the Garland W. Patch Collection, now belonging to Strawbery Banke, but augmented from other sources. An exhibit of three generations of Portsmouth woodworkers - Daniel Thurston (1776-1855, Samuel Kingsbury (1793-1880) and Samuel H. Kingsbury (1833-1917) provides both continuance and added items over a century of craftsmanship. This includes a receipt of sale of a number of Thurston's tools to his son-in-law, Kingsbury, in 1827 for $57.55. There is also an outstanding exhibit of boatbuilding.

A visit to Strawbery Banke is highly recommended. This will most certainly provide ideas as to how tools can be attractively shown. In my opinion this pleasing and informative display is the foremost woodworking tool exhibit to be seen in any non-profit museum in United States.

Preface to the Supplement and Second Edition

Approximately 1350 copies of the first edition were published. In spite of some rather carping and negative reviews from persons who might otherwise have constructively assisted, the book sold out in less than two years. Fortunately there were many favorable reviews and support from libraries, museums, historical societies, and enthusiastic response from the collectors.

In my opinion if such a text is to be informative and serviceable to its readers, it is essential to include numerous, clear, definitive and large photographs. Unfortunately, the increases in costs are proportional to the number published. This is the economic reason that very few commercially published books on such limited interest subjects contain so few photographic illustrations. Liberal use of photographs was accomplished in the first edition. In order to hold other expenses to a minimum I chose to present the text using an IBM selectric typewriter, rather than the more expensive type-set arrangement. Unfortunately due to my lack of professional training and pressure to meet a deadline, numerous typographical errors resulted. For this inconvenience I sincerely apologize. Hopefully an improvement has been achieved in this second edition. Type-setting does not always eliminate errors as noted in a recent book concerned with the same subject at this.

Admittedly being the author, editor and publisher is not a good arrangement. In order to save costs I have published my books without any professional counsel with my own design and layout. Unless a person has undertaken such a project, it is difficult to appreciate the exhausting, time comsuming problems and anxiety accompanying such a publication. A large prominant publisher, after considerable study of this book, stated that if they had produced it, the price would have to be twice mine. The point is that had I not made these efforts, it is very doubtful that this book would have ever been available with this detailed photographic presentation. It was indeed a very gratifying experience to receive so many letters of appreciation noting that this study had assisted collectors in organizing and assembling their planes to more meaningful significance.

It seems incredible how much information has been brought to my attention and has come to light by many scholarly collectors since the first edition. Through these encouragements, this supplement and second edition is now being offered, again with liberal photographic and documentary presentation. It is hoped that my continued original researches, together with material from many acknowledged collectors will provide new insights to this study. Much study remains to be made concerning American planemaking, particularly during the late 18th and early 19th Centuries. It is doubtful whether all this developments will be fully unraveled, but piece by piece collectors studying these artifacts bring to surface new information. The great variety of styles and innovations and designs achieved by these American craftsmen makes this a facinating study constantly revealing efforts "to build a beter mousetrap".

Indeed it would have been much easier for the reader of this second edition if I had entirely revised the text, presenting the new material in chronological sequence. However, it was not economically possible for me to undertake this task. It has been a great pleasure to share information, discuss and correspond matters concerning planes with many friends and fellow collectors. Throughout the text I have acknowledged these many contributions. Addtionally I would like to thank William L. Goodman for answering numerous questions and offering suggestions. Also thanks to my wife, Jane, for printing assistances, as well as counsel.

Kenneth D. Roberts   January 31, 1978

Chapter VI

New Insights into 18th Century Planemaking

Indeed it is difficult to report significant data about 18th Century planemakers without undertaking time-comsuming research and studies of local history and genealogical sources. Since much of the activity occurred in New England and other eastern states, this limits such historical studies to persons who can visit the scenes. It is almost impossible to obtain pertinent land deed records and wills from probate through correspondence. These craftsmen were so busy earning a living and for the most part unaware to their contributions very little significant records of their activities were recorded. Only scraps of information about them survive. Fortunately there are a few dedicated scholars who after time-consuming research dig out some facts and with educated guesses are able to relate an intelligent presentation. Gradually a realistic account develops from their work.

Unquestionably this subject is of great interest to many collectors and antiquarians. Many of the planes used by furniture makers, for moulding interiors in houses and other architectural applications originated from these craftsmen. There was considerable variation in sizes and shapes of the plane bodies, wedges and totes. Real artistic crafstmenship in in evidence. These distinguishing characteristics enable the collector to readily identify such planes as 18th Century manufacture, or at least early 19th. The shape of a wedge is often a clue. Fig. 1 (page 9) illustrates several 18th Century planes; several more are shown in Figs. 125 & 126. Plate XXXIII shows several tracing of wedges from the mid-18th through the late 19th Centuries.

Donald and Anne Wing, who wrote all of Chapter I, have graciously submitted the following update report of their continued studies since publishing the 1st Edition. A revision of Table I on page 14 includes some added working dates as well as the Northampton, Massachusetts planemaker, Benjamin Alford Edwards (b.1757, d.1822).

"Joseph Fuller of Providence, Rhode Island, can now be dated with certainty. He died on 6 May 1822 and in his estate inventory many tools are listed.[1] In the Providence *Gazette* of 18 May appears a notice of an auction of Fuller's "furniture, tools, and stock of a tool maker's shop."[2]

Fuller was born on 3 May in Lisbon, Connecticut (near Norwich)[3] and the date of his move to Providence is yet unknown, although he was a charter member of the Providence Association of Mechanics and Manufacturers in 1789. In his will, dated in Providence on 3 Novemeber 1821, he left a quarter of his estate to his adopted son, Joseph.[4] Apparently this is the man who is listed in the business directories as a blockmaker to the 1830's.

Also interesting are the close ties bewteen the Fullers and the Fields. The plane maker's son was named Joseph Field until his adoption,[5] and many Fields appear in the will. In the directory of 1841-42, the addresses given for Joseph Fuller (the son) and Isaac Field, another plane maker, are the same. More research should disclose the exact relationship here.

The will and estate inventory of Henry Wetherel have come to light also. His will, dated 20 December 1793 in Chatham, Connecticut, leaves to his son Henry his "blacksmith shoop [sic] and all my stock and tools relative to my trade in the different branches of it."[6] The inventory is dated 24 February 1797, indicating that he died shortly before that date. It is quite detailed but does not include any great number of planes, or any specific plane makers' tools such as floats or mother planes. In the types of woods that are listed, beech and birch, certainly the most commonly used for planes, are noticeably absent.[7]

It is our conclusion that Henry, Senior, who married in 1760 and made planes in Norton, Massachusetts, moved to Chatham sometime before 1790 and apparently made very few planes there, to judge from the scarcity of one -1 Chatham planes. Many planes with the two -11 stamp (we assume the son) have strong British characteristics, while others are questionable as to nationality; and so we believe that son Henry imported British planes and probably also manufactured some.

Plane maker B.A. Edwards of Northampton, Massachusetts, has been dated as being born in 1757 and dying in 1822. The will and inventory of Benjamin Alvord Edwards do not specify a plane makers, but he is the only B.A. Edwards in Northampton at the correct period.[8]

Some new clues relative to E. Briggs in Keene, New Hampshire have emerged. Two brothers, Elisha (m.1758, d.1803) and Eliphalet (b.1713, d.1780) Briggs moved with other settlers from the Wrentham-Norton (Mass.) area to Keene in the 1760's. Both were joiners. Elisha's son by the same name lived from 1774-1801, with little recorded information on him. Eliphalet's son, Eliphalet, lived from 1734-1776. His son by the same name was a cabinet maker and lived from 1765-1827. His sons, in turn, were also cabinet and chair makers.

Thus there are a good many possibilities for the plane maker among the various Elishas and Eliphalets. Since the planes with the E.Briggs in Keen stamp are definitely of 18th-century appearance, and since the word "in" is characteristic of the Rhode Island and southeastern Massachusetts are, it seems nearly ceratin that one among these men was the plane maker.[9] " (end of report by the Wings)

A recent interesting speculation suggests that the adjustable plow plane with thumbscrews for locking the fence arms through the body may have been a New England innovation.[10] The conventional English practice was with sliding wedge locks (keys) mortised into the side. The thumbscrews from the top were probably introduced about the turn of the 19th Century, or slightly earlier. This raises the question was the plow with screw arms and locking nuts also an innovation originating in New England? It appears that screw arm plows first appeared in New England between 1822 and 1838.[11] These were however made as late as 1872, see Note, Fig. 114, page 194.

191

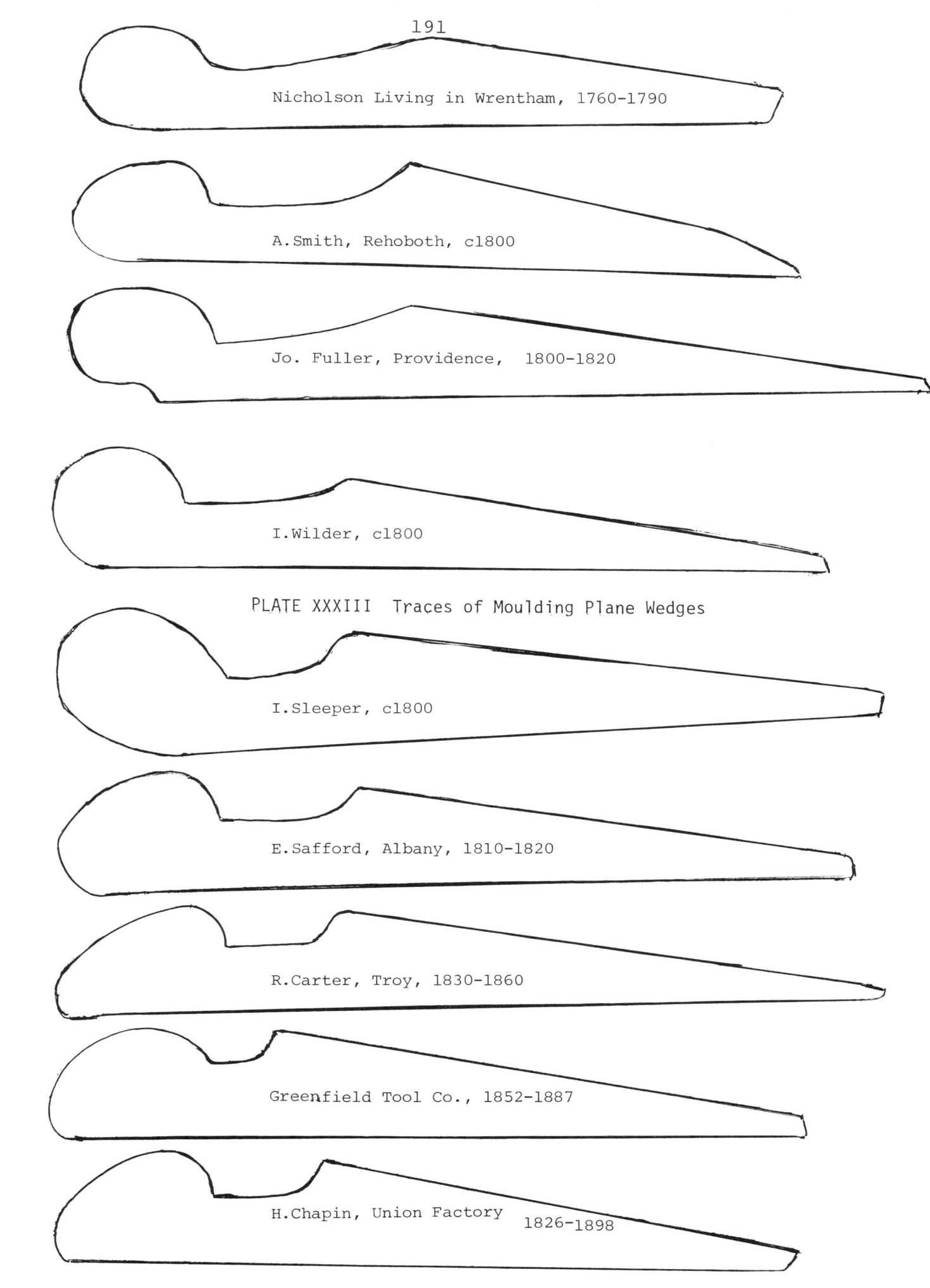

Nicholson Living in Wrentham, 1760-1790

A. Smith, Rehoboth, c1800

Jo. Fuller, Providence, 1800-1820

I. Wilder, c1800

PLATE XXXIII   Traces of Moulding Plane Wedges

I. Sleeper, c1800

E. Safford, Albany, 1810-1820

R. Carter, Troy, 1830-1860

Greenfield Tool Co., 1852-1887

H. Chapin, Union Factory   1826-1898

W.L. Goodman reports "screwed staves (fence arms) with wooden nuts . . . with 16th-century ploughs at Dresden"[12] However he points out that the essential difference between Continental and English plows was that the latter had arms attached to the fence (also American practice) while the former always had the arms attached to the plane body. Holtzapffel refers to screw arm plows as "German" (see p.175, which is page 486 Holtzapffel); whereas R.A. Salaman refers to these as "French or Screw-Stem Plough".[13] In United States the handled plow with screw arms was sometimes called "Empire Plow".[14] In any event the adjustable screw arm plow became the favorite in United States after 1850.

Those plane collectors who are particularly interested in history, design, patents, manufacturing, and other aspects of this tool may join the recently organized British-American Rykenological Society, known as B-ARS.[15] Their Bulletin, *PLANE TALK*, contains many interesting exchanges of information on a variety of plane subjects.

Perhaps the best manner to become familiar with 18th Century American planes is to study private and museum collections. To assist those whose locations make this difficult a liberal presentation of photographs of many different types of these planes follows in this Chapter. Unless otherwise mentioned all of these planes are in my own collection.

Fig. 113. 18th Century
Crown Moulding Plane
  Imprint: I.Walton/ IN READING   Photo: Courtesy of Museum of Our National Heritage Collection of Lexington Historical Society

NOTES - CHAPTER VI

1. Inventory of the Estate of Joseph Fuller, Providence City Hall, Providence, RI, Probate Records, #A-4698.
2. William H. Fuller, *Genealogy of Some Descendants of John Fuller of Ipswich* [Palmer. MA, 1914], p.232
3. *Ibid*
4. Will of Joseph Fuller, Providence City Hall, Providence, RI, Probate Records, v.13, p.111
5. William H. Fuller, *op. cit.*, p.111
6. Will of Henry Wetherel, Connecticut State Library, Hartford, CT, Probate Records, #339
7. Inventory of the Estate of Henry Wetherel, Connecticut State Library, Hartford, CT Probate Records, #340. Note: Further details on the Wetherels are to be found in *Plane Talk* [Bulletin of the British-American Rykenological Society], v.1, no.4, December 1976, p.3-4.
8. John S. Kebabian, *Chronicle of EAIA*, v.29, No.1, March 1976, p.14
9. John S. Kebabian and Richard S. Martin, "E. Briggs in Keen", seperate articles, *Plane Talk*, Bulletin of B-ARS, v.II, No.1, Spring 1977, p.2-3
10. R.D. Graham, jr., "The Yankee Plow?", article to be published in *Plane Talk*.
11. The earliest known price list of planes is that of D.& M. Copeland, Hartford, CT thought to be c.1822. This did not mention plows regulated by screw arms. The 1838 Price List of Collins of Ravena, OH noted screw arm plows. Emanual W. Carpenter of Lancaster, Pa. was granted patent No. 594, dated Feb.6, 1838 - Method of Constructing the Screw Arms for All Kinds of Planes Regulated with Screw Arms.
12. W.L. Goodman, *The History of Woodworking Tools*, [London, 1964], p. 108
13. R.A. Salaman, *Dictionary of Tools*, [London, 1975], p.346
14. *Illustrated Supplement to the Catalog . . . Bench Plane, Moulding Tools, Manufactured by the Arrowmammett Works*, [Middletown, CT; 1857], p. 11 Reprinted 1976 by Ken Roberts Publishing Co. See item No. 129 on page 6 of the Invoice List reproduced on page 143 this book.
15. The address of the Secretary of B-ARS, E.M. Sayward is 60 Harvest Lane, Levittown, N.Y. 11756.

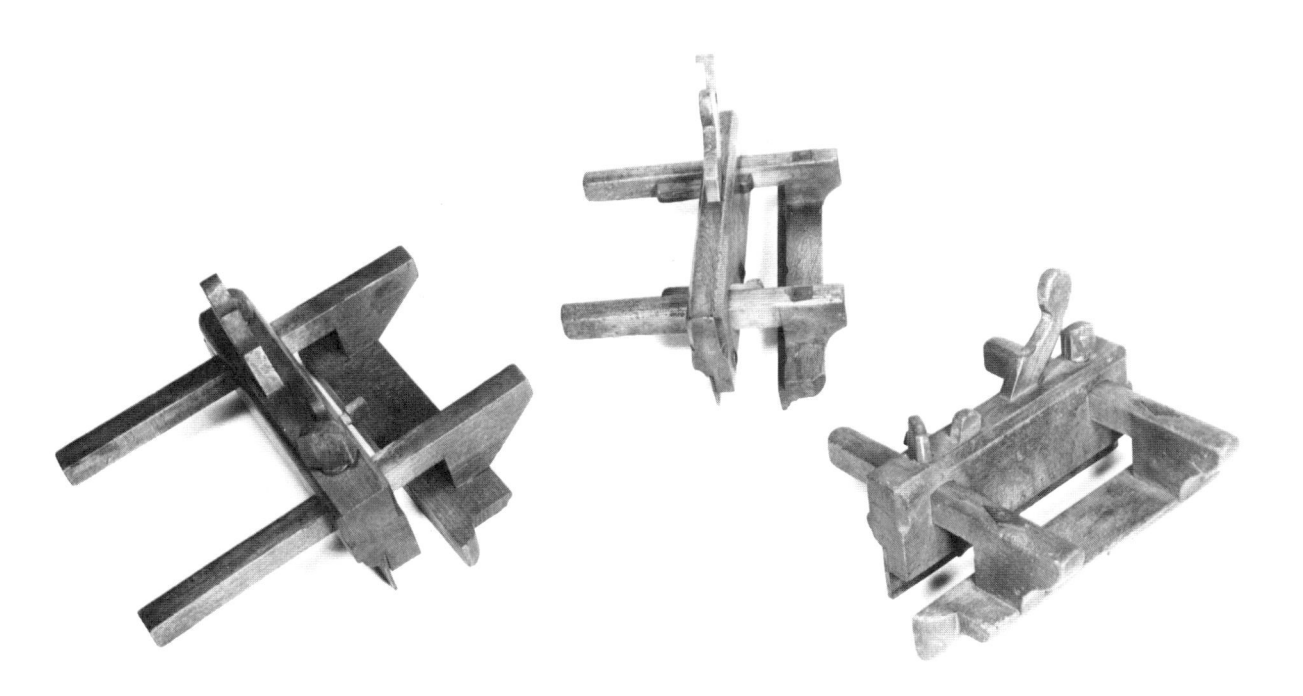

Fig. 114. 18th Century Plow Planes. Note: Although such slide arm plows with screw stops are generally early, 12 varities of these were offered by Greenfield Tool Co. (items $497-#508) *1872 Illustrated Catalogue of Joiners' Bench Planes and Moulding Tools*.

Fig. 115. Crown Moulding Planes - 18th Century
Left: 3-1/2" x 13"; Right: 4" x 13-1/2"

Fig. 116. 18th Century Bench Planes: Front to Back: 13-1/2" Jack; 22" Fore by I.Day; 30" Jointer by I.Day; 33" Long Jointer

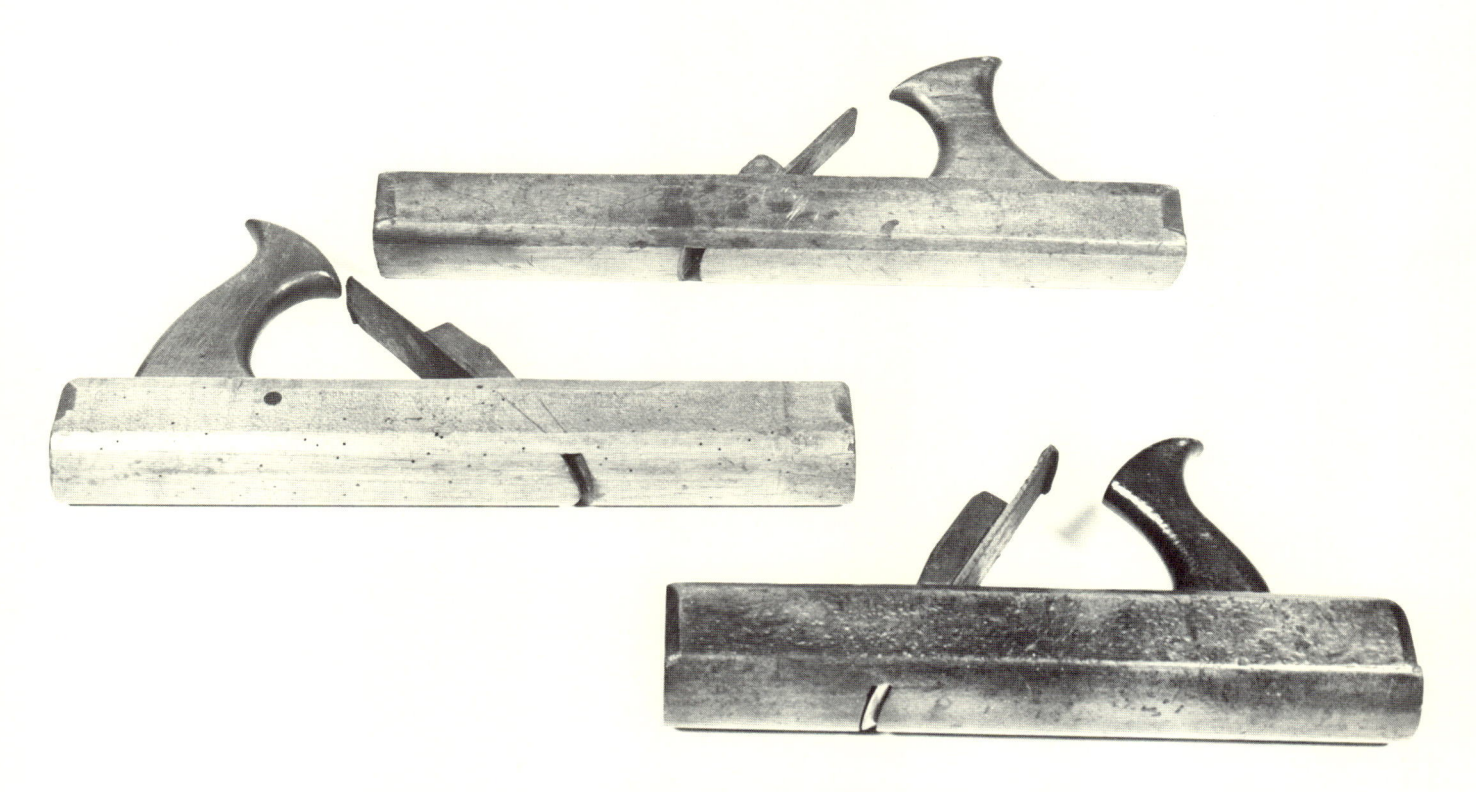

Fig. 117. 18th Century Bench Planes: Front to Back: 12" Gutter by Mutter, c.1791 London, England; 14-1/2" American Gutter; and 16-1/2" Jack.

Fig. 118. Early 2½"x14" Moulding Plane with Fence by WOOTHOUDT.
Photograph by William A. Downes

Fig. 119. 13-3/4" Tiger Maple Handled Moulding Plane (rear)
12-34" 18th Century Sash Plane (front)

Fig. 120. 18th Century 2¼"x14" Raising Plane by John Taber.

Fig. 121. Early Raising Plane 3-3/4"x14" Note: Iron Brackets and Wing Nuts.

Fig. 122. Halving Planes. Front: 10½" 18th Century with Tote
Back: 19th Century. H.Chapin UNION FACTORY; Moulding Plane Size.
[For description of halving planes; see page 104]

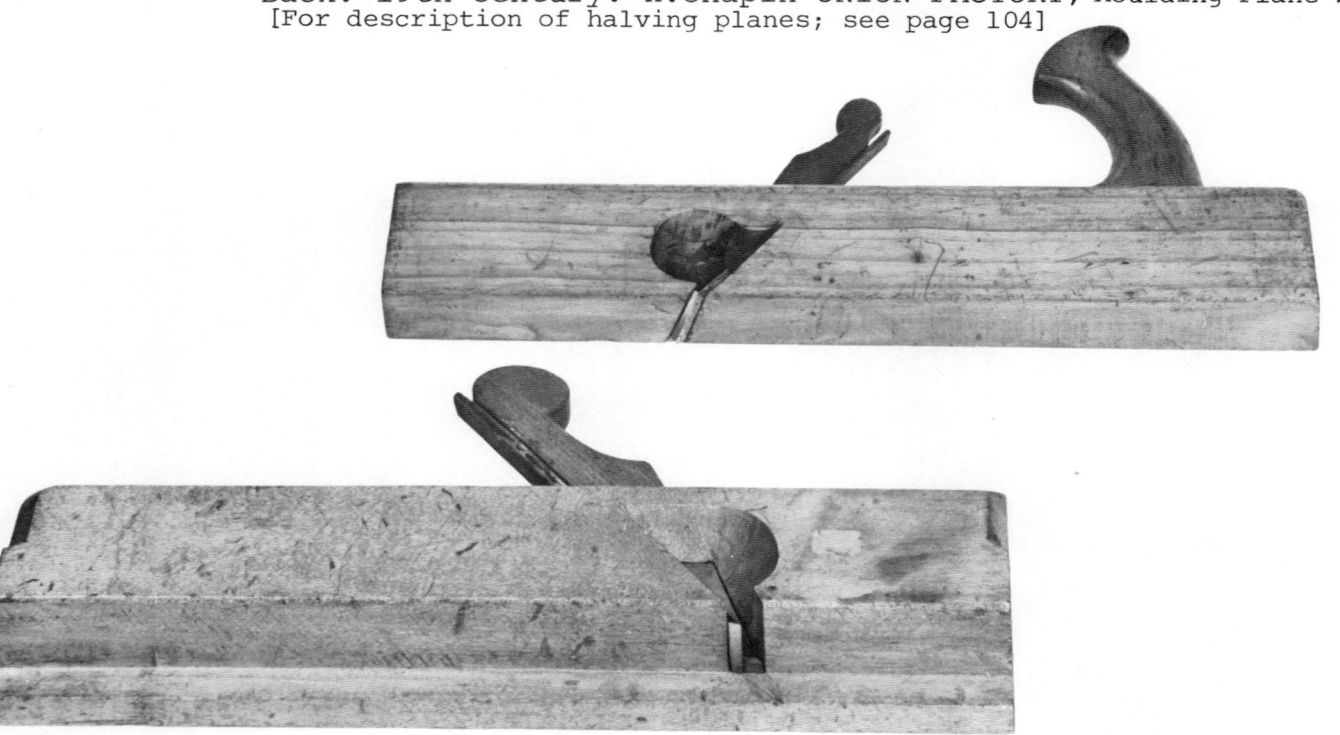

Fig. 123. 18th Century Rabbet Planes. Front: 1-1/2"x15" Square Iron
Back: 1-1/4"x15", skew iron.

Fig. 124 A.
Early Moving Filletster

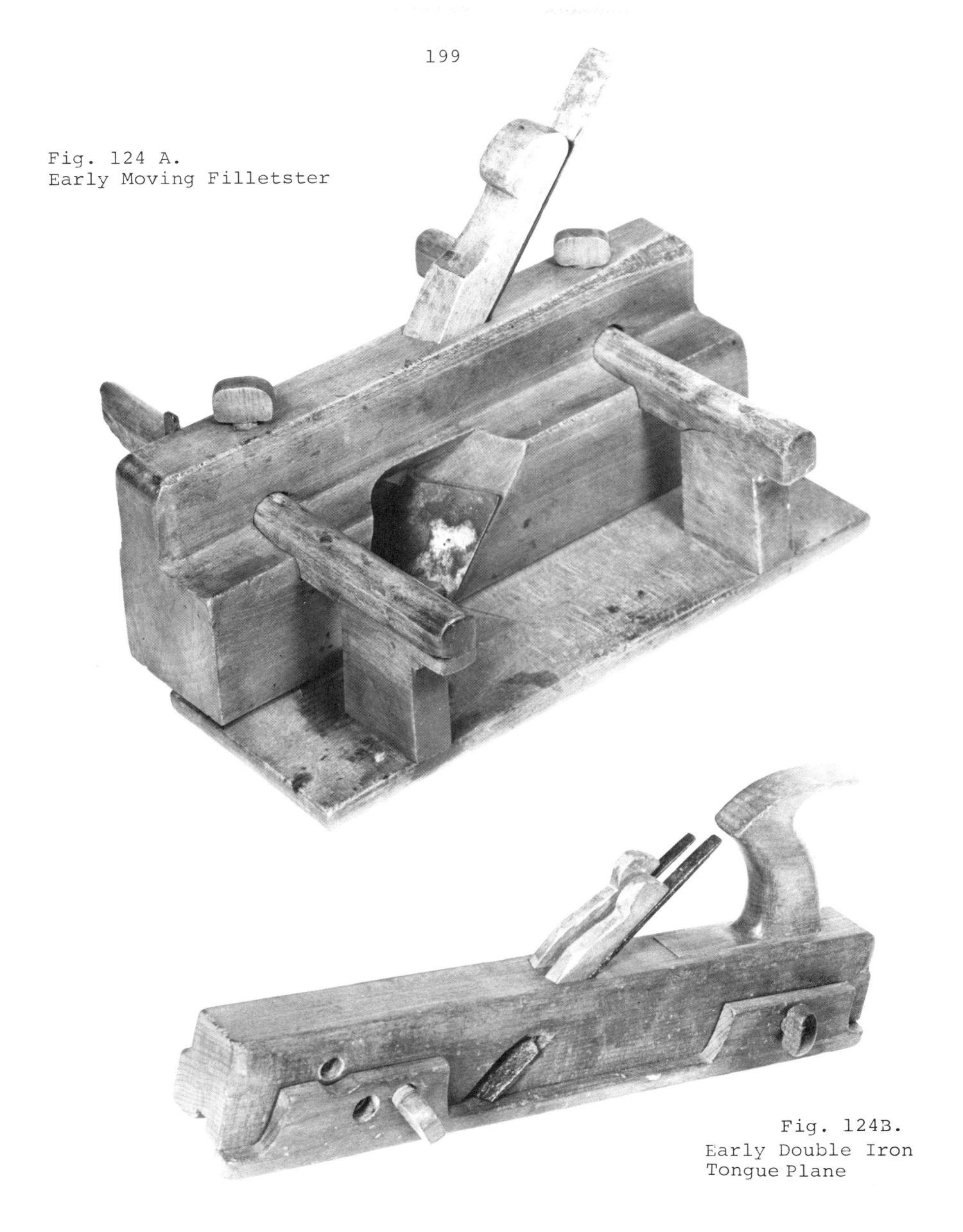

Fig. 124B.
Early Double Iron
Tongue Plane

Fig. 125 A. 18th Century Moulding Planes: Top: Pair of Tounge & Groove Plane by Sleeper; Bottom: Jn.Tower [left]; I.Wilder [right]

Fig. 125 B. 18th Century Moulding Planes: Top: Unknown Maker [left]; A.Smith [right] Bottom: F.Nicholson [left]; Unknown Maker [right]

Chapter VII

More About 19th Century Planemaking

Commercial planemaking was a relatively small operation previous to 1850. This chapter will relate some facts with illustrated examples about such a business conducted by a rather obscure planemaker, Joseph R. Tolman at Hanover, Massachusetts. This will be followed by some details concerning Leonard Bailey, his business in Boston and the development of the transitional planes. A price list of Kellogg's Bench and Moulding Planes and notices by the Greenfield Tool Co. are reproduced. The subject will be continued and chronologically presented in Chapter VIII relating the tenure of the Sandusky Tool Co.

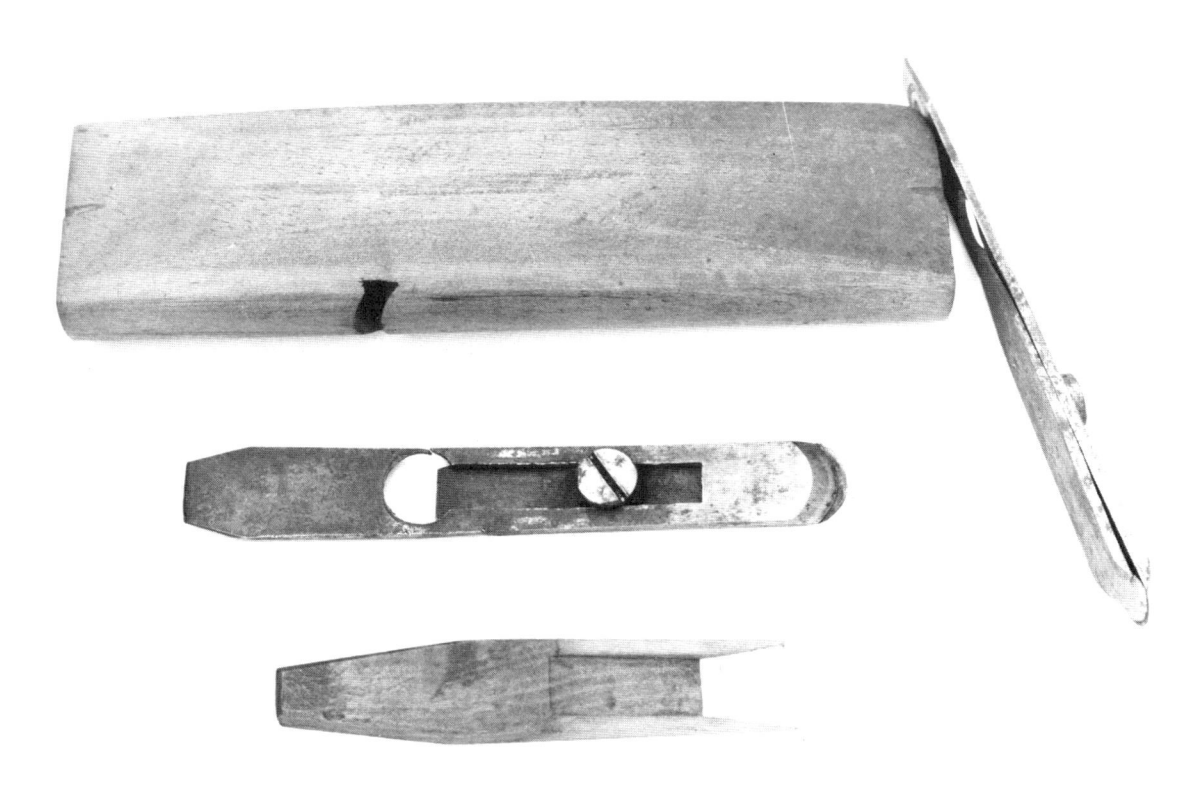

Fig. 126. Double Iron Round Plane by J.R.Tolman (9-3/8" long)

Most commercial planemakers by the middle third of the 19th Century followed conventional standards of sizes and shapes of planes. An exception was Joseph R. Tolman, who is believed to have first made planes at South Scituate, Massachusetts just before 1820.[1] While he is listed in the *Boston Almanac* for 1841 only at 115 Commercial Street, all imprints yet reported are J.R.Tolman/Hanover,Mass. While the majority of his spar, hollowing and rounding planes are the standard 9-3/8 inches in length, these usually have double irons and wedges similar to bench planes, as seen in Fig. 126 above.

Fig.127. Three Pairs of Hollowing and Rounding Planes by J.R.Tolman. Note the pronounced chamfer along the edges, probably for in-close work.

Fig.128. Fifteen Spar Planes. All with Double Irons.

All of the spar planes shown in Fig. 128 but one have the imprint of J.R.Tolman/Hanover,Mass. The other has imprint T.J.Tolman/Hanover,Mass., his son, who is believed to have taken over his father's business after his death in 1864. The fact that so many J.R.Tolman planes found are of the spar type strongly suggests that he specialized in making planes for shipbuilders. This was certainly extensively carried out in this area.

Fig. 129. Three Conventional Smoothing Planes and a 2¼" x 16" Razee Plane, all by J.R.Tolman, Hanover, Massachusetts.

Fig. 130 Double Iron Compass Rabbet and Hollowing Planes by J.R.Tolman

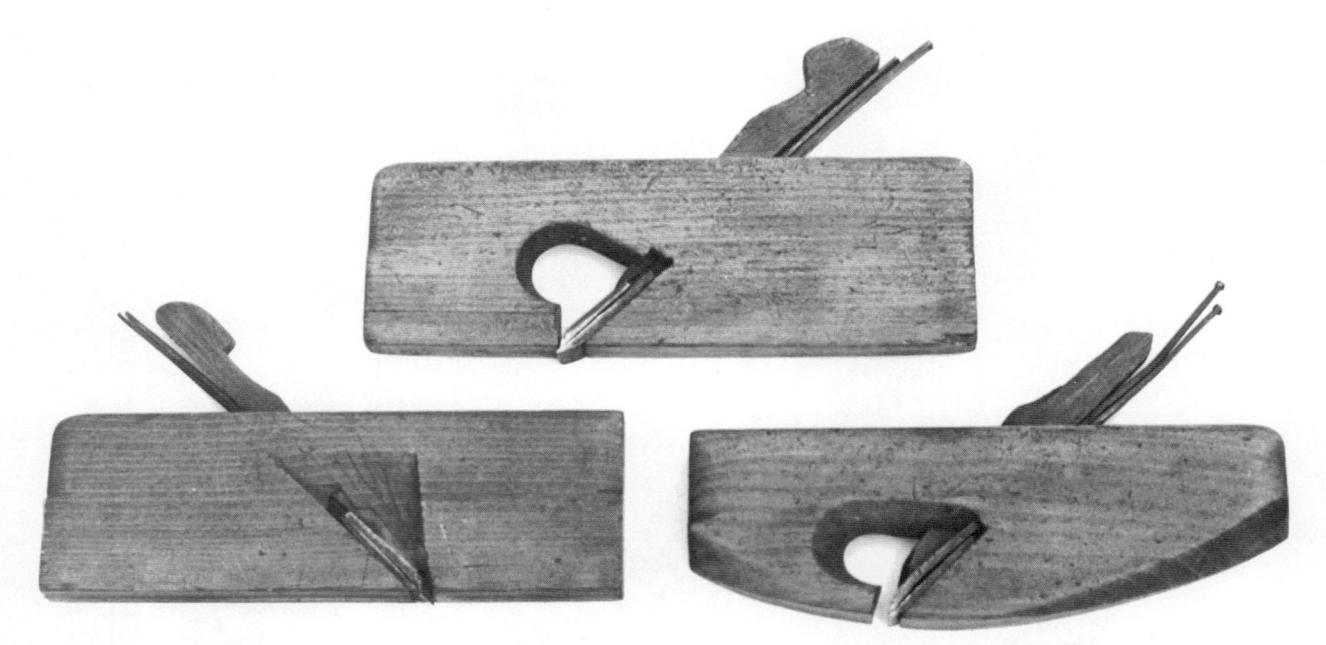

Fig. 131. Double Iron Planes by J.R.Tolman, Hanover, Massachusetts.
Top: Straight Rabbet. Lower right: Compass Rabbet, note
Chamfer for working around corners. Lower left: Center Bead.

Fig. 132. Two Bead Planes by J.R.Tolman, Hanover, Massachusetts.
Note the manner in which the side of the plane at the lower
left is cut away for chip removal. (Also   same on center bead
plane shown at lower left of Fig. 131.

Grateful acknowledgement is made to William A. Downes for making the photographs
of the Tolman Planes for Figs. 126 - 136.[except No. No.132 & No. 135]

Fig. 133. Rabbet Planes by J.R.Tolman, Hanover, Massachusetts.
Top: conventional 9-3/8" length, but with brass plate sole.
Plane at extreme right is 22" length. All double irons,1" wide.

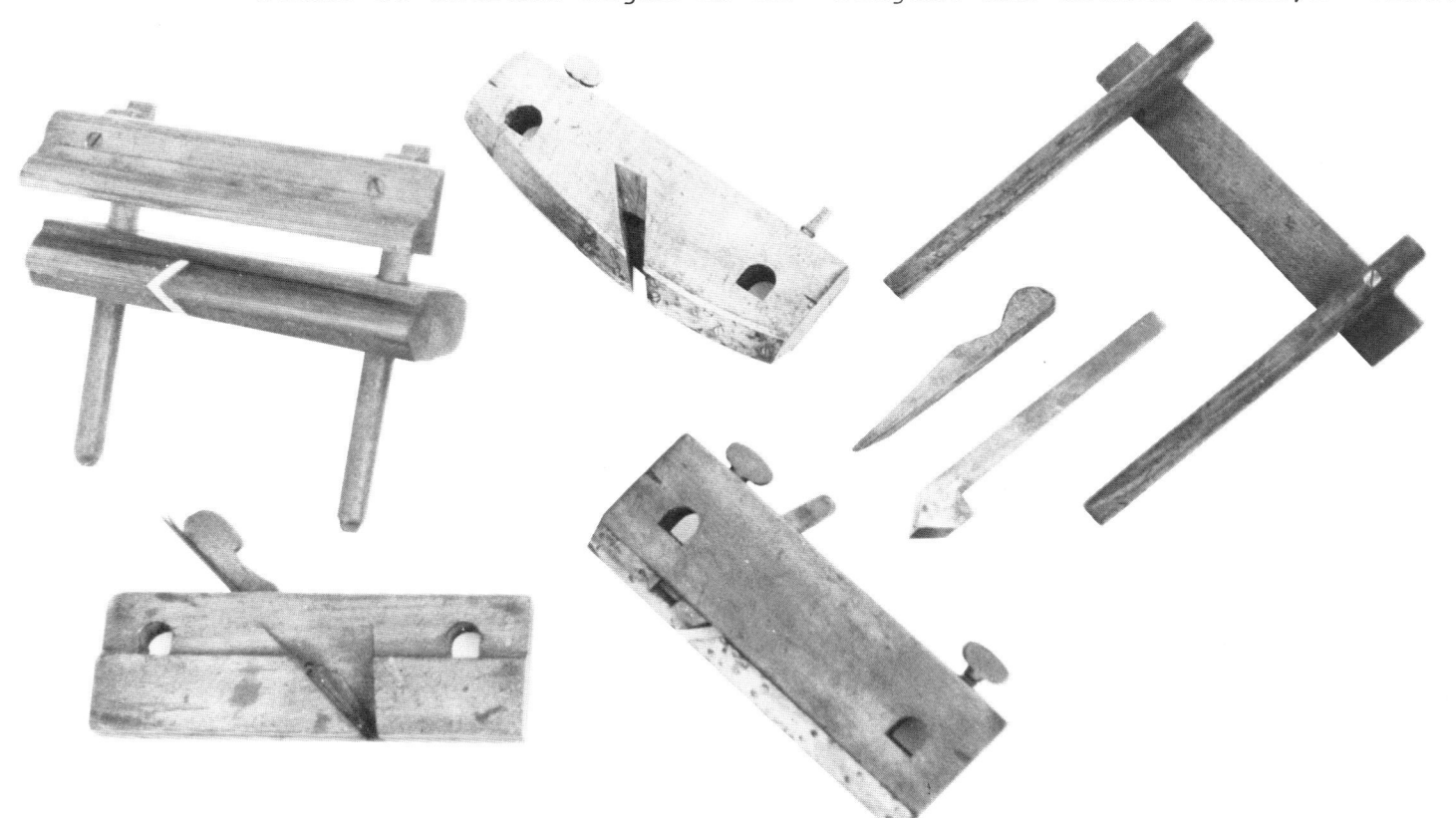

Fig. 134. Unique V-Grooved Plow Planes by J.R.Tolman, Hanover, Mass.
The lower center is a V-groove straight plane with metal plated sole; the upper center is a V-groove compass plane.also with metal sole. Both planes use the same common fence, wedge and iron shown in the upper right. The bead plane with double irons shown at the lower left also uses this fence. At the upper left is shown another V-groove plow with a boxwood wear strip dovetailed into the sole.

The obvious advantage of the double irons in these Tolman planes is a smoother finish results as a consequence of less chatter. Indeed it is very uncommon to find double iron moulding planes. A U.S.Letters Patent was awarded to T.J.Tolman on January 13,1857(#16412) for a Bench Plane. The drawing accompanying this patent showed a double iron square rabbet plane having an adjustable front piece on the sole in front of the iron in order to regulate the spacing. His claim was that this feature would produce "much smoother and nicer work". No mention was made of the double iron, which certainly contributed to this claim.

As part of their apprenticeship shipbuilders were taught to make their own planes. It is for this reason that many of the razee jacks, frequently made from lignum vitae, only bear an owner's name. A group of four 2¼" x 16" unmarked as to maker are shown in Fig. 135.

Fig. 135. A Group of 2¼" x 16" RazeeJack Planes. Top three are all lignum vitae. Bottom is beech, but a strip of lignum vitae has been glued to the sole Lignum vitae has superior wearing characteristics.

While on the subject of shipbuilder's planes, a unique adjustable sole compass plane made from an ordinary smoothing plane is shown in Fig. 136. A slot was cut above the sole from each end. Brass plates were inserted in the sole in order that it could be drawn upward through limited arc by tightening screws. This plane is obviously not factory made, but by some craftsman to suit his own needs. The stock appears to be sycamore and the wedge cherry. A somewhat similar wooden compass plane has been described by Richard Starr.[2]

Figure 136. Wood Adjustable Compass Plane. 9" long x 1-3/4" width.

Fig.137. Transitional Planes of T.D.Worrall's Patent. 8½" Smoothing Plane and 16" Jack by Lowell Plane & Tool Co., c.1856

The earliest of the so-called "transitional" planes (wood bottom) with cast iron superstructure; note page 51) were of types shown in Fig. 137. Both of these had irons stamped Multiform Moulding Plane Co., Boston, Mass. Note that the smoothing plane shown above has a knob and the front structure is slightly different than that of Fig.7, page 53.

PRICE LIST

OF

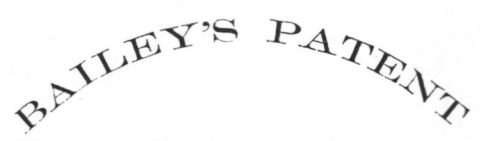

BAILEY'S PATENT

IRON AND WOOD

BENCH PLANES,

VENEER SCRAPERS AND SPOKE SHAVES.

MANUFACTURED BY

BAILEY, CHANY & CO.

No. 55 CAUSEWAY ST.,

Corner Lancaster,   Entrance, 40 Lancaster Street,

BOSTON, MASS.

IRON SPOKE SHAVES.

No.		Price per dozen.
1.	Patent Double Iron, Raised Handle	$6.00
2.	Patent Double Iron, Straight Handle	6 00
3.	Patent Adjustable, Raised Handle	7 00
4.	Patent Adjustable, Straight Handle	7.00
5.	Model Double Iron, Hollow Face	7.00
6.	Coopers' Spoke Shave, (Heavy)	13 00
6½.	Coopers' Spoke Shave, (Heavy), 4 inch cutter	15.00
7.	Coopers' Spoke Shave, (Light)	7.00
8.	Model Double Iron Shave	5.00
9.	Single Iron Shave, New Style	6.00
10.	Double Cutter, Hollow and Straight	7 00
11.	Patent Adjustable, New Style	7.50
12.	Scraper Spoke Shave	6.00

TRADE DISCOUNT,   20 PER CENT.
ON ORDERS EXCEEDING $100,   25 "

steel, of equal thickness throughout, tempered and ground by an improved process. We warrant it superior to any Plane Iron in the market. Each Plane is fitted in working order, and cannot fail to give entire satisfaction. Our improvements are all patented, the latest bearing dates of August 6th and December 24th, 1867.

BAILEY, CHANY & CO.

Plate XXXIV [First Half] Bailey, Chany & Co. Price List, c.1868
(From the Collection of Bob Ashcroft)

The next transitional planes were made by Leonard Bailey at Boston. (see page 52) According to Boston Directories Bailey formed a partnership with Jacob Chany, noted in the 1868 *Boston City Directory* as Bailey, Chany & Co.: "Planes and Spokeshaves" at 73 Haverill Street. However in the *Boston Business Directory* of 1868 they are noted at 57 Causeway making iron and wood planes, and in the 1869 at 55 Causeway. The partnership must have dissolved in 1869, as on May 19th that year, he signed an agreement with Stanley Rule & Level Co. for use of his patents. He then moved to New Britain to assume the position of superintendent at their factory. Apparently by error the firm Bailey, Chany & Co. was listed in the *New England Cities Business Directory* and *Boston Business Directory*, but not in *Boston City Directory* of 1870, at 55 Causeway, Boston. A four page price list of Bailey, Chany & Co. is shown as Plate XXXIV. This is not dated, but assumed to be 1868 or 1869. This indicated that transitional planes were made at Boston of the same sizes and prices as listed in the 1870 *Stanley Rule & Level Co. 1870 Price List* (see Plate XI, page 56). In the latter catalog the digit 2 has been placed before the Wood Planes #1-9 and a 3 before #10-14.

IRON PLANES.

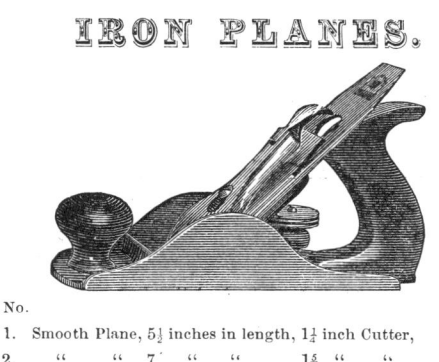

No.						Each.
1.	Smooth Plane, 5½ inches in length, 1¼ inch Cutter,					$5.00
2.	"	" 7 " "	1⅝ " "			6.00
3.	"	" 8 " "	1¾ " "			6.50
4.	"	" 9 " "	2 " "			7.00
5.	Jack	" 14 " "	2 " "			7.50
6.	Fore	" 18 " "	2⅜ " "			9.00
7.	Jointer,	" 22 " "	2⅜ " "			10.00
8.	"	" 24 " "	2⅝ " "			11.00
9.	Block	" 10 " "	2 " "			12.00
10.	Carriage Makers' Rabbet Plane, 14 inches in length, 2⅛ inch cutter,					7.50
11.	Belt Makers' Plane, 2⅜ inch cutter,					6.50
12.	Veneer Scraper, 3 inch cutter,					6.50

TRADE DISCOUNT, 10 PER CENT.
ON ORDERS EXCEEDING $100, 15 "

These tools meet with universal approbation from the best mechanics. For beauty of style and finish they are unequalled, and the great convenience in operating renders them the cheapest planes in use; they are *self-adjusting* in every respect, and each part, being made interchangeable, can be replaced at trifling expense. Both the Iron and Wood Planes are entirely independent

WOOD PLANES.

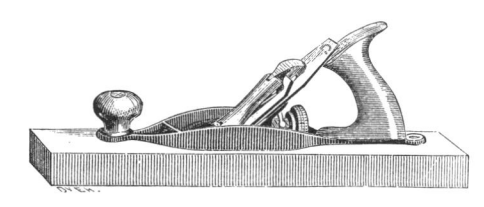

No.						Each.
1.	Smooth Plane, 7 inches in length, 1¾ inch cutter,					$3.00
2.	"	" 8 " "	1¾ " "			3 00
3.	"	" 9 " "	1¾ " "			3.00
4.	"	" 8 " "	2 " "			3 00
5.	Block	" 9½ " "	1¾ " "			3.00
6.	Jack	" 15 " "	2 " "			4.00
7.	"	" 15 " "	2¼ " "			4.00
8.	Fore	" 18 " "	2⅜ " "			4 50
9.	"	" 20 " "	2⅜ " "			4.50
10.	Jointer,	" 22 " "	2⅜ " "			4.75
11.	"	" 24 " "	2⅜ " "			4.75
12.	"	" 26 " "	2⅝ " "			5.50
13.	"	" 28 " "	2⅝ " "			5 50
14.	"	" 30 " "	2⅝ " "			5.75

TRADE DISCOUNT, 15 PER CENT.
ON ORDERS EXCEEDING $100, 20 "

in themselves, requiring neither hammer, screw-driver, nor wrench, to remove, replace or adjust the cutter Without removing the plane from the work, or either hand from the plane, by simply turning a screw, the cutter is adjusted to any thickness of shaving desired. We call particular attention to our new Patent Plane Iron, manufactured by us from the very best cast

Plate XXXIV [Second Half] Bailey, Chany & Co. Price list, c. 1868

LEONARD BAILEY,
Manufacturer of 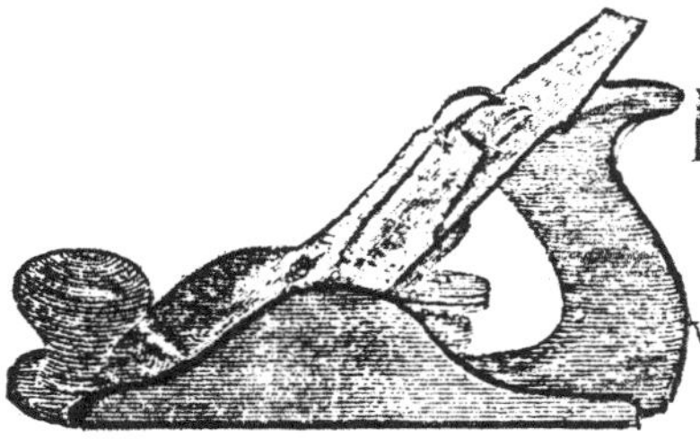
PATENT WOOD WORKING TOOLS,
Such as *Iron and Wood Bench-Planes,*
(Of all sizes and descriptions,)
VENEER-SCRAPERS, SPOKE-SHAVES, &c.,
73 HAVERHILL STREET,
BOSTON, MASS.

Plate XXXV Photocopy from page 71 Advertising Section of 1867 *New England Business Directory* [Boston]. Courtesy of William Hilton

The advertisement in Plate XXXV discloses that Bailey was making wood planes as early as 1867. These were probably of the transitional style and same as illustarted in Plate XXXIV. The cut for the metal plane in both of these Plates appears to be the same. Note that the screw adjustment for depthening regulation of the cutting iron is shown with vertical axis, which was soon thereafter changed to the horizontal position.

Plate XXXVI

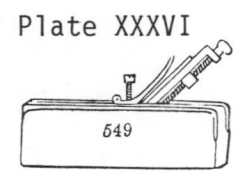

Illustration from 1857
General Catalogue of Engineer's & Mechanical Tools by Joseph Fenn, London [105 Newgate Street]

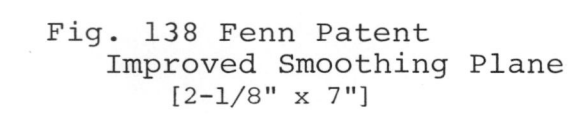

Fig. 138 Fenn Patent
Improved Smoothing Plane
[2-1/8" x 7"]

See Note No.22, page 222 for information about James Silcock's 1844 Patent in England for "Certain Improvements in Planes" This strongly indicates that his patent preceded those later in America for Combination Planes.

Fenn's Patent - Improved Smoothing Plane, c.1857
Fig. 139 Iron, Wood Body & Adjusting Mechanism & Holding Clamp

Bailey's Patent #67,398, August 6,1867 was his earliest for screw adjustment of the cutting iron. This showed a sketch of a wooden plane with cast iron superstructure. Bailey was not the first to apply such screw control for depth regulation. T.D.Worrall's Patent #17,951, issued ten years earlier on August 4,1857 showed such screw adjustment. Even this latter patent may have been preceeded by an arrangement used by Joseph Fenn, London, England a few years earlier.[3]

A recent acquisition is a 2-1/8" x 7" smoothing plane, shown in Figs. 138 & 139, with imprint Fenn/PATENT.[4] The cutting iron is 1½" wide and about 4" long and slotted to fit against a screw adjusting rod, having a brass wing-nut turn handle. This mechanism serves to adjust the depth of the plane iron resting in the bed. The special holding clamp, shown with the brass spring with tensioning regulation, at the right of Fig. 139, holds the iron in the bed and is held by two collars mounted into each side of the plane body. *The General Catalog of ENGINEERS' & MECHANICAL TOOLS*, manufactured and sold by Joseph Fenn, illustrates this as item No. 549 and noted this as *FENN'S Improved Double Iron SMOOTHING PLANE* (See Plate XXXVI)[5] and sold at 10s 6d. There appears to be some similarity between this and the 1857 Worrall mechanism, but the Fenn device appears to be a few years earlier.[21]

The sales of both iron and wood Bailey planes rapidly increased after this line was taken over by Stanley Rule & Level Co. A brochure distributed by this firm, dated January 1,1874, noted "over 60,000 sold". This was ten times greater than the reported 6000 sold during their first year offering these tools. Some of the larger wood plane firms took on lines of iron planes to compete with the Stanley Rule & Level Co. H.Chapin's Son (E.M.Chapin) advertised a smooth, jack and joiner plane in their 1874 Catalog, stating: "More than Fifty Thousand of the Iron Planes are already in use by our very best wood-workers, and their sale is constantly and largely increasing. The adjustable throat, the perfection of their work, the simple and convenient method of fastening the iron, the fact that they are the only iron Planes made in which ordinary bits can be used, and the price *TWENTY-FIVE PER CENT LESS*, than others, make these the favorite Planes among all classes of wood-workers" They also offered an iron block plane. This line of bench planes and the block plane appear to have been manufactured by the Metallic Plane Co. of Auburn,N.Y.[6] The Sandusky Tool Co. offered iron planes made under the Morris Patent, which is noted in the next Chapter. The Derby Plane Co. of Birmingham,Conn. also offered a line of iron planes.

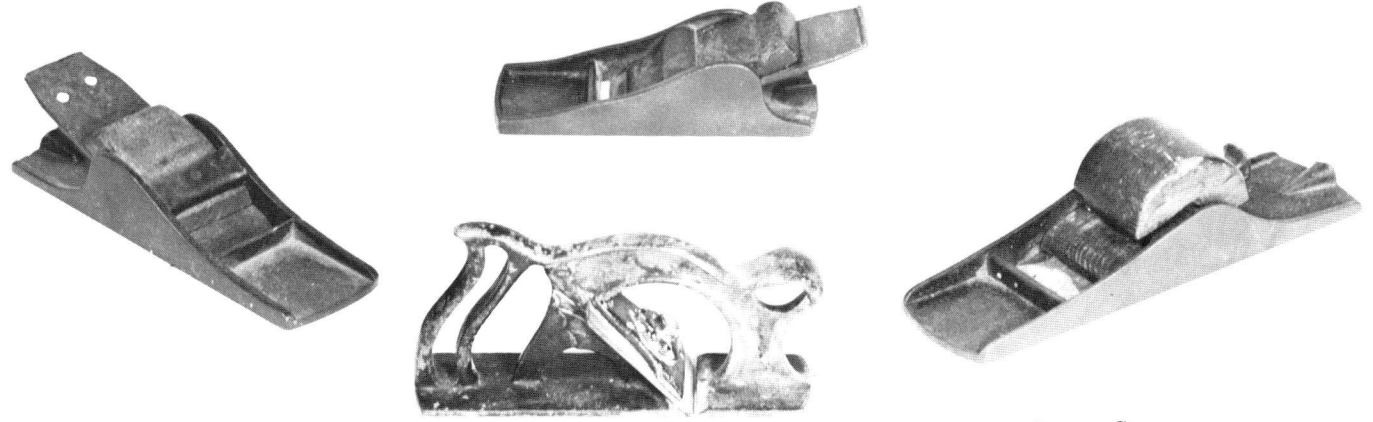

Fig.140. Iron Block Planes. Front center by Birmingham Plane Co. Other three by Metallic Plane Co., Auburn, New York.

Within ten years after Stanley Rule & Level Co. had taken over the Bailey planes, several competitive wooden 'transitional' planes had appeared on the market. Those made by Gage Tool Co. have been previously discussed (pages 62-64). The Standard Rule Co. of Unionville (borough of Farmington) Connecticut purchased rights to a patent jointly held by Solon and Arthur Rust.[7] (U.S. Patent #287,581, Sept.30,1883). This concerned a holding and adjusting device for a plane iron that was equally adapted to iron and wood bottom planes. This firm offered a line of wood bottom planes having the same sizes and numbers at Stanley Rule & Level Co., and at the same prices noted in the latter firms 1888 Catalogue.[8] Three pages from a Price List prepared by The Standard Rule Co. are shown in Plate XXXVII. Four of these planes are illustrated in Figs. 141 & 142.

Fig. 141
Standard Rule Co.
Wood Bench Planes
Top: No.32 - 24" Jointer
Middle: No.28 - 18" Fore
Bottom: No. 26 - 15" Jack

Fig. 142
Standard Rule Co.
No. 36 - 10" Jenny

Wood Planes.

Patented Oct. 30, 1883.

No. 21.	Smooth Plane, 7 inches in length, 1¾ inch Cutter,	$2.00
No. 22.	Smooth Plane, 8 inches in length, 1¾ inch Cutter,	2.00
No. 23.	Smooth Plane, 9 inches in length, 1¾ inch Cutter,	2.00
No. 24.	Smooth Plane, 8 inches in length, 2 inch Cutter,	2.00
No. 25.	Block Plane, 9½ inches in length, 1¾ inch Cutter.	2.00

Pat. Oct. 30, 1883.

No. 35.	Handle Smooth, 9 inches in length, 2 inch Cutter,	$2.50
No. 36.	Handle Smooth, 10 inches in length, 2⅜ inch Cutter,	2.75
No. 37.	Jenny Smooth, 13 inches in length, 2⅝ inch Cutter.	3.00

Pat. Oct. 30, 1883.

No. 26.	Jack Plane, 15 inches in length, 2 inch Cutter,	$2.25
No. 27.	Jack Plane, 15 inches in length, 2⅜ inch Cutter,	2.50
No. 28.	Fore Plane, 18 inches in length, 2⅜ inch Cutter,	2.75
No. 29.	Fore Plane, 20 inches in length, 2⅜ inch Cutter,	3.00
No. 30.	Jointer Plane, 22 inches in length, 2⅜ inch Cutter,	3.00
No. 31.	Jointer Plane, 24 inches in length, 2⅜ inch Cutter,	3.00
No. 32.	Jointer Plane, 26 inches in length, 2⅝ inch Cutter,	3.25
No. 33.	Jointer Plane, 28 inches in length, 2⅝ inch Cutter,	3.25
No. 34.	Jointer Plane, 30 inches in length, 2⅝ inch Cutter.	3.50

☞ Extra Plane Woods of every style can be supplied cheaply.

WE claim for the Standard Plane the most perfect adjustment of any similar tool in the market, inasmuch as it is positive and direct in its action, and the rocker which holds the iron and cap allows the iron to adjust itself in perfect line with the face of the plane.

The ordinary Plane Irons in general use, and which can be obtained at any hardware store, can be used in the adjustment, which is a decided advantage over Special Irons that need to be specially ordered, which causes delay and inconvenience. The Wood Plane is supplied with the same adjustment as the Iron Plane.

A trial of the Planes will convince any practical mechanic that it has no superior in the market. ALL Irons warranted.

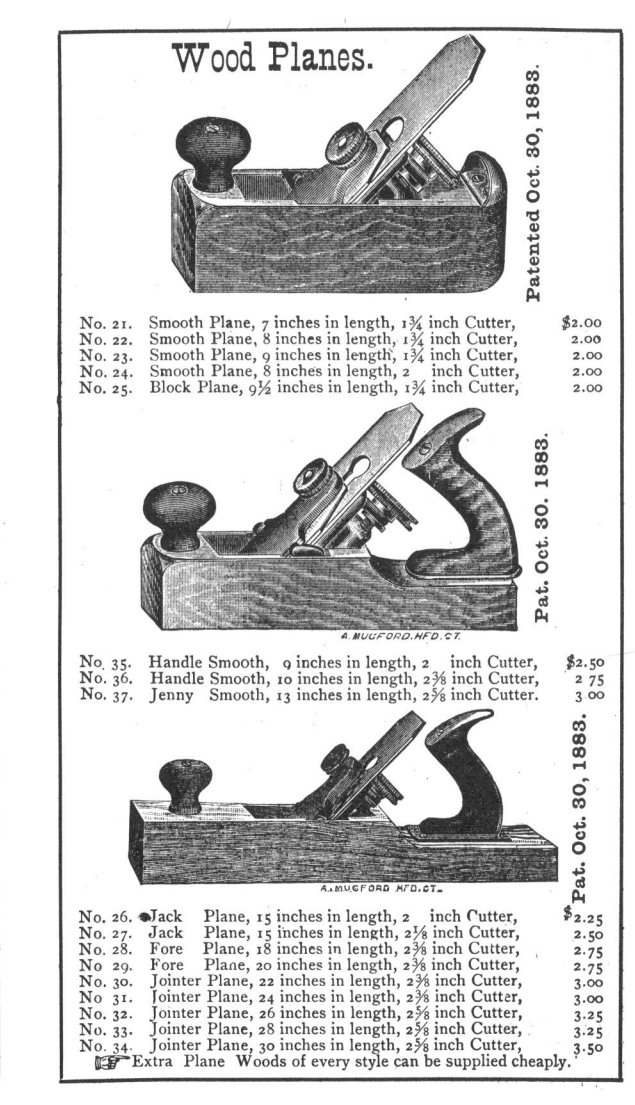

THE STANDARD
Iron and Wood Planes.

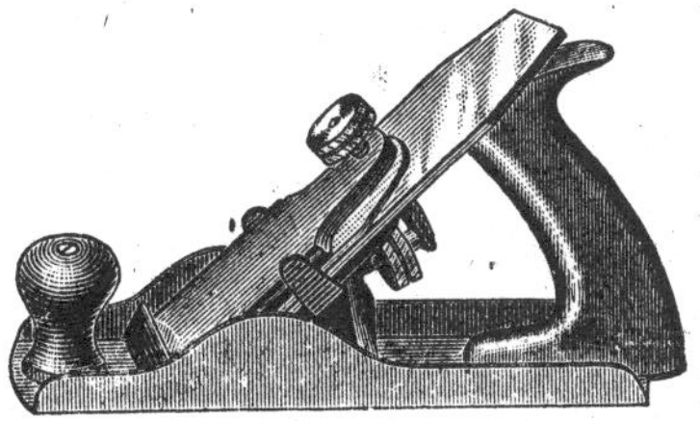

Pat. Oct. 30, 1883.

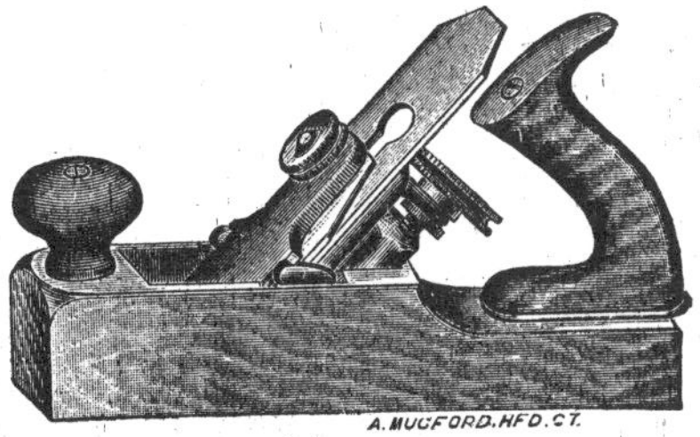

MANUFACTURED BY

❧THE STANDARD RULE CO.❧

MANUFACTURERS OF

Boxwood and Ivory Rules, Try Squares and T Bevels, Plumbs and Levels, Iron Planes, Etc.

UNIONVILLE, CONN.

DOWD & CO., PRINT, WINSTED, CONN.

Plate XXXVII – Three Pages from Standard Rule Co. Price List, c.1888
(From the Collection of J.Lee Murray, jr.)

THE BAILEY PATTERN ADJUSTABLE IRON AND WOOD PLANES.

These Planes have our Latest Improved methods for Adjusting the Cutter, and are finely finished and made from the best of material.

Every Plane is tested before it leaves the factory, and put in perfect working order. Nothing has been spared to make it a perfect tool of its kind.

The Cutters are warranted and will be replaced when failing from any fault of making.

---

68   THE UPSON NUT COMPANY.

The Bailey Pattern Adjustable Wood Planes.

Cutters Adjusted by a Lever.

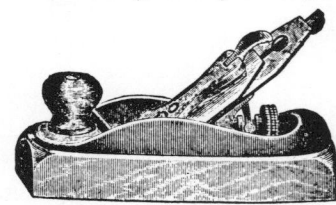

No.	Type	Length	Cutter	Price
21.	Smooth Plane,	7 inches in length,	1¾ inch Cutter, each,	$2 00
22.	"	8 "	1¾ "	2 00
23.	"	9 "	1¾ "	2 00
24.	"	8 "	2 "	2 00
25.	Block "	9½ "	1¾ "	2 00

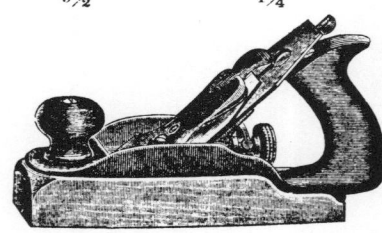

No.	Type	Length	Cutter	Price
35.	Handle Smooth,	9 inches in length,	2 inch Cutter, each,	$2 50
36.	"	10 "	2⅜ "	2 75
37.	Jenny "	13 "	2⅝ "	3 00

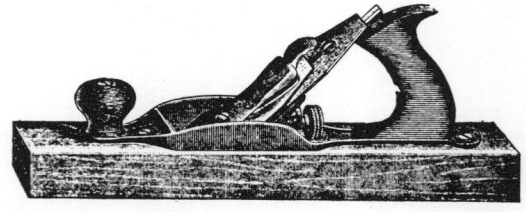

No.	Type	Length	Cutter	Price
26.	Jack Plane,	15 inches in length,	2 inch Cutter, each,	$2 25
27.	"	15 "	2⅛ "	2 50
28.	Fore "	18 "	2⅜ "	2 75
29.	"	20 "	2⅜ "	2 75
30.	Jointer "	22 "	2⅜ "	3 00
31.	"	24 "	2⅜ "	3 00
32.	"	26 "	2⅝ "	3 25
33.	"	28 "	2⅝ "	3 25
34.	"	30 "	2⅝ "	3 50

The Bailey Pattern Plane Irons.

Packed half dozen in a box.

Size,	1¼	1⅝	1¾	2	2⅛	2⅜	2⅝ inch.
Single Irons,	20	25	28	30	33	37	40 cents each.
Double "	40	45	50	55	60	65	70 " "

☞ Orders for Plane Irons should designate the No. of the Planes for which they are wanted.

The Standard Patent Adjustable Iron and Wood Planes,

MANUFACTURED ONLY BY

THE UPSON NUT COMPANY.

These Planes are of superior quality, both in material and finish.

The Cutter is the heavy cutter known to the trade, and is made from the best quality of steel, and warranted.

Every Plane is put in working order and tested before it leaves the factory. For a fine tool we can recommend it as second to none.

---

66   THE UPSON NUT COMPANY.

The Standard Patent Adjustable Wood Planes.

Cutters Adjusted by a Lever.

Patented October 30, 1883.

No.	Type	Length	Cutter	Price
21.	Smooth Plane,	7 inches in length,	1¾ inch Cutter, each,	$2 00
22.	" "	8 "	1¾ "	2 00
23.	" "	9 "	1¾ "	2 00
24.	" "	8 "	2 "	2 00
25.	Block "	9½ "	1¾ "	2 00

Patented October 30, 1883.

No.	Type	Length	Cutter	Price
35.	Handle Smooth,	9 inches in length,	2 inch Cutter, each,	$2 50
36.	" "	10 "	2⅜ "	2 75
37.	Jenny "	13 "	2⅝ "	3 00

Patented October 30, 1883.

No.	Type	Length	Cutter	Price
26.	Jack Plane,	15 inches in length,	2 inch Cutter, each,	$2 25
27.	" "	15 "	2⅛ "	2 50
28.	Fore "	18 "	2⅜ "	2 75
29.	" "	20 "	2⅜ "	2 75
30.	Jointer "	22 "	2⅜ "	3 00
31.	" "	24 "	2⅜ "	3 00
32.	" "	26 "	2⅝ "	3 25
33.	" "	28 "	2⅝ "	3 25
34.	" "	30 "	2⅝ "	3 50

☞ Extra Plane Woods of every style can be supplied **cheaply**.

Plate XXXIX - Page 66, Upson Nut Co. Catalog, 1890
Planes made under the Rust Patent
(Photocopy courtesy of the Connecticut State Library, Hartford, CT)

The Standard Rule Co. was established and incorporated at Farmington, Connecticut in 1872, occupying the second floor of the Bunnell shop in Unionville, employing about thirty persons.[9] The firm was capitalized at $40,000, but did not own any real estate.[10] Andrew S. Upson was the president and principal stockholder. He also had financial control and was president of the Upson Nut Co., capitalized at $250,000.[11] This was formerly the Union Nut Co. of Unionville, Connecticut. About 1872 a division of the Upson Nut Co. was also established in Cleveland, Ohio. George Karrmann affiliated with the Unionville firm in 1883.[12] He was granted U.S.Patent #410,710, September 10,1889 for a Bench Plane, which was assigned to the Upson Nut Co. of Farmington, Connecticut. This provided for a friction slide, screw adjustment for both depth control and lateral adjustment of the plane iron.[13] This was a means of circumventing the patents held by Stanley Rule & Level Co.[14] Upson Nut Co. soon offered a competitive line of transitional planes at the same prices and with the same numbers as those available from Stanley Rule & Level Co.[15] These are noted as the 'Bailey Pattern Adjustable Wood Planes' in the Upson Nut Co. 1890 Catalog.(see Plate XXXVIII.

Andrew Upson, president of both concerns, merged the Standard Rule Co. with the Upson Nut Co. (Unionville Division) probably between 1888 and 1890. Both lines of planes were continued. Those made under the Rusts' Patent were known as 'The Standard Patent Adjustable Wood Planes' and sold at the same prices as the other line of 'Bailey Pattern'. (see Plate XXXIX) It is not known how long Upson Nut continued to manufacture planes. The principal product of the firm was nut and bolt items, and the competition from Stanley Rule & Level Co. in planes probably made this line less profitable. Andrew Upson died in 1905. A large part of the firm's operations were transferred to Cleveland in 1911, and it is possible that planes were discontinued about this time. The former line of rules made by Standard Rule Co. were continued by Upson Nut at Unionville until 1922.[16]

Fig. 143. Transitional Jack Planes made under Mosher Patent.
Left: Union Manufacturing Co. Right: B Plane, Birmingham Plane Co.

Transitional planes were also manufactured in Connecticut by the Birmingham Plane Co. This firm is believed to have been a re-organization of the L.& C.Deforest concern at Birmingham, Conn.[17] about 1880. George D. Mosher assigned his plane patent, #413,300, granted October 22, 1889, to this firm. Co-incidentally Solon Rust of New Hartford, Conn. was also awarded a plane patent, #413,300, on the same date and also assigned this to the Birmingham Plane Co.[18] A 15" x 2-3/4" Jack Plane, with imprint "B.Plane/Patented/Oct.22,1889", and made by the Birmingham Plane Co. under the Mosher Patent, is illustrated in Fig. 143. The other plane in this photograph, shown to the left, bears imprint "No.27/Union/Pat. Oct.22,1889". This was made by the Union Manufacturing Co. at New Britain, Conn. who acquired the Birmingham Plane Co. about 1900, then called the Derby Plane Co. (see page 66). In 1920 the Union Manufacturing Co. was acquired by the Stanley Rule & Level Co. who discontinued this line of Union planes.

Fig. 144 - Pattern Maker's Plane with 12 Detachable Shoes
(Collection of James H. Cooley)

The iron stock, 2½" x 18½", shown in Fig. 144, without any of the wooden shoes, could be used alone as a jointer plane. The interchageable shoes and irons permitted variable arcs to be planed for working circles from 6 to 24 inches. The cutting irons accompaning this plane all have imprint of Charles Buck. This would date the plane 1873 - 1915.[19] An advertisement of such a Pattern Makers' Plane from the 1896 *Hammacher,Schlemmer & Co. Catalog* is illustrated in Plate XL, page 218.

MOULDING PLANES.

NOSING PLANES.

To ¾ in.	⅞ and 1 in.	1⅛ and 1¼ in.	1⅜ in.	1½ in.
.88	1.00	1.12	1.38	1.50

QUARTER HOLLOWS AND ROUNDS.

To 1 inch.	Over 1 inch.
75	.87½

RABBET PLANES—Skew or Square.

	Plain.	1 Spur.	2 Spur.
To 1 inch	75	1.00	1.25
To 1¼ "	84	1.09	1.34
To 1½ "	92	1.17	1.42
To 1¾ "	1.00	1.25	1.50
To 2 "	1.08	1.33	1.58

SASH AND COPING PLANES.

Furnished to order of various patterns.

SIDE RABBETS.

Side Rabbets, ...75c.

STAIR ROUNDS.

To ⅞ inch.	1 inch.
75c.	88c.

Discount on all Moulding Planes, 25 per cent.

Plows—with Moulson's Irons.

Screw arm—boxed fence—plated.

	Plain.	Handled.
Beech	7.50	9.50
Boxwood or Rosewood	9.50	11.50

For Brass Screw, Side Stops, add to list, ...50c.
Discount on all Plows, 30 per cent.

We would particularly call the attention of the trade to our Plows, which will be found to be the largest and most substantial in the market.

This manufactory of Planes has been in operation without cessation for fifty years, and is justly celebrated for its large stock of coarse grained, well-seasoned timber, unequalled in the country.

A PRICE LIST

OF

KELLOGG'S

Bench & Moulding

PLANES

SOLD BY

BURDITT & WILLIAMS,

Headquarters for New England,

No. 20 Dock Square,

BOSTON.

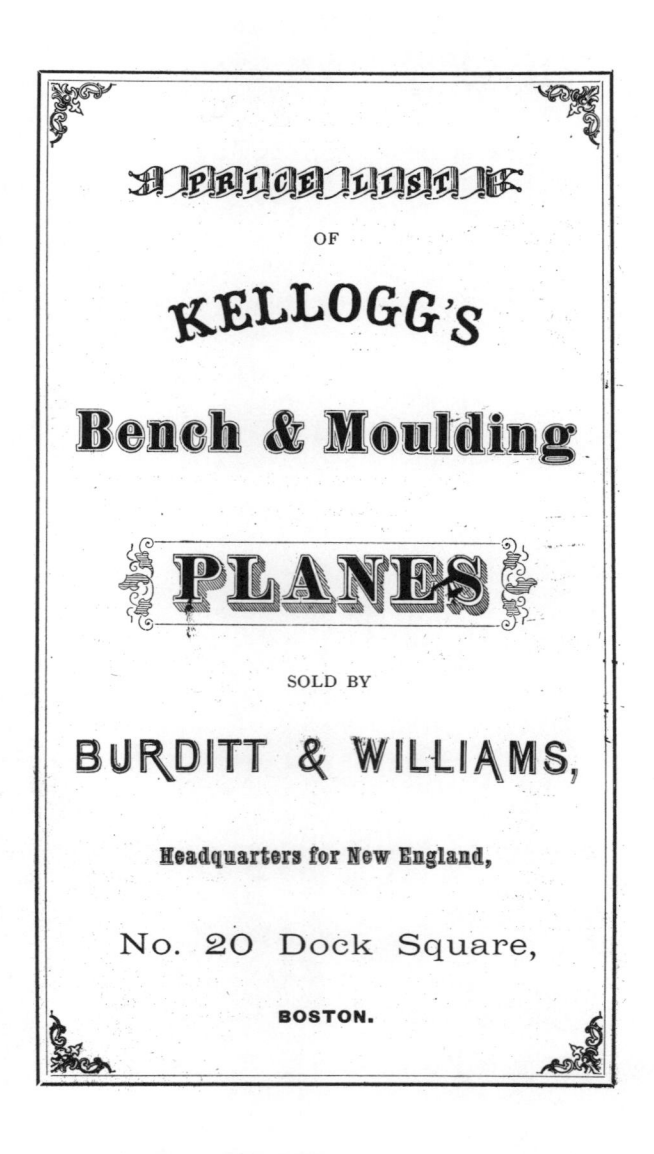

Plate XLI [First Half] Price List of Kellogg's Planes
(From the Collection of Bob Ashcroft)

PATTERN MAKERS' PLANE.

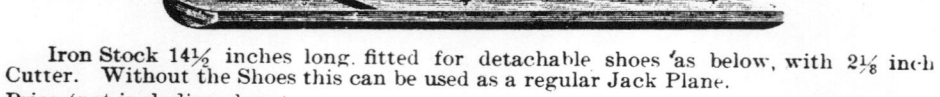

Iron Stock 14½ inches long, fitted for detachable shoes as below, with 2⅛ inch Cutter. Without the Shoes this can be used as a regular Jack Plane.
Price (not including shoes)..Each, $2.25

Each shoe is accompanied by a 2 inch iron. We carry shoes for 6, 9, 12, 18 and 24 inch circles...Each, $0.65

Plate XL - Pattern Makers' Plane

(Page 57, *1896 Hammacher, Schlemmer & Co. Catalog*)

BENCH PLANES.

MOULSON'S IRONS.

		Single Iron.	Double Iron.
Block Plane		1.00	
Smooth "	to 2⅛ inch	88	1.25
" "	2¼ inch		1.38
" "	2⅜ inch		1.42
" "	2½ inch		1.50
" "	Handled		2.00
Jack "		1.00	1.38
Fore "	22 inch	1.50	1.92
Jointer "	26 inch	1.67	2.08
" "	28 inch	1.75	2.25
" "	30 inch	2.00	2.50
Gutter "		1.25	
Tooth "		1.25	
Circular or Heel Plane		1.38	
Boxwood Block "		2.00	
" Smooth "			2.25

For the convenience of the trade, our Bench Planes are packed in cases as follows:

Block Planes,	36	in case.
Smooth "	36	"
Jack "	24	"
Fore "	12	"
Jointer "	6	"

Bench Planes, Double Iron, in sets of five, packed one set in case........ 8.05
Discount 20 per cent.

Premium Planes.

Same list as Common Bench Planes.

Selected stock, polished wood, ebony starts, in sets of five, packed one set in case........ 8.05
Discount

Razee or Ship Planes.

DOUBLE IRON.

Jack	Fore, 22 in.	Jointer, 26 in.	Jointer 28 in.
1.63	2.25	2.50	2.75

In sets of four, packed one set in case, consisting of Handled Smooth, Jack, Fore and Jointer,........ 8.38
Discount 20 per cent.

Premium Ship Planes.

Same list as Common Ship Planes.

Selected stock, polished wood, ebony starts, in sets of four, packed one in case, consisting of Handled Smooth, Jack, Fore and Jointer,........ 8.38
Discount

MOULDING PLANES.

BEAD PLANES.

	To ¾ in.	⅞ and 1 in.	1⅛ and 1¼ in.	1⅜ and 1½ in.
Common	67	88	1.00	1.25
Double	1.34	1.75		

BEAD PLANES—BOXED.

	To 5/16 in.	⅜ in.	½ in.	⅝ in.	¾ in.	⅞ and 1 in.
Common	84	92	1.00	1.08	1.17	1.25
Double	1.68	1.84	2.00	2.16	2.34	2.50

Two Iron Bead Planes furnished to order.

CENTRE BEADS.

	To ⅜ in.	½ in.	⅝ in.	¾ in.	1 in.
Single Boxed	84	92	92	92	
Solid "	92	1.00	1.08	1.17	1.25

DADOES.

Wood Side Stop.	Brass Side Stop.	Brass Screw Stop.
1.25	1.31	1.75

FILLETSTERS.

Common.	Side Stop.	Screw Stop.
1.75	2.00	2.75

Add for Cut	25
" Boxing	25
" Slide Arms	50
" Screw Arms	1.00
" Brass-tipped Arms	1.00

HOLLOWS AND ROUNDS.

Nos. 1 to 12, per pair	1.00
" 13 to 18, "	1.13
" 19 to 24, "	1.25
In half sets, 12 pair packed in case, No. 2 to 24, per case	13.13
In full " 24 " " " "	26.25

MATCH PLANES.

	To 1 in.	To 1¼ in.
Plated	2.00	
Handled and Plated	2.88	3.00

DOUBLE MATCH PLANES.

	To 1 in.	To 1¼ in.
Plated	2.00	
Handled and Plated	2.00	3.00

Plate XLI [Second Half] Price List of Kellogg's Planes
(From the Collection of Bob Ashcroft)

The price list, shown in Table XLI, is undated, but is believed to be c.1880, when the firm was under the management of William Kellogg. He was the son of James Kellogg of Amherst, Mass., who had established the business there about 1830. (see page 25) The prices listed are about 25% higher than those noted by the Sandusky Tool Co. and others at that time. However with the penned discount of "25 per cent" these prices are brought into line with competitors.

OFFICE OF THE
Greenfield Tool Company,
GREENFIELD, MASS.

RATES adopted by the "Plane Manufacturers' Association," at Kennard House, Cleveland, Ohio, December 18, 1872.

F. V. FOLLETT, Sec'y.　　　　　　　　　　　　　　　ALFRED THOMAS, Pres't.

	Page.	Discount.
Bench Planes, stamped "New York,"	3 & 4	15 & 5 per cent.
"　"　" "Greenfield Tool Co." Irons warranted.	3 to 15	15 " "
"　"　" without Irons,	70 to 71	15 " "
Moulding Tools, all kinds, best quality,	15 to 65	15 " "
Plows, " " "	49 to 52	15 " "
Bench and Hand Screws, all kinds, best quality,	67 to 69	net List.
Plane Irons, "Diamond Stamp,"	74 to 75	" "
Plane and Saw Handles,	69 to 70	20 " "
Rules, box-wood, ivory and miscellaneous,	76 to 78	30 & 10 " "
Try-Squares and Bevels,	79 to 80	25 & 10 " "
Plumbs and Levels, Pocket Levels, Level Glasses,	81 to 83	50 & 10 " "
Gauges	66 to 67	35 " "
Base Knobs	81	20 " "
Templets	65	25 " "

☞ Parties purchasing of us Planes and Plane Irons, previous to 1st July, 1873, of the net amounts as below, will be entitled to annexed credits on amounts so bought, viz:

On 300 dollars, a disount of 2 1-2 per cent. extra.
On 500 dollars, a discount of 5 per cent. extra.
On 2000 dollars and over, a discount of 5 and 2 1-2 per cent.

Terms, NET CASH. ALL BILLS, unpaid at expiration of 30 days from date of invoice, to be drawn for AT SIGHT, with exchange.

Goods delivered at Depot here. Boxes at cost. Prices subject to change without notice, and invoices made at prices ruling at time of shipment.

WE GUARANTY OUR PRICES AS LOW AND TERMS AS FAVORABLE as corresponding goods in the market, and confidently believe our friends will give us the same generous patronage as heretofore.

OX SHOES.

We are now manufacturing PARKER'S PATENT FORGED OX SHOES; the only article of the kind made, and we can unhesitatingly recommend them as superior to any hand-made Shoe.

Per 100 lbs., boxed and delivered at Depot here, $15,00.

☞ Parties purchasing previous to 1st July, 1873, the quantities as below, will be entitled to annexed credits on quantities so bought, viz:

On 500 lbs., ...5 per cent. discount.
On 1000 lbs., ...10 per cent. discount.
On 2000 lbs. and over, ...10 and 2 1-2 per cent. discount.

Very respectfully,　　　　GREENFIELD TOOL CO.

ALONZO PARKER, Treasurer.
B. S. PARKER, Secretary.

Plate XLII - 1873 Announcement by the Greenfield Tool Co.
(Collection of Bob Ashcroft)

A discount sheet, probably issued for the 1873 trade by the Greenfield Tool Co., is shown above as Plate XLII. This noted *"Rates adopted by the PLANE MANUFACTURERS' ASSOCIATION"* at Kennard House, Cleveland, Ohio, December 18, 1872. This seems reasonable indication that price fixing was then in effect among other large manufacturers: H.Chapin's Son; Auburn Tool Co.; Ohio Tool Co. and Sandusky Tool Co. Attention was called to a new product - OX SHOES.

The introduction to the 1869 *Illustrated Catalogue and Invoice Price List of Joiners' Bench Planes,*etc. *of the Greenfield Tool Co.* noted: - "The prices are those adopted by all the leading manufacturers two years since". This is further evidence that price fixing was prevalent. (see Plate IV, page 29)

GREENFIELD TOOL CO.

(*Proprietors "Greenfield Cutlery Co."*)

Manufacturers of

TABLE CUTLERY

IN GREAT VARIETY.

Butter and Fruit Knives!

NUT PICKS AND TABLE FORKS,

SILVER PLATED.

ALSO,

Solid Handled, Superfine Ivory, Extra Bone and Hard Rubber

TABLE KNIVES!

Sole Manufacturers of

PARKER'S PATENT FORGED CONCAVE OX SHOES.

THE ONLY SHOE THAT IS SELF FITTING.

ALSO,

Joiners' Bench and Moulding Planes

OF EVERY DESCRIPTION.

Plane Irons, Plow Bits, &c.

A. ALVORD, President. S. S. WARD, Treasurer.

WAREHOUSE:—New York, 85 Chambers Street.

FACTORIES AND PRINCIPAL OFFICE.

GREENFIELD, - - MASS.

Plate XLIII - Advertisement in *1881 Greenfield Directory*
(Photocopy courtesy of the Public Library, Greenfield, Mass.)

The above advertisement indicates an attempt to diversify products by the Greenfield Tool Co. in 1881. The firm had been among the principal plane manufacturers in the United States, but was then on the decline. The firm closed down after a serious fire in 1887. (see page 28). [20]

Notes - Chapter VII

1. L.N.Brundage,"J.R.Tolman, Planemaker", *Chronicle EAIA*,V.29,No.4,Dec.1976,p.70
2. Richard Starr,"A Wooden Compass Plane",*Chronicle EAIA*,V.30,No.4,Dec.1977,p.55-56
3. Rees's, *Encyclopedia* [Reprint: *Clocks,Watches & Chronometers,1819-20*] Original Section on Clock Tools,1807, indicated Joseph Fenn making such tools at 105 Newgate Street, London at that date.
4. A search of English patents by the Staff of the British Science Library Branch failed to reveal any patent of this nature issued to Jospeh Fenn. It is possible Fenn had purchased this patent from the inventor.
5. Grateful thanks are extended to Warren G. Ogden, jr. for furnishing a photocopy of this from his original of this Catalogue.
6. K.D. & J.W.Roberts,*New York Planemakers, etc.*,op.cit.,p.134 & Plate 115,p.135
7. Solon Rust was born in New Hartford, CT. He was apprenticed under H.Chapin and left about 1850 to work for L.DeForest at Birmingham,CT. He returned to work for H.Chapin's Son in 1864. On March 31,1868 he was granted a patent jointly with E.M.Chapin for an adjustable screw regulated plow plane. Later with his son,Arthur, he was granted several patents for various mechanisms for holding plane irons and bench planes. These were assigned to various plane firms through purchased rights. See: Roger Smith,*B-ARS PLANE TALK,Summer 1977*,V.II,No.2,p.7.
8. *1888 Stanley Rule & Level Co. Catalog*,Reprint 1975,Ken Roberts Publishing Co.
9. Mabel Hurlburt,*Farmington Town Clerks and Their Times*,[Hartford,CT,1945],p.345
10. Farmington,CT, Land Records, B66, p.676
11. Farmington Land Records, op. cit, B66, p.400. Grateful acknowledge is made to Mrs. Elizabeth Coykendall and Mr. Raymond Brooks of Unionville, CT for assistance and sharing historical data about these two concerns.
12. Farmington Land Records, B.66,p.336
13. The first attempt to control the lateral adjustment of the Bailey Plane was by J.A.Traut and H.Richards(U.S.Patent#176,152,April 16,1876) assigned to Stanley Rule & Level Co. and first applied to their line of "Liberty Bell" Planes. Improvements were made in joint patent by L.Mead and J.A.Traut(U.S. Patent #378.704,Feb.28,1888). The final arrangement was by J.A.Traut's Patent of July 24,1888 (U.S.Patent #386,509)
14. See page 33,*1888 Stanley Rule & Level Co.Catlog*,op.cit., see #8 above.
15. *ibid*, p.35
16. Rules were continued at Unionville until 1922 when this portion was purchased by three directors of the Stanley Rule & Level Co. who formed the Upson Rule Co. July 14,1922 and immediately sold it to the Stanley Rule & Level Co. Farmington, CT. Land Records.
17. Birmingham,Connecticut was the 19th Century name for the industrial area between the confluence of the Naugatuck and Housatonic Rivers that is today part of Derby. It was named Birmingaham because of the iron works there comparable to Birmingham, England. The Birmingham Plane Co. was on the west side of the Housatonic River and was then actually in the township of Huntington, which is now part of Shelton. (See A.Hughes and M.Allen, *Connecticut Name Places*, Connecticut Historical Society [Hartford,CT])
18. Both patents are sketched and described in the *Official Patent Gazette*, [Washington,DC], V.49, 1889; G.D.Mosher,pp.459-60; S.R.Rust, p.468.
19. *Buck Brothers 1890 Price List*,1976 Reprint,p.123,Ken Roberts Publishing Co.
20. *1872 Greenfield Tool Co. Catalog*, 1977 Reprint by Ken Roberts Publishing Co.
21. Recent research in England also indicates that there is a strong possibility that the combination plane, formerly thought to have been an American development from independent work by Phillips and Miller [see pages 73-74] 1867-70, was preceded by James Silcock, Birmingham by his Patent #10033 in England dated 1844, "Certain Improvements in Planes". This covered various combination operations for a metal plane with regulating stops as a double fillister for side,sash, back and skewed rabbet; grooving plough; dado; moulding and beading.See: Alan Beardmore, "Who Invented the Stanley Combination Plane"*Woodworker*[Hemel Hempstead,Herts,England] September 1976, pp. 258-261.

Chapter VIII

Ohio Planemaking and Sandusky Tool Co., 1869-1931

The movement of plane manufacturing from the east, mainly New England and New York State, to Ohio has been briefly discussed earlier. (See Pages 34 - 37). The progression in Ohio was Cincinnati, Chillicothe, Columbus and finally Sandusky. Throughout the 1850's and 1860's the leading firm was the Ohio Tool Co. at Columbus. However later this firm was to be outranked by the Sandusky Tool Co., established in 1869. While it was the last major firm to be formed for manufacturing wooden planes, it was also the last producing these when shut down in 1931.

The earliest Cincinnati Directory was published in 1819, two years before the first St. Louis and forty-one before the first at Chicago. In an historical sketch this noted: 15 cabinet making shops with 84 employees; 16 cooper shops with 50 employess; 9 coach builders with 33 employees; 4 chairmakers with 31 employees; 80 - 100 house carpenters and 60 - 70 boat carpenters. This extensive variety of woodworking manufacturing undoubtedly led to considerable demand of tools locally, as well as for sales and distribution to the west. James McGennis (sic, McGinnis) was noted as a planemaker at 6th Street between Plum and Western Row.[1]

Until 1850 most of the planemaking firms appear to be short lived with numerous changes in partnership. Separate imprints of J.Creagh have been noted on planes also having the imprint of another maker: J.Donaldson; also E.F.Seybold.[2] After Jesse Walker, planemaker who had come from New York, died, his widow, Ester Walker, carried on the business at 204 Main Street in 1829. Widow Catherine Seybold in 1853-55 continued the business of E.F.Seybold, 1836-52. Studies since the first Edition of this book have uncovered more new plane makers working at Cincinnati than any other location. (see Check List)

An example of a short duration firm is that of John Morrison who advertised four successive weeks in the Chillicothe, *Supporter & Scioto Gazette,* May/June 1826:

> PLANE MANUFACTORY
>
> John Morrison informs the public that he carries on *PLANE MAKING* opposite Messrs. Barr & Cambell's store. Mechanics wishing to purchase can be supplied with all kinds of Planes made in the best manner, and sold unusually low. All orders will be thankfully received and ounctually attended to.
> *May 11, 1826*

After his last advertisement in this paper June 8,1826, John Morrison was not to be heard from again.[3]

Sandusky, Ohio is located on the south shore of Lake Erie, approximately midway between Cleveland and Toledo. Incorporated in 1824 as Sandusky City, subsequently the latter word was dropped. Along with the rest of Erie County, and also Huron County, lying next south, this formed part of the so-called "Sufferers' Lands" of "Firelands", being the western most part of the Connecticut Western Reserve. The land in the "Firelands" was given out by the State of Connecticut to veterans, their familiies and descendants whose homes, buildings and crops had been ravaged during the Revolutionary War by invaders. Many of the place names and buildings have traces of Connecticut origins.

When the Ohio Canal system was built, it had been hoped in Sandusky that the route would be through the Sandusky and Scioto Rivers through to Columbus. However two seperate canals were built; one from Toledo to Cincinnati; the other from Cleveland to Marietta. Thus Sandusky, although having the best natural harbor of any city in Ohio on Lake Erie, lost out. Consequently Sandusky remained relatively small, while Cleveland and Toledo both subequently became metropolises.

In 1835 William Henry Harrison broke ground at Sandusky for what was to be Ohio's first railroad, the Mad River Rail Road. It extended southwesterly to Springfield, and eventually to Cincinnati. This afforded easy transportation from Lake Erie to the great Ohio-Mississippi-Missouri River system. Accordingly many European immigrants in travelling from New York, westward through the Eirie Canal, and by Boat from Buffalo passed through Sandusky. A number, especially from Germany, Austria-Hungary, and Italy decided to stay on at Sandusky.

In 1853 the Cleveland and Toledo Railroad built a pier track across a corner of Sandusky Bay, thereby creating sort of a Cove. According to old accounts, part of this "Cove" consisted of a pocket of stagnant water. As the city could not afford to fill this in, a thirty-year lease was granted to an entity known as the Sandusky Ship Yard, which apparently never built either a ship or a building on the site. In 1867 a woodworking firm known as Allen, Dorsey & Tenny acquired this lease. In 1868 this firm experimented with the manufacture of wooden planes. In 1869 the business was incorporated as Sandusky Tool Co., and was able to procure an extension of the lease until 1938. The lease was a nominal annual cash rental, but the lessee was obliged to fill in a specified portion of the stagnant water area every year. This filled-in area eventually became the site of the drying sheds and some of the lesser building of the Tool Company.

George Barney, Sr. was President of the newly organized Tool Company; Stephen W. Dorsey, superintendent; and L.H. Tenney, secretary and treasurer. Dorsey left the firm in 1851, while Tenney had left during the first year. J.A. Montgomery, who had previously supervised the manufacture of planes at Ohio Tool Co., was engaged to replace Dorsey. Montgomery designed automatic mortising machinery for making plane stocks that was used throughout the tenure of this Company. An example of his ingenious designs of woodworking machinery was a Picket Cutter illustrated in the 1877 Catalog, the earliest extant catalog of this firm.[4]

With abundant forests of the best hardwoods nearby, shipbuilding, wheel manufacturing, and other woodworking industries in general flourished during a long period in the area. The excellent harbor brought lumber from the pineries of Michigan, Wisconsin and Minnesota. Consequently tools for wood working were in high local demand. Additionally the shipping facilities by both water and railroad enabled prompt deliveries to the east west and south.

The title page and introduction to the 1877 Catalog are shown as Plates XLIV & XLV. Approximately half of the 67 pages in this Catalog were devoted to planes offering an extensive line of these tools as any competitive manufacturer supplied at this date. Indeed it was a credit to the progressive management, noted on Plate XLIV, that this firm had developed into a national leader within the short period of eight years of existence.

In addition to the complete line of bench and moulding planes, other significant items noted in this catalog were:

1. Morris Patent Iron Planes
2. Beech, Applewood, Boxwood, Rosewood and Ebony Plow Planes, the latter two being optionally furnished with ivory tips.
3. Self-regulating Plow Plane made from Box, Rosewood or Ebony, all optionally supplied with ivory tipped arms.
4. Warranted Plane Irons of Single and Double Styles, made from the Best English Cast Steel.
5. Silver Steel Clipper Irons with Full Polish, introduced by the firm during the Philadelphia Exhibition of 1876.
6. A line of Axes - Ohio, Yankee, Western and Double-Bit Patterns.
7. Picks, Mattocks, Sledges and Mason's Tools; also handles.
8. Schwehr's Improved German Hoe
9. Hand Screws and Cabinte Maker's Clamps.
10. Saw and Chisel Handles.
11. Cooper's Tools.
12. J.A. Montgomery's Patent Picket Cutter.

Albert Schwer developed machinery in the early 1870's for forging an eye-hoe blade from a single piece of steel. This was noted in the 1877 Catalog as "SCHWEHR'S IMPROVED GERMAN HOE". [5] His father, John Schwer, a blacksmith, had immigrated from Eschbach, Baden to Sandusky, and had taught his som how to hand forge such a hoe; wherin the handle fits into a D-shapped socket forged as an integral part of the blade. He received several patents on these machines, and thereafter received a royalty from the Tool Company for the rights to use them. He was given the position of Superintendent of the forge division. These same machines were still in use when production ceased in 1930.

ILLUSTRATED LIST

OF

PLANES, PLANE IRONS,

COOPERS' AND CABINET MAKERS' TOOLS, AXES,
PICKS, MATTOCKS, SLEDGES, HOES, STONE MASONS' AND MINERS' TOOLS, HAND
AND BENCH SCREWS, ALL KINDS OF HANDLES, MALLETS,
SCREW DRIVERS, SAW BUCKS, &C., &C.

MANUFACTURED BY

THE SANDUSKY TOOL CO.,

SANDUSKY, OHIO

GENERAL EASTERN AGENCY,

NO. 113 CHAMBERS STREET,

NEW YORK.

SANDUSKY:
REGISTER STEAM PRINTING ESTABLISHMENT,
1877.

Plate XLIV - Title Page 1877 Sandusky Tool Co. Catalogue

THE SANDUSKY TOOL COMPANY.

H. C. POST, Prest. and Treas.   J. A. MONTGOMERY, Supt.   J. P. KNIGHT, Sec'y.

SANDUSKY, OHIO, MARCH 1st, 1877.

GENTLEMEN :

We take pleasure in calling your attention to the extensive assortment of *first-class* tools, etc., manufactured by us, more perfectly illustrated and classified in this catalogue now presented, than in any other heretofore issued. Our aim will still be to excel in the uniform standard of all goods represented herewith. We are constantly making new improvements in machinery, whereby we are able to improve both style and finish of our goods to meet the especial wants of the trade and consumers.

OUR GOODS ARE FULLY WARRANTED.

We have added in this issue several new lines to which we call especial attention. We employ only skilled labor and every tool is inspected before being shipped.

Most respectfully soliciting your further valued commands, and tendering thanks for the patronage given us in the past, we remain,

Very truly,

SANDUSKY TOOL CO.

Plate XLV - Introduction to the 1877 Sandusky Tool Co. Catalogue

Fig. 145A - Top View Diamond Metallic Bench Plane
(E.H.Morris Patent - Photo courtesy of Raymond M.Smith)

Fig. 145B - Bottom View Diamond Metallic Bench Plane
(E.H.Morris Patent - Photo Courtesy of Raymond M.Smith)

As mentioned in the previous Chapter, Sandusky Tool Co. was among the firms soon to follow offering an iron bench plane to compete with the Bailey line sold by Stanley Rule & Level Co. The Diamond Metallic Bench Plane, made under the Morris Patent (Ellis H. Morris of Salem, Ohio: US Patent #109,037; Nov.8,1870)[6] was offered in a 10" smooth plane; a 16" jack; or a 22" jointer. The advantages of this construction, claimed in the patent, were a lighter metal plane with the web pattern of the sole and cheaper, since less metal was used. The illustrations above in Figs. 145A & B show the 22" jointer.[7]

The "Self-adjusting Plow Plane", illustrated in Fig. 146, has become among the most sought after tools among present plane collectors. It is not known whether this was patented, but it is somewhat similar to the E.Chapin-Solon Rust Patent, March 31,1868, made at H.Chapin's Son's Union Factory at Pine Meadow, Conn.[8] In any event this style was made at Sandusky Tool Co. in several woods from 1877, perhaps earlier, through the tenure of the firm. It is noted in their 1925 Catalog (Nos.138-143). Its manufacture required extreme precision techniques in making the threaded collar sleeves through which the guide arms slide. Indeed this is a remarkable tool!

The earliest known regulating screw adjustable plow was that of Israel White's January 9,1834 Patent. This is illustrated on a Broadside, Plate VI, page 33, which is dated November 12,1833, a few months before the patent was granted. The 1838 Patent of E.W.Carpenter of Lancaster, Pa. has been previously noted.[9]

Fig. 146 Self-Adjusting Boxwood Sandusky Tool Co. Plow

A brochure was published in 1879 noting various agricultural machinery offered by the firm. These were: Bruner Patent Corn Cultivator; Adams' Buckeye Land Roller; and Sandusky Horse Rake.(See Plate XLVI, page 230). Perhaps such manufacturing was an attempt to diversify products.

Mozart Gallup, a native of Connecticut, became a director, treasurer and assistant secretary of the firm on September 1,1880. He had started to work in 1874 as a bookkeeper. The 1885 Catalogue noted him as General Manager and Treasurer. (See Plate VIIIa, page 38) He became president, also retaining the position as General Manager, on September 14,1886. He continued to hold the office of president until his death on September 6,1923. In 1918 (his 88th year) he relinquished the office of general manager to his son, Frank M.Gallup.

The 1885 Catalogue (78 pages) showed a comparative listing of planes with model numbers made by Sandusky Tool Co.; Ohio Tool Co.; Auburn Tool Co.; Chapin Tool Co.; and the Greenfield Tool Co.[10] This listing is shown on pages 39 - 41. These were the leading manufacturers of wooden planes at this date. An unusual item illustrated on page 63 of the 1885 Catalogue was Kinney's Patent Guage Ripping Plane, shown in Plate XLVII, page 231.

THE

SANDUSKY TOOL COMPANY

SANDUSKY, OHIO,

MANUFACTURERS OF THE

BRUNER PATENT CORN CULTIVATOR

—THE—

SANDUSKY HORSE RAKE,

—AND THE—

ADAMS' BUCKEYE LAND ROLLER.

_____Agent,

SANDUSKY REGISTER PRESS.

ADAMS' Buckeye Land Roller!

PATENTED SEPT. 7th, 1875.

MANUFACTURED BY

SANDUSKY TOOL COMPANY
SANDUSKY, OHIO.

THE BEST ROLLER EXTANT.

READ! and consider a few of the many essential points which combine to make this implement in every way worthy of the confidence of the farmer.

1st. Its lightness of Draft.
2d. Its capacity for extra weights.
3d. Its Cast Iron bolted heads.
4th. Its Cast Steel Spring Seat.
5th. Its simplicity.
6th. Its Durability.

The Roller is in three sections which are made to adjust themselves to the ground. It is as easily turned as a wagon. The team only having the front Roller to turn. There being no strain on the horse's necks and no swinging of the tongue.

Plate XLVI - 1879 Brochure by Sandusky Tool Company Advertising Agricultural Machinery [Collection of Cliff Brown]

SANDUSKY TOOL COMPANY. 63

KINNEY'S PATENT GAUGE RIPPING PLANE.
SOMETHING NEW.

The above cut represents Kinney's Gauge Ripping Plane, the only tool manufactured in the world whereby thick or thin lumber can be ripped by hand with ease and precision. In the center of the gauge a small circular tooth cutter is so arranged as to be raised or lowered, by the thumb screw above, as the thickness of the lumber requires. In pushing the gauge over the board the cutter rotates, consequently cannot follow the grain of the timber. Can be adjusted to any width with ease. In ripping thick lumber, cut on both sides.

As this is the only Gauge Ripping Plane manufactured, it must of necessity have a very large sale, and dealers will have no trouble in selling them at a fair price.

	Price, each.	Per Dozen.
Kinney's Patent Gauge Ripping Plane—Beech,	$2.50	$24.00
" " " " "—Applewood,	2.75	27.00

KINNEY'S PATENT ROTARY MARKING GAUGE.

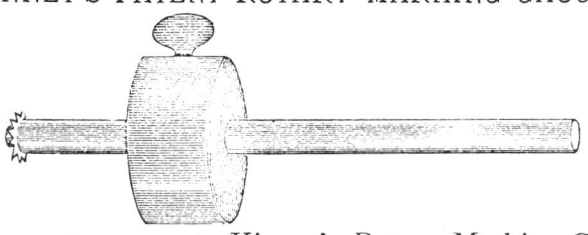

The above cut represents Kinney's Rotary Marking Gauge, for all mechanics working in wood; acknowledged by all to be the best in the world. Instead of a brad on end of shaft to do the work there is a fine toothed marker which rotates, enabling it to step over the grain, consequently it can not follow the grain of the timber. This gauge is also useful in slitting thin stuff. Sells at sight. All mechanics will have one.

These Gauges are put up in neat boxes of one dozen each, and sell readily at a fair price.

	Price, each.	Per Dozen.
Kinney's Rotary Marking Gauges—Bright Steel Rod,	50 c.	$4.00
" " " "—Nickel Plated, do.	75 c.	5.50

Plate XLVII - Kinney's Patent Gauge - Page 63, 1885 Sandusky Tool Co. Catalogue
[Photocopy courtesy of Ohio Historical Society Library, Columbus, Ohio]

Around 1890 Sandusky Tool Co. took over the account of Sargent & Co. and supplied this firm with most of their wooden planes for resale under the imprint and brand of "SARGENT & CO.". Previous to this date Sargent had obtained their wooden planes from H.Chapin's Son. [11] The 1871 *SARGENT & CO. CATALOGUE* noted "Agent for H.Chapin's Son's Planes" Their 1888 Catalogue listed and illustrated several brands of planes: "U.S." Bench Planes - Warranted; Sargent & Co.'s Bench Planes, "Kenewa" - Not Warranted; and "U.S" Miscellaneous Planes. It is believed that all brands were purchased from other manufacturers; some may have been from H.Chapin's Son; some from Sandusky Tool Co. In any event it is defintely known that later the Sandusky Tool Co. became a large supplier of planes to Sargent & Co. [12] It may have been that Gallup had previous Connecticut business relations with Sargent & Co., but more probable could offer a lower price.

Thomas A. Tully has pointed out the similarity between the Sandusky and Sargent imprints.[13] Another sales technique, probably introduced by Sandusky Tool Co. about this time, was imprinting some of their planes with *OGONTZ*, the name of an Indian chief of a tribe of Ottawas who lived in Sandusky.[14] Previously from information given to me, Ogontz was believed to have been a firm making planes in the Philadelphia area. Planes have since been reported with both imprints of Ogontz and Sandusky, as well as similiarities of such planes with only one of these imprints.[15] The 1877 *Sandusky Tool Co. Catalog* stated in regard to Ohio, Yankee and Western Axe Patterns:
" 'OGONTZ' quality $1.00 less per dozen" Whether planes stamped "OGONTZ" were of second quality or whether this was just a sale's 'gimmick', is not know. Certainly many planes with "OGONTZ" imprint have been observed with equal or better quality than surviving planes of Sandusky Tool Co.

An imprint that is occasionally reported is: "A.C.Bartlett's/ Ohio Planes". Variation of this imprint have recently been observed: "Bartlett's Ohio Planes/COLUMBUS" [16]; and "OHIO PLANE CO./ A.C.BARTLETT, Pres."[17] In both the 1895 and 1899 Catalogues of the Hibbard, Spencer, Bartlett & Co., Chicago, Illinois are listed "A.C.Bartlett's Ohio Bench Planes" and "A.C.Bartlett's Ohio Fancy Planes". Plate XLVIII notes the former from the 1899 Catalogue. Note that this also lists OGONTZ Bench Planes. In this same Edition A.C.Bartlett is listed among the vice-presidents and Directors of this firm. Previous to 1890 this merchandizing concern was Hibbard,Spencer & Co. It is suggested that the salemanship of Mr. Bartlett enabled him to align such a connection and become a partner in this firm at Chicago. In all probability A.C.Bartlett did not manufacture planes, but had a sale's office somewhere in Ohio and simply bought planes at the best price from both Ohio Tool Co. and later at Sandusky Tool Co.

Traces of Plane Imprints

HIBBARD, SPENCER, BARTLETT & CO.

A. C. BARTLETT'S OHIO BENCH PLANES.

No. 3.   No. 5.

Warranted Irons, Polished Lignum-vitæ Start.

No. 3—Smooth, 2 to 2¼ in., double irons, 8 in. long, - - - - - - - each $0.90
No. 5—Handled smooth, 2 to 2¼ in., double irons, 10½ in. long, - - - - - " 1.75
36 IN A CASE.

Warranted Irons, Polished Lignum-vitæ Start.

No. 10—Jack, 2 to 2¼ in., single irons, 16 in. long, - - - - - - - each $0.85
No. 13—Jack, 2 to 2¼ in., double irons, 16 in. long, - - - - - - - " 1.00
36 IN A CASE.

No. 19.   No. 25.

Warranted Irons, Polished Lignum-vitæ Start.

No. 19—Fore, 2⅜ to 2½ in., double irons, 22 in. long, - - - - - - each $1.40
No. 25—Jointer, 2½ to 2¾ in., double irons, 26 in. long, - - - - - " 1.50
No. 25—Jointer, 2½ to 2¾ in., double irons, 28 in. long, - - - - - " 1.60
No. 25—Jointer, 2½ to 2¾ in., double irons, 30 in. long, - - - - - " 1.75
FORE, 24. JOINTER, 20 IN A CASE.

OGONTZ.

Polished Ebony Start.

No. 6—Smooth, 2 to 2¼ in., double irons, 8 in. long, - - - - - - each $0.90
No. 12—Jack, 2 to 2¼ in., double irons, 16 in. long, - - - - - - " 1.00
No. 20—Fore, 2⅜ to 2½ in., double irons, 22 in. long, - - - - - - " 1.40
No. 30—Jointer, 2½ to 2¾ in., double irons, 26 in. long, - - - - - " 1.50
SMOOTH, 36; JACK, 36; FORE, 24; JOINTER, 20 IN A CASE.

Plate XLVIII - A.C.Bartlett's Ohio Bench Planes - 1899 Hibbard, Spencer, Bartlett & Co. Catalogue - Chicago, Illinois

An excellent account concerning the methods of manufacturing bench and moulding planes at Sandusky Tool Co., presumably as it was performed about 1920, appeared in the 1955 *Chronicle of EAIA*.[18] A statement in this, quoted from William Lorenzen,[19] noted: "The Sandusky Tool Co. had 36 plane maker's benches. These planemakers all worked piece work, and during the height of their operation produced some 1200 planes a day."

During the fifteen period of 1910 through 1924, the Corporate Records (See Table XV) a yearly average of approximately fifty-five thousand dollars of woodworking tools; slightly less than half that amount in hoes and garden tools; for total sales of about eighty-one thousand dollars; and with a payroll of just under half that figure. However over these years the firm losses were twenty-three thousand five hundred dollars; or an average yearly loss of sixteen hundred dollars.

Table XV - Operations of Sandusky Tool Company, 1910 - 1924
[Sales and Payroll in Thousands of Dollars]

Year	Wood Tools	Hoes	Total	Profit or Loss	Payroll
1910	62.2	37.2	99.4	+ 10.4	34.9
1911	63.8	34.3	98.0	+ 18.2	36.2
1912	66.6	38.7	105.3	− 11.1	36.3
1913	62.6	34.9	97.5	+ 8.5	37.7
1914	52.8	27.2	80.0	+ 5.1	35.1
1915	38.9	20.7	59.6	− 5.7	29.5
1916	46.3	38.4	84.7	+ 6.9	30.5
1917	41.0	35.1	76.1	− 4.3	34.5
1918	60.9	22.7	83.6	− 9.6	76.9
1919	72.9	14.3	87.2	− 17.7	
1920	60.3	24.6	84.9	+ 2.6	43.8
1921	34.4	13.8	48.2	− 5.3	43.8
1922	53.8	8.0	61.6	− 16.2	29.0
1923	56.3	14.1	70.3	− 4.6	37.4
1924	50.9	24.9	75.8	− 0.7	37.9
Total	823.8	388.9		− 23.5	543.5
Average	54.9	25.9		− 1.6	36.2

The same bleak financial situation faced the other two surviving plane manufacturing firms: Chapin-Stephens and Ohio-Auburn.[20] The market for wooden planes had about collapsed. The factors were the successes and competition from the iron and transitional iron-wood planes by Stanley Rule & Level Co., Sargent & Co., and several others; also automated machinery replaced much of the work formely done by hand planes. All three firms had failed to develop new products, and failure was inevitable. In the case of Sandusky Tool Co. aged management, probably with limited capital to re-invest were important contributing factors. Nevertheless Sandusky struggled on longest in the field.[21]

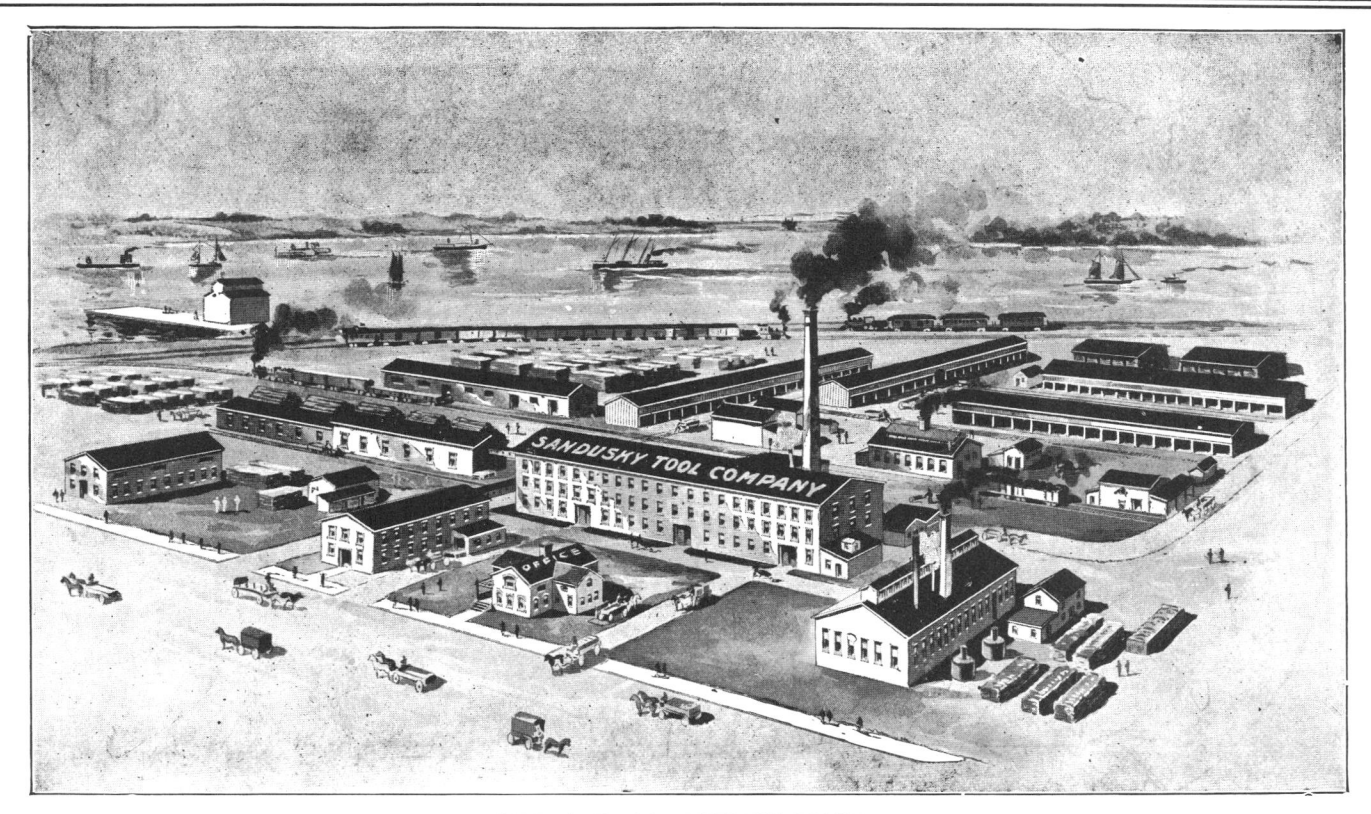

SANDUSKY TOOL COMPANY PLANT

Plate XLIX. Sketch of Sandusky Tool Co. from Catalogue No. 24

Catalogue #24, 75 pages, was published by the firm early in 1922. This announced William L. Allendorf, Vice-President, and Otto C. Holzaepfel, succeeding Frank M. Gallup, son of M. Gallup, as General Manager. This latter change was made January 9,1922. Allendorf was president of the Commercial Bank at Sandusky and was executor of the will of M. Gallup, president of Sandusky Tool Co.

The listing of planes in Catalogue No. 24 was substanially reduced from the 1885 Catalogue. However, two new items appeared: NEW IMPROVED ALUMINUM TOP BENCH PLANES (nine sizes in lengths of 7" to 30"), and WEATHER STRIP PLANES (Two varities: Special Rabbet or Meeting Rail Plane; and Special Grooving Plane with Metal Fence. Plane irons were noted "manufactured from the best cast steel and fully warranted", without any reference to English Cast Steel. A diversified line of hoes was offered consisting of the following patterns" planters'; Scovil; Lyndon; Original German (Schwer's); tobacco; grub or sprouting; oval eye grub; giant sizes; street cleaning; steel laid types; grape; rice; hilling; Hercules handled; cotton scraping and Erhardt's light garden.

In spite of the new Catalogue business declined. Losses continued to accumulate. Mozart Gallup, President of the firm, died September 6, 1923. He was replaced by William L. Allendorf on May 21, 1924, and the firm continued to struggle on. The "straw that about broke the camel's back" occurred on June 28, 1924.

The northeast corner of Sandusky was swept by a tornado during the afternoon of Saturday, June 28, 1924. The Sandusky Tool Co. was in the direct path of the tornado, and not a single building escaped without some damage. The three-story main building, constructed from native limestone, was unroofed, and the north wall of the third story was razed. The forge plant was also unroofed, all windows blown out and the line shafting blown down. Packing, shipping buildings and open end timber drying sheds were destroyed. While rebuilding appeared to be possible, in view of continued financial losses of the preceeding years, the Probate Court refused to permit money from the estate of M.Gallup to be invested on behalf of the Tool Co. For the next five months a skeleton crew filled what orders could be supplied from inventory and operated such machinery that could be run when the weather was favorable, but the old plant was in its dying gasp!

During the fall negotiations commenced, ending on December 10, 1925 with new ownership acquiring the old firm and incorporating as a new Sandusky Tool Co.[22] George A. Schwer was president; William F. Seitz, vice-president; Alden Seitz (his son), treasurer; and Wilbert G.Schwer (son of George), secretary and thereafter, general manager. Herculian efforts directed by George A.Schwer with rehiring men, consisting largely of the old employees, rehabilitated the plant within two months to operating condition. A new building equipped with new grinding machinery was constructed. The vast majority of these one hundred employees were in their sixties and seventies with two being in their eighties. "Their performance and dependability were a stinging rebuke to modern idea programs of compulsory retirement at 65, or even younger. We had little or no absenteeism, a very low record of industrial accidents (not withstanding the alarming absence of safety guards and measures throughout the ancient plant, practically no need for inspection of finished products to insure quality, and no gold bricking on the job."[23] What a credit indeed to combined efforts of management and labor for their securities.

After the plant became productive, Wilbert Schwer and Alden Seitz made a tour to the Middle Atlantic Seaboard area in June 1925. They visited customers of the old firm at Philadelphia, New York and southern New England. They also visited their only principal domestic plane competitor, Chapin-Stephens at New Hartford, Connecticut.[23] According to Wilbert Schwer, "unfortunately most of the conferences turned out to be nostalgic reminiscences of vast amounts of business done in the years gone by, but not one customer could offer much in the way of prospects for the future".[24] A summary of his report is presented in Table L.

Catalogue No. 25, compiled by Wilbert G. Schwer was published on September 1, 1925. This was the final catalog issued by the firm and probably the last wooden plane catalog to be published in the United States. The introduction to this appears as Plate L. This Catalogue was divided into three sections: Sandusky Semi-Steel and Adjustable Wood Bench Planes; Hoes and Forged Products; and Wood Tools. (Wood Planes and Plane Irons, etc.)[25]

Details of the Sandusky Semi Steel Planes are described in a brochure reproduced as Plate LI. U.S.Patent #1,696,584 was issued to Wilbert G. Schwer for this plane on December 25, 1928, which was assigned to the Sandusky Tool Corporation.

Table XVI - Summary of 1925 Trip to Middle Atlantic Seaboard [26]

1. Wooden planes were obsolescent almost to the point of being obsolete. The comparative few that were still being sold were only in the demand among aging wood workers and foreign born carpenters, who were accustomed to using such tools. The younger craftsmen were all all using metal bodied-planes. Furthermore our planes were not competitive in price with rather good quality planes being imported from Germany by such firms as Columbia Tool Co. of New York.

2. Wood hand screws were also on their way out. Such hand screws as were still being used were either of the Jorgensen type, having wooden jaws and steel spindles or else were all-metal clamps of various styles.

3. Since we were the only manufacturer of wooden planes left in this country, outside of Chapin-Stephens, which made its own plane irons, there was no market for our plane irons, except as used in our own planes, and this limited the number we could sell as replacements.

4. The hoe situation was a little brighter. While mechanization was well under way on farms and in the southern plantations, and far fewer hoes were being used than in years past, there still existed some volume. However, in addition to our leading competitor, The American Fork and Hoe Company (now True Temper, Inc.), there were perhaps some four or five other manufacturers. Likewise, quantities of European hoes, largely from Germany, but some from England, were coming into the country at prices we could not meet and such foreign-made hoes had practically driven us out of Latin America and other export markets which we formerly enjoyed. Last, but by no means least, our line of hoes was sadly deficient in not including "gooseneck" hoes, the type most in demand.

The "Sandusky" Adjustable Wood Bench Planes offered with wood bottoms (smoother, jack and fore planes with double irons) had the same adjusting mechanism as the Semi-Steel Bench Planes. Some incidental remarks concerning these Semi-Steel planes follow: [27]

"Semi-Steel was a selling gimmick that G,& C.Foundry used for years, and simply meant that 20 to 25% of steel was added to the usual gray-iron composition to give it high-strength. We,at the Tool Company, found it well suited for our metal plane bodies. The Foundry no longer stresses this name or point.

We had what the pattern makers call a "plate" for each size of plane body, so about four could be cast in a mold at one time. We had similar "plate" for casting the cap or slotted metal part that held the plane iron in place.

We machined the plane bodies on a No.2 Browne & Sharp milling machine, with a straddle-mill set up, one at a time. That wasn't too fast, but the demand for planes was not so brisk that we needed to go further. The caps were machined on the same machine,partly by jigs, and partly by obvious grinding and polishing operations.

The planes with wood bodies, but embodying the same internal mechanisms as our metal-body planes were not too successful, and we made comparatively few of them. Other plane manufacturers had the same experience with wood-body, metal-mechanism numbers.

You will note from the patent,I assigned my rights to the metal plane design to Sandusky Tool Corporation, which owned 100% by what is now True Temper, Inc. What they did with, I haven't the slightest idea. We did sell quite a lot of them during the brief time we made them"

The Sandusky Tool Company

ESTABLISHED 1868

GEORGE A. SCHWER, *President*

WILBERT G. SCHWER, *Secretary*

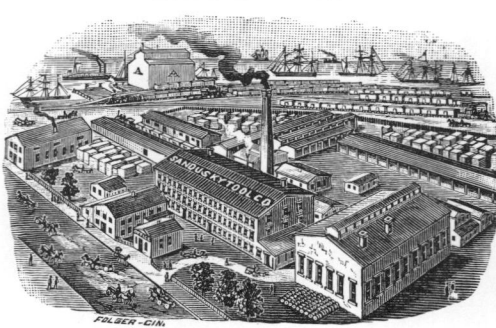

WILLIAM F. SEITZ, *Vice-President*

ALDEN SEITZ, *Treasurer*

SANDUSKY, OHIO, SEPT. 1, 1925.

To Our Customers:

We take pleasure in submitting for your examination our new catalog No. 25.

This catalog cancels all previously issued catalogs and bulletins, and we urge our customers to destroy all such printed matter and to order only from this catalog.

In addition to all of the well-known products we have been manufacturing for nearly sixty years, this catalog illustrates and describes many new products which we confidently expect will be of great interest to our customers.

We wish to emphasize the fact that our policies are progressive in every respect. We believe that we have brought our line of products thoroughly up-to-date with the additions shown in this catalog, and it will be our endeavor to keep abreast of the times by adding more and more lines every year.

We are prepared to quote attractive prices on special work of all kinds, and we earnestly solicit inquiries from our customers who are in the market for tools or hardware of any kind. Our plant presents a combination which is extremely unique, as we have a sawmill, woodworking shop, machine shop, forge shop, and a rolling and stamping mill, all under one roof. We are, consequently, well equipped for manufacturing a vast number of articles, and are always ready to place our facilities at the disposal of our customers.

All of our products are fully warranted as regards workmanship and materials, and we endeavor to give the best of service at all times.

Yours very truly,
THE SANDUSKY TOOL COMPANY.

Geo. A. Schwer
President.

Plate L - Introduction to the Sandusky Tool Co. Catalogue No. 25

SANDUSKY TOOL CORPORATION, SANDUSKY, OHIO, U. S. A.

SOLE MANUFACTURERS OF

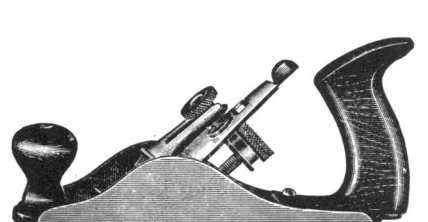

SANDUSKY SEMI-STEEL
PLANES

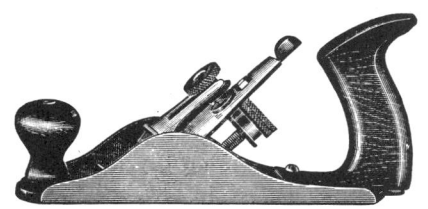

U. S. Patent Filed Oct. 14th, 1925
Serial No. 62,404.

Nos. 3S and 3SC

Type "S"—Smooth Bottom

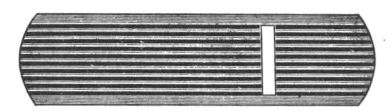

Type "SC"—Corrugated Bottom

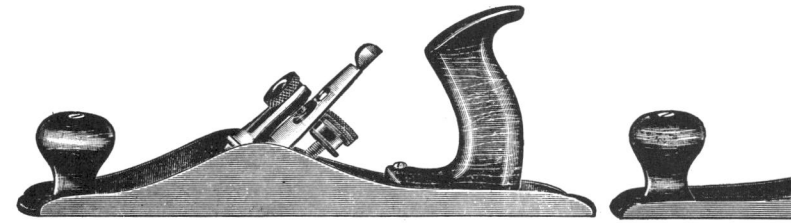

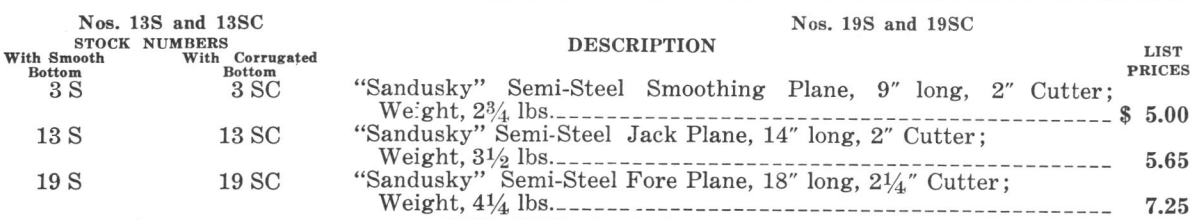

Nos. 13S and 13SC

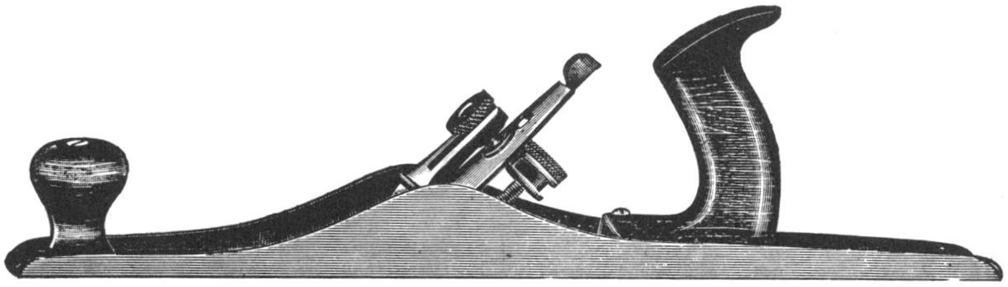

Nos. 19S and 19SC

STOCK NUMBERS		DESCRIPTION	LIST PRICES
With Smooth Bottom	With Corrugated Bottom		
3 S	3 SC	"Sandusky" Semi-Steel Smoothing Plane, 9" long, 2" Cutter; Weight, 2¾ lbs.	$ 5.00
13 S	13 SC	"Sandusky" Semi-Steel Jack Plane, 14" long, 2" Cutter; Weight, 3½ lbs.	5.65
19 S	19 SC	"Sandusky" Semi-Steel Fore Plane, 18" long, 2¼" Cutter; Weight, 4¼ lbs.	7.25

PACKED ONE PLANE IN A LABELED CARDBOARD BOX; TWELVE PLANES IN A CASE.
Sides and bottom brightly polished. Inside of body enameled with dark blue "Duco." Handles and knobs rosewood finish.

16 LESS PARTS.   12 POINTS OF SUPERIORITY.   READ THEM:

1. There are only 17 parts in a "Sandusky" Plane, as contrasted with 33 in the older types, and at the same time every necessary adjustment feature is retained.
2. Having fewer parts than the old-style iron plane, the "Sandusky" Plane is lighter in weight, and, consequently, less fatiguing to the user.
3. All of the fragile, easily-broken parts found in the older metal planes have been eliminated.
4. The adjusting mechanism of the "Sandusky" Plane is made entirely of steel, and is practically indestructible.
5. The adjusting mechanism is positive. There is no slippage or lost motion such as is found in the older types of iron planes.
6. The adjustment of a "Sandusky" Plane is simple. Anyone can "set" the plane after a moment's examination, without instructions or directions.
7. The entire plane can be assembled or taken apart in an instant with the single retaining nut.
8. The "Sandusky" Plane is properly balanced. The peculiar construction of the adjusting mechanism throws the weight forward, making the forward end the heavier, and causing the face of the plane to adhere to the wood with a minimum of effort.
9. The adjustment is absolutely rigid. When the retaining nut (located above the cutter) is tightened firmly, the cutting edge might be struck with a hammer without affecting the adjustment in the slightest degree. The cutter cannot chatter even when used against the hardest woods.
10. The "Sandusky" Plane contains the same type of heavy, wedge-shaped, non-chattering cutter (or plane iron) that has gained international renown in "Sandusky" Wood Planes during the last sixty years. This cutter will take and retain a much finer cutting edge than the thin irons used in most iron planes. The cap is so constructed as to make the cutter a double iron, and the distance of the cap from the cutting edge is automatically adjusted by regulating the depth of the cut in the manner described below.
11. The body of the "Sandusky" Plane is made of a special alloy of Semi-Steel, consisting of 85% gray iron, 10% steel, and 5% Mayari iron. This produces a very tough, close-grained metal, similar to that used in the cylinder blocks of high-grade automobile engines.
12. There is, after all, only one REAL plane maker—the man who has spent years as a maker of wood planes. Good machinists can make the parts of an iron plane and assemble them, but they have no conception of the delicate adjustments which must be made to a plane before it is ready for work requiring precision. Every "Sandusky" Semi-Steel Plane leaving our plant has had its cutter whetted up on a fine oil-stone, and has been thoroughly adjusted, and rigorously tested and inspected by wood plane makers with forty-five years' experience. This is the finest guaranty of satisfaction we could provide, and one which is not obtainable with any other metal plane on the market.

Plate LI - Sandusky Semi-Steel Planes - Sandusky Tool Corporation Advertisement

SANDUSKY TOOL CORPORATION

BUSINESS FOUNDED 1868

Mr. Kenneth D. Roberts,
Fitzwilliam, N. H., 03447.

Dear Mr. Roberts: **Sandusky, Ohio, U. S. A.,** November 10, 1977

This letter is written on a specimen of a four-page letterhead which we used to answer simple requests for information on our best-selling items. Also enclosed is my last spare copy of Catalog No. 25. From the list prices, we used to give discounts of 25-20% (i.e. 40%) to our best customers, such as Sargent & Co., Hibbard-Spencer-Bartlett, etc.; 25% to still smaller jobbers; and 10% to what I would call "general store" dealers, meaning retail establishments. The name "A.C. Bartlett" I remember well.

Catalog No. 24 was in use before we took over after the Tornado of 1924. We also had a Spanish language equivalent of Catalog No. 24. Yes, we had some Latin-American business, and we were occasionally visited by buyers, from Latin-American countries. Their technology was twenty or more years behind ours, so they still used some of our kinds of tools, although they had their own manufacturers, too.

My friend, Alden Seitz, who was treasurer of the Tool Company (and who is still living), and I, made an exploratory trip to our Atlantic seaboard customers in June, 1925, and stopped off to visit Frank Chapin (President of Chapin-Stephens) at Pine Meadow. He received us most cordially, and showed us all through his plant, which resembled ours generally, but was considerably smaller. He presented us each with a small, folding ivory pocket rule, as a momento of our visit. Incidentally, we thereafter regularly bought his wooden marking guages, (which he apparently made from scrap,) and sold them to our customers under our own name.

During the summer of 1925, I wrote Catalog No. 25, which was published in September, 1925. (By coincidence, the printer who published it, became my father-in-law ten years later.)

My grandfather, Albert Schwehr, -(spelling changed back to original "Schwer" in 1909) had patents on his hoe-making machinery, dating from the 1870's, and I had a patent on our semi-steel bench plane (US Patent # 1,696,584; Dec. 25, 1928). Undoubtedly J. A. Montgomery took out patents on some of his ingenious plane-making machinery, but I do not know that. As far as I know, no patents were held by the Tool Company covering wooden planes.

You will note from the patent that I assigned my rights in the metal plane design to Sandusky Tool Corporation, which was owned 100% by what is now True Temper, Inc. What they did with it I haven't the slightest idea. We did sell quite a lot of these planes, during the brief time we made them.

During my time (latter part of 1924 through 1929) we never used the name "OGONTZ", but it is quite possible, even probable, that it may have been used years ago. The name 'Ogontz' is the distinctive name of a chief of a tribe of Ottawas who lived in Sandusky. He was a great friend of Jay Cooke, noted Civil War financeer, who also originated in Sandusky.

During my time, we simply sold our so-called "cull" planes, without any brand on them at all, in job lots to dealers in such merchandise. They were "culls" or "seconds" only because they had a knot or some other imperfection in the wood which did not in any way impair their complete usefulness.

I really loved the old Tool Company. I fear that, had I been born in a time when it was still a paying business, and if I had had the same opportunity that I had in 1924-1929, I might have been content to be a small-time manufacturer, working, for a very modest salary. One thing I liked, was the versatility that I had to exercise. I wore a great many "hats" in the discharge of my $55 a week job: Office Manager; Plant Manager; Order Clerk; Comptroller; Cost Accountant; Purchasing Agent; Billing Clerk; Timber Buyer; Draftsman and Designer; Foreign Correspondent. I still remember when.

Cordially,

Wilbert G. Schwer

Plate LII - Letter from Wilbert G. Schwer on Sandusky Tool Co. Stationery

THE SANDUSKY TOOL COMPANY, Sandusky, Ohio

"SANDUSKY" SEMI-STEEL BENCH PLANES

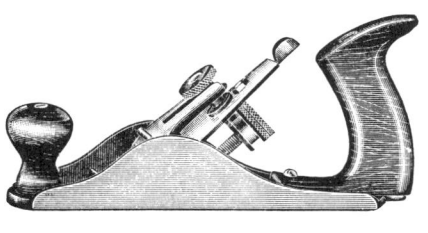

Nos. 3S and 3SC

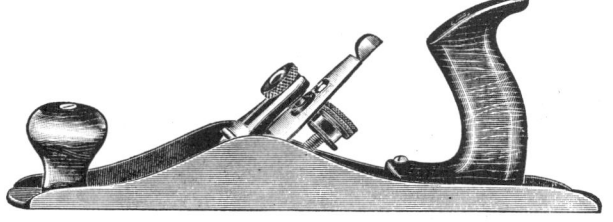

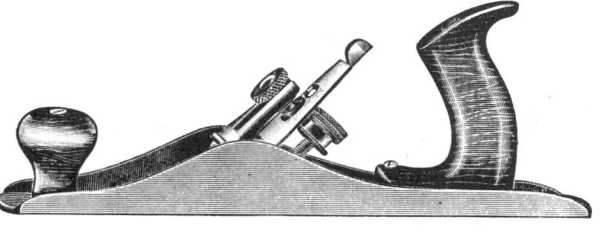

Nos. 13S and 13SC

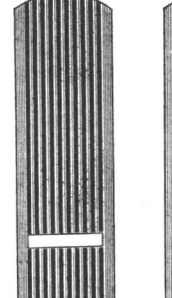

Corrugated Bottom  — Smooth Bottom

No.		Price Each
3-S	Semi-Steel Smoothing Plane, 9″ long, 2″ double iron; with smooth bottom	$5.00
13-S	Semi-Steel Jack Plane, 14″ long, 2″ double iron; with smooth bottom	5.65
19-S	Semi-Steel Fore Plane, 18″ long, 2¼″ double iron; with smooth bottom	7.25
3-SC	Semi-Steel Smoothing Plane, 9″ long, 2″ double iron; with corrugated bottom	5.00
13-SC	Semi-Steel Jack Plane, 14″ long, 2″ double iron; with corrugated bottom	5.65
19-SC	Semi-Steel Fore Plane, 18″ long, 2¼″ double iron; with corrugated bottom	7.25

SMOOTHING PLANES
1½″ to 2¼″ Irons

Nos. 1 and 3 — No. 5

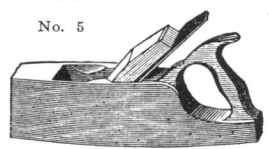

1—Single-Iron Smoothing Plane	$1.60
3—Double-Iron Smoothing Plane	2.00
5—Double-Iron Handled Smooth Plane	3.90

No. 06 HORNED SMOOTH, JACK, & SCRUB PLANES

No. 06 Horned Smooth

Single-Iron, Horned Smooth Plane	$2.70
Double-Iron, Horned Smooth Plane	2.80
Single-Iron, Horned Jack Plane	3.20
Double-Iron, Horned Jack Plane	3.30
Horned Scrub Plane	2.80

JACK PLANES

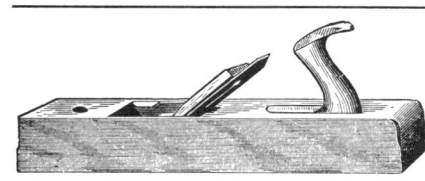

Nos. 10 and 13

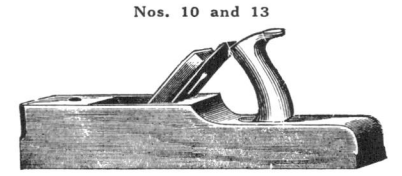

No. 15

No.		Price Each
10	Single-Iron Jack Plane	$1.80
13	Double-Iron Jack Plane	2.30
15	Double-Iron Jack Plane, with Razee Handle	2.70

FORE PLANES and JOINTER PLANES
2⅜″ and 2½″ Irons

19—Double-Iron, Fore Plane, 22 inches long	$3.80
21—Double-Iron, Fore Plane, 22 inches long, with Razee Handle	4.30
25—Double-Iron, Jointer Plane:	

Length	24″	26″	28″	30″
Price Each	$4.00	4.00	4.30	4.80

No. 36 TOOTH PLANES
2⅛″ Irons

Price Each $3.20

SIDE BEAD PLANES

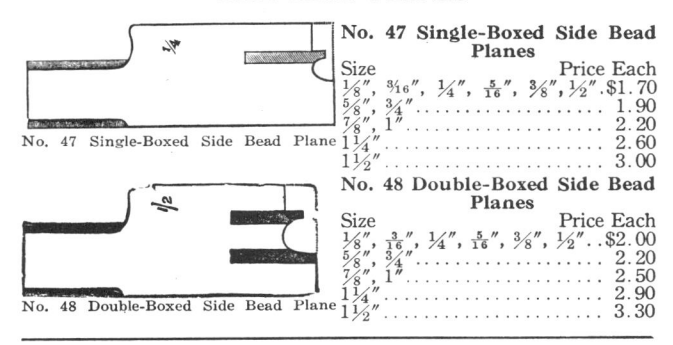

No. 47 Single-Boxed Side Bead Plane

No. 47 Single-Boxed Side Bead Planes

Size	Price Each
⅛″, 3/16″, ¼″, 5/16″, ⅜″, ½″	$1.70
⅝″, ¾″	1.90
⅞″, 1″	2.20
1¼″	2.60
1½″	3.00

No. 48 Double-Boxed Side Bead Plane

No. 48 Double-Boxed Side Bead Planes

Size	Price Each
⅛″, 3/16″, ¼″, 5/16″, ⅜″, ½″	$2.00
⅝″, ¾″	2.20
⅞″, 1″	2.50
1¼″	2.90
1½″	3.30

No. 51 CENTER BEAD PLANES

No. 51 Center Bead Plane

Double Boxed Center Bead Planes

Size	Price Each
⅛″, 3/16″, ¼″, 5/16″, ⅜″, ½″	$2.00
⅝″, ¾″	2.20
⅞″, 1″	2.50

No. 92 HOLLOW AND ROUND PLANES

No. 92 Hollow and Round Planes

Size No.	Size	Diameter of Circle	Price per Pair
1	¼″	½″	$3.20
2	⅜″	¾″	3.20
3	½″	1″	3.20
4	⅝″	1¼″	3.20
5	¾″	1½″	3.20
6	⅞″	1¾″	3.20
7	1″	2″	3.60
8	1⅛″	2¼″	3.60
9	1¼″	2½″	3.60

DADO PLANES

No. 62 Dado Plane

No.		Price Each
60	Dado, Brass Side Stop	$3.20
	¼″, ⅜″, ½″, ⅝″, ¾″, ⅞″, 1″.	
62	Dado, Screw Stop	$4.40
	¼″, ⅜″, ½″, ⅝″, ¾″, ⅞″, 1″.	

FILLETSTER PLANES

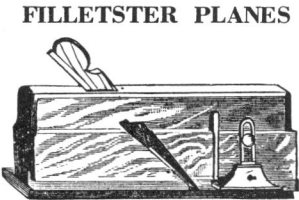

No. 68 Filletster Plane

No.		Price Each
65	Filletster Plane	$3.20
66	Filletster, with Cutter	3.60
67	Filletster, with Cutter and Brass Side Stop	4.00
68	Filletster, with Cutter and Brass Side Stop, Boxed	5.30
69	Filletster, with Cutter and Brass Screw Stop, Boxed	7.00

Plate LIII - Page 2 of Four Page Sandusky Tool Co. Brochure

THE SANDUSKY TOOL COMPANY, Sandusky, Ohio

MATCH PLANES

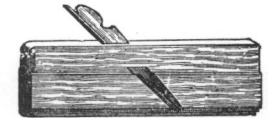

One Pair No. 100 MATCH PLANES

No.		Price per Pair
99—Board Match Planes, Twin or Separate, ⅜″, ½″, ⅝″, ¾″, ⅞″, and 1″		$4.40
100—Board Match Planes, Twin or Separate, Plated, ⅜″, ½″, ⅝″, ¾″, ⅞″, and 1″		$5.00

NOSING PLANES

No. 111 Nosing Planes with One Iron

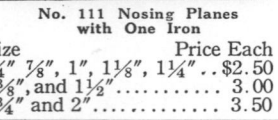

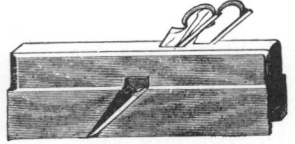

Size	Price Each
¾″, ⅞″, 1″, 1⅛″, 1¼″	$2.50
1⅜″, and 1½″	3.00
1¾″ and 2″	3.50

No. 113 Nosing Planes with Two Irons

Size	Price Each
¾″, ⅞″, 1″, 1⅛″, 1¼″	$3.20
1⅜″ and 1½″	3.70
1¾″ and 2″	4.20

No. 146 SKEW RABBET PLANES

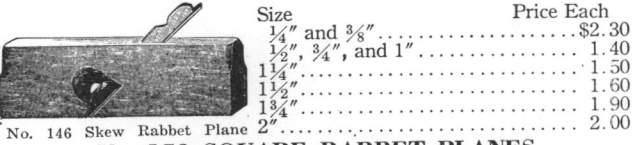

Size	Price Each
¼″ and ⅜″	$2.30
½″, ¾″, and 1″	1.40
1¼″	1.50
1½″	1.60
1¾″	1.90
2″	2.00

No. 146 Skew Rabbet Plane

No. 150 SQUARE RABBET PLANES
Same sizes and prices as Skew Rabbet Planes.

BUCK RABBET PLANES
With Handle and Two Cutters

No. 149 Buck Rabbet Plane, Skew

No. 149—With Center Handle

Size	Price Each
1″, 1¼″, 1½″, 1¾″, and 2″	$3.80
2¼″ and 2½″	4.50

No. 149½—With Side Handle

Size	Price Each
1″, 1¼″, 1½″, 1¾″, and 2″	$4.20
2¼″ and 2½″	4.90

In addition to the planes shown here, we manufacture many other styles and sizes, including a full line of special planes for installing weather strips.

WOOD BENCH — PLANE IRONS
We can furnish plane irons for any types of wood planes.

Single Iron **DOUBLE IRONS** Cut Iron 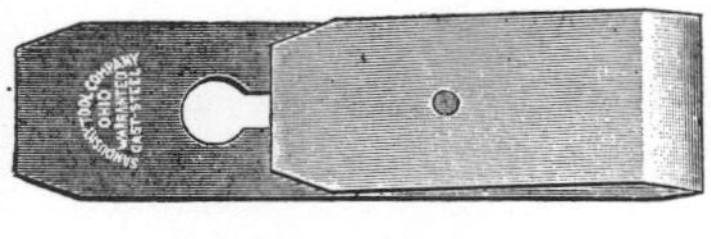 Double Iron
SINGLE IRONS and **CUT IRONS** Without Caps

Size in inches	1½″	1⅝″	1¾″	1⅞″	2″	2⅛″	2¼″	2⅜″	2½″	2⅝″	2¾″	3″
Per Dozen	$11.00	12.00	12.00	12.50	12.90	13.20	14.00	14.80	16.40	18.00	20.30	23.40

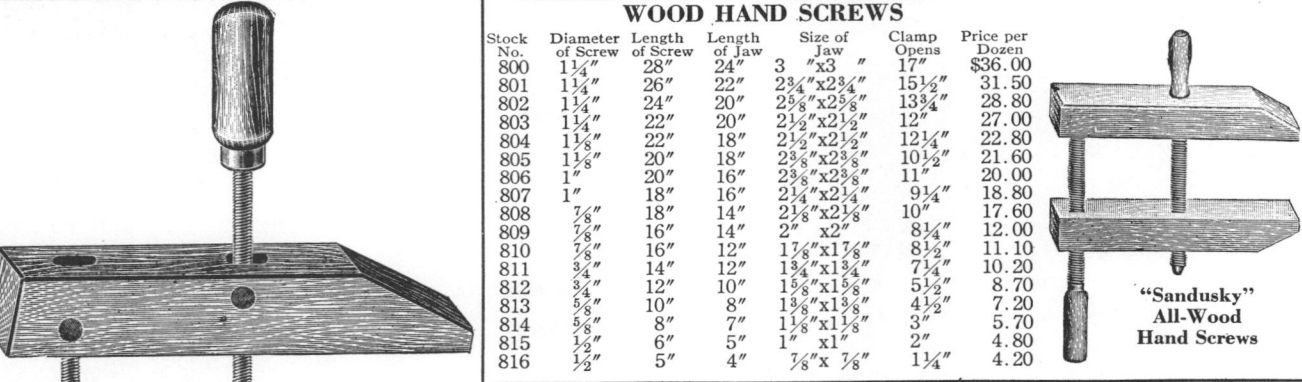

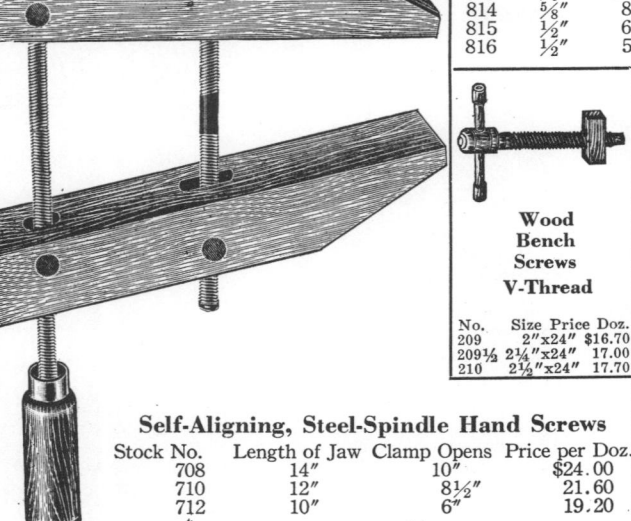

Size in inches	1½″	1⅝″	1¾″	1⅞″	2″	2⅛″	2¼″	2⅜″	2½″	2⅝″	2¾″	3″
Per Dozen	$8.00	9.00	9.00	9.50	9.90	10.30	11.00	11.80	12.70	14.30	16.60	19.70

WOOD HAND SCREWS

Stock No.	Diameter of Screw	Length of Screw	Length of Jaw	Size of Jaw	Clamp Opens	Price per Dozen
800	1¼″	28″	24″	3″x3″	17″	$36.00
801	1¼″	26″	22″	2¾″x2¾″	15½″	31.50
802	1¼″	24″	20″	2⅝″x2⅝″	13¾″	28.80
803	1¼″	22″	20″	2½″x2½″	12″	27.00
804	1⅛″	22″	18″	2½″x2½″	12¼″	22.80
805	1⅛″	20″	18″	2⅜″x2⅜″	10½″	21.60
806	1″	20″	16″	2⅜″x2⅜″	11″	20.00
807	1″	18″	16″	2¼″x2¼″	9¼″	18.80
808	⅞″	18″	14″	2⅛″x2⅛″	10″	17.60
809	⅞″	16″	14″	2″x2″	8¼″	12.00
810	⅞″	16″	12″	1⅞″x1⅞″	8½″	11.10
811	¾″	14″	12″	1¾″x1¾″	7¼″	10.20
812	¾″	12″	10″	1⅝″x1⅝″	5½″	8.70
813	⅝″	10″	8″	1⅜″x1⅜″	4½″	7.20
814	⅝″	8″	7″	1⅛″x1⅛″	3″	5.70
815	½″	6″	5″	1″x1″	2″	4.80
816	½″	5″	4″	⅞″x⅞″	1¼″	4.20

"Sandusky" All-Wood Hand Screws

Wood Bench Screws V-Thread

No.	Size	Price Doz.
209	2″x24″	$16.70
209½	2¼″x24″	17.00
210	2½″x24″	17.70

Self-Aligning, Steel-Spindle Hand Screws

Stock No.	Length of Jaw	Clamp Opens	Price per Doz.
708	14″	10″	$24.00
710	12″	8½″	21.60
712	10″	6″	19.20

IRON BENCH SCREWS

Stock No.		Price per Doz.
309	Iron Bench Screw, with Moveable Collar, Double Thread, Wrought Steel Screw, and Wood Handle; Size, 1″x16″	$14.40

Plate LIV - Page 3 of Four Page Brochure of Sandusky Tool Company

THE SANDUSKY TOOL COMPANY, Sandusky, Ohio

PLANTERS' EYE HOES
(NOT HANDLED)

Planters' Pattern    Scovil Pattern    Lyndon Pattern

PLANTERS' PATTERN HOES

Nos.	4/0	3/0	2/0	1/0	1	2	3	4	5	6
Wdth.of Blade	5½"	6"	6½"	7"	7½"	8"	8½"	9"	9½"	10"
Price per Doz.	$5.50	$5.50	$5.50	$5.75	$6.00	$6.50	$7.00	$7.50	$8.00	$8.50

SCOVIL AND LYNDON PATTERN HOES

Nos.	4/0	3/0	2/0	1/0	1	2	3	4	5	6
Wdth.of Blade	5½"	6"	6½"	7"	7½"	8"	8½"	9"	9½"	10"
Price per Doz.	$5.75	$5.75	$5.75	$6.00	$6.25	$6.75	$7.25	$7.75	$8.25	$8.75

OVAL-EYE GRUB or SPROUTING HOES
(NOT HANDLED)

PRICE LIST

Nos.	7/0	6/0	5/0	4/0
Width of Blade	4"	4½"	5"	5½"
Price per Dozen	$6.50	$7.00	$7.50	$8.00

GERMAN PATTERN HANDLED SQUARE-EYE HOES
56-inch Handles

When sold without handles, these hoes have the same prices as Planter's Pattern Hoes.

Nos.	4/0	3/0	2/0	1/0	1	2	3	4
Width of Blade	5½"	6"	6½"	7"	7½"	8"	8½"	9"
Price per Doz.	$8.50	$9.00	$9.50	$10.00	$10.75	$11.50	$12.25	$13.00

German Pattern Handled Square-Eye Grub or Sprouting Hoes
4-ft. Handles

When sold without handles, these hoes have the same prices as Oval Eye Grub or Sprouting Hoes.

Nos.	7/0	6/0	5/0	4/0
Width of Blade	4"	4½"	5"	5½"
Price per Dozen	$9.00	$9.50	$10.00	$10.50

HANDLED GRAPE HOES
4-ft. Handles

Price per Dozen $15.00

HANDLED SIDEWALK CLEANERS
4½-ft. Handles
PRICE LIST

Nos.	1	2
Width of Blade	7½"	8"
Price per Doz.	$10.00	$10.40

Nos.	3	4
Width of Blade	8½"	9"
Price per Doz.	$10.80	$11.20

"HERCULES" HANDLED HOES

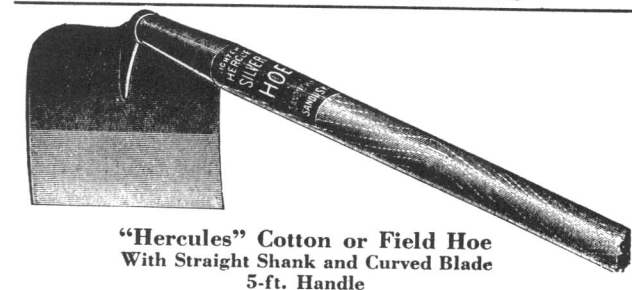

"Hercules" Cotton or Field Hoe
With Straight Shank and Curved Blade
5-ft. Handle

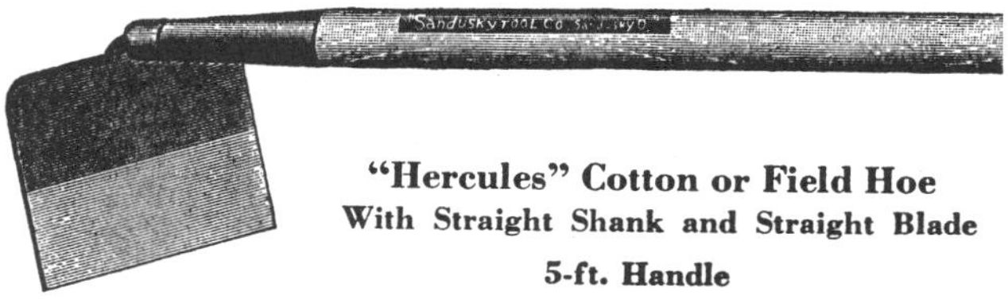

"Hercules" Cotton or Field Hoe
With Straight Shank and Straight Blade
5-ft. Handle

"Hercules" Cotton or Field Hoe
With Goose-Neck Shank and Straight Blade
5-ft. Handle

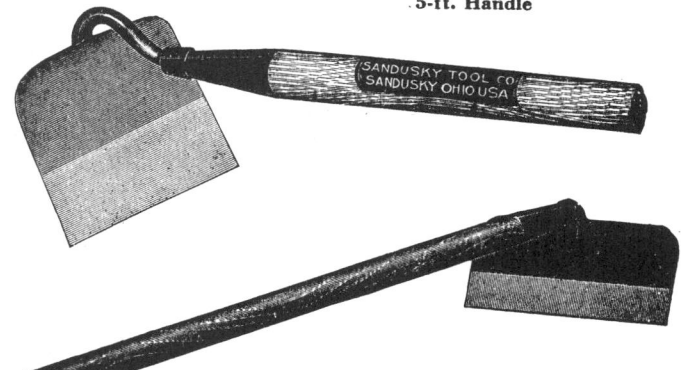

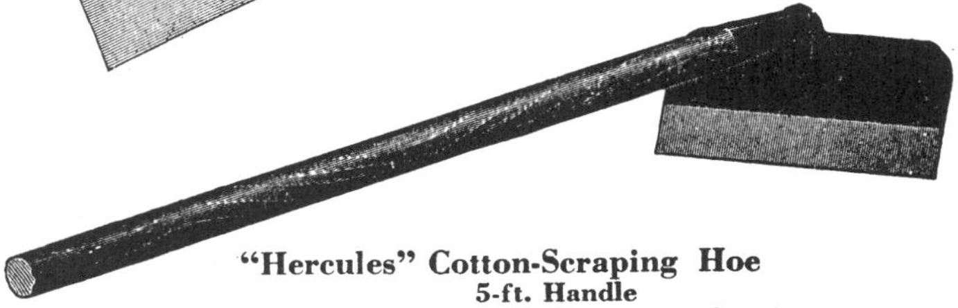

"Hercules" Cotton-Scraping Hoe
5-ft. Handle
(Price List applying to the four types above)

Nos.	3/0	2/0	1/0	1	2	3	4	5	6
Width of Blade	6"	6½"	7"	7½"	8"	8½"	9"	9½"	10"
Price per Doz.	$9.60	10.00	10.40	10.80	11.20	11.60	12.00	12.40	12.80

"Hercules" Meadow Hoes
(Full Polished)
5-ft. Handles

PRICE LIST

Nos.	1	2	3	4	5	6
Width of Blade	7½"	8"	8½"	9"	9½"	10"
Price per Dozen	$10.20	$10.60	$11.00	$11.40	$11.80	$12.20

Hercules Regular Goose-Neck Hoes
4½-ft. Handle

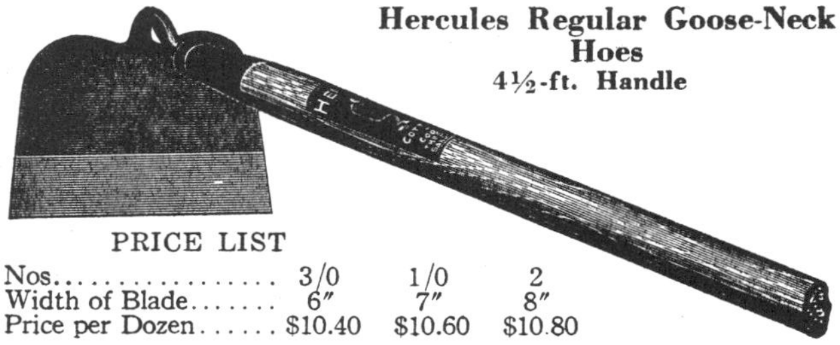

PRICE LIST

Nos.	3/0	1/0	2
Width of Blade	6"	7"	8"
Price per Dozen	$10.40	$10.60	$10.80

THE PRICES SHOWN ABOVE ARE FOR ONE-HALF OR ONE-THIRD POLISHED HOES IN NATURAL OIL FINISH

Plate LV - Page 4 of Four Page Brochure by Sandusky Tool Co.

A letter from Wilbert G. Schwer, accompanied by a four page brochure, are presented in Plates LII - LV. This brochure was used by the new firm to answer prospective inquiries about their products. The letter (see plate LII) summarizes some of Mr. Schwer's experience with the Sandusky Tool Co. In spite of vigorous sales' programs, advertising, and low cost production, the level of business and profits were most discouraging to management.

According to a survey made by Wilbert G. Schwer, ten types of planes accounted for 90% of all the planes listed in the Catalogue No. 25. A summary of this distribution is presented in Table XVII.[27]

Table XVII - Distribution of Types of Planes sold in 1925.

Stock Nos.		Catalog Page	Percent of Sales
146	Skew Rabbet Planes, all sizes	55	25.0
182-3-4.etc.	Weather Strip Planes (*)	61	16.4
3	Double-Iron Smoothing Planes	31	12.9
13	Double-Iron Jack Planes	31	10.1
92	Hollow & Round PLanes, all sizes	50	9.3
150	Square Rabbet Planes, all sizes	56	6.2
47	Single Boxed Side Bead Planes, all sizes	37	5.9
99	Board Match Planes, all sizes	51	1.8
113	Nosing Planes, with two irons, all sizes	53	1.3
19	Double-Iron Fore Planes	32	1.1
	Total		90.0
	All other sizes and tyes of planes		10.0

(*) Weather strip planes were usually made to the customers' specifications so should probably be considered as special purpose planes.

Note: The above statistics were taken from the sales for the first ten months of 1925, and the new semi-steel planes were not on the market until the end of that period, and no figures were available as to their sales.

As a consequence of the trip to the east in 1925, it was found out that the No. 185 Marking Gauge could be purchased from Chapin-Stevens at five cents each. Since the material was worth that amount, these gauges were purchased from this competitor and shipped out with a Sandusky Tool Co. label. The price noted in the Catalog was $2.40 per dozen, or twenty cents each.

A mythical situation had developed in Sandusky that the land leased to the Tool Co. was to expire in 1937. The City proposed to construct an attractive public waterfront area, to be known as Battery Park on the site of the Tool Co. In 1925 this political propaganda developed into a hassle between the then City Manager and the Tool Co. The upshot of this was the Tool Co. was deniend an extension of the ficticious lease for a twenty-five year period. If the management could have obtained an extension of the lease, they had considered investing capital into the firm for manufacturing new products.

Faced with discouraging business conditions and the inability to procur an extension of the lease, management accepted an offer from the American Fork and Hoe Co., now True Temper, Inc., and sold out "lock, stock and barrel". The new owners incorporated as Sandusky Tool Corporation, a wholly owned subsidiary, and took over complete direction on March 1,1926. While George A. Schwer was elected president of the new firm, from that time he was not active in that business. Since the new parent company had no one in its organization familiar with the plane business, Wilbert G. Schwer continued as secretary and plant manager until 1929.[28] The buildings were stripped from machinery and ultimately sold to the city in February 1931. The buildings of the Tool Co. were torn down, the heavy lintel stones and window sills were used at the entrance of the cove and to construct a small jetty and for fill at the Park. Thus ended the Chapter!

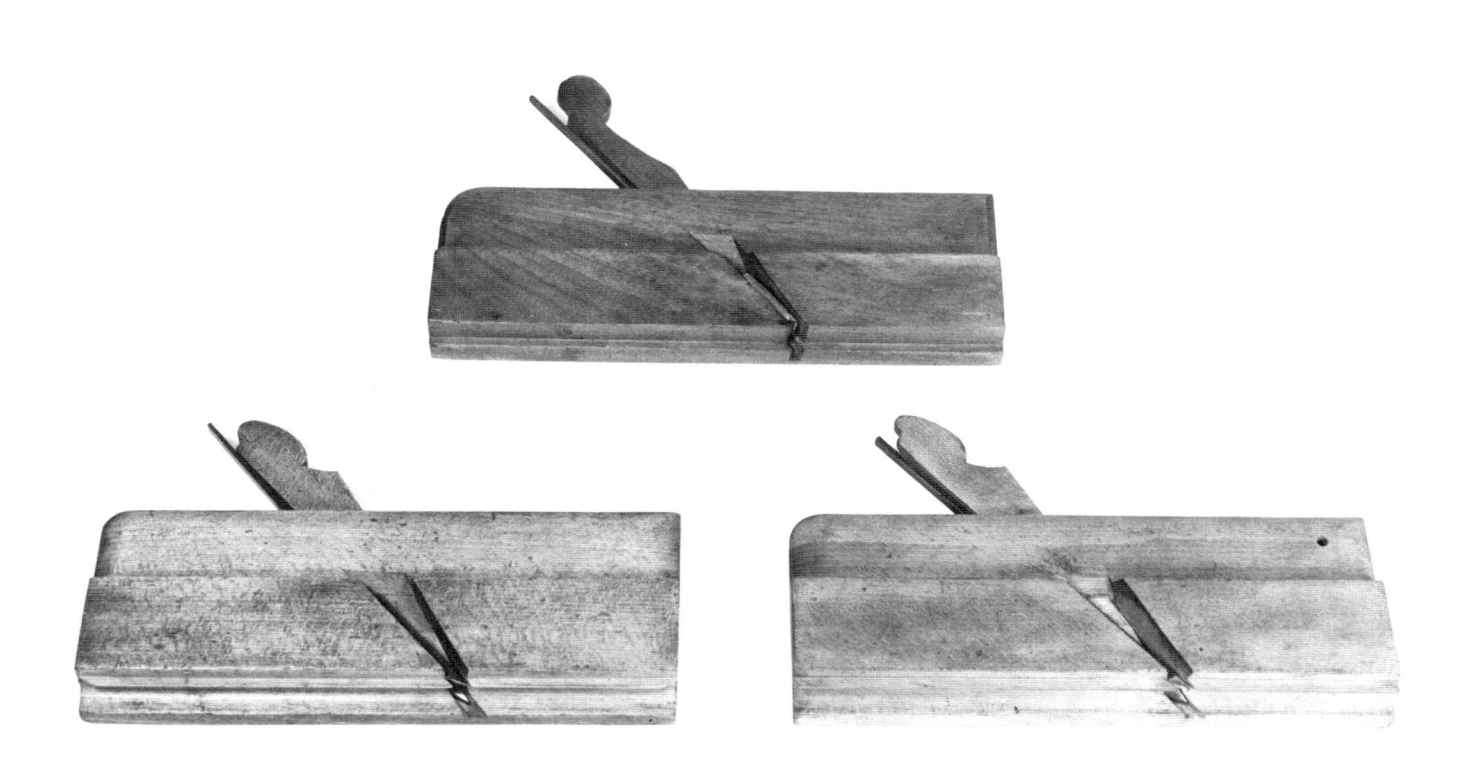

Fig. 147. Moulding Planes with Notched Wedges (see p.7)
 Top: Jo.Fuller, Providence, c.1800; Bottom: Sandusky Tool Co.,c.1900.
 Plane at left has imprint Sandusky Tool Co. in sheild (see Note No.13, Fig.2) Plane at right has imprint Sargent & Co. in same sheild design. (see Note 13, Fig.4)

Notes - Chapter VIII

Grateful acknowledgemnt is expressed to Wilbert G. Schwer for his assistance and loan of materials in writing this Chapter. Numerous details were abstracted from his manuscript - The Sandusky Tool Company Story. A copy of this is at the Sandusky Library. It was a real privilege to have access of first hand accounts from a knowledgeable person who was on the scene. Additionally he answered many questions by correspondence. The date of his Manuscript is February 1967.

1. Rabbet plane, collection of Addison Clipson.
2. Respectively from the collections of Ray Smith and Gil Gandenberger.
3. Correspondence from John R.Grabb, Dec.22,1977.
4. The *1877 Sandusky Tool Co. Catalogue* has been reprinted by this Publisher, Jan.1978
5. The original spelling of this family name was Schwer, but Albert Schwer upon linguistic advice had changed it to SCHWEHR. Later the family reverted to the original SCHWER. However the hoes were marked SCHWEHR's Patent.
6. E.H.Morris was also granted a Patent for Improvement in Moulding Planes on March 21,1871. This consisted of a combination plane stock to take different cutters. At that date he resided in Canton, Ohio.
7. R.M.Smith, *Chronicle of EAIA*, V.29,No.2,June 1976, p.28.
8. US Patent No.76,051 for an Improvement in Carpenters' Planes. This had a central screw with turn handle and two guiding arms each side on the adjusting screw. William Kimberley of Highgate, near Birmingham,England was granted Her Majesty's Patent,Nov.22,1887,"Improvement in Plough and Sash Fillister Planes for a similar arrangement.
9. See Note 11, p.194.
10. The *1885 Sandusky Tool Co. Catalogue* is in the collection of the Ohio Historical Society Library, Columbus, Ohio.
11. In 1866 H.Chapin sold his plane business at the Union Factory to his two sons, Edward M.and George W.Chapin, who continued the firm as H.Chapin's Sons. In 1868 George sold his interest to Edward, who continued as H.Chapin's Son until his death in 1897 when the firm name was changed to H.Chapin's Son & Co.
12. Correspondence with Wilbert G.Schwer, November 1, 1977.
13. Thomas A.Tully, *Chronicle of EAIA*, V.30,No.3, September 1977, pp.45-46
14. The indian chief's name was OGONTZ. He was sort of 'mentor' to Jay Cooke when the latter was a boy at Sandusky. Jay Cooke financed the Union side of the Civil War. He thought so much of Ogantz that he named his estate at Philadelphia OGONTZ.
15. Thomas Tully, op.cit.,see Note No. 13 above.
16. Collection of Addison Clipson.
17. Collection of Kendall Bassett.
18. F.H.Wildung, op.cit.,see Note No.73, p.46.
19. Mr. W.Lorenzen was Shippimg Clerk,scheduled production and was assistant to the General Manager,Otto Holzaepfel,during the early 1920's. Correspondence Wilbert G. Schwer, January 1978.
20. The Auburn Tool Co. merged with the Ohio Tool Co. Nov.14,1893 and continued as the Ohio Tool Co. until closing in 1921 at Charleston, W.Virgina.
21. Sandusky Tool Co. probably ceased plane manufacturing late in 1929 or early in 1930. Stanley Rule and Level Co. purchased the Chapin-Stevens Co. December 31, 1928 and closed down all manufacturing at this New Hartford,Conn. factory.
22. Ohio Corporation, No. 116,448
23. W.G.Schwer, Manuscript - The Sandusky Tool Co. Story,Feb.1967,pp.10-11.
24. *ibid*, p.14
25. *Sandusky Tool Co. Catalogue No.25,* has been reprinted by Ken Roberts Publishing Co. January 1978.
26. W.G.Schwer, Manuscript, op. cit., p.14.
27. Correspondence with W.G.Schwer, Nov.10, 1977.
28. Since June 1930, Wilbert G. Schwer has been active,engaged in the practice of law at Sandusky, Ohio.

Chapter IX

Window Sash Planes

The frame in which the glass panes are held to form a window is called the sash. The moulded strips in which the individual panes are supported and morticed into the sash are called muntin or sash bars. The outside surfaces of the sash bars are made with rabbeted sections to hold the panes by glazing. The inside sections are more decorative, having ovalo, ogee, Gothic or bevel mouldings. Both these inside (left) and outside (right) surface simultaneously cut by sash planes are illustrated in Plate LVI.[1]

Plate LVI - Sash Plane Section from 1857 Illustrated Supplement Arrowmammett Catalogue of Bench Planes and Moulding Tools, Middletown, CT.

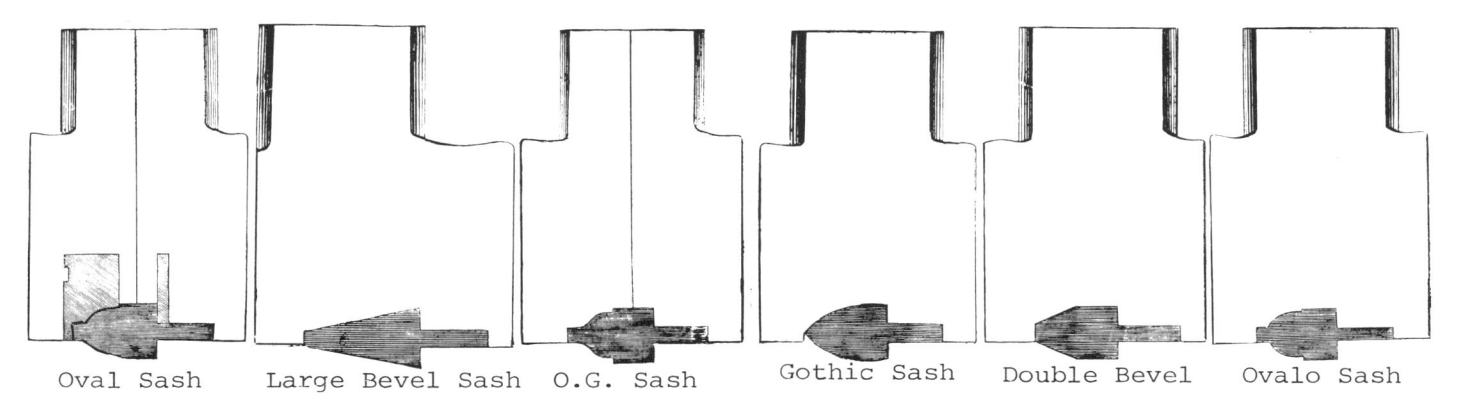

Oval Sash   Large Bevel Sash   O.G. Sash   Gothic Sash   Double Bevel   Ovalo Sash

During the 18th Century both the inside and outside sections of sash bars and sash frame edges were shaped by planes. Automated sash and door mortising machinery began to appear in the United States by the mid-1830's and to replace such work formerly accomplished by hand planing.[2] Those readers that are not acquainted with window construction might benefit from studying sections in *Dictionary of Tools*.[3]

In England during the mid-19th Century the conventional practice for making window sash was to first form the rabbeted section using a sash fillister (preferred English spelling). The rabbeted "stuff" was then held in a 'sticking board' on the bench. The inside section was then planed after selecting a moulding plane of appropriate shape. A template was used to ascertain uniform size of this moulding. Fig. 148 illustrates a sash fillister (Routledge & Son, Birmingham) at the right[the fence has been reversed to show the brass stop], a pair of "lamb's tongue" sash moulding planes (Kirk & Heathcott, No.31 Norfolk Lane, Sheffield) at the left and a sash template at the center. Formerly it has been thought that two sash moulding planes were employed; No.1 for roughing out; and No.2 for finishing. However, recent studies by W.L. Goodman have shown that No.1 was used for the sash bars and No.2 for the sash frame, the latter having slightly deeper contour than the former. This allowed for more light to be transmitted through the window frame.[4]

Fig. 148. Left to Right. Pair of English Sash Planes, Sash Template. Sash Fillister

A detailed description and use of the sash fillister appears in *The Mechanics Companion*. See Section 21, page 163 this book. There were two forms of the sash fillister; one with the mouth on the right side of the plane which throws the shavings on the bench, and one with the mouth on the left side, which throws the shavings off the bench. The former had a rebate on the left side of the sole, opposite the mouth, which acted as a stop when the depth of the rebate on the sash bar had been planed. (See Section 22, p.164) The latter usually had a seperate brass side stop, similar to that used with a moving filletster and also had a nicker and wedge. (SeeSection 23, page 164) This type is also illustrated above in Fig. 148, but the fence has been reversed in this photograph in order to more clearly see the brass stop and nicker.

On the matter of sash filletster (preferred American spelling), an error was made in the 1st Edition in labeling the plane shown in Fig. 78, p.121 by this name. Mercer's earlier error in this connection was inadvertently followed.[5] The particular plane shown in Fig. 78 is a wood screw manually adjustable sash plane. While my error has been corrected in this 2nd Edition, it is suggested that 1st Edition copies be accordingly changed to the proper label.

Although not very commonly found today, sash filletsters were made in America at least until 1858. Six varities were offered in the *1858 Arrowmammett Works Catalogue* [see items#157-162,page 7 invoice list (page 143)]. Two types (items#218 & 219) were offered *Hermon Chapin's 1853 Catalogue & Invoice Price List*. Perhaps this type of plane was widely disgarded after this date. In any event those that have survived seem to be limited to the 18th and early 19th Centuries. Such a sash plane is shown in Fig.149. This plane is 9 inches long, has the mouth on the left side and throws the shavings off the bench.[6] It can therefore be considered Nicholoson Type 2. (see Section 23, p.104). This has the imprint J.Stiles/New York, and was made between 1768-1775.

A sash filletster with mouth on the right side which throws the shavings on the bench (Nicholson Type 1) by Amos Wheaton, Philadelphia c.1795, is shown in Fig. 150. Note that both of these planes have fence adjustmant by wedges, rather than the later screw arms.

Fig. 149. Sash Filletster by J.Stiles/NEW YORK, c.1768 - 1775

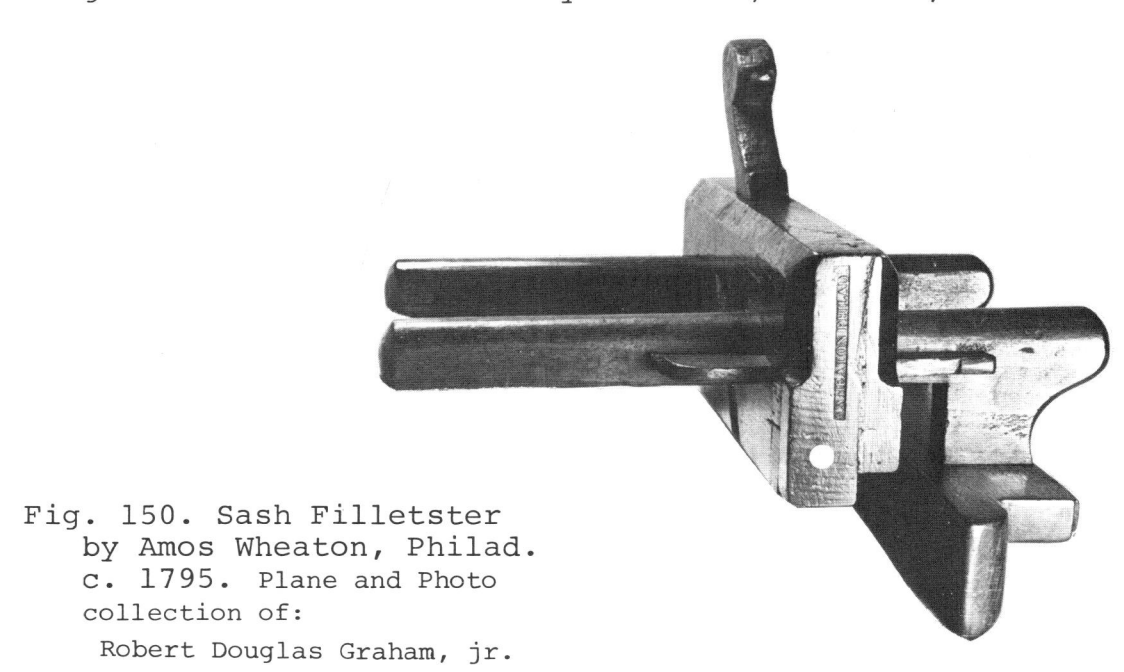

Fig. 150. Sash Filletster by Amos Wheaton, Philad. c. 1795. Plane and Photo collection of:
Robert Douglas Graham, jr.

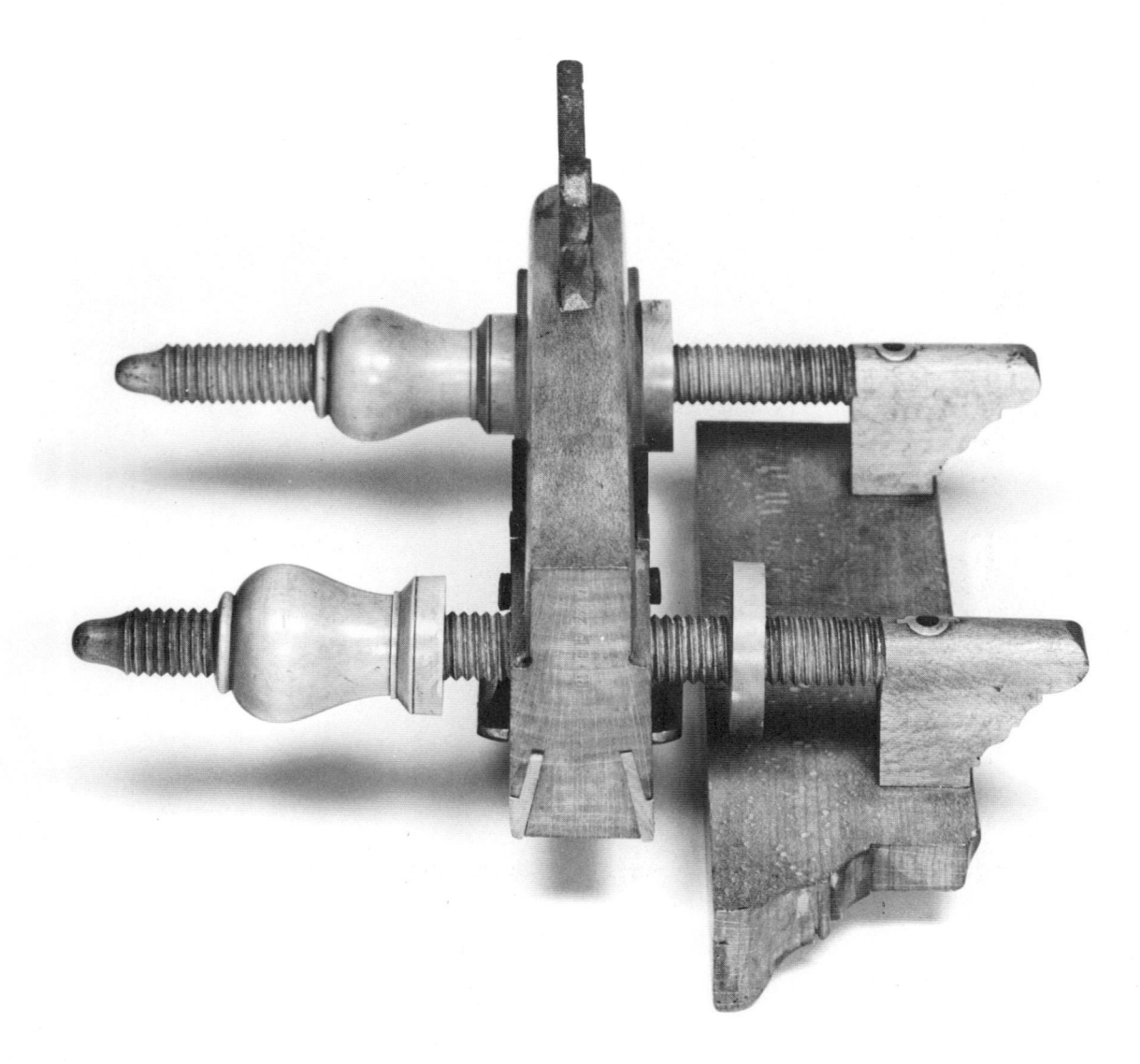

Fig. 151. Combination Sash and Moving Filletster by Reed, Utica, N.Y.
[Collection of James Cooley]

A very rare American plane, combination sash and moving filletster, is shown in Fig. 151. This has its mouth on the left, skewed to the left, and throws the shavings on the bench; therefore, a Type No. 1 Nicholoson sash filletster. Note that both stops are screw sliding brass inserts on each side. Of course only one stop is used at one time; the right side when used as a moving filletster for conventional rabbet work; while the left stop when used as a sash filletster. Note both working edges of the sole are shoulder boxed. This plane bears the imprint REED/Utica, N.Y. John Reed was trained in Wales.[7] He immigrated to Utica in 1820, continuing to make planes there until 1867.

Such planes were made in England and called "Double Fillister to do both Side and Sash Work".[8] This type of plane is illustrated in the 1899 *Alex Mathieson Wood Working Tools Catalogue*.[9] In general fancier sash sections were made in Great Britain than United States, which may account for the simplicity of American sash planes. A section illustrating sash mouldings used in Great Britain from page 196 of this *Mathieson's Catalogue* is shown on the last page, 314, of this text.

Fig. 152. Single Iron "Stick and Rabbet" American Sash Planes.

In the late 18th and early 19th Centuries in America, the more common form of sash plane was 12 to 14 inches in length, 1 to 2¼ inches in width, having a single iron, usually an open tote, and simultaneously cut both the rabbet and sash moulding on one side of the sash bar. The bottom plane illustrated in Fig. 152 is a typical example. Note the distinctive shaped tote, the chamfer around the side and ends, and the manner that the handle was pegged from the side. All of these are characteristics of 18th Century American planes. The plane at the top of Fig. 152 is also 13½ inches in length, but is made from a single piece of wood with a closed handle. Again the chamfer suggests either 18th or early 19th Century manufacture. Was this single iron "stick and rabbet" design a New England development? Or was this developed earlier in England? Based only on my observations todate of English planes, it would appear that this was an innovation developed in New England and not practiced in England until late in the 19th Century.[11] Another 18th Century sash plane of this type (12½" x 1-3/4") is shown at the bottom of Fig. 153. The top sash plane in the same illustration shows a most unusual double iron with single wedge with separator. This offered advantage of independent sharpening of the irons. The chamfer on this plane and style of tote indicates early 18th Century manufacture.

252

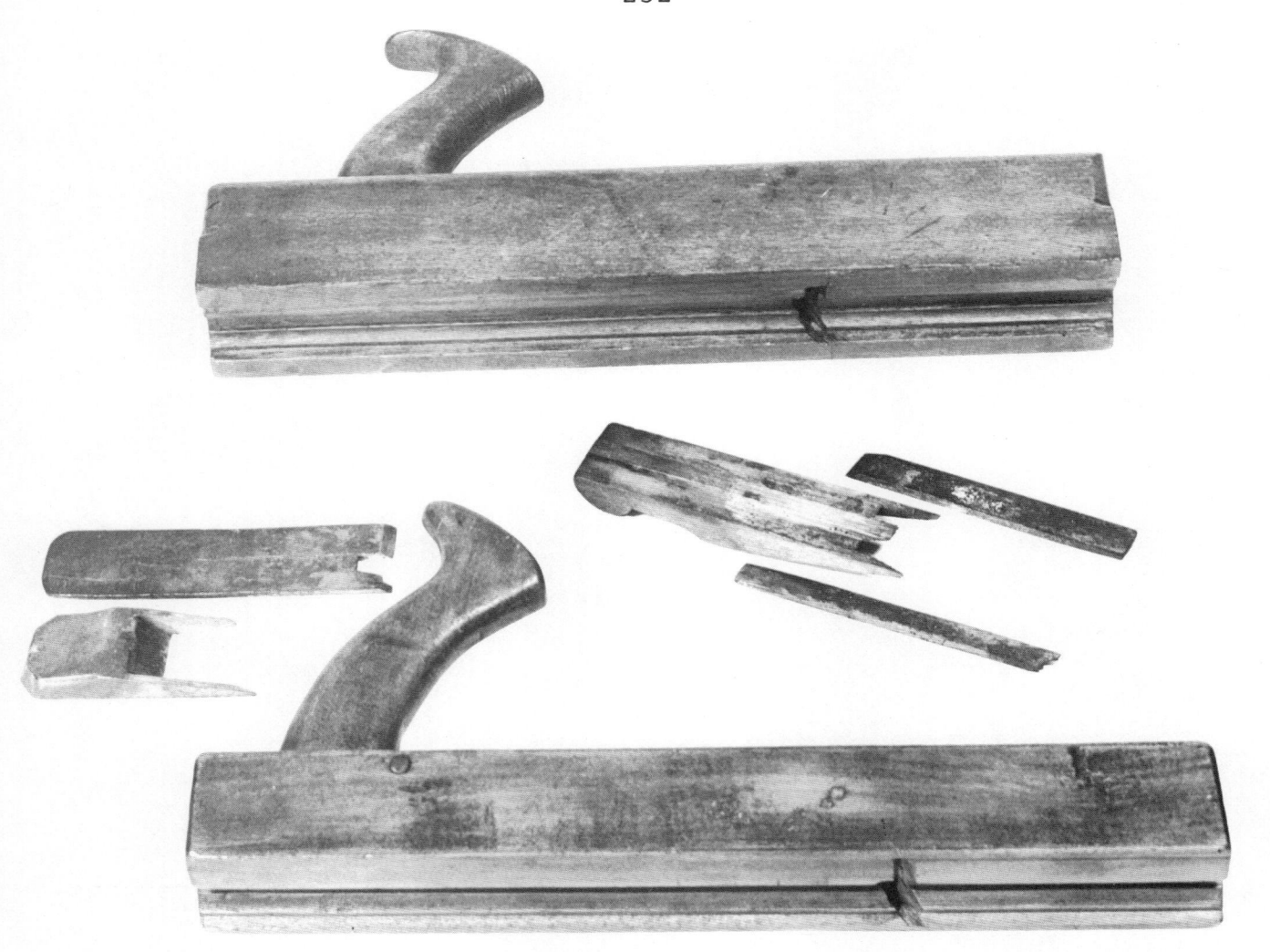

Fig. 153. Single (bottom) and Double (top) Iron American Sash Planes.

About the turn of the 18th Century such sash planes were made shorter, 10 inches in length and without handles, similar to conventional moulding planes. An example of such a late 18th Century sash plane is shown below in Fig. 154.

Fig. 154. Late 18th Century Sash Plane, 10" in length

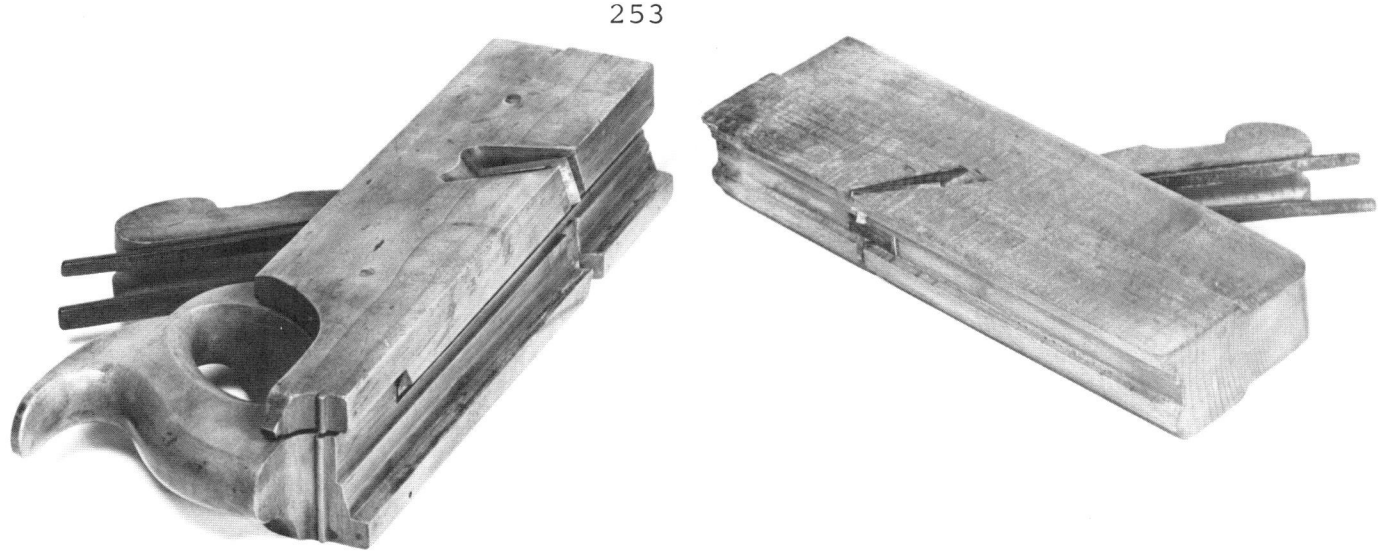

Fig. 155. Double Iron American Sash Planes

Early in the 19th Century sash planes were made the same lengths as conventional moulding planes both with single and double irons. An advantage of the latter skewed the irons slightly in opposite directions, which improved finish of cut. It would be quite impossible to skew single iron sash plane, as the improvement gained on one side would ruin the cutting gained on the opposite side. A 9-3/8" length double iron sash plane is shown above to the right in Fig. 155 without handle; and a double iron handled sash plane at the left. Note the irons in the latter are slightly skewed. This plane was made from cherry rather than the conventional beech and shows artistic workmanship. The rabbet section was made separately from the sash section, and held to the latter by two iron screws. A wood spacer could be inserted bewteen these two planes to conform to the desired width of sash being planed.

By the 1820's such double iron sash planes were being offered in United States with wooden screw arms holding the two sections together and with a self-regulating mechanism to adjust seperation without using a spacer. Three screw adjustable sash planes are shown in Fig. 156. The planes shown to the left and center are self-regulating types, while the one to the right is manually adjusting and requires a spacer to set seperation. The one at the far left was probably made in the 1820's and was dowelled from the bottom. The center plane was made about mid-19th Century and was dowelled from the top. Note that all of these irons are skewed in opposite directions in each plane.

The operation of the self adjusting mechanism can be understood by examination of Fig. 157. At the bottom is shown the two sections of the plane at the left of Fig.156 taken appart. The screw arms fit into the sash section at the right, through collars that are dowelled from the bottom into a slot. This permits them to be turned but not withdrawn .(see separate screw pin with slot cut into collar at center) When the screw is turned from the outside and the planes are together, the sash section remains in the same position but the rabbet section must move away. Thus the distance bewteen the two planes can be self-regulated. Tapered guide dowels above the screws assist to hold the plane rigid. The screw sash at the top of Fig. 157 is a manually adjustable type and required a spacer to set the separation between the two planes.

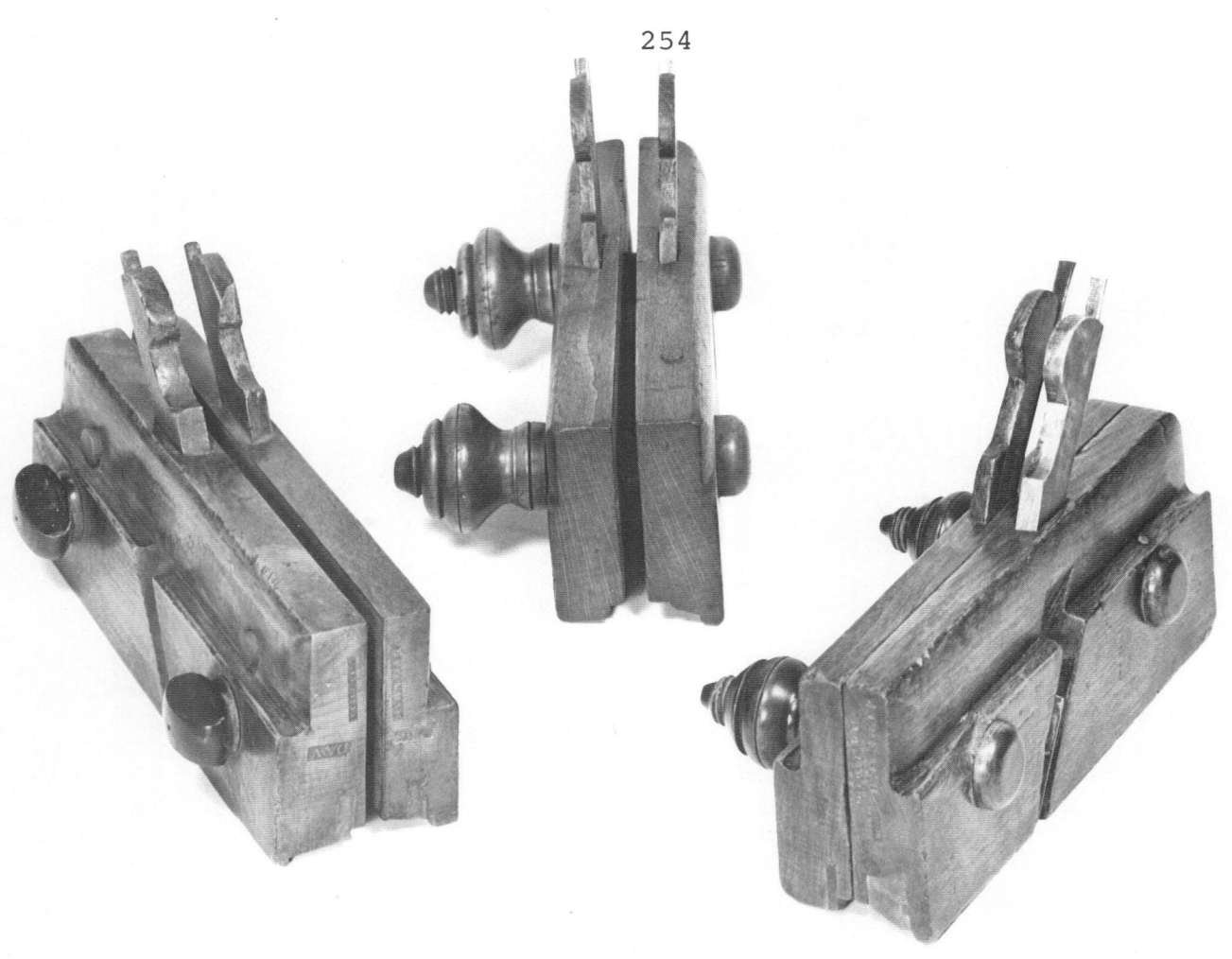

Fig. 156. Wood Screw Adjusting Double Iron Sash Planes

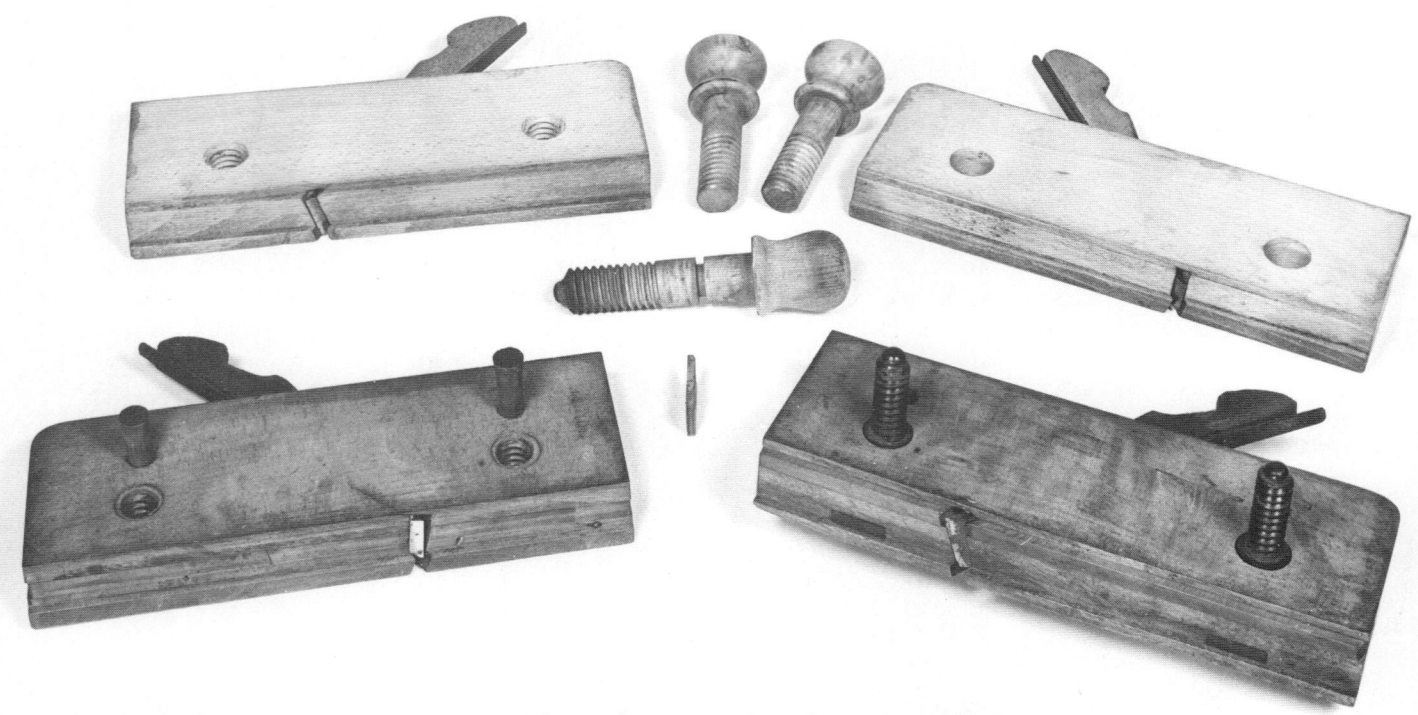

Fig. 157. Wood Screw Adjusting Sash Planes Taken Apart.

Fig. 158. Diamond Pad, Iron Screw, Self-Regulating Sash Plane (left)
Double-Iron Sash Plane (right)

    About 1830 self-regulating sash planes were offered with iron screws with either diamond or brass (round) pads. These are both described and illustrated on page 121. (Fig.77.) Fig. 158 (left) shows such a sash plane by M.Crannell, Albany. In making such planes it is evident that both the sash and rabbet sections are fully cut into the sole before then sawing the two sections into separate planes. Note that the M.Crannell imprint has been partially removed during this seperation; also note the interruptions, but continuance of the annual rings across the separation. The sash plane at the right by Kennedy & White, New York, though equipped with the diamond pads, was never separated into the two sections. Neither the diamond and brass pad iron screw self-regulating nor the wood screw adjustable sash planes ever became very popular in England. However both of these syles were made in Scotland. Apparently the English preferred to use the sash fillister and separate sash moulding planes. A rather rare English double-iron "stick-and-rebate" plane is showin in Fig. 159. This plane, 13¼' x 2¼", bears imprint W.Watkins/Bradford. His working dates there are 1879-88.

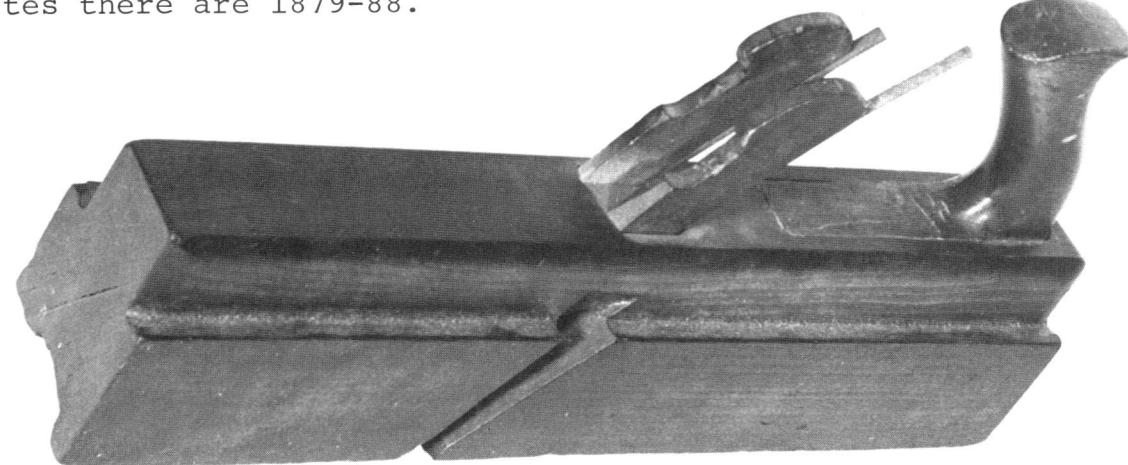

Fig.159. English Double Iron Sash Plane by W.Watkins, Bradford.

A recent article concerning sash coping planes presented some new insights in window frame making.[10] The author, Robert D. Graham, Jr., has graciously submitted the following text and sketch regarding their use. This contribution is very much appreciated and here acknowledged.

"The American sash plane, which is referred to in British parlance as a 'sash plane to stick and rebate', is quite rarely encountered in England, where moulding and rabbeting were normally carried out in separate operations. It is not the only common form found in America, but examples are found marked with imprints of known 18th Century American planemakers. The sash coping plane, which was apparently more commonly used in American than England, was made and used at least as early as the early part of the 19th Century. The use of coping planes has been hinted at, but the actual proceedure never full described in tool literature; 19th Century catalogs are of little help; nor do contemporary "how-to-do-it" books shed any light on the subject. Having had the good fortune to have acquired a matching set of sash and sash coping planes, made by A.CUMINGS/BOSTON in new condition, curiosity prompted me to conduct several experiments using these planes.

The first experiment was to make a coped joint between the stile and rail of a sash. This joint was quite easily made using the coping plane in the manner illustrated. (See Plate LVII). Some 19th Century planemakers offered coping planes in two forms; single and double. Because the plane stock works against the tenon of the rail, the double coping plane in this instance has the advantage of providing a more convenient hand grip. Various styles of single and double coping planes are shown at the bottom of the illustration.

It must be pointed out that the coping plane is not essential to window making. There are other methods (which certainly pre-date coping planes) which combine mitering and scribing (coping) with a gouge. The advantage of the coping plane may be that it makes possible a production line process whereby a large number of rails may be coped at a single setup. This writer found it very convenient to clamp a number of rails to the bench, cut the tenons all at one time with the help of a raising plane, and then cope all the rails at once. Using this method very uniform rails for any number of windows of equal size may be turned out in short order.

Another suggested use of the coping plane remains perhaps less resolved; the coping of sash bars at the point where they intersect the rails and stiles. This is the method used today in machine made sash work. It can also be done using a sash coping plane and the same production setup as described for coping the rails. It is of course necessary that the coping be done before the bars are moulded in order to prevent splintering. It can be done, but was it done? At least one early coping plane made by W.Raymond (bottom right in illustration) will only work against a wide tenon, as on a rail; there is little tenon on a sash bar to work against".

Double coping planes are illustrated in Fig. 160. The one at the right was made by T.Tileston, Boston and is the most uncommon 60° construction. The one at the left is an unknown make, but from the chamfer judged to have been made during the late 18th Century.

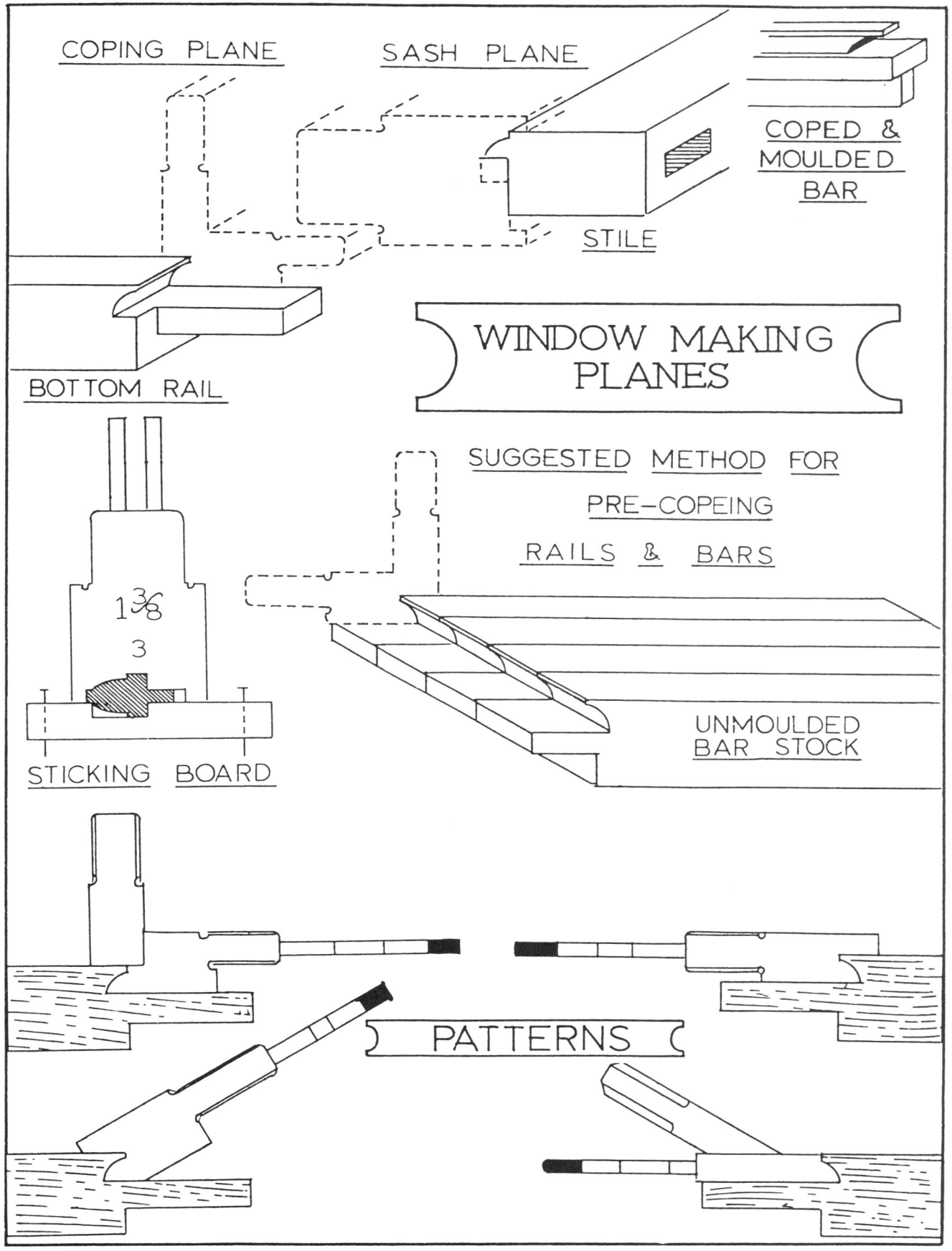

Plate LVII - Window Making Planes - Drawn by Robert D. Graham, Jr.

NOTES - Chapter IX

1. *1857 Illustrated Supplement Arrowmammett Works, Middletown, Conn. Bench Planes & Moulding Tool Catalog*, Reprinted by Ken Roberts Publishing Co., 1976, pp.14-15.
2. K.D.& J.W.Roberts,*New York Planemakers, op.cit.*,p.44.
3. R.A.Salaman,*Dictionary of Tools, op.cit.*, Window making, pp.519-20; sash planes, pp.345-55; sash fillisters, pp.327-28.
4. Correspondence from William L.Goodman, November 1977
5. H.C.Mercer, *Ancient Carpenters' Tools*,[Doylestown,Pa.,1928], p.133, Fig.126
6. K.D.& J.W.Roberts,*New York Planemakers, op.cit.*, Plate 12,p.15
7. *ibid*, p.35   8. *Alex Mathieson & Son Wood Working Tool Catalogue*
9. Reprinted Ken Roberts Publishing Co., 1975, p.3,No.17
10. R.D.Graham,jr., *Plane Talk*, B-ARS, V.1,No.4, Dec.1976, p.9
11. Recently I had suggested to W.L.Goodman that this type of plane was an American development limited to fairly simple mouldings used in United States. Mr.Goodman confirmed that indeed was strong evidence and this may well be an American design, used later in England and more frequently in Scotland, but a firm answer would require further research.

Fig. 160. Sash Coping Planes. Left: Unmarked 18th Century Manuafacture. Right: T.Tileston, Boston; Rare 60° Frame.

Chapter X

Moulding and Miscellaneous Planes

    This Chapter will comment and illustrate a few more varities of moulding planes. A few unusual miscellaneous types of planes will follow with additional illustrations and discussion.

    In general before American Empire Designs started, c.1815, complex mouldings had more pronounced curvature changes than the later Greek Revival style. Consequently moulding planes of this earlier period had wider surface variations than the later patterns which followed specified size increments. A group of five moulding planes of the period 1800 - 1825 illustrate this point in Fig. 161 below.

Fig. 161. Complex Moulding Planes of American Manufacture, 1800 - 1825.

    The use of such complex moulding planes in 'shooting stuff on the bench' required considerable expertise and judgement on the person holding and pushing the plane. Holtzapffel's *Mechanical Manipulation and Turning* discusses the use of such molding planes. (see pages 176-179 this book). The subject of <u>spring</u>, angular deviation, is noted on page 493. Robert D. Graham, jr. has recently written an article explaining some of the complications of this subject. His article was published in *Plane Talk* [Bulletin of the B-ARS, V.II, No.2, Summer 1977, p.14-16] He has prepared a two page summary of this with another two pages of diagrams that follow. Grateful acknowledgement is again expressed to Mr. Graham for his interests and support in submitting this material.

SPRING
by
Robert D. Graham, Jr.

Illustrated in figure (1) are accurate representations of two actual moulders designed to cut very similar mouldings comprised of a cyma reversa and astrigal. The example on the left--imprint GEORGE CARPENTER--is quite different than most complex moulders of British or American make in that it is intended to be used in a position perpendicular to the work rather than canted--as with the JO'FULLER example--which was standard practice in the eighteenth and nineteenth centuries. The amount of declination from the vertical usually ranges from 15 to 30 degrees and is known as spring.

Because if the slight disparity in overall widths of these two planes, it is not evident in the illustration that the width of the stock of the FULLER example is proportionally greater than the width of the CARPENTER example. This disproportion is to be expected when comparing canted versus uncanted moulders made to produce a profile of any given width.

This statement concerning the increased width of the canted moulder would on first thought seem to be erroneous, because if one imagines a rabbet plane canted 30 degrees to a baseline (fig. 2, a...b) one will of course say that the body of the canted plane is narrower than the profile produced and that the effect is even more pronounced as the angle is increased. Of course, no one would advocate the practicability of canting rabbet planes, but the illustration does give us, with a little help from Pythagoras, the opportunity to form the following axiom which will shed some light on the situation encountered when canting moulders:

> The distance between two parallel lines (the sides of our moulder) intersenting fixed points on a baseline is greatest when the lines are themselves perpendicular to the baseline.

When we apply these criteria to moulders it at once becomes evident that, because of the nature of the moulding's profile, we are dealing with a baseline that is itself canted. The rather typical moulding (fig. 3) which sticks on one inch and sticks down one half inch happens to have a baseline tilted to 25 degrees which corresponds exactly with the amount of spring designed into the canted moulder represented in the same figure. The parallel sides of this moulder are therefore perpendicular to the baseline of the moulding and it follows that a moulder with this degree of spring will be of the maximum width for the moulding depicted. Therefore, a savings of material, both wood and metal, would be effected by constructing the moulding so that it worked straight down. An un-sprung moulder is also superimposed in the same figure which would have an overall reduction in width of 11 per cent and a reduction of about 18 per cent in the width of the iron.

It is frequently, but not always, the case that the baseline of a moulder corresponds closely to the baseline of the moulding which it will produce--this is the reason that most canted moulders will stand straight up on our shelves. If the spring is either more or less than the angle of the baseline, the body of the moulder will be relatively thinner than it would be if the spring and the baseline corresponded exactly, but if the spring is very great, 35 degrees or

fig. 1

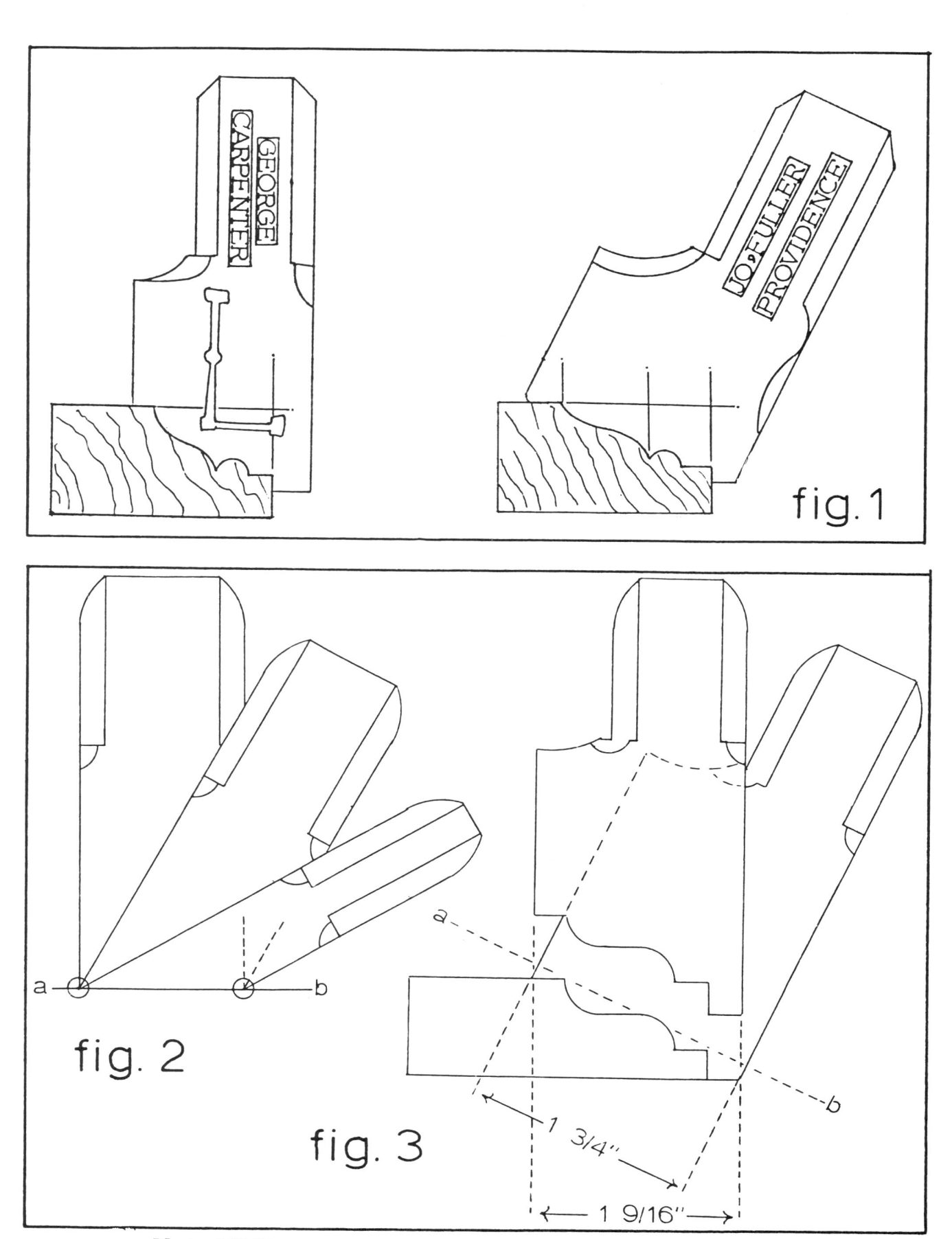

fig. 2

fig. 3

1 3/4"

1 9/16"

Plate LVIII Drawn by Robert D. Graham, jr.

more, the angle made between the side of the moulder and the shoulder will become quite accute, and the stock will have to be made thicker to strengthen the shoulder.

While the moulder which works straight down usually has the advantage of being less bulky, the moulder with spring has several very important advantages which more than compensate for any shortcomings discussed so far. Perhaps, the most obvious of these advantages is the improvement made in the cutting action of the iron. When dealing with a profile such as a ogee, canting the plane--and thereby the iron--removes from the cutting edge to a large extent those parts of the profile which, were a vertical iron used, would scrape rather than cut (fig. 4a). This of course applies only to a moulding profile with a canted baseline; when we are dealing with a semicircular profile, such as a bead or astrigal, the baseline is horizontal, and canting the iron would be detrimental in that it would remove the inherant deficiency from one side of the profile while compounding it on the opposite side (fig. 4b). The result would be an iron with which it would be difficult, or impossible, to produce an accurate moulding--the moulder would tend to vary from its intended line because of the resulting drag on one side.

Improved directional control is a very great attribute gained from building spring into a moulder. This can be illustrated by means of two identical ovalos (fig. 5) wouked by two moulders of different design. When working the moulding straight down there is a natural tendency for the moulder to work away from the stuff being worked. This is caused in part from the less efficient cutting, which produces drag, on the vertical parts of the profile and in part from the slope of the profile. Great care, and considerable effort, is necessary to maintain constant contact between the fence of the plane and the work. But, by canting the moulder so that it becomes nearly perpendicular to the baseline of the moulding, the combined forces (represented in the illustration by arrows) expended by the worker to push forward, down, and to maintain the fence in contact with the work are consolidated and directed in nearly one plane which corresponds to the vertical axis of the moulder and is perpendicular to the baseline of the moulding being produced.

Yet another advantage of springing has been pointed out by Philip Walker. This one, which has to do with producing a uniform mouth gap on planes with a vertical profile, is a bit hard to relate by either description or illustration. I think, as a starting point, it helps to illustrate a smoothing plane in various conditions of wear and in converted form (fig. 6). In (6a) the mouth of the new plane is narrow and uniform. In (6b) the plane is quite worn down, and because the throat becomes wider as it nears thw top of the stock, the mouth is now too wide to do good work. In (6c) a new smoother has been converted to field panels. Because the profile now has some height to it, it is as if the plane was worn down on only one side, so that the mouth is not uniform. But, if starting from scratch, a proper fielding plane is made to work perpendicular to the baseline (6d), the mouth is uniform.

This same problem is encountered when making the mouths of moulders. If the plane is to work straight down, the mouth gap will be much wider than is desirable on the upper parts of the moulding (6e) unless elaborate contouring of the throat is done. By springing the plane to correspond to the baseline (6f) these variations are considerably reduced.

263

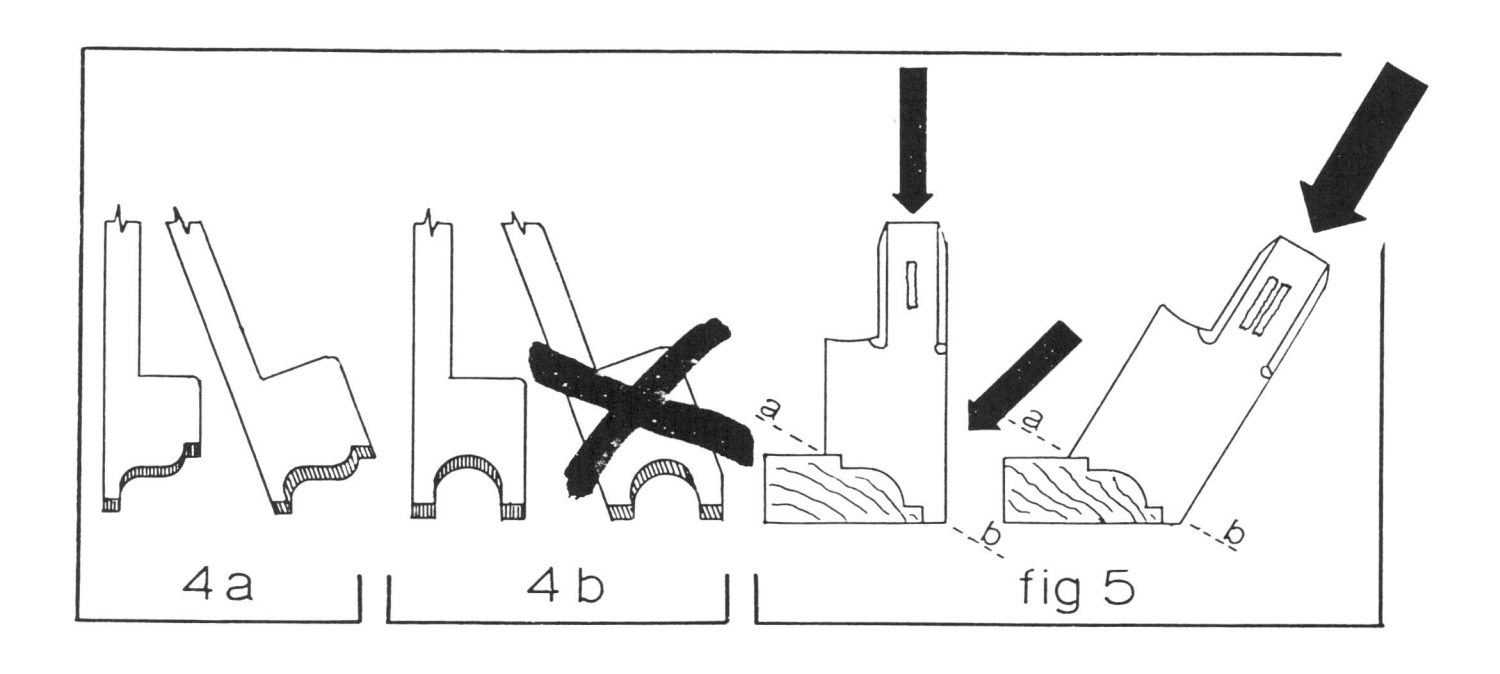

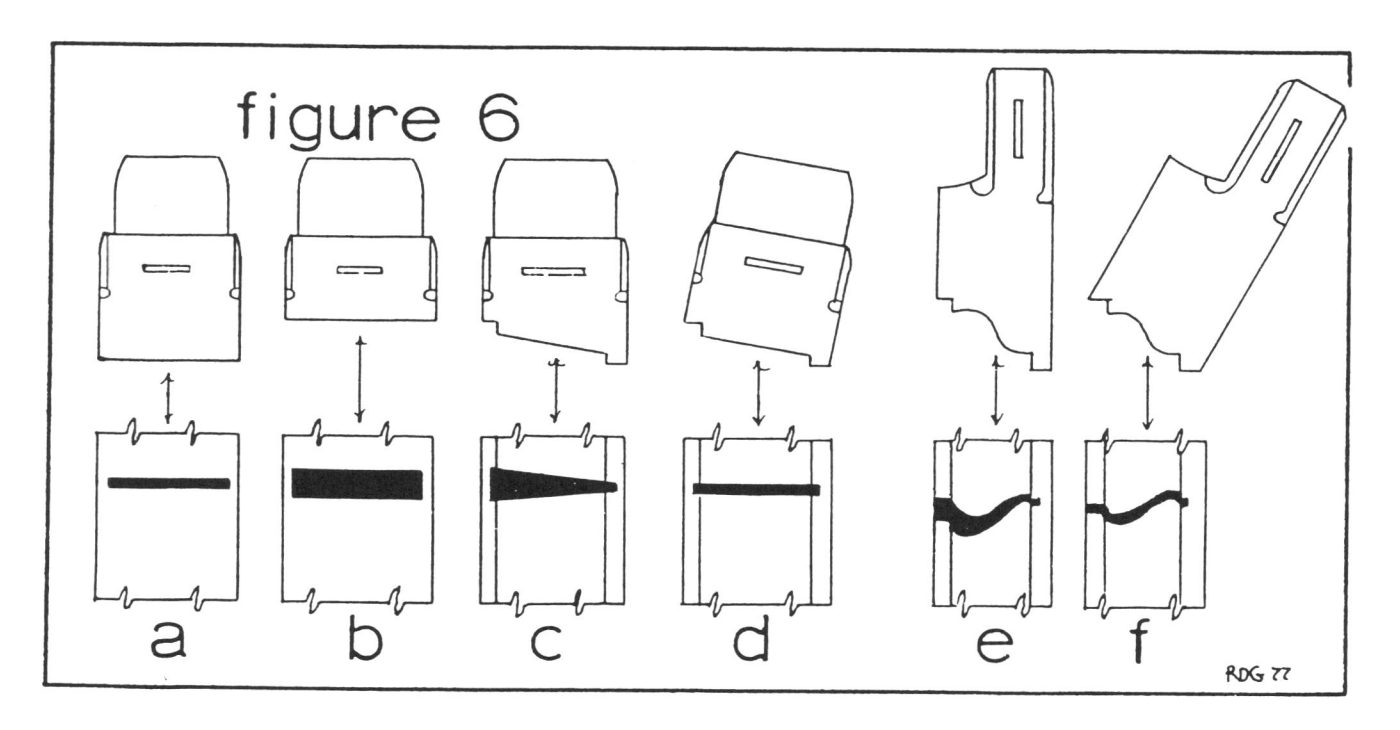

Plate LIX - Drawn by Robert D. Graham, jr.

Fig. 162 A & B. Handle Added to Standard Complex Moulding Plane.
Assists in both Line-up and shooting the moulding on the bench.

Fig. 163 A & B. 4" x 15" Crown Moulding Plane by Bensen & Parry, Albany.
2-1/4" x 6½" Double Iron Complex Moulding Plane [Front] by
C. Fuller - Causeway St. - Boston.

Fig. 164. 3" x 9" O.G.(left) and 1" x 9½" O.G. (right) Moulding Planes

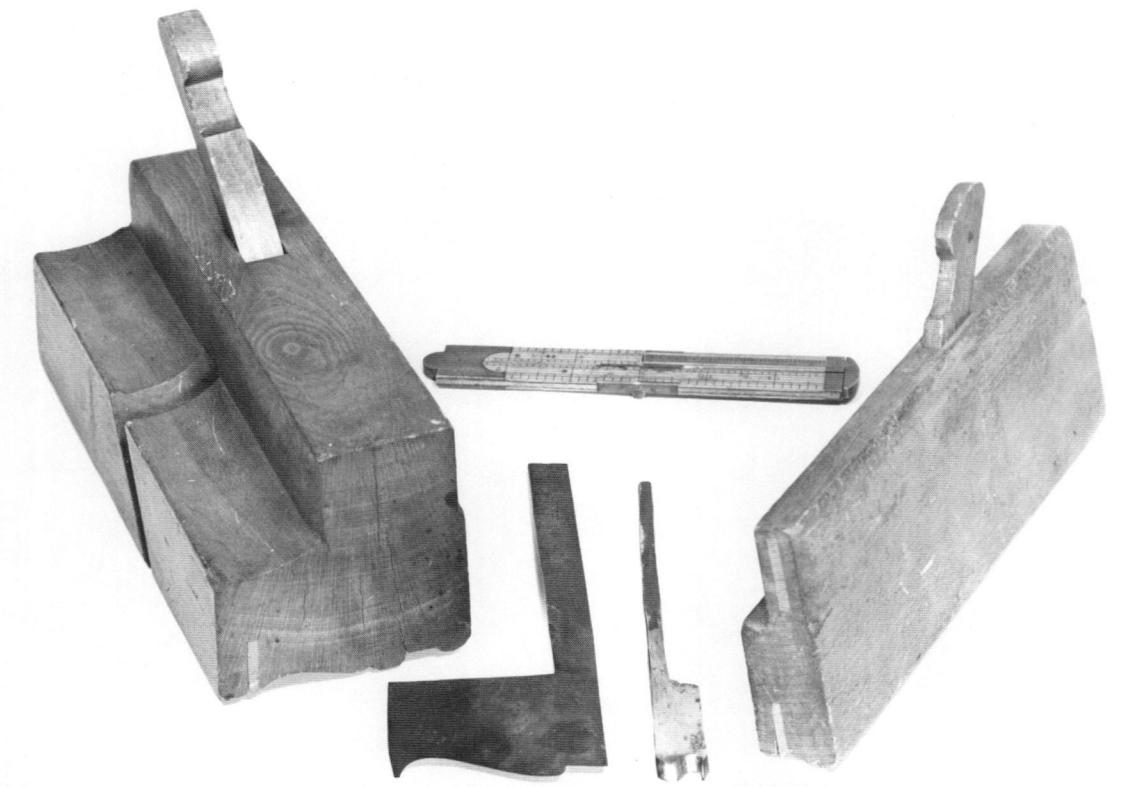

Fig. 165. Wide and Narrow Complex Moulding Planes. Left: 3-1/4" x 9-1/2" Reed/Utica; Right: 1" x 9-1/2" R.Carter/Troy.

Fig. 166. Crown Moulding Planes. Left: 5" x 18" Marked 1844
Right: 4-1/2" x 15" I.D.Gilman.

Fig. 167. Crown Moulding Planes. Left: 4-1/4" x 14-3/4"; C.W.Holder & Co.; Bloomington, Ill.[listed in 1855-56 Bloomington Directory as Hardware Dealer]; Right: 4-1/2" x 14-1/2" F.Gray.

Fig. 168. 3" x 15" Handled Complex Moulding Planes. Top: I.D.Gilman; Bottom Left: T.Tileston,Boston; Bottom Right: T.Tileston, Boston.

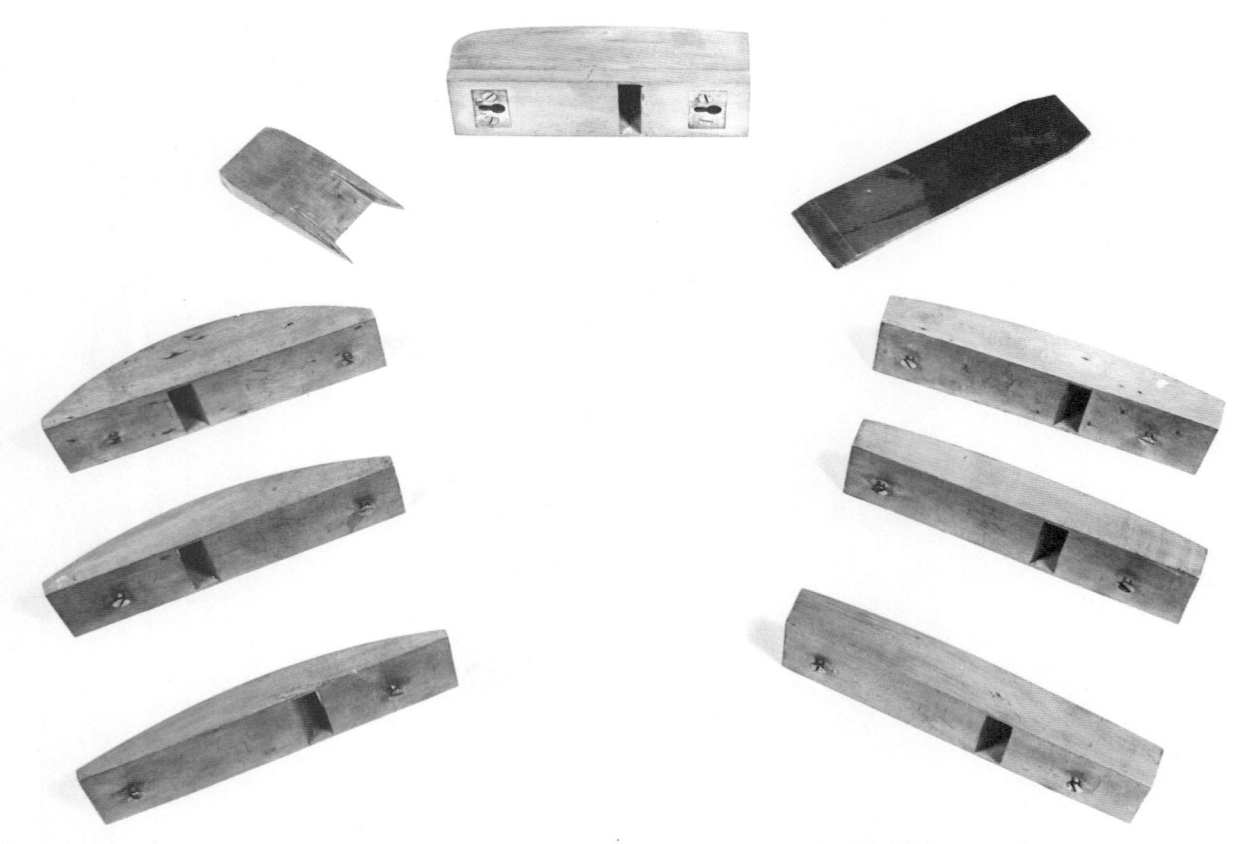

Fig. 169. Boxwood Compass Plane with Six Interchangeable Soles. [2-1/4" x 5-1/2"]

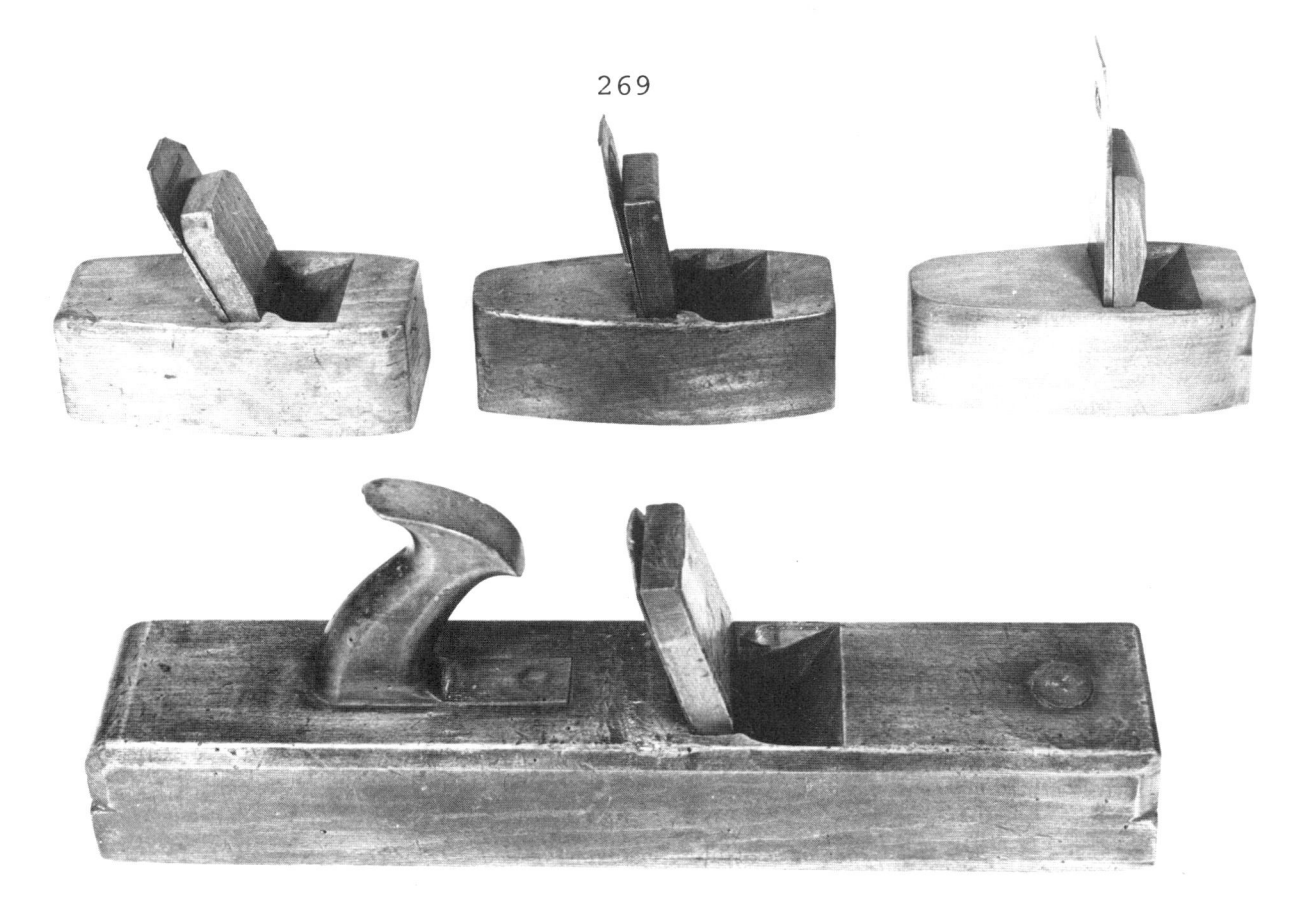

Fig. 170. Toothing Planes - Not all Toothing Planes have same angle of iron.
Front: English 3" x 17" Jack Size with Toothing Iron.

Fig. 171. Plane for Bevel Edges. 3" x 16". Imprint of Hayden/Syracuse, N.Y.
US Patent #6304, April 10, 1849 by William H. Blye DeRuyter, N.Y.
[Collection of James Cooley]

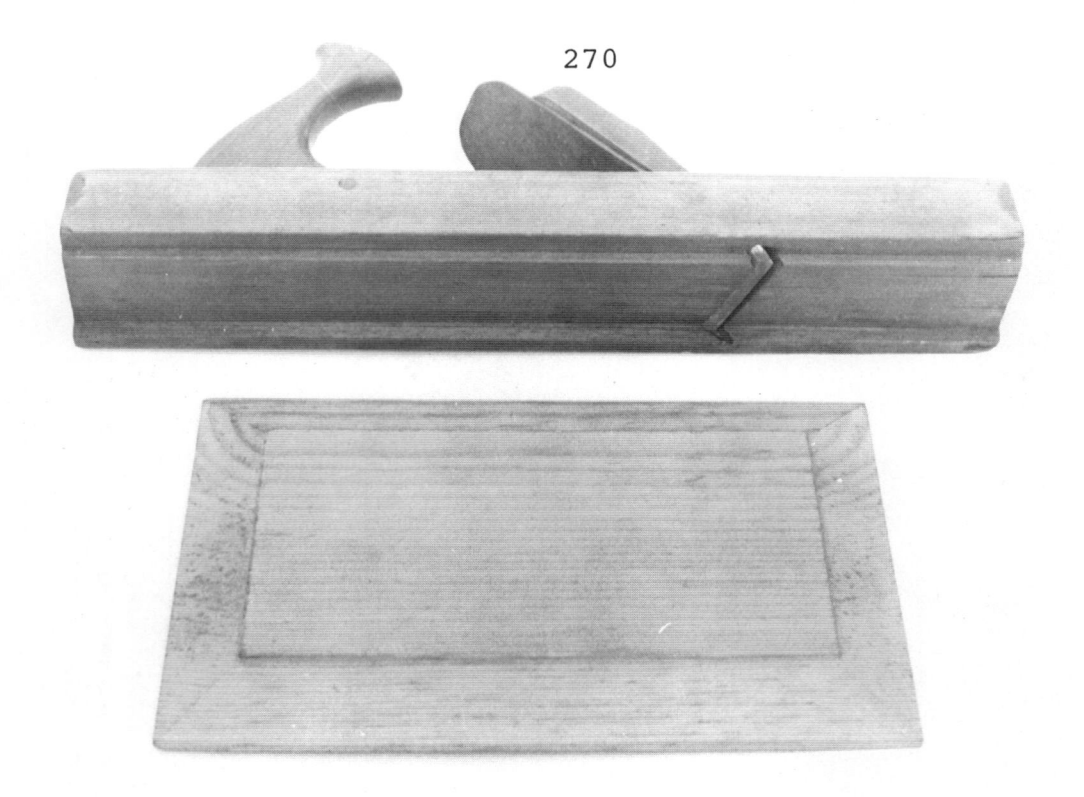

Fig. 172. 2" x 13" 18th Century Panel Plane [no Maker Imprint]

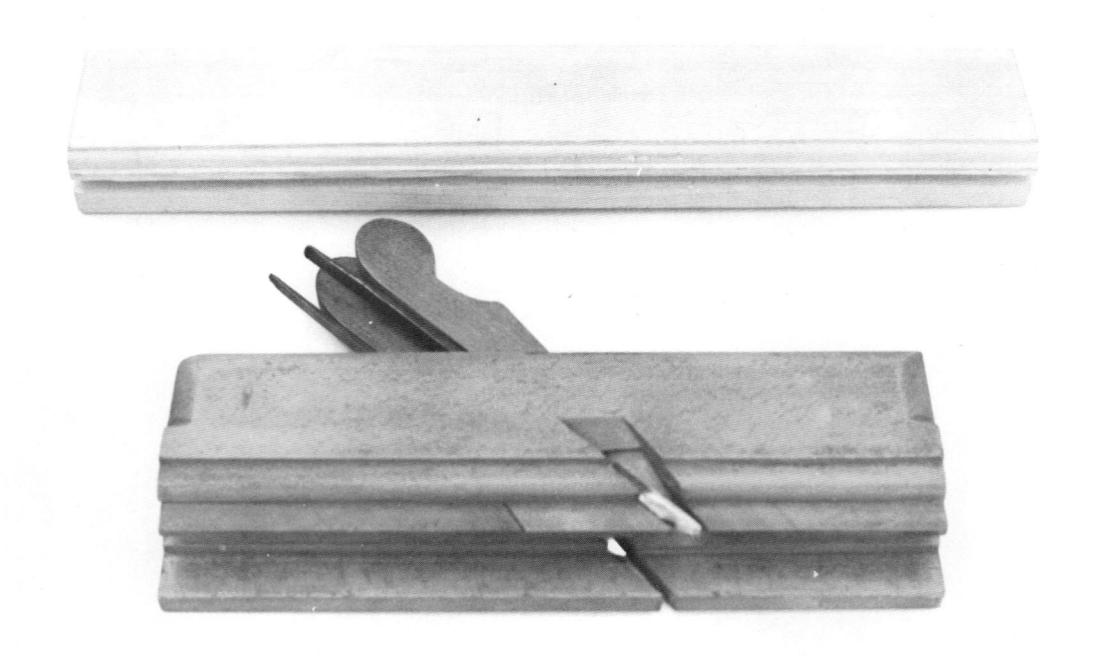

Fig. 173. Combined Moulding and Grooving Plane. 9-1/2" length, J.Woods.

Raising and panel planes were previously discussed on page 101. A rather unique double-iron plane which simultaneously cuts the groove in the stile and the moulding thereon is illustrated above in Fig. 173. The plane has an imprint: J.Woods, presently of unknown location, but from the shape of the wedges, it is most certainly early 19th Century, if not late 18th. When the groove is cut to full depth, it is brought to a stop and the side moulding has been fully developed. A very sensible arrangement. Strange that it is not seen more frequently.

Fig. 174. Planes of Figs. 172 & 173 in Action.

Fig. 175. Panel set in Stile with Planes Adjacent.

Photographs Figs. 172 - 175 Courtesy of William A. Downes.

Fig. 176. Handled Rabbet Planes. Left: 2" x 16"; Reed/UTICA; Beveled for Side Clearance of Handle. Center: Chapin-Stephens - No Handle Clearance.- 1-1/2" Right: 2" x 16"; H.Chapin - Union Factory; Handle Off-set for Clearance.

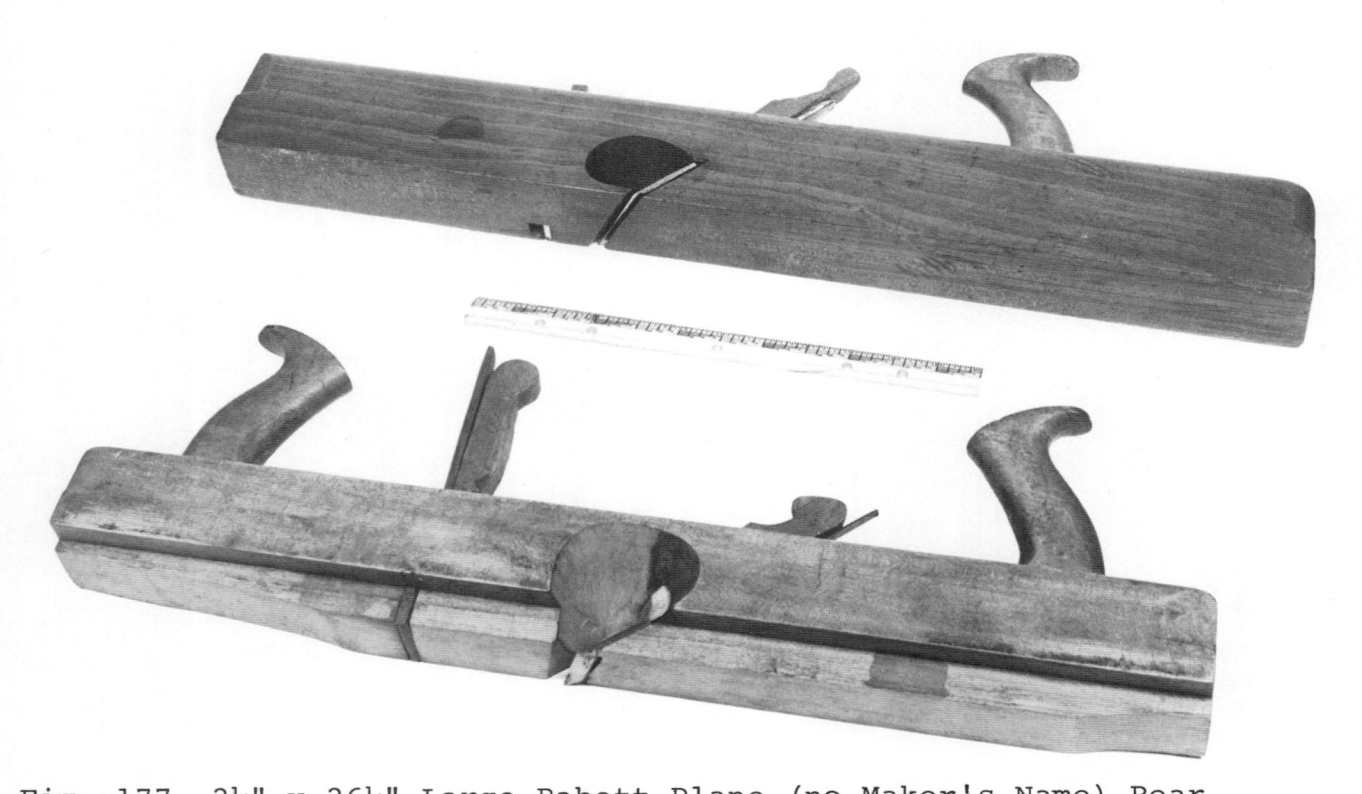

Fig. 177. 2¼" x 26½" Large Rabett Plane (no Maker's Name) Rear.

1⅓" x 22" Large Dado Two Handled Plane. No Maker's Name.
Front -   [Collection of James Cooley, as is plane at left, Fig.176]

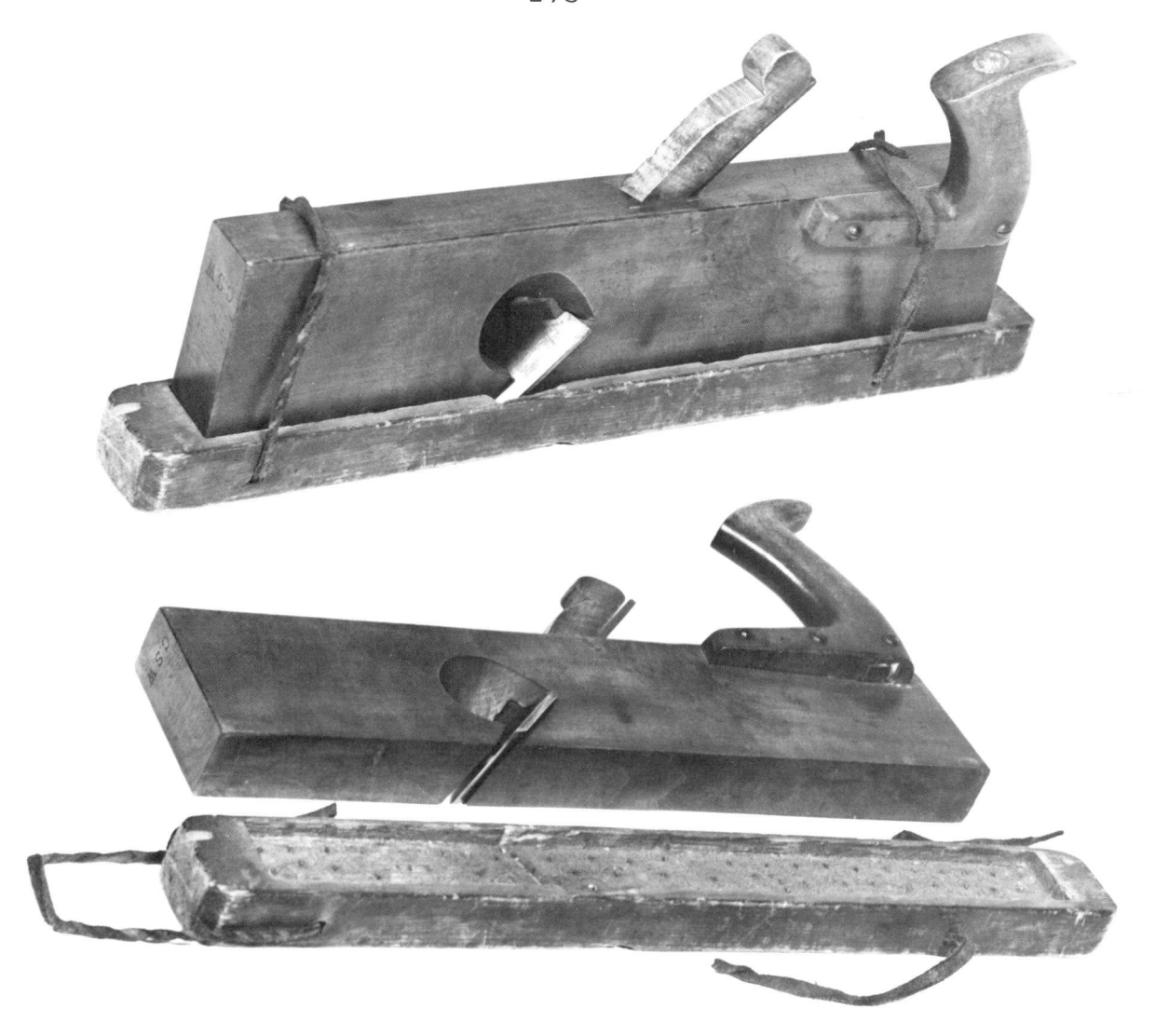

Fig. 178. 2" x 15" Rabbet Plane with Protective Case. Note: Off-set Handle for Side-Clearance.

Fig. 179. Combination Tongue & Groove Double Iron Planes. [Matched set in One]
Left: Handled. Right: Non-handled.
[Plane at left, collection of James Cooley]

SHOOTING PLANES.

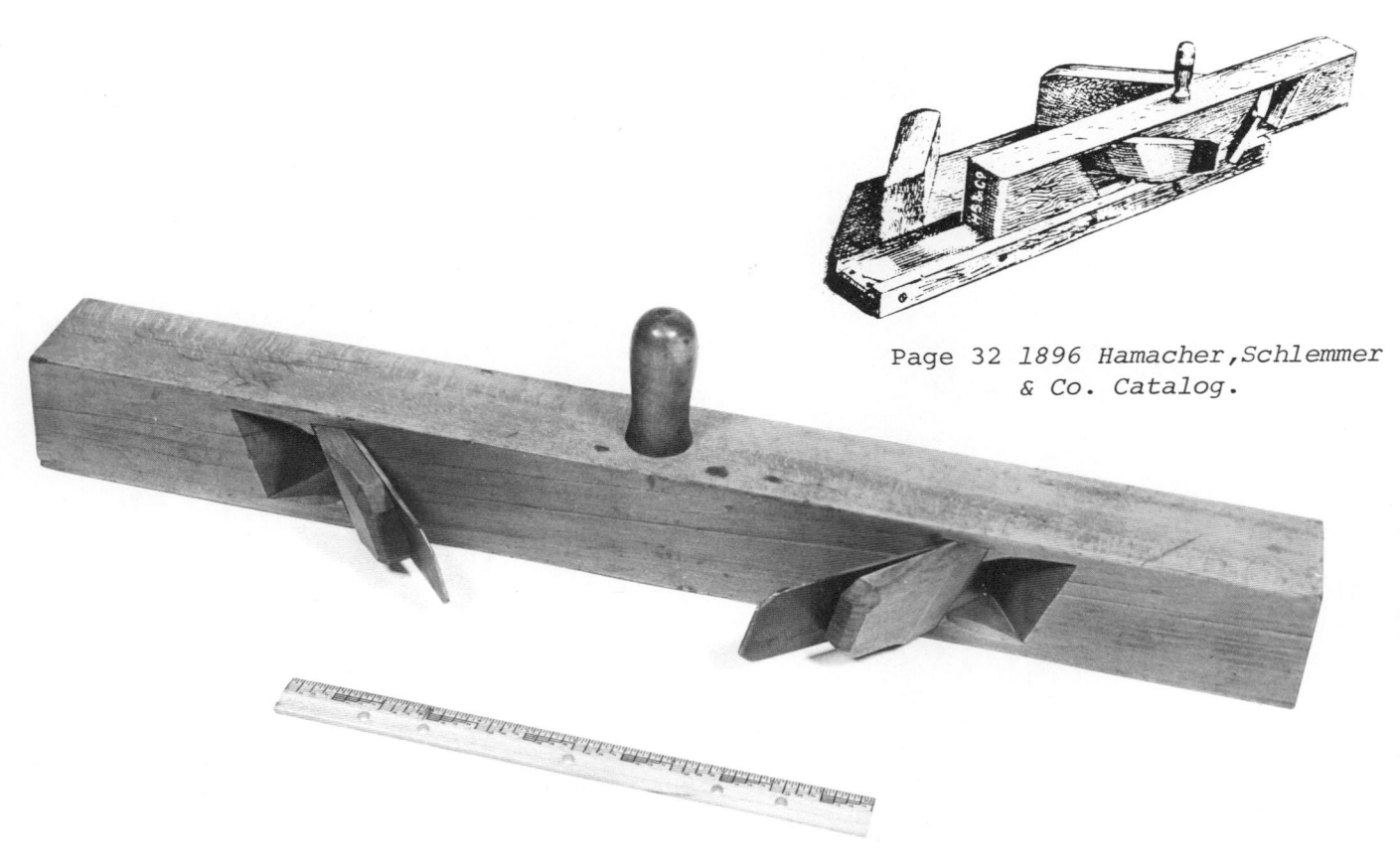

Page 32 *1896 Hamacher, Schlemmer & Co. Catalog.*

Fig. 180. 3" x 28½" Shooting Plane. No Maker's Name.

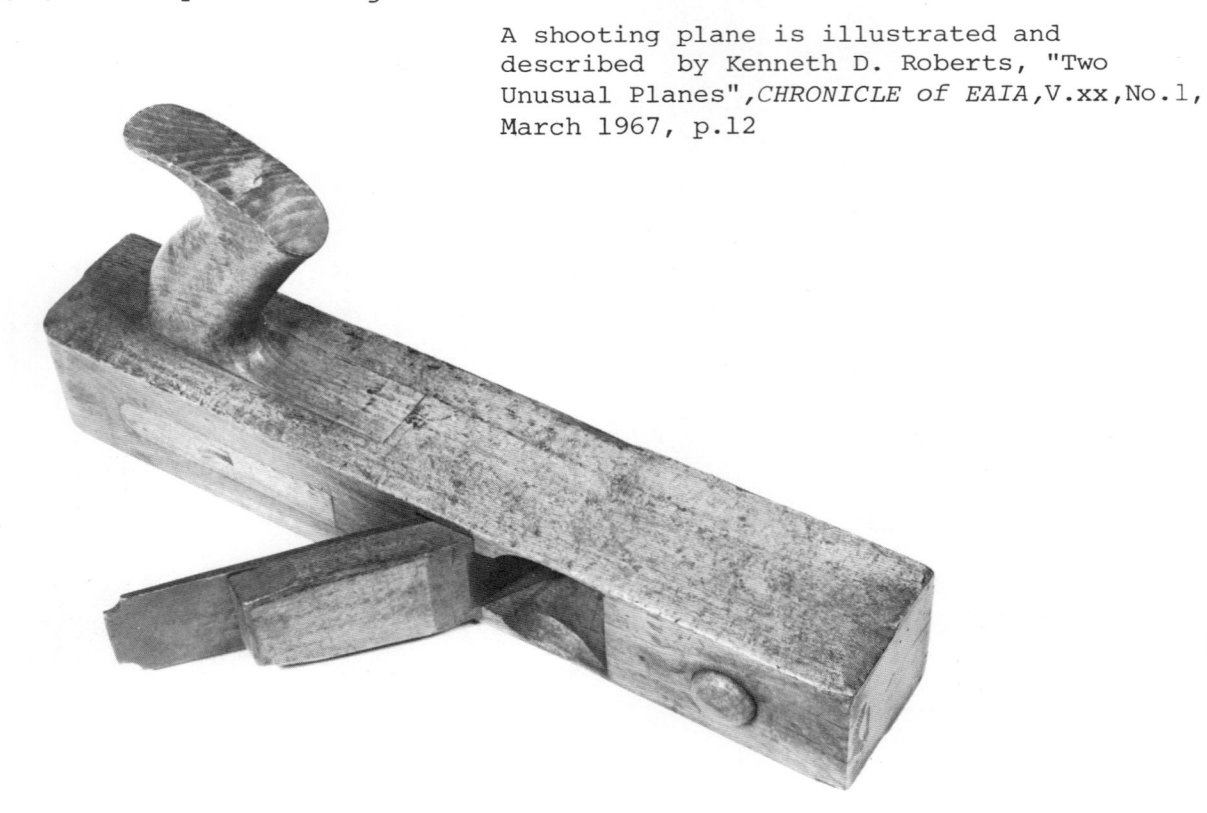

A shooting plane is illustrated and described by Kenneth D. Roberts, "Two Unusual Planes", *CHRONICLE of EAIA*, V.xx, No.1, March 1967, p.12

Fig. 181. 2¼" x 12" Jack Plane Converted into Shooting Plane. H. Chapin - Union Factory New Hartford, Connecticut.

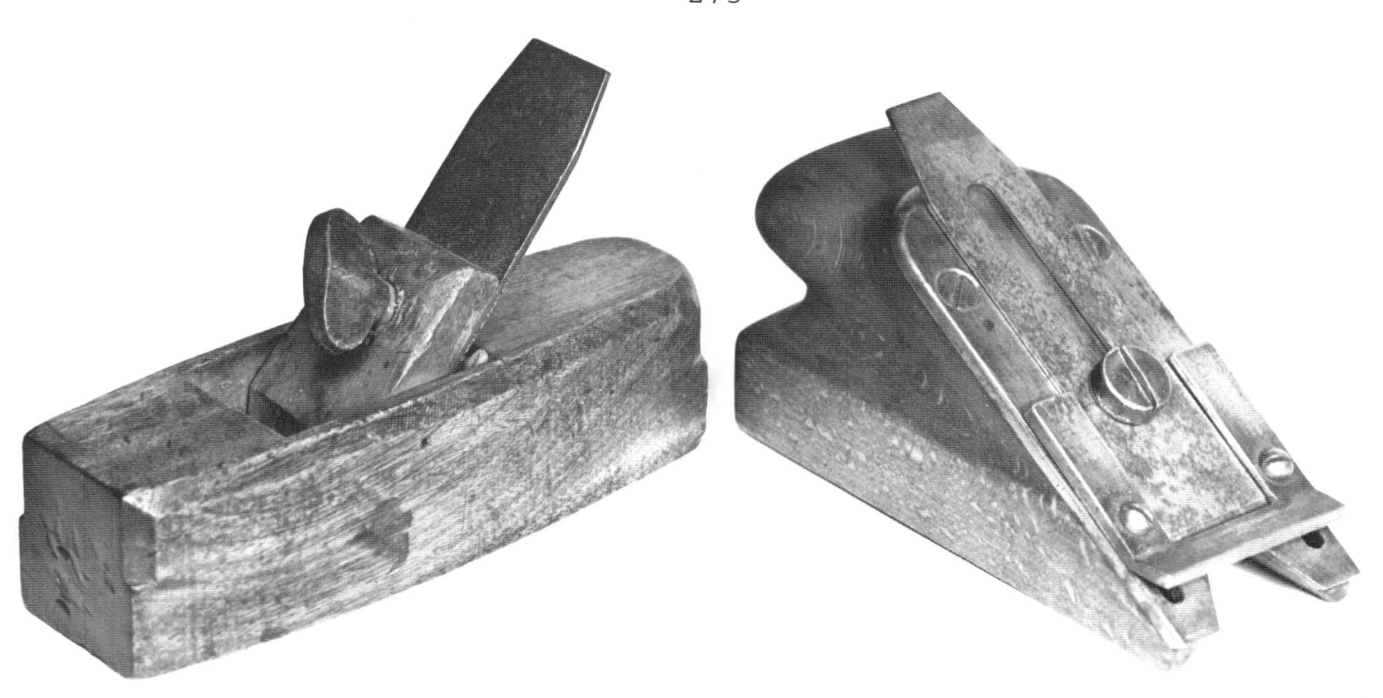

Fig. 182. 1-3/4" x 6½" Smoother with Thumb-screw Wedge (left)
2-1/4" x 5-3/4" Chamfer Plane

Fig. 183. 2¼" x 12½" Iron cased, Wood-filled American Mitre Plane

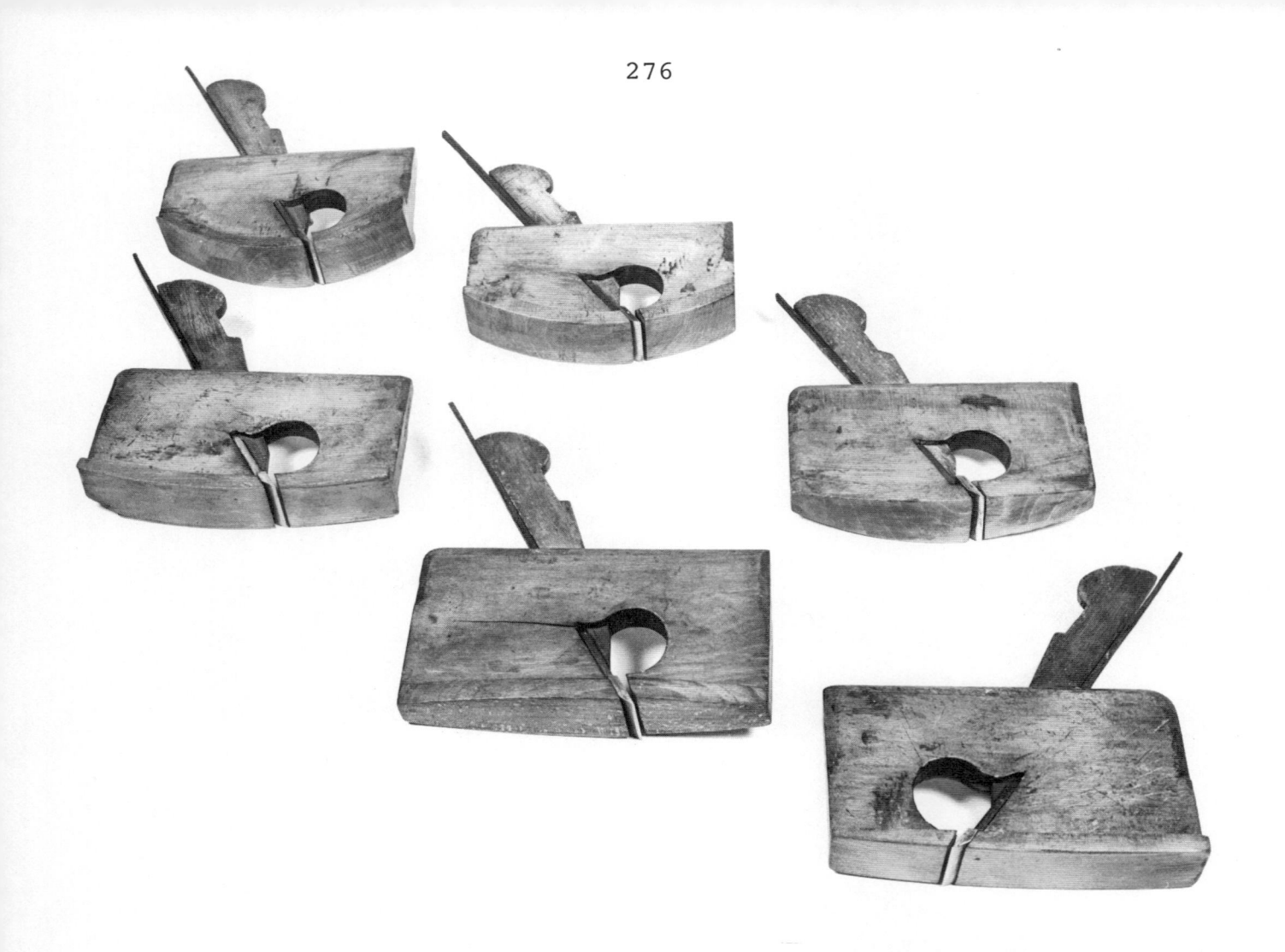

Fig. 184. 6" T-Compass Carriage Maker's Planes.

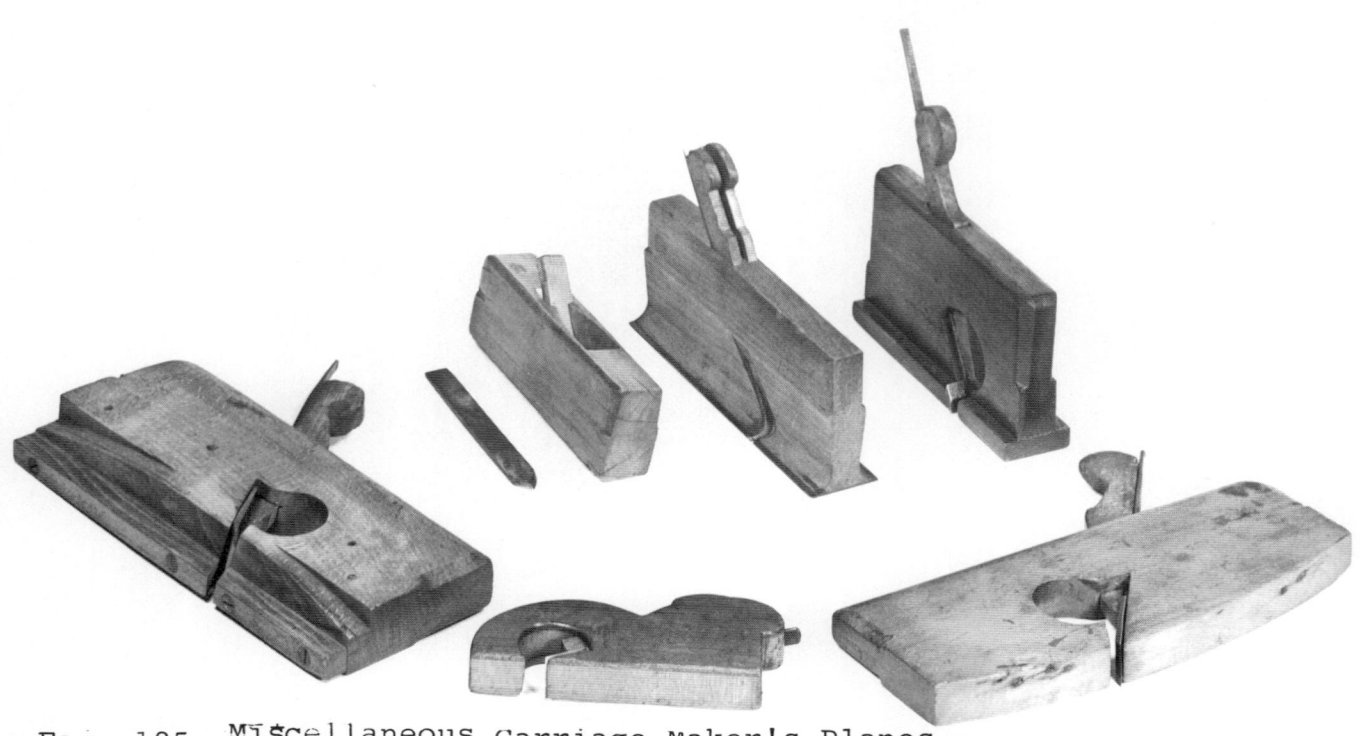

Fig. 185 Miscellaneous Carriage Maker's Planes

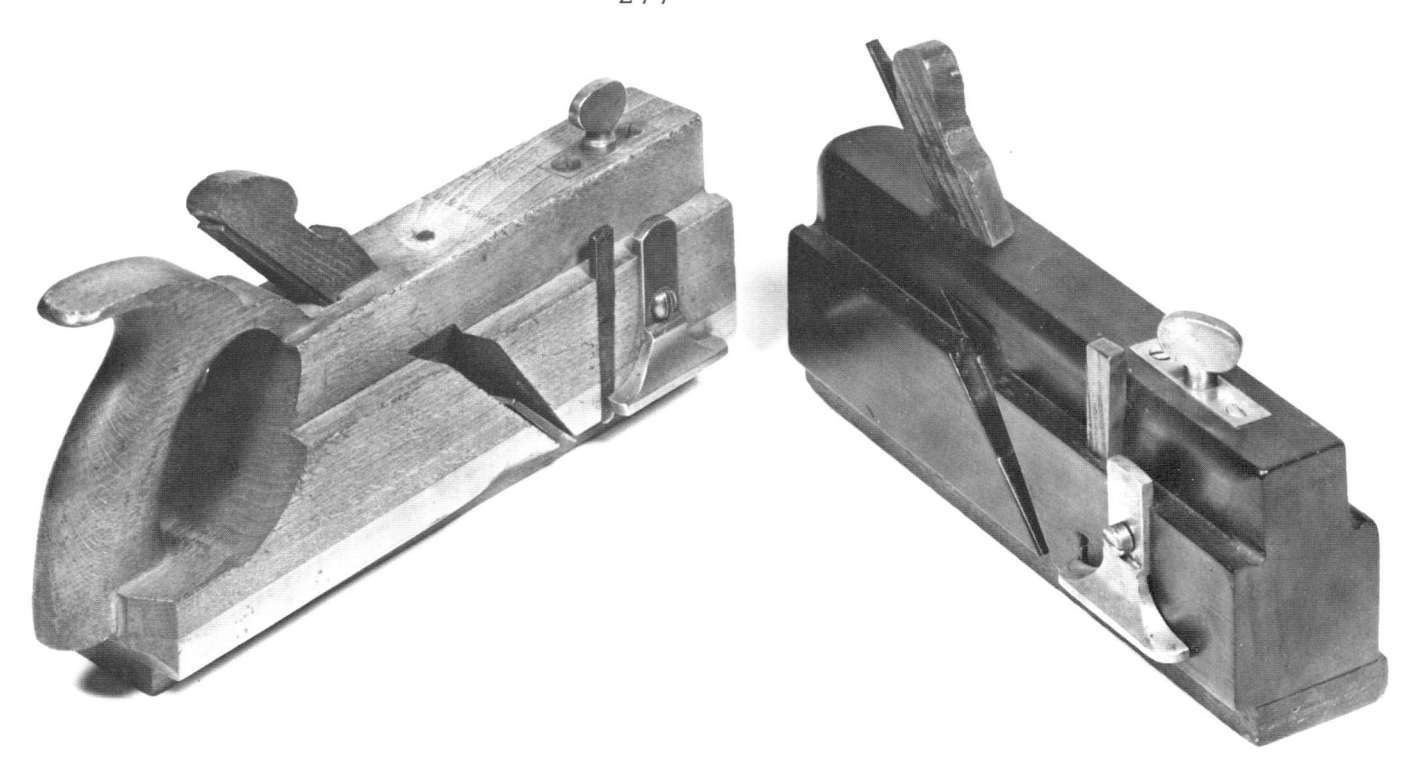

Fig. 186. 2¼" x 10" Handled Moving Filletster. G.W.Denison,Wintrop,Conn.[left]
2" x 9½" Ebony Moving Filletster. J.Hannan[New York, N.Y.] [right]

Fig. 187. 2¼" x 12" Handle Screw-Arm Rosewood Moving Filletser. Made by Taber Plane Co., New Bedford,Mass. Overprint stamped: Homer,Bishop & Co.,Boston,Mass.

Fig. 188. Fancy Screw Adjustable Plow Planes. Left: Ebony Handle & Boxwood Body by LeDeforest, Birmingham, CT. Right: Cocobola & Boxwood Fence by Shelton & Osborne Mfg. Co., Birmingham, Ct.

Fig. 189. 3/8" Dado Plane by Auburn Tool Co. with Screw-Arm Fence.

V. Check List of 19th Century American and Canadian Makers or Firms
[also planes made in Great Britain and imported or brought to United States and Canada during the 19th Century]

The following Check List of Planemakers includes manufacturers and/or dealers. The principal source of these names is obtained from a compilation of imprints appearing on the front top end of planes. Names preceded with an asterisk (*) are firms obtained from a Directory listing or some other primary source and of whom todate an imprint has not been reported.

Imprints of maker's names on artifacts apparently began with English trade guilds early in the seventeenth century during the reign of Charles I. The practice of stamping a maker's name, also frequently with an address and the word *Warranted*, was continued during the 18th and 19th centuries in America. (See: Fig.4, Chapter II) Typical 19th century imprints on planes are illustrated in Plate XXXII. [See: Kenneth D. and Jane W. Roberts, "The Identification and Classification of American Wooden Planes, *Chronicle of EAIA*, v.XIX, No.2, June 1966, p.18] Several imprints from New York planes are illustrated in our previous work, *Planemakers, etc*.[pp. 145-190]. The method of reproducing these imprints, developed by Jane W. Roberts, is explained in Appendix H, *Planemakers,etc*.[p.230].

It is often extremely difficult to distinguish between a possible maker and an owner's imprint. Some of the latter were as fancy as these used by makers and merchants. When a name is accompanied with an address or *warranted*, in all probability such was a planemaker even though documentation through printed records may not yet have been established. Dealers or merchants sometime added their own imprint to those of the makers from whom planes were purchased. In some instances dealers purchased planes without any imprint and applied their own stamp.

Both an alphabetical and geographical listing of each name has been tabulated, The latter is divided into the following subdivisions:

```
    I. - New England States              VI. - Canada
   II. - New York State                 VII. - Great Britain & Ireland
  III. - Middle Eastern States                 (England & Scotland)
         (NJ; PA; & MD)                VIII. - Partial Addresses
   IV. - Southern States                 IX. - Firms without Addresses
         (KY; LA; MS; TN; & VA)          X. - Names Alone of Probable
    V. - Midwestern States                     Plane Makers
         (IN;IL;IA;MI;MN;OH;MO;WI)
```

The listing of British imprints (VII) are those found in the United States and Canada observed and reported up until 1970. It is believed that these planes were brought over or imported previously to the 20th Century. Since 1970 antique dealers and importers have brought many English planes to this country, so further additions to this category would be questionable in regard to 19th Century usage.

Group IX, Firms without Addresses, are imprints that have been reported from at least two widely seperated localities to insure such are not owner names, but ordered or taken to such locations. Names alone are imprints personally examined by the author and thought to be planemakers, but may possibly in some instances be owners' imprints. It requires a great deal of experience for such judgement.

While this list is incomplete, it is believed that the names of the most important manufacturers who operated in the United States during the 19th century are included. Undoubtedly individual makers and smaller firms will be reported in the future and certainly many imprints of dealers and merchants will also emerge, particularly in mid-western locations.

Plate XXXII - Typical 19th Century Imprints on Planes.

Other Imprints are Illustrated on Frontispiece

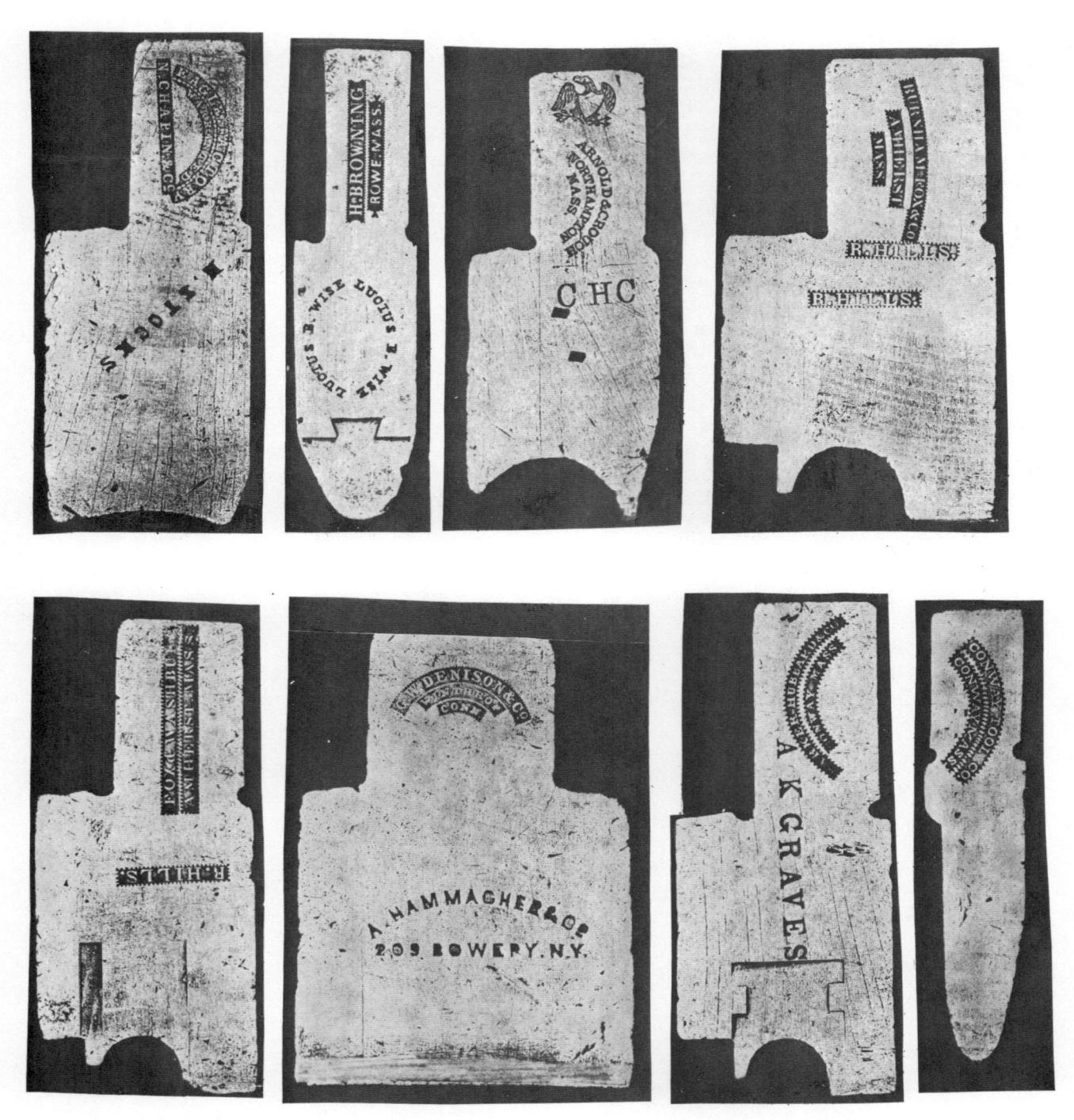

Technique for recording these Tool Imprints noted in Appendix H, page 230 *Planemaking and Other Edge Tool Enterprises in New York State in the Nineteenth Century.* [Kenneth D. and Jane W. Roberts, Cooperstown, N.Y., 1971]

V - Check List of 19th Century American and Canadian Makers and Firms

I - NEW ENGLAND

MAINE

Bangor
- B. Morril
- P. B. Rider — -1839

Berwick
- L. P. Holmes

Brunswick
- J. P. Storer

Libson Falls
- S. Plummer

Gardner [West]
- D. Fuller

Portland
- J. Bradford — -1849-75-
- J. L. B. Hersey — -1849-

Thomaston
- J. H. Winslow

Waldoboro
- L. S. Soule

Waterville
- J. C. Jewett

VERMONT

Bethel
- *Newton & Dewey — 1857

Bellow Falls
- Dewey & Brown

Burlington
- J. Herrick — 1842-44

Cabot
- H. Russel

Jamaica
- E. C. Pierce

Montpelier
- *Preston Trow — 1842-43

Wilmington
- H. H. Read

Town Unknown
- John Morton

NEW HAMPSHIRE

- C. W. Roads

Amherst
- M. H. Milton

Canaan

Concord
- P. Sargent — -1856-

Dublin
- R. Piper

Hudson
- Cyrus Weaver — -1849-
- W. Warren — -1860-

NEW HAMPSHIRE [Continued]

Keene
- Briggs [probable 18th Century]
- Knowlton & Stone, D. [through 20th C.]
- E. Rugg

Littleton
- D. P. Sanborn — -1856

Manchester
- D. Sargent

Milford
- Addison Heald — 1868-95
- A. Heald & Co.
- A. Heald & Son — -1875-95

Nashua
- Eayrs & Co.
- D. Sargent
- C. Warren — -1844 -1864-72

Wolfboro
- A. M. Piper

Location Unknown
- Warren & Heald [probable Nashua or Milford]

RHODE ISLAND

Cumberland
- David Clark — 18th C.

Pawtucket
- Bodman & Hussey
- T. E. Smith

Providence
- Jon. Ballou — 18th C.
- Battey & Eddy — -1841-42
- Issac S. Battey — -1841-55
- L. B. Bigelow — 1852-53
- J. E. Child — 1852-75
- S. Cumings — -1828-
- I. Field — -1828-57
- Jo. Fuller — 18th C. -1824
- Fuller & Field — 1842
- J. R. Gale — -1832-
- Cumings & Gale — -1832-
- J. Lindenberger — -1797-1817
- P. H. Manchester — 1843-57
- Miller
- Olney
- J. W. Pearce — 1852-75
- Providence Tool Co., D. — -1860-

Warren
- N. L. Barrus — -1849-

Woonsocket
- C. Darling & Co.

MASSACHUSETTS
Amherst
Amherst Tool Co.	
Burnham, Fox & Co.	1842-44
Geo. Burnham, Jr.	-1849-
H.Church [South Amherst]	-1833-
E.P.Dickinson	1869-79
Fox & Washburn	1840-42
G.Fox	
L.Fox & Son	-1835-
S.Hastings	
S.& H.Hills	1829-30
Hills & Wolcott	-1829-
W.S.Howland	1852-60
J.Kellogg	1849-
J.Kellogg & Co.	
J.Kellogg & Son	-1865-
*Wm.Kellogg	-1875-
Kellogg, Fox & Washburn	1839-40
E.P.Nutting [So.Amherst]	-1852-56
Truman Nutting [So.Amherst]	1831-57
C.H.Rhoads	
W.L.Washburn	

Ashfield
A.Kelly & Co.
R.A.Kelly & Co.

Boston
Thos.L.Appleton	1878-92
Bailey, Chany & Co.	1868-69
Leonard Bailey	1861-64
G.A.Benton	1858-76
John Bradford	1841-75
B.Callender & Co.	1862-87
*William Cooley	1846-49
*Cooley & Montgomery	1844-45
Corey, Brooks & Co.	
A.Cumings	1848-51
*S.R.Cummings	1872
F.Curtis	
N.Curtis	
C.Fuller, Causeway St.	1852-56
" , Pine St.	1867-72
" , Waltham St.	1873-87
L.Gardner	1846-54
Gardner & Appleton	
Gardner & Brazer	1825
Gardner & Murdock	1825-45
P.A.Gladwin & Co.	1865-82
Gladwin & Appleton	1873-77
Albert S. Haven	
Homer, Bishop & Co., D.	
W.Hull	1847-48
*Hull & Montgomery	1845-46
L.Little [prob. began 18thC.-early 19th]	
*Macumber, Bigelow & Douse, D.	
Montgomery	1848
Montgomery & Woodbridge	1847

Boston (Continued)
Multiform Plane Co.	1858-59
*J.Myers, 2nd [So.Boston]	1858
N.Phillips	
*Lemuel T. Pope	1841
M.Read	1842-44
*Read & Cummings [sic]	1845-46
*James Rumrell	1852-61
H.M.Sanders & Co.	
J.S.Stevens	1836-60
T.Tileston	1820-65
*Joseph R. Tolman	1841
Tucker & Appleton	1868-71
A.J.Wilkinson & Co., D.	1842-73
E.C.Woodbridge	1851-52

Bridgewater
C.C.Harlow	-1875-

Chelsea
Thos.Appleton	See Boston
G.A.Benton	" "
Gladwin & Appleton	" "
Tucker & Appleton	" "
*Thomas Vaugn	

Chesterfield
*S.Tower	1856

Conway
Conway Tool Co.	1850-51
Parker, Hubbard & Co.	1842-49

Cummington
Melvin Copeland	-1849-
J.Lovell	1852-82
H.L.Narramore	
A.P.Parson	-1875-
Thomas Porter	

Dedham
S. Doggett	[18th Century]
I.Pike	[" "]

Fairhaven
Wing H. Taber	-1833-

Fall River
J.W.Pearce	-1859-53-
P.M.Peckham	-1853-

Goshen
*H.Barnes	-1856
H.Barrus & Co.	1854-59
C.C.Dresser	1854-56
H.L.Naramore	1865-72
Union Tool Co.	1852-54

Greenfield
Greenfield Tool Co.	1851-87

Hanover
J.R.Tolman	-1849-
T.J.Tolman	-1864-

Hingham
Benjamin Parker	-1849-

Holliston
I.Iones [J.Jones] probably 18th C.

MASSACHUSETTS (Continued)
Hopkinton
*H.Adams	1856
*William Adams	1856

Huntington
M.Copeland	1842-56-
Copeland & Co.	probably 1856-
J.E. & G.M.Lindsey	1856-79

Lanesboro
E.Newell

Lawrence
W.H.Duston

Leeds
E.Newell

Lowell
Chase,Sargent & Shattung	
Fielding & Bartlett	
*Ansel Fish	-1853-56-
L.W.Hapgood	
Daniel Lovejoy	-1870-71-
Lowell Plane & Tool Co.	
John Pettingell	-1875-
Walden J. Pettingell	
C.Prescott	-1832-33-
Jacob Rogers & Co	
A.Smith	
Wing H. Taber	-1849-56-

Mansfield
S.B.Schenck	-1853-

Medway
I.Iones[J.Jones]	probably 18th C.

Mendon
E.Taft	18th C.

Middleboro
E.Clark	18th C.

New Bedford
B.D.Hathaway	
Lamb & Brownell	
J.H.Lamb	-1869-74-
W.G.Lamb	-1869-
A.M.Smith	-1834-
J.W.Smith	-1856-
J.M.Taber	-1852-75
L.H.Taber	1832-52
N.Taber	-1790-1839
Taber Plane Co.	1866-92

Newton
B.Piper	1881-

Northampton
Arnold & Crouch	
J.D.Kellogg	
Peck & Crouch	
S. Pomeroy	18th C.
H. Wells	

Norton
Hussey,Bodman & Co.
C.D. & O.H.Lord	-1875-
H.Wetherel	c.1764

Norwich
Hills & Richards

Pittsfield
P.Brooks & Co.	
Wm. Brown	-1849-
M.Sweet	-1826-29-
J.Webb	
J. & W. Webb	
W.Webb	
Webb & Gamwell	

Reading
I.Walton	-1764-

Rehoboth
A.Smith	18th C.
E.Smith	

Rowe
H.Browning	1852-55
Wm. D.Swain	c.1856

Salem
Charles Odel

Southampton
Davis & Lester

South Orange
A.Barnes

South Scituate
James Merritt	
Tolman & Merritt	c.1864

Springfield
H.Crane	-1867-75-
Griswold & Dickinson	
Hill Swinselle	
H.Hills	-1849-
S. & H. Hills	
Hills & Winship	-1837-
Hills & Wolcott	
F.Richards & Co.	
Smith & Stewart	-1875-

Stockbridge
Wm.S.Davis	-1849-

Taunton
Wm.Woodward	early 19th C.

Waltham
Richardson Bros.

Westfield
N.Chapin, Eagle Factory	-1849-
Marshall & Brown	

Williamsburg
James Mfg. Co.	
H.L.James	-1855-
H.Wells	1852-56

Worcester

F.J. Gouch	1848-67
Sanborn & Co.	
Sanborn & Gouch	1845-46
E. Smith	1862-75

Worthington

E.C. Ring [Ringville]	-1855-
E. & T. Ring & Co.	-1849-
L. & T. Ring & Co.	
I.E. Sanderson	1852-53

Wrentham

C.E. Chelor	1758-75
F. Nicholson	c.1750
I. Nicholson	c.1760-90

CONNECTICUT

Barkhamsted [Riverton]

Alfred Alford Plane Co.	1853-64
Phoenix Co. [Hitchcocksville]	-1856-61

Bridgeport

John T. Platt	-1868-

Birmingham [now Derby]

L. Deforest	c.1850
*L. & C.H. Deforest	1860
Simeon Deforest	-1849-56-
Birmingham Plane Co.	-1862-89-

Chatham [now Portland]

H. Wetherell [1]	early 19th C.

Cornwall

Charles Gardner	-1857-58-

Derby

Linson Deforest	-1850-60-
Wm.F. Gilbert	
Derby Plane Mfg. Co.	-1894-98-

East Haddam

Wm.H. Goodspeed	-1875

East Hartford

J.J. Bowles	-1838-43
P. Brooks	
Burnham	
Burnham Brothers	

Glastonbury

Obed Andrus	-1857-71
James Killam	1822-60
Lyman Killam	-1857-58-

Hartford

L.B. Bidwell	1844-48
D. Copeland	c.1820-
D. & M. Copeland	c.1822-25
M. Copeland	c.1831-
M. & A. Copeland	c.1826-31
Giddings & Meek	
L. Kennedy [Sr.]	1809-42
L. Kennedy & Co. [Jr.]	1845
*Kennedy & Bragaw	1844-46
*Kennedy & Way	1838-43
K. & C.	

Hartford (Continued)

J.T. Loomis	1847-63
Willis Thrall & Son, D.	1860-95

Huntington

Birmingham Plane Co.	-1862-89-

Middletown

Baldwin Tool Co.	1841-57-
*N.H. Closson	-1849-58-
*M. Nelson	-1849-
Savage & Carter	-1849-
*S.D. Vansands	-1849-
H. Wetherell	early 19th C.

Meriden

*N.F. Hart & Co.	-1857-58-

New Britain

Stanley Rule & Level	1870-1941
Union Manufcaturing Co,	1890-1921

New Hartford

*Copeland [D.] & Chapin [H.]	1825-29
H. Chapin [Union Factory]	1829-66
*H. Chapin's Sons	1866-68
*H. Chapin's Son	1868-97
*H. Chapin's Son & Co.	1898-1901
Chapin-Stephens Co.	1901-29
*Clark & Wiswall	-1856-
Eagle Factory	
Warner & Driggs [Phoenix Fact.]	-1853
Wm. Warner	-1849-51-
G. & N.J. Ward	

New Haven

J.E. Bassett, D. in business 1784	
Baldwin Beecher	-1850-53
Beecher & Addis	1850-53
F.S. Bradley & Co.	1866-91
C.P. Brown	
I. Hammond	-1840-45
E. Hoadley	
Kenewa Tool Co. [Imprint of Sargent]	
Mathewman & Co.	1872-76
C. Morehouse	-1840-46
David Pond	1853-63
W.H. Pond [Wadsworth H.]	1844-81
W.H. Pond [William H.]	1847-67
Pond & Briggs	1868-69
Pond, Malcolm & Welles	
Sargent & Co.	c.1890-1930-
Union Works	
G. Wolcott	

New London

*B.F. & J. Beckwith	-1857-60-
*Samuel Dennis	-1849-74-
*Harris & Ames	-1857-58-

Norwalk

*E.V.A. Chichester	-1856-65-

Norwich

C.W. Holden	-1850-75-
*Peoples Machine Works	-1866-

CONNECTICUT (Continued)

Salisbury (Chapinsville)
Bird French	-1849-

Saugatuck (now Westport)
Doscher Plane & Tool Co.	-1886-1902-

Saybrook
C.& S.Bulkley	-1850-
G.W.Denison & Co. (Winthrop)	1869-90
John Denison	-1850-66-
J.& L.Denison	
L.Denison	
James W.Mason	-1869-8--

Unionville (Farmington)
Standard Rule Co.	1884-88
Upson Nut Co.	1888-90-

Vernon
*A.W.Tracy	-1856-60-

Wallingford
Joel Fenn & Co.	-1849-
P.A.Gladwin & Co.	
Gladwin & Platts	
Sawheag Works	-1850-51-

Windsor Locks
Wm.Muir & Co.

Winsted
Winsted Plane Co.	1851-56

II - NEW YORK

Albany
E.Baldwin		1807-17
D.Bensen		1832-47
Bensen & Crannell	D.& M.	1844-62
Bensen & M'Call		1842
Bensen & Mockridge		1830-31
Bensen & Munsel		1849-50
Bensen & Parry		1838-39
*Joseph Coughtry		1891-97
Matthew Crannell	D.& M.	1862-92
John Gibson		1823-52
Joseph Gibson		1839-46
J.& J.Gibson		1837-38
Issac Jones		1891-95
*Leonard Kenny(also,Kenney)		1818-19
Thos. J.McCall		
John S.Parry		1833-41
Samuel Randall		1833-34
Randall & Bensen		1827-29
*Randall & Co.		1840-41
Randall & Cook		1835-39
*Randall & Shepard		1826
Simeon Rowell		1820-28
Rowell & Gibson		1824-28
*Rowell & Kenney		1821-24
Elias Safford		-1813-21
Daniel M. Shepard		1827-28

Ashford
E.Moses	-1850-

Auburn
Auburn Tool Co.		1864-93
Barker & Baldwin	D.	1850-57
Casey & Co.		1857
Casey,Clark & Co.		1864
Casey,Kitchel & Co.		1847-58
Dunham & M'Master		1821-25
Easterly & Co.		1866-68
Ensenore Works		1857
Excelsior Works		1867
A.Howland & Co.		1869-74
T.J.M'Master & Co.		1825-29
Z.J.M'Master & Co.		1846-47
New York Tool Co.		1864-93
Ohio Tool Co.		1993-1907
Owasco Tool Co.		-1875-
Scioto Works		1893-1907
J.A.Sex & Co.		
Watrous & Osborne	D.	-1850-
Young & M'Master		1838-43

Binghamton
G.W.Gregory	D.	

Brooklyn
John C. Duryea		1836-49
*G.H.Dwenger		1847-56
Richard W.Hendrickson	D.& M.	1869-70
*John S.Parry		1842-54
D.Shiverick & Co.		
*David Schiverick		1865-67
*Shiverick & Malcolm		1853-64

Buffalo
George Axe		1855-80
*Robert Bingham		1864-65
Orrin Edgerton		1836-47
E.F.Folger & Co.	D.	1849-57
Holton & Crane	D.	
*Michael Lang		1858-71
Pratt & Co.	D.	1836-50
Thomson Brothers	D.	1847-59
Wm.A.Thomson	D.	1836-46
L.& I.J.White		1837-1928

Concord
John Sanderson	1852-70-

Delhi
Archibald Inglis	1850-76

Deposit
Edward Moses	-1850-

Dundee
M.B.Tidey	-1834-

Elmira
Wm.H.Spaulding [also,Spalding]

Hastings
Moses	-1850

NEW YORK (Continued)
Hudson
Cornelius Tobey		-1792-1807
J.I.Tobey		-1827-

Ithaca
A. M.Seaman		1826-92
Nathaniel Spaulding		-1869-70-
Treman Bros.	D.	1849-57
Treman,King & Co.	D.	1857-1900

Johnstown
Lyman Scovill		-1837-38-

Kingston
J.J.Styles (also,J.Stiles)		-1820-76

Little Falls
George Ashley	D.	-1845-70-
Harris & Shepherd	D.	1864-69

Lockport
Lockport Edge Tool Co.		1860-70

Lansingburgh
C.Allen		18th.C.

McLean
Nathaniel Spaulding		-1824-50

Middletown
Israel O. Beattie		-1861-72-

Newport
Enos Robbins		-1850-55-

New Lebanon
J.Kendall		-1835-

New York City
H.Adams & Co.		
Consider Alford		1812-17
A.& E.Baldwin		1830-41
Elbridge G.Baldwin		1830-50
Enos Baldwin		1817-29
Samuel S. Barry	D.	1827-41
J.W.Barron		
Barry & Way	D.	1842-47
*Barry,Way & Sherman	D.	1847
Wm.E.Belch	D.	1833-64
Bewley [Thos,& Edmund]		1822-32
*John Bornhoeft		1850
Wm.Bryce & Co.	D.	1846-73
Burger & Baumgard	D.	1877-1900
C.T. & Co.		
Cassebeer,Reed & Co.	D.	1878-83
David W.Cation		1835-44
T.S.& Clark		
Colunbia (Wood) Tool Co.		-1925-
*Luther G.Conklin		-1831-
E.L.Cooper & Co.	D.	1863-73
Joseph Coughtry		1849-50
Wm.Cuddy	D.	1841-54
*Moses H.Davis		1842-44
Davis & King		
*Linson DeForest		1857-58
DeValcourt (John C.& Charles)		1827-36
Martin Doscher	D.	1879-91
Douglas		-1796
Peter Duryee	D.	1841-67
Eclipse Tool Co.		1901-02
J.W.Farr		1832-51
Chalers Fletcher	D.& M.	1857-83
John W.Gibbs		1829-33
Gibbs & Cation		1834
Gilbert,Sweet & Lyon	D.	1887-89
*Gottfried Goebbel		1855-57
Thos.Grant		18th.C.
*Jacob Green		1850-54
A.Hammacher & Co.	D.	1864-84
Hammacher,Schlemmer & Co.	D.	1855-1900
James Hannan	D. & M.	1849-55
J.W.Harron		1867-1917
Robert Harron		1844-65
Hegney & Boilerman		
Richard W.Hendrickson	D.& M.	1859-67
John Hill/Tool Store	D.	1813-52
Robert Hoey		1834-37
Hoey & Taber		1836-40
Wm.F.Hoffman		
*Benjamin P.Hubbell		1852-54
*Henry A.James		1851
Jordon Hardware Corp.		
Kennedy,Barry & Way	D.	1841
Kennedy & White		1822-40
Josiah King		1835-87
E.R.Krum	D.	1869-96
*Charles S.Little	D.& M.	-1846-72
W.H.Livingston & Co.	D.	1840-66
Mannebach		1858-98
Luke Marley		1820-56
Martin & Corey	D.	1857-65
*James W.Mason		1874-78
Merritt & Co.	D.	-1842-60
Albert G. Moore		1856-61
Nathusius,Kegler & Morrison	D.	1859-76
Andrew Newell		1885-1905
Osborne & Little		-1846
John S.Parry		-1832-
J.Pearce		
*James H.Perry	D.	-1832-
John H. Perry		1850-63
Quackenbush,Townsend & Co.	D.	1865-92
Reed & Auerbacher	D.	1884-1910
*W.Schlemmer & Co.	D.	1871-72
Ashbel Searl	D.	1849-53
Cornelius S. See		1829-46
Sherman Bros	D.	1853-73
Sickels,Sweet & Lyon	D.	
Smith.Lyon & Field	D.	
*Phineas Smith	D.& M.	1855-96
James Stiles [also,Styles]		1768-75
*Wing H. Taber		1841-42
Charles Tollner	D.	1851-61
*C.Tollner & A.Hammacher	D.	1862-63

New York City (Continued)
Ward & Fletcher		1852-53
Wm.Ward	D.& M.	1850-72
Wm.Way	D.	1848
Way & Co.	D.	1853-59
Way & Sherman	D.	1849-52
J.& W.Webb		
Wm.Williams		1843-47
*Henry Wilson		1852-54
Wood's Tool Store	D.	1831-55

Ogdensburgh
*R.C.Bailey		1850

Oswego
Wheeler & Allen [also,Allin]	D.	1857-61
R.Woodford & Co.	D.	1839-55

Poughkeepsie
John G. Sandkuhl	1850-84

Rochester
*Barton & Babcock	1834
*Barton & Belden	1845
*Barton & Milliner	1863
Barton & Smith	1842
David R. Barton	1832-75
Wm.B.Bryan	D.& M. 1834-54
*Ira Belden	D.& M. 1846-53
Benton,Evans & Co.	1834-38
H.Bush	1831-33
Crane & Scott	1866-67
E.Evans	1834-40
E.& J.Evans	1841-85
Gregg & Hamilton	

Rome
*George Stedman	1859-73
Wardwell & Co.	D. -1851-1900-
Pell & Wright	

Salina
*Lyman Nolton	-1850-

Syracuse
Charles Carter		1856-59
Joseph T. Hayden		-1850-51-
D.S. & S.P.Geer	D.	-1853-54-
*Hayden & Norton		-1850-51

Troy
Edward Carter	D.& M.	1848-97
E.& C.Carter		1849-53
R.Carter	D.& M.	1831-61
R.& C.Carter		1847-48
R.& L.Carter		1842-46
Charles S.Rowell		-1832-
Simeon Rowell		1828-32
J.M.Warren & Co.	D.	1845-1900

Singsing
T.Z.M'Master & Co.	1829-38
Z.J.M'Master & Co.	1839-43

Utica
Collins & Robbins	c.1830
R.J.Collins	1831-37

Utica (Continued)
L.Kennedy Jr.	1825-32
John Reed	1820-68
Gideon Wolcott	-1832-

Watertown
B.F.Berry	1834-35
Lorenzo Case	c.1850
Gleason & Wood	c.1860
Albert L. Gleason	1859-82
J.Lord	c.1823-65
C.S.See	
W.W.Wood & Bro.	c.1870

Location Unknown
American Plane Co.
Buffalo Tool Co.
Cayudutta Factory
Cayuga, N.Y.
CR& W. NY Co.
Empire Tool Co.
Genesee Tool Co.
Jordon Hardware Corp.
New York Tool Works
D.Rogers, N.Y.
Troy Tool Co.

III Other Middle East States

New Jersey

Camden
N.Norton

Jersey City
M.Luttgen

New Brunswick
S.C. Cook

Newark
D.T.Andrus [also,Andruss]		-1831-
Samuel E. Farrand		-1831
A.Mockridge		1830-70
Mockridge & Francis	D.& M.	1845-70
Mockrige & Son		1873-98
James Searing		1835-39
*John D. Searing		1835-49

Vineland
Gage Tool Co.	1883-1920

Pennsylvania

Lancaster
Samuel Auxer	
E.W.Carpenter	-1859-
D.Heiss	
Kieffer & Auxer	

Manheim
J.F.Bauder

Philadelphia
Barber & Ross	
John Bell	1829-51
S.H.Bibighaus	1840-67

Philadelphia (Continued)

Biddle & Co.	
R.& W.C.Biddle	-1840-
Booth,Mills & Co.	-1873-
R.W.Booth	-1846-47-
W.Brooks	-1791-1807
*George Butler	1819-35
*John Butler	1795-1830
*A.J.Colton D.& M.	1861-76-
D.Colton	-1839-75
D.Colton & B.Sheneman D.& M.	1847-50
J.Colton	1837-76-
M.Deter	
T.Donoho	1854
Elder & Son	
Field & Hardie	
Glenn & Duff	
*George Goldsmith	1809-53
Thos. Goldsmith	1801-37
Wm. Goldsmith	-1839-69
W.Grinel	
*J.F.Jones	1825-35
J.T.Jones	1831-46
Kneass	
Mander & Dillon	-1865-
Martin	-1785-1801
James W.Massey	1808-30
*Samuel Massey	1818
Thos. Napier	-1785-1810
R.A.Parrish	1807-45
E.W.Pennell	-1839-59
Pennell & Miller	
Richards	
B.Sheneman	1846-67
B.Sheneman & Bro.	1860
B.& T.J.Sheneman	1860
Edward Sheneman	1863
Wm. Souder	1823-53
John Spayd	1860
Spayd & Bell	
John Veit	1857-99
A.Wheaton	19th.C.
*Charollete White[late Isreal]	1840
George White	1818-22
Henry G.White	1851-58
Israel White	1831-39
I. & I.White	
Jacob White	1818-43
*White & Grinnell	1818
Williams' Universal Plane	1864
R.Wright	
Yarnall & McClure	

Pittsburgh

J.Chappell
W.Evens
Whitmore & Wolff

Pittsburgh (Continued)

Whitmore,Wolff,Duff & Co.
Joseph Woodwell & Co.

MARYLAND
Baltimore

Atkinson	-1829-35 & -1840-42
Atkinson & Co.	1837-
*Atkinson & Chapin	1836
JN⁰ M. Barkley	1816-24
Baltimore Plane Co.	after1883
Barkley & Hughes	
J.S.Brown	-1842
J.T.Brown	-1824-43-
E.Caldwell	-1840-56-
N.Camper	-1851-56 & 1859-80
Carlin & Fulton/Sole Agents Baltimore Plane Co.	1883-
P.Chapin	-1835-36 & 1843-56
Chapin & Kendall	-1833-
G.Freeburger, Jr.	-1849-51-
B.Huff	-1849-51-
J.Keller	-1796-1808-
H.L.Kendall	-1849-&1859-
*H.L.Kendall & Co.	1860-
Kendall [Thomas]	-1831-33 & -1835-42
*Kendall & M'Cubbin	1837-
*Kendall & Schroeder	1858-
R.W.Maccubbin	-1840- & 1845-58-
E.I.Matthews	
Wm. C.Ross	1863-68-
*Robert Schroeder	1860-
A.B.Seidenstricker	-1870-72
W.Vance	-1799-1833-
*John T.West	1874
Wiseman & Ross	-1842-43-
Geo.W.Young Jr. & Co.	-1870-
*Young & Seidenstricker	1868

WASHINGTON, D.C.

Bridge
Wm.P.Webb

IV - SOUTHERN STATES

KENTUCKY
Georgetown

I.Vanzant

Louisville

T.Atkinson
O.T.Bull
W.L.Epperson
T.Fugate & J.Conover
A.McBride
W.W.Richey
N.H.Stout
Stout & Richey
Woodruff & McBride

LOUISIANA   New Orleans

Chas. Gaines
P.A.Lanauze

MISSISSIPPI   Natchez

Jno. B. Quegles
              Vicksburg
J.A.Peale & Co.

TENNESSEE   Memphis

R.T.Lamb

VIRGINIA
              Wheeling
Anderson Laing & Co.
Wm.Steele & Co.   -1839-51-
              Petersburg
Q.& W.C.Morton
              Norfolk
E.Tabb & Co.

   V - MIDWESTERN STATES

ILLINOIS
              Alton
Nelson & Hayner
Root & Platt
Ryan & Bros.
Topping & Bro.
              Bloomington
C.W.Holder & Co.   D.   -1855-56-
              Chicago
W.Blair & Co.
S.Deschauer   -1864
W.F.Dominick
J.& A.Fish
*Hibbard,Spencer,Bartlett & Co.-1899-
J.Mattson
A.R.& G.H.Miller
A.H.Newbold
Sears,Roebuck & Co. late 19th C. -1930
Tuttle,Hibbard & Co.   D.
              Jacksonsville
Ayers & Co.
              Jonesboro
Wiley & Frick
              Quincy
L.& C.M.Bull
              Springfield
B.F.Fox

INDIANA
              Ft.Wayne
B.W.Oakley & Som   D.   1869-78
Oakley & French   D.   -1858-73

INDIANA (Continued)
              Indianapolis
J.R.Vajen
              Madison
J.Burnet
              New Albany
S.Cook & Co.
J.Gilmer
T.Stout
S.P.Woodruff
              Richmond
Peters & Trimble
              Terre Haute
S.Cook & Co.
S.H.Potter

IOWA
              Davenport
Powell & Child
              Evansville
Babcock Brothers
C.S.Wells   c.1860
              Ft. Demoin [Des Moines]
Sanford & Co.   1857-71
              Muscatine
Geo. Mahan

MICHIGAN
              Detroit
Buhl,Ducharme & Co.
J.P.Cook
H.H.Knapp
A.H.Newbould   c.1840-50
B.B.& W.R.Noyes
T.B.Rayl & Co.
J.M.Slater
M.H.Webster

MINNESOTA   Minneapolis
I.L.Penney

MISSOURI   St.Louis
G.Bremerman
Child,Farr & Co.
Child,Pratt & Co.
Hall & Hynson
J.Hall
Hunt & Wiseman
Hynson
E.F.Kraft & Co.
A.Meier & Co.
Meyer & Schulze
Henry Miller
Julius Morisse
Shapleigh,Day & Co.
E.C.Simmons [Keen Kutter]
M.Stout also M.& N.H.Stout
Wilson & Bros.

OHIO Chillicothe
Denning & Campbell	D.	-1843-56
John Morrison		1826
D.A.Schutte	D.	-1850-55

Cincinnati
W.Baum & Co.		1850-52
R.W.Booth	D.	1848-80
F.C.Brandt	D.	c1850-70
L.R.Carter		-1834-
Carter,Donelson & Co.		-1831-32
Carter,Donelson & Fugate		-1831-
*John Conover		1829
J.Creagh		-1834-50
Creagh & Richards		-1829-
Creagh & Williams		-1831-32
*Cunningham & Co.		1853-54-
J.Donaldson		-1824-34
Thos. Fugate		-1830-46-
*James Galbreath		1850
*David N.Garrison		1829-40
Glaescher & Co.	D.	1879-89
G.W.Glaescher	D.	1859-79
N.H.Harris & Co.	D.	1856-57
T.A.Heim		
Heim & Smith		1849-50
G.Herder	D.	1844-70
Thomas Holliday & Co.	D.	1866-77
Holliday & Smith	D.	1855-81
*Hullings		1843-44
*Hullings & Kemper		-1842-
B.King & T.Fugtae		-1827-28
Kolp		1839-1850
L.Krause	D.	1850-59
Kuhlmann Hdwe.Co.	D.	1889-1920
R.Lang		1842-43
H.A.Langhurst	D.	1866-80
B.Lape		1842-46-
F.Lender		-1839-50
J.H.Lohr	D.	1858-71
J.Lyon		-1834-40
Lyon & Hall		1840
Lyon,McKinnell & Co.		1842-45
Lyon & Smith		1848-51-
J.McGinnis		1819
McKinnell & Co.		1848-50
Mead & Shelton		1853-55
Miller & Probasco		1834
Moon & Laby		
Oakley & French	D.	-1858-73
*Abel Pearson	D.	1850
B.Phillips		-1836-50
T.& A.Pickering	D.	1866-75
Queen City Tool Co.	D.	
T.J.Richards		-1831-32-
Rickard		1831
H.Rohrkasse & Co.	D.	1848-57
G.Roseboom		-1843-48

Cincinnati (Continued)
G.& W.H.Roseboom		-1843-52
Roseboom & Magill		1855
*Roseboom & Smith		1853-54
*Roseboom & Thomas		1853-54
C.B.Schaefer & Co.		1850-52
Schaefer & Cobb		-1853-54
E.F.Seybold		1836-52
C.Seybold (Catherine,late E.F.)		1853-55
Seybold & Spencer		
John Seymour		c1855
S.Sloop		1839-40
C.J.Smith & Co.		1849-59
J.H.Smith		
J.& C.Smith	D.	1851-52
T.D. & Co.		1842-65
Hiram Taylor		1844-65
John C.Taylor		1850-61
J.Taylor/H.Taylor		1851-57
Theising & Evans	D.	1850
F.Underwood/C.B.Schaefer		1854-57
D.Walker		-1830-
*Ester Waker (late Jesse)		1829
J. Walker		1824-29
*Walker & Hall		1831
R.A.Ward		1836-37
J.L.Wayne & Son		
*Josiah Wiggins		1850
*Wiggins & Peifer		1850
Young & Holiday		1850-51

Cleveland
Kellog & Hastings	-1846-48-
F.B.Marble	-1845-53
Marble & Smith	
A.& W.Marsh	
J.G.Steiger	-1863-64-
J.J.Vinal	-18453-
G.Worthington	

Columbus
Buttles & Runyon	-1844-
E.W.Case	
A.Copeland	
Gere,Abbott & Co.	
Hall,Case & Co.	-1850-
P.Hayden & Co.	-1847-
J.M.McCune & Co.	
Ohio Tool Co.	1851-1913
Scioto Works (brand of Ohio Tool Co.)	

Dayton
J.Bracelin	-1858-
D.N.Garrison	-1853-54-
Holcom & Slentz (East Dayton)	
Rogers & Fowler	-1856-57-

Mason
*J.M.Babbitt	-1856
*S.Hastings	
*J.H.Verbryck	-1853-

OHIO (Continued)
Kingston
J.Zimmerman -1839-
Jackson
H.White
N.Libson
J.Starr
Ohio City
J.Rumbaugh
P.S.Francisco
Ravena
Collins
Griffin
Sandusky
A.C.Bartlett's Ohio Planes
Ogantz (brand of Sandusky Tool Co.)
Sandusky Tool Co. 1869-1931
Ohio Plane Co. (A.C.Bartlett,pres.)
Springfield
Runyon & King -1852-
Tiffin City
J.M.Naylor & Co.
Troy
J.Richmond
Vernon
I.S.Allen
Warren
R.H.Barnum
Charles White -1853-54-
White & Spear
Xenia
E.Fillmore
Zanesville
H.& W.T.Carey

WISCONSIN Milwaukee
Edwin Clark
L.Kennedy 1848-49
H. Jo.Nazro & Co. 1848-59
P.Weber & Co.

VI - IMPRINTS OF PLANES MADE IN CANADA

NEW BRUNSWICK
I.F.Burpee, St.John 1865-1877
J.R.Goggin Hardware,Chatham D.1875-1900
Thomas McAvity,St.John D.
Willis, St.John 1865-66
Robert Moir

ONTARIO
Dryburgh, N.E.Hope
J.Dryburgh, Bright
J.Bailie,Toronto
Juson & Co, Hamilton -1864-66
J.P.Milliner & Co., Kingston 1857-58
Tho. Machin, Toronto
Ontario Tool Co.

ONTARIO (Continued)
Vokes Hardware Co.,Ltd,Toronto 1894-1934
Wood, Hamilton

QUEBEC PROVINCE
S.Dalpe, Roxton Pond 1868-94
J.Dawson, Montreal 1867-89
V.A.Emond Quebec City 1867-89
W.C.McDonald,Montreal
A.Monty (also Monte),Roxton Pond 1896-1928
Morland Tool Co., Montreal
Quebec Steam Plane Factory,Quebec 1889-
Roxton Pond Tool Co. 1876-1884
Wallace, Montreal
S.F. Willard, Roxton Pond 1876-84

VII - IMPRINTS found in U.S.A. before 1970
of English Manufactured Planes

England - Bath
Farmer
Smith
Stothert
Stothert & Walker
Birmingham
Amess
Atkin & Son/Sheffield Works
Birch & Son/Warranted
I.Briscoe
H.Brown
Brown & Barnard
Charles & Co.
Thomas Cauldwell
Cox & Luckman
I.Cox
G.Davis
L.Davis
W.Fellows
B.Frogatt
Jenkins & Clark
Darbey. . . I Briscoe
D.Kimberley & Sons
Martin & Shaw
T.Mackenzie
Wm. Moss
H.C.Parkes
W. Parkes
S.Powell
D.Preston
E.Preston & Sons
Routledge
Staniforth & Ford
F.Street
L.Tompinson
S.Tompinson
Bradford
T.Underwood
W.Watkins

ENGLISH IMPRINTS (Continued)

Bristol
T.J.Gardner
S.Green
W.Greenslade
Jn.Hall
W.Haw
Holbrook

Carlisle
Jno.Cockbain

Exeter
R.Davis

Hull
S.King
King & Compe
King & Peach
Spence & King

Lambeth
Buck   [District of London]

Leeds
W.Anderson
Bewley
W.Simpson
I.Teal
W.Thackery/Armley Yorks
Trenam
J.Willey/ N.Swinegate

Liverpool
Ja.Clarke
Fairclough
John J.Harley
Hayes
Moore
Taylor & Son
S.Lunt

London
Ames
J.Ames
Archer/ 45 Goodge St.
Berry/ 6 Long Lane
J.Buck/ 91 Waterloo Road
Buck & Hickman
Bywater
Casebourne
J.Connolly
D.Cook
I.Cogdell
Copley
R.Dabbs
I[J.]Davis
J.Dixon
J.Dukes
Fitkin
Gabriel
John Green [I.Green]
Hambleton
Higgs

LONDON (Continued)
H.& J.Hill
I.Long
I.Lund
Lyms
Madox
Rd. Melhuish Ltd.
Moon/ Martin's Lane
   [also,Lincoln Inn Field]
Mosley late Mutter
Mosley & Son
John Mosley & Son
Mutter
Nelson/ 122 Edgeware Rd.
C.Nurse & Co.
Phillipson
Preston & Son
John Rogers
G.Sampson
G.Shaw/ 95 Hackeby St.
Shepley
Shepley & Brain
Sims
I.Sym
Stokoe
J.Tadgell
Tucker
S.Tyzack & Sons
R.Wooding

Manchester
Arthington
Chapple late Wilcox
Dyson & Son
W.Edwards
Gleave
Hatersich

Newcastle Upon Tyne
Cowell & Chapman
J.Miller/ 73 Clayton St.

Norwich
Griffiths

Nottingham
Axe & Hields
Hields

Sheffield
Wm.Brookes & Sons
D.Flather & Sons
John Gilbert
W.Hasler
Heathcott
W.Large
W.Marples & Sons
C.T.Skelton & Co.
Turner

Sunderland
E.G.Fitzackerley

ENGLISH IMPRINTS (Continued)
Worcester
J.Barnes
Barnes
York
W.Dibb
B.Dyson
Middleton
Varvill/ Ebor Works
Varvill & Son

Locations in England Unkown
J.Clark
I.Cutwell
Fisher
J.Forbes
I.Iohnson
Lourie
Manners
Parsons
H.Rogers Sons & Co.

North Ireland - Belfast
S.Keller

SCOTLAND - Aberdeen
James Reid
Dundee
Dryburgh
Kinnear
A.Wallace
Edinburgh
Arthur
A.Donaldson
Peter MacKay & Co.
A.Mathieson & Co.
Melville
Thos.Napier
Scobie & McIntosh
Stewart
Wilson & Co.
Glasgow
Aristine Tool Co.
Bennett & Burley
Carrick & Craig
T.Chapman
Currie
J.Dobie
John Elsworth
Grossman Keen & Co.
Chas.F. Loftus
Hogg
Peter MacKay & Co.
McPherson Bros.
Marshall
Moir
Morison

SCOTLAND (Continued) Glasgow
D.Temple
Wm.Tomlinson
Wilson
Perth
D.Mallock & Son
D.Mallock
McVicar
McGlasen

REPUBLIC of IRELAND - Dublin
Booth
Kennan & Son

VIII - FIRM NAMES WITH PARTIAL ADDRESSES

Aird/ Prichton
Geo.Allen/ Warrington
Allen & Eldridge/ So. WmsTown
G.P.Bancroft/ Granville
Barnabas/ Niles
A.G.Christen/ Bern
Crane/ Kingston
I.Davies/ Holdbrook
G.Harder/ Main B.T.
O.Kurz/ Berlin
LaChappelle/ Strassburg
J.Lock/ Bennington
M.Long/ Reading
J.P.Lyne & Son/ Carlisle
Middleton/ Newark
Missouri Premium H.C.& T.
J.D.Miller/ Bridgeport
Morley & Jenkins/ Kingston
G.Mundorff/ Berlin
W.E.Perry/ W.Haven
Plutte & Becker/ Hamburg
Sale & Griggs/ Davenport
G.Shaw/ 95 Hackney St.
D.Stoner/ Brunswick
E.Thomas/ Holdbrook
Thompson/ Stuben
J.H.Timken/ Bremen
R.Wells/ Trenton
J.R.West/ Easton

IX - FIRM NAMES WITHOUT ADDRESSES

Achushnet Works
J.Andruss
Beck & Co.
Blackstone Works
I.F.Brodhead
Brown Tool Co.
C.F.Buckeley & Co.
A.Chance Son & Co.
Charles & Duff

Firm Names Without Addresses (Continued)   X - Names Alone
[possible makers or firms]

Chester Tool Co.	Abbot
Chip A Way	A.Adams
Cormier/ Garanti Veritable	Aetzler
D.O.Crane	Album 63
I.Darrly	O.R.Aldrich
H.Davidson	Allans
E.& C. Co.	J.Angermyer
Eagle Mng. Co.	WmArmstrong
R.Eastburn	A.Aubrey
B.Eddy/ Warranted	Austin
S.Gardner & Co.	R.Barnes
C.M.Gere/ Warranted	Ts.Barrand
E.Gere	S.A.Barstow
Glock & Tallmadge	D.Bassett
Wm.Greves & Sons	I.Bear
H.& Bros.	J.B.Bell
H.C. & Co.	W.Bell
Handcock Tool Co.	A.Benjamin [18th C.]
J.Harrison & Co.	E.Berry
Humphrey & Sterns	Bohney
J.Hussey	W.S.Bonham
D.Jarvis	Bourt
W.E.Johnson & Co.	W.Boyd
Judkins Bros.	A.Boyden
Kampman & Co.	A.Boyer
S.Killum	J.Blocksidge
King & Cunningham	J.H.Brandow
D.Lines	N.Briggs
N.Little	O.H.Brooks
G.Long	B.Brown
G.W.Manning	F.Cabot
Mechanics Tool Co.	R.Campbell
J.Milton	L.Cantin
A.Morton & Co.	P.Chase
Ohio King	I.Clark [18th C.]
Owens & Barkley	U.Clap [late 18th or early 19th C.]
Owings & Roy	T.Clark
Pagel & Ferguson	H.M.Cole
B.Paine [late Shepley & Co.]	M.Colt
J.T.Plimley & Co.	Cristelkn
W.Raymond [18th C.]	D.Cutler
Ryland Ostrum & Co.	J.W.Darling
S.H.Mfg. Co.	D.Davis
I. Sleeper [late 18th C or early 19th C.]	I.Day [18th C.]
Spencer	S.Dean
I.Veal	W.Delly
W.Bros. & Co.	T.Delve
L.G.Wells	A.Dow
White River Works	A.W.Elliot
Whittier & Spear	Rich.D.Field
J.Woods	S.Felch
	L.Ferry [18th C.]
	R.R.Finch
	J.Fleetwood
	C.W.Foot

X - **Names Alone** (Continued)

M.French
N.French
J.Geard
N.Gere
J.C.Gifford
J.Gladding, Jr.
J.Goodbrake
J.G.Goodhue
Jn.Gordon
Jo.Gramling
F.Gray
G.Harwood
L.Hawes
J.L.Haynes
Iacob Heiss
Co. Hendrin
A.Hide   [18th C.]
M.F.Higley
Hoadley
J.Hovey
C.M.Howland
D.Hubbard
J.Hunt
W.C.Isaacs
J.Janssen [also;-sin]
S.E.Jones
R.Jonson
E.A.Judkins
C.Keene
I.Kent
S.Kimball [18th C.]
John Kintzel
M.Knieram
J.Kratz
S.Law
R.S.Layton
S.Leonard
Iacob Lening
H.Libhart
C.Lindenberger
London
C.Long
D.Long
J.A.Lundgren
J.B.Mack
Wm.Mapier
E.J.McRonald
J.Mead [18th C.]
J.Minot
L.Merrill
D.Mitchell
Z.Morgan,Jr.
A.P.Morrill
A.Morse
J.Morse

T.Morse
F.N.Mower
J.J.Nash
Jn.Nevinson
N.Nutting
Ed.Paine
J.Parkhurst
F.Pearson
Peeler
J.C.Poor
W.Powell
D.Presprey
J.Randell
Raudet
L.Rich
P.Rogers [18th C.]
S.Root
Roxton
Runched
R.Safford
R.Sanderson
J.Schauer
Seller
W.Schultz
A.W.Shillinglaw
H.Simmons
S.Sleeper
P.Small
J.Smiley
C.S.Smith
E.Smith/H.O.Smith
Sneth
W.Sniff
Snow
C.Spann
O.A.Spear
Speyers
A.Spicer
O.Spicer
H.Sprague
J.A.Sraft
R.C.Starr
Stoeker
F.Stones
Mutter G. Sudd
D.Sweet
John Taber [18th]
Tasker
D.Taylor
J.Thomas
D.Thompson [18th]
J.Tough
Jn.Tower
L.Tyler
R.Wall

J.Waltz
D.Warner
L.Warner
R.Waters
S.Wentworth   [18th C.]
Weeden
L.Weeler
Whitehaven
I.Wilder   [18th C.]
D.Wilson
Isaac Willey
I.Wiser
B.Wollam
Woothoudt

ALPHABETICAL LISTING OF MAKERS, FIRMS & IMPRINTS

Names are noted with locations as to town and state or country with reference to previous listings. VIII refers to probable firms with partially known address. IX refers to probable firms or makers with unknown address; X refers to possible maker or firm from studies of imprints reported; * indicates a directory listing with no imprint of maker or firm yet reported.

Abbot, X
Achushnet Works, IX
A.Adams, X
*H.Adams, Hopkinton, MA
H.Adams, New York, NY
*William Adams, Hopkinton, MA
T.Atkinson, Louisville, KY
Aetzler, X
Aird/ Prichton, VIII
Album 63, X
A.Aubrey, X
O.R.Aldrich, X
Alford, New York, NY
Alford Plane Co., Barkhamsted, CT
Geo. Allen, Warrington, VIII
Allans, X
I.S.Allen, Vernon, OH
Allen & Eldridge, So.Wmstown, VIII
C.Allen, Lansingburgh, NY
American Plane Co., New York
Ames, London, England
J.Ames, London, England
Amess, Birmingham, England
Amherst Tool Co., Amherst, MA
Anderson & Laing, Wheeling, VA
W.Anderson, Leeds, England
D.T.Andrus, Newark, NJ
J.Andruss, IX
Obed Andrus, S.Glastenbury[sic] CT
J.Angermyer, X
Thos.L.Appleton, Boston & Chelsea, MA
Archer, London, England
Aristine Tool Co., Glasgow, Scotland
Wm.Armstrong, X
Arnold & Crouch, Northampton, MA
Arthington, Manchester, England
Arthur, Edinburgh, Scotland
G.Ashley, Little Falls, NY
Atkin & Son, Birmingham, England
Atkinson, Baltimore, MD
*Atkinson & Chapin, Baltimore, MD
Atkinson & Co., Baltimore. MD
T.Atkinson, Louisville, KY
A.Aubrey, X
Auburn Tool Co., Auburn, NY
Austin, X
Samuel Auxer, Lancaster, PA
Axe & Hields, Nottingham, England
G.Axe, Buffalo, NY

Ayers & Co., Jacksonville, IL
*J.M.Babbit, Mason, OH
Babcock Bros., Evansville, IA
J.Bagley, X
*Leonard Bailey, Boston, MA
*Bailey, Chany & Co., Boston, MA
*R.C.Bailey, Oswegatchie, N.Y.
J.Bailie, Toronto, Canada
E.Baldwin, Albany, NY
Elbridge Baldwin, New York, NY
Enos Baldwin, New York, NY
A.& E.Baldwin, New York, NY
Baldwin Tool Co., Middletown, CT
Jon Ballou, Providence, RI
Baltimore Plane Co., Baltimore, MD
G.P.Bancroft, Granville, VIII
Barber & Ross, Philadelphia. PA
Barker & Baldwin, Auburn, NY
JNo M.Barkley, Baltimore, MD
Barkley & Hughes, Baltimore, MD
Barnabas, Niles, VIII
Barnes, Worcester, England
A.Barnes, So.Orange, MA
*Hiram Barnes, Goshen, MA
J.Barnes, Worcester, England
R.Barnes, X
R.H.Barnum, Warren, OH
Ts.Barrand, X
H.Barrus & Co., Goshen, MA
N.L.Barrus, Warren, RI
S.S.Barry, New York, NY
Barry & Way, New York, NY
*Barry, Way & Sherman, New York, NY
S.A.Barstow, X
D.R.Barton, Rochester, NY
*Barton & Babcock, Rochester, NY
*Barton & Belden, Rochester, NY
*Barton & Milliner, Rochester, NY
Barton & Smith, Rochester, NY
D.Bassett, X
*J.E.Bassett, New Haven, CT
*I.S.Battey, Providence, RI
*Battey & Eddy, Providence, RI
J.F.Bauder, Manheim, PA
W.Baum & Co., Cincinnati, OH
I.Bear, X
Isreal O.Beattie, Middletown, NY
Baldwin Beecher, New Haven, CT
Beacher & Addis, New Haven, CT

Beck & Co., IX
*B.F.& J.Beckwith, New London, CT
W.E. Belch, New York, NY
*Ira Belden, Rochester, NY
John Bell, Philadelphia, PA
J.B.Bell, X
W.Bell, X
A.Benjamin, X
Bennett & Burley, Glasgow, Scotland
Bensen & Crannell, Albany, NY
Bensen & M'Call, Albany, NY
Bensen & Mockridge, Albany, NY
Bensen & Munsel, Albany, NY
Bensen & Parry, Albany, NY
David Bensen, Albany, NY
G.A.Benton, Boston, MA
Benton, Evans & Co., Rochester, NY
Berry, London, England
B.F.Berry, Watertown, NY
E.Berry, X
Bewley, New York, NY
Bewley, Leeds, England
Biddle & Co., Philadelphia, PA
R.& W.C.Biddle & Co., Philadelphia, PA
S.H.Bibighaus, Philadelphia, PA
L.B.Bidwell, Hartford, CT
L.B.Bigelow, Providence, RI
*Robert Bingham, Buffalo, NY
Birch & Son, Birmingham, England
Birmingham Plane Co., Derby, CT
Blackstone Works, IX
W.Blair & Co., Chicago, IL
J.Blocksidge, X
Bodman & Hussey, Pawtucket, RI
Bohney, X
W.S.Bonham, X
Booth, Dublin, Ireland
Booth, Mills & Co., Philadelphia, PA
R.W.Booth, Cincinnati, OH
R.W.Booth, Philadelphia, PA
*John Bornhoeft, New York, NY
Bourt, X
J.J.Bowles, East Hartford, CT
W.Boyd, X
A.Boyden, X
A.Boyer, X
J.Bracelin, Dayton, OH
J.Bradford, Portland, ME
John Bradford, Boston, MA
F.S.Bradley & Co., New Haven, CT
J.H.Brandow, X
F.C.Brandt, Cincinnati, OH
G.Bremerman, St. Louis, MO
Bridge, Washington, D.C.
Briggs, Keene, NH
N.Briggs, X
I.Briscoe, Birmingham, England
I.F.Broadhead, IX

Wm.Brookes & Sons, Sheffield, England
O.Brooks, X
P.Brooks, East Hartford, CT
P.Brooks & Co., Pittsfield, MA
W.Brooks, Philadelphia. PA
Brown Tool Co., IX
Brown & Barnard, Birmingham, England
B.Brown, X
C.P.Brown, New Haven, CT
H.Brown, Birmingham, England
J.S. [also I.S.]Brown, Baltimore, MD
J.T.Brown, Baltimore, MD
J.W.Brown & Co., Boston, MA
L.Brown, Baltimore, MD
Wm.Brown, Pittsfield, MA
H.Browning, Rowe, MA
W.W.Bryan, Rochester, NY
W.Bryce & Co., New York, NY
Buck, Lambeth, London, England
Buck & Hickman, London, England
J.Buck, London, England
Buffalo, Tool Co., New York
Buhl, Ducharme & Co., Detroit, MI
C.F.Bulkeley & Co., IX
C.& S.Bulkley, Saybrook, CT
O.T.Bull, Louisville, KY
L. & C.H. Bull, Quincy, IL
Burger & Baumgard, New York, NY
J.Burnet, Madison, IN
Burnham, East Hartford, CT
Burnham Brothers, East Hartford, CT
Geo.Burnham, jr., Amherst, MA
Burnham, Fox & Co., Amherst, MA
I.& F.Burpee, St.John, N.B., Canada
H.Bush, Rochester, NY
*George Butler, Philadelphia, PA
*John Butler, Philadelphia, PA
Buttles & Runyon, Columbus, OH
Bywater, London, England
C.T.& Co., New York
F.Cabot, X
E.Caldwell, Baltimore, MD
B.Callender & Co., Boston, MA
R.Campbell, X
N.Camper, Baltimore, MD
L.Cantin, X
H.& W.T.Carey, Xenia, OH
Carlin & Fulton, Baltimore, MD
E.W.Carpenter, Lancaster, PA
Carrick & Craig, Glasgow, Scotland
Carter, Donelson & Co., Cincinnati, OH
Carter, Donelson & Fugate, Cincinnati, OH
C.Carter, Syracuse, NY
Edward Carter, Troy, NY
E.& C.Carter, Troy, NY
L.R.Carter, Cincinnati, OH
R.Carter, Troy, NY
R.& C. Carter, Troy, NY

R.& L.Carter, Troy, NY
E.W.Case, Columbus, OH
L.Case, Watertown, NY
Casebourne, London, England
Casey & Co., Auburn, NY
Casey,Clark & Co., Auburn, NY
Casey, Kitchel & Co., Auburn, NY
Cassebeer Reed & Co., New York, NY
*Cation, New York, NY
Cauldwall, Birmingham, England
Cayudutta Factory, New York
Cayuga, New York
A.Chance Son & Co., IX
Chapin & Kendall, Baltimore, MD
*E.M.Chapin, New Hartford, CT
H.Chapin/Union Factory New Hartford, CT
*H.Chapin Son ['s], New Hartford, CT
N.Chapin/Eagle Factory, Westfield, MA
P.Chapin, Baltimore, MD
Chapin-Stephens & Co., New Hartford, CT
T.Chapman, Glasgow, Scotland
Chapple, Manchester, England
J.Chappell, Pittsburgh, PA
Charles & Co., Birmingham, England
Charles & Duff, IX
P.Chase, X
Chase,Sargent & Shattuck, Lowell, MA
C.E.Chelor, Wrentham, MA
Chester Tool Co., IX
*E.V.A.Chichester, Norwalk, CT
J.E.Child, Providence, RI
Child,Farr & Co., St.Louis, MO
Child,Pratt & Co., St.Louis, MO
Chip A Way, IX
A.G.Christen, Bern, VIII
H.Church, S.Amherst, MA
U.Clap, X
*Clark & Wiswall, New Hartford, CT
E.Clark, Middleboro, MA
*Edwin Clark, Milwaukee, WI
I.Clark, X
J.Clark, England
T.Clark, X
Ja.Clarke, Liverpool, England
E.Clifford, X
*N.H.Closson, Middletown,
Jno. Cockbain, Carlisle, England
I.Cogdell, London, England
H.M.Cole, X
Collins, Ravenna, OH
Collins & Robbins, Utica, NY
M.Colt, X
*A.J.Colton, Philadelphia, PA
D.Colton, Philadelphia, PA
J.Colton, Philadelphia, PA
D.Colton & B.Sheneman, Philadelphia, PA
Columbia Tool Co., New York, NY
Luther G.Conklin, New York, NY

John Conover, Cincinnati, OH
J.Connolly, London, England
Conway Tool Co., Conway, MA
D.Cook, London, England
J.Cook, Terre Haute, IN
S.C.Cook, New Brunswick, NJ
S.Cook & Co., New Albany, IN
J.P.Cook, Detroit, MI
*Wm.Cooley, Boston, MA
*Cooley & Montgomery, Boston, MA
E.L.Cooper, New York, NY
Copeland & Co., Huntington, MA
A.Copeland, Columbus, OH
D.Copeland, Hartford, CT
D.& M.Copeland, Hartford, CT
M.Copeland, Hartford, CT & Huntington, MA
M. & A. Copeland, Hartford, CT
*Copeland & Chapin, New Hartford, CT
Copley, London, England
Corey Brooks & Co., Boston, MA
Cormier, X
J.Coughtry, Albany & New York, NY
Cowell & Chapman, New Castle, England
Cox & Luckman, Birmingham, England
I.Cox, Birmingham, England
Crane & Scott, Rochester, NY
D.O.Crane, IX
Crane, Kingston, VIII
H.Crane, Springfield, MA
M.Crannell, Albany, NY
*John Crawford, Mason, OH
Creagh & Richards, Cincinnati, OH
Creagh & Williams, Cincinnati, OH
J.Creagh, Cincinnati, OH
Cristelkn, X
W.Cuddy, New York, NY
*Cumings [sic:Cummings] & Gale, Providence, RI
A.Cummings[sic:Cumings] Boston, MA
S.Cumings, Providence. RI
S.R.Cummings, Boston, MA
Cunningham & Co., Cincinnati, OH
Currie, Glasgow, Scotland
F.Curtis, Boston, MA
N.Curtis, Boston, MA
D.Cutler, X
I.Cutwell, England
Rd.Dabbs, London, England
S.Dalpe, Roxton Pond, P.Q., Canada
Darby..I.Driscoe, Birmingham, England
C.Darling, Woonsocket, RI
J.W.Darling, X
I.Darrly, X
H.Davidson, X
I.Davies, Holdbrook, VIII
Davis & King, New York, NY
*Davis & Lester, Southampton, MA
D.Davis, X
G.Davis, Birmingham, England

I.[J.]Davis, London, England
M.Davis, New York, NY
R.Davis, Exeter, England
*Wm.S.Davis, Stockbridge, MA
I.Day, X
J.Dawson, Montreal, P.Q., Canada
S.Dean, X
S.DeForest, Birmingham, CT
*Linson Deforest, New York, NY
Linson Deforest, Birmingham, CT
W.Delley, X
T.Delve, X
G.W.Denison & Co., Saybrook, CT
John Denison, Saybrook, CT
J.& L.Denison, Saybrook, CT
L.Denison, Saybrook, CT
Denning & Campbell, Chillicothe, OH
Samuel Dennis, New London, CT
Derby Plane Co., Derby, CT
S.Deschauer, Chicago, IL
M.Deter, Philadelphia, PA
DeValcourt, New York, NY
Dewey & Brown, Bellows Falls, VT
W.Dibb, York, England
E.P.Dickinson, Amherst, MA
J.Dixon, London, England
J.Dobie, Glasgow, Scotland
S.Doggett, Denham, MA
W.F.Dominick, Chicago. IL
A.Donaldson, Edinburgh, Scotland
J.Donaldson, Cincinnati, OH
T.Donoho, Philadelphia, PA
Doscher Plane Co., Saugatuck, CT
Martin Doscher, New York, NY
Douglas[s], New York, NY
A.Dow, X
C.C.Dresser, Goshen, MA
Dryburgh, Dundee, Scotland
Dryburgh, N.E.Hope, Ontario, Canada
Dryburgh, Bright, Ontario, Canada
B.Dyson, York, England
J.Dukes, London, England
Dunham & M'Master, Auburn, NY
J.C.Duryea, Brooklyn, NY
Peter Duryee, New York, NY
W.H.Duston, Lawrence, MA
*G.H.Dwenger, Brooklyn, New York
Dyson & Son, Manchester, England
E.& C. Co., IX
Eagle Factory, New Hartford, CT
R. Eastburn, IX
Easterly & Co., Auburn, NY
Eayrs, Nashua, NH
Eclipse Tool Co., New York, NY
B.Eddy, IX
O.Edgerton, Buffalo, NY
W.Edwards, Manchester, England
Elder & Son, Philadelphia, PA

A.W.Elliot, X
John Elsworth, Glasgow, Scotland
V.A.Emond, Quebec, Canada
Empire Tool Co., New York
Ensenore Woks, Auburn, NY
W.L.Epperson, Louisville, KY
E.Evans, Rochester, NY
E.& J.Evans, Rochester, NY
Excelsior Works, Auburn, NY
Fairclough. Liverpool. England
Farmer, Bath, England
J.W.Farr, New York, NY
Samuel E. Farrand, Newark. NJ
S.Felch, X
W.Fellows, Birmingham, England
Joel Fenn & Co., Wallingford, CT
L.Ferry, X
I.Field, Providence, RI
Field & Hardie, Philadelphia, PA
Rich.D.Field, X
Field & Bartlett, Lowell, MA
*Ansel Fish, Lowell, MA
J.& A. Fish, Chicago, IL
Fisher, England
Fitkin, London, England
E.G.Fitzackerley, Sunderland, England
D.Flather & Sons, Sheffield, England
J.Fleetwood, X
Charles Fletcher, New York. NY
E.F.Folger & Co., Buffalo, NY
C.W.Foot, X
J.Forbes, England
B.F.Fox, Springfield, IL
Fox & Washburn, Amherst, MA
G.Fox, Amherst, MA
L.Fox & Son, Amherst, MA
P.S.Francisco, Ohio City, OH
G.Freeburger, jr, Baltimore, MD
Bird French, Salisbury, CT
M.French, X
N.French, X
B.Frogatt, Birmingham, England
*Thos.Fugate, Cincinnati, OH
T.Fugate & J.Conover. Louisville, KY
C.Fuller, Boston, MA
David Fuller, West Gardner, ME
Jo.Fuller, Providence, RI
*Fuller & Field, Providence, RI
Gabriel, London, England
Gage Tool Co., Vineland, NJ
Charles C. Gaines, New Orleans, LA
*James Galbreth, Cincinnati, OH
J.R.Gale, Providence, RI
Gardner & Appleton, Boston, MA
Gardner & Brazer, Boston, MA
Gardner & Murdock, Boston, MA
*Charles Gardner, Cornwall, CT
L.Gardner, Boston, MA

S.Gardner & Co., IX
T.J.Gardner, Bristol, England
D.N.Garrison, Cincinnati & Dayton, OH
J.Geard, X
Genesee Tool Co., New York
Gere, Abbot & Co., Columbus, OH
C.M.Gere, IX
E.Gere, IX
N.Gere, X
Gibbs & Cation, New York, NY
John W.Gibbs. New York, NY
John Gibson, Albany, NY
Joseph Gibson, Albany, NY
J.& J.Gibson, Albany, NY
Giddings & Meek, Hartford, CT
J.C.Gifford, X
Gilbert, Sweet & Lyon, New York, NY
John Gilbert, Sheffield, England
W.F.Gilbert, Derby, CT
J.Gilmer, New Albany, IN
J.Gladding, jr., X
Gladwin & Appleton, Boston, MA
Gladwin & Platts, Wallingford, CT
P.A.Gladwin & Co., Wallingtford, CT
P.A.Gladwin & Co., Boston, MA
Glaescher, Cincinnati, OH
A.L.Gleason, Watertown, NY
Gleason & Wood, Watertown, NY
Gleave, Manchester, England
Glenn & Duff, Philadelphia, PA
Glock & Talmadge, IX
J.R.Goggin, Chatham,N.B., Canada
*Gottfried Goebbel, New York, NY
*G.Goldsmith, Philadelphia, PA
T.Goldsmith, Philadelphia, PA
Wm.Goldsmith, Philadelphia, PA
J.Goodbrake, X
J.G.Goodhue, X
*Wm.H.Goodspeed, East Haddam, CT
Jn.Gordon, X
F.J.Gouch, Worcester, MA
Jo.Gramling, X
Tho.Grant, New York, NY
F.Gray, X
I.Green, London, England [John Green]
*Jacob Green, New York, NY
S.Green, Bristol, England
Greenfield Tool Co., Greenfield, MA
W.Greenslade, Bristol, England
Gregg & Hamilton, Rochester, NY
Gregory, Binghampton, NY
Wm.Greves & Sons, IX
Griffin, Ravenna, OH
Griffiths, Norwich, England
W.Grinel, Philadelphia, PA
Griswold & Dickinson, Springfield, MA
Grossman,Keen & Co., Glasgow, Scotland
H.& Bros., IX

H.C. & Co., IX
Hall, Case & Co., Columbus, OH
Hall & Hynson, St. Louis, MO
J.Hall, St. Louis, MO
Jn.Hall, Bristol, England
Hambleton, London, England
Hammacher,Schlemmer & Co., New York, NY
A.Hammacher & Co., New York, NY
I.Hammond, New Haven, CT
Handcock Tool Co., IX
J.Hannan, New York, NY
L.W.Hapgood, Lowell, MA
G.Harder, VIII
John J.Harley, Liverpool, England
C.C.Harlow, Bridgewater, MA
*Harris & Ames, New London, CT
Harris & Shepperd, Little Falls, NY
N.Harris & Co., Cincinnati, OH
J.Harrison & Co., IX
J.W.Harron, New York, NY
Robert Harron, New York, NY
*N.F.Hart, Meriden, CT
G.Harwood, X
W.Hasler, Sheffield, England
S.Hastings, Amherst, MA
*S.Hastings, Mason, OH
B.D.Hathaway, New Bedford, MA
Hathersich, Manchester, England
Albert S.Haven, Boston, MA
W.Haw, Bristol, England
L.Hawes, X
Hayden, Syracuse, NY
*Hayden & Nolton, Syracuse, NY
P.Hayden & Co., Columbus, OH
Hayes, Liverpool, England
J.L.Haynes, X
Addison Heald, Milford, NH
A.Heald & Co., Milford, NH
A.Heald & Son, Milford, NH
Heathcott, Sheffield, England
T.A.Heim, Cincinnati, OH
Heim & Smith, Cincinnati, OH
D.Heiss, Lancaster, PA
Iacob [Jacob] Heiss, X
R.W.Hendrickson,Brooklyn & New York, NY
Co. Hendrin, X
Hegney & Boilerman, New York, NY
G.Herder, Cincinnati, OH
J.Herrick, Burlington, VT
J.L.B.Hersey, Portland, ME
J.H.Heupel & Co., Cincinnati, OH
A.Hide, X
Hields, Nottingham, England
Higgs, London, England
M.F.Higley, X
H.& J.Hill, London, England
John Hill, New York, NY
Hill Swinselle, Springfield, MA

Hills & Richards, Norwich, MA
Hills & Winship, Springfield, MA
Hills & Wolcott, Amherst, MA
Hills & Wolcott, Springfield, MA
H.Hills, Springfield, MA
S.& H.Hills, Amherst, MA
Hoadley, X
E.Hoadley, New Haven, CT
R.Hoey, New York, NY
Hoey & Taber, New York, NY
Thos.Holliday, Cincinnati, OH
W.Hoffman, New York, NY
Hogg, Glasgow, Scotland
Holbrook, Bristol, England
C.W.Holden, Norwich, MA
Holcomb & Slentz, E.Dayton, OH
Holliday & Smith, Cincinnati, OH
T.Holliday, Cincinnati, OH
L.P.Holmes, Berwick, ME
Homer, Bishop & Co., Boston, MA
Horton & Crane, Buffalo, NY
I.Hovey, X
A.Howland & Co, Auburn, NY
C.M.Howland, X
W.S.Howland, Amherst, MA
D.Hubbard, X
*Benjamin P.Hubbell, New York, NY
B.Huff, Baltimore, MD
W.Hull, Boston, MA
*Hull & Montgomery, Boston, MA
Hullings, Cincinnati, OH
*Hullings & Kemper, Cincinnati, OH
Humphrey & Sterns, IX
Hunt & Wiseman, St. Louis, MO
J.Hunt, X
Hussey, Bodman & Co., Norton, MA
J.Hussey, IX
Hynson, St. Louis, MO
A.Inglis, Delhi, NY
I.Iohnson, England
I.Iones, Holliston, MA
I.Iones, Medway, MA
W.C.Isaacs, X
James Mfg. Co., Williamsburg, MA
*Henry A. James, New York, NY
H.L.James, Williamsburg, MA
J.Janssen, X [also, -sin]
D.Jarvis, IX
Jenkins & Clark, Birmingham, England
J.C.Jewett, Waterville, ME
W.E.Johnson & Co., IX
E.Jones, X
Isaac Jones, Albany, NY
J.F.Jones, Philadelphia, PA
J.T.Jones, Philadelphia, PA
S.E.Jones, X
T.Jones, Philadelphia, PA
R.Jonson, X

Jordon Hardware Corp., New York, NY
Judkins Bros., IX
E.A.Judkins, X
Juson & Co., Hamilton, Ontario, Canada
K.& C., Hartford, CT
Kampman & Co., IX
C.Keene, X
John Keller, Baltimore. MD
S.Keller, Belfast, North Ireland
Kellog & Hastings, Cleveland, OH
Kellogg, Fox & Washburn, Amherst, MA
J.Kellogg, Amherst, MA
J.Kellogg & Co., Amherst, MA
J.Kellogg & Son, Amherst, MA
J.D.Kellogg, Northampton, MA
*Wm.Kellogg, Amherst, MA
A.Kelly & Co., Ashfield, MA
R.A.Kelly & Co., Ashfield, MA
H.L.Kendall, Baltimore, MD
H.L.Kendall & Co., Baltimore, MD
J.Kendall, N.Lebanon, NY
Kendall [Thomas], Baltimore, MD
*Kendall & M'Cubbin, Baltimore, MD
*Kendall & Schroeder, Baltimore, MD
Kenewa Tool Co. New Haven, CT
Kennan & Son, Dublin, North Ireland
Kennedy, Utica, NY
Kennedy & Co., Hartford, CT
*Kennedy & Bragaw, Hartford, CT
*Kennedy & Way, Hartford, CT
Kennedy & White, New York, NY
Kennedy, Barry & Way, New York, NY
L.Kennedy [sr.], Hartford, CT
L.Kennedy [jr.], Milwaukee, WI
*Leonard Kennedy [jr.], Albany, NY
L.Kenny, Albany, NY
I.Kent, X
Kieffer & Auxer, Lancaster, PA
J.Killam, Glastenbury [sic], CT
*Lyman Killam, Glastonbury, CT
S.Killum, IX
S.Kimball, X
D.Kimberly & Sons, Birmingham, England
Josiah King, New York, NY
S.King, Hull, England
King & Compe, Hull, England
King & Cunningham, IX
King & Fugate, Cincinnati, OH
King & Peach, Hull, England
Kinnear, Dundee, Scotland
John Kintzel, X
H.H.Knapp, Detroit, MI
Kneass, Philadelphia, PA
M.Knieram, X
Knowlton & Stone, Keene, NH
J.Kolp, Cincinnati, OH
E.F.Kraft & Co., St. Louis, MO
L.Krause, Cincinnati, OH

J.Kratz, X
E.R.Krumm, New York, NY
Kulmann Hdwe. Co., Cincinnati, OH
O.Kurtz, Berlin, VIII
LaChappelle, Strassburg, VIII
Lamb & Brownell, New Bedford, MA
J.H.Lamb, New Bedford, MA
W.G.Lamb, New Bedford, MA
R.T. Lamb, Memphis, TN
P.A.Lanauze, New Orleans, LA
*Michael Lang, Buffalo, NY
R.Lang, Cincinnati, OH
H.Langhurst, Cincinnati, OH
B.Lape, Cincinnati, OH
W.Large, Sheffield, England
S.Law, X
R.S.Layton, X
Iacob Lening, X
S.Leonard, X
F. Lender, Cincinnati, OH
H.Libhart, X
C.Lindenberger, X
Lindenberger, Providence, RI
J.E. & G.M.Lindsey, Huntington, MA
D.Lines, IX
*Charles S.Little, Boston, MA
L.Little, Boston, MA
N.Little, X
Wm. H.Livingston, New York, NY
J.Lock, X
Lockport Edge Tool Co., Lockport, NY
Chas.F.Loftus, Glasgow. Scotland
J.H.Lohr, Cincinnati, OH
London, X
C.Long, X
D.Long, X
G.Long, IX
I.Long, London, England
M.Long, Reading, VIII
J.Lord, Watertown, NY
J.T.Loomis, Hartford, CT
C.D. & O.H.Lord, Norton, MA
Lourie, England
D.Lovejoy, Lowell, MA
J.Lovell, Cummington, MA
Lowell Plane & Tool Co., Lowell, MA
I.Lund, London, England
J.A.Lundgren, X
S.Lunt, Liverpool, England
M.Luttgen, Jersey City, NJ
Lyms, London, England
J.P. Lyne & Son, Carlisle, VIII
J.Lyon, Cincinnati, OH
Lyon,McKinnell & Co., Cincinnati, OH
Lyon & Hall, Cincinnati, OH
Lyon & Smith, Cincinnati, OH
F.M.Lynch
R.W. Maccubbin Baltimore. MD

Thos.Machin, Toronto, Ontario, Canada
J.B.Mack, X
Peter Mackay & Co., Edinburgh, Scotland
Peter Mackay & Co., Glasgow, Scotland
T.Mackenzie, Birmingham, England
Macomber,Bigelow & Dowse, Boston, MA
Madox, London, England
Geog. Mahan, Muscatine, IA
D.Mallock, Perth, Scotland
D.Mallock & Son, Perth, Scotland
P.H.Manchester, Providence, RI
Mander & Dillon, Philadelphia, PA
Mannebach Bros., New York, NY
Manners, England
G.W.Manning, IX
Wm.Mapier, X
Marble & Smith, Cleveland, OH
F.B.Marble, Cleveland, OH
Marley, New York, NY
Wm.Marples & Sons, Sheffield,England
Alex Marshall, Glasgow, Scotland
A.& W.Marsh, Cleveland, OH
Marshall & Brown, Westfield, MA
Martin, Philadelphia, PA
Martin & Corey, New York, NY
Martin & Shaw, Birmingham, England
*James W.Mason, Saybrook, CT
*James W.Mason, New York, NY
Massey, Philadelphia, PA
*Samuel Massey, Philadelphia, PA
Mathewman & Co., New Haven, CT
A.Mathieson,Edinburgh, Scotland
A.Mathieson, Glasgow, Scotland
E.I.Matthews, Baltimore, MD
J.Mattson, Chicago, IL
A.McBride, Louisville, KY
Thos.J.McCall, Albany, NY
J.M.McCune, Columbus, OH
W.C.McDonald, Montreal, P.Q., Canada
J.McGinnis, Cincinnati, OH
McKinnel & Co., Cincinnati, OH
McGlasshan,Perth, Scotland
T.J.McMaster & Co., Auburn, NY
T.J.McMaster & Co., Singsing, NY
Z.J.McMaster & Co., Auburn, NY
Z.J.McMaster & Co., Singsing, NY
McPherson Bros., Glasgow, Scotland
E.J.McRonald, X
McVicar, Perth, Scotland
J.Mead, X
Mechanics Tool Co., IX
A. Meier& Co., St. Louis, MO
Rd. Melhuish Ltd., London, England
Alex.Melville, Edinburgh, Scotland
L.Merrill,X
Merritt, Co., New York, NY
James Merritt,So.Scituate, MA
Mead,Shelton & Co., Cincinnati, OH

Meyer & Schulze. St. Louis, MO
Middleton, York, England
Middleton, Newark, VIII
J.F.Millard, Roxton Pond,P.Q., Canada
J.P.Millener & Co.,Kingston,Ont.,Canada
Miller,Providence, RI
A.R. & G.H. Miller, Chicago, IL
Henry Miller, St. Louis, MO
J.Miller, New Castle Upon Tyme,England
J.D.Miller, Bridgeport, VIII
W.W.Miller, St.Louis, MO
Miller & Probasco, Cincinnati, OH
J.Milton, IX
M.H.Milton, Canaan, NH
J.Minot, X
Missouri Premium/ H.C. & T., VIII
D.Mitchell, X
A.Mockridge, Newark, NJ
Mockridge & Francis, Newark, NJ
Mockridge & Son, Newark, NJ
Moir, Glasgow, Scotland
Robert Moir, New Brunswick, Canada
A.Monte[also,Monty],Roxton Pond,P.Q.,Canada
Montgomery, Boston, MA
Montgomery & Woodbridge, Boston, MA
Moon, London, England
Moon & Laby, Cincinnati, OH
Moore, Liverpool, England
A.G.Moore, New York, NY
C.Morehouse, New Haven, CT
Z.Morgan, jr., X
Morison, Glasgow, Scotland
Julius Morisee, St. Louis, MO
Moreland Tool Co., Montreal, P.Q.,Canada
Morley & Jenkins, Kingston, VIII
A.P.Morrill, X
B.Morrill, Bangor, ME
John Morrison, Chillicothe, OH
A.Morse, X
J.Morse, X
T.Morse, X
A.Morton & Co., IX
John Morton, Vermont
Moseley late Mutter, London, England
John Moseley & Son, London, England
Moses, Hasting, NY
E.Moses, Deposit, NY.
E.Moses, Asford, NY
Wm.Moss, Birmingham, England
F.N.Mower, X
Wm.Muir, Windsor Locks, CT
Multiform Plane Co., Boston, MA
G.Mundorff, Berlin, VIII
Mutter, London, England
Jeremiah Myers,2nd., So.Boston, MA
Thos. Napier, Edinburgh, Scotland
Thos. Napier, Philadelphia, PA
H.L.Naramore, Cummington & Goshen, MA

J.J.Nash, X
Nathusius,Kegler & Morrison, New York, NY
John M. Naylor & Co., Tiffin City, OH
H.Jo.Nazro & Co., Milwaukee, WI
Thos. Negus & Son, New York, NY
Nelson, London, England
Nelson & Hayner, Alton, IL
*M.Nelson, Middletown, CT
Jn. Nevinson, X
A.H.Newbold, Chicago, IL
A.H.Newbould[sic,Newbold],Detroit, MI
Andrew Newell, New York, NY
E.Newell, Lanesboro & Leeds, MA
New York Tool Co., Auburn, NY
New York Works, New York
F.Nicholson, Wrentham, MA
I.Nicholson, Wrentham, MA
*L.Nolton, Salina, NY
N.Norton, Camden, NJ
B.B. & W.R. Noyes, Detroit, MI
C.Nurse & Co., London, England
E.P.Nutting, SO. Amherst, MA
N.Nutting, X
Truman Nutting, Amherst. MA
Oakley & French, Fort Wayne, IN
B.W.Oakley & Son, Fort Wayne, IN
Ogontz Tool Co., Sandusky, OH
Ohio King, IX
Ohio Plane Co.[A.C.Bartlett]
   probably Sandusky Tool Co.
Ohio Tool Co., Columbus, OH
Ohio Tool Co., Auburn, NY
Olney, Providence, RI
Ontario Tool Co.,Ontario, Canada
Owasco Tool Co., Auburn, NY
Owens & Barkley, IX
Owings & Roy, IX
Pagels & Ferguson, IX
B.Paine, IX
Ed. Paine, X
Benjamin Parker, Hingham, MA
Parker,Hubbard & Co., Conway, MA
H.C.Parkes, Birmingham, England
W.Parkes, Birmingham, England
J.Parkhurst, X
R.A.Parrish, Philadelphia, PA
John S.Parry. Albany, NY
Parson, England
A.P.Parsons, Cummington, MA
J.A.Peale & Co., Vicksburg, MS
J.Pearce, Fall River, MA
J.Pearce, New York, NY
J. W. Pearce, Providence, RI
*Abel Pearson, Cincinnati, OH
F.Pearson, X
Peck & Crouch, Northampton, MA
P.M.Peckham, Fall River, MA
Peeler, X

Pennell & Miller, Philadelphia, PA
E.W.Pennell, Philadelphia. PA
I.L.Penney, Minneapolis, MN
*Peoples Machine Works, Norwich, CT
*James H.Perry, New York, NY
John H.Perry, New York, NY
Peters & Trimble. Richmond, IN
John Pettingell, Lowell, MA
Walden J. Pettingell, Lowell, MA
N.Phillips, Boston, MA
P.Phillips, Cincinnati, OH
Phillipson, London, England
Phoenix Company, Barkhamsted, CT
T.A.Pickering, Cincinnati, OH
E.C.Pierce, Jamaica, VT
I.Pike, Dedham, MA
B.Piper, Newton, MA
R Piper, Dublin, NH
S.Plummer, Lisbon Falls, ME
*J.T.Platt, Bridgeport, CT
J.T.Plimley & Co., IX
Plutte & Becker, Hamburg, VIII
S.Pomeroy, Northampton, MA
David Pond, New Haven, CT
Wadsworth H.Pond, New Haven, CT
William H. Pond, New Haven, CT
Pond & Briggs, New Haven, CT
J.C.Poor, X
*L.T.Pope, Boston, MA
Thomas Potter, Cummington, MA
S.H.Porter, Terre Haute, IN
Powell & Child, Davenport. IA
S.Powell, Birmingham, England
Pratt & Co., Buffalo, NY
C.Prescott, Lowell, MA
D.Presprey, X
Preston & Son, London, England
D.Preston, Birmingham, England
Edw.Preston & Sons, Birmingham, England
Providence Tool Co., Providence. RI
Quackenbush,Townsend & Co., New York, NY
Jno.B.Quegles, Natchez, MS
Queen City Tool Co., Cincinnati, OH
Quebec Steam Plane Factory,Quebec,Canada
Randall & Benson, Albany, NY
Randall & Co., Albany, NY
Randall & Cook, Albany, NY
*Randall & Shepard, Albany, NY
S.Randall, Albany, NY
J.Randell, X
Raudet, X
T.B.Rayl & Co., Detroit, MI
W.Raymond, IX
*Read & Cummings, Boston, MA
H.H.Read,Wilmington, VT
M.Read, Boston, MA
Reed & Auerbacher, New York, NY
John Reed, Utica, NY

James Reid, Aberdeen, Scotland
C.H.Rhoads, Amherst, MA
L.Rich, X
T.J.Richards, Cincinnati, OH
Richards, Philadlphia, PA
F.Richards & Co, Springfield, MA
Richardson Brothers, Waltham, MA
W.W.Richey, Louisville, KY
J.Richmond, Troy, OH
P.B.Rider, Bangor, ME
E.C.Ring, Ringville, MA
E.&T.Ring & Co., Worthington, MA
L.&T.Ring & Co.,Worthington, MA
E.Robbins, Newport, NY
D.Rogers, New York
H.Rogers Sons & Co., England
Rogers & Fowler, Dayton, OH
Jacob Rogers & Co., Lowell, MA
John Rogers, London, England
P.Rogers, X
H.Rohrkasse, Cincinnati, OH
S.Root, X
Root & Platt, Alton, IL
G.Roseboom, Cincinnati, OH
G.& W.H.Roseboom, Cincinnati, OH
Roseboom & Magill, Cincinnati, OH
*Roseboom & Smith , Cincinnati, OH
*Roseboom & Thomas, Cincinnati, OH
William C.Ross, Baltimore, MD
Routledge, Birmingham, England
C.S.Rowell, Troy, NY
S.Rowell, Troy & Albany, NY
Rowell & Gibson, Albany, NY
*Rowell & Kenny, Albany, NY
Roxton, X
Roxton Pond Tool Co, P.Q., Canada
E.Rugg, Keene, NH
J.Rumbaugh, Ohio City, OH
*J.Rumrell, Boston, MA
Runched, X
Runyon & King, Springfield, OH
H.Russel, Cabot, VT
Ryan & Bros., Alton, IL
Ryland Ostrum & Co., IX
S.H.Mfg. Co., IX
E.Safford, Albany, NY
R.Safford, X
Sale & Griggs, Davenport, VIII
G.Sampson, London, England
Sanborn & Co., Worcester, MA
Sanborn & Gouch, Worcester, MA
D.P.Sanborn, Littleton, NH
I.E.Sanderson, Worthington, MA
J.Sanderson, Concord, NY
R.Sanderson, X
Sanford & Co., Ft.Demoin, IA
G.Sandkuhl, Poughkeepsie, NY
Sandusky Tool Co., Sandusky, OH

Sargent & Co., New Haven, CT
D.Sargent, Manchester & Nashua, NH
P.Sargent, Concord, NH
Savage & Carter, Middletown, CT
Sawheag Works, Wallingford, CT
Schaefer & Cobb, Cincinnati, OH
C.Schaefer, Cincinnati, OH
J.Schauer, X
S.B.Schenck, Mansfield, MA
*W.Schlemmer & Co., New York, NY
*Robert Schroeder, Baltimore, MD
W.Shultz, X
D.A.Schutte, Cillicothe, OH
Scioto Works, Auburn, NY
Scioto Works, Columbus, OH
Scobie & McIntosh, Edinburgh, Scotland
W.Scott, Pittsburgh, PA
L.Scovill, Johnstown, NY
A.M.Seaman, Ithaca, NY
James, Searing, Newark, NJ
A.Searl, New York, NY
C.S.See, New York & Watertown, NY
Sears,Roebuck & Co., Chicago, IL
A.B.Seidenstricker, Baltimore, MD
A.B.Seidenstricker & Co., Baltimore, MD
Seller, X
J.A.Sex & Co., Auburn, NY
C.Seybold, Cincinnati, OH
E.F.Seybold, Cincinnati, OH
John Seymour, Cincinnati, OH
Shapleigh,Day & Co., St. Louis, MO
G.Shaw, VIII
B.Sheneman, Philadelphia, PA
*B.& T.J.Sheneman, Philadelphia, PA
B.Sheneman & Bro., Philadelphia, PA
*Edward Sheneman, Philadelphia, PA
Daniel M. Shepard, Albany, NY
Shepley, London, England
Shepley & Brain, London, England
Sherman Bros., New York, NY
Shillinglaw, X
Shiverick, Brooklyn, NY
Shiverick-Malcolm, Brooklyn, NY
Sickel,Sweet & Lyon, New York, NY
Simpson, Leeds, England
E.C.Simmons, St.Louis, MO
H.Simmons, X
Sims, London, England
C.T.Skelton & Co., Sheffield, England
J.M.Slater, Detroit, MI
I.Sleeper, IX
S.Sleeper, X
S.Sloop, Cincinnati, OH
P.Small, X
J.Smiley, X
Smith, Bath, England
Smith,Lyon & Field, New York, NY
Smith & Stewart, Springfield, MA
A.Smith, Lowell, MA

A.Smith, Rehoboth, MA
A.M.Smith, New Bedford, MA
C.S.Smith, X
C.J.Smith, Cincinnati, OH
E.Smith, Rehoboth & Worcester, MA
E.Smith/ H.O.Smith, X
J.& C.Smith, Cincinnati, OH
J.H.Smith, Cincinnati, OH
J.W.Smith, New Bedford, MA
*Phineas Smith, New York, NY
T.E.Smith, Pawtucket, RI
Sneth, X
W.Sniff, X
Snow, X
*Wm.Souder, Philadelphia, PA
L.S.Soule, Waldoboro, ME
C.Spann, X
N.Spaulding, Ithaca, NY
N.Spaulding, McLean, NY
W.H.Spaulding, Elmira, NY
John Spayd, Philadlephia, PA
Spayd & Bell, Philadelphia, PA
O.A.Spear, X
Spence & King, Hull, England
Spencer, IX
Speyers, X
A.Spicer, X
H.Sprague, X
J.A.Sraft, X
Staniforth & Ford, Birmingham, England
Standard Rule Co., Unionville, CT
Stanley Rule & Level Co., New Britain, CT
J.Starr, New Lisbon, OH
R.C.Starr, X
*George Stedman, Rome, NY
W.Steele & Co., Wheeling, VA
J.G.Steiger, Cleveland, OH
J.S.Stevens, Boston, MA
Stewart, Edinburgh, Scotland
J.Stiles, New York, NY
J.Stiles, Kingston, NY
Stoeker, X
Stokoe, London, England
D.Stoner, Brunswick, VIII
F.Stines, X
J.P.Storer, Brunswick, ME
Stothert, Bath, England
Stothert & Walker, Bath, England
M.&N.H.Stout, St. Louis, MO
N.H.Stout, Louisville, KY
Stout & Richey, Louisville, KY
T.Stout, New Albany, IN
F.Street, Birmingham, England
J.J.Styles, Kingston, NY
Mutter G. Sudd, X
Wm.D.Swain, Rowe. MA
D.Sweet, X
M.Sweet, Pittsfield, MA
I.Sym, London, England

T.D.& Co., Cincinnati, OH
E.Tabb & Co., Norfolk, VA
Taber Plane Co., New Bedford, MA
J.M.Taber, New Bedford, MA
John Taber, X
L.H.Taber, New Bedford, MA
*W.H.Taber, NEw York, NY
Wing H. Taber, Fairhaven, MA
Wing H. Taber, Lowell, MA
J.Tadgell, London, England
E.Taft, Mendon. MA
Tasker, X
Taylor & Son, Liverpool, England
D.Taylor, X
*Hiram Taylor, Cincinnati, OH
*John C. Taylor, Cincinnati, OH
J./H. Taylor, Cincinnati, OH
I.Teal, Leeds, England
D.Temple, Glasgow,Scotland
W.Thackeray, Leeds, England
Theising & Evans, Cincinnati, OH
E.Thomas, X
D.Thompson, X
Thompson, Stuben, VIII
Thomson Bros., Buffalo, NY
Wm.A.Thomson, Buffalo, NY
Willis Thrall & Son, Hartford, CT
T.Tileston,Boston, MA
J.H.Timken, Bremen. VIII
C.Tobey, Hudson, NY
J.I.Tobey, Hudson, NY
C.Tollner, New York, NY
*C.Tollner & Hammacher, New York, NY
Tolman & Merritt, So.Scituate, MA
J.R.Tolman, Boston & Hanover, MA
T.J.Tolman, Hanover, MA
L.Tomkinson, Birmingham, England
S.Tomkinson, Birmingham, England
WM.Tomlinson, Glasgow, Scotland
Topping & Bro., Alton, IL
J.Tough, X
JN.Tower, X
*S.Tower, Chesterfield. MA
*A.W.Tracy, Vernon, CT
Treman & Bros., Ithaca, NY
*Treman,King & Co, Ithaca, NY
Trenam, Leeds, England
Troy Tool Co., New York
Tucker, London, England
Tucker & Appleton, Boston, MA
Turner, Sheffield, England
Tuttle, Hibbard & Co., Chicago, IL
L.Tyler, X
S.Tyzack & Sons, London, England
Underwood & Schaefer, Cincinnati, OH
T.Underwood, Bradford, England
Union Factory, New Hartford, CT
Union Manufacturing Co, New Britain, CT
Union Tool Co., Goshen, MA

Union Works, New Haven, CT
Upson Nut Co., Unionville, CT
J.R.Vajen, Indianapolis, IN
Wm.Vance, Baltimore, MD
*S.D.Vansands, Middletown, CT
I.Vanzant, Georgetown, KY
Varvill, York, England
Varvill & Son, York, England
*Thomas Vaugn, Chelsea, MA
I.Veal, IX
John Veit, Philadelphia, PA
*J.H.Verbryck, Mason OH
J.J.Vinal, Cleveland, OH
Vokes Hardware Co.Ltd., Toronto,Canada
W.Bro.& Co., IX
D.Walker, Cincinnati, OH
J.Walker, Cincinnati, OH
Walker & Hall, Cincinnati, OH
R.Wall, X
Wallace, Montreal, P.Q., Canada
A.Wallace, Dundee, Scotland
I.Walton, Reading, MA
J.Waltz, X
R.D.Ward, Cincinnati, OH
Ward & Chapin, Baltimore, MD
Ward & Fletcher, New York, NY
G.& N.J.Ward, New Hartford, CT
William Ward, New York, NY
Wardwell & Co., Rome, NY
D.Warner, X
L.Warner, X
Wm.Warner, New Hartford, CT
Warner & Driggs, New Hartford, CT
C.Warren, Nashua, NH
J.M.Warren, Troy, NY
W.Warren, Hudson, NH
Warren & Heald, NH
W.L.Washburn, Amherst, MA
R.Waters, X
W.Watkins, Bradford, England
Watrous & Osborne, Auburn, NY
J.L.Waynes & Son, Cincinnati, OH
William Way, New York, NY
Way & Co., New York, NY
Way & Sherman, New York, NY.
Cyrus Weaver, Hudson, NH
Webb & Gamwell, Pittsfield, MA
J.Webb, Pittsfield. MA
J.& W.Webb,New York, NY
J.& W.Webb, Pittsfield, MA
W.Webb, Pittsfield, MA
Wm.P.Webb, Washington, D.C
Webb & Baker, Pittsfield, MA
P.Weber & Co., Milwaukee, WI
M.H.Webster, Detroit, MI
Weeden, X
C.S.Wells, Evansville, IA
H.Wells, Northampton, MA
H.Wells, Williamsburgh, MA

L.G.Wells, IX
L.G.& R.Wells, IX
R.Wells, Trenton, VIII
S.Wentworth, X
J.R.West, Easton, VIII
John T.West, Baltimore, MD
H.Wetherel [sr.],Norton, MA
          & Chatham, CT
H.Wetherell, [jr.], Chatham, CT
          & Middletown, CT
A.Wheaton, Philadelphia, PA
I.Wheeler & Allen, Oswego, NY
L.Wheeler, X
White & Grinnell, Philadelphia, PA
White & Spear, Warren, OH
Charles White, Warren, OH
*Charolette White, Philadelphia, PA
G.White, Philadelphia, PA
Henry G.White, Philadelphia, PA
H.W.White, Jackson, Ohio
Israel White, Philadelphia. PA
I.I.White, Philadelphia, PA
*Jacob White, Philadelphia, PA
L.& I.J.White, Buffalo, NY
Whitmore & Wolff, Pittsburgh, PA
Whitemore,Wolff,Duff & Co., Pitts.,PA
Whittier & Spear, IX
Josiah Wiggins, Cincinnati,OH
Wiggins & Peiffer, Cincinnati, OH
A.J.Wilkinson & Co., Boston, MA
Wiley & Frick, Jonesboro, IL
S.F.Willard, Roxton Pond, P.Q.,Canada
Isaac Wiley, X
J.Willey, Leeds, England
Williams Universal Plane, Philadelphia, PA
W.Williams, New York, NY
Willis, St.John, New Brunswick, Canada
Wilson, Glasgow, Scotland
Wilson & Bros., St. Louis. MO
Wilson & Co., Edinburgh, Scotland
D.Wilson, X
*Henry Wilson, New York, NY
J.H.Winslow, Thomaston, ME
Winsted Plane Co., Winsted, CT
Wiseman & Ross,Baltimore, MD
I.Wiser, X
R.Wooding, London, England
G.Wolcott, New Haven, CT & Utica, NY
B.Wollam, X
J.Woods, IX
Wood, Hamilton, Ontario, Canada
Wood's Tool Store, New York, NY
*W.W.Wood & Bro., Watertown, NY
E.C.Woodbridge, Boston, MA
R.Woodford & Co., Oswego, NY
H.Woodruff & McBride, Louisville, KY
S.P.Woodruff, New Albany, IN
Wm.Woodward, Taunton, MA
Joseph Woodweil & Co., Pittsburgh, PA

Woothoudt, X
G.Worthington, Cleveland, OH
R.Wright, Philadelphia, PA
Yarnall & McClure, Philadelphia, PA
Geo.W.Young, jr. & Co., Baltimore, MD
Young & Holiday, Cincinnati, OH
Young & McMaster, Auburn, NY
*Young & Seidenstricker, Baltimore, MD
J.Zimmerman, Kingston,Ontario,Canada

The following names appeared in the geographical listing, but inadvertently were not included in the alphabetical listing.

David Clark, Cumberland, RI
T.S. & Clarke, New York, NY
R.J. Collins, Utica, NY
W. Evens, Pittsburgh, PA
E. Fillmore, Xenia, OH
G.H. Glaesher, Cincinnati, OH
Charles Odel, Salem, MA
W.E. Perry/ W.Haven, VIII
Phoenix Factory, New Hartford, CT
Pond, Malcoml & Welles, New Haven, CT
W.Powell, X
Rickard, Cincinnati, OH
H.M.Sanders & Co., Boston, MA
*John D. Searing, Newark, NJ
O. Spicer, X
E. Thomas, Holdrook, VIII
White River Works, IX
Whitehaven, X
  I.Wilder, X

The names of makers and firms who do not appear on these listings will undoubtedly be reported in the future by observations from serious collectors. My guess is that the majority of imprints that will be reported will be firms or dealers for the most part operating in the mid-western or western parts of the United States.

For those who are interested in being advised of newly reported imprints, it is suggested that they join the B-ARS. See Note No. 15, page 193.

EAIA Members who contributed information on Plane imprints, 1st Editon

A.H. Barben	Thelma M. LaVergne
Willis Barshied, Jr.	Samuel K. Lessey
*Kendall H. Bassett	Joseph Link
James A. Beam	Floyd J. Locher
Mark H. Beecher	R.D. Morris
D. V. Beede	George E. Murphy
W.P. Blodgett	Paul Musch, Jr.
Davis S. Brown	George M. Mustybrook
R.K. Brunner	Waleter Nashert
Donald H. Buttel	Donald R. Paschall
Robert H. Carlson	Harry J. Patton
E.W. Carson	Ralph A. Prince
*James A. Cooley	Joseph H. Ptaszek
Harvey E. Cooley	Peter Reed
Thomas J. Currier	Raymond M. Richardson
Barnet Delson	J. Paul Rideout
Edward Durell	Ivan S. Risley
Ole E. Fietland	Jane W. Roberts
John R. Gerwig, Jr.	Lee Roberts
Kenneth Gleason	Alva Russell
Victor B. Goodrich, Jr.	Robert J. Scott
*John R. Grabb	Eric Sloane
*Robert D. Graham, Jr.	Patricia E. Smith
Howard Groh	*Raymond M. Smith
Frederick G. Hardenbrook	William M. Stanton
Harold J. Hayes	J. Norrish Thorne
J.L. Henderson	Raymond R. Townsend
*William B. Hilton	Leroy C. Voss
Charles F. Hummel	J.P. Walker
Leslie M. Keating	Elwood J. Way
John S. Kebabian	Wallace P. Wetzel
*Paul B. Kebabian	*Donald Wing
James A. Keillor	L.Merrill Yoder
K.C. Larabee	*Also assisted with 2nd Edition

Additional Persons who assisted with 2nd Edition.

Seth Burchard	E.C. Martin
Addison Clipson	Bob Ochenas
Bill Curtis	C.Garland Rainey
Bill Eviston	Roger Smith
Gill Gandenberger	Bryan Sutton
Richard E. Hay	Anne Wing
Donald A. Krauss	

Particular thanks and acknowledgement are made to Richard Hay for his help with Baltimore planemakers; Addison Clipson, Bill Eviston, Gil Gandenberger and Ray Smith for assitance with Cincinnati and Ohio; and Bryan Sutton for documented dates of Canadian makers.

Sincere appreciations are expressed to Donald and Anne Wing for their material concerning 18th Century New England planemakers; Wilbert G. Schwer for his help with Sandusky Tool Co., Bob Graham for contributions on sash coping planes and spring and Bill Downes for photographic assistances.

LIST OF ILLUSTRATIONS [2nd Edition]

Figure Number	Title	Page
112	Plane Exhibit. Peter Lowd House. Strawbery Banke.	187
113	Crown Moulding Plane. I.Walton/IN READING	192
114	18th Century Plow Planes.	193
115	Crown Moulding Planes - 18th Century	194
116	18th Century Bench Planes	195
117	18th Century Bench Planes	195
118	Moulding Plane with Fence by Woothoudt	196
119	Tiger Maple Moulding Plane and 18th Century Sash Plane	196
120	18th Century Raising Plane by John Taber	197
121	Early Raising Plane	197
122	Halving Planes - 18th Century & 19th Century	198
123	18th Century Rabbet Planes	198
124A	Early Moving Filletster	199
124B	Early Double Iron Grooving Plane	199
125	18th Century Moulding Planes	200
126	Double Iron Round Plane by J.R.Tolman	201
127	Three Pairs of Hollowing and Rounding Planes by J.R.Tolman	202
128	Fifteen Spar Planes with Double Irons by J.R.Tolman	202
129	Smoothing Planes and a Razee by J.R.Tolman	203
130	Double Iron Compass and Hollowing Planes by J.R.Tolman	203
131	Double Iron Planes by J.R.Tolman	204
132	Two bead Planes by J.R.Tolman	204
133	Rabbet Planes by J.R.Tolman	205
134	Unique V-Grooving Plow Planes by J.R.Tolman	205
135	Lignum Vitae Razee Jack Planes	206
136	Wood Adjustable Compass Plane	207
137	T.D.Worrall's Patent Transitional Planes	207
138	Fenn Patent Improved Smoothing Plane	210
139	Iron,Wood Body & Adjusting Mechanism - Fenn Patent Plane	210
140	Iron Block Planes	211
141	Wood Bench Planes - Standard Rule Co.	212
142	Standard Rule Co. - 10" Jenny No. 36	212
143	Transitional Planes Made under Mosher Patent	216
144	Pattern Maker's Plane with 12 Detachable Shoes	217
145	Morris Diamond Metallic Bench Plane	228
146	Self-Adjusting Boxwood Sandusky Tool Co. Plow	229
147	Moulding Planes with Notched Wedges	245
148	English Sash Planes, Sash Template and Sash Fillister	248
149	Sash Filletster by J.Stiles/New York c.1768-1775	249
150	Sash Filletsrer by Amos Wheaton/ Philad.,c1795	249
151	Combination Sash & Moving Filletster by J.Reed/Utica,N.Y.	250
152	Single Iron "Stick and Rabbet" American Sash Planes	251
153	Single and Double Iron American Sash Planes	252
154	Late 18th Century Sash Plane	252
155	Double Iron American Sash Plane	253
156	Wood Screw Adjusting Sash Double Iron Planes	254
157	Wood Screw Adjusting Sash Planes Taken Apart	254
158	Diamond Pad Self-Regulating Sash Plane	255
159	English Double Iron Sash Plane by W.Watkins, Bradford	255
160	Sash Coping Planes	258
161	Complex Moulding Planes of American Manufacture,1800-1825	259
162	Handle Added to Standard Complex Moulding Plane	264
163	Crown Moulding Planes	265
164	O.G. Moulding Planes	266
165	Wide and Narrow Complex Moulding Planes	

Number	Title	Page
166	Crown Moulding Planes	267
167	Crown Moulding Planes	267
168	Handled Complex Moulding Planes	268
169	Boxwood Compass Plane with Six Interchangeable Soles	268
170	Toothing Planes	269
171	Plane for Bevel Edges	269
172	18th Century Panel Plane	270
173	Combined Moulding and Grooving Plane	270
174	Planes of Figs, 172 & 173 in Action	271
175	Panel Set in Stile with Planes Adjacent	271
176	Handled Rabbet Plane	272
177	Large Rabbet Plane and Large Dado Two Handled Plane	272
178	Rabbet Plane with Protective Case	273
179	Combination Tongue & Groove Double Iron Planes	273
180	Shooting Plane	274
181	Jack Converted into Shooting Plane	274
182	Smoother with Thumb Screw Wedge	275
183	Iron Cased, Wood filled American Mitre Plane	275
184	6" T-Compass Carriage Maker's Planes	276
185	Miscellaneous Carriage Maker's Planes	276
186	Moving Filletster Planes	277
187	Handle Screw-Arm Rosewood Moving Filletster	277
188	Fancy Screw-Arm Adjustable Plow Planes	278
189	Dado Plane with Adjustable Screw-Arm Fence	278

LIST OF PLATES

XXXIII	Traces of Moulding Plane Wedges	191
XXXIV	Bailey, Chany Co. Price List, c.1868	207-208
XXXV	1867 Boston Directory Advertisement of Leonard Bailey	209
XXXVI	Improved Smoothing Plane - 1857 Fenn Catalogue - London	210
XXXVII	Three Pages from Standard Rule Co. Catalogue	213
XXXVIII	Upson Nut Catalogue, page 68	214
XXXIX	Upson Nut Catalogue, page 66	215
XL	Pattern Maker's Plane, 1896 Hamacher, Schlemmer Co. Catalogue	218
XLI	Kellogg's Plane Price List	218-219
XLII	1873 Announcement by Greenfield Tool Co.	220
XLIII	1881 Directory Advertisment of Greenfield Tool Co.	221
XLIV	Title Page 1877 Sandusky Tool Co Catalogue	226
XLV	Introduction to 1877 Sandusky Tool Co. Catalogue	227
XLVI	Advertising Brochure Sandusky Tool Co.	230
XLVII	Kinney's Patent Guage - 1880 Sandusky Tool Co. Catalogue	231
XLVIII	A.C.Bartlett's Ohio Planes, 1899 Hibbard, Spencer, Bartlett & Co.	233
XLIX	Sketch of Sandusky Tool Co., Catalogue #24	235
L	Introduction to 1925 Sandusky Tool Co. Catalogue	238
LI	Sandusky Semi-Steel Planes	239
LII-LV	Sandusky Tool Co. Brochure	240-243
LVI	Sash Planes from 1857 Illustrated Supplement Arrowmammett	247
LVII	Window Making Planes	257
LVIII	Spring	261
LIX	Spring	263

TABLES

XV	Operations Sandusky Tool Co., 1910 - 1924	234
XVI	Summary of 1925 Eastern Trip Sandusky Tool Co.	237
XVII	Distribution of Plane Sales 1925	244

INDEX

The Index is divided into three Sections: I. Authors and Publications; II. Subject Matter; and III Types of Planes. Only the names in the ten chapters are indexed. The Check List provides both a geographical and an alphabetical listing of the planemakers and firms. Illustrations, plates and tables for the first five chapters are listed in the front pages, vi - viii, and for the last five chapters pages 309-310. The types of planes appearing in the *1858 Arrowmammett Works Catalogue*, Appendix I, and in various other illustrations from trade cataloges are not indexed.

I - Authors and Publications

Arrowmammett Works 1858 Catalogue: 141 - 153
Chronicle of EAIA: 79, 83, 84, 89, 90, 92, 94, 98, 105, 112, 114, 125, 190, 201, 207, 228, 232, 234, 274
Goodman, W.: 1 - 3, 8, 50, 193, 247, 251
Holtzapffel: 3, 4, 79, 82 - 84, 90, 112, 114, 125, 168 - 181, 192, 259
Jenkins, J.: 134
Kilby, K.: 134
Knight, E.: 4
Mercer, H.: 1, 248
Moxon, J.: 1, 3
Nicholson, P.: -1 - 3, 79, 83, 90, 98, 105, 112, 114, 119, 120, 130, 131, 132, 134, 140
Plane Talk [B-ARS]: 190, 192, 256, 259
Rees, A.: 3, 211
Rempel, J.: 106
Salaman, R.: 1, 79, 83, 84, 89, 90, 94, 98, 103, 105, 106, 112, 119, 120, 125, 130, 131, 132, 134, 140, 192, 247, 258
Sandusky Tool Co. Catalogues: 38 - 41, 225 - 227, 238
Stanley Rule & Level Co. Catalogues: 56 - 57
Welsh, P. 51

II - Subject Matter

Advertisements: 17, 21, 22, 30, 31, 33, 35, 36, 38 - 41, 54 - 57, 64, 65, 67, 71, 73 - 75, 208, 209, 213 - 215, 218 - 221, 223 230 233, 239 - 243
Blocks [Ship]: 18
Brass: 18
Cast Steel: 43, 44, 65
Clocks: 18, 43, 47
Coopering: 48, 134 - 139
Daniel, T.: 48
England: 1 - 5, 8.9. 16, 18, 20, 43. 50, 66, 110, 130, 133, 210, 211, 247, 248, 251, 255, 269
Fay, J. 49
Fenn, J.: 210, 211
Floats: 30, 42
Flooring: 49
Furniture: 47, 189
Gab: 42
Hammacher, Schlemmer & Co., 59, 64, 274
Honeyman Hardware: 74
Imprints: Frontispiece, 8, 279, 280
Joints: 95, 97
Locher, F. 59, 60
Mead, C.: 72
Miller, C.: 71, 72
Montgomery Ward: 68, 74
Museums: 183 - 187
Page, G.: 49
Panel: 47, 101, 270, 271
Patents: 32, 33, 50 - 53, 59, 62, 66, 68 70, 72, 94, 132, 210 - 212, 213, 217 225, 228, 231, 236, 246, 269
Philips, R.: 70, 72, 210
Plane Irons: 7, 8, 20, 32, 42 - 44, 50, 82, 83, 90, 91, 113, 225, 237
[sharpening]: 159, 180, 181
Planemakers:
    Alford, C.: 16
    Andruss, O.: 19, 32, 151
    Appleton, T.: 28
    Arnold & Crouch: 19, 26, 152
    Baldwin, A.: 19, 23
    Baldwin, E.: 16, 19
    Barrus, H.: 26, 27
    Bartlett, A.C.: 232, 233
    Barton, D.: 32, 43
    Bailey, L.: 52 - 54, 72, 201, 209, 211
    Bailey, Chany & Co.: 52, 208, 209
    Ballou, I.: 8. 9, 12 - 14
    Beardsley: C.: 50
    Bell, J.: 32
    Bensen & Crannell: 34
    Bensen & Parry: 265
    Bewley, R.: 110
    Bibighaus, J.: 5, 32
    Bowles, J.: 5
    Brett, C.: 9, 13, 14
    Bridges: 59, 62
    Briggs, E.: 14, 190
    Brooks, W.: 16
    Browning, H.: 26
    Burnham, G.: 23, 25, 27
    Burrowes, E.: 74, 76

Butler, J.: 16
Carpenter, S.: 42
Carter, R.: 34. 191
Chapin, E.: 174
Chapin, H.: 5, 18, 23, 27, 92, 102, 104, 110, 191
Chapin, N.: 19. 26
Chapin, P.: 19, 30 - 32, 118
Cogdel, J.: 9
Collins,: 5, 36
Colton, D.: 110
Copeland, D.: 18, 25
Copeland, D.& M.: 5, 17, 18
Copeland, M.: 25, 123
Copeland, M.& A.: 18
Copeland & Chapin: 26
Creagh, J.: 34, 36
Creagh & Rickard: 35
Dean, B.: 14
Denison, J.: 5, 20, 21, 23, 93
Denison, L.: 20
Denning & Campbell: 36
Doggett, S.: 14
Dunham & McMaster: 34
Benjamin Alford Edwards: 14, 189
Ferry, A.: 50, 54
Foster, W. 50, 54
Fowler, J.: 7, 8, 10, 14
Fox, H.: 23
Fox, L.: 23, 24
Fugate, T.: 34, 35
Fuller, C.: 28, 59, 61, 126-27, 265
Fuller, J.: 8, 10, 14, 16, 189-91, 245
Gabriel, C.: 8
Gage, J.: 59, 62
Gladwin, P.: 28, 94
Goldsmith, G.: 16
Goldsmith, T.: 16
Grant, T.: 9
Hall, Case & Co.: 93
Harrow, R.: 19, 152
Hayden, P.: 37
Heald, A: 28
Heiss, D.: 125
Hills, Winship.: 19
Holmes, J.: 14
Holly, B.: 3, 50
Howes, S.: 53
James, H.: 27
Karrmann, J.: 66, 214
Kennedy, L.: 16, 17, 34, 35
Kennedy, S.: 16
Killam, J.: 20, 23
Kellogg, J.: 23 - 25, 27
Kellogg, W.: 24, 25, 218, 219
King, J.: 84
Knowles, H.: 50, 51, 54
Lindsey, J.& G.: 28
Little, L.: 14

Lindenberger, S.: 10, 14
Loughborough, W.: 50, 54, 68
Lyon, J. 34
Lyon, McKinnel & Co.: 36
Maccubbin, R.: 32, 110
McMaster., T: 110
Mander & Dillon: 131, 132
Massey, S.: 16
Mockridge & Francis: 32
Mockridge, H. 32
Napier, T.: 7, 9, 16
Narrowmore, H.: 28
Nicholson, F.: 8, 9, 12-14, 191
Nicholson, J.: 12, 14, 125
Nutting, T.: 23, 25
Palmer, N.: 50
Parker, A. 27
Parrish, R. 16
Pike, I.: 14
Pond, W.: 19, 20, 23, 152
Randall & Cook: 108
Richard, H.: 54, 59
Ring, E.& T.: 26, 27
Roseboom, G.: 152
Safford, E.: 16, 191
Sanford, L.: 54
Seidenstricker, A.: 19, 152
Seybold, C.: 42, 223
Seybold, E.: 36, 223
Sheneman, B.: 152
Sleeper, I.: 14, 191, 200
Smith, A.: 7, 9, 13, 14, 191, 200
Smith, E.: 14
Stevens, J.: 28
Taber, J.: 14
Taber, N.: 14
Taft, N.: 14
Thayer, B.: 23
Tidey, M.: 53
Tolman, J.R.: 201 - 205
Tolman, T.J.: 202, 206
Traut, J.: 52. 54, 59, 72, 73
Vance, N.: 16
Walton, I.: 14, 192
Warner, W.: 22, 23
Wells, J. 17, 42
Wetherell[1], 10, 11, 13, 14, 190
White, C.: 42
White, G.: 16
White, I.: 32, 33
White & Spear,: 36
Wilder, I.: 191, 200
Willey, J.: 5
Worral, T.: 51, 53, 68, 70, 207

Planemaking Factories
    Arrowmammett Works: 5, 19, 79, 82, 84, 89, 90, 92, 94, 105, 106, 112, 118 - 121, 125, 128, 130, 132 - 135, 141 - 153, 192

Planemaking Factories (continued)
   Auburn Tool Co.: 32, 34, 37, 39 - 41, 66, 234
   Alford Plane Co.: 20
   Baldwin Tool Co. [See: Arrowmammett Works]
   D.R.Barton Tool Co.: 5, 74
   Birmingham Plane Co.: 216
   Conway Tool Co.: 26, 27
   Copeland & Co.: 27
   Chapin-Stephens Co.: 20, 74, 76, 234, 240
   Derby Plane Co.: 66
   Eagle Factory: 19, 26
   Globe Co.: 19, 20
   Greenfield Tool Co.: 5, 26 - 29, 39 - 41, 191, 193, 220, 221
   Kellogg: 24 - 26, 218, 219
   Lowell Plane Co.: 51, 68, 207
   Middletown Tool Co.: 20, 43
   Ohio Tool Co.: 32, 37, 39 - 41, 66, 68, 69, 234
   Phoenix Co.: 20
   Pratt & Co.: 5
   Sandusky Tool Co.: 5, 37 - 42, 223 - 246
   Sargent & Co.: 5, 65, 66 - 68, 232
   Sawheag Works: 20, 22
   Standard Rule Co.: 2]2, 213, 215
   Stanley Rule & Level Co.: 5, 44, 50, 52, 54, 56, 57, 66, 68, 71 - 74, 76, 133, 134, 208, 216, 217
   Union Factory: 5, 17 - 19, 39 - 41, 102, 104
   Union Manufacturing Co.: 66, 68, 69, 217
   Upson Nut Co.: 66, 69, 214 - 216
   Warner & Driggs: 19, 20
   White, L.& I.J.: 32, 43, 135
   Winstead Plane Co.: 20

Planemaking in Various States
   Connecticut: 5, 7, 10, 12, 17, 19, 21 - 23, 47, 190, 212 - 217, 237, 240
   Massachusetts: 5, 7, 10, 12 - 14, 23 - 28, 190, 201 - 209, 218 - 221
   New York: 5, 9, 16, 28, 32, 34, 248, 249
   Maryland: 5, 16, 17
   New Hampshire: 28, 187
   New Jersey: 32
   Ohio: 7, 32, 34 - 37, 223 - 246
   Pennsylvania: 9, 16, 32, 33
   Rhode Island: 7, 12, 13, 19, 189

Planing Machine: 48, 49
Rogers, C.: 49
Sash: 49, 247 - 258
Sash Templates: 124, 248
Sears Roebuck: 68, 69
Smith's Key [Sheffield]: 4, 5, 43
Spring: 178, 259 - 263
Terry, E.: 18, 47
Wedges: 7, 189, 191, 245
Whitney, B.: 49
Whitney, E.: 18

Wood Moulding Mills: 48, 49
Woodworth, W.: 48, 49

III. Types of Planes

Bailey: 44, 50, 52, 54 - 56, 58 - 61, 66, 69, 74, 75, 211, 212, 214
Beading: 73, 74, 106, 108 - 111, 166, 167, 204
Bench: 1, 4, 10, 11, 17, 30, 53, 56 - 58, 62, 74, 79 - 82, 84, 160, 169, 195, 212, 233
Bevel: 171
Block: 39, 60, 61, 84, 85, 160, 275
Bull Horn: 80, 84, 85
Carriage Maker's:
   Smooth: 80, 139
   Plain Rabbet: 80, 140, 276
   T-Rabbet: 80, 140, 276
Chamfer: 80, 131, 132, 275
Combination: 70 - 75, 216, 222
Compass: 80, 131, 156, 169, 203 - 205, 207, 268
Coping: 122 - 124, 256 - 258
Core Box, 80, 132
Coopers
   Croze: 80, 138, 176
   Jointer: 80, 138, 176
   Howell: 80, 137, 139
   Chamfer: 137, 139
Cornice or Crown Moulding: 125 - 128, 190, 265, 267
Dado: 68, 72 - 74, 80, 90, 105, 156, 166, 272, 278
Filletster: 3, 4, 68, 71 - 73, 80, 97, 98, 100, 121, 155, 161 - 163, 174, 175, 277
Fore: 1 - 4, 56, 57, 63 - 65, 68, 80, 81
Forkstaff: 130, 156, 160
Gage: 59, 62 - 64, 212
Grooving: 1, 3, 4, 72, 76, 79, 80, 90, 156, 166, 169, 174, 176, 270, 273
Gutter: 80, 129, 130, 195
Halfing: 80, 104, 198
Hollows & Rounds: 1, 2, 4, 74, 80, 112, 113, 167, 178, 202
Instrument Maker's: 80, 84, 86, 87
Jack: 1 - 4, 50, 56 - 60, 79 - 82, 89, 155 - 157, 170, 195, 206
[using: 95]
Jenny: 56, 59, 60, 61, 212
Jointer [Joynter]: 1 - 4, 56 - 58, 60, 63 - 68, 80, 156, 160, 170, 180 - 182
Liberty Bell: 57 - 59, 61, 74
Long: 2 - 4, 156, 159, 170, 116
Match: 68, 71, 73, 80, 94, 95, 96, 273
Metal [cast iron]: 51, 70 - 75, 211, 275
Mitre: 59, 61, 80, 84, 85
Moulding: 1 - 4, 10, 17, 31, 49, 68, 74, 79, 80, 106 - 111, 114 - 118, 157, 169, 196, 200, 245, 259, 266, 268
Mother Plane: 10, 12, 190

Types of Planes [continued]
  Ogee: 1, 4, 80, 107, 114 - 116, 266
  Nosing: 74, 80, 110, 111
  Panel: 80, 101 - 103, 170, 270, 271
  Pattern Maker's: 217, 218
  Plow: 1 - 4, 11, 32, 33, 68, 70 - 73, 80
    90 - 93, 155, 156, 165, 175, 190, 192,
    193, 205, 229, 278
  Pump: 80, 129, 130
  Rabbet: 1, 2, 4, 57, 59, 68, 71 - 74, 80,
    90, 97 - 100, 156, 160, 164, 170, 176,
    198 - 203 - 205, 272, 273
  Rabbet [side]: 80, 104, 156, 157, 165, 177
  Raising: 102, 103, 197
  Razee: [ship planes]: 59, 66, 74, 80,
    89, 203, 206

Routing: 80, 133, 175
Sash: 80, 120, 121, 155, 163, 164, 247-258
Sash Filletster: 164, 247 - 250
Shooting Board: 274
Slitting: 73, 80, 133
Smooth: 1 - 4, 56 - 68, 79 - 84, 86, 89,
  155, 156, 182, 203
Snipes' Bill: 1, 2, 4, 80, 109, 119
Spar : [mast]: 80, 130, 202
Toothing: 80, 84, 86, 170
Toy: 80, 84, 86,
Transition: 51 - 61, 66, 68, 69, 207, 208,
  212, 216, 217
Trying: 3, 4, 30, 32, 155, 159, 170
Weather Strip: 21, 244

ERRATA 1st Edition

Page 13, Caption Fig. 4, Change Chatham, Mass. to Chatham, Conn.
Page 14, Table I. Change Brigss to Briggs
Page 20, 2nd Paragraph, 10th line; Change 1868-1874 to 1868-1890.
Page 42, Table VII; Change dates of dissolved Greenfield Tool Co. from 1883 to 1887;
    and Sandusky Tool Co. from 1926 to 1931.
Page 47, Last line; Change Petents to Patents.
Page 61, Last line, Change No.22 to No. 122.
Page 99, Figure 46. A rabbet plane with square iron has been placed at the
    top, the present two top lowered and the present bottom plane removed.
Page 111, Caption Fig. 61; Change bead to torus.
Page 121, Last line; Change sash filletster to screw arm adjustable sash plane.
    Make same change in Caption to Fig. 78.

Fancy Sash Sections Typical of Use in Great Britain. From *Alex. Mathieson & Sons, Ltd. Catalogue of Wood Working Tools*, [Eigth Edition, 1899, Edinburgh], p. 196